*Hundreds of yarns to laugh at,
to treasure ...
Words and music to sing out every
beloved ballad and song!*

Enjoy the plain stuff of history ... the practical wisdom of a nation. From early tales of witches to the folk humor of our own times—all the sayings, beliefs and customs since the birth of America.

They're now collected in a book to read again and again—for the legendary heroes and badmen, the funny stories and classic songs. All in one highly hailed volume of unprecedented scope.

A Treasury of American Folklore—with a Foreword by Carl Sandburg—is also a respected work of scholarship, and an invaluable tool for all students of American history and folklore.

"Would appeal to every variety of taste."
—*Journal of American Folklore*

"Comes nearer to ... the traditional roots of American culture than any other one-volume work."
—*Southern Folklore Quarterly*

A TREASURY OF
AMERICAN
FOLKLORE

STORIES, BALLADS, AND
TRADITIONS OF THE PEOPLE

Edited by
B. A. BOTKIN

Foreword by
CARL SANDBURG

Specially abridged and with a new
introduction by Joseph Leach

A TREASURY OF AMERICAN FOLKLORE

*A Bantam Book / published by arrangement with
Crown Publishers, Inc.*

PRINTING HISTORY
*Crown edition published May 1948
31 printings through September 1976
A Selection of Preferred Choice Bookplan August 1978
Bantam abridged edition / January 1981*

ISBN 0-553-14149-X

Published simultaneously in the United States and Canada

Bantam Books are published by Bantam Books, Inc. Its trademark, consisting of the words "Bantam Books" and the por-
trayal of a bantam, is Registered in U.S. Patent and Trademark
Office and in other countries. Marca Registrada. Bantam
Books, Inc., 666 Fifth Avenue, New York, New York 10103.

CONTENTS

III. KILLERS

IV. FREE LANCES

II. THE SKY'S THE LIMIT

III. LOCAL CRACKS AND SLAMS

PART THREE: JESTERS

I. PRANKS AND TRICKS

PART FOUR: LIARS

I. YARNS AND TALL TALES

II. FROM THE LIARS' BENCH

PART FIVE: FOLK TALES AND LEGENDS

I. ANIMAL TALES

FOREWORD

WE HAVE heard of the boy and his sister coming home from school to tell their mother, "We learned today we have been talking prose all our lives and we didn't know it." Likewise many of us grown-ups have talked off a lot of folklore in our lives and we didn't know it was folklore—and if we had known it wouldn't have made much difference. You can't stop 'em from telling it even if they politely warn you beforehand, "Stop me if you've heard this." They (or we?) are irrepressible as the tenacious debating opponent of whom A. Lincoln said in 1858 that the only way you could make him quit would be "to stop his mouth with a corn cob."

So here we have nothing less than an encyclopedia of the folklore of America. An encyclopedia is where you get up into box car numbers. There have been small fry collections of folklore we might say, but this one is a big shot. It will pass the time, furnish laughter, provide entertainment. And then besides giving you the company of nice, darnfool yarn spinners, it will give you something of the feel of American history, of the gloom chasers that moved many a good man who fought fire and flood, varmints and vermin, as region after region filled with the settlers and homesteaders who proclaimed, "We are breaking sod for unnumbered millions to come."

And now that the days of those pioneers are passed, we have cities and skyscraping structures of steel and concrete that would have amazed them, motion pictures and radio transmissions that some would have declared "plumb ridiculous," not to mention the tractors which can plow without mules and the storm-proof all-steel buggies and wagons that do better than a mile a minute without a horse to pull.

And this smart later generation of youth has its folklore and our encyclopedia has plenty of specimens of Little Audrey, of Knock Knock, Who's There?, of the little moron who being told he was dead ordered that he should be moved into the living room.

Something rather sweetly modern and quite impossible to see as coming alive out of any former generation is such a story as the editor dug out of "Chicago Industrial Folklore," by Jack Conroy. There it was hiding out in the Manuscripts of the Federal Writers' Project of the Works Progress Administration for the State of Illinois. It tells about Slappy Hooper, the World's Biggest, Fastest and Bestest Sign Painter and is a fresh modern masterpiece worth standing alongside the well-liked antiques which will not fail to be passed along from generation to generation.

A longtime book is this. One reading won't do for it. There are places in it where good fools have such love for other good fools that they must trade the follies and whims of their imaginations, to help forget their troubles, even their tragedies.

Excellent authority tells us that the right laughter is medicine to weary bones. And on many a page here one may find the droll smile or the rocking laughter that moved many a humble and honest struggler on American soil as he studied, with whatever of mind he had, what the present of his country was—and what the future might be.

The people or the folk of the present hour that is and of the future that is to be, many and many of them are seen here in their toil, laughter and struggle, are heard and made known in part in the heaped-up and sprawling materials of this book. It breathes of the human diversity of these United States.

CARL SANDBURG

PREFACE

I

WHEN I began to think of a book of American folklore, I thought of all the good songs and stories and all the good talk that would go into it, and of what a richly human and entertaining book it would be. A book of American folklore, I thought, should be as big as this country of ours—as American as Davy Crockett and as universal as Brer Rabbit. For when one thinks of American folklore one thinks not only of the folklore of American life—the traditions that have sprung up on American soil—but also of the literature of folklore—the migratory traditions that have found a home here.

Because folklore is so elemental and folk songs and stories are such good neighbors and pleasant companions, it is hard to understand why American folklore is not more widely known and appreciated. For this the word "folklore" is partly responsible. Folklore is the scholar's word for something that is as simple and natural as singing songs and spinning yarns among the folk who know the nature and the meaning but not the name—and certainly not the scholarship—of folklore. Because the word denotes both the material and its study, and has come to stand more for the study of the thing than for the thing itself, folklore, in fact, seems to have become the possession of the few who study it rather than of the many who make or use it.

The essence of folklore, however, is something that cannot be contained in a definition but that grows upon one with folklore experience. Old songs, old stories, old sayings, old beliefs, customs, and practices—the mindskills and handskills that have been handed down so long that they seem to have a life of their own, a life that cannot be destroyed by print but that constantly has to get back to the spoken word to be renewed; patterned by common experience; varied by individual repetition, inventive or forgetful; and cherished because somehow characteristic or expressive: all this, for want of a better word, is folklore.

Complementary to the "Stop me if you've heard this" aspect of folklore is the trait implied in the comeback: "That's not the way I heard it." For what makes a thing folklore is not only that you have heard it before yet want to hear it again, because it is different, but also that you want to tell it again in your own way, because it is anybody's property. On the one hand, repeated retelling establishes confidence in the rightness of what is said and how it is said. On the other hand, the beauty of a folk lyric, tune, story, or saying is that, if you don't like it, you can always change it, and, if *you* don't, someone else will.

But if folklore is old wine in new bottles, it is also new wine in old bottles. It says not only, "Back where I come from," but also, "Where do we go from here?" If this book is intended to bring the reader back to anything, it is not to the "good old days" but to an enjoyment and understanding of living American folklore for what it is and what it is worth. This is an experience in which Americans as compared with other peoples are sadly deficient. Perhaps it is because we are not one people but many peoples in one, and a young people, who have grown up too close to the machine age. The industrial folk tales and songs in this book are evidence enough that machinery does not destroy folklore. Rather, in our rapid development from a rural and agricultural to an urban and industrial folk, we have become estranged from the folklore of the past, which we cannot help feeling a little self-conscious or antiquarian about, without yet being able to recognize or appreciate the folklore of the present.

Perhaps the best way to understand the songs and stories in this book is in terms of a species of living literature which has no fixed form (in this respect differing from the classics, which it resembles in permanence and universality of appeal) and which is constantly shifting back and forth between written and unwritten tradition. Since print tends to freeze a song or a story, folklore is most alive or at home out of print, and in its purest form is associated with the "grapevine" and the bookless world. But that does not make it synonymous with illiteracy or ignorance, nor is it true that the educated do not also have their lore, or that lore ceases to be lore as soon as it is written down or published. Folk literature differs from the rest of literature only in its history: its author is the original "forgotten man."

Not only does folklore shift, but it changes as it shifts, between the top and bottom layers of culture. As it gets nearer to the world of professional poets and story-tellers, it tends to shape about itself a formal "literary" tradition of its own, as in the great collections of legends and folk tales that have come down to us from ancient and medieval times and have been pored over by scholars. But alongside of this more classic folk literature, which has acquired scholarly prestige and which gives and takes erudition, is the humbler and homelier folk literature of everyday life and the common man—today's people's literature (which the older folk literature may once have been). The difference between the two (a difference perhaps only of degree) is the difference, say, between the English and Scottish ballads and the "Dust Bowl Ballads" of Woody Guthrie.

This range of variation within the folklore field is a source of both strength and weakness. For while it enables folklore perpetually to rebuild itself from the ground up, it creates a kind of class-consciousness among folklorists. Thus the British folk-song and folk-dance expert, Cecil J. Sharp, while very much taken with the vigor and beauty of our mountain songs and dances, was unable to see in our cowboy songs anything but the fact that the "cowboy has been despoiled of his inheritance of traditional song" and has "nothing behind him" and nothing but "himself and his daily occupations to sing about, and that in a self-centered, self-conscious way, e.g., 'The cowboy's life is a dreadful life'; 'I'm a poor lonesome cowboy'; 'I'm a lonely bull-whacker,' and so forth."

Further complicating and diversifying the picture is a third quantity, midway between "folk" and "academic"—the "popular." The latter is distinguished by its wider and more passing acceptance, the result of transmission through such "timely" media as stage, press, radio, and films. Yet the so-called lively arts—jazz, vaudeville, burlesque, comic strips, animated cartoons, pulps—often have a folk basis or give rise to new folk creations, such as Mickey Mouse and Donald Duck. Many of the innovations of popular lore are associated with new inventions: e.g., the Ford joke and the gremlins. At the same time many of our modern gags have an ancient and honorable, if somewhat wheezy, lineage. The one about the two Irishmen, the Hebrew, and the baloney ("The Three Dreams") goes back to the twelfth century, while Little Moron jokes are as old as the Turkish Nasreddin.

Also close to folk sources but to be distinguished from folk literature proper is literature about the folk. This ranges from old-timers' reminiscences (one of the best examples of which in this book is Martha L. Smith's "Going to God's Country") and homespun humor and verse to local color and regional stories and sketches, all of which throw light on the folk and folklore backgrounds, culminating in that small body of masterpieces of "folk art" mined out of the collective experience and imagination by writers, known and unknown, who have succeeded in identifying themselves with their folk tradition.

II

It would be possible to get a good idea of American folklore by reading the fifty-seven volumes of the *Journal of American Folklore*. Since, however, writers of all kinds are always making use of folklore in one way or another, sometimes when one least expects it, one can turn up a surprising amount of good folklore simply by going through books, magazines, and newspapers. The present collection is a generous sampling, selected and arranged according to the interpretative principle of relating the material to certain folk motifs, such as hero-worship, boasting, pranking, jesting, "artistic" lying, and the like. By further relating these activities to certain regional and occupational groupings, the book is designed to reveal the cultural pattern of which American folklore is a part.

The term "American folklore" is employed here in the sense that one speaks of American literature, language, humor, etc., as an expression of the land, the people, and their experience. The same images and symbols have permeated all parts of this expression, so that folklore, literature, language, and humor are inseparable. "American folklore" is a much narrower and yet more definite concept than "folklore in America," which includes not only all the Americas but European folklore in America. For practical purposes, because I have had to draw the line somewhere, I have limited myself to folklore in the English idiom in the United States, excluding necessarily the Indian and foreign-language minorities. It is with considerable regret, and not with any intention of over-stressing the Anglo-Saxon element, that I have had to dispense with the contrast of these "strips, stripes, and streaks of color." But for the resultant loss of diversity there may be a compensating gain in unity. Even within these limits I have collected a great deal more than I could find room for.

In order to keep the book further in hand, two tests were applied to all selections: readability, with an emphasis on literary and especially narrative interest, and permanence and breadth of appeal. Articles and collections of data being ruled out, customs and beliefs are represented only as they enter into song and story. According to my conception of folklore as the stuff that travels and the stuff that sticks—the basic principle of selection—I have had to leave out much good material valuable as social history rather than as folklore or purely local in interest. At the same time, a certain amount of stuff that travels without sticking or that sticks without traveling has been included as representative of folklore in the making.

In dealing with such a large mass of material from so many different sources and of so many different types and tones, it sometimes becomes difficult to see the woods for the trees. If I have chopped down a few trees here and lopped off a few branches there, it is also to clear a path through the wilderness. If I have preferred a little looseness to too much tightness of selection and arrangement, it is because I believe a smoother flow is achieved thereby and also because I have wanted to give the mass effect of thousands of unknown singers and story-tellers.

To vary the pace and to show both the discrete and the discursive folk imagination at work, short and long pieces have been intermingled in varying proportions. In those cases in which a song or a story might have served more than one purpose, it has been placed where it seems to have the most effect. In the same way, I have chosen versions which seem to me most effective, though the reader will probably think of versions he likes better, possibly because he knows them better. I should like to hear of these, too. Wherever possible and desirable, I have preferred the earlier sources, though there are seldom, if ever, "original" sources for folklore. In the matter of text, I have left spelling, punctuation, etc., alone, in spite of inconsistencies, except where they might get in the way of the reader. Original titles have been retained for complete pieces, but in the case of excerpts no attempt has been made to distinguish between original and added titles.

In the amount and nature of the introductory comment (in solid type) by the editor, two rules have been observed: (1) Where material is already available in other books, as in the various types of folk tales and folk songs, the comment has been kept to a minimum; where the material is fairly fresh, as in the first four parts of the book, more comment has been deemed necessary. (2) The approach has been broadly literary and social rather than strictly folkloristic. All uninitialed footnotes are by the editor.

III

Although for the most part I have preferred to let American folklore speak for itself, in one respect it is necessary to distinguish between folklore as we find it and folklore as we believe it ought to be. Folklore as we find it perpetuates human ignorance, perversity, and depravity along with human wisdom and goodness. Historically we cannot deny or condone this baser side of folklore—and yet we may understand and condemn it as we condemn other manifestations of human error.

Folklore, like life itself, in Santayana's phrase, is animal in its origins and spiritual in its possible fruit. Much of the animalism, of course, does not appear here except by implication because of the taboos surrounding print. What does come through, however, often in violent contradiction of our modern social standards, is the essential viciousness of many of our folk heroes, stories, and expressions, especially in their treatment of minorities—Indians, Negroes, Mexicans, Chinese, etc.

In stories of anti-social humor and "necktie justice"— "Trimming a Darky's Heel," "Roy Bean and the Chinaman"— the narrator inevitably reflects the prejudices belonging to his and his hero's race and class. Such stories stick because they have the tang of life and are a historical comment. They should be preserved not to perpetuate but to reveal and correct the errors and evils they narrate. With this perspective the whole of folklore may become an instrument for understanding and good will.

A word should be said here about the movement that seeks to make folklore the basis of an entire social or art tradition. One can forgive "folksiness" almost everything—its nostalgia, its quaintness, its cuteness—but not its clannishness, which is next to chauvinism, and which speaks of folklore in terms of the "racial heritage" or insists that a particular folk group or body of tradition is "superior" or "pure." On the other hand, it is not necessary to go to the opposite extreme and to deny the importance of folklore and even a healthy provincialism, as one of the ingredients, though not necessarily the most important ingredient, of a well-rounded culture. It is hoped that, while preserving this normal view of folklore, the book may serve as an inspiration and a source-book for writers, teachers, and all others who are concerned with the materials of an American culture.

For the rest, I have tried to let the material flow as it will in shaping itself about our ways of thinking and feeling in America, much as the literature of American folklore may be said to shape itself about the folklore of American life. In this way I have sought to give not only an American view of folklore but a folk's-eye view of America. By going to almost every form and medium of writing about America as well as to the regular folklore publications, I have hoped to give a broader and more living conception of American folklore than is to be gained from any single line of approach.

IV

The source of each selection is indicated in a note at the foot of the page on which the selection begins. Where several selections appear on the same page, the sources are indicated in the same order. These source notes constitute at once a complete list of acknowledgments and a selected bibliography. Special thanks are due to those who have contributed unpublished material, and to the Federal Writers' Project, for which much of this material was originally written.

Grateful acknowledgments are due to the many authors and publishers, selections from whose publications are included in this book. An exhaustive effort has been made to locate all persons having any rights or interests in this material, and to clear reprint permissions. If any required acknowledgments have been omitted or any rights overlooked, it is by accident and forgiveness is desired.

In addition to those who have read or discussed with me various parts of the book at one time or another during the four years in which it took shape, the following have been close to the work as a whole:

Paul R. ("Febold Feboldson") Beath, especially in the first compilation;

Gertrude Botkin, my wife, who shared the labor with me from first to last;

Hugo V. Buonagurio, who made the music drawings;

Crown Publishers, consistently sympathetic in their encouragement and support;

Edmund Fuller, who first suggested the idea and name of

A Treasury of American Folklore and saw it through to the end;

Bertha Krantz, his assistant, who handled the permissions and served as a steadying influence;

Charles Seeger, who served as music consultant for the book.

Finally, without the collections of the Library of Congress, with which my work as Fellow in Folklore as well as folk-song archivist has brought me in close contact, this book would not have been possible.

B. A. BOTKIN

Washington, D.C.
March, 1944

INTRODUCTION

I

IN LAUNCHING his new *Treasury of American Folklore* in 1944, Benjamin A. Botkin said that he wanted his anthology to be "as big as this country of ours, as American as Davy Crockett and as universal as Brer Rabbit." The 900-page volume was indeed a Moby Dick of a book. Its contents ranged the whole forty-eight states from Maine to California, from the Canada line to Key West—"from hell to breakfast," as a Texas folk saying would put it.

The challenge for me as Botkin's abridger has been to retain a sense of his whale but to restrain it in waters of a reasonable, more practical size for the 1980's. Yet the restraints afford me a chance to make plain the significant core of Botkin's original book that his own editorial comments never quite delineated. This core was detected only by the astute reader who, between guffaws and shivers and knee-slapping laughter, caught the implications of the big story that Botkin was trying to tell.

To consider the book as an unfolding story is to see the characters and plot and setting as Botkin always perceived them when he focused his thoughts on American life. To him the plot was as plain as Mt. Rushmore's four noses and as long as American history, the setting was as wide as the North American continent and the characters numbered into the millions. That thousands of readers, sensing that story, drove it onto the best-seller charts and welcomed it as a Book of the Month Club bonus brought Botkin a deep satisfaction. That many scholars welcomed the book for its freshness, its broadened sense of the American "folk," sweetened his pride in the book he had wrought. That many analytically minded scholars and critics, missing his point, met the book with hostile dismay, troubled him.

Botkin's low-keyed editorial comments were partly to blame for academia's mixed reception, but it was his rather controversial concept of "folklore" that caused most of the scholarly skirmish. The fact that the dustup is still going on tells quite a tale about all of us folks in general.

II

Like happy hounds in a dogfight, colleague lined up against colleague, friend squared off against friend, into two sharply drawn camps. The bone of contention was what, in the professors' judgments, had Botkin achieved or attempted to show or simply never finished—or what had his grand title *A Treasury of American Folklore* promised and what had his thick volume delivered. Through all the tempest Botkin never complained and never explained himself either. For his *Treasury* had found a sales market that no other editorial judgment in America had ever imagined: a nationwide audience hungry for lusty American brags, legends, jokes, and songs, for a reassuring light on themselves as a people and their threatened, uneasy place on the planet.

The time, please recall, was the war-weary spring of 1944, two months before D-Day and the invasion of Europe, when once again American men were risking their lives for their country in battle. And American women and parents at home were praying that the sunshine of victory would soon light up their menfolks' journey back home.

Botkin's *Treasury* spoke straight to that market's concerns, and the popular press quickly took note. The new anthology, said the *Christian Science Monitor*, celebrates America's "tremendous physical vitality," her "heartiness, kindliness, and genuine interest in people" for which she is "known today the world over."[1]* *The New York Times* relished Botkin's display that America's folklore is "full of space and irreverence, portraying a mythical and hoped-for society in which nothing is impossible."[2] The *Saturday Review* celebrated the fact that Botkin's persistent labor in a field often dismissed as a "lowly," unrecognized "bi-product of American civilization" was now offering to the American people new pleasure in the "often rough and raucous output" of a "new people in a new land."[3] Applauding the book's "terse good humor," the *Weekly Book Review* welcomed the new anthol-

* Numbered reference notes begin on page 573.

ogy's lack of "academic tone" with which too much of American folklore had been "burdened in the recent past by assorted professors and thesis-hunting graduate students."[4]

The first verdicts in the professional journals were equally favorable. Wayland Hand's review in the *Journal of American Folklore* found the book "the first serious attempt to provide a general anthology of American folklore." Its scores of selections from folk materials "would appeal to every variety of taste." To compensate the editor and publisher for making the book available, "may the demand for the book . . . not cease until a broad cross section of Americans may come to know and treasure it."[5]

Arthur Palmer Hudson declared in the *Southern Folklore Quarterly* that Botkin's *Treasury* "comes nearer to representing the traditional roots of American culture than any other one-volume work has come. It is a book for the American people."[6]

Outcries from scholars *against* Botkin were slower in coming, but come they did, with a vengeance. Richard M. Dorson dismissed the whole book as "a scrapbook" lacking all "philosophical unity," the product of a method lacking "proper discrimination" and "system."[7] If any one word succinctly labeled its contents, wrote Dorson, that word should be "fakelore," at best. In that same camp, the *New Yorker* grumbled that Botkin's "enormous enthusiasm" for his subject perhaps explained his book's need for "more editorial discrimination."[8]

Nobody doubted Botkin's enthusiasm. But many readers, especially the scholar-professors, did question Botkin's methods of research, the criteria he had applied in hunting his quarry and in deciding what to discard in the bush as unfit and what to bring back as trophies worth publishing. Botkin might have disarmed some of his fellow folklorists if he had tried to establish his standards in a more definite way and in a more prominent place than his book's friendly, informal front pages. For in letting his choices speak for themselves, Botkin left it to his readers to decide what he meant by the word "folk," by the word "folklore," and how he had determined that a source was "valid," that a piece was "authentic."

Lacking precise definitions, Botkin's book charged into a linguistic thicket of definitions long held in scholarly repute. The term "folklore" was invented in 1846 by an English scholar, W. J. Thoms, as label for "the intellectual remains of earlier cultures surviving in the traditions of the peasant class,"⁹ and "loving studies of old customs, usages, and superstitions."¹⁰ Ever since, the usefulness of Thoms's word has been recognized wherever English was spoken and written, both among laymen and among scholars. But in the passage of time it has taken on so many popular shadings, so many esoteric refinements, that to use the word at all among academics poses problems. To be clear to his audience, the user must first specify which connotation he wishes to imply, which meaning out of all the possible meanings he wishes to pinpoint.

The trouble with "folklore," the word, stemmed in part from its parent stem, "folk," a word no less hard to define to the satisfaction of all. From one speaker's lips "folk" might mean a peasant, illiterate group; and from another's, any group possessing at least one viewpoint or interest or condition in common. The trouble was only compounded by the word "lore." To one user "lore" might mean a group's anonymously created body of knowledge, beliefs, customs, values, and songs—"the material that is handed on by tradition, either by word of mouth or by custom and practice."¹¹ But to another, "lore" might mean any group's agreed-upon ways of looking at and dealing with life, expressed and passed on in print or in some other medium, no matter who originally thought them or said them or sang them, and no matter how much the wordings and forms might change as they moved across distance and time.

The definitions upon which Botkin built his *Treasury of American Folklore* (and its spin-off regional treatments) satisfied thousands of readers through all thirty-two printings and three separate editions the book had enjoyed by 1979. For such general readers Botkin's definitions weren't then and aren't now important. If you, for example, opened this volume for pleasure—for a good read—precise definitions would only divert your attention away from the color and fun. If you are the person, however, who studies the *meanings* of "folklore," a word that one frustrated linguist finally defined as "what folklorists study,"¹² a statement here, at long last in this book's long career, can be helpful.

III

Botkin's word "folk," to begin with. Botkin lays aside all questions of age or longevity or social position or literacy or sophistication. A "folk" group is any group that thinks of

itself as distinct, as possessing a core of shared experiences
and outlook, a store of convictions and assumptions. From
its members' sense of their "in-ness," their separate identity,
springs its ways of expression, its meanings, its assumptions,
its rituals, its "lore." In this sense, everybody holds member-
ship in some kind of "folk" group—no matter how large or
how small—which to his satisfaction gives him a sense of
himself.

Given his meaning for "folk," Botkin rejects all questions
of origination or authorship or means of transmittal when he
defines "folklore." To him, folklore is what a group takes as
its expression of meaning, truth, and amusement, "what people
say about themselves in their own way and words."[13] And
what makes a thing folklore is its "tellable, listenable, and
repeatable quality, close to mother wit and common experience, heightened by popular fantasy," and—he might have
added to defend many items he includes in this book—that it
is "said acceptably well, oftentimes by educated, professional
writers."

As to his method of hunting and gathering, Botkin did not
in the strict sense plow wide and dig deep in "the field." He
did not go to "the folk." He winnowed instead the rich
harvest of materials made available by those who had gone
to the folk and transcribed and recorded their tellings and
singings. His search was mostly in libraries among the
volumes and shelves of such major American folklore collections as that in the Library of Congress. As a collector, he
brought to light, in many respects for the first time, "folklore"
that for want of his kind of energy and purpose had lain
unknown, untold, and unsung to the literate public.

IV

Bearing his definitions in mind, anyone reading his pages
now will readily see how his meanings of "folk" and "folklore"
give a shape to his book. The book's table of contents does
pose a problem, however. Since his table lists pieces by *lore
types* and by *subjects* ("Heroes and Boasters," "Tall Talk,"
and "Humorous Anecdotes and Jests," to cite three examples),
not *folk groups*, his concept of "folk" may be lost on many
a scholar-reader. Lacking a diamond-hard definition of "folk,"
the book appears to lack precise, authentic "folklore."

The "folks" represented in Botkin's pages compose a large
company. The company would have been even larger if, as

he explained in his original introduction, space had allowed him to include all the American folks that he saw. This fact, plus his sense of his intended readers' anti-German, anti-Japanese concerns in 1944, led him to concentrate upon lore in the English language, to feature the Anglo-Saxon white elements and their companion black and red elements in the national scene, and to omit—except for incidental references —all other ethnic-linguistic groups: American Indians, Asiatic Americans, Latin Americans, and the many European American folks still preserving their separate lores in their old tongues.

What folks does Botkin include? In one respect or another, at least the following: political groups, America's on-the-move pioneers, age groups, occupational groups, religious groups, regional and state groups, rural groups, city groups, social groups. In featuring the lore of these folks, he illustrates their sense of themselves, the figures they take as their heroes and villains, the sayings they use with each other, their notion of "others" outside. The following examples are a foretaste:

Political lore: Davy Crockett's campaigning among his backwoods constituents for Congress by shouting, "Ain't I the yaller flower of the forest! And I am all brimstone but the head and ears, and that's aquafortis!" Replies his listener, "Stranger, you are a beauty; and if I know'd your name, I'd vote for you next election." Says Crockett, "I'm that same David Crockett. You know what I'm made of. I can kill more lickur, fool more varmints, and cool out more men than any man you can find in all Kentucky." Says his listener, "Good morning, stranger—I'm satisfied."

Pioneer lore: (a) For all the high-spirited droves heading west in covered wagons sporting "Frisco or Bust!" and "Pike's Peak or Bust!" there was many a disillusioned party drag-tailing east, their wagons moaning "Busted—By Thunder!" (b) And "Oh, don't you remember sweet Betsey from Pike,/ Who crossed the big mountains with her lover Ike,/ With two yoke of cattle, a large yellow dog,/ A tall shanghai rooster and one spotted hog." (c) And "Oh, what was your name in the States?/ Was it Thompson or Johnson or Bates?/ Did you murder your wife/ And fly for your life?/ Say, what was your name in the States?"

The lore of an age group: (a) the tale of a long-legged boy "sparking" a farmer's daughter when the hostile father came in with a shotgun; the boy jumped through a window and running across the cabbage patch scared up a rabbit; in about two leaps the boy caught up with the rabbit, kicked it high in the air, and grunted, "Git out of the road and let somebody run that knows how." (b) And the prank among schoolboys, called making a fellow walk "Spanish." "You catch him by the collar and the slack of his pants behind and make him step along on the tips of his toes, feeling very awkward and helpless," while the other fellows roll around on the ground, laughing their heads off.

The lore of working folks: (a) The flatboatmen on the big rivers with their hero, Mike Fink: "I'm a Salt River roarer! I'm a reg'lar screamer from the ol' Massassip'! I can out-run, out-jump, out-shoot, out-brag, an' out-fight ary man on both sides the river from Pittsburgh to New Orleans an' back ag'in to St. Louiee. Come on you bargers, you milk-white mechanics, I ain't had a fight for two days an' I'm spilein' for exercise. Cock-a-doodle-do!" (b) And the west Texas cowboys with their Pecos Bill, whose mother, a sturdy pioneer woman, had killed forty-five Indians with a broom-handle and weaned baby Bill on moonshine liquor when he was three days old. He cut his teeth on a bowie-knife, and his first playmates were bears and big catamounts. (c) And the Minnesota lumberjacks with their hero Paul Bunyan, who on the Fourth of July was upset when a big rain was about to spoil his party. He swam straight up through a solid pillar of rain and "turned the dam thing off."

The lore of religious folks: (a) As told by a black Baptist preacher: "De Methodiss, my bruddren, is like de grasshopper —hoppin', all de time hoppin'—hop into heaven, hop out, hop into heaven, hop out. But, my bruddren, de Baptiss, when he get to heaven, *he's dar*!" (b) And a Mormon as seen by a gentile: Buffalo Bill, Pawnee Bill, and Three Dollar Bill were out hunting an Indian war party that had captured a Mormon emigrant, his seventeen wives, and his fifty-one kids. "There they are," sings out one of the Bills. That night, Buffalo Bill slipped into camp, put the seventeen wives on his pony and started off for Ft. Hays, Kansas. Pawnee Bill gathered up the fifty-one kids on his pony and started after Buffalo Bill. Three Dollar Bill offered the same favor to the Mormon himself, but the old man was so happy over his capture—presumably since it freed him from seventeen wives and an army of kids —he chose to stay with the Indians.

The lore of folks who define themselves by their home place: (a) The Texan who sings, "Oh, give me a home where the buffalo roam,/ Where the deer and the antelope play,/ Where seldom is heard a discouraging word,/And the skies are not cloudy all day." And the other Texan who hollers, "With my tarantula boots made of alligator-skin, and my centipede hunting-shirt made of tanned rattlesnakes' hides, I have escaped pretty well, but these don't protect you against the stinging scorpions, 'cow killers,' and scaly-back chinches, that crawl about at night when you are asleep! The only way to keep them at a distance is to 'chaw' tobacco and drink whisky, and that is the reason the Temperance Society never flourished much in Texas." (b) Or the case of the Chicago gangster's funeral in Florida. When the coffin was opened at the grave-side to give all the mourners one final look and the beautiful Florida sunshine streamed in, up rose the corpse yelling his head off and feeling around for his gun. "The bystanders had to kill him again before they could go on with the funeral." (c) California's climate troubles: "It is so healthy we had to shoot a man in order to start a graveyard." (d) Or the Kentucky backwoodsman's dislike of the Yankee peddler: "You might as well try to hold a greased eel as a live Yankee."

The lore of folks that define themselves by reference to race: (a) Somebody killed a Chinaman and was brought before the white Texan Judge Roy Bean, who leafed through two or three law books, then turned the culprit loose, explaining that "he'd be damned if he could find any law against killing a Chinaman." (b) When Mike Fink, for target practice, shot off the heel of a barefooted black man, he crowed, to the great delight of his friends, "I've jest altered his breed, and arter this his posterity kin wear the neatest kind of a boot!" (c) Or the Florida rope-skipping rhyme: "Johnny gave me apples,/Johnny gave me pears,/Johnny gave me fifteen cents/And kissed me on the stairs./I'd rather wash the dishes,/I'd rather scrub the floor,/I'd rather kiss a nigger boy/Behind the kitchen door." (d) Or the Mississippi black's explanation of his skin color: "All folks was born black, an' dem what's turned white, dey jest had more sense," for when the Angel of the Lord came down and told all the people to go wash in the stream, most people just held back and laughed. The ones that rushed into the water came out white. The ones that held back either stayed black or were so slow slipping into the water that most of the water was gone. What was left was only enough to turn them light-colored in spots: the palms of their hands and the soles of their feet.

The lore of folks that define themselves by how much they know: (a) A fine city man with a brand-new buggy and a prizewinning team got lost on a country road. "Hello," he called to a boy chopping cotton nearby. "Where does this road go to?" "Hain't never seed it go nowhars," says the boy. "Well, then," calls the man, "how far is it to the next town?" "Don't know; never measured it." "You don't know anything," says the man; "you certainly are the biggest fool I ever saw." Boy gives a long look at the man. "I know I ain't lost." (b) Algernon McGoodle, the track star from Yale, came out to rest on an Arizona sheep ranch. The rancher told him to help round up the lambs. Algernon put in a hard day; but at sundown, the Yalie came to the house, panting, "I ran every one of those damn lambs back into the band every time they tried to get away." To the sheepman's howls of laughter, Al had brought in forty-seven jackrabbits and sixteen cottontails.

V

In perusing this big collection, you will quickly encounter the notion in Botkin that helped create the scholarly skirmish about him. "Whenever I have drawn upon professional storytellers and humorists," he remarks in a later folklore anthology,[14] "I have done so because they are good storytellers as well as folk artists." If his use of art/literature by Mark Twain, Joel Chandler Harris, and Washington Irving runs counter to the concept of folklore as "unwritten tradition," Botkin points out that in an age of print, even when originally oral, folklore "sooner or later finds it way into print and does not therefore cease to be folklore." In fact, Botkin declared, print may be the most accurate, true-to-the-folk way to capture and keep the wisdom and insights of "those who have gone before us." If professional, educated talents could record and express *this sense of the folk* especially clearly, so much the better for all. The *sense* of the folk was, in his view, the essential heart of the matter.

Such Botkin manifestoes as these fanned the sparks of dismay in his enemy's camp into flames. "What the state paper is to the historian and creative work to the literary scholar, the oral traditional text is—or should be—to the student of folklore," wrote Richard M. Dorson.[15] "Folklore" is spurious that is "transmitted largely by print, broadcasting, or other commercial and organized means," added Jan Harold Brunvand.[16] A scholar cannot discuss and appraise the aesthetics of oral style if the sources at his disposal mingle the spoken words of an informant with the written intrusions of an editor." Lacking the traditional text, painstakingly gathered and transcribed and/or recorded, fresh and verbatim, from the folk sources themselves, how could one know that "the beliefs and values revealed in folklore are accurate testimonials" of a given culture "if an alien hand has refined and 'improved the raw texts?' "[17]

And, Dorson continued, if a printed source is to be used at all by a legitimate specialist, it would have to pass many a test: "Is it analogous to field collected reports, does it come from a publication close to the grass roots, does its style indicate a spoken rather than a literary manner, is the purpose of the writer to report rather than to invent?"[18] If a piece or a collection of printed versions could not survive such a test, it could only be labeled "fakelore." Such a rhapsodic, undigested heap of materials was little more than a self-conscious effort to speak in the voice "not of the folk but of the mass culture."[19]

Over the years, Botkin himself became a rather celebrated cause among many folklorists who defined his terms and his field and his audience largely his way. Their enthusiasm for his *Treasury* and its later regional offshoots stemmed mostly from their recognizing an intention in Botkin, as observer of American "folk" life, that precise traditional analysts like Dorson and company could not accept.

Herbert Halpert, president of the American Folklore Society in 1955, spoke to this point in his presidential address. Among the several complaints that some scholar-folklorists voiced against Botkin, said Halpert, including the irritating fact that "so many non-folklorists enjoy his books," was his failure to be more specific about "what he is trying to do," about his interest in showing how folk themes bounce back and forth between print and oral tradition, in trying to show social history and social attitudes, and in analyzing the complex interplay between folklore, popular lore, and formal literature."[20]

It was a fact nevertheless, Halpert continued, that Botkin as a popularizer had put all professional folklorists into his debt for catching the imagination of many young people who later became graduate students in folklore. Just as significantly, Botkin had turned up unsuspected proof that folklore is as "fascinating to other people as it is to the specialist" and had interested publishers of popular books and magazines in feeding this new public's huge appetite "for the human qualities in folklore."[21]

Echoing the hoorays for Botkin, in 1966 Bruce Jackson's *Folklore and Society: Essays in Honor of Benj. A. Botkin* clarified an additional value that Botkin's theories of folk and folklore had served. "I'm not sure what is the cause—perhaps it is the competitiveness of the academic milieu—but there is a peculiar tendency for some humanities to try to be sciences,"[22] for imposing judgments upon human nature's mercurial quirks through means that could only apply to exact laboratory disciplines. "Of all the humanistic fields," Jackson declared, folklore should be "the last to lose contact with the real world, to get so enveloped in technology and terminology and theory that it has meaning only in relation to itself."[23] The final true value of folklore, Jackson continued, is that it tries not to freeze all the warmth of the voices of folks speaking through it but to let "them turn on enough of their own lights so we can see what they're doing, and from that perhaps infer why, and from that perhaps learn something about ourselves as well."[24] More than a matter of studying verbal structures and tale types and the provenance of subjects that scholars debate and write books about, folklore is, as Botkin said all along, "people saying things, doing things, playing, and making do."[25]

One note can be added to Jackson's encomiums: Botkin's including some pieces not yet accepted as folklore serves a useful purpose. Since "folklore," in Botkin's opinion, is always in process, that which is widely popular and that which reflects the tastes and the interests of "the mass culture" may well become "lore." Hence, his including the story of Tom Sawyer's fence-painting scheme.

To cite only a few possible examples out of our own time: Elvis Presley, John F. Kennedy, Martin Luther King, Jr., Bill Mauldin's Willie and Joe, Li'l Abner, Charlie Brown—these are types of the raw stuff, in this general sense, out of which authentic lore can develop. Just as the Casey Jones song, which Botkin includes as lore of railroading men, was once a writer's invention, so too may "Mighty Reggie," an Associated Press writer's invention in 1978, become lore of American baseball players and fans. In twelve four-line stanzas, the AP's anonymous poet details the tense moment during the 1978 World Series in Los Angeles when the Dodgers' rookie pitcher, Bob Welch, faced the Yankees' great batter, Reggie Jackson. The score stood 4–3, two out, one inning left to play, when "fifty thousand voices cheered, as Welch gripped ball in mitt. One hundred thousand eyes watched Reggie rub his bat and spit." Welch's first pitch was "a blazer. Reggie missed it clean." And "fifty thousand throats responded with a Dodger scream." Seven fastballs later, the count was three and two; "no shootout on a dusty street out here in the Far West could match the scene: a famous bat; a kid put to the test." And then the kid rears back, he lets a fastball fly. . . . For New York and Los Angeles, for Dodgers and Yankees, the final stanza says everything:

> "Ah, the lights still shine on Broadway,
>   but there isn't any doubt:
> The Big Apple has no joy left.
>   Mighty Reggie has struck out."[26]

VI

Except for one final point, this would seem a good note on which to conclude these remarks and to wish you godspeed in reading what lies ahead. That final point—Botkin's unique contributions—merits more than a glance. For one thing, in compiling his book, Botkin made certain that his editorial comments and footnote citations fully suggested valuable leads for other pursuers of American lore. For another, in bringing to light so many hundreds of items, he made available a rich trove of American cultural materials appropriate for many uses: for the schoolteacher needing new teaching resources, for the fiction writer needing authentic detail (character types, character traits, speech rhythms and diction, mannerisms, events), for the speech maker needing punch lines, for the historian needing fresh illustrations of the human side of his story, for the layman needing a sense of his American roots, for the tired business man needing a good book of jokes, and for anyone—of whatever slant and persuasion—wanting an occasional dip into folklore's version of truth and the human condition, which as *Time* magazine's Frank Trippett said recently, "is always handy to have around for nourishment and entertainment, in case the present goes dry."[27]

Beyond these needs what do these pages hold for the reader whom Botkin kept uppermost in his mind? The answer involves his major notion of American folk. If Botkin's book plumbs "the deepest springs of American yeoman culture," as Haldeen Braddy affirms that it does,[28] if John West is correct that the very essence of folklore study "has to be the folk," as well as the lore,[29] then one must, in reaching a verdict regarding Botkin's accomplishment, view askance the Dorson suggestion that *A Treasury of American Folklore* has no "philosophical unity." The fact is that the book does have a philosophical unity.

V.S. Pritchett, reviewing the London edition (*The American People in Their Satires, Legends, Tall Tales, Traditions, Ballads and Songs*) in 1946, recognized Botkin's "philosophical unity." In the United States it had long been clear, Pritchett declared, that conditions had been favorable to the making of a modern lore. "The waves of exploration, each leaving behind it a pungent wreckage on the new tide-mark, an epic quality in the life of the pioneer, the cowboy, the men of the gold rush, the miners, the builders of the transcontinental railways; the freedom from the restraints of a traditional culture"[30] have produced—perhaps to the surprise of the many-colored-many-tongued Americans themselves— a new *national* folk.

That new *national* American folk is the heart of Botkin's big book. To see that vast new national folk is to see a single folk group encompassing many smaller folk groups: the folk of a region, a state, a county, a city, a neighborhood, a cross-roads, a town block; the folk of a church, a parish, a work-shop, a campus, a playground, a team, a class in a schoolroom, a family.

Spotlighting this national folk that like a great hen gathers her little chicks under her wings, *A Treasury of American Folklore* becomes a vast mural of composite faces painted with many sorts of brush strokes and pigments, a blending of a mighty chorus of voices—all depicting one thing. Now streamlined a bit, the book's original worth for the 1940's may be renewed for us of the 1980's who, in our time and condition, resemble those readers more than a little. If any one thing above all makes any group self-aware, gives any one folk its sense of itself as coherent, vital, unique, that thing is danger and threat from outside. American folks of the 1980's do have their threats. Energy crises, rampant economic competition in the world markets, military threats in the Middle East and Afghanistan, the dollar's shrinking purchasing power abroad: such threatening dark clouds in our sky cause us, like Botkin's original readers, to ponder who we have been and are and will become.

Botkin points out that American society never became the world's great melting pot, stirring its human ethnic ingredients into one color and speech. Instead, he offers a folklorist's proof that American society has become a great folk—made up of folks. If we are hardly one nation under one god, we are a nation under one flag, the united folks of America. It is to this body of readers that Benjamin Botkin's *A Treasury of American Folklore* tells its story anew.

—JOSEPH LEACH

The University of Texas at El Paso
April 1, 1980

Part One

Heroes and Boasters

I

BACKWOODS BOASTERS

1. The "Irrepressible Backwoodsman"

HERO tales tell us more about a people than perhaps any other tales. For, as admirable or exceptional men, heroes embody the qualities that we most admire or desire in ourselves. So we begin with the heroes as our most potent folk symbols and most reliable touchstones of a people's "choice."

In every age heroes arise from a people's dream of greatness or from homage to the great and near-great. In other times and places heroes received their sanction from religion or mythology as they derived their being or their powers from a world other than our own. Lacking a body of true myth and ritual, Americans conceive of their heroes, save for vague demigods of the Paul Bunyan type, as strictly of this world, however much they may take us out of it.

In modern times, especially in a democracy, hero myths and hero worship have become inextricably mixed. From a universal need of models larger than life or "desire to be ruled by strength and ability," Americans choose or create heroes in their own image. In a complex industrial society, hero-making goes on at various levels, so that every walk of life and almost every occupation have their heroes. Essentially, however, American heroes are of three main types: the poor boy who makes good, the good boy gone wrong, and the kind that is too good or too bad to be true. Thus, on the one hand, the schoolbooks and popular literature of edification draw upon the ranks of leaders—explorers, pioneers, soldiers, statesmen, inventors, and industrialists—for patron saints and tutelary geniuses, to inspire love of country or teach the ethics of success. On the other hand, the dime-novel concealed behind the geography book glorifies the gentlemen on horseback and the demons with the six-shooter. Midway between these two extremes is an American fairyland of strong men and giants who perform the impossible.

A composite picture of the American hero would show him to be a plain, tough, practical fellow, equally good at a bargain or a fight, a star-performer on the job and a hell-raiser off it, and something of a salesman and a showman, with a flair for prodigious stories, jokes, and stunts and a general capacity for putting himself over. Our nearest approach to a national myth, explaining and justifying the many contradictions in our heroes, is the frontier or pioneer myth. This reconciles the primitive virtues of brute strength, courage, and cunning with the economic virtues of thrift, hard work, and perseverance.

The backwoodsman was the first of our tall men, whose words were tall talk and whose deeds were tall tales. Romantic fiction has made much of his fierce, wild courage and independence and his "rough diamond" chivalry as well as of his skill with the rifle. "That murderous weapon," wrote Audubon of the Kentucky hunters, "is the means of procuring them subsistence during all their wild and extensive rambles, and is the source of their principal sports and pleasures." It also brought them into national prominence in the Battle of New Orleans, January 8, 1815. "Tough as a hickory," these "coonskin voters" helped put "Old Hickory" in the White House thirteen years later. In May, 1822, seven years after the battle, before a New Orleans audience of stamping, clapping, whooping flatboatmen and keelboatmen (many of whom had fought under Jackson), Noah Ludlow, the comedian, sang a song which marked the passing of the backwoodsman from history into legend. This was "The Hunters of Kentucky." By this time, too, the backwoodsman had emerged into his later phases. Like Mike Fink, the hunter had become a riverman; and beyond the Mississippi, following his free, wild way of living, he was to revert once more, like Mike Fink, to hunting and trapping.

In pursuit of game, skins, scalps, land, or adventure, the backwoodsman followed the shifting fringe of settlement, marching ahead of civilization or running away from it. As a picaresque type, the footloose adventurer, he illustrates what Lucy Lockwood Hazard calls the "dwindling of the hero," from the godlike or kinglike to the average human and subhuman level.

2. THE LION OF THE WEST

More and more, as the country was settled, the backwoods-man's motto became, in the words of the picaresque Simon Suggs, "It is good for a man to be shifty in a new country." To be shifty in a new country meant beating the other fellow to it. For a society that cannot support a large population puts a premium on outdoing—out-running, out-licking, and out-hollering—one's neighbor. Men with the bark on must also be men of gumption and gusto, who could talk, as well as walk, tall into and out of scrapes, rows, and sprees.

Boasting—the epic brag—has always been part of the trappings of the hero. The strong man of the Beowulf type or the medieval knight would gird himself for combat and inspire confidence in his followers by rehearsing his exploits in big talk. In his "paradise of puffers," however, the backwoods boaster tended to boast in terms of the future rather than of the past, and seemed more interested in making claims than in living up to them. Moreover, since boasting, like bombast, contains in itself the seeds of its own travesty, it became hard to distinguish bragging from windy laughing at bragging and serious from mock or burlesque boasts.

From his noise the boaster became known as a roarer or screamer. Because the qualities of the horse and the alligator seemed most fitting to the animal antics and noises of the ring-tailed roarer, the alligator horse or half-horse, half-alligator became his emblem. "It is an old remark," writes Washington Irving, "that persons of Indian mixture are half civilized, half savage, and half devil—a third half being provided for their particular convenience. It is for similar reasons, and probably with equal truth, that the backwoodsmen of Kentucky are styled half man, half horse, and half alligator, by the settlers on the Mississippi, and held accordingly in great respect and abhorrence."[1] Perhaps the best literary description we have of the strange breed in action is Robert Montgomery Bird's por-trayal of the Salt River roarer,[2] Roaring Ralph Stackpole, rascally horse thief and stentorian braggart, in *Nick of the Woods* (1837).

Like the first successful Yankee character—Jonathan, in Royall Tyler's *The Contrast* (1787)—the first full-length por-trait of the ring-tailed roarer was a stage creation. This was Colonel Nimrod Wildfire, the hero of James K. Paulding's

lost prize-play, *The Lion of the West*,[3] which was produced
at the Park Theatre, New York City, on April 25, 1831. The
rôle of Colonel Wildfire, "a raw Kentuckian recently elected
to Congress," was created by James J. Hackett, the "rising
young comedian" and donor of the prize, who was also responsible for the names of the play and the hero. Wildfire was
acclaimed as a contribution to the gallery of native American
types (along with Hackett's Solomon Swap), and, through
two rewritings of the play over a period of twenty years, remained one of the most successful rôles of the actor's career.

The one surviving speech of the play appears in several
newspaper, almanac, and jokebook versions, attributed now
to Colonel Wildfire and now to the meteoric Davy Crockett,
who in 1831 was nearing the end of his second term in Congress. According to Paulding's son and biographer, the play-
wright disclaimed any intention of a take-off of that "well-
known personage,"[4] eliciting from him the following reply:

Washington City, 22nd Decr. 1830.

Sir your letter of the 15 Inst was handed to me this day by my
friend Mr. Wilde—the newspaper publications to which you refer
I have never seen; and if I had I should not have taken the reference
to myself in exclusion of many who fill offices and who are as untaught as I am. I thank you however for your civility in assuring
me that you had no reference to my peculiarites. The frankness of
your letter induces me to say a declaration from you to that effect
was not necessary to convince me that you were incapable of
wounding the feelings of a strainger and unlettered man who had
never injured you—your charecter for letters and as a gentleman is
not altogethar unknown to me.

I have the honor with
great respects &c—
DAVID CROCKETT.[5]

Whatever Paulding's intentions, the actor's interpretation
and the public's acceptance of Wildfire must have profited by
the resemblance between the two lions of the West, even to
Crockett's taking a bow at a performance of the play. Thus
the wood-engraving of Crockett on the cover of the 1837
almanac is virtually indistinguishable from the cut of Hackett
in the rôle of Wildfire.[6] Following the Crockett version of the
Wildfire speech, the author of the *Sketches and Eccentricities
of Col. David Crockett, of West Tennessee* (1833), has this
to say of the play:

This scene, with some slight alteration, has been attributed I understand to an imaginary character, Colonel Wildfire. This I have not seen. But I am unwilling that the *hard earnings* of Crockett should be given to another.

Such curious coincidences and correspondences illustrate the way in which folklore becomes mixed with life and literature, and also point to the fact that many Crockett stories may have had their source in current anecdotes and been identified with other characters.

3. DAVY CROCKETT

If the prevailing rusticity of American folk heroes may be said to constitute one of their chief attractions, then none of them is more attractive than Davy Crockett, the prime example of the country boy who made good. "Crockett was rude and uncouth," writes one of his admirers, "but honest and heroic. To the homely sense of the backwoodsman, he joined a spirit as brave and chivalrous as any that followed the banner of the Black Prince against the infidel."[7] His rise to fame serves as a peg on which to hang the moral, "You can't keep a good man down."

It is certainly a very curious phase of American and especially of western character, which is exhibited in the ease and promptness with which the colonel passes from one act of the singular drama of his life to another. Yesterday a rough bear-hunter, today, a member of the legislature, to-morrow about to become a member of Congress, and the fearless opponent of his old commander, General Jackson.

Such sudden and successful advances in life are scarcely seen except in our own country, where perfect freedom opens a boundless field to enterprise and perseverance.[8]

Although in his own day Crockett's name was a household word for his jokes as well as his achievements, the image of the "Colonel" that endures to-day is not that of a national political figure or the martyr of the Alamo but that of the comic backwoodsman. While historians of the American epic may, with Frank Norris, deplore the fact that "Crockett is the hero only of a 'funny story' about a sagacious coon,"[9] the epic's loss is humor's gain. The transformation of this prototype of the forks-of-the-creek philosopher and grass-roots politician into the archetype of the protean, wandering, legendary, American hero of the Munchausen-Eulenspiegel breed is an important and fascinating chapter in the annals of American hero-making.

In the "gentleman from the cane" the ring-tailed roarer is superimposed upon the comic backwoodsman, who is essentially the droll Yankee with more guts and gusto and less guile, to become the "gamecock of the wilderness." Because of his many-sidedness, his lively, humorous, homespun figure has supplanted the romantic frontiersman of the Daniel Boone type as the "heroic version of the poor-white," and rivals many another American hero. Thus, in his gumption he outdoes his older contemporary, Mike Fink, whom he resembles as game-hog and Indian-fighter but to whose tough guy he plays the smart aleck among backwoods boasters. In his rôle of cracker-box philosopher and story-telling politician, the coonskin Congressman anticipates Lincoln, although with Crockett story-telling was a business rather than an art—the business of being a wag and a good fellow.

While electioneering, the colonel always conciliates every crowd into which he may be thrown by the narration of some anecdote. It is his manner, more than the anecdote, which delights you. . . .

Pursuing this course, he laughs away any prejudice which may exist against him; and having created a favourable impression, enforces his claims by local arguments, showing the bearing which great national questions have upon the interests of the persons whom he wishes to represent. This mode, together with the faculty of being a boon companion to every one he meets, generally enables him to accomplish his object.[10]

The anecdotes of Crockett's Washington adventures show the "irrepressible backwoodsman" playing up to the accepted notion of himself as the rustic wag and wisecracker, a rôle in which he seems to have been the victim partly of his own ambition and good nature and partly of the designs of political friends and foes. Yet in his speeches in Congress, where he served three terms between 1827 and 1835, he is a sincere, plain-spoken champion of the people, with an occasional stroke of hard-hitting sarcasm:

Sirs, I do not consider it good sense to be sitting here passing laws for Andrew Jackson to laugh at; it is not even good nonsense . . . out of those that the President has got about him, I have never seen but one honest countenance since I have been here, and he has just resigned.[11]

In the autobiographical comic prose epics ascribed to him (1833–1836), he becomes "our first Southern humorist." From now on, laughter gains the ascendancy, and horse sense gives way to horseplay. Posthumously, he plays the buffoon in the "Crockett" almanacs (1835–1856), where his heroics are swallowed up in slapstick and hokum. Hoax, legend, myth, and caricature, he thus runs the gamut from the poor but honest farmer who made good by his own wits and go-aheadativeness ("Be sure you are always right, then go ahead") to the demigod who "totes the thunder in his fist and flings the lightning from his fingers." Somewhere between these two extremes the real Crockett has been lost. Even the stock figure of the backwoods bully and boaster yields to the riproaring superman of the jokebooks, whose tedium is relieved by an occasional flash of vernacular prose poetry and comic sublimity, as in "Crockett's Morning Hunt." Folk memories of Crockett linger in occasional hunting yarns of the South.[12]

Throughout the following sketches Crockett is essentially the hunter in pursuit of ever bigger and better game, from varmints and politicians to the challenging elements. Nowhere is backwoods mythology more alive than in Crockett's encounters with his animal friends and foes, in which Crockett is half-varmint and every varmint is half-Crockett.

4. MIKE FINK

In one of the Crockett almanacs we read of a shooting match between Crockett and Mike Fink ("a helliferocious fellow" and "an almighty fine shot"), in which the former lost by default. First, Crockett aimed at a cat sitting on the top rail of Mike's potato patch at a distance of about a hundred and fifty yards, and "the ball cut off both the old tom cat's ears close to his head, and shaved the hair off clean across the skull, as slick as if I'd done it with a razor, and the critter never stirred, nor knew he'd lost his ears till he tried to scratch 'em." Next, Mike aimed at a sow with a litter of pigs around her, "away off furder than the eend of the world" and kept "loading and firing for dear life, till he hadn't left one of them pigs enough tail to make a toothpick on." Then Crockett mended Mike's shot, which had left one of the pigs about an inch of tail, and cut it off as if it "had been drove in with a hammer."

That made Mike a kinder sorter wrothy, and he sends a ball after his wife as she was going to the spring after a gourd full of water, and knocked half her comb out of her head, without stirring a hair, and calls out to her to stop for me to take a blizzard at what was left on it. The angeliferous critter stood still as a scarecrow in a cornfield, for she'd got used to Mike's tricks by long practice.

"No, no, Mike," sez I, "Davy Crockett's hand would be sure to shake if his iron war pointed within a hundred mile of a shemale, and I give up beat, Mike."

These feats of markmanship are in the true Mike Fink tradition, which ranged from driving nails with bullets to shooting tin cups and scalp locks from heads. Mike's unique claim to fame among deadshots lay in the fact that most of his shooting wagers were sadistic pranks. For as a bully and cut-up hell-bent for fun Mike had more in common with the pseudo bad men of the West than he had with the river pirates and common ruffians among whom he moved. Unlike the frontier rascals who thought that "even a crime might take on the aspect of a good joke," Mike was one to carry a joke to the point of being a crime. He was quite impartial in his choice of victims, shooting off a Negro's heel because he disliked its shape or forcing his woman to lie down in a pile of leaves to which he set fire, to cure her of looking at other men.

Born of Scotch-Irish parents at old Fort Pitt in 1770, Mike Fink in his youth acquired a reputation as an Indian scout and the best shot in Pittsburgh. As the country filled up and the Indians were pushed across the Lakes and beyond the Mississippi, wrote Morgan Neville, in "The Last of the Boatmen" (1829), many of the scouts, "from a strong attachment to their erratic mode of life, joined the boatmen, then just becoming a distinct class." Among them he soon distinguished himself not only as the "king of the keelboatmen," known as the Snag on the Mississippi and the Snapping Turtle on the Ohio, but also as the "demigod of the rivers," in whom according the Bernard DeVoto, "Casanova, together with Paul Bunyan, merges into Thor."[13]

It was the perpetual fight of the boatmen with the river that made them "reckless savages." Among the various types of river craft the keelboat offered the greatest challenge to the boatman's strength, skill, and endurance.

In ascending the river, it was a continued series of toil, rendered more irksome by the snail like rate, at which they moved. The boat was propelled by poles, against which the shoulder was placed; and the whole strength and skill of the individual was applied in this manner. As the boatmen moved along the running board, with their heads nearly touching the plank on which they walked, the effect produced on the mind of an observer was similar to that on beholding the ox, rocking before an overloaded cart. Their bodies, naked to their waist, for the purpose of moving with greater ease, and of enjoying the breeze of the river, were exposed to the burning suns of summer, and to the rain of autumn. After a hard day's push, they would take their "fillee," or ration of whisky, and having swallowed a miserable supper of meat half burnt, and of bread half baked, stretch themselves without covering, on the deck, and slumber till the steersman's call invited them to the morning "fillee." Notwithstanding this, the boatman's life had charms as irresistible as those presented by the splendid illusions of the stage. Sons abandoned the comfortable farms of their fathers, and apprentices fled from the service of their masters. There was a captivation in the idea of "going down the river"; and the youthful boatman who had "pushed a keel" from New Orleans, felt all the pride of a young merchant after his first voyage to an English sea port. From an exclusive association together, they had formed a kind of slang peculiar to themselves; and from the constant exercise of wit, with the "squatters" on shore, and the crews of other boats, they acquired a quickness, and smartness of vulgar retort, that was quite amusing. The frequent battles they were engaged in with the boatmen of different parts of the river, and with the less civilized inhabitants of the lower Ohio, and Mississippi, invested them with that ferocious reputation, which has made them spoken of throughout Europe.[14]

In the same year that Noah Ludlow introduced "The Hunters of Kentucky" to the people of New Orleans, Mike Fink became one of Ashley's men in the service of the Mountain Fur Company. For, as the supremacy of the steamboat was established, the flatboatmen and keelboatmen turned to other fields. Some went to work on the steamboats, others became raftsmen, and still others like Mike Fink joined the trapping and trading expeditions that crossed the Rockies. At Fort Henry in Montana this champion marksman, fighter, drinker, lover, boaster, and jester was "killed in a skrimmage," in which his various types of prowess were called into play.

The Hunters of Kentucky*

Hunters of Kentucky.

1. Ye gentlemen and ladies fair who grace this famous city, Just
2. We are a hardy freeborn race, each man to fear a stranger, What-

lis - ten if you've time to spare, while I rehearse a dit - ty; And
e'er the game, we join in chase, despising toil and dan - ger, And

for an op-por - tu - ni - ty, conceive yourselves quite lucky, For
if a daring foe an-noys, whate'er his strength and forces, We'll

'tis not often here you see a hun-ter from Ken-tucky,
show him that Kentucky boys are "al-li - ga - tor horses."

O Ken-tuck-y, the hunters of Ken-tuck-y.
O Ken-tuck-y, '&c.

O Ken-tuck-y, the hun-ters of Ken - tuck-y.

Facsimile from *The Amateur's Song Book*, Boston, 1843.

---

* From *Melodies, Duets, Trios, Songs, and Ballads, Pastoral, Amatory, Sentimental, Patriotic, Religious, and Miscellaneous.* Together with Metrical Epistles, Tales and Recitations, by Samuel Woodworth, pp. 221–223. New York: James M. Campbell. 1826.

11

I s'pose you've read it in the prints,
　　How Packenham attempted
To make Old Hickory Jackson wince,
　　But soon his scheme repented;
For we with rifles ready cock'd,
　　Thought such occasion lucky,
And soon around the General flock'd
　　The hunters of Kentucky.
　　　　Oh! Kentucky, &c.

You've heard, I s'pose, how New-Orleans
　　Is famed for wealth and beauty—
There's girls of every hue, it seems,
　　From snowy white to sooty;
So Packenham he made his brags,
　　If he in fight was lucky,
He'd have their girls and cotton bags,
　　In spite of Old Kentucky.
　　　　Oh! Kentucky, &c.

But JACKSON, he was wide awake,
　　And wasn't scared at trifles;
For well he knew what aim we take,
　　With our Kentucky rifles;
So he led us down to Cypress swamp,
　　The ground was low and mucky;
There stood John Bull, in martial pomp,
　　And here was Old Kentucky.
　　　　Oh! Kentucky, &c.

A bank was raised to hide our breast,
　　Not that we thought of dying,
But then we always like to rest,
　　Unless the game is flying;
Behind it stood our little force—
　　None wished it to be greater,
For every man was half a horse,
　　And half an alligator.
　　　　Oh! Kentucky, &c.

They did not let our patience tire,
　　Before they showed their faces—
We did not choose to waste our fire,
　　So snugly kept our places;

But when so near we saw them wink,
　　We thought it time to stop them;
And 'twould have done you good, I think,
　　To see Kentucky pop them.
　　　　Oh! Kentucky, &c.

They found at last 'twas vain to fight
　　Where lead was all their booty,
And so they wisely took to flight,
　　And left us all the beauty.
And now, if danger e'er annoys,
　　Remember what our trade is,
Just send for us Kentucky boys,
　　And we'll protect you, Ladies.
　　　　Oh! Kentucky, &c.

Roaring Ralph Stackpole*

"CUNNEL," said he, "you're a man in authority, and my superior officer; wharfo' thar' can be no scalping between us. But my name's Tom Dowdle, the rag-man!" he screamed, suddenly skipping into the thickest of the throng, and sounding a note of defiance; "my name's Tom Dowdle, the rag-man, and I'm for any man that insults me! log-leg or leather-breeches, green-shirt or blanket-coat, land-trotter or river-roller,—I'm the man for a massacree!" Then giving himself a twirl upon his foot that would have done credit to a dancing-master, he proceeded to other antic demonstrations of hostility, which when performed in after years on the banks of the Lower Mississippi, by himself and his worthy imitators, were, we suspect, the cause of their receiving the name of the mighty alligator. It is said, by naturalists, of this monstrous reptile, that he delights, when the returning warmth of spring has brought his fellows from their holes, and placed them basking along the banks of a swampy lagoon, to dart into the centre of the expanse, and challenge the whole field to combat. He roars, he blows the water from his nostrils, he lashes

---

* From *Nick of the Woods, or The Jibbenainosay, A Tale of Kentucky*, by Robert Montgomery Bird, Vol. I, pp. 58–59. Philadelphia: Carey, Lea & Blanchard. 1837.

it with his tail, he whirls round and round, churning the water into foam; until, having worked himself into a proper fury, he darts back again to the shore, to seek an antagonist. Had the gallant captain of horse-thieves boasted the blood, as he afterwards did the name, of an "alligator half-breed," he could scarce have conducted himself in a way more worthy of his parentage. He leaped into the centre of the throng, where, having found elbow-room for his purpose, he performed the gyration mentioned before, following it up by other feats expressive of his hostile humor. He flapped his wings and crowed, until every chanticleer in the settlement replied to the note of battle; he snorted and neighed like a horse; he bellowed like a bull; he barked like a dog; he yelled like an Indian; he whined like a panther; he howled like a wolf; until one would have thought he was a living menagerie, comprising within his single body the spirit of every animal noted for its love of conflict. Then, not content with such a display of readiness to fight the field, he darted from the centre of the area allowed him for his exercise, and invited the lookers-on individually to battle. "Whar's your buffalo-bull," he cried, "to cross horns with the roarer of Salt River? Whar's your full-blood colt that can shake a saddle off? H'yar's an old nag can kick off the top of a buck-eye! Whar's your cat of the Knobs? your wolf of the Rolling Prairies? H'yar's the old brown b'ar can claw the bark off a gum-tree! H'yar's a man for you, Tom Bruce! Same to you, Sim Roberts! to you, Jimmy Big-nose! to you, and to you, and to you! Ar'n't I a ring-tailed squealer? Can go down Salt on my back, and swim up the Ohio! Whar's the man to fight Roaring Ralph Stackpole?"

A Vote for Crockett*

"I HAD taken old Betsy," said he, "and straggled off to the banks of the Mississippi river; and meeting with no game, I didn't like it. I felt mighty wolfish about the head and ears, and thought I would spile if I wasn't kivured up in salt, for I hadn't had a fight in ten days; and I cum acrost a fellow floatin' down stream settin' in the stern of his boat fast asleep.

---

* From *Sketches and Eccentricities of Col. David Crockett, of West Tennessee*, pp. 44–145. New York: Printed and Published by J. & J. Harper. 1833.

Said I, 'Hello, stranger! if you don't take keer your boat will run away with you'—and he looked up; and said he, 'I don't value you.' He looked up at me slantendicler, and I looked down upon him slantendicler; and he took out a chaw of turbaccur, and said he, 'I don't value you that.' Said I, 'Cum ashore, I can whip you—I've been trying to git a fight all the mornin' '; and the varmint flapped his wings and crowed like a chicken. I ris up, shook my mane, and neighed like a horse. He run his boat plump head foremost ashore. I stood still and sot my triggurs, that is, took off my shurt, and tied my galluses around my waist—and at it we went. He was a right smart coon, but hardly a bait for such a fellur as me. I put it to him mighty droll. In ten minutes he yelled enough, and swore I was a ripstavur. Said I, 'Ain't I the yaller flower of the forest! And I am all brimstone but the head and ears, and that's aquafortis.' Said he, 'Stranger, you are a beauty: and if I know'd your name, I'd vote for you next election.' Said I, 'I'm that same David Crockett. You know what I'm made of. I've got the closest shootin' rifle, the best 'coon dog, the biggest ticlur, and the ruffest racking horse in the district. I can kill more lickur, fool more varmints, and cool out more men than any man you can find in all Kentucky.' Said he, 'Good mornin', stranger—I'm satisfied.' Said I, 'Good mornin', sir; I feel much better since our meetin' '; but after I got away a piece, I said, "Hello, friend, don't forget that vote.' "

The Ballad of Davy Crockett*

Now, don't you want to know some — thing con-cern-in'
Where it was I come from and where I got my learn-in? Oh, the
world is made of mud out o' the Mis-sis-sip-pi Riv-er! The

* From *American Ballads and Folk Songs*, collected and compiled by John A. Lomax and Alan Lomax, pp. 251–253. Copyright, 1934, by The Macmillan Company. New York. Adapted from "The Ballad of Davy Crockett," by Julia Beazley, in *Texas and Southwestern Lore*, Publications of the Texas Folk-Lore Society, Number VI (1927), edited by J. Frank Dobie, pp. 205–206.

sun's a ball of fox-fire, as well you may dis-civ-er.

Chorus

Take the la-dies out at night. They shine so bright They

make the world light when the moon is out of sight.

And so one day as I was goin' a-spoonin'
I met Colonel Davy, and he was goin' a-coonin'.
Says I, "Where's your gun?" "I ain' got none."
"How you goin' kill a coon when you haven't got a gun?"

Says he, "Pompcalf, just follow after Davy,
And he'll soon show you how to grin a coon crazy."
I followed on a piece and thar sot a squirrel,
A-settin' on a log and a-eatin' sheep sorrel.

When Davy did that see, he looked around at me,
Saying, "All I want now is a brace agin your knee."
And thar I braced a great big sinner.
He grinned six times hard enough to git his dinner!

The critter on the log didn't seem to mind him—
Jest kep' a-settin' thar and wouldn't look behind him.
Then it was he said, "The critter must be dead.
See the bark a-flyin' all around the critter's head?"

I walked right up the truth to disciver.
Drot! It was a pine knot so hard it made me shiver.
Says he, "Pompcalf, don't you begin to laugh—
I'll pin back your ears, and bite you half in half!"

I flung down my gun and all my ammunition.
Says I, "Davy Crockett, I can cool your ambition!"
He throwed back his head and he blowed like a steamer.
Says he, "Pompcalf, I'm a Tennessee screamer!"

Then we locked horns and we wallered in the thorns.
I never had such a fight since the hour I was born.
We fought a day and a night and then agreed to drop it.
I was purty badly whipped—and so was Davy Crockett.

I looked all around and found my head a-missin'—
He'd bit off my head and I had swallered his'n!
Then we did agree to let each other be;
I was too much for him, and he was too much for me.

The Coon-Skin Trick*

WHILE on the subject of election matters, I will just relate a little anecdote about myself, which will show the people to the East how we manage these things on the frontiers. It was when I first run for Congress; I was then in favor of the Hero [Andrew Jackson], for he had chalked out his course so sleek in his letter to the Tennessee legislature that, like Sam Patch, says I, "There can be no mistake in him," and so I went ahead. No one dreamt about the monster and the deposits at that time, and so, as I afterward found, many like myself were taken in by these fair promises, which were worth about as much as a flash in the pan when you have a fair shot at a fat bear.

But I am losing sight of my story. Well, I started off to the Cross Roads dressed in my hunting shirt, and my rifle on my shoulder. Many of our constituents had assembled there to get a taste of the quality of the candidates at orating. Job Snelling, a gander-shanked Yankee, who had been caught somewhere about Plymouth Bay, and been shipped to the West with a cargo of codfish and rum, erected a large shantee, and set up shop for the occasion. A large posse of the voters had assembled before I arrived, and my opponent had already made considerable headway with his speechifying and his treating, when they spied me about a rifle shot from camp, sauntering along as if I was not a party in business. "There comes Crockett," cried one. "Let us hear the colonel," cried another; and so I mounted the stump that had been cut down for the occasion, and began to bushwhack in the most approved style.

I had not been up long before there was such an uproar in the crowd that I could not hear my own voice, and some of my constituents let me know that they could not listen to me on such a dry subject as the welfare of the nation until they had something to drink, and that I must treat them. Accordingly I jumped down from the rostrum, and led the way to the shantee, followed by my constituents, shouting, "Huzza for Crockett!" and "Crockett forever!"

When we entered the shantee Job was busy dealing out his rum in a style that showed he was making a good day's work

* From *Life of Colonel David Crockett*, Written by Himself, pp. 240–245. Philadelphia: G. G. Evans. 1860.

of it, and I called for a quart of the best; but the crooked crittur returned no other answer than by pointing to a board over the bar, on which he had chalked in large letters, *"Pay to-day and trust to-morrow."* Now that idea brought me up all standing; it was a sort of cornering in which there was no back-out, for ready money in the West, in those times, was the shyest thing in all natur, and it was most particularly shy with me on that occasion.

The voters, seeing my predicament, fell off to the other side, and I was left deserted and alone, as the Government will be, when he no longer has any offices to bestow. I saw as plain as day that the tide of popular opinion was against me, and that unless I got some rum speedily I should lose my election as sure as there are snakes in Virginny; and it must be done soon, or even burnt brandy wouldn't save me. So I walked away from the shantee, but in another guess sort from the way I entered it, for on this occasion I had no train after me, and not a voice shouted, "Huzza for Crockett!" Popularity sometimes depends on a very small matter indeed; in this particular it was worth a quart of New England rum, and no more.

Well, knowing that a crisis was at hand, I struck into the woods, with my rifle on my shoulder, my best friend in time of need; and, as good fortune would have it, I had not been out more than a quarter of an hour before I treed a fat coon, and in the pulling of a trigger he lay dead at the foot of the tree. I soon whipped his hairy jacket off his back, and again bent my steps towards the shantee, and walked up to the bar, but not alone, for this time I had half a dozen of my constituents at my heels. I threw down the coon-skin upon the counter, and called for a quart, and Job, though busy dealing out rum, forgot to point at his chalked rules and regulations; for he knew that a coon was as good a legal tender for a quart in the West as a New York shilling any day in the year.

My constituents now flocked about me, and cried, "Huzza for Crockett!" "Crockett forever!" and finding the tide had taken a turn, I told them several yarns to get them in a good humor; and having soon dispatched the value of the coon, I went out and mounted the stump without opposition, and a clear majority of the voters followed me to hear what I had to offer for the good of the nation. Before I was half through one of my constituents moved that they would hear the balance of my speech after they had washed down the first part with some more of Job Snelling's extract of cornstalk and molasses, and the question being put, it was carried unanimously. It wasn't considered necessary to tell the yeas and nays, so we adjourned to the shantee, and on the way I began to reckon that the fate of the nation pretty much depended upon my shooting another coon.

While standing at the bar, feeling sort of bashful while Job's rules and regulations stared me in the face, I cast down my eyes, and discovered one end of the coon-skin sticking between the logs that supported the bar. Job had slung it there in the hurry of business. I gave it a sort of quick jerk, and it followed my hand as natural as if I had been the rightful owner. I slapped it on the counter, and Job, little dreaming that he was barking up the wrong tree, shoved along another bottle, which my constituents quickly disposed of with great good humor, for some of them saw the trick; and then we withdrew to the rostrum to discuss the affairs of the nation.

I don't know how it was, but the voters soon became dry again, and nothing would do but we must adjourn to the shantee; and as luck would have it, the coon-skin was still sticking between the logs, as if Job had flung it there on purpose to tempt me. I was not slow in raising it to the counter, the rum followed, of course, and I wish I may be shot if I didn't, before the day was over, get ten quarts for the same identical skin, and from a fellow, too, who in those parts was considered as sharp as a steel trap and as bright as a pewter button.

This joke secured me my election, for it soon circulated like smoke among my constituents, and they allowed, with one accord, that the man who could get the whip hand of Job Snelling in fair trade, could outwit Old Nick himself, and was the real grit for them in Congress. Job was by no means popular; he boasted of always being wide awake, and that any one who could take him in was free to do so, for he came from a stock that, sleeping or waking, had always one eye open, and the other not more than half closed. The whole family were geniuses. His father was the inventor of wooden nutmegs, by which Job said he might have made a fortune, if he had only taken out a patent and kept the business in his own hands; his mother, Patience, manufactured the first white oak pumpkin seeds of the mammoth kind, and turned a pretty penny the first season; and his aunt Prudence was the first to discover that corn husks, steeped into tobacco water, would make as handsome Spanish wrappers as ever came from Havana, and that oak leaves would answer all the purpose of filling, for no one could discover the difference except the man who smoked them, and then it would be too late to make a stir about it. Job himself bragged of having made some useful discoveries, the most profitable of which was the art of converting mahogany sawdust into cayenne pepper, which he said was a profitable and safe business; for the people have been so long accustomed to having dust thrown in their eyes that there wasn't much danger of being found out.

The way I got to the blind side of the Yankee merchant was pretty generally known before election day, and the result was that my opponent might as well have whistled jigs to a milestone as attempt to beat up for votes in that district. I beat him out and out, quite back into the old year, and there was scarce enough left of him, after the canvass was over, to make a small grease spot. He disappeared without even leaving a mark behind; and such will be the fate of Adam Huntsman, if there is a fair fight and no gouging.

After the election was over, I sent Snelling the price of the rum, but took good care to keep the fact from the knowledge of my constituents. Job refused the money, and sent me word that it did him good to be taken in occasionally, as it served to brighten his ideas; but I afterwards learnt when he found out the trick that had been played upon him, he put all the rum I had ordered in his bill against my opponent, who, being elated with the speeches he had made on the affairs of the nation, could not descend to examine into the particulars of a bill of a vendor of rum in the small way.

Speech of Colonel Crockett in Congress*

"MR. SPEAKER.

Who—Who—Whoop—Bow—Wow—Wow—Yough. I say, Mr. Speaker; I've had a speech in soak this six months, and it has swelled me like a drowned horse; if I don't deliver it I shall burst and smash the windows. The gentleman from Massachusetts [Mr. Everett] talks of summing up the merits of the question, but I'll sum up my own. In one word I'm a screamer, and have got the roughest racking horse, the pret-

---

* From *Davy Crockett's Almanac, of Wild Sports in the West, Life in the Backwoods, & Sketches of Texas*, Vol. I, No. 3, 1837, p. 40. Nashville, Tennessee: Published by the heirs of Col. Crockett.

tiest sister, the surest rifle and the ugliest dog in the district. I'm a leetle the savagest crittur you ever *did see*. My father can whip any man in Kentucky, and I can lick my father. I can outspeak any man on this floor, and give him two hours start. I can run faster, dive deeper, stay longer under, and come out drier, than any *chap* this side the big *Swamp*. I can outlook a panther and outstare a flash of lightning, tote a steamboat on my back and play at rough and tumble with a lion, and an occasional kick from a *zebra*. To sum up all in one word *I'm a horse*. Goliah was a pretty hard colt but I could choke him. I can take the rag off—frighten the old folks—astonish the natives—and beat the Dutch all to smash —make nothing of sleeping under a blanket of snow—and don't mind being frozen more than a rotten apple.

"Congress allows *lemonade* to the members and has it charged under the head of stationery—I move also that *whiskey* be allowed under the item of *fuel*. For *bitters* I can suck away at a noggin of aquafortis, sweetened with brimstone, stirred with a lightning rod, and skimmed with a hurricane. I've soaked my head and shoulders in Salt River, so much that I'm always corned. I can walk like an ox, run like a fox, swim like an eel, yell like an Indian, fight like a devil, spout like an earthquake, make love like a mad bull, and swallow a nigger whole without choking if you butter his head and pin his ears back."

Crockett's Morning Hunt*

ONE January morning it was so all-screwen-up cold that the forest trees war so stiff that they couldn't shake, and the very day-break froze fast as it war tryin' to dawn. The tinder-box in my cabin would no more ketch fire than a sunk raft at the bottom o' the sea. Seein' that daylight war so far behind time, I thought creation war in a fair way for freezin' fast.

"So," thinks I, "I must strike a leetle fire from my fingers, light my pipe, travel out a few leagues, and see about it."

Then I brought my knuckles together like two thunder clouds, but the sparks froze up afore I could begin to collect 'em—so out I walked, and endeavored to keep myself unfriz

---

* From *Davy Crockett, American Comic Legend*, selected and edited by Richard M. Dorson, pp. 16–17. Copyright, 1939, by Rockland Editions. New York. Reprinted from the 1854 Crockett Almanac (New York, Cozans).

by goin' at a hop, step and jump gait, and whistlin' the tune of "fire in the mountains!" as I went along in three double quick time. Well, arter I had walked about twenty-five miles up the peak o' Daybreak Hill, I soon discovered what war the matter. The airth had actually friz fast in her axis, and couldn't turn round; the sun had got jammed between two cakes o' ice under the wheels, an' thar he had bin shinin' and workin' to get loose, till he friz fast in his cold sweat.

"C-r-e-a-t-i-o-n!" thought I, "this are the toughest sort o' suspension, and it mustn't be endured—somethin' must be done, or human creation is done for."

It war then so antedeluvian and premature cold that upper and lower teeth an' tongue war all collapsed together as tight as a friz oyster. I took a fresh twenty pound bear off o' my back that I'd picked up on the road, an' beat the animal agin the ice till the hot ile began to walk out on him at all sides. I then took an' held him over the airth's axes, an' squeezed him till I thaw'd 'em loose, poured about a ton on it over the sun's face, give the airth's cog-wheel one kick backward, till I got the sun loose—whistled "Push along, keep movin'!" an' in about fifteen seconds the airth gin a grunt, and begun movin' —the sun walked up beautiful, salutin' me with sich a wind o' gratitude that it made me sneeze. I lit my pipe by the blaze o' his top-knot, shouldered my bear, an' walked home, introducin' the people to fresh daylight with a piece of sunrise in my pocket, with which I cooked my bear steaks, an' enjoyed one o' the best breakfasts I had tasted for some time. If I didn't, jist wake some mornin' and go with me to the office o' sunrise!

The Shooting of the Cup*

A FEW hours brought us to one of those stopping points, known by the name of "wooding places." It was situated immediately above Letart's Falls. The boat, obedient to the wheel of the pilot, made a graceful sweep towards the island above the chute, and rounding to, approached the wood pile. As the boat drew near the shore, the escape steam reverberated through the forest and hills, like the chafed bellowing

* From "The Last of the Boatmen," by N. [Morgan Neville], in *The Western Souvenir*, A Christmas and New Year's Gift for 1829, edited by James Hall, pp. 110–114. Cincinnati: Published by N. and G. Guilford. [1828?]

of the caged tiger. The root of a tree, concealed beneath the water, prevented the boat from getting sufficiently near the bank, and it became necessary to use the paddles to take a different position.

"Back out! Mannee! and try it again!" exclaimed a voice from the shore. "Throw your pole wide—and brace off! or you'll run against a snag!"

This was a kind of language long familiar to us on the Ohio. It was a sample of the slang of the keel-boatmen.

The speaker was immediately cheered by a dozen of voices from the deck; and I recognized in him the person of an old acquaintance, familiarly known to me from my boyhood. He was leaning carelessly against a large beech; and, as his left arm negligently pressed a rifle to his side, presented a figure, that Salvator would have chosen from a million, as a model for his wild and gloomy pencil. His stature was upwards of six feet, his proportions perfectly symmetrical, and exhibiting the evidence of Herculean powers. To a stranger, he would have seemed a complete mulatto. Long exposure to the sun and weather on the lower Ohio and Mississippi had changed his skin; and, but for the fine European cast of his countenance, he might have passed for the principal warrior of some powerful tribe. Although at least fifty years of age, his hair was as black as the wing of the raven. Next to his skin he wore a red flannel shirt, covered by a blue capot, ornamented with white fringe. On his feet were moccasins, and a broad leathern belt, from which hung, suspended in a sheath, a large knife, encircled his waist.

As soon as the steam boat became stationary, the cabin passengers jumped on shore. On ascending the bank, the figure I have just described advanced to offer me his hand.

"How are you, Mike?" said I.

"How goes it?" replied the boatman—grasping my hand with a squeeze, that I can compare to nothing, but that of a blacksmith's vise.

"I am glad to see you, Mannee!"—continued he in his abrupt manner. "I am going to shoot at the tin cup for a quart—off hand—and you must be judge."

I understood Mike at once, and on any other occasion, should have remonstrated, and prevented the daring trial of skill. But I was accompanied by a couple of English tourists, who had scarcely ever been beyond the sound of Bow Bells; and who were travelling post over the United States to make up a book of observation, on our manners and customs.

There were, also, among the passengers, a few bloods from Philadelphia and Baltimore, who could conceive of nothing equal to Chestnut or Howard streets; and who expressed great disappointment, at not being able to find terrapins and oysters at every village—marvellously lauding the comforts of Rubicum's. My tramontane pride was aroused; and I resolved to give them an opportunity of seeing a Western Lion—for such Mike undoubtedly was—in all his glory. The philanthropist may start, and accuse me of want of humanity. I deny the charge, and refer for apology to one of the best understood principles of human nature.

Mike, followed by several of his crew, led the way to a beech grove, some little distance from the landing. I invited my fellow passengers to witness the scene.—On arriving at the spot, a stout, bull-headed boatman, dressed in a hunting shirt—but bare-footed—in whom I recognized a younger brother of Mike, drew a line with his toe; and stepping off thirty yards—turned round fronting his brother—took a tin cup, which hung from his belt, and placed it on his head. Although I had seen this feat performed before I acknowledge, I felt uneasy, whilst this silent preparation was going on. But I had not much time for reflection; for this second Albert exclaimed—

"Blaze away, Mike! and let's have the quart."

My "compagnons de voyage," as soon as they recovered from the first effect of their astonishment, exhibited a disposition to interfere. But Mike, throwing back his left leg, levelled his rifle at the head of his brother. In this horizontal position the weapon remained for some seconds as immovable, as if the arm which held it, was affected by no pulsation.

"Elevate your piece a little lower, Mike! or you will pay the corn," cried the imperturbable brother.

I know not if the advice was obeyed or not; but the sharp crack of the rifle immediately followed, and the cup flew off thirty or forty yards—rendered unfit for future service. There was a cry of admiration from the strangers, who pressed forward to see if the foolhardy boatman was really safe. He remained as immovable, as if he had been a figure hewn out of stone. He had not even winked, when the ball struck the cup within two inches of his skull.

"Mike has won!" I exclaimed; and my decision was the signal which, according to their rules, permitted him of the target to move from his position. No more sensation was exhibited among the boatmen, than if a common wager had been won. The bet being decided, they hurried back to their boat, giving me and my friends an invitation to partake of "the treat." We declined, and took leave of the thoughtless creatures. In a few minutes afterwards, we observed their "Keel" wheeling into the current,—the gigantic form of Mike, bestriding the large steering oar, and the others arranging themselves in their places in front of the cabin, that extended nearly the whole length of the boat, covering merchandize of immense value. As they left the shore, they gave the Indian yell; and broke out into a sort of unconnected chorus—commencing with—

> "Hard upon the beech oar!—
> She moves too slow!
> All the way to Shawneetown,
> Long while ago."

Trimming a Darky's Heel*

IN THE early days of St. Louis, before the roar of commerce or manufactures had drowned the free laugh and merry song of the jolly keel boatmen, those primitive navigators of the "Father of Waters" tied up their crafts beneath the bluff, which then, eighty feet in height, rose perpendicular from the water's edge in front of the city. On top of the bluff then, as now, a number of *doggeries* [drinking places] held forth their temptations to the hardy navigator, and they were often the scene of the wildest kind of revelry.

At that time *Mike Fink*, the chief among keel boatmen, was trading to St. Louis, and he frequently *awoke* the inhabitants by his wild freaks and daredevil sprees. Mike was celebrated for the skill with which he used the *rifle*—then the constant companion of western men. It was his boast that he could "best shoot whar he'd a mind to with his *Betsy*," as he familiarly termed his "shooting iron," and his companions, for the pleasure of noting his skill, or exhibiting it to some stranger, would often put him to the severest kind of tests.

One day, while lying upon the deck of his boat below the St. Louis bluff, with two or three companions, the conversation turned upon Mike's last shot; and one of the party ven-

---

* By Solitaire [John S. Robb]. From *The Saint Louis Weekly Reveille*, Vol. III (January 25, 1847), No. 29, p. 1147.

tured the opinion that his skill was departing. This aroused
the boatmen into a controversy, and from their conversation
might be learned the manner of the shot which was the subject of dispute. It was thus: One of the party, at a distance of
one hundred yards, had placed a tin cup between his knees,
and Mike had, at that distance, bored the center of the cup.

"I'll swar I don't hold that cup agin for you, Mike," remarked the doubter, "for thus is the delicatest kind of a
trimble comin' in your hand, and, some of these *yur* days,
you'll miss the cup clear."

"Miss thunder!" shouted Mike; "why, you consarned corn-
dodger mill, it war you that had the trimbles, and when I
gin old Bets the wakin' tetch, you *squatted* es ef her bark
war agoin' to bite you!"

"Oh, well," was the reply, "thar's mor'n one way of gettin'
out of a skunk hole, and ef you kin pass the trimbles off on
me, why, you kin *pass*, that's all; but I ain't goin' to trust you
with a sight at my paddles agin at an hundred paces, that's
sartin."

"Why, you scary varmint," answers Mike, bouncing to his
feet and reaching for *Betsy*, which stood by the cabin door
of the boat, "jest pint out a muskeeter, at a hundred yards,
and I'll nip off his right hinder eend claw, at the second jint,
afore he kin hum *Oh, don't!*"

"Hit a musketeer, ha, ha!" was the tantalizing response of
the others; "why, you couldn't hit the hinder part of that
nigger's heel up thar on the bluff, 'thout damagin' the bone,
and that ain't no shot to crow about."

The negro referred to was seated at the very edge of the
bluff, astride of a flour barrel, and one foot hung over the
edge. The distance was over a hundred yards, but Mike instantly raised his rifle, with the remark: "I'll jest trim that
feller's heel so he kin wear a decent boot!" and off went *Betsy*.

The negro jumped from his seat, and uttered a yell of pain,
as if, indeed, his whole heel had been trimmed off, and Mike
stood a moment with his rifle listening to the negro's voice,
as if endeavoring to define from the sound whether he was
really seriously hurt. At last the boatman who had been
doubting Mike's present skill remarked:

"You kin *leave*, now, Mike, fur that darky's master will be
arter you with a sharp stick;" and then he further added as a
taunt—"I knowed Betsy was feelin' for that nigger's bones
jest by the way you held her!"

Mike now became a little wrathy, and appeared inclined

to use *his* bones upon the tormentor, but some of the others advised him to hold on—that he would have a chance to exercise them upon the constable. In a short time an officer appeared with a warrant, but as soon as Mike looked at him he gave up the thought of either flight or resistance, and quietly remarked to his companions that the officer was a clever fellow, and "a small *hoss* in a fight."

"The only way you kin work him is to fool him," says Mike, "and he's a weazel in that bisness hisself!"

The warrant was produced by the officer and read to the offender, who signified his assent to the demand for his body, and told the representative of the law to lead the way. He did so, and when about to step off the boat he cast his eye back, supposing that Mike was following him, yet a little suspicious. The movement was a prudent one, for he discovered the tail of Mike's hunting shirt at the very moment the owner was retreating into the small cabin at the rear of the boat, which was immediately locked on the inside! All the boatmen, as if by previous concert, began to leave their craft, each bearing away upon his shoulder any loose implement lying about, with which an entrance into the cabin could be forced. The officer paused a moment, and then went to the cabin door, which he commenced persuading the offender to open, and save him the trouble of forcing it. He received no answer, but heard a horrible rustling within. At length getting out of patience, he remarked aloud:

"Well, if you won't open the door I can burn you out!" and he commenced striking fire with a pocket tinder box. The door immediately flew open, and there stood a boatman in Mike's dress; but it *wasn't Mike!*

"You ain't arter me, are you, *hoss?*" inquired the boatman.

The officer, without reply, stepped inside of the small cabin and looked around. There appeared to be no place to hide a figure as large as Mike, and there was a fellow dressed just like him. The thought immediately came uppermost in the officer's mind, that the offender had changed coats outside, while his back was turned to go off the boat, and one of the parties that had walked off was Mike in disguise! He was about to step out when a moccasin-covered heel, sticking out of a hole in a large mattress, attracted his attention, and when he touched it the heel vanished. He put his hand in to feel, and Mike burst out in a hoarse laugh!

"Quit your ticklin'!" shouted he. "Consarn your cunnin' pictur', I'll *gin in* 'thout a struggle."

The other boatman now joined in the laugh, as he helped the officer to pull Mike out of his hiding place. He had changed his garments *inside* the cabin instead of outside. A crowd of the boatmen also gathered around, and they all adjourned to the bluff, where, after taking drinks, they started in a body for the magistrate's office, who, by the way, was one of the early French settlers.

"Ah, ha!" he exclaimed, as the party entered the door; "here is ze men of ze boat, raisin' ze *diable* once more time. I shall not know what to do wiz *him*, by gar. Vat is de mattair now?"

"Why, Squire," broke in Mike, "I've jest come up with the Colonel to collect a small bill offen you!"

"You shall collect ze bill from *me*?" inquired the Justice. "What for you do the city good to de amount of von bill? Ah, ha! You kick up your *heel* and raise de batter and de salt of de whole town wiz your noise so much as we nevair get some sleep in de night!"

All eagerly gathered around to hear what Mike would reply, for his having a bill against the Justice was news to the crowd.

"You jest hit the pint, Squire," said Mike, "when you said that thar word *heel*! I want you to pay me fur trimmin' the heel of one of your town niggers! I've jest altered his breed, and arter this his posterity kin warr the neatest kind of a boot!"

The boatmen burst into a yell of laughter, and the magistrate into a corresponding state of wrath. He sputtered French and English with such rapidity that it was impossible to understand either.

"Leave ze court, you ras*kells* of ze boat!" shouted the Squire above the noise. "*Allez vous-en, vous* rogues, I shall nevair ave nosing to do wiz you. You ave treat ze court wiz *grand contempt.*"

The boatmen, all but Mike, had retired to the outside of the door, where they were still laughing, when Mike again, with a sober and solemn phiz, remarked to the Squire:

"Well, old dad, ef you allays raise *h-ll* in this way fur a little laffin' that's done in your court, I'll be cussed ef I gin you any more of my cases!"

Another roar from the boatmen hailed this remark.

"Constable, clear ze court, in *une* instant, right avay! *Les sacre diables* of ze river, no know nosing about how to treat wiz de law. I shall ave nosing to do wiz de whole what you call pile of ze rogues!"

"I ain't agoin' to stand any more sich law as this," remarked Mike. "Consarn my pictur' ef I don't leave the town!"

"Go to ze *devil*!" shouted the magistrate.

"I won't," says Mike; "mabbe he's anuther French Jestis!"

Amid a torrent of words and laughter Mike retreated to his boat, where he paid the officer for his trouble, and sent a handful of silver to the darky to extract the pain from his shortened heel.

II

PSEUDO BAD MEN

WITH the passing of the keelboat many of Mike Fink's tribe became raftsmen, joining the new crew of hardy adventurers that brought the forests down to the towns in the form of rafts, put together in "cribs" of logs or boards and then taken apart to be sold.

"The typical raftsman," writes Charles Edward Russell, in *A-Rafting on the Mississip'* (1928), "was reckless, dissolute, daring and all that, but he was more; he was humorous with a style of humor all his own and largely his own language in which to frame it; emotional at bottom, sophisticated on the surface; a singer, a dancer, an improviser of wild yarns, ready with fist, dagger, or pistol; something of a poet, curiously responsive to charitable appeals, something of a Lothario, something of a pirate, something of a blackguard, and in profanity equipped with resources incomparable for richness of invention and competence of authority."

Lumber rafting on the Upper Mississippi lasted roughly from 1840 to 1915; but the old-time raftsman began to disappear when the raft-boat, or steamboat used to tow or push rafts, came in, about 1865. The hardihood of the raftsman of the floating days tended to be measured by the strength of his whisky, which was so powerful that it would take the hair off a buffalo robe. Or, to cite another school of thought on the buffalo robe test, Mike Fink "drank so much whisky that he destroyed the coating of his stomach, and the doctor told him that before he could get well, he would need a new coat for it. Mike thought the thing over, and said, when he had a new coat for his stomach, he would have one that would stand the whisky; and he made up his mind that a buffalo robe with the hair on it was just the thing, and so he sat down, and swallowed it. He could drink any amount of whisky after that, and never so much as wink."[1]

But when a buffalo robe failed as a stomach lining, oqueejum did the trick. Something of the toughness of the raftsman and the humor of his invention may be gleaned from the following advice of one raftsman to another:

"Hey! Don't let that stuff drop like that on your boots!" I heard one raftsman say to another that was passing him a bottle. "I spilt some on my new shore shoes last week and it ate the uppers clean off down to the soles."

"Was them shoes tanned with oqueejum?" asked the other in a quietly interested way, as if he were seeking scientific knowledge.

"No, sir. That there leather was tanned with the best hemlock bark, and the shoes cost me $3 in Red Wing."

"Now, say, my friend"—gently remonstrative—"don't you know better than to buy leather tanned with hemlock? What you want is leather tanned with oqueejum and then whisky can't eat it. You see, whisky and hemlock, they get together on social terms, same's you and me, and then the whisky does its deadly work and swallers the leather. But whisky and oqueejum's enemies, and when they meet whisky gets licked every time. That's why I keep my stomach lined with it. Oqueejum's made from the bamjam tree which grows in India to a height of more than a thousand feet. Its wood is so hard they have to cut it with a cold chisel. It stands to reason that it's stronger than hemlock. Try some on your stomach and then your liquor won't get to your head like this."[2]

The hardihood of the raftsman tended also to be measured by his boasting. In the famous raft scene in *Life on the Mississippi* (1874), which gives us our first glimpse of Huck Finn, Mark Twain has immortalized the "screamer." The "screamer" is the ring-tailed roarer grown maudlin, who boasts out of his weakness rather than his strength. He is the bogus bad man, who has already been glimpsed in the canebrake cockalorum and in the cock-of-the-walk pose of Mike Fink.

West of the Mississippi the scream of the backwoods boaster and bully passed into the howl of the pseudo or mock bad man, who, in his boasting chants and yells, proclaimed his intestinal fortitude with more and more weird anatomical details. In addition to the usual animal traits he claimed a mythical animal nurse and a more than usual endowment of teeth and other hard substance in his makeup. Crockett, too, it will be recalled, boasted of being "half chicken hawk and steel-trap" and of his wilderness birthplace—"born in a cane brake, cradled in a sap trough, and clouted with coon skins."

No one liked to play bad man more than the cowboy on a spree; and from his favorite interjection, "Whoopee!," originally a call to animals, "making whoopee" has become a general term for carousing. But if a would-be desperado announced that it was his time to howl, this was chiefly for the benefit of the uninitiated. For the rest knew that with the true bad man or killer the rule was: "Shoot first and talk afterward."[3]

On the frontier, however, "apparent rage" and "vigorous language" had their uses in bluffing or blustering one's way out of a tight place as well as in letting off steam. By such devices an Iowa squatter is reported to have got rid of a prospective settler from Illinois "who casually remonstrated against any one holding more than one claim and not even that 'unless he lived on it' ":

"My name, Sir, is Simeon Cragin. I own *fourteen* claims, and if any man jumps one of them I will shoot him down at once, Sir. I am a gentleman, Sir, and a scholar. I was educated in Bangor, have been in the United States army and served my country faithfully—am the discoverer of the Wopsey—can ride a grizzly bear, or whip any *human* that ever crossed the Mississippi; and if you dare jump one of my claims, die you must."[4]

The dramatized bad man yells not only lean heavily on one another but also become mixed with literary or semi-literary parodies and burlesques. Such, frankly, is "The Bad Man from the Brazos," beginning:

I'm a blizzard from the Brazos on a tear, hear me hoot;
I'm a lifter of the flowing locks of hair, hear me toot;
    I'm a rocker from the Rockies
    And of all the town the talk is,
"He's a pirate from the Pampas on the shoot."[5]

Fink's Brag*

I'M A Salt River roarer! I'm a ring-tailed squealer! I'm a reg'lar screamer from the ol' Massassip'! WHOOP! I'm the very infant that refused his milk before its eyes were open, and called out for a bottle of old Rye! I love the women an' I'm chockful o' fight! I'm half wild horse and half cock-eyed alligator and the rest o' me is crooked snags an' red-hot snappin' turkle. I can hit like fourth-proof lightnin' an' every lick I make in the woods lets in an acre o' sunshine. I can out-run, out-jump, out-shoot, out-brag, out-drink, an' out-fight, rough-an'-tumble, no holts barred, ary man on both sides the river from Pittsburgh to New Orleans an' back ag'in to St. Louiee. Come on, you flatters, you bargers, you milk-white mechanics, an' see how tough I am to chaw! I ain't had a fight for two days an' I'm spilein' for exercise. Cock-a-doodle-do!

Bully of Salt River**

THE bully of Salt River war named Skippoweth Branch. He slept in his hat, chawed his vittles with his foreteeth, and could scream through his nose. He sunned himself in a thunder storm, went to meeting on two horses, never turned out for man or beast; and was sworn to lick every thing he saw, except his own father and mother. He would walk ten miles, at any time of day or night, for a fight. He called himself the great oak that grows half its length underground, and turns up its roots unexpected. He sometimes took the name of floating iron and melted pewter, red hot cannon balls, and Big Snag of the Desert. He said he lived on the mountains and eat thunder, that he had a neckcloth at home made of double chain lightning, and that he could never come to his full height till the clouds were lifted a peace. He called himself a west wind full of prickles, a dose for old Kaintuck and a drawing plaster for the Allegheny mountains. The fact is he

---

* From Mike Fink, King of Mississippi Keelboatmen, by Walter Blair and Franklin J. Meine, pp. 105–106. Copyright, 1933, by Henry Holt & Company, Inc. New York.

** From Mince Pie for the Million. Philadelphia and New York: Turner & Fisher. 1846.

war too smart to live long, and screamed himself to death, one night, to show his spirrit. I knowed him when he war a boy, and seed him when he war a man, and went to his funeral when he war ded. He war the pride of the country, and could outscream seven catamounts tied together.

Billy Earthquake*

As WE were passing by the court-house, a real "screamer from the Nob," about six feet four in height, commenced the following tirade:—"This is *me*, and no mistake! Billy Earthquake, Esq., commonly called Little Billy, all the way from No'th Fork of Muddy Run! I'm a small specimen, as you see, a remote circumstance, a mere yearling; but cuss me if I ain't of the true imported breed, and I can whip any man in this section of the country. Whoop! won't *nobody* come out and fight me? Come out, some of you, and die decently, for I'm spileing for a fight, I hain't had one for more than a week, and if you don't come out I'm flyblowed before sundown, to a certingty. So come up to taw!

"Maybe you don't know who Little Billy is? I'll tell you. I'm a poor man, it's a fact, and smell like a wet dog; but I can't be run over. I'm the identical individual that grinned a whole menagerie out of countenance, and made the ribbed nose baboon hang down his head and blush. W-h-o-o-p! I'm the chap that towed the Broad-horn up Salt River, where the snags were so thick that the fish couldn't swim without rubbing their scales off!—fact, and if any one denies it, just let 'em make their will! Cock-a-doodle-doo!

"Maybe you never heard of the time the horse kicked me, and put both his hips out of jint—if it ain't true, cut me up for catfish bait! W-h-o-o-p! I'm the very infant that refused its milk before its eyes were open, and called out for a bottle of old Rye! W-h-o-o-p! I'm that little Cupid! Talk about grinning the bark off a tree!—'tain't nothing; one squint of mine at a bull's heel would blister it. O, I'm one of your toughest sort,— live for ever, and then turn to a white oak post. I'm the ginewine article, a real double acting engine, and I can out-

* From *An American Glossary*, Being an Attempt to Illustrate Certain Americanisms upon Historical Principles, by Richard H. Thornton, Vol. II, pp. 969–970. Philadelphia: J. B. Lippincott Company. 1912. Reprinted from a Florida newspaper, about the year 1840.

run, out-jump, out-swim, chaw more tobacco and spit less, and drink more whiskey and keep soberer than any man in these localities. If that don't make 'em fight (walking off in disgust) nothing will. I wish I may be kiln-dried and split up into wooden shoe-pegs, if I believe there's a chap among 'em that's got courage enough to collar a hen!"

Bad Man Yells*

A CERTAIN class of chant-like yells emphasizing the badness of the man yelling them belongs to the lore of the bad man, I suppose, though oftener than not they originated in a spirit of mockery. The cowboy liked to "yip" them out when he was playing bad man—for the cowboy was truly "the playboy of the western world." Here is a yell that "hard customers" from the country around Harrisburg and Houston used to give fifty years ago. My father, who was a very quiet man, used to quote it to enforce his contempt for the "fly-up-the-creeks" from whom he learned it.

> Raised in a canebrake,
> Fed in a hog trough,
> Suckled by a she bear,
> The click of a six-shooter is music to my ear!
>   Wh-o-o-o-p-ee!

> The further up the creek you go
> The worse they get,
> And I come from the head of it!
>   Wh-o-o-o-p-ee!

Another boast, adapted to a Texas river, was as follows:

> Born high up on the Guadalupe,
> Raised on a thorny prickly pear,
> Quarrelled with alligators,
> And fought grizzly bears!

A. J. Sowell, who knew Texas frontier life as few men who have written of it knew it, says in his *Rangers and Pioneers*

---

* From "Ballads and Songs of the Frontier Folk," by J. Frank Dobie, *Texas and Southwestern Lore*, Publications of the Texas Folk-Lore Society, Number VI, edited by J. Frank Dobie, pp. 149–150. Copyright, 1927, by the Texas Folk-Lore Society. Austin.

of Texas (San Antonio, 1884, page 330): "Occasionally in some Western village, you will hear a voice ring out on the night air in words something like these: 'Wild and woolly,' 'Hard to curry,' 'Raised a pet but gone wild,' 'Walked the Chisholm Trail backwards,' 'Fought Indians and killed buffalo,' 'Hide out, little ones,' and then you may expect a few shots from a revolver. It is a cowboy out on a little spree, but likely he will not hurt anyone, as some friend who is sober generally comes to him, relieves him of his pistol, and all is soon quiet again." Sowell adds that such yelling cowboys were exceptions.

The Boasting Drunk in Dodge*

WHEN a group of cowboys reached Dodge City from Texas, they had not slept in a bed for months; nor had they shaved or enjoyed a hot bath or a haircut. Their clothing was dirty, often ragged. They had not seen a woman perhaps for half a year. The saloons of Dodge never shut their doors (on the opening day the proprietor threw away the keys). The red lights in back of the saloons beckoned. First the cowboys got rid of their extra hair, bought new outfits of clothing, and then they tanked up. They were ready to go. Some were quiet in their dissipation. Others talked—perhaps to keep up their courage—as does the "Boasting Drunk." Dodge was the toughest town known in 1883.

Raised on six-shooters till I get big enough to eat ground shotguns,
When I'm cool I warm the Gulf of Mexico and bathe therein,
When I'm hot there's an equinoxical breeze that fans me fevered
    brow,
The moans of widows and orphans is music to me melancholy soul.

Me the boy that chewed the wad the goat eat that butted the goat
    off the bridge,

---

* From *Cowboy Songs and Other Frontier Ballads*, collected by John A. Lomax and Alan Lomax, pp. 135–136. Revised and Enlarged. Copyright, 1910, 1916, 1938, by The Macmillan Company; 1938, by John A. Lomax. New York.
Cf.:

Raised in a canebrake, and suckled by a lion,
Head like a bombshell and teeth made out of iron;
Nine rows of jaw teeth and holes punched for more.
I come from ourang-a-tang where the bullfrogs jump
    from north to south.
—*Cowboy Songs and Other Frontier Ballads*, collected
by John A. Lomax and Alan Lomax, p. 63.

Born in the Rocky Mountains, suckled by a grizzly bear,
Ninety-nine rows of jaw teeth and not a single hair.

Thirty-two inches 'tween the eyes and they feed me with a shovel,
Mount the wild ass and leap from crag to crag,
And roar like laughter in a tomb,
Jump from precipice to precipice and back to pice again.

Snatched him bald-headed and spit on the place where the hair
    come off;
Take a leg off him and beat him over the head with the bloody
    end of it,
Slap his head up to a peak and then knock the peak off,
Take his eye out and eat it for a grape.

Gimme one hundred yards start and I'll run plumb to Honolulu
    without even wettin' my feet,
Shoulder five hundred bushel of shot and wade through solid rocks
    up to my shoulder blades.
Any damn man don't believe it . . .

I'll lick him on a sheep hide and never tromp on the tail,
Knock a belch out of him that'll whiz like a nail,
Knock a belch out of him longer'n a rail,
Sharp enough to stick a pig with.

Other Cowboy Boasting Chants*

I'm wild and woolly
And full of fleas;
Ain't never been curried
Below the knees.
I'm a wild she wolf
From Bitter Creek,
And it's my time
To h-o-w-l, whoop-i-e-e-ee.

Wasp nests and yaller jackets,
The higher you pitch, the sweeter my navy tastes.
Born on the Guadalupe,
Ten miles below Duck Pond,
Raised in the Rocky Mountains.
Hang one spur where the collar works
And the other where the crupper works.

---

* From *American Ballads and Folk Songs*, collected and compiled by John A. Lomax and Alan Lomax, pp. 382–383. Copyright, 1934, by The Macmillan Company. New York.

Four rows of jaw teeth
And holes punched for more;
Steel ribs and iron backbone,
And tail put on with screws,
Double dew-clawed,
Knock-kneed and bandy-shanked,
Nine rows of teeth,
And holes punched for more.

III

KILLERS

1. WILD BILL HICKOK

THE line of Western heroes is an unbroken one. As a boy in La Salle County, Illinois, James Butler Hickok, born the year after Crockett died, like him killed wolves for bounty, and idolized Kit Carson, who later praised him for his fearlessness. And when he was twenty, according to tradition, Wild Bill came to the aid of an eleven-year-old boy, named Will Cody, who was being rough-handled by his companions in Lew Simpson's wagon train. Wild Bill's prowess in knock-down and drag-out fighting and in marksmanship recall the feats of Mike Fink. On his first job as a towpath driver on the Illinois and Michigan Canal, he emerged as the victor of a fist fight that lasted over an hour, beginning on the towpath and ending in the water with his adversary nearly drowned. "I allers shoot well," he told George Ward Nichols, "but I come ter be perfeck in the mountains by shootin at a dime for a mark, at bets of half a dollar a shot." As a killer Wild Bill has been the subject of much controversy. Was he a gun fighter, who fought fair, or a gunman, who didn't? As a legend, he eclipses Bat Masterson, Wyatt Earp, and other marshalls who were also "bad men."

The killer arose out of the turbulent conditions of the frontier, where "the six-shooter was the law of the land," and a man shot to kill if self-preservation demanded that he kill or be killed. Since a split second, in which one got the drop on one's adversary, might mean the difference between these two alternatives, the mastery went to the man who combined agility of movement and steadiness of nerve, such as were required for drawing quickly and shooting straight, with coolness of head. " 'Whenever you get into a row,' said Wild Bill, 'be sure and not shoot too quick. Take time. I've known many a feller slip up for shootin' in a hurry.' "

The law of the six-shooter was based on an utter disregard for human life, which elevated murder to a cold-blooded science. " 'As ter killing men,' said Wild Bill, 'I never thought much about it. The most of the men I have killed it was one or t'other of us, and at sich times, you don't stop to think; and what's the use after it's all over?' " And as to how he got into fights: " 'D——d if I can tell . . . but you know a man must defend his honor.' " Again: " 'That I have killed men, I admit, but never unless in absolute self-defence, or in the performance of an official duty. I never, in my life, took any mean advantage of an enemy. Yet, understand,' he added, 'I never allow a man to get the drop on me.' "[1]

Thus, when confronted by a desperado with a gun in each hand, Bill stepped back, with upraised hand: " 'Don't shoot him—he's only in fun!' he called out. Mulvey turned, expecting to confront a deputy approaching from behind. In the instant that his attention was distracted Bill snatched out a revolver and dropped him with a bullet in the brain."[2]

Although no seasoned trouper like Buffalo Bill, with whom he appeared briefly in Ned Buntline's melodrama, *The Scouts of the Prairie*, in 1873, Wild Bill displayed considerable showmanship in living up to his early-acquired reputation as a "bad man to fool with." George Ward Nichols' account of his fabulous exploits was probably no more extravagant than Wild Bill's conception of himself. For throughout his varied career as stage-coach driver, Civil War sharpshooter and spy, Indian fighter, scout, guide, and peace officer, Wild Bill helped create his own legend by combining a certain amount of pose with a sense of his own mission. Thus do heroes both during and after their lifetime make it easier for the folklorist and harder for the historian.

Wild Bill's reputation as a bad man to fool with rested on his reputation as a gunfighter and this in turn on his use of all those tricks of gunplay which old-timers attribute to the pseudo bad man and the fancy shooter, such as carrying two guns, shooting from the hip, and "fanning" (firing a revolver by brushing back the hammer with the palm of the left hand). Whether this show of daredeviltry and flashiness were due to courage or the lack of it, Wild Bill made the most of it, while at the same time taking no chances. The result was such myths as the "McCanles massacre" and such stunts as simultaneously killing two assailants who had entered by opposite doors of a restaurant. He could do this not because he "had eyes in the back of his head, or some sixth sense," but because he "drew his pistols, both of them, with a movement almost quicker than the eye could perceive, and with one he killed the man in front of him, and at the same time with the other gun hand resting on the opposite shoulder he killed the man behind him, looking through the mirror" over the front door.[3]

His good looks and gallantry, plus his taste for fancy clothes, also gained for him the reputation of a lady-killer. Mrs. Cody was entranced at the actuality, as she had been terrified at the prospect, of meeting him.

I could have danced the Highland Fling, I believe, so happy was I to find mildness where I had been led to believe would be the most murderous of persons. Instinctively I looked for revolvers. There were none, not even the slightest bulge at the hips of the Prince Albert he wore. I was happier than ever. We danced. And I must confess that we danced and danced again until Will laughingly put a stop to it.[4]

There was no end of miracles. Many of his hair-raising exploits during the war involved his well-trained horse, Black Nell (reminiscent of the marvelous steeds of earlier heroes), whose "trick of dropping quick" saved his life time and again. With the warriors and tribal chieftains of other heroic ages this "prince of pistoleers" was linked not only by his saga of daring challenges, thrilling combats, and miraculous escapes but also by his tragic doom. In fact, the fairies presided at his death as well as at his birth. Even his remains, as evidenced at the time of their exhumation for reburial underwent the miracle of natural embalming.

2. BILLY THE KID

The superman among killers was Billy the Kid, whose golden legend has grown out of all proportion to the few sordid facts of his short, lightning-swift career. Born as

William H. Bonney in New York City in 1859, he was brought to Kansas at the age of three; at twelve killed his first man in Silver City, New Mexico, for insulting his mother; after a series of wanderings and crimes in Arizona, Mexico, Texas and New Mexico, joined the Murphy-Dolan faction in the Lincoln County war; made a sensational escape from his captors at Lincoln; and while visiting his sweetheart at Fort Sumner was shot in the dark by Sheriff Pat Garrett. This bare outline has been filled in by old-timers, journalists, and dime-novelists with some of the most lurid and fantastic traditions and fictions that the popular imagination has ever concocted. Both the hero-worshippers and the debunkers have had a field day with the apocrypha of the "Southwest's most famous desperado" and "best-loved hero in the state's history"—the "darling of the common people." The list of twenty-one killings in twenty-one years which was the Kid's boast has been repeatedly revised downward, conservative estimates ranging from twelve to three. And the reputedly handsome, generous daredevil stands unmasked by his only authentic photograph, according to one unsympathetic critic, as "a nondescript, adenoidal, weasel-eyed, narrow-chested, stoop-shouldered, repulsive-looking creature with all the outward appearance of a cretin."[5]

His dual personality has made him something of an enigma, which has fascinated his biographers. According to Pat Garrett:

The Kid had a lurking devil in him. It was a good-humored, jovial imp, or a cruel and blood-thirsty fiend, as circumstances prompted. Circumstances favored the worser angel, and the Kid fell.

The two sides of his nature met in a curious "nerveless imperturbability," which Walter Noble Burns analyzes as "a sub-zero vacuum—devoid of all human emotions."

"A little while before we made a dash for our lives, the Kid rolled a cigarette. I watched him. It seemed just then as if he had about a minute and a half to live. But when he poured the tobacco from his pouch into the cigarette paper he did not spill a flake. His hand was as steady as steel. A blazing chunk of roof fell on the table beside him, barely missing his head. "Much obliged," he said; and he bent over and lighted his cigarette from the flame. Then he looked at me and grinned as if he thought that was a good joke. He didn't roll that cigarette because he was nervous but because he wanted a good smoke. You could tell by the way he inhaled the smoke and let it roll out of his mouth that he was getting real pleasure out of it. If you had seen Billy the Kid roll that cigarette and smoke it, señor, you would have known at once that he was a brave man."[6]

Like many another Western gun fighter—Wild Bill, Jesse James—Billy the Kid was killed without a chance to fight for his life. An extra touch of tragic irony is added to the Kid's fate by the fact that his slayer was, up to the time of his appointment as sheriff, a good friend. As his biographer Pat Garrett was a good friend after the Kid's death, too. And by his death the Kid did Garrett a good turn. Partly because of the fame of his victim and partly because of the special kind of courage that it took to carry out his assignment, Pat Garrett became a hero in his own right, as not the greatest (Wild Bill's title) but the "last great sheriff of the old frontier."

By writing his *Authentic Life of Billy the Kid*, Pat Garrett also tried to kill the monstrous lies that sprang up after Billy the Kid's death. But as late as 1926 the rumor persisted that the Kid was still alive, as reported in an El Paso paper for June 24:

Leland V. Gardiner . . . believes Billy the Kid, notorious outlaw of pioneer days, still lives, and has thought so for the past ten years, he said. He is not the El Pasoan, however, who communicated his belief to the New Mexico Historical Society. That informant said he had seen the Kid about ten years ago (in an eastern city).

"I am not certain, but believe I have seen the Kid," said Mr. Gardiner. "I am told that he is on an isolated ranch within 500 miles of El Paso. When strangers come to the ranch he disappears until they are gone. . . . He can't take chances on being detected."[7]

3. JESSE JAMES AND OTHERS

Similar rumors have dogged the memory of Jesse James, and no less than seventeen persons, according to his granddaughter, have claimed to be the "original Jesse James." As Billy the Kid was the child of the cattle rustling wars, so Jesse James was the product of the bloody border warfare of Western Missouri and Eastern Kansas, beginning with the conflict over the Free Soil issue, passing into Civil War bushwhacking, and culminating in postbellum outlawry. As a boy on a Missouri farm, Jesse played at shooting or hanging Jim Lane or John Brown. In his youth, it will be recalled, Wild Bill Hickok was a member of Jim Lane's Red Legs and had his cabin burned down in retaliation by Missouri border ruffians; and Buffalo Bill's father, Isaac Cody, was likewise involved in the free-state cause. In 1863 what had been a game became for Jesse a life-and-death affair. While ploughing in a cornfield, he was seized and lashed with a rope by a squad of Federal militia, who nearly hanged his step-father and subsequently arrested and jailed his mother and sister. Joining the guerrillas under "Bloody Bill" Anderson, he was outlawed at the close of the war. Whether or not they were "driven" to crime by "persecution," he and his brother Frank and their cousins, the four Younger boys, all ex-guerrillas, turned to robbing banks and trains for a livelihood.

This background in sectional conflict and civil strife perhaps helped to make Jesse James stand out in the popular imagination as a symbol of revolt and protest against the forces of tyranny and injustice. For most Americans he represents the Robin Hood tradition of the "good bad man," certain aspects of which are seen in Billy the Kid. In his bland, quixotic humor and impish wiliness, however, the Kid, like Wild Bill Hickok, has more in common with the tradition of the "cheerful rogue," which has given us "bad boys" and "bad good men" from Robin Hood and Tyl Eulenspiegel to Huckleberry Finn. Jesse James, on the other hand,

> robbed from the rich and he gave to the poor,
> He'd a hand and a heart and a brain.

And he all but achieved martyrdom through death by treachery. These lines, reminiscent of the refrain of the ballad, were inscribed on his monument at his mother's request:

> Murdered by a Traitor and Coward Whose
> Name Is Not Worthy to Appear Here

The classic instance of Jesse James' chivalry is the episode in which he paid off the mortgage for a poor widow and then stole the money back from the mortgage owner. The same story is told of Sam Bass, the "Texas Robin Hood," who was also a victim of the treachery of one of his own men—the best example of the good boy gone wrong.

The last Robin Hood of the Southwest was Charley ("Pretty Boy") Floyd, of Sallisaw, Oklahoma, described as a "nice, soft-spoken boy, good to his mother," with a special grudge against bankers and sheriffs.

It was his custom . . . to inform the sheriffs ahead of time when he was about to rob a bank, and it was so well known that he would rather pot a sheriff any day than rob a bank that nowadays the sheriffs invariably locked themselves in and barred the doors or left town as the date approached. The list of sheriffs and deputies whom "Pretty Boy" had shot in the head—he never shot except at the head and there was only one record of his missing—was desperately long.[8]

Wild Bill*

I. My First Meeting with Wild Bill

LET me at once describe the personal appearance of the famous Scout of the Plains, William Hitchcock, called "Wild Bill," who now advanced toward me, fixing his clear gray eyes on mine in a quick, interrogative way, as if to take "my measure."

The result seemed favorable, for he held forth a small, muscular hand in a frank, open manner. As I looked at him I thought his the handsomest *physique* I had ever seen. In its exquisite manly proportions it recalled the antique. It was a figure Ward would delight to model as a companion to his "Indian."

Bill stood six feet and an inch in his bright yellow moccasins. A deer-skin shirt, or frock it might be called, hung jauntily over his shoulders, and revealed a chest whose breadth and depth were remarkable. These lungs had had growth in some twenty years of the free air of the Rocky Mountains. His small, round waist was girthed by a belt which held two of Colt's navy revolvers. His legs sloped gradually from the compact thigh to the feet, which were small, and turned inward as he walked. There was a singular grace and dignity of carriage about that figure which would have called your attention meet it where you would. The head which crowned it was now covered by a large sombrero, underneath which there shone out a quiet, manly face; so gentle is its expression as he greets you as utterly to belie the history of its owner, yet it is not a face to be trifled with. The lips thin and sensitive,

* From "Wild Bill" [by George Ward Nichols], *Harper's New Monthly Magazine*, Vol. XXXIV (February, 1867), No. CCI, pp. 273–285.

the jaw not too square, the cheek bones slightly prominent, a mass of fine dark hair falls below the neck to the shoulders. The eyes, now that you are in friendly intercourse, are as gentle as a woman's. In truth, the woman nature seems prominent throughout, and you would not believe that you were looking into eyes that have pointed the way to death to hundreds of men. Yes, Wild Bill with his own hands has killed hundreds of men. Of that I have not a doubt. "He shoots to kill," as they say on the border.

In vain did I examine the scout's face for some evidence of murderous propensity. It was a gentle face, and singular only in the sharp angle of the eye, and without any physiognomical reason for the opinion, I have thought his wonderful accuracy of aim was indicated by this peculiarity. He told me, however, to use his own words:

"I allers shoot well; but I come ter be perfeck in the mountains by shootin at a dime for a mark, at bets of half a dollar a shot. And then until the war I never drank liquor nor smoked," he continued, with a melancholy expression; "war is demoralizing, it is."

Captain Honesty was right. I was very curious to see "Wild Bill, the Scout," who, a few days before my arrival in Springfield in a duel at noonday in the public square, at fifty paces, had sent one of Colt's pistol-balls through the heart of a returned Confederate soldier.

Whenever I had met an officer or soldier who had served in the Southwest I heard of Wild Bill and his exploits, until these stories became so frequent and of such an extraordinary character as quite to outstrip personal knowledge of adventure by camp and field; and the hero of those strange tales took shape in my mind as did Jack the Giant Killer or Sinbad the Sailor in childhood days. As then, I now had the most implicit faith in the existance of the individual; but how one man could accomplish such prodigies of strength and feats of daring was a continued wonder.

II. THE DUEL WITH DAVE TUTT

Bill was born of Northern parents in the State of Illinois. He ran away from home when a boy, and wandered out upon the plains and into the mountains. For fifteen years he lived with the trappers, hunting and fishing. When the war broke out he returned to the States and entered the Union service. No man probably was ever better fitted for scouting than he.

Joined to his tremendous strength he was an unequalled horseman; he was a perfect marksman; he had a keen sight, and a constitution which had no limit of endurance. He was cool to audacity, brave to rashness, always possessed of himself under the most critical circumstances; and, above all, was such a master in the knowledge of woodcraft that it might have been termed a science with him—a knowledge which, with the soldier, is priceless beyond description. Some of Bill's adventures during the war will be related hereafter.

The main features of the story of the duel was [*sic*] told me by Captain Honesty, who was unprejudiced, if it is possible to find an unbiased mind in a town of 3000 people after a fight has taken place. I will give the story in his words:

"They say Bill's wild. Now he isn't any sich thing. I've known him goin on ter ten year, and he's as civil a disposed person as you'll find he-e-arabouts. But he won't be put upon.

"I'll tell yer how it happened. But come inter the office; thar's a good many round hy'ar as sides with Tutt—the man that's shot. But I tell yer 'twas a far fight. Take some whisky? No! Well, I will, if yer'l excuse me.

"You see," continued the Captain, setting the empty glass on the table in an emphatic way, "Bill was up in his room a-playin seven-up, or four-hand, or some of them pesky games. Bill refused ter play with Tutt, who was a professional gambler. Yer see, Bill was a scout on our side durin the war, and Tutt was a reb scout. Bill had killed Dave Tutt's mate, and, atween one thing and another, there war an onusual hard feelin atwixt 'em.

"Ever sin Dave come back he had tried to pick a row with Bill; so Bill wouldn't play cards with him any more. But Dave stood over the man who was gambling with Bill and lent the feller money. Bill won about two hundred dollars, which made Tutt spiteful mad. Bime-by, he says to Bill:

" 'Bill, you've got plenty of money—pay me that forty dollars yer owe me in that horse trade.'

"And Bill paid him. Then he said:

" 'Yer owe me thirty-five dollars more; yer lost it playing with me t'other night.'

"Dave's style was right provoking; but Bill answered him perfectly gentlemanly:

" 'I think yer wrong, Dave. It's only twenty-five dollars. I have a memorandum of it in my pocket down stairs. Ef it's thirty-five dollars I'll give it yer.'

"Now Bill's watch was lying on the table. Dave took up the watch, put it in his pocket, and said: 'I'll keep this yere watch till yer pay me that thirty-five dollars.'

"This made Bill shooting mad; fur, don't yer see, Colonel, it was a-doubting his honor like, so he got up and looked Dave in the eyes, and said to him: 'I don't want ter make a row in this house. It's a decent house, and I don't want ter injure the keeper. You'd better put that watch back on the table.'

"But Dave grinned at Bill mighty ugly, and walked off with the watch, and kept it several days. All this time Dave's friends were spurring Bill on ter fight; there was no end ter the talk. They blackguarded him in an underhand sort of a way, and tried ter get up a scrimmage, and then they thought they could lay him out. Yer see Bill has enemies all about. He's settled the accounts of a heap of men who lived round here. This is about the only place in Missouri whar a reb can come back and live, and ter tell yer the truth, Colonel—" and the Captain, with an involuntary movement, hitched up his revolver-belt, as he said, with expressive significance, "they don't stay long round here!

"Well, as I was saying, these rebs don't like ter see a man walking round town who they knew in the reb army as one of their men, who they now know was on our side, all the time he was sending us information, sometimes from Pap Price's own head-quarters. But they couldn't provoke Bill inter a row, for he's afeard of hisself when he gits *awful* mad; and he allers left his shootin irons in his room when he went out. One day these cusses drew their pistols on him and dared him to fight, and then they told him that Tutt was a-goin ter pack that watch across the squar next day at noon.

"I heard of this, for every body was talking about it on the street, and so I went after Bill, and found him in his room, cleaning and greasing and loading his revolvers.

" 'Now, Bill,' says I, 'you're goin ter git inter a fight.'

" 'Don't you bother yerself, Captain,' says he. 'It's not the first time I have been in a fight; and these d—d hounds have put on me long enough. You don't want me ter give up my honor, do yer?'

" 'No, Bill,' says I, 'yer must keep yer honor.'

"Next day, about noon, Bill went down to the squar. He had said that Dave Tutt shouldn't pack that watch across the squar unless dead men could walk.

"When Bill got onter the squar he found a crowd standin in the corner of the street by which he entered the squar, which is from the south, yer know. In this crowd he saw a lot of Tutt's friends; some were cousins of his'n, just back from the reb army; and they jeered him, and boasted that Dave was a-goin to pack that watch across the squar as he promised.

"Then Bill saw Tutt standin near the courthouse, which yer remember is on the west side, so that the crowd war behind Bill.

"Just then Tutt, who war alone, started from the courthouse and walked out into the squar, and Bill moved away from the crowd toward the west side of the squar. Bout fifteen paces brought them opposite to each other, and about fifty yards apart. Tutt then showed his pistol. Bill had kept a sharp eye on him, and before Tutt could pint it Bill had his'n out.

"At that moment you could have heard a pin drop in that squar. Both Tutt and Bill fired, but one discharge followed the other so quick that it's hard to say which went off first. Tutt was a famous shot, but he missed this time; the ball from his pistol went over Bill's head. The instant Bill fired, without waitin ter see ef he had hit Tutt, he wheeled on his heels and pointed his pistol at Tutt's friends, who had already drawn their weepons.

" 'Aren't yer satisfied, gentlemen?' cried Bill, as cool as an alligator. 'Put up your shootin-irons, or there'll be more dead men here.' And they put 'em up, and said it war a far fight."

"What became of Tutt?" I asked of the Captain, who had stopped at this point of his story, and was very deliberately engaged in refilling his empty glass.

"Oh! Dave? He was as plucky a feller as ever drew trigger; but, Lord bless yer! it was no use. Bill never shoots twice at the same man, and his ball went through Dave's heart. He stood stock-still for a second or two, then raised his arm as if ter fire again, then he swayed a little, staggered three or four steps and then fell dead.

"Bill and his friends wanted ter have the thing done regular, so we went up ter the Justice, and Bill delivered himself up. A jury was drawn; Bill was tried and cleared the next day. It was proved that it was a case of self-defense. Don't yer see, Colonel?"

I answered that I was afraid that I did not see that point very clearly.

"Well, well!" he replied, with an air of compassion, "you haven't drunk any whisky, that's what's the matter with yer." And then, putting his hand on my shoulder with a half-mysterious, half-conscious look in his face, he muttered, in a whisper:

"*The fact is, thar was an undercurrent of a woman in that fight!*"

[The following conversation took place that afternoon at the hotel.—B. A. B.]

I had a curiosity, which was not an idle one, to hear what this man had to say about his duel with Tutt, and I asked him:

"Do you not regret killing Tutt? You surely do not like to kill men?"

"As ter killing men," he replied, "I never thought much about it. The most of the men I have killed it was one or t'other of us, and at sich times you don't stop to think; and what's the use after it's all over? As for Tutt, I had rather not have killed him, for I want ter settle down quiet here now. But thar's been hard feeling between us a long while. I wanted ter keep out of that fight; but he tried to degrade me, and I couldn't stand that, you know, for I am a fighting man, you know."

A cloud passed over the speaker's face for a moment as he continued:

"And there was a cause of quarrel between us which people round here don't know about. One of us had to die; and the secret died with him."

"Why did you not wait to see if your ball had hit him? Why did you turn round so quickly?"

The scout fixed his gray eyes on mine, striking his leg with his riding-whip, as he answered.

"I *knew* he was a dead man. I never miss a shot. I turned on the crowd because I was sure they would shoot me if they saw him fall."

"The people about here tell me you are a quiet, civil man. How is it you get into these fights?"

"D—d if I can tell," he replied, with a puzzled look which at once gave place to a proud, defiant expression as he continued—"but you know a man must defend his honor."

"Yes," I admitted, with some hesitation, remembering that I was not in Boston but on the border, and that the code of honor and mode of redress differ slightly in the one place from those of the other.

Billy the Kid*

I. The People Remember the Kid

If you would learn in what affectionate regard the people of New Mexico cherish the memory of Billy the Kid to-day, you have but to journey in leisurely fashion through the Billy the Kid country. Every one will have a story to tell you of his courage, generosity, loyalty, lightheartedness, engaging boyishness. More than likely you yourself will fall under the spell of these kindly tales and, before you are aware, find yourself warming with romantic sympathy to the idealized picture of heroic and adventurous youth.

Sit, for instance, on one of the benches under the shade trees in the old square at Santa Fé where the wagon caravans used to end their long journey across the plains. Here the rich and poor of this ancient capital of the land of mañana and sunshine come every day to while away an hour and smoke and talk politics. Mention Billy the Kid to some leisurely burgher. Instantly his face will light up; he will cease his tirade against graft and corruption in high places and go off into interminable anecdotes. Yes, Billy the Kid lived here in Santa Fé when he was a boy. Many a time when he was an outlaw with a price on his head, he rode into town and danced all night at the dance hall over on Gallisteo Street. The house is still there; the pink adobe with the blue door and window shutters. Did the police attempt to arrest him? Not much. Those blue-coated fellows valued their hides. Why, that boy wasn't afraid of the devil. Say, once over at Anton Chico. . . .

Or drop into some little adobe home in Puerta de Luna. Or in Santa Rosa. Or on the Hondo. Or anywhere between the Ratons and Seven Rivers. Perhaps the Mexican housewife will serve you with frijoles and tortillas and coffee with goat's milk. If you are wise in the ways of Mexicans, you will tear off a fragment of tortilla and, cupping it between your fingers, use it as a spoon to eat your frijoles that are red with chili pepper and swimming in soup rich with fat bacon grease. But between mouthfuls of these beans of the gods—and you will be ready to swear they are that, else you are no connoisseur

---

* From *The Saga of Billy the Kid*, by Walter Noble Burns, pp. 64–69. Copyright, 1925, by Doubleday, Page & Company. Garden City, New York.

in beans—don't forget to make some casual reference to Billy the Kid. Then watch the face of your hostess. At mention of the magic name, she will smile softly and dreamlight will come into her eyes.

"Billee the Keed? Ah, you have hear of heem? He was one gran' boy, señor. All Mexican pepul his friend. You nevair hear a Mexican say one word against Billee the Keed. Everybody love that boy. He was so kind-hearted, so generous, so brave. And so 'andsome. *Nombre de Dios!* Every leetle señorita was crazy about heem. They all try to catch that Billee the Keed for their sweetheart. Ah, many a pretty *muchacha* cry her eyes out when he is keel; and when she count her beads at Mass, she add a prayer for good measure for his soul to rest in peace. Poor Billee the Keed! He was good boy—*muy valiente, muy caballero.*"

Or ask Frank Coe about him. You will find him a white-haired old man now on his fruit ranch in Ruidoso Cañon. He fought in the Lincoln County war by the Kid's side and as he tells his story you may sit in a rocking chair under the cottonwoods while the Ruidoso River sings its pleasant tune just back of the rambling, one-story adobe ranch house.

"Billy the Kid," says Coe, "lived with me for a while soon after he came to Lincoln County in the fall of 1877. Just a little before he went to work for Tunstall on the Feliz. No, he didn't work for me. Just lived with me. Riding the chuck line. Didn't have anywhere else special to stay just then. He did a lot of hunting that winter. Billy was a great hunter, and the hills hereabouts were full of wild turkey, deer, and cinnamon bear. Billy could hit a bear's eye so far away I could hardly see the bear.

"He was only eighteen years old, as nice-looking a young fellow as you'd care to meet, and certainly mighty pleasant company. Many a night he and I have sat up before a pine-knot fire swapping yarns. Yes, he had killed quite a few men even then, but it didn't seem to weigh on him. None at all. Ghosts, I reckon, never bothered Billy. He was about as cheerful a little hombre as I ever ran across. Not the grim, sullen kind; but full of talk, and it seemed to me he was laughing half his time.

"You never saw such shooting as that lad could do. Not a dead shot. I've heard about these dead shots but I never happened to meet one. Billy was the best shot with a six-shooter I ever saw, but he missed sometimes. Jesse Evans, who fought on the Murphy side, used to brag that he was as good a shot as the Kid, but I never thought so, and I knew Jesse and have seen him shoot. Jesse, by the way, used to say, too, that he wasn't afraid of Billy the Kid. Which was just another one of his brags. He was scared to death of the Kid, and once when they met in Lincoln, Billy made him take water and made him like it. Billy used to do a whole lot of practice shooting around the ranch, and had the barn peppered full of holes. I have heard people say they have seen him empty his shooter at a hat tossed about twenty feet into the air and hit it six times before it struck the ground. I won't say he couldn't do it, but I never saw him do it. One of his favourite stunts was to shoot at snowbirds sitting on fence posts along the road as he rode by with his horse at a gallop. Sometimes he would kill half-a-dozen birds one after the other; and then he would miss a few. His average was about one in three. And I'd say that was mighty good shooting.

"Billy had had a little schooling, and he could read and write as well as anybody else around here. I never saw him reading any books, but he was a great hand to read newspapers whenever he could get hold of any. He absorbed a lot of education from his newspaper reading. He didn't talk like a backwoodsman. I don't suppose he knew much about the rules of grammar, but he didn't make the common, glaring mistakes of ignorant people. His speech was that of an intelligent and fairly well educated man. He had a clean mind; his conversation was never coarse or vulgar; and while most of the men with whom he associated swore like pirates, he rarely used an oath.

"He was a free-hearted, generous boy. He'd give a friend the shirt off his back. His money came easy when it came; but sometimes it didn't come. He was a gambler and, like all gamblers, his life was chicken one day and feathers the next, a pocketful of money to-day and broke to-morrow. Monte was his favourite game; he banked the game or bucked it, depending on his finances. He was as slick a dealer as ever threw a card, and as a player, he was shrewd, usually lucky, and bet 'em high—the limit on every turn. While he stayed with me, he broke a Mexican monte bank every little while down the cañon at San Patricio. If he happened to lose, he'd take it like a good gambler and, like as not, crack a joke and walk away whistling with his hands rammed in his empty pockets. Losing his money never made him mad. To tell the truth, I never saw Billy the Kid mad in my life, and I knew him several years.

"Think what you please, the Kid had a lot of principle. He was about as honest a fellow as I ever knew outside of some loose notions about rustling cattle. This was stealing, of course, but I don't believe it struck him exactly that way. It didn't seem to have any personal element in it. There were the cattle running loose on the plains without any owner in sight or sign of ownership, except the brands, seeming like part of the landscape. Billy, being in his fashion a sort of potentate ruling a large portion of the landscape with his six-shooter, felt, I suppose, like he had a sort of proprietary claim on those cattle, and it didn't seem to him like robbery—not exactly—to run them off and cash in on them at the nearest market. That's at least one way of figuring it out. But as for other lowdown kinds of theft like sticking up a lonely traveller on the highway, or burglarizing a house, or picking pockets, he was just as much above that sort of thing as you or me. I'd have trusted him with the last dollar I had in the world. One thing is certain, he never stole a cent in his life from a friend."

II. The "War of Billy the Kid"

The tacit defiance of law, the reign of terror and bloodshed inaugurated by The Kid were met in a determined manner by the proper authorities. On June 15th, 1879, Marion Turner, deputy sheriff of Lincoln county, had a warrant placed in his hands for the arrest of The Kid for the murder of Morton Baker, McCluskey, Brady and Hindman. Turner was not only a very brave but a very wise man. He knew that the man for whom he had a warrant was a desperate character, and therefore desperate measures were resorted to to effect his capture. Turner organized a posse of thirty-five men, consisting principally of ranchmen and cowboys of the anti-Chisum faction. In adopting this course Turner not only took advantage of the general horror which every man would feel at the cold-blooded murders, but also of the peculiar and intense hatred entertained against The Kid and his gang by those who conceived their rights had been trampled on by Chisum. The posse was not a very large one, but every man in the crowd was an expert handler of the rifle and could be depended on in an emergency. As emergencies were very liable to arise, this readiness and nerviness was a good and important factor of the problem.

On the seventeenth day of June, after being out two days,

Turner and his posse came upon The Kid and his sixty-three men. The place where they met was in a narrow cañon at the mouth of a range of low foot hills. To the right was a thickly wooded expanse, to the left huge boulders, with here and there a straggling pine tree, while in front ran a small stream which had its source ten miles distant, to the north. The Kid's party had made their camp five miles up the stream, and had come down to the place where it left the hills in order to reconnoiter, when they were met by Turner's posse. The former divided, one division running back to protect their camp, and the other remaining to confront the posse, each side thus being evenly balanced. Turner halted nearly a hundred yards from where The Kid was standing, and arranging his forces in the best possible manner with each man's hand on his rifle, stepped out a few steps from the ranks and read his warrant. To the requisition a defiant answer was returned to the effect that they would never get him, dead or alive; whereupon Turner ordered his men to arrest him. They advanced at a double-quick, on horseback, but The Kid, wishing to avoid a fight until he could effect a junction with the remainder of his gang, as well as secure a better position, hastily retreated. Seeing his purpose the order was given to fire, but the aim of the posse was rendered uncertain by the motion of their horses and only two men were hit, one being seriously and the other fatally wounded. None of the Sheriff's party were touched by the return fusillade. The fight continued in this way for five miles, neither side scoring another fatal shot. A decided stand was made at the camp and Turner drew off for consultation. At the camp all was bustle and confusion. A rude embankment had been thrown up, behind which The Kid, his men, their horses and pack animals were waiting to receive the expected onslaught. The consultation between Turner and his men resulted in the employment of strategy. They retired a short distance and halted just on the edge of the wood. Ten of the party formed a line along its edge and the other twenty-five dashed into the wood with the intention of making a circuit and coming in upon the gang from the rear. This was easily accomplished, provided the ruse was successful, because The Kid's camp joined the woods on the right. The danger of the undertaking lay in the fact that if the plan was discovered the little party of ten would fall an easy prey to a foe outnumbering them six to one. The minutes that succeeded the departure of the twenty-five were anxious ones to those who remained. Every movement of the

enemy was watched and a show of preparation for renewing
the conflict was kept up. Five minutes had passed. The detour
should have been made in that time. The Kid appeared at the
head of his men and began to file out of the camp, confident
of the superiority of numbers and his own charmed life. At this
moment, and not a second too soon, a yell was heard from
behind. Turner had flanked them. They turned, and another
yell was heard. The ten who had guarded the operation of
their comrades rushed up the stream. A deadly fire was poured
in from two sides, and for a moment all was confusion and
panic. At this juncture The Kid dashed forward, and calling
upon his men to rally broke through the opposing force, killing
one of them and slightly wounding two more. He was followed
by Turner, the Nemesis. Volley after volley was fired. The
flight was so rapid that neither the dead nor the wounded were
cared for. On! On! in feverish haste. Crossing and recrossing
the little stream, turning to fire and then savagely spurring
their horses forward, they fairly flew. Of the sixty-five men
whom The Kid led into the cañon only forty escaped alive,
while Turner lost but five. The odds had changed, and they
were not as favorable to the desperado. Across the plain,
dodging hither and thither, now advancing, then retreating, the
two forces went, each wreaking vengeance on the other, each
paying old scores and getting even with bitter enemies.
Strange as it may seem, this running fight lasted two days,
with scarcely a stop for food or water. The forces by this time
had become considerably reduced, numbering but twenty-five
each. Lieut. Col. Dudley, of the famous 9th Cavalry (colored),
learning that re-enforcements were being sent to The Kid,
took two companies of his regiment and went to Turner's
assistance. As luck would have it Dudley was first on the
ground and The Kid and his gang at once retreated towards
Lincoln which was but a few miles distant. They took shelter
in McSwain's house, one of the most elegantly furnished
dwellings in the Territory, in which only the most fashionable
were wont to enter. The cavalry rushed up but were repulsed
and fell back. Again the line was formed, this time on foot, and
an advance was made. The fight raged furiously. It was a
question of annihilation for one side or the other, and every
man fought like a demon. Port holes were cut and rifle balls
sent from them with unerring aim. The house became a fort
and the garden surrounding it a battlefield. During the battle
Mrs. McSwain encouraged the garrison by playing martial airs
on her piano, and singing inspiring battle songs. The besieging

posse soon got the range of the piano from its sound, and shot it to pieces with their heavy buffalo rifles, the wife of McSwain narrowly escaping. This siege was of three days' duration. On the third day of the fight Turner, being convinced that they could not be conquered by legitimate warfare, ordered the house to be fired by throwing bucketfuls of blazing coal oil on the roof and inside through the windows. This precipitated the crisis, and about dusk of the third day the desperadoes made a rush for their horses with the intention of thereby effecting an escape. A hand to hand combat ensued in which twelve of The Kid's men and two of Turner's posse were killed, McSwain being among the number. During the rush from the burning house, Tom O'Fallaher, a "pard" of The Kid's, young, and from San Antonio, Texas, noticed a friend fall. Although a storm of balls and buckshot rained around him he coolly stopped, picked up his comrade and was about to carry him out when he noticed that he was dead. Throwing the body down he drew a sword and fought his way out. This brave fellow was afterwards killed by deputy sheriff Garrett's posse, shortly after the capture of The Kid.

The leader of the gang, The Kid, seemed to bear a charmed existence. A hundred bullets were speeded towards him and not one reached the mark. He escaped without a scratch, and with barely a dozen men fled, hotly pursued but never caught. Immediately after this fearful flight he reorganized his followers, received accessions to his cause, and was again in condition to make the average New Mexican go to bed with a feeling of insecurity. The Kid in the meanwhile had added five names to his death-roll. It now numbered eleven.

III. DEATH OF BILLY THE KID*

In March, 1881, a Deputy United States Marshal by the name of John W. Poe arrived in the booming mining camp of White Oaks. He had been sent to New Mexico by the Cattlemen's Association of the Texas Panhandle. Cattle King Charlie Goodnight, being the president of the association, had selected Mr. Poe as the proper man to put a stop to the stealing of Panhandle cattle by "Billy the Kid" and gang.

After the "Kid's" escape, Pat Garrett went to White Oaks and deputized John W. Poe to assist him in rounding up the "Kid."

---

* From *History of "Billy the Kid,"* by Chas. A. Siringo, pp. 124–133. Copyright, 1920, by Chas. A. Siringo.

From now on Mr. Poe made trips out in the mountains trying to locate the young outlaw. The "Kid's" best friends argued that he was "nobody's fool," and would not remain in the United States, when the Old Mexico border was so near. They didn't realize that little Cupid was shooting his tender young heart full of love-darts, straight from the heart of pretty little Miss Dulcinea del Toboso, of Fort Sumner.

Early in July, Pat Garrett received a letter from an acquaintance by the name of Brazil, in Fort Sumner, advising him that the "Kid" was hanging around there. Garrett at once wrote Brazil to meet him about dark on the night of July 13th at the mouth of the Taiban arroyo, below Fort Sumner.

Now the sheriff took his trusted deputy, John W. Poe, and rode to Roswell, on the Rio Pecos. There they were joined by one of Mr. Garrett's fearless cowboy deputies, "Kip" McKinnie, who had been raised near Uvalde, Texas.

Together the three law officers rode up the river towards Fort Sumner, a distance of eighty miles. They arrived at the mouth of Taiban arroyo an hour after dark of July 13th, but Brazil was not there to meet them. The night was spent sleeping on their saddle blankets.

The next morning Garrett sent Mr. Poe, who was a stranger in the country, and for that reason would not be suspicioned, into Fort Sumner, five miles north, to find out what he could on the sly, about the "Kid's" presence. From Fort Sumner he was to go to Sunny Side, six miles north, to interview a merchant by the name of Mr. Rudolph. Then when the moon was rising, to meet Garrett and McKinnie at La Punta de la Glorietta, about four miles north of Fort Sumner.

Failing to find out anything of importance about the "Kid," John W. Poe met his two companions at the appointed place, and they rode into Fort Sumner.

It was about eleven o'clock, and the moon was shining brightly, when the officers rode into an old orchard and concealed their horses. Now the three continued afoot to the home of Pete Maxwell, a wealthy stockman, who was a friend to both Garrett and the "Kid." He lived in a long, one-story adobe building, which had been the U. S. officers' quarters when the soldiers were stationed there. The house fronted south, and had a wide covered porch in front. The grassy front yard was surrounded by a picket fence.

As Pat Garrett had courted his wife and married her in this town, he knew every foot of the ground, even to Pete Maxwell's private bed room.

On reaching the picket gate, near the corner room, which Pete Maxwell always occupied, Garrett told his two deputies to wait there until after he had a talk with half-breed Pete Maxwell.

The night being hot, Pete Maxwell's door stood wide open, and Garrett walked in.

A short time previous, "Billy the Kid" had arrived from a sheep camp out in the hills. Back of the Maxwell home lived a Mexican servant, who was a warm friend to the "Kid." Here "Billy the Kid" always found late newspapers, placed there by loving hands, for his special benefit.

This old servant had gone to bed. The "Kid" lit a lamp, then pulled off his coat and boots. Now he glanced over the papers to see if his name was mentioned. Finding nothing of interest in the newspapers, he asked the old servant to get up and cook him some supper, as he was very hungry.

Getting up, the servant told him there was no meat in the house. The "Kid" remarked that he would go and get some from Pete Maxwell.

Now he picked up a butcher knife from the table to cut the meat with, and started, bare-footed and bare-headed.

The "Kid" passed within a few feet of the end of the porch where sat John W. Poe and Kip McKinnie. The latter had raised up, when his spur rattled, which attracted the "Kid's" attention. At the same moment Mr. Poe stood up in the small open gateway leading from the street to the end of the porch. They supposed the man coming towards them, only partly dressed, was a servant, or possibly Pete Maxwell.

The "Kid" had pulled his pistol, and so had John Poe, who by that time was almost within arm's reach of the "Kid."

With pistol pointing at Poe, at the same time asking in Spanish: "Quien es?" (Who is that?), he backed into Pete Maxwell's room. He had repeated the above question several times. On entering the room, "Billy the Kid" walked up to within a few feet of Pat Garrett, who was sitting on Maxwell's bed, and asked: "Who are they, Pete?"

Now discovering that a man sat on Pete's bed, the "Kid" with raised pistol pointing towards the bed, began backing across the room.

Pete Maxwell whispered to the sheriff. "That's him, Pat." By this time the "Kid" had backed to a streak of moonlight coming through the south window, asking: "Quien es?" (Who's that?)

Garrett raised his pistol and fired. Then cocked the pistol

again and it went off accidentally, putting a hole in the ceiling, or wall.

Now the sheriff sprang out of the door onto the porch, where stood his two deputies with drawn pistols.

Soon after, Pete Maxwell ran out, and came very near getting a ball from Poe's pistol. Garrett struck the pistol upward, saying: "Don't shoot Maxwell!"

A lighted candle was secured from the mother of Pete Maxwell, who occupied a nearby room, and the dead body of "Billy the Kid" was found stretched out on his back with a bullet wound in his breast, just above the heart. At the right hand lay a Colt's-.41 calibre pistol, and at his left a butcher knife.

Now the native people began to collect,—many of them being warm friends of the "Kid's." Garrett allowed them to take the body across the street to a carpenter shop, where it was laid out on a bench. Then lighted candles were placed around the remains of what was once the bravest, and coolest young outlaw who ever trod the face of the earth.

The next day, this, once mother's darling, was buried by the side of his chum, Tom O'Phalliard, in the old military cemetery.

He was killed at midnight, July 14th, 1881, being just twenty-one years, seven months and twenty-one days of age, and had killed twenty-one men, not including Indians, which he said didn't count as human beings.

IV. Song of Billy the Kid*

I'll sing you a true song of Billy the Kid, I'll sing of the desperate deeds that he did Way out in New Mexico long, long a—

---

* From *American Ballads and Folk Songs*, collected and compiled by John A. Lomax and Alan Lomax, pp. 137–138. Copyright, 1934, by The Macmillan Company. New York.

go When a man's on—ly chance was his own for—ty four.

When Billy the Kid was a very young lad,
In old Silver City he went to the bad;
Way out in the West with a gun in his hand
At the age of twelve years he first killed his man.

Fair Mexican maidens play guitars and sing
A song about Billy, their boy bandit king,
How ere his young manhood had reached its sad end
He'd a notch on his pistol for twenty-one men.

'Twas on the same night when poor Billy died
He said to his friends: "I am not satisfied;
There are twenty-one men I have put bullets through
And Sheriff Pat Garrett must make twenty-two."

Now, this is how Billy the Kid met his fate:
The bright moon was shining, the hour was late.
Shot down by Pat Garrett, who once was his friend,
The young outlaw's life had now come to its end.

There's many a man with a face fine and fair
Who starts out in life with a chance to be square,
But just like poor Billy he wanders astray
And loses his life in the very same way.

Jesse James

I. BALLAD OF JESSE JAMES*

Jes—se James was a lad who killed man—ya man. He
robbed the Glen—dale train. He stole from the rich and he
gave to the poor, He'd a hand and a heart and a brain.
Chorus
Jes—se had a wife to mourn for his life, Three

* From *Singing Cowboy*, A Book of Western Songs, collected and edited
by Margaret Larkin, pp. 158–159. Copyright, 1931, by Alfred A. Knopf, Inc.
New York.

It was Robert Ford, that dirty little coward,
I wonder how he does feel,
For he ate of Jesse's bread and he slept in Jesse's bed,
Then he laid Jesse James in his grave.

Jesse was a man, a friend to the poor.
He'd never see a man suffer pain,
And with his brother Frank he robbed the Chicago bank,
And stopped the Glendale train.

It was on a Wednesday night, the moon was shining bright,
He stopped the Glendale train,
And the people all did say for many miles away,
It was robbed by Frank and Jesse James.

It was on a Saturday night, Jesse was at home,
Talking to his family brave,
Robert Ford came along like a thief in the night,
And laid Jesse James in his grave.

The people held their breath when they heard of Jesse's death,
And wondered how he ever came to die,
It was one of the gang called little Robert Ford,
That shot Jesse James on the sly.

Jesse went to his rest with hand on his breast,
The devil will be upon his knee,
He was born one day in the county of Shea
And he came of a solitary race.

This song was made by Billy Gashade,[9]
As soon as the news did arrive,
He said there was no man with the law in his hand
Could take Jesse James when alive.

Jesse had a wife to mourn for his life,
Three children, they were brave,
But that dirty little coward that shot Mister Howard,
Has laid Jesse James in his grave.

II. JESSE JAMES AND THE POOR WIDOW*

"One day," says Sam Allender, "Frank James told me that on a certain occasion he and his pals were traveling on horseback somewhere in northern Missouri. It being about noon, they were hungry. They pulled off the main road and found a lone woman in charge of a small farmhouse. They asked her if she could supply them with something to eat.

"At first the woman hesitated. The men displayed money and assured her they would be glad to pay for what they ate. She then proceeded to prepare such scant food as she had on hand. As she was making coffee and cooking eggs, the James crowd sat around the room. They noticed that she was weeping; tears were rolling down her cheeks, sobs were heaving her bosom.

" 'Jesse,' said Frank in telling me the story, 'was always tender-hearted—couldn't stand a woman's tears. He asked her why she was crying. She tried to smile it off, and said that seeing us men around the house reminded her of the happy time when her husband was living and had other men now and then helping him do the farm work; she was just thinking how sadly things had changed since his death, and that was what made her cry, so she said.

" 'Jesse kept on asking questions. The woman said she had several children at school, some miles down the road; there was a mortgage on her farm, she went on to say, for $1,400; it was overdue; and this was the last day of grace.

" ' "Aha!" said Jesse, "and so that's really what's making you cry—you're afraid you're going to lose your home. I see."

" 'Yes, that was it, she admitted. That very afternoon, said the weeping widow, the man who held the mortgage was coming out from town to demand his money. He was a hardhearted old miser, she stated, and she didn't have a dollar to apply on the debt. The man would be sure to foreclose and turn her and her helpless little ones out.

" ' "Huh!" said Jesse, "that so?" his eyes blinking fast and furiously. "Well, now ma'am, I don't know about that; I—well, now, I think maybe you won't lose your farm after all."

" 'The widow looked rather puzzled. She put the food on the table and all of us sat down and turned to. After we

* From *The Rise and Fall of Jesse James*, by Robertus Love, pp. 289–292. Copyright, 1926, by Robertus Love. New York: G. P. Putnam's Sons.

finished eating, Jesse produced a sack and counted out on the table $1,400.

" ' "Here, lady," said Jesse, "you take this money and pay off your mortgage."

" 'The lady was amazed. "I can't ever pay you back," she said, "and so I won't borrow it."

" ' "But it's no loan," said Jesse; "it's a gift."

" 'The widow said she couldn't believe it was anything but a dream—things never happened that way—but Jesse assured her it was no dream; the money was good money and it was for her use. Jesse then sat down and wrote out a form of receipt, which he had the woman copy in her own handwriting. He put the original into his pocket, so that his handwriting wouldn't get into other hands. Jesse instructed the woman to pay the mortgage-holder the $1,400 and have him sign the receipt—in ink. He then handed her a handful of cash for her immediate needs.

" 'Jesse asked the grateful widow to describe the man who held the mortgage. She did so, telling the kind of rig he drove and about what hour she expected him, and the road by which he would come out from town. We then bade her good day and mounted our horses. The widow was still weeping, but weeping for joy.

" 'We rode some distance from the house and hid in the bushes beside the rocky road along which the mortgage man was to come in his buggy. Presently we saw him driving toward the widow's house, and pretty soon driving back, looking prosperous. He was humming "Old Dan Tucker was a fine old feller" as he came opposite. We stepped out into the road, held him up and recovered the $1,400.'

"I asked Frank James," said Sam Allender, "if they had any more difficulty in getting the money on that occasion than they had had on the occasion when they first acquired it; and he replied, with a laugh:

" 'Now, Sam, I'm not being sweated.' "

Sam Bass

I. THE SAM BASS LEGEND*

SOON after his death, relics of Sam Bass began to crop up in nearly every town of central and northern Texas. If all the "authentic" Bass guns could be gathered in one place, they would stock an arsenal. A contemporary newspaper supported the claim of Milt Tucker, of Georgetown, that Bass gave him his gun when captured. Other guns owned by two Rangers, Dick Ware and John L. Banister, were also said to have been surrendered by Bass when captured. A fourth gun for which the same claim was made was sold at auction in Austin soon afterwards. Sam's cartridge belt, with a few unused bullets, was given to the University of Texas Library. His compass went to Captain Dan W. Roberts, of the Texas Rangers, while Captain June Peak retained the bowie knife taken from the body of Arkansas Johnson at Salt Creek. Horns of steers said to have been killed by Bass were sold at fancy prices, and a carpenter at Snyder nailed to the top of his tool chest a horseshoe supposed to have been worn by the Denton mare.

G. W. Allen, a mule-team freighter and storekeeper in Old Round Rock, possessed a hat said to have been given him by Sam Bass. Another headpiece, described as "the identical hat which Sam Bass wore at the time of his capture," was displayed at the bar of the El Paso Hotel at Fourth and Main, Fort Worth, about three weeks after Sam was buried. The hat was a limp one with a low crown and a wide brim. The owner, C. A. Sparks, traveling agent for a St. Louis wholesale hat firm, said Bass gave him the hat; and he showed corroborative statements from citizens of Round Rock.

Near Belton, people pointed to live oaks in which Bass was said to have shot his initials while riding at full speed. In Round Rock, Henry Koppel and his successors showed visitors the bandits' bullet marks in the store, and the Sam Bass Cafe was opened across the street. Every cave within a wide area was said to have been a hiding place for the outlaw band. Boy Scouts from Denton have explored a cave at Pilot Knob, imagining they were in the brigands' rendezvous; and a wild recess in the hills of Palo Pinto County has become known as

* From *Sam Bass*, by Wayne Gard, pp. 239–247. Copyright, 1936, by Wayne Gard. Boston and New York: The Houghton Mifflin Company.

Sam Bass Hollow. Longhorn Cavern, about forty miles west of Georgetown, had been widely advertised as a former haunt of the famous outlaw, though it is doubtful if he ever was within thirty-five miles of the place.

Thickets, as well as caves, have been pointed out as the desperado's hiding places; Bass hideouts in Texas have become almost as numerous as George Washington beds in Virginia. On their way back to Denton County from their fourth Texas train robbery at Mesquite, Sam and his regulars were said to have hidden for a day or two in a bois d'arc thicket just north of Dallas, on what later became the campus of Southern Methodist University. A short distance west of this thicket, the story goes, a Negro youngster named Bob was looking after a herd of hogs when a stranger approached on a horse and asked what he was doing.

"Herdin' hogs, suh," the boy replied.

"Do you know who I am?" the rider asked.

"No, suh, ah sho don't, suh."

"I'm Sam Bass!"

This statement almost paralyzed the youngster, whose fear was not lessened when Bass whipped out a gun, pointed it at Bob, then returned it to the holster.

"Boy, I ought to kill you," he said. "But I won't. There are men following me. When they get here, you tell them I've gone toward the Trinity River."

The bandit then rode off to the north, and Bob ran in the opposite direction until out of breath. As he stopped to rest, a posse headed by Sheriff Marion Moon rode up; and the frightened boy told them Bass had ridden westward, toward the river.

Many of the legends that took root in cattle camps and hearthsides magnified Sam's crimes as well as the size of his loot. Most of these stories were as fictitious as that of the Texas verse writer who described Bass as stealing a pig when the Indiana youth was only ten years old. More plausible was the Denton County story that, at the outset of his robbing career, Sam tried to hold up Henry Hill, of Little Elm. Hill, who went by the name of Rawhide, was building a cotton gin and had gone to Dallas to obtain money for wages and other expenses. Returning to Lewisville by train, he hired a livery horse and started home. Sam and two companions waylaid him and, after an exciting chase, shot his horse from under him. At this, Hill grabbed his saddle-bags containing the money and took refuge in a nearby farmhouse. The amateur robbers then gave up the pursuit and rode away.

Although sheriffs and Rangers seldom sighted him, legendary encounters with the elusive Sam were reported from many places. Once he stopped a Negro near Cove Hollow and asked him to trade horses, but the well-mounted darky refused.

"Do you know who I am?" asked the brigand. "I'm Sam Bass!"

At this news, the Negro tumbled off his horse and began to run for his life. Sam called him back, however, and—after the saddles were changed—handed him seventy-five dollars.

Until he ran short of money at the last, Bass always paid well for his fresh mounts—usually with gold stolen from the Union Pacific express at Big Springs.

Once he stopped a cattleman in the northern part of Dallas County and asked for chewing tobacco. "You can buy more, but I can't," he explained. The rancher handed over a plug; and Sam cut off a piece, returning the remainder with a half dollar.

Bass then offered fifty dollars for the man's horse, but he replied that he had paid only half that amount for the nag.

"That's all right; I'll take that mule of yours to make up the difference," said Sam.

A trade was made, and both men went off well satisfied.

Some of the stories have to do with banks Sam tried to rob or thought of robbing, but didn't. Although court testimony indicated that Bass sent Billy Scott to inspect the bank at Weatherford, legend has it that the desperado led his whole band there to look over the financial situation. They found Jim Couts, the trigger-fingered banker, seated on the curb in front of his place on the south side of the square. Sam already was acquainted with the rugged financier, and the setup didn't look promising. For some time, the bandit leader sat on a drygoods box and whittled while his men walked up and down in front of the bank. Later, they decided that before they could rob the bank they would have to kill Couts. As they didn't want to undertake that job, they mounted their horses and rode away.

The generosity of Sam with the twenty-dollar gold pieces he brought back from the big train robbery in Nebraska gave him fame as a Robin Hood even while he was living; and after his death the stories of his giving and spending were enlarged. Payments of twenty dollars for a dozen eggs or a pan of warm biscuits were reported from many directions. On one occasion, he was said to have stopped with his outlaw band at the farm home of a Denton County widow. Against the woman's wishes, the robbers stayed overnight; but Bass told his men that the widow was a lady and must be treated as such. The men behaved themselves and did no drinking; and when they left the next morning, Bass paid the widow fifty dollars.

Many stories were told at the expense of those who pursued the outlaw band. A cocky young Breckenridge lawyer was said to have led a heavily armed posse against Bass, whom he expected to capture by nightfall. But when the pursuers found the desperado, Sam refused to flee, and therefore the posse could not chase him. Rather than to approach too close to the notorious gunman, the men in the posse rode home and reported that Bass could not be found.

From Breckenridge came also the tale of a young detective who arrived with the announcement that he was going to kill Sam Bass. Walking along the road toward the supposed hideout of the brigands, he received a lift from a man in a buggy. He explained his mission to the driver, who asked if he would know Sam Bass if he saw him.

"No," answered the detective.

"Well, you're riding with him now," his companion calmly remarked.

The detective then began trembling and begging for his life and telling of his wife and children at home. He was released, and this was the last time he went out looking for Sam Bass.

However, another amateur detective in Breckenridge was said to have given a better account of himself. This young fellow, who roomed at the town's only hotel, began talking about capturing Bass when the outlaws were rumored to be camping in Stephens County. Not rating this self-appointed detective's courage as highly as they might, several young fellows of the town decided to play a trick on him by impersonating the train-robber band and giving the pursuer a big scare when he was decoyed in their direction. A young newspaper editor, Homer Davenport, agreed to lead the detective to a place in the country where the others would be hidden.

As the editor led the bandit-catcher up a hillside, shots were fired by the pranksters from behind rocks at the summit, and the two men started to run back. The editor fell on his rifle, as planned, and called out that he was killed. After running a little farther, the detective suddenly turned around and marched deliberately back to the supposed corpse, pistol in hand. Muttering, "I can't leave a man like that," he began firing at the men he took for brigands hiding behind the rocks —firing to kill. Not until the corpse rolled off to join the fleeing townsmen did he see through the trick. It was two days before Davenport mustered enough courage to resume his meals at the hotel.

The most persistent of all the Bass legends have been those of buried gold. A Denton saloonkeeper was said to have buried six hundred dollars' worth of Sam's double-eagles at a spot within the town; and thirty thousand dollars of his loot was reported buried in Montague County, northwest of Denton. A cave near McNeil, a few miles south of Round Rock, and another in Llano County were also said to have received some of his stolen treasure. For more than half a century, men armed with maps and spades—and sometimes with divining rods—have been looking for chests of gold they believed Sam buried.

One of the earliest stories of the outlaw's buried riches came from a young farmer, Henry Chapman, who lived near Springtown, in Parker County. In January, 1879, Chapman was riding a mule through the woods from Harrison's gin, at the pool on Clear Fork, to Squire Milliner's place near the mouth of Salt Creek. At a point near Skeen's Peak, his mule became scared, gave a hard lurch, and broke the saddle girth. While he was dismounted, mending the girth, Chapman discovered a pile of fresh dirt covered with pieces of brush. He supposed at first that some fellow had been enticed into the woods and murdered, but he was curious enough to remove the brush and loose earth.

Within a few minutes, as he related afterwards, he unearthed a walnut box big enough to hold a bushel and a half. The box was crammed with gold and silver coins, including many twenty-dollar gold pieces. His first impulse was to fill his pockets, but he remembered that he had a sack under his saddle. He quickly procured this sack and began to fill it with treasure from the walnut box.

As the coins were clinking into the sack, Chapman happened to look up and was terrified to see eight men advancing upon him with guns leveled at his head. As he was unarmed he hastily mounted his mule and galloped off. He never saw the gunmen again, but he was sure they were associates of Sam Bass, who had come back for treasure they had helped the outlaw bury in the previous summer.

From Austin to the Red River, caves were searched for gold the robber chieftain was supposed to have buried, but none was found. Before long, maps and diagrams began to appear. Several years after the turn of the century, N. B. Hamilton, a Round Rock liveryman, was in Mexico and obtained from an American there a map that showed just where the Bass treasure was buried. Hamilton brought the map back to Round Rock and let two of his friends, B. H. Allen and George Townsley, into the secret. The map indicated that the treasure was hidden in a hollow tree on the old Leander and Liberty Hill road, two miles northwest of Round Rock. Equipped with axes and lanterns, the men went to the scene late at night and chopped down the tree. The only metallic substance they found, however, was a single rusty nail. The next morning, people who passed along the road wondered why the tree-trunk had been chopped to bits and none of the wood carried away.

Two decades later, other men with other maps were observed digging for Sam's gold in the neighborhood of Cove Hollow, more than forty miles northwest of Denton. As late as January, 1928, feverish treasure-hunters carried the search into the city of Dallas. The searchers had seen an old penciled map that showed where Sam had buried two hundred thousand dollars' worth of gold bullion and other valuables. The hiding place was under a forked stump near a spring on the west side of Trinity River. The spot was located, and for several weeks nocturnal excavations were made on a section of the river bluff, owned by Marcus Plowman, two blocks north of the Oak Cliff end of the Houston Street viaduct.

Stackalee*

HE WAS BORN WITH A VEIL OVER HIS FACE

> Gypsy told Stack's mother,
> Told her like a friend,
> Your double-jinted baby
> Won't come to no good end.

* By Onah L. Spencer. From *Direction*, Vol. IV (Summer, 1941), No. 5, pp. 14–17. Copyright, 1941, by Direction, Inc.

AND the gypsy woman shore said a hatful, cause it all come out that very way. And how comes Stackalee's mother to call in the fawchin teller was cause he come kickin into this wide world double-jinted, and with a full set of teeth. But what scared her most was he had a veil over his face, and everybody knows that babies born with veils on their faces kin see ghosts and raise 41 kinds of hell.

SOLD HIS SOUL TO THE DEVIL

And so when Stackalee growed up he got to be an awful rascal and rounder wit lots of triflin women and he staid drunk all the time. One dark night as he come staggerin down the road the devil popped up real sudden, like a grinnin jumpin jack. He carried Stackalee into the grave yahd and bought his soul. And that's how come Stack could go round doin things no other livin man could do, such as:

Makin himself so little he could git into a bottle on a shelf and you could look at him settin there—yes suh! And fillin a small bottle full of water and settin it in a big glass jar where it would sink to the bottom till he began to talk to it and make it rare up and drap back just howsoever he wanted it to. And by walkin barefoot on hot slag out of a pig iron furnace and never gittin burned and eatin all the hot fire you could hand him without burning his stummick and changin hisself into a mountain or varmint. Some old timers lowed they knowed him personal and that his favorite night time shape was a prowlin wolf. That's how it come they used to sing that old song about him:

> Stackalee didn't wear no shoe;
> Couldn't tell his track from horse or mule.

THE MAGIC HAT

You see, it happened like this: Stack was crazy about Stetson hats; specially them great big five gallon hats with dimples in the crown. And he had a whole row of em hangin on pegs and you could look at em along the wall of his rickety shanty on Market Street in St. Louis, where he lived with his woman, Stack o' Dollars, that I'm goin to tell you about later.

He had a dimpled and lemon colored yaller hat, and a black Sunday one with two white eyes to wear to funerals with his new brogans, and lots of other ones, all kinds and colors.

But his favorite was an oxblood magic hat that folks claim he made from the raw hide of a man-eatin panther that the devil had skinned alive. And like I told you, how come Stack to have it was because he had sold his soul to old Scratch. You see, Satan heard about Stack's weakness, so he met him that dark night and took him into the grave yahd where he coaxed him into tradin his soul, promisin him he could do all kinds of magic and devilish things long as he wore that oxblood Stetson and didn't let it get away from him. And that's the way the devil fixed it so when Stack did lose it he would lose his head, and kill a good citizen, and run right smack into his doom.

HIS GIRL FRIEND

Now Stackalee had a girl friend and her name was Stack o' Dollars. She blew into St. Louis off Cincinnati's old Bucktown on the Levee where she used to run gamblin games at a saloon there called the Silver Moon, long, long ago; and she always bet her whole stack of silver dollars.

> She walked into the Silver Moon
> Stacked her dollars, mountain high;
> Says they call me Stack o' Dollars
> Cause my limit is the sky.

She had two diamond teeth with gold fillin and when she opened her mouth with a sunburst smile, didn't they glitter! Proud of them sparklers, too, cause they shined like flashlights. Wouldn't pawn em, even to get old Stackalee out on bond. And since they was fastened to her haid they was safe cause she was a fat mama with the meat shakin on her bones and she didn't need no man for a bouncer. She feared nothin and nobody. Her motto was: "Come clean, or come dirty and get cleaned." She could put a knot on a bully's haid so big that he wouldn't know whether the knot was on him or he was on the knot.

She had a full bosom, wore an eight-gallon Stetson, smoked cheroots, and was tougher than Big Mag of Chicago's old Cheyenne District. She ruled the levees with her big fist, and even old double-jinted Stackalee, big enough to go bear huntin with a willow switch, had to light out when they had them Saturday night fist fights, cause she would roll up her sleeves and begin smackin him around till their shanty shook like when Joshua fit the battle of Jericho and the walls come tumblin down. But she was good-hearted, though, when she was sober; and old long tall Stack who was a gambler with plenty of good-lookin browns claimed he like her cause she whupped him so good.

STACKALEE GOES WEST

Now like I told you, Stack was popular with the women folks cause he could whup the blues on a guitar, and beat out boogie woogie music piano bass and the like of that, but what they liked about him most was he was so stout he could squeeze the breath out of em almost. And his favorite one was a voodoo queen down in New Orleans French market.

Any way, the women got to braggin on him bein so stout that they reckoned he could even give old Jesse James a good tussle. So Stack, with his gun handle filled with notches, knowed there was a reward out for him for men he had washed away. He lowed he was lucky 'count of his magic Stetson to keep in hidin, but he figgered he had better light out while the goin was good. So he thought he would just look up old Jesse James and give him a trial.

> Stackalee went out West,
> Met Jesse James, and did his best.

Yes, sir, that fool even got mixed up with Jesse James. But Jesse was too much for him—turned old Stack every way but *loose*. And Lord knows what might not have happened to Stack if the devil hadn't come down the road in a cloud of dust that got in Jesse's eyes. Leastwise, it might have saved the city of San Francisco and it might have kept old Stack from gettin into all them other amazin things I'm goin to tell you about later. And leastwise the devil wouldn't have changed hisself to look like Billy Lyons and get poor innercent Billy killed.

STACKALEE CHANGES HIMSELF INTO A HORSE

Anyway, after the devil had saved him from Jesse James, Stack, knowin the law was hot after him, lit out again, headin west. And it was on the way over the mountains that he run into two cullud deputies on the lookout for him in order to collect the $5,000 reward offered for his arrest. So Stack set

down to swap a few words with 'em between two big mountains[10] before they had caught on who he was. Then he told
em he didn't aim to hurt em, he just wanted to know what
their names was. When they told him, that sucker hauled out
his forty-five and shot their initials in their hats, changed
hisself into a horse, and galloped away with a lot of little
baby red devils ridin on his back. And did them deputies run
the other direction! They knowed it was Satan's work and they
thought maybe Stack was the devil hisself.

> Tell you the truth!
> Think I'm lyin?
> Had to run sideways
> To keep from flyin.

So skeered they tore out through a graveyahd, knockin
tombstones over like ten pins in a bowlin alley. And so Stack
he held his sides laughin, and set down between them two big
mountains and thought and thought, and finally made up his
mind to go on to Frisco, where he was later called "the black
Samson."

How Old Scratch Tricked Stackalee

It was in the year of eight-een hun-dred
and six-ty-one In St. Lou-is on Mar-ket St. where
Stack-a-lee was born. Ev' — ry-bo-dy's
talk-in 'bout Stack-a-lee. It was
on one cold and frost—y night When
Stack-a-lee and Bil-ly Ly-ons had one aw-ful fight,
All a-bout an old Stet-son hat

The White Elephant Barrel House was wrecked that night;
Gutters full of beer and whisky; it was an awful sight.

Jewelry and rings of the purest solid gold
Scattered over the dance and gamblin hall.

The can can dancers they rushed for the door
When Billy cried, "Oh, please, Stack, don't shoot me no more."

"Have mercy," Billy groaned. "Oh, please spare my life;
I've got two little babies and an innocent wife."

Stack says, "God bless your children, damn your wife!
You stole my magic Stetson; I'm gonna steal your life."

"But," says Billy, "I always treated you like a man.
'Tain't nothin to that old Stetson but the greasy band."

He shot poor Billy once, he shot him twice,
And the third time Billy pleaded, "Please go tell my wife."

Yes, Stackalee, the gambler, everybody knowed his name;
Made his livin hollerin high, low, jack and the game.

Meantime the sergeant strapped on his big forty-five,
Says, "Now we'll bring in this bad man, dead or alive."

And brass-buttoned policemen all dressed in blue
Came down the sidewalk marchin two by two.

Sent for the wagon and it hurried and come
Loaded with pistols and a big gatling gun.

At midnight on that stormy night there came an awful wail—
Billy Lyons and a graveyard ghost outside the city jail.

"Jailer, jailer," says Stack, "I can't sleep.
For around my bedside poor Billy Lyons still creeps.

"He comes in shape of a lion with a blue steel in his hand,
For he knows I'll stand and fight if he comes in shape of man."

Stackalee went to sleep that night by the city clock bell,
Dreaming the devil had come all the way up from hell.

Red devil was sayin, "You better hunt your hole;
I've hurried here from hell just to get your soul."

Stackalee told him, "Yes, maybe you're right,
But I'll give even you one hell of a fight."

When they got into the scuffle, I heard the devil shout,
"Come and get this bad man before he puts my fire out."

The next time I seed the devil he was scramblin up the wall,
Yellin, "Come an get this bad man fore he mops up with us all."

Then here come Stack's woman runnin, says, "Daddy, I love you
    true;
See what beer, whisky, and smokin hop has brought you to.

"But before I'll let you lay in there, I'll put my life in pawn."
She hurried and got Stackalee out on a five thousand dollar bond.

Stackalee said, "Ain't but one thing that grieves my mind.
When they take me away, babe, I leave you behind."

But the woman he really loved was a voodoo queen
From Creole French market, way down in New Orleans.

He laid down at home that night, took a good night's rest,
Arrived in court at nine o'clock to hear the coroner's inquest.

Crowds jammed the sidewalk, far as you could see,
Tryin to get a good look at tough Stackalee.

Over the cold, dead body Stackalee he did bend,
Then he turned and faced those twelve jury men.

The judge says, "Stackalee, I would spare your life,
But I know you're a bad man; I can see it in your red eyes."

The jury heard the witnesses, and they didn't say no more;
They crowded into the jury room, and the messenger closed the door.

The jury came to agreement, the clerk he wrote it down,
And everybody was whisperin, "He's penitentiary bound."

When the jury walked out, Stackalee didn't budge.
They wrapped the verdict and passed it to the judge.

Judge looked over his glasses, says, "Mr. Bad Man Stackalee,
The jury finds you guilty of murder in the first degree."

Now the trial's come to an end, how the folks gave cheers;
Bad Stackalee was sent down to Jefferson pen for seventy-five years.

Now late at night you can hear him in his cell,
Arguin with the devil to keep from goin to hell.

And the other convicts whisper, "Watcha know about that?
Gonna burn in hell forever over an old Stetson hat!"
Everybody's talkin 'bout Stackalee.

IV

FREE LANCES

1. ROY BEAN

THE thin and shifting line that separated law enforcement from law-breaking in the West permitted not only a peace officer like Wild Bill to become known as a "killer" but also a comic scalawag like Roy Bean to become known as the "Law West of the Pecos." A Kentuckian by birth, he counted the art of bluff as part of his backwoods heritage; and in his late fifties, after knocking about California, New Mexico, and Texas, playing for small stakes as adventurer and jack-of-all-trades—saloon-keeper, ranger, bull-whacker, blockade-runner, wood merchant—he gave up fortune-hunting and sought the limelight. In the lawless waste of the Trans-Pecos country he followed the construction of a new line on the Southern Pacific Railroad as camp saloon-keeper, first at Vinegarroon and then at Langtry, where in 1883 the tracks were joined and Bean moved in as a squatter on the railroad right of way. With some 8,000 workers on their hands, the railroad contractors learned the truth of the saying that "West of the Pecos there is no law" and called in the Texas Rangers to help counteract crime. On August 2, 1882, Roy Bean got himself appointed justice of the peace, on a hunch that it might be doubly profitable to preside over both the barroom and the bar of justice. From then until his death in 1903, he held court in the "Jersey Lily" saloon, named, like the town, for the English actress, whom Bean never met but who visited the place after his death.

The judge who specialized in finable cases and kept most of the fines was not uncommon in the West,[1] but Roy Bean was the most famous example of the type. In fact, even during his lifetime his legend reached such proportions that his brother Sam wrote of him:

You may have graduated at Yale or Harvard and carry a number of diplomas, but if you have not seen or heard of Judge Roy Bean of Texas you are groping in darkness and there yet remains a large space to be filled in your classical head.[2]

There was plenty of precedent for Roy Bean in the usual Western "Law" or sheriff, who was "judge, jury, and executioner" all in one, and in frontier vigilantism. In fact, he had had first-hand knowledge of the latter when he narrowly escaped from hanging for killing a rival in a love affair in California. And the many anecdotes of his shady business dealings before he became the "Law West of the Pecos" testify to the native shrewdness and bluster which enabled him to dispose of cases in his own way. At any rate, the red rope-burn that he wore about his permanently stiff neck, usually hidden by a bandana, was his only diploma, and his only law book was the *Revised Statutes of Texas* for 1876. But he inspired respect for the law with his two six-shooters and such bizarre punishments as the use of the bear-and-stake method for sobering up drunks, while the stories of his weird decisions and judgments entertained the newspaper public and have become classics of the Southwest bench and bar. In his comic rôle of fining-judge Roy Bean rivals the famous "hanging judge" of Fort Smith, Arkansas, Isaac C. Parker.

"Hear ye! Hear ye! This honorable court is now in session, and if anybody wants a snort before we start step up to the bar and name your poison."

"It is the judgment of this court that you are hereby tried and convicted of illegally and unlawfully committing certain grave offences against the peace and dignity of the State of Texas, particularly in my bailiwick, to wit: drunk and disorderly, and being Law West of the Pecos, I fine you two dollars; then get the hell out of here and never show yourself in this court again."[3]

2. BIG-FOOT WALLACE

Your true Western original was an unassuming fellow, free from sham heroics, who, though six feet two in his moccasin feet, and head and shoulders above the rest as fighter and story-teller, was yet "guileless and unsuspicious as a child, and whenever . . . in conflict with the shrewd, calculating man of business, . . . as helpless as a 'stranded whale.' " This is the stuff of which "provincial heroes" are made; and such was William A. ("Big-Foot"[4]) Wallace, born in Virginia, in 1816, and noted as a Texas scout and ranger. Like Buffalo Bill, he lived through the cycle of the West and saw the frontier pass; and although he would not have presumed to say with the former, "I stood between savagery and civilization most all my early days," in his later days, when he went back East for a visit, he was perfectly capable of seeing the humor of the "savagery" of civilization. *The Adventures of Big-Foot Wallace*, by John C. Duval, "first Texas man of letters," who served with Big-Foot in Jack Hays' company of Texas Rangers, is the result of a happy collaboration between a provincial hero and a provincial writer. "Always free and at home with himself," writes J. Frank Dobie,[5] "Big-Foot seems to have opened up to Duval with utmost gusto; and Duval took the bridle off him, slapped his rump with his reins and told him to hist his heels to heaven." Although the two are pretty well mixed, "Duval emerges an artist, and Big-Foot emerges robust, as natural as daylight, and as 'red-blooded' as a maverick yearling. . . . By virtue of Duval's narrative he remains the saltiest, rollickiest, most genial, most individualistic pioneer Indian fighter, Mexican layer-out, and lone-wolf dweller of the open range that Texas has ever had."

In the last portion of the book the lone-wolf character of Big-Foot is seen at its best by contrast with the settlements and with his "fish out of water" experience on the farm, proving that "You can take the boy out of the wilderness but you can't take the wilderness out of him" and that "innocence abroad" is still one of the best devices of satire.

Roy Bean, Law West of the Pecos

I. NECKTIE JUSTICE*

"Hear ye! Hear ye! This honorable court's now in session; and if any galoot wants a snort afore we start, let him step up to the bar and name his pizen. Oscar, serve the gentlemen." Thus did Judge Bean open court to try one Carlos Robles, an opening typical of his original procedure.

"Carlos Robles," he said solemnly after witnesses and hangers-on had downed their liquor, "it is the findin' of this

* From *Vinegarroon*, The Saga of Judge Roy Bean, "Law West of the Pecos," by Ruel McDaniel, pp. 83–89. Copyright, 1936, by Ruel McDaniel. Kingsport, Tenn.: Southern Publishers.

court that you are charged with a grave offense against the peace and dignity of the law West of the Pecos and the State of Texas, to wit: cattle-rustlin'. Guilty or not guilty?"

Not being able to speak or comprehend English, Robles merely grunted.

"Court accepts yore plea of guilt. The jury will now deliberate; and if it brings a verdict short of hangin' it'll be declared in contempt. Gentlemen, is yore verdict ready?"

The twelve nondescript citizens cleared their throats in unison. "It is, your honor," several spoke.

"Thank you, gentlemen. Stand up, Carlos Robles, and receive yore sentence. You got anything to say why judgment shouldn't be passed on you in this court?"

Of course Carlos had not, in view of the fact that he had only the vaguest idea of what was transpiring.

"Carlos Robles," Judge Roy continued, his voice almost quaking with the solemnity of the occasion, "you been tried by twelve true and good men, not men of yore peers, but as high above you as heaven is of hell; and they've said you're guilty of rustlin' cattle.

"Time will pass and seasons will come and go; Spring with its wavin' green grass and heaps of sweet-smellin' flowers on every hill and in every dale. Then will come sultry Summer, with her shimmerin' heat-waves on the baked horizon; and Fall, with her yeller harvest-moon and the hills growin' brown and golden under a sinkin' sun; and finally Winter, with its bitin', whinin' wind, and all the land will be mantled with snow. But you won't be here to see any of 'em, Carlos Robles; not by a dam' sight, because it's the order of this court that you be took to the nearest tree and hanged by the neck till you're dead, dead, dead, you olive-colored son-of-a-billy-goat!"

The Law West of the Pecos could be cruel in administering his brand of justice; but he was cruel only when he deemed the accused and the crime fully warranting such cruelty. He more frequently tempered justice with his own peculiar brand of mercy, especially if there was any means by which he could profit by that mercy.

One afternoon several ranchmen brought in a twenty-year-old boy accused of horse-stealing. They demanded that he be tried and dealt with according to the enormity of the crime.

Judge Bean duly opened court. He appointed six men as jurors, the actual number meaning nothing to him and depending entirely upon men available. He would not appoint just any citizens to jury duty. They must be good customers

of the liquid bar at the other end of the shack during inter-
missions, or their services as jurors no longer were desirable
or acceptable. Every transaction must be made to return the
utmost in profit, and non-drinking jurors were strictly dead
timber.

"Hear ye! This honorable court is again in session. Anyone
wishin' a snort, have it now. This here prisoner is charged with
the grave offense of stealin' a horse and Oscar, where are the
witnesses?" the Law West of the Pecos opened. He appreciated
his own sense of humor in varying his court openings to
relieve the monotony; but he seldom varied to the extent of
omitting the invitation to participate in a snort at the other bar.

"We caught him in the act of stealin' the animal," the
ranchman testified. "He admitted his intentions."

"That right, young feller? You was stealin' the cayuse?"

The young prisoner dropped his head, unruly red hair
tumbling down over his high forehead. "Yes, your honor," he
mumbled.

"Gentlemen of the jury," His Honor instructed, "the accused pleads guilty to horse theft. You know as well as I do
the penalty. I'm ready for yore verdict." And it was promptly
forthcoming.

Gravely the judge passed sentence. "If there's any last word,
or anything, I'll give you a few minutes," he told the pale
Easterner, thus extending an infrequent favor.

"I would like to write a note—to my mother back in
Pennsylvania," the doomed prisoner mumbled with obvious
emotion. "Thank you."

"Oscar, fetch the prisoner a piece of wrappin' paper and
a pencil. I think we got a pencil back there behind that row
of bottles." Bean gently handed the convicted thief these
writing facilities, got up and tendered him the beer barrel and
rickety table from which sentence had just been passed. Then
he took a position directly behind the boy so that he could
watch over his shoulder at what he wrote.

The victim wrote at length in apology for the grief and
trouble he had caused his mother and earnestly sought her
forgiveness. "In small part perhaps I can repay you for the
money I have cost you in keeping me out of trouble. Enclosed
is $400, which I've saved. I want you—."

Judge Bean started, cleared his throat, cut in at this point.
"By gobs!" he exclaimed, "gentlemen, I got a feelin' there's
been a miscarriage of justice, in this case. I hereby declare it
re-opened. Face the bar, young man."

The prisoner removed himself from the beer keg and stood erect in front of the judicial bench, befuddled at this sudden turn.

"After all, that wasn't much of a cayuse the lad tried to steal; and he didn't actually steal him. So I rule it's a finable case. I hereby fine the accused three hundred dollars and get to hell outer this country afore I change my mind!"

The boy gladly enough paid three hundred of his four hundred dollars and assured the court that the next setting sun would find his brow well beyond El Rio Pecos.

Practically every cattleman and law-abiding citizen of the Bean bailiwick had an indefinite appointment as deputy constable to the Law West of the Pecos. Thus any citizen who apprehended any person in the act of committing a crime or suspected any of crime had authority to bring him on forthwith for trial. Bean consistently encouraged such co-operation, for the more business they brought before the court, the greater the financial returns for the whole establishment. Naturally it was understood that such arresting constables did not in any manner participate in the fee accruing from such cases created by them. This doubtless was the only justice court in the State of Texas wherein only one official received all fees collected by the office.

Under authority as deputy constable, Reb Wise, Pecos rancher, brought in a cattle rustler on a hot August afternoon when business at the refreshment counter was exceptionally brisk. It was all both Roy and Oscar could do to handle the trade. Consequently Bean looked up with sour expression when Deputy Constable Wise approached the bar and informed the judge that a prisoner was awaiting attention at the bar of justice.

"What's he charged with, Reb?" Roy asked, opening another foaming bottle of Triple-X beer.

"Cattle-rustlin', yuhr honor," Reb replied.

"Whose cattle?"

"Mine."

"You positive he's guilty, Reb?"

"Positive? Say, Judge, I caught him with a runnin' iron on one of my finest calves!" the rancher replied with emphasis.

For the first time Roy glanced up at the scowling prisoner. He noticed blood dripping from his left ear. "Who plugged his ear?" he inquired.

"I did, yuhr honor, when he wouldn't stop."

"You ought'n shot at his head, Reb. You could 'a' killed

him; and that would 'a' been bad, because he wouldn't have been saved for the punishment he deserves. You real shore he's guilty?"

"Didn't I say, Judge, I caught him runnin' a brand on my stuff?"

"All right then," the judge said. "What'll it be for you, feller?" to a newcomer at the bar, ". . . All right then. The court finds the accused guilty as charged; and as there ain't no worse punishment I know of right handy, I hereby sentence him to be hung. Reb, I'm busy's hell here. You and some of yore compadres take him out and tie his neck to some handy limb—some place where his cronies'll be positive to see him; and that's my rulin'. Court's adjourned and what'll it be for you down there, Slim?"

II. ROY BEAN, CORONER*

The story that everybody knows about Roy Bean the coroner comes from another bridge accident which happened a little earlier than this.

It was a Sunday afternoon in February, 1892. A number of bridge carpenters from the Pecos project had come up to pass the day at the Jersey Lily, among them a quiet fellow named Pat O'Brien who didn't care much for the carousing and hell raising that was going on. Towards evening he decided to take a walk. There were no shady lanes or pasture paths in those parts so he started off down the railroad tracks, a smile on his face and a six-shooter in his hip pocket. Why he wanted the weapon is not clear. Maybe he was from the East. Easterners were more careful about this article of dress than native Texans.

When he got to the Myers Canyon bridge, three miles east of Langtry, a heavy wind was blowing as usual down the draw, and one gust was strong enough to take him off his feet and land him at the bottom where the sharp rocks ended his career. Section workers and track walkers were always very careful when they crossed this bridge, but the stranger never suspected his danger until it was too late.

That evening he was found and Roy was notified. He and Jim King (now Del Rio) went out in a buckboard, brought the body back, and laid it out on the table in the saloon.

* From *Roy Bean, Law West of the Pecos*, by C. L. Sonnichsen, pp. 119–123, 126–128, 154, 168–173. Copyright, 1943, by C. L. Sonnichsen. New York: The Macmillan Company.

Nobody knew who the man was beyond his name, so they searched him for identification and in so doing found the six-shooter and forty dollars.

"Now," said Coroner Bean, "I've got to bury this poor devil and it's hard digging in these rocks. I hereby fine this defendant forty dollars for carrying concealed weapons."

Turning to Jim King he added, "Don't you think that's the way to handle it, Jimmy?" Jimmy thought so, and Roy had no idea that he had made a historic decision, but one man told another and pretty soon Texas was chuckling again at Roy Bean's way of conducting his business. The San Antonio *Express* got hold of the story of Roy's verdict in March and passed it on to the world.

"Gentlemen," said Roy to the jury and onlookers, "there is nothing to find out how that man came to his death. He fell from the bridge and that's all there is about it. But there is one thing that is not so plain, and that is what was he doing with that gun? Of course he is dead and can't explain, but that ain't the fault of the law; it's his own misfortune. Justice is justice, and law is law, and as he can't offer no satisfactory explanation of the matter I shall be obliged to fine him forty dollars for carrying on or about his person that pistol. Because a man chooses to put on a pair of wings is no reason why the great State of Texas should not have what is coming to her all the same."

III. Roy Bean and the Chinaman

It is time now to talk about Roy Bean's affair with the Chinaman. The earliest and shortest version of the story appeared in the El Paso *Daily Times* for June 2, 1884.

Here is the latest on Roy Bean:
Somebody killed a Chinaman and was brought up standing before the irrepressible Roy, who looked through two or three dilapidated law books from stem to stern, and finally turned the culprit loose remarking that he'd be d—d if he could find any law against killing a Chinaman.

That is the core of what has become, after fifty years, one of the best known anecdotes ever to come out of the Southwest. The time must have been about the beginning of 1883 (the ends of track were joined in January). From the west hundreds of Chinese laborers were building. From the east came the Irish and other brawny sons of Europe. The white laborers hated the Chinese for their willingness to work for low wages, their saving ways, their squeaking gibberish, and their love of peace. More killings than one occurred when the gangs from east and west got close enough to rub elbows and cut throats, and there were many narrow escapes. For example take the night in 1882 when the Irish, who had built almost to the east side of the Pecos, got involved in a celebration, and decided their lives would be wasted unless they crossed over to where the Chinese were camped on the west bank and cut off a few pigtails. They knew that a Chinaman did not like to fight and would not fight under ordinary provocation, but would give a satisfactory performance if his pigtail were cut off. So these drunk and joyful Irishmen organized themselves and were all ready to start out when the foreman interfered and averted a race riot by a very slim margin.

Even so, many Chinamen lost their lives by one means or another and were buried where they fell. Later the bones of many of them were collected and sent back to the west coast by Chinese friends who came in for the purpose.

Usually the Americans concerned themselves very little about whether a Chinaman lived or died, but somehow the historic case under discussion was brought to Roy Bean for judgment and he turned the Irishman loose, as most Americans in West Texas would have been glad of an excuse to do. On account of the feeling between the Chinese and the other laborers it would have been easy to start a race riot just then, and Roy knew it. Besides, as he once said, there were about two hundred of the toughest white men in the world around the saloon and they might have lynched him if he hadn't let the Irishman go free. His decision was merely his own peculiar way of preserving law and order, at the same time protecting the health of Judge Bean, but the ruling had the real gamy Western tang and stuck in men's minds. The story not merely lived; it grew. By 1899 it was getting into the newspaper exchanges this way:

At Langtry, Tex., says the San Francisco Wave, Squire Roy Bean, who administers justice and keeps the leading saloon, had to sit in judgment on a railroad clerk who had killed Ah Ling, a laundry man for, as he claimed, insulting him. The man was arrested and brought before magistrate Bean, who listened to the evidence, which was given by the accused himself, and then proceeded to turn the pages of the revised statutes: "This here book, which is a Texas law book," he announced, "says that hommyside is th' killin' of a human, male ur female. They is many kinds of hommyside—murder, manslaughter, plain hommyside, negl'gent hommyside, justifi'ble hommyside an' praiseworthy hommyside. They is three kinds of humans—white men, niggers, and Mexicans. It stan's to reason thet if a Chinym'n was human, killin' of him would come under th' head of praiseworthy hommyside. The pris'ner is discharged on condition that he pays f'r havin' th' Chinee buried."

In print and out of print the story went around, gathering details and variations. In the last ten years it has been reprinted a dozen times, and every fresh book about the old days in the Southwest tells it a new way. In 1934, F. H. Bushick put out this version in his book *Glamorous Days:*

Some cavalry soldier in passing through that way, it was thought, had lost his sabre. One of the bridge gang found it. When it was brought into camp nobody wanted the old corn cutter except this Irishman who took a shine to it because he had once been a soldier himself. He ground up the old blade and kept it as a handy weapon, he being a storekeeper of iron supplies, a responsible sort of job.

This Irishman was in the habit of now and then stealing a pie from the cook. The chink got to missing his pies and finally lay for the Irishman and caught him red handed. Armed with a big butcher knife, the Chink attacked the Irishman, who ran and got his old sabre and returned to the fray. He made just one pass at the chink with his sabre and cut off his head as clean as if the Lord High Executioner of China had done the job.

A ranger arrested the Irishman and took him before Judge Bean.

The most remarkable variation of all appeared in 1931 in Tom Rynning's book *Gun Notches.* Tom was an old cavalry man and peace officer who knew Roy, and this is the way he tells it:

Once Roy's son shot and killed a Chinaman because he charged too much for his laundry or something serious like that, and of course young Bean was tried before his old man. Naturally Roy wanted to give his boy as easy a deal as the law would allow, but he was a square-shooter and if his son turned out guilty of a misdemeanor or anything like that, it was a cinch he'd wrap it to him just like he was a stranger.

So the judge opened court with the usual formalities, throwing out a couple of drunks who wouldn't quit snoring during the proceedings, and started the justice mill to grinding. On account of his own kin being up for trial, and all the customers watching him more interested than usual, he went about things mighty careful and legal-like.

As a rule he give his decisions right out of his deep knowledge of the law, for he'd been a J. P. for a year or more then; but this time he figured he had to dig into the Unabridged Statutes of 1846, or somewheres round that date.

He hooked his spectacles onto his handsome big red nose and begun reading the law book out loud so's everybody could see he wasn't keeping any ace in the hole. And damned if he didn't read those Texas statutes from cover to cover, cussing every cow-puncher awake that went to sleep on him and refusing to let any of them go to the bar for a drink during that long spell of court.

When he'd waded plumb through the Texas law from murder to cow brands, in about two hours or so, those cowpunchers and rustlers had got a darned sight more legal knowledge screwed into their skulls than lots of the tin-horn lawyers of the state ever knew. In fact, they was a plumb nuisance after that, some of them spouting their information about Texas law by the hour every time they got drunked up and could get some unfortunate dogie to stand hitched long enough to pour it into him by the gallon.

"And there she is, gentlemen," says Roy Bean, when he'd got through. "That's the full unexpurgated law of the great State of Texas up to 1873, and it ain't noways likely there's been any fundamental changes run into since.

"The complete statutes of this here state from the Alamo on ahead, and there ain't a damned line in it nowheres that makes it illegal to kill a Chinaman. The defendant is discharged."

The Adventures of Big-Foot Wallace*

I. SKETCH OF WALLACE'S LIFE

William A. Wallace was born in Lexington, Rockbridge County, Virginia, in the year 1816. He went to Texas in 1836, a few months after the battle of San Jacinto, for the purpose, he says, of taking pay out of the Mexicans for the murder of his brother and his cousin, Major Wallace, both of whom fell at "Fannin's Massacre." He says he believes accounts with them are now about square.

He landed first at Galveston, which consisted then of six groceries and an old stranded hulk of a steamboat, used as a hotel, and for a berth in which he paid at the rate of three dollars per day. From Galveston, Wallace went on to La Grange, then a frontier village, where he resided until the

---

* From *The Adventures of Big-Foot Wallace, the Texas Ranger and Hunter,* by John C. Duval, pp. xiv–xv, 221–222, 229–254, 281–291. Copyright, 1870, by J. W. Burke & Co. Macon, Georgia.

spring of 1839, when he moved to Austin, just before the seat of government was established at that place. He remained at Austin until the spring of 1840, when finding that the country was settling up around him too fast to suit his notions, he went over to San Antonio, where he resided until he entered the service.

He was at the battle of the Salado, in the fall of 1842, when General Woll came in and captured San Antonio. The fight began about 11 o'clock in the day, and lasted until night. General Woll had fourteen hundred men, and the Texans one hundred and ninety-seven, under Caldwell (commonly known as "Old Paint"). Between eighty and one hundred Mexicans were killed, while the Texans lost only one man (Jett). Forty men, however, from La Grange, under Captain Dawson, who were endeavoring to form a junction with them, were surrounded and captured by the Mexicans, who massacred them all as soon as they had surrendered their arms.

In the fall of 1842, he volunteered in the "Mier Expedition," an account of which appears in this volume. After his return from Mexico, he joined Colonel Jack Hays's Ranging Company, the first ever regularly enlisted in the service of the "old Republic," and was with it in many of those desperate encounters with the Comanches and other Indians, in which Hays, Walker, McCulloch, and Chevalier gained their reputations as successful Indian-fighters.

When the Mexican war broke out in 1846, Wallace joined Colonel Hays's regiment of mounted volunteers, and was with it at the storming of Monterey, where he says he took "full toll" out of the Mexicans for killing his brother and cousin at Goliad in 1836.

After the Mexican war ended, he had command of a Ranging Company for some time, and did good service in protecting the frontiers of the State from the incursions of the savages. Subsequently he had charge of the mail from San Antonio to El Paso, and, though often waylaid and attacked by the Indians, he always brought it through in safety.

II. How Big-Foot Wallace Got His Name

It was while we were prisoners at the City of Mexico that I acquired the name of "Big-Foot," which has stuck to me like Texas mud ever since. It happened in this way: Some of the foreign residents of the city, observing that we were almost in a shoeless condition, made up by contribution among themselves a sufficient sum to purchase a pair of shoes for each of us. Every one was fitted with a suitable pair except myself; but I searched in vain every shop and "tienda" in the city for even a pair of No. 11's, though 12's fit me best, and finally I had no alternative left me but to buy the leather and have a pair put up on purpose for me by a "zapatero," or go barefooted. The Mexicans are generally a small people compared with the Americans, and their feet are still smaller in proportion; consequently they were much astonished at the size of mine, and from that time forward, and as long as I remained in the city, I was known among them as "Big-Foot."

I flatter myself, however, that my foot is not a very large one, taking into consideration the fact that I am just six feet two inches in height, and weigh upward of two hundred pounds net. But, even if it were otherwise, there is nothing dishonorable in the appellation, and I would rather be called "Big-Foot Wallace" than "Lying Wallace," or "Thieving Wallace." Such handles to my name would not be agreeable.

III. The St. Charles Tavern

The St. Charles "Tavern"—How He Registered His Name— Wallace Is Afraid of a Fire—He Breakfasts at the St. Charles, and Gets Up an Excitement—The Bill of Fare—Fried Bull-frogs.

. . . I went to the St. Charles tavern, to hunt up quarters for the night, as I had been told it was the best in the city, and I was determined to have the best of everything going while I was on my travels. Some one had pointed the tavern out to me in the daytime, and as it was but a little way off, I soon came to it, and went up the broad steps in front, and then into a room where several men were putting their names down in a book.

I asked a fellow standing behind the railing at a desk, if the landlord was in, as I wanted to see him. He laughed a little, though I didn't see anything funny in the question, and told me the landlord was out just then, but that he would attend to any business I might have with him. I told him all I wanted was a room to sleep in, and as much "grub" as I could eat as long as I staid in New Orleans.

"Certainly," said he, "you can be accommodated. Will you please register your name?"

I took the pen and wrote down "Big-Foot Wallace" in the

first column, "Buffalo-Bull Ranch, Texas," in the second, and "Old Virginny" in the third. Then the clerk, or whoever he was, struck something that sounded like a clock, and a fellow jumped up from the corner of the room, and came up to where we were.

"Show this gentleman to No. 395," and he handed the waiter a little piece of candle that didn't look to me nigh long enough to last us through three hundred and ninety-five rooms. But the whole tavern was lighted up with little brass knobs, that made every place as bright as day.

The waiter took me up one pair of stairs, and then up another and another, until I thought I was in a fair way to get to heaven at last, providing my breath didn't fail me. We then wound about through half a dozen lanes and alleys, until at last we came to No. 395. The waiter unlocked the door, lit my candle, and told me good night.

"Stop a minute, my friend," said I; "if this tavern should catch fire to-night, how am I to find my way back again to where we started from?"

"Oh," said he, "there's no danger of fire, for it is all built of rock; and besides, it's insured."

"Devil trust it," said I, "with that gas stuff burning all over it. If it can set fire to a brass knob, why can't it burn a rock, too? I'd rather trust myself in a dry prairie, with a stiff 'norther' blowing, and the grass waist high, and hostile Indians all around: my chances of being roasted alive wouldn't be half as good as they are up here in No. 395; and besides," said I, "I'm not insured!"

"Well," said he, "if the house catches fire, all you've got to do is to pull that string hanging down there with the tassel on the end of it, which rings a bell, and I'll come up and show you the road down."

"Look here, my friend," said I, "you can't satisfy me in that way. This is room 395, and I suppose there's at least 395 more of 'em, and when 790 bells are all ringing at the same time, how are you going to tell which one is mine? You might as well try to tell the bellowing of a particular buffalo-bull in a gang of ten thousand. No, sir; you stay up here with me, and when the row commences, if you are lucky enough to find your way down, I won't be far behind you."

"Well," said he, "when my watch is up, which will be in about half an hour, I'll come back."

"'Nough said," I replied, "and I'll stand treat in the morning."

So I turned into bed, and in five minutes was fast asleep. I never knew whether the fellow came back or not, but I suppose he did, for he claimed the "treat" off me the first thing in the morning. I gave him a brand-new fifty-cent piece, and he said he'd like to take the job by the week at half the price: so I engaged him regularly at twenty-five cents a night, and considered it dirt-cheap at that.

I made an early start in the morning, for I knew I had a crooked way to travel and a dim trail to follow; and about 9 o'clock I found myself in the room where I had registered my name the night before, and feeling considerably snappish after my long tramp.

I inquired of one of the porters sitting there, how long it was till breakfast. He said any time I wanted it, and showed me the way into the breakfast-room. It was almost as large as a small prairie, and, instead of one long table, as we have in our taverns at home, there were at least forty or fifty little round ones scattered about all over it.

Being of rather a social disposition, although I have lived so much in the woods by myself, and seeing a tolerably jovial little party of ladies and gentlemen sitting around one of these tables, I walked up and took a seat with them. I saw in a minute I wasn't welcome, for the gentlemen looked as ill-natured as a sulky bull, and the ladies all tittered; but I pretended not to notice it, and called to one of the waiters who was running round, to bring me a pound or so of beefsteak and the "condiments."

At this, one of the men spoke up, and said "he presumed I was under a mistake, as that was a private table."

"Yes, sir," said I, "I am. I presumed you were gentlemen; and as to this being a private table, all I have to say is, it's the first one I ever saw in a 'public house.' However," I continued, "I've no wish to force my company where it isn't wanted," and I got up and took a seat at another table.

If a man had spoken to me at a tavern in Texas the way that chap did, I would have introduced him to "Old Butch" at once; but thinks I, maybe things are different here, and I bothered myself no more about it.

There was nothing to eat on the table where I had taken a seat but a plate of butter and a bowl of sugar; but in a minute or so a waiter stepped up and handed me a paper. I took it, folded it up, and laid it on the table.

"My friend," says I, "I'm 'remarkable' hungry just now,

and I'll read that after I get something to eat, if you say there's anything special in it."

After a little while he says, "What'll you have for breakfast, sir?"

"Well," I answered, "anything that's fat and juicy. What have you got cooked?"

"If you'll read the 'bill of fare,'" says he, "you can see for yourself."

"Well! let's have it," said I.

"That's it you have just folded up and laid on the table there," he replied.

"Oh, yes," said I. "I understand now;" and I picked it up, and the first thing I saw on it was *"Café au lait,"* "and it's late enough too for it, heaven knows," said I; "for I am used to taking a quart cup every morning just at daybreak!"

"What else?" said the waiter, and I read on:

"Pâté du fois gras"—some sort of yerbs, thought I, and I never went high on greens, especially for breakfast. I found most of the names of the things on the "bill of fare" were French, or some other foreign lingo, and they were all Greek to me; but, to make the waiter believe I knew very well what they were, only I wasn't partial to their sort of "grub," I told him to bring me some "crapeau fricassee" and "gumbo filet," and I wish I may never take another "chaw" of tobacco if he did not bring me a plateful of fried bull-frogs' legs, and another full of their spawn, just the same sort of slimy, ropy stuff you see around the edges of shallow ponds. I might have known that everything French had frog in it in some shape or other, just as certain as "Chili pepper" is found in everything the Mexicans cook. However, I made out a tolerable breakfast on other things, but would have been much better satisfied if I could have had four or five pounds of roasted buffalo-meat and a *"marrow gut."*

IV. The Quadroon Ball

Wallace Meets with an Adventure—Goes to a Quadroon Ball, and Teaches Them "the Stampede"—Wallace Takes a "White Lion," and Pays for It—Has His Fortune Told—What Followed.

After breakfast, I loaded my pipe and took a seat on the front porch, with my legs hoisted up on the iron railings, and while I was sitting there puffing away, as comfortable as an old sow in a mud-hole on a hot day, a young woman came along on the opposite side of the street, and stopped awhile to look at some pictures in a window. Presently she looked up and beckoned me to come to her! I couldn't believe my eyes at first, but she kept on motioning her hand to me until I knew there was no mistake about it.

I thought maybe she takes me for some acquaintance of hers, and I'll go down and let her know she is on the wrong trail, just to see how foolish she will look when she finds she has been making so familiar with a stranger. So I went down the steps and crossed over to where she was standing. When I got up close to her I noticed that her dress didn't look overly neat, and that her eyes were as red as if she had been on a burst for the last week. I made her a polite bow, however, and remarked that I supposed she was mistaken; but before I could finish my speech, which I had "cut and dried," like the politicians, she ran up to me and grabbed me by the hand.

"Oh, bosh!" said she, "not a bit of it: you are the hardest fellow to take a hint I ever saw. I've been beckoning to you for the last half hour. Come along, Johnny Green, I want to introduce you to some particular friends of mine."

"My name ain't Johnny Green," said I, trying to get my hand loose from her; but she held on to it like a vise.

"Oh! never mind that," said she; "come along with me, and we'll have a jolly time of it."

Thinks I, if you ain't a brazen piece I never saw one; for all the time she was talking she kept dragging me on, though there were half a dozen fellows on the stoop of the tavern, killing themselves laughing at us. This made me desperate, and I jerked my hand away by main force, though I hated to serve anything like a woman in such a rough way.

"Won't you go?" said she.

"No," said I, "not just now; I haven't time."

"Well," she answered, "if you won't go, I reckon you won't refuse to 'treat.' "

"Certainly not," said I. "What'll you take—a lemonade, or an ice-cream?"

"To the old boy," said she, "with your lemonades and ice-cream! I'll take a glass of brandy with a little schnapps in it."

"There," said I, and I threw her a slick quarter; "that'll buy you one;" and I turned on my heel and made tracks for the tavern as fast as I could.

Geminy! what a "cussin' " she gave me as I went! I thought

I had heard the rangers on the frontiers of Texas make use of pretty hard language, but they couldn't hold a candle to that young woman. The farther I went the louder she "cussed," and I never got out of hearing of her until I found my way at last up to 395, where I bolted myself in, and never came out till dinner-time.

V

MIRACLE MEN

1. COMIC DEMIGODS

WHEN the heroes of history go, the demigods arrive. As the ring-tailed roarer is a comic version of the frontiersman who wrestles single-handed with the wilderness, so our tinkering demigods are the comic culture heroes of an industrial civilization who account for its wonders. Their miracles are also the pranks of trickster heroes, whose huge laughs provide much the same sort of comic relief as our comic strips. "All mythical heroes have been exaggerations," says Max Eastman, "but they have been serious ones. America came too late for that. ... That is the natively American thing—not that her primitive humor is exaggerative, but that her primitive exaggerations were humorous."[1]

A typical American demigod is Pecos Bill, the culture hero of the cowboy, who is said to have "invented most of the things connected with the cow business." At the same time his affinity with the wild men of the West is attested by his title of the "king killer of the bad men." His toughness is of the kind that was the boast of the pseudo bad men: "He cut his teeth on a bowie knife, and his earliest playfellows were the bears and catamounts of East Texas." In the Davy Crockett tradition are his fights with two grizzly bears, which he hugged to death; with a rattlesnake, which he used as a lariat to spin at Gila monsters; and with a mountain lion, which soon hollered for mercy and let Bill ride him "a hundred feet at a jump . . . quirtin' him down the flank with the rattlesnake." He is the boasting cowboy par excellence; and his cyclone variant of the theme of the horse that couldn't be ridden and the cowboy that couldn't be thrown is only a little less poetic than Badger Clark's High-Chin Bob version. In the latter's poem of "The Glory Trail" (also recorded from tradition by John A. Lomax) Bob ropes a mountain lion; and since neither would or could let go, they continue together through eternity—a ghost rider on a ghost horse leading a ghost lion in a noose. Pecos Bill's death is a caricature of the death of a hero, caused, according to one version, by putting "fish-hooks and barbed wire in his toddy."

In a slightly different key is the "saga of inadvertence" of Bowleg Bill, whose fool stunts and outlandish exploits are more the result of happy accidents—"uncommon happenquences"—than of design. His reckless playfulness links him with Pecos Bill, but this "gawdamnedest intelligent fool" outdoes the other in the "larger lunacy" of his antics. As a sea-going cowboy and an "inland furriner" he combines the freak-ishness of a hybrid with the innocence of the greenhorn, though in this case a greenhorn who teaches the old hands some new tricks. Of the breed of pet trout and rattlesnakes is Piccolo the whistling whale; and the bronco that could not be broken turns up again in Slickbritches the Hoss-Mackerel.

The American genius for invention has produced its hero in Paul Bunyan. Although he handles nature like a toy and accounts for the bigness of certain American geographical features, such as Puget Sound, he is primarily a work giant whose job is to invent logging. By reason of his having to start from scratch, there is something primordial about him; but unlike most Titans, he combines brain with brawn, and employs both for the good of mankind. He has gone a long way from the giant of nursery tales whose chief purpose was to scare little children and be slain by the hero.

Just as the "mightiest of loggers" appears in other settings and guises as Tony Beaver, Kemp Morgan, Finn MacCool, and Febold Feboldson, so his exploits are essentially prodigious lies of the Munchausen variety, which are much older than the heroes themselves. The "key stories" in the Bunyan cycle may be matched by hundreds of Old World parallels in Stith Thompson's *Motif-Index of Folk-Literature*.

Tales of the Paul Bunyan type originated as separate anecdotes or "gags" exchanged in competitive bragging or lying contests and involving "sells" and the pranking of greenhorns. "The best authorities," writes W. B. Laughead (and in this the experts all agree), "never recounted Paul Bunyan's exploits in narrative form. They made their statements more impressive by dropping them casually, in an offhand way, as if in reference to actual events of common knowledge." Such remarks often began with a phrase of reminiscence or reminder: "Time I was with Paul up in the Big Onion country ——"; "That happened the year I went up for Paul Bunyan"; "Did you ever hear of the —— that Paul Bunyan ——?"

James Stevens traces the mythical Paul Bunyan to a French-Canadian logger named Paul Bunyon, who won a reputation as a prodigious fighter in the Papineau Rebellion against the Queen in 1837, and later became famous as the boss of a logging camp—"he fight like hell, he work like hell, and he pack like hell."[2] But whatever his historical origins, if any, Paul Bunyan—the superman in a world of suger-gadgets—has become an American symbol of bigness and a proverbial character on which to tack an extravagant anecdote. Although the tradition has spread to many other occupations—the oil fields, the wheat fields, and construction jobs, Paul Bunyan tales are told popularly, outside of the industry more than within it, and depend for their effect upon pure exaggeration rather than upon occupational coloring.

The first appearance of Paul Bunyan in print seems to have been an advertising man's idea. In 1914 the Red River Lumber Company issued a booklet of tales which has since gone through twelve editions, gradually incorporating more and more advertising matter along with the original stories. To-day Paul Bunyan is the company's trademark and "stands for the quality and service you have the right to expect from Paul Bunyan." The author and illustrator of these booklets, W. B. Laughead, who claims to have invented many of the names of characters and who is given credit for initiating the preservation of the Paul Bunyan stories, has never made clear whether Paul Bunyan dreamed up the lumber business or *vice versa*.[3] In 1914 also appeared Douglas Malloch's poem "The Round River Drive," published in *The American Lumberman*, to be followed in 1916 by the first scholarly investigation of the legends by K. Bernice Stewart and Homer A. Watt, in 1919 by the "first continuous narrative" of Ida Virginia Turney, and in 1924 by Esther Shephard's volume. In the same year James Stevens began to publish his dressed-up versions for readers who do not like their folklore raw. How much of

Paul Bunyan is folklore and how much of it is literature is still an open question. But in the absence of authentic oral versions, scholars give credence to the view that he is, if not actually a hoax, at least the product of downward transmission.[4]

Paul Bunyan has been the inspiration of other demigods who are probable inventions, such as Tony Beaver, the West Virginia lumberjack hero of *Up Eel River* (1928), by Margaret Prescott Montague, and Febold Feboldson, the plains hero. On the origins of the latter Paul R. Beath writes:[5]

I first became aware of Febold Feboldson when stories of him were appearing regularly in the Gothenburg, Nebraska, *Times.* As I recall this was in 1927 or 1928 while I was undergraduate at the University of Illinois. About this time I read James Stevens' *Paul Bunyan* and immediately spotted the similarity. It was during this period that I started contributing an occasional story to the *Times* during my summer vacations which I spent in Nebraska. The stories were mostly adaptations of those I had heard around town with elaborations and embellishments to fit what I conceived to be Febold's character, i. e., an indomitable Swedish pioneer who could surmount any difficulty.

I must add here that as a boy and young man I worked as night clerk in a hotel in Gothenburg where I heard literally thousands of stories told by travelling salesmen and other garrulous wayfarers. I suppose I received clues to many of the stories I used from this ever flowing stream. At one time, after I had read the Canterbury Tales in college, I contemplated a modern set based on this hotel experience.

. . . Don Holmes of the *Times* told me that the character had been created by Wayne T. Carroll, a local lumber dealer, who wrote a column under the name of Watt Tell in the now defunct Gothenburg *Independent.* This series, to the best of my knowledge, began about 1923. Later Carroll used Febold in advertising he wrote for his lumber company. Lumber magazines were the first to use Paul Bunyan and it seems obvious to me that Febold was patterned after Paul Bunyan. But Febold could never have been a lumber hero, because there are no trees on the Great Plains. So Febold became a hero wrestling with the adversities of the plains— tornadoes, drouths, extreme hot and cold, Indians, politicians, and disease.

Because I have published Febold the widest of any of his first champions—that is, Carroll, Holmes, and myself—I have been accused of creating him. I did not. Febold, a pioneer Swede, and all his nephews were in existence when I came upon the legend. Febold, the fabulous uncle, had already gone to his reward by retiring to California like a good middlewesterner. His exploits seemed always to be recounted by someone who knew him in the old days, usually his nephews, Bergstrom Stromberg, Herebold Farvardson, Hjalmar Hjalmarson, and Eldad Johnson. For some reason there was always a contemporary of Febold called Eldad Johnson's grandfather. The only historical basis for any of these characters is that Olof Bergstrom is Bergstrom Stromberg, . . . the immigration from Gothenburg, Sweden, to Nebraska of a band of Swedes [having been] led by Olof Bergstrom who founded both Stromberg (the reverse of his true name) and Gothenburg in the state of Nebraska. It is my opinion that Carroll had this man in mind, because tales of him were current when I was a boy. He had a most hectic career. He married a Swedish singer on one of his periodic returns to the old country; she later committed suicide. He worked for the Union Pacific selling railroad land to the incoming immigrants. He killed a man and was acquitted. He was said to have disappeared.

In 1928 these stories "caught on." Not only did Don write them, but contributions began coming in from the *Times* readers. From 1928 to 1933 at least one Febold story appeared in the *Times* without a break from week to week, a total of 260 stories.

Mr. Beath's account throws light on the making of legendary heroes. The early stages of the process are clearly reflected in the Febold stories, where the central conception of a heroic character has not yet attained full growth and tends to fall apart into the *disjecta membra* of tall stories.

2. STRONG MEN AND STAR PERFORMERS

Although American legendary heroes like Paul Bunyan and the other work giants are occupational heroes, they are industrial pioneers rather than industrialists. Thus Paul Bunyan represents the days before the timber beast became a timber mechanic and Old Stormalong, the days of wooden ships and iron men. Under the influence of the machine the hero undergoes a change. The work boss is supplanted by the ordinary worker, who distinguishes himself not so much for innovations as for doing a good job of whatever he is doing. He is a strong man or a star performer with tragic and social rather than comic significance. The tragedy usually results from his being overcome by a superior force—the machine. Thus John Henry dies in a contest with a steam drill and Casey Jones in a train wreck with one hand on the whistle cord and the other on the airbrake lever; while Joe Magarac offers himself up as a sacrifice to make better steel.

Originally a flesh-and-blood hero of the rock-tunnel gangs,

the great steel-driver who died with his hammer in his hand while competing with a steam-drill at Big Bend Tunnel on the Chesapeake and Ohio Railroad in West Virginia in 1870, John Henry has become a legendary and mythical figure with various symbolic significances. In folk song tradition the "tiny epic of man's last stand against the machine" has produced a work song (the hammer song), a ballad, and a social song or blues, in which the central theme of the drilling contest has attracted to itself double meaning stanzas and conventional ballad lines and motifs. The few John Henry tales that have been recovered are of the Paul Bunyan type, elaborating the hero's size, strength, skill, and prowess with food, women, etc. As the tradition moved west, other kinds of labor were substituted for tunnel construction, until in Roark Bradford's version John Henry becomes the champion cotton picker, roustabout, and railroad man with more than a touch of the bad man and boaster or "big mouth."

"I'm f'm de Black River country," said John Henry, "and I kin roust what I kin git my hands on. But dat don't make me no rouster. I'm f'm de Black River country whar de sun don't never shine. My home ain't hyar, and I'm fixin' to git around."

". . . 'Scuse me for laughin', Cap'm," he said, "but dat tawk do sound funny. Dat winch might work like ten good men, but how about John Henry? I burned out all de men you got, and I kin burn dat steam winch out, too.

"So th'ow down another stage for me, so I kin git some action. I'll roll more cotton on de *Big Jim White* den you kin wid dat steam winch, 'cause I'm John Henry and I'm six foot tall and my strenk can't hit de bottom. Maybe de women fool me bad, and maybe, too, de gamblers. Maybe de happy dust cross me up and de preacher put me in de dozens. But rollin' cotton ain't nothin' but work, and can't nobody fool me. So stand back, you bullies, and gimme some room, and watch me roll dat cotton. I'll clean dat boat befo' de sun goes down or my name ain't John Henry."

The supreme symbol of industrial strength is Joe Magarac, who comments thus on his name and nature: "Sure! Magarac. Joe. Dat's me. All I do is eatit and workit same lak jackass donkey." He symbolizes not only the power of steel but the power of the men behind the steel, the human basis of our basic industry.

There is no glory comparable to poured iron or poured steel. The gushing out of fiery metal from a great wheel-like container seems like the beginning of Creation. This black container of molten iron is twenty feet high. A ladle advances on an overhead railway. It travels to the container of molten iron. It moves forward on its track and then laterally and then down. The black container swings around slowly on its axle as a man presses a lever.

Then follows the sudden magnificence of poured metal. Like giant fireworks, a thousand sparks fly from it, a river of white fire throwing off cascades of stars, a fiery shower on all sides. On a greasy platform above the ladle are the men who operate it. They look down with indifference into its seething deadly brightness.

My guide said: "A man fell into that once, and they buried him and all the tons of metal. Right here they held the burial service."

The story of the man who fell into the vat of molten metal and became part of it obsesses the men's minds. I have heard it told in different ways.

They tell you of a man made into iron rails, of another who went into the structure of great buildings.

This story is as old as time. There was a great bell once which was cast and re-cast and would not ring true until a human being was sacrificed to it.[6]

———◆———

The Saga of Pecos Bill*

IT is highly probable that Paul Bunyan, whose exploits were told in a recent number of *The Century Magazine*, and Pecos Bill, mythical cow-boy hero of the Southwest, were blood brothers. At all events, they can meet on one common ground: they were both fathered by a liar.

Pecos Bill is not a new-comer in the Southwest. His mighty deeds have been sung for generations by the men of the range. In my boyhood days in west Texas I first heard of Bill, and in later years I have often listened to chapters of his history told around the chuck-wagon by gravely mendacious cow-boys.

The stranger in cattle-land usually hears of Bill if he shows an incautious curiosity about the cow business. Some old-timer is sure to remark mournfully:

"Ranchin' ain't what it was in the days Bill staked out New Mexico."

If the visitor walks into the trap and inquires further about

---

* By Edward O'Reilly. From *The Century Magazine*, Vol. 106 (October, 1923, No. 6), pp. 827–833. Copyright, 1923, by The Century Co.

Bill, he is sure to receive an assortment of misinformation that every cow-hand delights in unloading on the unwary.

Although Bill has been quoted in a number of Western stories, the real history of his wondrous deeds has never been printed. I have here collected a few of the tales about him which will doubtless be familiar to cow-men, but deserve to be passed on to a larger audience.

Bill invented most of the things connected with the cow business. He was a mighty man of valor, the king killer of the bad men, and it was Bill who taught the broncho how to buck. It is a matter of record that he dug the Rio Grande one dry year when he grew tired of packin' water from the Gulf of Mexico.

According to the most veracious historians, Bill was born about the time Sam Houston discovered Texas. His mother was a sturdy pioneer woman who once killed forty-five Indians with a broom-handle, and weaned him on moonshine liquor when he was three days old. He cut his teeth on a bowie-knife, and his earliest playfellows were the bears and catamounts of east Texas.

When Bill was about a year old, another family moved into the country, and located about fifty miles down the river. His father decided the place was gettin' too crowded, and packed his family in a wagon and headed west.

One day after they crossed the Pecos River, Bill fell out of the wagon. As there were sixteen or seventeen other children in the family, his parents didn't miss him for four or five weeks, and then it was too late to try to find him.

That's how Bill came to grow up with the coyotes along the Pecos. He soon learned the coyote language, and used to hunt with them and sit on the hills and howl at night. Being so young when he got lost, he always thought he was a coyote. That's where he learned to kill deer by runnin' them to death.

One day when he was about ten years old a cow-boy came along just when Bill had matched a fight with two grizzly bears. Bill hugged the bears to death, tore off a hind leg, and was just settin' down to breakfast when this cow-boy loped up and asked him what he meant by runnin' around naked that way among the varmints.

"Why, because I am a varmint," Bill told him. "I'm a coyote."

The cow-boy argued with him that he was a human, but Bill wouldn't believe him.

"Ain't I got fleas?" he insisted. "And don't I howl around all night, like a respectable coyote should do?"

"That don't prove nothin'," the cow-boy answered. "All Texans have fleas, and most of them howl. Did you ever see a coyote that didn't have a tail? Well, you ain't got no tail; so that proves you ain't a varmint."

Bill looked, and, sure enough, he didn't have a tail.

"You sure got me out on a limb," says Bill. "I never noticed that before. It shows what higher education will do for a man. I believe you're right. Lead me to them humans, and I'll throw in with them."

Bill went to town with this cow-hand, and in due time he got to enjoyin' all the pleasant vices of mankind, and decided that he certainly was a human. He got to runnin' with the wild bunch, and sunk lower and lower, until finally he became a cow-boy.

It wasn't long until he was famous as a bad man. He invented the six-shooter and train-robbin' and most of the crimes popular in the old days of the West. He didn't invent cow-stealin'. That was discovered by King David in the Bible, but Bill improved on it.

There is no way of tellin' just how many men Bill did kill. Deep down he had a tender heart, however, and never killed women or children, or tourists out of season. He never scalped his victims; he was too civilized for that. He used to skin them gently and tan their hides.

It wasn't long before Bill had killed all the bad men in west Texas, massacred all the Indians, and eat all the buffalo. So he decided to migrate to a new country where hard men still thrived and a man could pass the time away.

He saddled up his horse and hit for the West. One day he met an old trapper and told him what he was lookin' for.

"I want the hardest cow outfit in the world," he says. "Not one of these ordinary cow-stealin', Mexican-shootin' bunches of amateurs, but a real hard herd of hand-picked hellions that make murder a fine art and take some proper pride in their slaughter."

"Stranger, you're headed in the right direction," answers the trapper. "Keep right on down this draw for a couple of hundred miles, and you'll find that very outfit. They're so hard they can kick fire out of a flint rock with their bare toes."

Bill single-footed down that draw for about a hundred miles that afternoon; then he met with an accident. His horse stubbed his toe on a mountain and broke his leg, leavin' Bill afoot.

He slung his saddle over his shoulder and set off hikin' down that draw, cussin' and a-swearin'. Profanity was a gift with Bill.

All at once a big ten-foot rattlesnake quiled up in his path, set his tail to singin', and allowed he'd like to match a fight. Bill laid down his saddle, and just to be fair about it, he gave the snake the first three bites. Then he waded into that reptile and everlastingly frailed the pizen out of him.

By and by that old rattler yelled for mercy, and admitted that when it came to fightin', Bill started where he let off. So Bill picked up his saddle and started on, carryin' the snake in his hand and spinnin' it in short loops at the Gila monsters.

About fifty miles further on, a big old mountain-lion jumped off a cliff and lit all spraddled out on Bill's neck. This was no ordinary lion. It weighed more than three steers and a yearlin', and was the very same lion the State of Nuevo León was named after down in old Mexico.

Kind of chucklin' to himself, Bill laid down his saddle and his snake and went into action. In a minute the fur was flyin' down the cañon until it darkened the sun. The way Bill knocked the animosity out of that lion was a shame. In about three minutes that lion hollered:

"I'll give up, Bill. Can't you take a joke?"

Bill let him up, and then he cinched the saddle on him and went down that cañon whoopin' and yellin', ridin' that lion a hundred feet at a jump, and quirtin' him down the flank with the rattlesnake.

It wasn't long before he saw a chuck-wagon with a bunch of cow-boys squattin' around it. He rode up to that wagon, splittin' the air with his war-whoops, with that old lion a-screechin', and that snake singin' his rattles.

When he came to the fire he grabbed the old cougar by the ear, jerked him back on his haunches, stepped off him, hung his snake around his neck, and looked the outfit over. Them cow-boys sat there sayin' less than nothin.'

Bill was hungry, and seein' a boilerful of beans cookin' on the fire, he scooped up a few handfuls and swallowed them, washin' them down with a few gallons of boilin' coffee out of the pot. Wipin' his mouth on a handful of prickly-pear cactus, Bill turned to the cow-boys and asked:

"Who the hell is boss around here?"

A big fellow about eight feet tall, with seven pistols and nine bowie-knives in his belt, rose up and, takin' off his hat, said:

"Stranger, I was; but you be."

Bill had many adventures with this outfit. It was about this time he staked out New Mexico, and used Arizona for a calf-pasture. It was here that he found his noted horse Widow-Maker. He raised him from a colt on nitroglycerin and dynamite, and Bill was the only man that could throw a leg over him.

There wasn't anythin' that Bill couldn't ride, although I have heard of one occasion when he was thrown. He made a bet that he could ride an Oklahoma cyclone slick-heeled, without a saddle.

He met the cyclone, the worst that was ever known, up on the Kansas line. Bill eared that tornado down and climbed on its back. That cyclone did some pitchin' that is unbelievable, if it were not vouched for by many reliable witnesses.

Down across Texas it went sunfishin', back-flippin', side-windin', knockin' down mountains, blowin' the holes out of the ground, and tyin' rivers into knots. The Staked Plains used to be heavily timbered until that big wind swiped the trees off and left it a bare prairie.

Bill just sat up there, thumbin' that cyclone in the withers, floppin' it across the ears with his hat, and rollin' a cigarette with one hand. He rode it through three States, but over in Arizona it got him.

When it saw it couldn't throw him, it rained out from under him. This is proved by the fact that it washed out the Grand Cañon. Bill came down over in California. The spot where he lit is now known as Death Valley, a hole in the ground more than one hundred feet below sea-level, and the print of his hip-pockets can still be seen in the granite.

I have heard this story disputed in some of its details. Some historians claim that Bill wasn't thrown; that he slid down on a streak of lightnin' without knockin' the ashes off his cigarette. It is also claimed that the Grand Cañon was dug by Bill one week when he went prospectin'; but the best authorities insist on the first version. They argue that that streak of lightnin' story comes from the habit he always had of usin' one to light his cigarette.

Bill was a great roper. In fact, he invented ropin'. Old-timers who admit they knew him say that his rope was as long as the equator, although the more conservative say that it was at least two feet shorter on one end. He used to rope a herd of cattle at one throw.

This skill once saved the life of a friend. The friend had tried to ride Widow-Maker one day, and was thrown so high he came down on top of Pike's Peak. He was in the middle of a bad fix, because he couldn't get down, and seemed doomed to a lingerin' death on high.

Bill came to the rescue, and usin' only a short calf-loop, he roped his friend around the neck and jerked him down to safety in the valley, twenty thousand feet below. This man was always grateful, and became Bill's horse-wrangler at the time he staked out New Mexico.

In his idle moments in New Mexico Bill amused himself puttin' thorns on the trees and horns on the toads. It was on this ranch he dug the Rio Grande and invented the centipede and the tarantula as a joke on his friends.

When the cow business was dull, Pecos Bill occasionally embarked in other ventures; for instance, at one time he took a contract to supply the S. P. Railroad with wood. He hired a few hundred Mexicans to chop and haul the wood to the railroad line. As pay for the job, Bill gave each Mexican one fourth of the wood he hauled.

These Mexicans are funny people. After they received their share of the wood they didn't know what to do with it; so Bill took it off their hands and never charged them a cent.

On another occasion Bill took the job of buildin' the line fence that forms the boundary from El Paso across to the Pacific. He rounded up a herd of prairie-dogs and set them to dig holes, which by nature a prairie-dog likes to do.

Whenever one of them finished a nice hole and settled down to live in it, Bill evicted him and stuck a fence-post in the hole. Everybody admired his foresight except the prairie-dogs, and who cares what a prairie-dog thinks?

Old Bill was always a very truthful man. To prove this, the cow-boys repeat one of his stories, which Bill claimed happened to him. Nobody ever disputed him; that is, no one who is alive now.

He threw in with a bunch of Kiowa Indians one time on a little huntin'-trip. It was about the time the buffalo were getting scarce, and Bill was huntin' with his famous squatter-hound named Norther.

Norther would run down a buffalo and hold him by the ear until Bill came up and skinned him alive. Then he would turn it loose to grow a new hide. The scheme worked all right in the summer, but in the winter most of them caught colds and died.

The stories of Bill's love-affairs are especially numerous. One of them may be told. It is the sad tale of the fate of his bride, a winsome little maiden called Slue-Foot Sue. She was a famous rider herself, and Bill lost his heart when he saw her riding a catfish down the Rio Grande with only a surcingle. You must remember that the catfish in the Rio Grande are bigger than whales and twice as active.

Sue made a sad mistake, however, when she insisted on ridin' Widow-Maker on her weddin'-day. The old horse threw her so high she had to duck her head to let the moon go by. Unfortunately, she was wearin' her weddin'-gown, and in those days the women wore those big steel-spring bustles.

Well, when Sue lit, she naturally bounced, and every time she came down she bounced again. It was an awful sad sight to see Bill implorin' her to quit her bouncin' and not be so nervous; but Sue kept right on, up and down, weepin', and throwin' kisses to her distracted lover, and carryin' on as a bride naturally would do under those circumstances.

She bounced for three days and four nights, and Bill finally had to shoot her to keep her from starvin' to death. It was mighty tragic. Bill never got over it. Of course he married lots of women after that. In fact, it was one of his weaknesses; but none of them filled the place in his heart once held by Slue-Foot Sue, his bouncin' bride.

There is a great difference of opinion as to the manner of Bill's demise. Many claim that it was his drinkin' habits that killed him. You see, Bill got so that liquor didn't have any kick for him, and he fell into the habit of drinkin' strychnine and other forms of wolf pizen.

Even the wolf bait lost its effect, and he got to puttin' fish-hooks and barbed wire in his toddy. It was the barbed wire that finally killed him. It rusted his interior and gave him indigestion. He wasted away to a mere skeleton, weighin' not more than two tons; then up and died, and went to his infernal reward.

Many of the border bards who knew Pecos Bill at his best have a different account of his death.

They say that he met a man from Boston one day, wearing a mail-order cow-boy outfit, and askin' fool questions about the West; and poor old Bill laid down and laughed himself to death.

Old Stormalong, the Deep-Water Sailorman*

"CERTAINLY, I 'member Old Stormalong," said the oldest skipper on Cape Cod. "I was a 'prentice fust on his ship and later on I was Second when he was bosun on the *Courser*, out o' Boston. *That* was a ship, a wooden ship with iron men on her decks, a ship that aint been eekaled by these hoity-toity steamboats. No, sir, an' never will. Donald McKay built that ship just because he found one sailorman who could handle her as she should be handled. But, you're aimin' to hear about a sailorman an' not about ships.

"Only t'other day a young whippersnapper was a-telling me about Stormie sayin' as how he was fourteen fathoms tall. I've heared other tales about his height. I know! He was jes' four fathoms from the deck to the bridge of his nose.

"He was the first sailorman to have the letters 'A. B.' after his name. Those were jes' his 'nitials, put after his name on the ship's log just the same as always. Alfred Bulltop Storm-along was the name he gave his first skipper. The old man looked him over and says:

"'A. B. S. Able-Bodied Sailor. By your size and strength they should measure the talents of all other seamen.'

"It makes me pretee mad when I see some of the horn-swogglers of today with these letters after their names. They are only feeble imitators o' the greatest o' all deep-water sailormen.

"You landsmen know very little about real sailormen, that is, blue-water sailors. This chap Stormalong was not only a sailorman for all waters, he was a whaler too. I mind the time we was anchored in the middle of the North 'Lantic finishin' off a right whale. The lookout sights a school off to the east'ard and Stormie, the bosun, gives the order to h'ist the mudhook. All hands for'ard but not a h'ist. The hook 'ud give a bit and then it 'ud sink right back into the mud. Seemed to be hands clutchin' it and draggin' it out o' our hands. Once we got it clear o' the bottom and almost shipped it when we seed what was wrong. Nothin' short of an octopus

* From *Here's Audacity! American Legendary Heroes*, by Frank Shay, pp. 17–31. Copyright, 1930, by Frank Shay. New York: The Macaulay Company.

was wropped all 'round that mudhook. He was holdin' the anchor with half of his tenacles and with the other half hangin' on to the seaweed on the bottom.

"The mate yelled 'vast heavin'' and went back to tell the skipper. When the old man came for'ard to see for himself he was just in time to see Stormie go overboard with his sheath knife in his teeth. He went below the su'face and there began a terrific struggle. The water was churned and splashed about so that old hooker jes' rolled about like she was beam to the wind. All of us was sure our bosun had been tore 'part by the octopus. The struggle went on for about a quarter of an hour when Stormie's head came to the su'face. Some one called out to throw him a line but before one could be brought he had grabbed the anchor chain and came hand over hand to the deck. The strugglin' in the water kept on for a while but moved away from the ship.

" 'All right,' yelled Stormie, 'all hands lean on it and bring it home.'

"After the anchor was shipped I asked him what he had done to the octopus.

" 'Jes' tied his arms in knots. Double Carrick bends. It'll take him a month o' Sundays to untie them.'

"There was one peculiar thing about Stormalong that was due to his size. He was as loyal to his ship as any sailorman until he saw a bigger one. Then he'd get peevish an' sullen until he had signed aboard the bigger ship. His biggest complaint was that ships weren't built big enough for a full sized man.

"Well, the ship we were on at that time was *Lady of the Sea*, finest and fastest of the sea packets. Even that didn't satisfy him. He wanted a bigger ship or he'd go farmin'. Once he said to us as we sat 'round the forebitt:

" 'When this hooker gets to port I'm goin' to put an oar over my shoulder and I'm goin' to start walkin' 'way from salt water. I'm goin' to keep right on walkin' until some hairlegger says to me, "What's that funny stick you have on your shoulder, matey?" an' right there I'm goin' to settle down and dig potaters.'

" 'Yes,' said the Third-in-Command, skeptically, 'what potaters are you goin' to dig?'

" 'Regular and proper spuds, fresh ones, not like the dead potaters you get on his hooker,' said the Sailor Who Was Tired of the Sea.

" 'Got to plant them first,' said the Third. 'Then you got to hoe them, pick the bugs off'n them, spray them, hoe them some more. You got to irrigate them, too. Best irrigater for potatoes is the sweat off'n your brow. Just dig so hard and fast that the sweat rolls down along your nose and drops on the plant. Much harder'n holystoning the deck which, by the way, you'll begin on jus' as soon as you turn to in the mornin'.'

" 'Nothin' can be as hard as holystoning a deck,' observed Stormie.

" 'Compared with sailoring,' I cuts in, 'farmin' comes under the headin' of hard labor. The best part o' farmin', I'll admit, is that all the hard work comes in fine weather while with sailorin' it's jes' t'other way 'bout.'

"For the rest of that trip Stormalong was moody and pre-occupied. He had been on the ship for over a year, a very long time for him, without seeing a bigger ship. When the ship hit Boston Stormie signed off. He came on deck with his duffel bag over his shoulder.

" 'Where you goin'?' I asks him.

" 'Farmin',' says he.

"Then he heaves the bag over the rail and follows it to the wharf. The crew of the *Lady of the Sea* just stood along the rail and gaped.

2

"Several years later when we were again lined against the wharf at Boston a big, tall man was seen coming down the wharf.

" 'Stormie, or I'm a fool,' says I to myself.

"The big man came over the side and sure enough it was Alfred Bulltop Stormalong. There was a change immediately apparent. He was taller than ever but the flesh hung in dew-laps all over him and his eyes showed the marks of great suffering. Too, he looked hungrily at the sea. He breathed deep breaths of the salt air and in a few minutes seemed to regain some of his old spirit.

" 'Stormie, where 'a' you been?' I asks him.

" 'Farmin',' says he.

" 'How'd you like it?' I goes on.

" 'Terrible,' says he. 'Nothin' but green grass an' trees an' hills an' hot work. Nary a breeze or the smell o' the sea. Never a storm to make a man pull out all the best that's in him. Nothin' but zephyrs an' a hot sun an' pushin' on a plow. All my muscles were made for pullin' an' on a farm there's nothin' to do but push. Sailorin's the best job after all.'

"He signed on for his old job of boatswain and after taking on water we got under way. We cruised about the Caribbean Sea taking on and discharging shipments for over six months. Then we made for Boston Harbor.

"Stormie was a loyal sailor until he saw a bigger ship and the *Lady of the Sea* was the biggest ship sailing the Atlantic. At least we thought she was but just before we got to Barnegat we came across what first appeared to be a mirage. She was just the biggest ship ever built and I heard the skipper say to the mate that she was Donald McKay's dream come to life. Her lines were perfect, her cloth pure white and hung on silver masts. She rolled lazily on a sea that made us bump about like a cork. I saw Stormie at the rail gazing in goggle-eyed admiration.

"'Must take a million ordinary sailors to man her,' he gasped. 'Yes, sir! One million at the least. Well, I guess I'll be leavin' this packet.'

"The next mornin' we were without a bosun. The best explanation we could give was that during the night he had gone over the side and swum to the big ship. For a second time Stormalong had gone out of my life.

"After the *Lady of the Sea* discharged her cargo in Boston we got word that they were signing on a crew for a new ship, the *Courser*. I applied for a place as second mate and was signed on. We were told to report to a ship at the end of the wharf that was acting as a tender for the *Courser* which was too big to enter Boston Harbor.

"The next morning we boarded the tender and were taken out to the *Courser*. She was none other than the big ship we had seen from the *Lady of the Sea*, the ship that Stormie had gone over the side for. She looked like a ship that might have been built for a race of men of Stormalong's stature. The first thing that caught my eye as my feet hit the deck was a stableful of horses.

"'Horse boat, huh!' I said.

"'Horse boat nothin',' said the man in charge of the tender. 'Those horses are for the men on watch.'

"Believe it or not. That ship was so big that all officers and men on watch were mounted on horses. Manalive, her rigging was so immense that no living man could take her in at a single glance. Her masts penetrated the clouds and the top sections were on hinges so they could be bent over to let the sun and moon pass. Her sails were so big that the builders had to take all the able-bodied sailmakers out in the Sahara Desert to find room to sew them. Young men who were sent aloft usually came down as gray-beards. The skipper had to order all hands aloft six days before a storm. Every yard and every block and tackle had bunkhouses and cooks' galleys built into them to accommodate the men who worked aloft. She carried over six hundred men and some of the sailormen never saw all their shipmates. Once the Old Man, who gave his orders through a megaphone, ordered all hands forward. It took the after crew a week to get there and then over thirty were killed in the crush. Some of the men got lost because they had not taken the precaution to bring their compasses with them.

"The *Courser* was so big that she had to keep to the oceans, there was no harbor big enough for her to turn about it. Her wheel was so big it took thirty-two men working in unison to turn her and early in the cruise it was found that Stormalong was the only man aboard who could make her answer the wheel promptly. When we had to take on or discharge a cargo a whole fleet of ordinary ships used to come out and we would transship our load.

"But she was a great ship. There never was a storm great enough to cause her any real discomfort.

"There was one that caused us a bit of worry. One of those September gales that chivvy us in the North Atlantic. She was so big that the Skipper just let her ride out any storm, knowing that no matter how big a blow it was the *Courser* could weather it. Well, this was some storm, and we bobbed about like a regular sized vessel all over that ocean. Worst of it was that the clouds and fog made it so dark we couldn't make where we were at. This went on for over a fortnight when we awoke to see the sun bright and shining. The bosun put his mouth to his megaphone and shouted:

> Rise and shine
> For the Black Ball Line

and all hands turned to. There was Stormalong at the wheel holding her true to what he thought was her course. After the Captain and all the mates had 'taken the sun' and figured it out on paper they told us we were somewhere in the North Sea and headed south. That meant trouble. The *Courser* could never get through the English Channel and it meant that we'd pile up against the cliffs of Dover or on the French coast. You see, the North Sea wasn't big enough for us to turn around in. The skipper and the mates had a consultation and decided as they could not turn around to take a chance of easing through the Channel. The officers rode across the poop of that ship on their horses, yelling orders and squinting their eyes along the ship's sides. Stormie was at the wheel and the only man who could see everything at once. Just as they got to the point between Calais and the cliffs of Dover all sails were reefed and the skipper was ready to order the men to take to the boats. He looked back at Stormie and saw that the man at the wheel was calm and steady.

" 'Will she make it?' yelled the skipper through his megaphone.

" 'I think so!' answered the man at the wheel. 'May scrape a bit o' paint off'n our sides but she'll go through.'

"Then, squinting first along the port side an' then the starboard, he called to the man on the poop deck:

" 'Better send all hands over and soap the sides, put an extry heavy coat on the starboard.'

"The skipper got the whole crew plastering the sides with the best soap he had and the big ship eased through just as sweet as honey. But it's all due to the soap that we did get through. It was such a tight fit that the cliffs at Dover scraped every bit of soap off the starboard side. Ever since then the cliffs at that point have been pure white. That was from the *Courser*'s soap and the action of the waves. Sometime when you are in the channel take a look at the waves. They are still a bit foamy from the soap.

"When the Old Man saw we had gotten through he called all hands forward to splice the main brace, which meant in nautical terms, to come and have a drink of grog.

"The *Courser* kept right on going but after a few hours we got into shallow water and we had to jettison all of our ballast. We threw so much overboard that you can still see the piles of dirt. The English call them the Channel Islands.

"In all the time I knew her the *Courser* had but one other storm that troubled her. Strange to relate but it was another September gale, one of those lads that generally does so much damage around Florida. The *Courser* was down among the Caribbees and the storm whipped her about pretty badly. The Skipper wasn't as much afraid of losing his ship as he was of hitting one of the islands and knocking it and the inhabitants into kingdom come. The ship just missed Haiti and headed west by south like a broncho with the bit in his teeth. Right down the Gulf she went until she came to Darien and without asking anybody's permission went right through the Isthmus. The *Courser* found herself out in the Pacific Ocean. The only eye-witnesses of the destruction outside the crew were a couple of army officers who had been sent down by the United States to make surveys for a canal. And right in front of their eyes a ship comes along and digs it for them. Naturally they took all the credit but the truth of it is Old Stormalong and the *Courser* dug that ditch."

The Oldest Skipper on Cape Cod paused in his narrative to yawn and give his cronies a chance.

"All I ever knowed about him," said another, "was that he took his whale soup in a Cape Cod dory, that his fav'rite meat was shark. He liked ostrich eggs for breakfast and then he would lie back on the deck and pick his teeth with an eighteen foot oar."

"Skippers came and skippers went," said the Oldest Skipper on Cape Cod, "but Stormie stuck to the *Courser* to the end. He died while we were discharging a cargo from the middle of the Gulf of Mexico."

Paul Bunyan

I. WHO MADE PAUL BUNYAN?*

WHO made Paul Bunyan, who gave him birth as a myth, who joked him into life as the Master Lumberjack, who fashioned him forth as an apparition easing the hours of men amid axes and trees, saws and lumber? The people, the bookless people, they made Paul and had him alive long before he got into the books for those who read. He grew up in shanties, around the hot stoves of winter, among socks and mittens drying, in the smell of tobacco smoke and the roar of laughter mocking the outside weather. And some of Paul came overseas in wooden bunks below decks in sailing vessels. And some of Paul is old as the hills, young as the alphabet.

The Pacific Ocean froze over in the winter of the Blue Snow and Paul Bunyan had long teams of oxen hauling regular white snow

---

* From *The People, Yes,* by Carl Sandburg, pp. 97–99. Copyright, 1936, by Harcourt, Brace and Company, Inc. New York.

over from China. This was the winter Paul gave a party to the Seven Axmen. Paul fixed a granite floor sunk two hundred feet deep for them to dance on. Still, it tipped and tilted as the dance went on. And because the Seven Axmen refused to take off their hob-nailed boots, the sparks from the nails of their dancing feet lit up the place so that Paul didn't light the kerosene lamps. No women being on the Big Onion river at that time the Seven Axmen had to dance with each other, the one left over in each set taking Paul as a partner. The commotion of the dancing that night brought on an earthquake and the Big Onion river moved over three counties to the east.

One year when it rained from St. Patrick's Day till the Fourth of July, Paul Bunyan got disgusted because his celebration of the Fourth was spoiled. He dived into Lake Superior and swam to where a solid pillar of water was coming down. He dived under this pillar, swam up into it and climbed with powerful swimming strokes, was gone about an hour, came splashing down, and as the rain stopped, he explained, "I turned the dam thing off." This is told in the Big North Woods and on the Great Lakes, with many particulars.

Two mosquitoes lighted on one of Paul Bunyan's oxen, killed it, ate it, cleaned the bones, and sat on a grub shanty picking their teeth as Paul came along. Paul sent to Australia for two special bumble bees to kill these mosquitoes. But the bees and the mosquitoes intermarried; their children had stingers on both ends. And things kept getting worse till Paul brought a big boatload of sorghum up from Louisiana and while all the bee-mosquitoes were eating at the sweet sorghum he floated them down to the Gulf of Mexico. They got so fat that it was easy to drown them all between New Orleans and Galveston.

Paul logged on the Little Gimlet in Oregon one winter. The cook stove at that camp covered an acre of ground. They fastened the side of a hog on each snowshoe and four men used to skate on the griddle while the cook flipped the pancakes. The eating table was three miles long; elevators carried the cakes to the ends of the table where boys on bicycles rode back and forth on a path down the center of the table dropping the cakes where called for.

Benny, the Little Blue Ox of Paul Bunyan, grew two feet every time Paul looked at him, when a youngster. The barn was gone one morning and they found it on Benny's back; he grew out of it in a night. One night he kept pawing and bellowing for more pancakes, till there were two hundred men at the cook shanty stove trying to keep him fed. About breakfast time Benny broke loose, tore down the cook shanty, ate all the pancakes piled up for the loggers' breakfast. And after that Benny made his mistake; he ate the red hot stove; and that finished him. This is only one of the hot stove stories told in the North Woods.

II. THE WHISTLING RIVER*

It seems that some years before the winter of the Blue Snow (which every old logger remembers because of a heavy fall of bright blue snow which melted to ink, giving folks the idea of writing stories like these, so they tell) Ol' Paul was logging on what was then known as the Whistling River. It got its name from the fact that every morning, right on the dot, at nineteen minutes after five, and every night at ten minutes past six, it r'ared up to a height of two hundred and seventy-three feet and let loose a whistle that could be heard for a distance of six hundred and three miles in any direction.

Of course, if one man listening by himself can hear that far, it seems reasonable to suppose that two men listening together can hear it just twice as far. They tell me that even as far away as Alaska, most every camp had from two to four whistle-listeners (as many as were needed to hear the whistle without straining), who got two bits a listen and did nothing but listen for the right time, especially quitting time.

However, it seems that the river was famous for more than its whistling, for it was known as the orneriest river that ever ran between two banks. It seemed to take a fiendish delight in tying whole rafts of good saw logs into more plain and fancy knots than forty-three old sailors even knew the names of. It was an old "side winder" for fair. Even so, it is unlikely that Ol' Paul would ever have bothered with it, if it had left his beard alone.

It happened this way. It seems that Ol' Paul is sitting on a low hill one afternoon, combing his great curly beard with a pine tree, while he plans his winter operations. All of a sudden like, and without a word of warning, the river h'ists itself up on its hind legs and squirts about four thousand five hundred and nineteen gallons of river water straight in the center of Ol' Paul's whiskers.

Naturally Paul's considerably startled, but says nothing, figuring that if he pays it no mind, it'll go 'way and leave him be. But no sooner does he get settled back with his thinking

---

* From *Ol' Paul, The Mighty Logger*, by Glen Rounds, pp. [III] 19–41; [IV], 42–51; [V], 117–133. Copyright, 1936, by Holiday House, Inc. New York.

and combing again, than the durn river squirts some more! This time, along with the water, it throws in for good measure a batch of mud turtles, thirteen large carp, a couple of drowned muskrat, and half a raft of last year's saw logs. By this time Ol' Paul is pretty mad, and he jumps up and lets loose a yell that causes a landslide out near Pike's Peak, and startles a barber in Missouri so he cuts half the hair off the minister's toupee, causing somewhat of a stir thereabouts. Paul stomps around waving his arms for a spell, and allows:

"By the Gee-Jumpin' John Henry and the Great Horn Spoon, I'll tame that river or bust a gallus tryin'."

He goes over to another hill and sits down to think out a way to tame a river, forgetting his winter operations entirely. He sits there for three days and forty-seven hours without moving, thinking at top speed all the while, and finally comes to the conclusion that the best thing to do is to take out the kinks. But he knows that taking the kinks out of a river as tricky as this one is apt to be quite a chore, so he keeps on sitting there while he figures out ways and means. Of course, he could dig a new channel and run the river through that, but that was never Paul's way. He liked to figure out new ways of doing things, even if they were harder.

Meanwhile he's gotten a mite hungry, so he hollers down to camp for Sourdough Sam to bring him up a little popcorn, of which he is very fond. So Sam hitches up a four-horse team while his helpers are popping the corn, and soon arrives at Paul's feet with a wagon load.

Paul eats popcorn and thinks. The faster he thinks the faster he eats, and the faster he eats the faster he thinks, until finally his hands are moving so fast that nothing shows but a blur, and they make a wind that is uprooting trees all around him. His chewing sounds like a couple hundred coffee grinders all going at once. In practically no time at all the ground for three miles and a quarter in every direction is covered to a depth of eighteen inches with popcorn scraps, and several thousand small birds and animals, seeing the ground all white and the air filled with what looks like snowflakes, conclude that a blizzard is upon them and immediately freeze to death, furnishing the men with pot pies for some days.

But to get back to Ol' Paul's problem. Just before the popcorn is all gone, he decides that the only practical solution is to hitch Babe, the Mighty Blue Ox, to the river and let him yank it straight.

Babe was so strong that he could pull mighty near anything

that could be hitched to. His exact size, as I said before, is not known, for although it is said that he stood ninety-three hands high, it's not known whether that meant ordinary logger's hands, or hands the size of Paul's, which, of course, would be something else again.

However, they tell of an eagle that had been in the habit of roosting on the tip of Babe's right horn, suddenly deciding to fly to the other. Columbus Day, it was, when he started. He flew steadily, so they say, night and day, fair weather and foul, until his wing feathers were worn down to pinfeathers and a new set grew to replace them. In all, he seems to have worn out seventeen sets of feathers on the trip, and from reaching up to brush the sweat out of his eyes so much, had worn all the feathers off the top of his head, becoming completely bald, as are all of his descendants to this day. Finally the courageous bird won through, reaching the brass ball on the tip of the left horn on the seventeenth of March. He waved a wing weakly at the cheering lumberjacks and 'lowed as how he'd of made it sooner but for the head winds.

But the problem is how to hitch Babe to the river, as it's a well-known fact that an ordinary log chain and skid hook will not hold water. So after a light lunch of three sides of barbecued beef, half a wagon load of potatoes, carrots and a few other odds and ends, Ol' Paul goes down to the blacksmith shop and gets Ole, the Big Swede, to help him look through the big instruction book that came with the woods and tells how to do most everything under the sun. But though Paul reads the book through from front to back twice while Ole reads it from back to front, and they both read it once from bottom to top, they find nary a word about how to hook onto a river. However, they do find an old almanac stuck between the pages and get so busy reading up on the weather for the coming year, and a lot of fancy ailments of one kind and another that it's supper time before they know it, and the problem's still unsolved. So Paul decides that the only practical thing to do is to invent a rigging of some kind himself.

At any rate he has to do something, as every time he hears the river whistle, it makes him so mad he's fit to be tied, which interferes with his work more than something. No one can do their best under such conditions.

Being as how this was sort of a special problem, he thought it out in a special way. Paul was like that. As he always thought best when he walked, he had the men survey a circle about thirty miles in diameter to walk around. This was so that if he was quite a while thinking it out he wouldn't be finding himself way down in Australia when he'd finished.

When everything is ready, he sets his old fur cap tight on his head, clasps his hands behind him, and starts walking and thinking. He thinks and walks. The faster he walks the faster he thinks. He makes a complete circle every half hour. By morning he's worn a path that is knee-deep even on him, and he has to call the men to herd the stock away and keep them from falling in and getting crippled. Three days later he thinks it out, but he's worn himself down so deep that it takes a day and a half to get a ladder built that will reach down that far. When he does get out, he doesn't even wait for breakfast, but whistles for Babe and tears right out across the hills to the north.

The men have no idea what he intends to do, but they know from experience that it'll be good, so they cheer till their throats are so sore they have to stay around the mess hall drinking Paul's private barrel of cough syrup till supper time. And after that they go to bed and sleep very soundly.

Paul and the Ox travel plenty fast, covering twenty-four townships at a stride, and the wind from their passing raises a dust that doesn't even begin to settle for some months. There are those who claim that the present dust storms are nothing more or less than that same dust just beginning to get back to earth—but that's a matter of opinion. About noon, as they near the North Pole, they begin to see blizzard tracks, and in a short time are in the very heart of their summer feeding grounds. Taking a sack from his shoulder, Paul digs out materials for a box trap, which he sets near a well-traveled blizzard trail, and baits with fresh icicles from the top of the North Pole. Then he goes away to eat his lunch, but not until he's carefully brushed out his tracks—a trick he later taught the Indians.

After lunch he amuses himself for a while by throwing huge chunks of ice into the water for Babe to retrieve, but he soon has to whistle the great beast out, as every time he jumps into the water he causes such a splash that a tidal wave threatens Galveston, Texas, which at that time was inhabited by nobody in particular. Some of the ice he threw in is still floating around the ocean, causing plenty of excitement for the iceberg patrol.

About two o'clock he goes back to his blizzard trap and discovers that he has caught seven half-grown blizzards and one grizzled old nor'wester, which is raising considerable fuss and bids fair to trample the young ones before he can get them out. But he finally manages to get a pair of half-grown ones in his sack and turns the others lose.

About midnight he gets back to camp, and hollers at Ole, the Big Swede:

"Build me the biggest log chain that's ever been built, while I stake out these dadblasted blizzards! We're goin' to warp it to 'er proper, come mornin'."

Then he goes down to the foot of the river and pickets one of the blizzards to a tree on the bank, then crosses and ties the other directly opposite. Right away the river begins to freeze. In ten minutes the slush ice reaches nearly from bank to bank, and the blizzards are not yet really warmed to their work, either. Paul watches for a few minutes, and then goes back to camp to warm up, feeling mighty well satisfied with the way things are working out.

In the morning the river has a tough time r'aring up for what it maybe knows to be its last whistle, for its foot is frozen solid for more than seventeen miles. The blizzards have really done the business.

By the time breakfast is over, the great chain's ready and Babe all harnessed. Paul quick-like wraps one end of the chain seventy-two times around the foot of the river, and hitches Babe to the other. Warning the men to stand clear, he shouts at the Ox to pull. But though the great beast strains till his tongue hangs out, pulling the chain out into a solid bar some seven and a half miles long, and sinks knee-deep in the solid rock, the river stubbornly refuses to budge, hanging onto its kinks like a snake in a gopher hole. Seeing this, Ol' Paul grabs the chain and, letting loose a holler that blows the tarpaper off the shacks in the Nebraska sandhills, he and the Ox together give a mighty yank that jerks the river loose from end to end, and start hauling it out across the prairie so fast that it smokes.

After a time Paul comes back and sights along the river, which now is as straight as a gun barrel. But he doesn't have long to admire his work, for he soon finds he has another problem on his hands. You see, it's this way. A straight river is naturally much shorter than a crooked one, and now all the miles and miles of extra river that used to be in the kinks are running wild out on the prairie. This galls the farmers in those parts more than a little. So it looks like Paul had better figure something out, and mighty soon at that, for already he can see clouds of dust the prairie folks are raising as they come at top speed to claim damages.

After three minutes of extra deep thought he sends a crew to camp to bring his big cross-cut saw and a lot of baling wire. He saws the river into nine-mile lengths and the men roll it up like linoleum and tie it with the wire. Some say he used these later when he logged off the desert, rolling out as many lengths as he needed to float his logs. But that's another story.

But his troubles with the Whistling River were not all over. It seems that being straightened sort of took the gimp out of the river, and from that day on it refused to whistle even a bird call. And as Paul had gotten into the habit of depending on the whistle to wake up the men in the morning, things were a mite upset.

First he hired an official getter-upper who rode through the camp on a horse, and beat a triangle. But the camp was so big that it took three hours and seventy-odd minutes to make the trip. Naturally some of the men were called too early and some too late. It's hard to say what might have happened if Squeaky Swanson hadn't showed up about that time. His speaking voice was a thin squeak, but when he hollered he could be heard clear out to Kansas on a still day. So every morning he stood outside the cookshack and hollered the blankets off every bunk in camp. Naturally the men didn't stay in bed long after the blankets were off them, what with the cold wind and all, so Squeaky was a great success and for years did nothing but holler in the mornings.

Febold Feboldson

I. REAL AMERICAN WEATHER*

SOMEBODY ought to do something about the weather. It's downright disgraceful that in most parts of the United States the climate is of foreign origin. Florida and California brazenly boast of Mediterranean sunshine. Winter resorts in the Adirondacks are only imitations of those in Switzerland. Even the famous blizzard of 1888 came from Siberia. In fact, there's only one place where you can get real, genuine, American

---

* By Paul R. Beath. From *Nebraska Folklore Pamphlets*, Number Five, pp. 2–3. Lincoln: Federal Writers' Project of the Works Progress Administration for the State of Nebraska. July 1, 1937.

weather, and that's on the great plains between the Mississippi and the Rockies.

In the early days, I guess, it was even more American than it is now. At least that's what Bergstrom Stromberg says. He's way past ninety and has seen some big weather in his day. Besides, he's heard all about the climate of the early days directly from his uncle, the famous Febold Feboldson. Febold was the first white settler west of the Mississippi, not counting Spaniards and Frenchmen who don't count anyway.

Take 1848 for instance. That was the year the Petrified Snow covered the plains all summer and held up the '48ers in their gold rush to California with the result that they became '49ers. At that time Febold was operating an ox train between San Francisco and Kansas City, because the snow prevented him from doing anything else.

Since Febold was the only plainsman able to make the trip that year, the '48ers appealed to him for help. His secret was to load up with sand from Death Valley, California. The sands of the desert never grow cold, nor did Febold and his oxen. The sand he sold to the gold rushers at fifty dollars a bushel, and they were glad to get it.

Then the '49ers began to swarm over the snow-covered plains in their prairie schooners. But before they reached the Rockies the jolting of the wagons scattered the sand and covered up every bit of the Petrified Snow. And that's the reason, according to Bergstrom Stromberg, that the prairies are so all fired hot in the summer.

Febold cursed himself twenty times a day for twenty years for selling the '48ers that sand. Then he spent the next twenty years trying various schemes to moderate the climate. He finally gave up in disgust and moved to California. Thus he set an example which all good Middlewesterners have followed ever since.

Or take the popcorn ball. There's a genuine American product. Most people think that someone invented the popcorn ball, but it's actually a product of the American weather. It invented itself, so to speak, on Bergstrom Stromberg's ranch in the early days when Febold owned the place.

It was during that peculiar year known as the Year of the Striped Weather which came between the years of the Big Rain and the Great Heat. This year the weather was both hot and rainy. There was a mile strip of scorching sunshine and then a mile strip of rain. It so happened that on Febold's farm there were both kinds of weather. The sun shone on his cornfield until the corn began to pop, while the rain washed the syrup out of his sugar cane.

Now the cane field was on a hill and the cornfield was in a valley. The syrup flowed downhill into the popped corn and rolled it into great balls. Bergstrom says some of them were hundreds of feet high and looked like big tennis balls from a distance. You never see any of them now, because the grasshoppers ate them all up in one day, July 21, 1874.

But the Great Fog, I suppose, was the biggest piece of American weather that ever hit the great plains. It followed the year of the Great Heat which killed off the Dirtyleg Indians and Paul Bunyan's Blue Ox. Near the end of that remarkable year, according to Bergstrom Stromberg, it began to rain and kept it up for the proverbial forty days and forty nights.

"But nary a drop of water hit the ground," said Bergstrom.

"Then what became of it?" I asked.

"Why, it turned into steam, of course. That there rain had no more chance of hittin' the ground than you have of spittin' into a blast furnace."

This steam, as Bergstrom tells it, cooled enough to turn into fog. The whole country was fogbound. It was so thick that people had to go around in pairs, one to hold the fog apart while the other walked through it. The pioneer ranchers didn't need to water their stock. The cattle would simply drink the fog. It looked funny to see pigs with their noses up in the air rooting for fish and frogs. But the dirt farmers were as mad as the stockmen were happy. The sun couldn't shine through the fog and the seeds didn't know which way was up. So they grew downward.

Things were getting pretty serious. All the farmers had just about decided to go to California when Febold came to their rescue. He hit upon the idea of importing some English fog-cutters from London. But the English were so slow that Febold didn't get his fog-cutters until Thanksgiving, and then the fog had turned to slush. He finally got to work and cut up the fog and slush into long strips which he laid along the roads so as not to spoil the fields. In course of time the dust covered up the roads and today you can hardly tell where Febold buried the Great Fog.

But many a rural mail carrier has cursed Febold and his English fog-cutters. For every spring when it rains or thaws, that old fog comes seeping up and makes rivers of mud out of all the country roads.

John Henry

I. John Henry, the Hero*

ALL questions of authenticity of the John Henry tradition fade into insignificance before the incontrovertible fact that for his countless admirers John Henry is a reality. To them he will always be a hero, an idol, a symbol of the "natural" man.

It is often charged against the Negro that he glorifies his tough characters, his "bad men." But when one considers that the Negro has had little opportunity to develop outside the fields of labor and hell-raising, this tendency is not surprising. Bad men are nearly always interesting, and, incidentally, no one can sing of them any more heartily than the white man. But a working man fits into the drab scene of everyday life, and it is a miracle if he achieves any sort of notoriety by his hard labor. John Henry, then, is a hero indeed. With his hammer and his determination to prove his superiority over a machine, he made a name for himself in folk history. His superstrength, his grit, his endurance, and his martyrdom appeal to something fundamental in the heart of the common man. John Henry stands for something which the pick-and-shovel Negro idolizes—brute strength. He epitomizes the tragedy of man versus machine. In laying down his life for the sake of convincing himself and others that he could beat a machine, he did something which many a Negro would gladly do. The whole thing is a sort of alluring tragedy which appeals strongly to one's egotism.

So strong, indeed, has been the admiration, the envy, of other men for John Henry that some have tried to repeat his drama. I have no doubt but that some of these John Henry episodes said to have happened at so many places throughout the country (the Alabama episode, for instance) are based on real incidents in which would-be John Henrys did their best to put themselves beside the god of the hammer.

Mention John Henry to a group of Negro working men and the chances are that you start an admiration contest. The rare man who intimates that *he* could beat John Henry is laughed down by his fellows. "Why man," said a true John Henryite

---

* From *John Henry: Tracking Down a Negro Legend*, by Guy B. Johnson, pp. 142–146. Copyright, 1929, by The University of North Carolina Press. Chapel Hill.

on such an occasion, "John Henry could take that hammer between his teeth and drive with his hands tied and beat you like all git-out." "Yes, Lawd," affirmed another, "that man had a stroke like a Alabama mule." "They tells me," said a third, "that he used to keep six men runnin' just to carry his drills back and forth from the man that sharpened 'em." And so on until no one could think of anything else to say about him.

F. P. Barker, an old Alabama steel driver who claimed to have known John Henry, said, "I could drive from both shoulders myself, and I was as far behind John Henry as the moon is behind the sun. The world has not yet produced a man to whip steel like John Henry."

A young woman in Georgia concluded an account of John Henry's life as follows:

When he died people came from all parts of the world to see this Famous man John Henry. His wife had it engraved on his tombstone.

his Epitah [sic]
"Here lies the steel driving man."

John Henry has a way of cropping up at unexpected times and places. I was standing on the street at Chapel Hill one night in a throng of people gathered to hear the Dempsey-Sharkey fight on the radio. When things looked bad for Dempsey, a Negro man who stood near me began to show his displeasure. "If they'd put old Jack Johnson in there," he said, "he'd lay that Sharkey man out." At the end of the round we discussed colored prize fighters. Suddenly he came out with, "I'll tell you another colored man would've made a real prize-fighter—that's John Henry. Yessir, anybody that could handle a thirty-pound hammer like that man could would make a sure-'nough fighter."

There is, on the whole, a surprisingly small amount of exaggeration in the stories about John Henry told by those who worship at his shrine. Occasionally you hear that John Henry used a thirty-pound hammer or that he wore out six shakers on the day of the famous contest or that his statue has been carved in solid rock at the portal of Big Bend Tunnel, but around John Henry there has not yet grown up a body of fantastic lore like that which surrounds certain other folk characters—Paul Bunyan, for example. The only really bizarre tale I have ever heard about John Henry is one which Professor Howard W. Odum obtained from a construction-camp Negro at Chapel Hill three years ago. I repeat it here just as it was published in *Negro Workday Songs*.

One day John Henry lef' rock quarry on way to camp an' had to go through woods an' fiel'. Well, he met big black bear an' didn't do nothin' but shoot 'im wid his bow an' arrer, an' arrer went clean through bear an' stuck in big tree on other side. So John Henry pulls arrer out of tree an' pull so hard he falls back 'gainst 'nother tree which is so full o' flitterjacks, an' first tree is full o' honey, an' in pullin' arrer out o' one he shaken down honey, an' in fallin' 'gainst other he shaken down flitterjacks. Well, John Henry set there an' et honey an' flitterjacks, an' after while when he went to get up to go, button pop off'n his pants an' kill a rabbit mo' 'n a hundred ya'ds on other side o' de tree. An' so up jumped brown baked pig wid sack o' biscuits on his back, an' John Henry et him too.

So John Henry gits up to go on through woods to camp for supper, 'caus he 'bout to be late an' he mighty hongry for his supper. John Henry sees lake down hill an' thinks he'll get him a drink o' water, 'cause he's thirsty, too, after eatin' honey an' flitterjacks an' brown roast pig an' biscuits, still he's hongry yet. An' so he goes down to git drink water an' finds lake ain't nothin' but lake o' honey, an' out in middle dat lake ain't nothin' but tree full o' biscuits. An' so John Henry don't do nothin' but drink dat lake o' honey dry. An' he et the tree full o' biscuits, too. An' so 'bout that time it begin' to git dark, an' John Henry sees light on hill an' he think maybe he can git sumpin to eat, 'cause he's mighty hongry after big day drillin'. So he look 'roun' an' see light on hill an' runs up to house where light is an' ast people livin' dere, why'n hell dey don't give him sumpin to eat, 'cause he ain't had much. An' so he et dat, too.

Gee-hee, hee, dat nigger could eat! But dat ain't all, cap'n. Dat nigger could wuk mo' 'n he could eat. He's greates' steel driller ever live, regular giaunt, he was; could drill wid his hammer mo' 'n two steam drills, an' some say mo' 'n ten. Always beggin' boss to git 'im bigger hammer. John Henry was cut out fer big giaunt driller. One day when he was jes' few weeks ol' settin' on his mammy's knee he commence cryin' an' his mommer say, "John Henry, whut's matter, little son?" An' he up an' say right den an' dere dat nine-poun'

hammer be death o' him. An' sho' 'nough he grow up right
'way into bigges' steel driller worl' ever see. Why dis I's tellin'
you now wus jes' when he's young fellow; waits til' I tells
you 'bout his drillin' in mountains an' in Pennsylvania. An'
so one day he drill all way from Rome, Georgia, to D'catur,
mo' 'n a hundred miles drillin' in one day, an' I ain't sure dat
was his bes' day. No, I ain't sure dat was his bes' day.

But, boss, John Henry was a regular boy, not lak some o'
dese gianuts you read 'bout not likin' wimmin an' nothin'.
John Henry love to come to town same as any other nigger,
only mo' so. Co'se he's mo' important an' all dat, an' co'se
he had mo' wimmin 'an anybody else. Some say mo' 'n ten,
but as to dat I don't know. I means, boss, mo' wimmin 'an
ten men, 'cause, Lawd, I specs he had mo' 'n thousand wimmin. An' John Henry was a great co'tin man, too, cap'n. Always was dat way. Why, one day when he settin' by his pa'
in san' out in front o' de house, jes' few weeks old, wimmin
come along an' claim him fer deir man. An' dat's funny, too,
but it sho' was dat way all his life. An' so when he come to
die John Henry had mo' wimmin, all dressed in red an' blue
an' all dem fine colors come to see him dead, if it las' thing
dey do, an' was mighty sad sight, people all standin' 'roun',
both cullud an' white.

II. John Henry*

* From *American Ballads and Folk Songs*, collected and compiled by John
A. Lomax and Alan Lomax, pp. 5–9. Copyright, 1934, by the Macmillan
Company. New York.

John Henry, he had a woman,
Her name was Mary Magdalene,
She would go to de tunnel and sing for John,
Jes' to hear John Henry's hammer ring,
Lawd, Lawd, jes' to hear John Henry's hammer ring.

John Henry had a li'l woman,
Her name was Lucy Ann,
John Henry took sick an' had to go to bed,
Lucy Ann drove steel like a man,
Lawd, Lawd, Lucy Ann drove steel like a man.

Cap'n says to John Henry,
"Gonna bring me a steam drill 'round,
Gonna take dat steam drill out on de job,
Gonna whop dat steel on down,
Lawd, Lawd, gonna whop dat steel on down."

John Henry tol' his cap'n,
Lightnin' was in his eye:
"Cap'n, bet yo' las' red cent on me,
Fo' I'll beat it to de bottom or I'll die,
Lawd, Lawd, I'll beat it to de bottom or I'll die."

Sun shine hot an' burnin',
Wer'n't no breeze a-tall,
Sweat ran down like water down a hill,
Dat day John Henry let his hammer fall,
Lawd, Lawd, dat day John Henry let his hammer fall.

John Henry went to de tunnel,
An' dey put him in de lead to drive;
De rock so tall an' John Henry so small,
Dat he lied down his hammer an' he cried,
Lawd, Lawd, dat he lied down his hammer an' he cried.

John Henry started on de right hand,
De steam drill started on de lef'—
"Before I'd let dis steam drill beat me down,
I'd hammer my fool self to death,
Lawd, Lawd, I'd hammer my fool self to death."

White man tol' John Henry,
"Nigger, damn yo' soul,
You might beat dis steam an' drill of mine,
When de rocks in dis mountain turn to gol',
Lawd, Lawd, when de rocks in dis mountain turn to gol'."

John Henry said to his shaker,
"Nigger, why don' you sing?
I'm throwin' twelve poun's from my hips on down,
Jes' listen to de col' steel ring,
Lawd, Lawd, jes' listen to de col' steel ring."

Oh, de captain said to John Henry,
"I b'lieve this mountain's sinkin' in."
John Henry said to his captain, oh my!
"Ain' nothin' but my hammer suckin' win',
Lawd, Lawd, ain' nothin' but my hammer suckin' win'."

John Henry tol' his shaker,
"Shaker, you better pray,
For, if I miss dis six-foot steel,
Tomorrow'll be yo' buryin' day,
Lawd, Lawd, tomorrow'll be yo' buryin' day."

John Henry tol' his captain,
"Looka yonder what I see—
Yo' drill's done broke an' yo' hole's done choke,
An' you cain' drive steel like me,
Lawd, Lawd, an' you cain' drive steel like me."

De man dat invented de steam drill,
Thought he was mighty fine.
John Henry drove his fifteen feet,
An' de steam drill only made nine,
Lawd, Lawd, an' de steam drill only made nine.

De hammer dat John Henry swung
It weighed over nine pound;
He broke a rib in his lef'-han' side,
An' his intrels fell on de groun',
Lawd, Lawd, an' his intrels fell on de groun'.

John Henry was hammerin' on de mountain,
An' his hammer was strikin' fire,
He drove so hard till he broke his pore heart,
An' he lied down his hammer an' he died,
Lawd, Lawd, he lied down his hammer an' he died.

All de womens in de Wes',
When he heared of John Henry's death,
Stood in de rain, flagged de eas'-boun' train,
Goin' where John Henry fell dead,
Lawd, Lawd, goin' where John Henry fell dead.

John Henry's li'l mother,
She was all dressed in red,
She jumped in bed, covered up her head,
Said she didn' know her son was dead,
Lawd, Lawd, didn' know her son was dead.

John Henry had a pretty li'l woman,
An' de dress she wo' was blue,
An' de las' words she said to him:
"John Henry, I've been true to you,
Lawd, Lawd, John Henry, I've been true to you."

Casey Jones

I. CASEY JONES, ENGINEER*

ON the last day of April [1928] occurs the 28th anniversary of the death of Casey Jones,—probably the most famous of a long line of locomotive engineer heroes who have died at their post of duty, one hand on the whistle and the other on the airbrake lever. Casey Jones' fame rests on a series of nondescript verses, which can hardly be called poetry. They were written by Wallace Saunders, a Negro engine wiper who had been a close friend of the famous engineer, and who sang them to a jigging melody all his own.

Mrs. Casey Jones still lives in Jackson, Tenn. She has two sons and a daughter. Charles Jones, her younger son, lives in Jackson; Lloyd, the older son, is with a Memphis auto agency; and her daughter, Mrs. George McKenzie, lives at Tuscaloosa, Ala.

Although 41 years have flitted by since Miss Janie Brady said "I do" and became the bride of John Luther (Casey) Jones, Mrs. Jones still keeps green the memory of that glad occasion. Today, still on the sunny side of 60, the plump blond woman with her cheery smile tells graphically the story of how her husband was killed, and how Wallace Saunders composed the original air and words that later swept the country for years as the epic ballad of the railroader.

"My husband's real name was John Luther Jones," she told her latest interviewer. "He was a lovable lad—6 feet 4½ inches in height, dark-haired and gray-eyed. Always he was in good humor and his Irish heart was as big as his body. All

---

* From *Erie Railroad Magazine*, Vol. 24 (April, 1928), No. 2, pp. 13, 44.

the railroaders were fond of Casey, and his wiper, Wallace Saunders, just worshipped the ground he walked on."

The interviewer asked Mrs. Jones how her husband got the nickname Casey.

"Oh, I supposed everyone knew that!" she replied. "He got it from the town of Cayce, Kentucky, near which he was born. The name of the town is locally pronounced in two syllables, exactly like 'Casey.' "

Mrs. Jones remembers Wallace Saunders very well, although she has not seen him for years.

"Wallace's admiration for Casey was little short of idolatry," she said. "He used to brag mightily about Mr. Jones even when Casey was only a freight engineer."

Casey Jones was known far and wide among railroad men, for his peculiar skill with a locomotive whistle.

"You see," said Mrs. Jones, "he established a sort of trade mark for himself by his inimitable method of blowing a whistle. It was a kind of long-drawn-out note that he created, beginning softly, then rising, then dying away almost to a whisper. People living along the Illinois Central right of way between Jackson and Water Valley would turn over in their beds late at night and say: 'There goes Casey Jones,' as he roared by."

After he had put in several years as freight and passenger engineer between Jackson and Water Valley, Casey was transferred early in 1900 to the Memphis-Canton (Miss.) run as throttle-puller of the Illinois Central's crack "Cannon-ball" train.

Casey and his fireman, Sim Webb, rolled into Memphis from Canton about 10 o'clock Sunday night, April 29. They went to the checking-in office and were preparing to go to their homes when Casey heard somebody call out: "Joe Lewis has just been taken with cramps and can't take his train out tonight."

"I'll double back and pull Lewis' old No. 638," Casey volunteered.

At 11 o'clock that rainy Sunday night Casey and Sim Webb clambered aboard the big engine and eased her out of the station and through the South Memphis yards.

> "All the switchmen knew by the engine's moans
> That the man at the throttle was Casey Jones."

Four o'clock of the 30th of April. The little town of Vaughn, Miss. A long, winding curve just above the town, and a long sidetrack beginning about where the curve ended.

"There's a freight train on the siding," Casey yelled across to Sim Webb.

Knowing the siding there was a long one, and having passed many other freights on it, Casey figured he would do the same this night.

But there were two separate sections of a very long train on the sidetrack this night. And the rear one was a little too long to get all its length off the main line onto the siding. The freight train crews figured on "sawing by"; that is as soon as the passenger train passed the front part of the first train, it would move forward and the rear freight would move up, thus clearing the main track.

But Casey's speed—about fifty miles an hour—was more than the freight crews bargained for.

But when old 638 was within a hundred feet of the end of the siding the horrified eyes of Casey Jones and Sim Webb beheld through the gloom the looming shape of several box-cars in motion, swinging across from the main line to the side-track. In a flash both knew there was no earthly way of preventing a smashup.

"Jump, Sim, and save yourself!" was Casey's last order to his fireman. As for himself, Casey threw his engine in reverse and applied the airbrakes—all any engineer could do, and rode roaring 638 into a holocaust of crashing wood that splintered like match boxes. Sim Webb jumped, fell into some bushes and was not injured.

When they took Casey's body from the wreckage (old 638 had plowed through the cars and caboose and turned over on her side a short distance beyond) they found one hand on the whistle cord, the other on the airbrake lever.

"I remember," Sim Webb told Casey's widow, "that as I jumped Casey held down the whistle in a long, piercing scream. I think he must have had in mind to warn the freight conductor in the caboose so he could jump."

Probably no individual, excepting a member of Casey's family, was more affected by the sad news than Wallace Saunders.

A few days later he was going about singing a song to a melody all his own. The air had a lilt that caught the fancy of every one who heard it. But Wallace, honest old soul, had no idea of doing more than singing it as a sort of tribute to his white friend's memory.

But one day a song writer passed through Jackson and heard the song and the details of Casey's tragic death. He went off and changed the words, but retained the lilting refrain and the name of Casey Jones. That was about 1902.

II. THE "CASEY JONES" SONG*

Four years ago the Erie Railroad Magazine gathered up the real story of Casey's life and death, as told by his widow, who still lives in Jackson, Tenn. The article was reprinted in railroad magazines and newspapers all over the world and has brought a continuous stream of letters ever since. Scores of correspondents have sent in various versions of the Casey Jones song, not only in English but in French, German and even in the language of the native laborers on the South African railways.

Every branch of railroading has at least one version of the song. The hobo jungles and the I.W.W. song books contribute others. Still others come from the campfires and boarding cars of construction gangs, and several weird and often unprintable variations were composed by doughboys in France during the world war.

Come all you round-ers for I want you to hear The
sto—ry told of a brave en—gi—neer;
Ca—sey Jones was the round-er's name, On a
heav-y six—eight wheel-er he rode to fame.

Caller called Jones about half-past four,
Jones kissed his wife at the station door,
Climbed into the cab with the orders in his hand,
Says, "This is my trip to the promised land."

* *Erie Railroad Magazine*, Vol. 28 (April, 1932), No. 2, p. 12. The present text (*ibid.*, Vol. 24, April, 1928, No. 2, p. 12), like the tune, is traditional, differing from the popular song version principally in the absence of the chorus. Copyright 1909 by Newton & Seibert. Copyright renewed. By permission of Shapiro, Bernstein & Co., Inc.

Through South Memphis yards on the fly,
He heard the fireman say, "You've got a white-eye,"
All the switchmen knew by the engine's moans,
That the man at the throttle was Casey Jones.

It had been raining for more than a week,
The railroad track was like the bed of a creek.
They rated him down to a thirty mile gait,
Threw the south-bound mail about eight hours late.

Fireman says, "Casey, you're runnin' too fast,
You run the block signal the last station you passed."
Jones says, "Yes, I think we can make it though,
For she steams much better than ever I knew."

Jones says, "Fireman, don't you fret,
Keep knockin' at the firedoor, don't give up yet;
I'm goin' to run her till she leaves the rail
Or make it on time with the south-bound mail."

Around the curve and a-down the dump
Two locomotives were a-bound to bump.
Fireman hollered, "Jones, it's just ahead,
We might jump and make it but we'll all be dead."

'Twas around this curve he saw a passenger train;
Something happened in Casey's brain;
Fireman jumped off, but Casey stayed on,
He's a good engineer but he's dead and gone—

Poor Casey was always all right,
He stuck to his post both day and night;
They loved to hear the whistle of Old Number Three
As he came into Memphis on the old K.C.

Headaches and heartaches and all kinds of pain
Are not apart from a railroad train;
Tales that are earnest, noble and gran'
Belong to the life of a railroad man.

The Saga of Joe Magarac: Steelman*

WHILE working in the steel mills along the Monongahela valley of Pennsylvania, I often heard one of the many Slavs

* By Owen Francis. From *Scribner's Magazine*, Vol. XC (November, 1931), No. 5, pp. 505–511. Copyright, 1931, by Charles Scribner's Sons.

who worked in the mills call one of his fellow-workers "*magarac*." Knowing that literally translated the word *magarac* meant jackass, but knowing also, from the tone of voice and the manner in which it was used, that it was seldom used derisively, I questioned my Hunkie leverman as to its meaning as understood by the Hunkie workers. He gave me a vivid explanation. He said:

"Magarac! Dat is mans who is joost same lak jackass donkey. Dat is mans what joost lak eatit and workit, dats all."

Pointing a finger toward another of his race, a huge Hunkie by the name of Mike, who was walking from the open hearth, he yelled:

"Hay! Magarac!"

At once, Mike's thumbs went to his ears, and with palms outspread his hands waved back and forth while he brayed lustily in the best imitation of a donkey that he could give.

"See," my leverman said, "dere is *magarac*. Dat is Joe Magarac for sure."

Then they both laughed and spoke in their mother tongue, which I did not understand.

It was evident enough there was some definite reason for the use of the word, and obviously that reason was, to their way of thinking, very humorous.

By working for a considerable number of years with a Hunkie on my either side, by sitting many evenings in their homes, and, since turning my thoughts to writing, by spending a good deal of my time with them, I have been fortunate enough to hear considerably more about Mr. Joe Magarac.

I find that Joe Magarac is a man living only in the imagination of the Hunkie steel-mill worker. He is to the Hunkie what Paul Bunyan is to the woodsman and Old Stormalong is to the men of the sea. With his active imagination and his childlike delight in tales of greatness, the Hunkie has created stories with Joe Magarac as the hero that may in the future become folklore of our country. Conceived in the minds of Hunkie steel-mill workers, he belongs to the mills as do the furnaces and the rolling-mills. Although the stories of Joe Magarac are sagas, they have no tangible connection so far as I have been able to find, with the folklore of any of the countries which sent the Hunkie to these United States. It seems that the Hunkie, with the same adaptability that has made him into the best worker within our shores, has created a character and has woven about him a legend which admirably fits the environment in which he, the Hunkie, has been placed. Basically, the stories of Joe Magarac are as much a part of the American scene as steel itself.

I did not hear the story which I have set down here as accurately as I have been able, at one time. Some of it I heard in the mill; some of it while sitting on the hill above the mill on pleasant Sunday afternoons; the most of it while sitting in Agnes's kitchen with Hunkie friends at my side and well-filled tin cups of prune-jack before us.

The saga of Joe Magarac is more typical of the Hunkie than any tale or incident or description I might write. It shows his sense of humor, his ambitions, his love of his work, and, in general, shows what I know the Hunkie to be: a good-natured, peace- and home-loving worker.

THE HOME OF JOE MAGARAC

Joe Magarac was workit every day and every night at mill and same lak before he was makit rails with hands. Pretty soon dat pile of rails in yard get bigger and bigger for Joe Magarac is workit so hard and after coople months yard was full, everyplace was rails. When Joe Magarac see dat he joost laughit and workit harder as ever. So one day roller-boss he comit up from down by finishing mills and he say to Joe Magarac who was workit by his furnace in open hearth. Roller-boss he say:

"Well, Joe Magarac, I guess we gone shut mill down early dis week. Dis time we catch plenty rails everyplace and we no catch many orders. So by Gods, we gone shut mill down Thursday night and we no start 'em up again until Monday morning. Mebbe you gone put slow heat in furnace: you tell stockman give you fifty-ton stock. You put 'em in stock and give furnace slow fire so dat she keepit warm and be ready for start 'em up on Monday."

Joe Magarac he act lak he gone say something and den he no say nothing and roller-boss tink everyting gone be all right dis time and he gone away.

When next Monday comit mans gone back to work for open hearth. Den dey see dat Joe Magarac is not workit on furnace dat morning. Everyplace dey lookit and dey no see Joe anyplace. 'Nother mans was workit on Noomber Seven and pretty soon when Noomber Seven was ready for tap 'em out melter-boss gone down to platform to see what kind steel dat slow heat makit. He was standit by ingot mould and pretty soon he hear voice what say:

"How she lookit dis time?"

Melter-boss lookit 'round and he no see nobody and den dat voice say again:

"It's me, Joe Magarac. I'm inside ladle."

Melter-boss turn around and he lookit inside ladle and he see Joe. Joe was sitting inside ladle with hot steel boiling up around neck. Melter-boss was scared lak anyting and he say:

"What the hells you do in dere, Joe Magarac? Better you gone crawl out dat ladle right 'way or I tink maybe for sure dat she gone melt you up."

Joe Magarac close one eyes for melter-boss and he say:

"Dats fine. Dats good business, dats joost what I wanit. By Gods, I be sick dis time of mill what shut down on Thursday and no start 'em up again until Monday. What the hells I gone do all time mill is shut down anyway? I hear big boss say dat he was gone makit two, three good heats steel so dat he gone have best steel what we can makit for buildit new mill dis place. Dey gone tear down dis old mills and makit new ones what is gone be best mills in whole Monongahela valley, what gone be best mills in whole world. Den by Gods, I get plan: I gone joomp in furnace when steel is melted down and dey gone melt 'em up, who was made from steel, to makit steel to makit dat mills. Now Mr. Boss you gone listen for me and I gone tell you someting. You gone take dis ladle steel what has me inside and you gone pour 'em out in ingot mould and den you gone roll 'em out and makit beam, channel, and maybe one, two piece angle and you gone take dat steel and makit new mills. You do lak I say for you and you gone see you gone have best mills for anyplace. Good-by."

Den Joe Magarac sit back down in ladle and hold his chin down in boiling steel until he was all melted up. Pretty soon dey pour him out in ingot mould.

Well, after dey roll 'em out dat heat and dey cut 'em up dey see dat dis time dey have best steel what was ever made. Oh, my, dat steel was smooth and straight and it no have seam or pipe nothing. Den melter-boss he gone 'round for everybody and he say:

"Now we gone have best mills for sure. You see dat steel? By Gods, nobody ever see steel lak dat before and dats joost because Joe Magarac he makit dat steel. Sure, he's inside and now we gone takit dat beam and dat channel and we gone build finest mills what ever was."

Dey do lak melter-boss say and dat is why all young boys

want to go for mill, and dat is why when somebody call Hunkie *magarac* he only laughit and feel proud as anyting, and dat is why we catch the best mill for anyplace, ya damn right!

VI

PATRON SAINTS

ON THE purely patriotic level our heroes are apt to be too good to be true. Such is the case with that "typically good man," Washington, whose integrity is traditionally taught by means of what the Doubter in the Sazerac Lying Club characterizes as the "doggonedest biggest lie as was ever told in this here Club." Yet in spite of more robust and even backwoodsy traits and episodes in young manhood, the juvenile Washington of Parson Weems' cherry-tree legend is of a piece with the "supercilious postage-stamp" likeness that the older Washington has become in the hearts of his countrymen.

As human being and folk hero, as American image and symbol, Lincoln is more satisfying. His "log cabin to White House" career fits the Horatio Alger pattern (which is essentially the fairy-tale pattern) of the poor boy who makes good; his genius as a folk story-teller helped in the making of his own legend; and he suffered the martyrdom which is the hero's apotheosis. He is also the perfect exemplar of the Freudian formula which sees in his homeliness the potentiality of our own impotence and of the American democratic creed of the self-made man. ("Any boy can become President.") Rather than too good to be true, Lincoln was great because he was not afraid to be common.

Although Americans as a rule have clung less tenaciously to the ideal of the good life than to that of the useful one, following Mr. Hoover's "American way" of "stimulating their ingenuity to solve their own problems," the doctrine of plain living and high thinking has produced spiritual heroes—saints and martyrs in whom self-abnegation is combined with service. That saints are not far from cranks is seen in the fanatic Johnny Appleseed, whose resemblance to Saint Francis is balanced by his likeness to a Yankee peddler, as the primitive Christian in him merged with the footloose type of hero. His "benevolent monomania" of "planting appleseeds in remote places" has overshadowed his less beneficent fixation of sowing the seed of dog-fennel, from a belief that it possessed valuable anti-malarial virtues. His inner meaning as a mystical pioneer cast in the unique rôle of a savior among wastrels is the intent of these lines written to be spoken in a pageant:

"My name is Johnny Appleseed. I lived in this part of the country a long time ago, when it had hardly been touched. I liked the Indians and I liked the white people and I liked the animals, and I didn't hurt any of them. I planted seeds and set out apple trees for the settlers and I took care of them. I told the people about God, and I tried to be a good man myself. I tried to be a good American, on this land we had found. Maybe I was, a little. Maybe I'm not dead yet."[1]

"I Cannot Tell a Lie"*

NEVER did the wise Ulysses take more pains with his beloved Telemachus, than did Mr. Washington with George, to inspire him with an *early love of truth.* "Truth, George," said he, "is the loveliest quality of youth. I would ride fifty miles, my son, to see the little boy whose heart is so *honest,* and his lips so *pure,* that we may depend on every word he says. O how lovely does such a child appear in the eyes of everybody! his parents doat on him. His relations glory in him. They are constantly praising him to their children, whom they beg to imitate him. They are often sending for him to visit them; and receive him, when he comes, with as much joy as if he were a little angel, come to set pretty examples to their children.

"But, Oh! how different, George, is the case with the boy who is given to lying, that nobody can believe a word he says! He is looked at with aversion wherever he goes, and parents

* From *The Life of George Washington,* by Mason Locke Weems (fifth edition), 1806.

dread to see him come among their children. Oh, George! my son! rather than see you come to this pass, dear as you are to my heart, gladly would I assist to nail you up in your little coffin, and follow you to your grave. Hard, indeed, would it be to me to give up my son, whose little feet are always so ready to run about with me, and whose fondly looking eyes, and sweet prattle make so large a part of my happiness. But still I would give him up, rather than see him a common liar."

"Pa," said George very seriously, "do I ever tell lies?"

"No, George, I *thank* God you do not, my son; and I rejoice in the hope you never will. At least, you shall never, from me, have cause to be guilty of so shameful a thing. Many parents, indeed, even compel their children to this vile practice, by barbarously beating them for every little fault: hence, on the next offence, the little terrified creature slips out a *lie!* just to escape the rod. But as to yourself George, you know I have *always* told you, and now tell you again, that, whenever by accident, you do anything wrong, which must often be the case, as you are but a poor little boy yet, without *experience* or *knowledge*, you must never tell a falsehood to conceal it; but come *bravely* up, my son, like a *little* man, and tell me of it: and, instead of beating you, George, I will but the more honour and love you for it, my dear."

This, you'll say, was sowing good seed!—Yes, it was: and the crop, thank God, was, as I believe it ever will be, where a man acts the true parent, that is, the *Guardian Angel*, by his child.

The following anecdote is a *case in point*. It is too valuable to be lost, and too true to be doubted; for it was communicated to me by the same excellent lady to whom I am indebted for the last.

"When George," said she, "was about six years old, he was made the wealthy master of a *hatchet!* of which, like most little boys, he was immoderately fond, and was constantly going about chopping every thing that came in his way. One day, in the garden, where he often amused himself hacking his mother's pea-sticks, he unluckily tried the edge of his hatchet on the body of a beautiful young English cherry-tree, which he barked so terribly, that I don't believe the tree ever got the better of it. The next morning the old gentleman, finding out what had befallen his tree, which, by the by, was a great favourite, came into the house; and with much warmth asked for the mischievous author, declaring at the same time, that he would not have taken five guineas for his tree. Nobody could tell him anything about it. Presently George and his hatchet made their appearance. *'George,'* said his father, 'do you know who killed that beautiful little cherry tree yonder in the garden?' This was a *tough question;* and George staggered under it for a moment; but quickly recovered himself: and looking at his father, with the sweet face of youth brightened with the inexpressible charm of all-conquering truth, he bravely cried out, 'I can't tell a lie, Pa; you know I can't tell a lie. I did cut it with my hatchet.'—'Run to my arms, you dearest boy,' cried his father in transports, 'run to my arms; glad am I, George, that you killed my tree; for you have paid me for it a thousand fold. Such an act of heroism in my son is more worth than a thousand trees, though blossomed with silver, and their fruits of purest gold.' "

It was in this way by interesting at once both his *heart* and *head*, that Mr. Washington conducted George with great ease and pleasure along the happy paths of virtue.

Honest Abe

I. The Young Store-Keeper*

As a clerk he proved honest and efficient, and my readers will be interested in some illustrations of the former trait which I find in Dr. Holland's interesting volume.

One day a woman came into the store and purchased sundry articles. They footed up two dollars and six and a quarter cents, or the young clerk thought they did. We do not hear nowadays of six and a quarter cents, but this was a coin borrowed from the Spanish currency, and was well known in my own boyhood.

The bill was paid, and the woman was entirely satisfied. But the young store-keeper, not feeling quite sure as to the accuracy of his calculation, added up the items once more. To his dismay he found that the sum total should have been but two dollars.

"I've made her pay six and a quarter cents too much," said Abe, disturbed.

* From *Abraham Lincoln, The Backwoods Boy;* or How a Young Rail-Splitter Became President, by Horatio Alger, Jr., pp. 64–66. Copyright, 1883, by Horatio Alger, Jr. New York: John R. Anderson & Henry S. Allen.

It was a trifle, and many clerks would have dismissed it as such. But Abe was too conscientious for that.

"The money must be paid back," he decided.

This would have been easy enough had the woman lived "just round the corner," but, as the young man knew, she lived between two and three miles away. This, however, did not alter the matter. It was night, but he closed and locked the store, and walked to the residence of his customer. Arrived there, he explained the matter, paid over the six and a quarter cents, and returned satisfied. If I were a capitalist, I would be willing to lend money to such a young man without security.

Here is another illustration of young Lincoln's strict honesty:

A woman entered the store and asked for half a pound of tea.

The young clerk weighed it out, and handed it to her in a parcel. This was the last sale of the day.

The next morning, when commencing his duties, Abe discovered a four-ounce weight on the scales. It flashed upon him at once that he had used this in the sale of the night previous, and so, of course, given his customer short weight. I am afraid that there are many country merchants who would not have been much worried by this discovery. Not so the young clerk in whom we are interested. He weighed out the balance of the half pound, shut up store, and carried it to the defrauded customer. I think my young readers will begin to see that the name so often given, in later times, to President Lincoln, of "Honest Old Abe," was well deserved. A man who begins by strict honesty in his youth is not likely to change as he grows older, and mercantile honesty is some guarantee of political honesty.

II. Spell "Defied!"*

"Spell *defied*!"

This question was put to a class in spelling by the master.

The first pupil in the straggling line of backwoods boys and girls who stood up in class, answered with some hesitation: "D-e-f-i-d-e, defied."

The master frowned.

"Next!" he called sharply.

* *Ibid.*, pp. 34–35.

The next improved upon the effort of the first speller, and in a confident tone answered:

"D-e-f-y-d-e."

"Wrong again! The next may try it," said the teacher.

"D-e-f-y-d!" said the third scholar.

"Worse and worse! You are entitled to a medal!" said Crawford, sarcastically. "Next!"

"D-e-f-y-e-d!" was the next attempt.

"Really, you do me great credit," said the teacher, a frown gathering on his brow. "You can't spell an easy word of two syllables. It is shameful. I'll keep the whole class in all the rest of the day, if necessary, till the word is spelled correctly."

It now became the turn of a young girl named Roby, who was a favorite with Abe. She was a pretty girl, but, nevertheless, the terrible word puzzled her. In her perplexity she chanced to turn toward the seat at the window occupied by her long-legged friend, Abe.

Abe was perhaps the best speller in school. A word like defied was easy enough to him, and he wanted to help the girl through.

As Miss Roby looked at him she saw a smile upon his face, as he significantly touched his *eye* with his finger. The girl took the hint, and spelled the word correctly.

"Right at last!" said Master Crawford, whose back was turned, and who had not seen Abe's dumb show. "It's lucky for you all that one of the class knew how to spell, or I would have kept my word, and kept you all in."

III. WORKING OUT A BOOK*

All the information we can obtain about this early time is interesting, for it was then that Abe was laying the foundation of his future eminence. His mind and character were slowly developing, and shaping themselves for the future.

From Mr. Lamon's Life I quote a paragraph which will throw light upon his habits and tastes at the age of seventeen:

"Abe loved to lie under a shade-tree, or up in the loft of the cabin, and read, cipher, and scribble. At night he sat by the chimney 'jamb,' and ciphered by the light of the fire, on the wooden fire-shovel. When the shovel was fairly covered, he would shave it off with Tom Lincoln's drawing-knife, and begin again. In the day-time he used boards for the same

* *Ibid.*, pp. 38–42.

purpose, out of doors, and went through the shaving process everlastingly. His step-mother repeats often that 'he read every book he could lay his hands on.' She says, 'Abe read diligently. He read every book he could lay his hands on, and when he came across a passage that struck him, he would write it down on boards if he had no paper, and keep it there until he did get paper. Then he would rewrite it, look at it, repeat it. He had a copy-book, a kind of scrap-book, in which he put down all things, and thus preserved them.'"

I am tempted also to quote a reminiscence of John Hanks, who lived with the Lincolns from the time Abe was fourteen to the time he became eighteen years of age: "When Lincoln —Abe—and I returned to the house from work, he would go to the cupboard, snatch a piece of corn-bread, take down a book, sit down on a chair, cock his legs up as high as his head, and read. He and I worked barefooted, grubbed it, ploughed, mowed, and cradled together; ploughed corn, gathered it, and shucked corn. Abraham read constantly when he had opportunity."

It may well be supposed, however, that the books upon which Abe could lay hands were few in number. There were no libraries, either public or private, in the neighborhood, and he was obliged to read what he could get rather than those which he would have chosen, had he been able to select from a large collection. Still, it is a matter of interest to know what books he actually did read at this formative period. Some of them certainly were worth reading, such as "Aesop's Fables," "Robinson Crusoe," "Pilgrim's Progress," a History of the United States, and Weems' "Life of Washington." The last book Abe borrowed from a neighbor, old Josiah Crawford (I follow the statement of Mr. Lamon, rather than of Dr. Holland, who says it was Master Crawford, his teacher). When not reading it, he laid it away in a part of the cabin where he thought it would be free from harm, but it so happened that just behind the shelf on which he placed it was a great crack between the logs of the wall. One night a storm came up suddenly, the rain beat in through the crevice, and soaked the borrowed book through and through. The book was almost utterly spoiled. Abe felt very uneasy, for a book was valuable in his eyes, as well as in the eyes of its owner.

He took the damaged volume and trudged over to Mr. Crawford's in some perplexity and mortification.

"Well, Abe, what brings you over so early?" said Mr. Crawford.

"I've got some bad news for you," answered Abe, with lengthened face.

"Bad news! What is it?"

"You know the book you lent me—the 'Life of Washington?' "

"Yes, yes."

"Well, the rain last night spoiled it," and Abe showed the book, wet to a pulp inside, at the same time explaining how it had been injured.

"It's too bad, I vum! You'd ought to pay for it, Abe. You must have been dreadful careless!"

"I'd pay for it if I had any money, Mr. Crawford."

"If you've got no money, you can work it out," said Crawford.

"I'll do whatever you think right."

So it was arranged that Abe should work three days for Crawford, "pulling fodder," the value of his labor being rated at twenty-five cents a day. As the book had cost seventy-five cents this would be regarded as satisfactory. So Abe worked his three days, and discharged the debt. Mr. Lamon is disposed to find fault with Crawford for exacting this penalty, but it appears to me only equitable, and I am glad to think that Abe was willing to act honorably in the matter.

Johnny Appleseed: A Pioneer Hero*

THE "far West" is rapidly becoming only a traditional designation: railroads have destroyed the romance of frontier life, or have surrounded it with so many appliances of civilization that the pioneer character is rapidly becoming mythical. The men and women who obtain their groceries and dry-goods from New York by rail in a few hours have nothing in common with those who, fifty years ago, "packed" salt a hundred miles to make their mush palatable, and could only exchange corn and wheat for molasses and calico by making long and perilous voyages in flat-boats down the Ohio and Mississippi rivers to New Orleans. Two generations of frontier lives have accumulated stores of narratives which, like the small but beautiful tributaries of great rivers, are forgotten in the broad sweep of the larger current of history. The march of Titans

* By W. D. Haley. From *Harper's New Monthly Magazine*, Vol. XLIII (November, 1871), No. CCLVIII, pp. 830–836.

sometimes tramples out the memory of smaller but more useful lives, and sensational glare often eclipses more modest but
purer lights. This has been the case in the popular demand
for the dime novel dilutions of Fenimore Cooper's romances
of border life, which have preserved the records of Indian
rapine and atrocity as the only memorials of pioneer history.
But the early days of Western settlement witnessed sublimer
heroisms than those of human torture, and nobler victories
than those of the tomahawk and scalping-knife.

Among the heroes of endurance that was voluntary, and
of action that was creative and not sanguinary, there was one
man whose name, seldom mentioned now save by some of the
few surviving pioneers, deserves to be perpetuated.

The first reliable trace of our modest hero finds him in the
Territory of Ohio, in 1801, with a horse-load of apple seeds,
which he planted in various places on and about the borders
of Licking Creek, the first orchard thus originated by him
being on the farm of Isaac Stadden, in what is now known
as Licking County, in the State of Ohio. During the five
succeeding years, although he was undoubtedly following the
same strange occupation, we have no authentic account of
his movements until we reach a pleasant spring day in 1806,
when a pioneer settler in Jefferson County, Ohio, noticed a
peculiar craft, with a remarkable occupant and a curious
cargo, slowly dropping down with the current of the Ohio
River. It was "Johnny Appleseed," by which name Jonathan
Chapman was afterward known in every log-cabin from the
Ohio River to the Northern lakes, and westward to the
prairies of what is now the State of Indiana. With two canoes
lashed together he was transporting a load of apple seeds to
the Western frontier, for the purpose of creating orchards
on the farthest verge of white settlements. With his canoes
he passed down the Ohio to Marietta, where he entered the
Muskingum, ascending the stream of that river until he
reached the mouth of the Walhonding, or White Woman
Creek, and still onward, up the Mohican, into the Black Fork,
to the head of navigation, in the region now known as Ash-
land and Richland counties, on the line of the Pittsburgh and
Fort Wayne Railroad, in Ohio. A long and toilsome voyage
it was, as a glance at the map will show, and must have occupied a great deal of time, as the lonely traveler stopped at
every inviting spot to plant the seeds and make his infant
nurseries. These are the first well-authenticated facts in the
history of Jonathan Chapman, whose birth, there is good

reason for believing, occurred in Boston, Massachusetts, in 1775. According to this, which was his own statement in one of his less reticent moods, he was, at the time of his appearance on Licking Creek, twenty-six years of age, and whether impelled in his eccentricities by some absolute misery of the heart which could only find relief in incessant motion, or governed by a benevolent monomania, his whole after-life was devoted to the work of planting apple seeds in remote places. The seeds he gathered from the cider-presses of Western Pennsylvania; but his canoe voyage in 1806 appears to have been the only occasion upon which he adopted that method of transporting them, as all his subsequent journeys were made on foot. Having planted his stock of seeds, he would return to Pennsylvania for a fresh supply, and, as sacks made of any less substantial fabric would not endure the hard usage of the long trip through forests dense with underbrush and briers, he provided himself with leathern bags. Securely packed, the seeds were conveyed, sometimes on the back of a horse, and not unfrequently on his own shoulders, either over a part of the old Indian trail that led from Fort Duquesne to Detroit, by way of Fort Sandusky, or over what is styled in the appendix to "Hutchins's History of Boguet's Expedition in 1764" the "second route through the widerness of Ohio," which would require him to traverse a distance of one hundred and sixty-six miles in a west-northwest direction from Fort Duquesne in order to reach the Black Fork of the Mohican.

This region, although it is now densely populated, still possesses a romantic beauty that railroads and bustling towns can not obliterate—a country of forest-clad hills and green valleys, through which numerous bright streams flow on their way to the Ohio; but when Johnny Appleseed reached some lonely log-cabin he would find himself in a veritable wilderness. The old settlers say that the margins of the streams, near which the first settlements were generally made, were thickly covered with low, matted growth of small timber, while nearer to the water was a rank mass of long grass, interlaced with morning-glory and wild pea vines, among which funereal willows and clustering alders stood like sentinels on the outpost of civilization. The hills, that rise almost to the dignity of mountains, were crowned with forest trees, and in the coverts were innumerable bears, wolves, deer, and droves of wild hogs, that were as ferocious as any beast of prey. In the grass the massasauga and other venomous reptiles lurked in such numbers that a settler named Chandler has left the fact on record that during the first season of his residence, while mowing a little prairie which formed part of his land, he killed over two hundred black rattlesnakes in an area that would involve an average destruction of one of these reptiles for each rod of land. The frontiersman, who felt himself sufficiently protected by his rifle against wild beasts and hostile Indians, found it necessary to guard against the attacks of the insidious enemies in the grass by wrapping bandages of dried grass around his buckskin leggings and moccasins; but Johnny would shoulder his bag of apple seeds, and with bare feet penetrate to some remote spot that combined picturesqueness and fertility of soil, and there he would plant his seeds, place a slight inclosure around the place, and leave them to grow until the trees were large enough to be transplanted by the settlers, who, in the mean time, would have made their clearings in the vicinity. The sites chosen by him are, many of them, well known, and are such as an artist or a poet would select—open places on the loamy lands that border the creeks—rich, secluded spots, hemmed in by giant trees, picturesque now, but fifty years ago, with their wild surroundings and the primal silence, they must have been tenfold more so.

In personal appearance Chapman was a small, wiry man, full of restless activity; he had long dark hair, a scanty beard that was never shaved, and keen black eyes that sparkled with a peculiar brightness. His dress was of the oddest description. Generally, even in the coldest weather, he went barefooted, but sometimes, for his long journeys, he would make himself a rude pair of sandals; at other times he would wear any cast-off foot-covering he chanced to find—a boot on one foot and an old brogan or a moccasin on the other. It appears to have been a matter of conscience with him never to purchase shoes, although he was rarely without money enough to do so. On one occasion, in an unusually cold November, while he was traveling barefooted through mud and snow, a settler who happened to possess a pair of shoes that were too small for his own use forced their acceptance upon Johnny, declaring that it was sinful for a human being to travel with naked feet in such weather. A few days afterward the donor was in the village that has since become the thriving city of Mansfield, and met his beneficiary contentedly plodding along with his feet bare and half frozen. With some degree of anger he inquired for the cause of such foolish conduct, and received for reply that Johnny had overtaken a poor, barefooted family moving Westward, and as they appeared to be in much greater need of clothing than he was, he had given them the shoes. His dress was generally composed of cast-off clothing, that he had taken in payment for apple-trees; and as the pioneers were far less extravagant than their descendants in such matters, the homespun and buckskin garments that they discarded would not be very elegant or serviceable. In his later years, however, he seems to have thought that even this kind of second-hand raiment was too luxurious, as his principal garment was made of a coffee sack, in which he cut holes for his head and arms to pass through, and pronounced it "a very serviceable cloak, and as good clothing as any man need wear." In the matter of head-gear his taste was equally unique; his first experiment was with a tin vessel that served to cook his mush, but this was open to the objection that it did not protect his eyes from the beams of the sun; so he constructed a hat of pasteboard with an immense peak in front, and having thus secured an article that combined usefulness with economy, it became his permanent fashion.

Thus strangely clad, he was perpetually wandering through forests and morasses, and suddenly appearing in white settlements and Indian villages; but there must have been some rare force of gentle goodness dwelling in his looks and breathing in his words, for it is the testimony of all who knew him that, notwithstanding his ridiculous attire, he was always treated with the greatest respect by the rudest frontiersman, and, what is a better test, the boys of the settlements forbore to jeer at him. With grown-up people and boys he was usually reticent, but manifested great affection for little girls, always having pieces of ribbon and gay calico to give to his little favorites. Many a grandmother in Ohio and Indiana can remember the presents she received when a child from poor homeless Johnny Appleseed. When he consented to eat with any family he would never sit down to the table until he was assured that there was an ample supply for the children; and his sympathy for their youthful troubles and his kindness toward them made him friends among all the juveniles of the borders.

In 1838—thirty-seven years after his appearance on Licking Creek—Johnny noticed that civilization, wealth, and population were pressing into the wilderness of Ohio. Hitherto he had easily kept just in advance of the wave of settlement; but now towns and churches were making their appearance, and even, at long intervals, the stage-driver's horn broke the silence of the grand old forests, and he felt that his work was done in the region in which he had labored so long. He visited every house, and took a solemn farewell of all the families. The little girls who had been delighted with his gifts of fragments of calico and ribbons had become sober matrons, and the boys who had wondered at his ability to bear the pain caused by running needles into his flesh were heads of families. With parting words of admonition he left them, and turned his steps steadily toward the setting sun.

During the succeeding nine years he pursued his eccentric avocation on the western border of Ohio and in Indiana. In the summer of 1847, when his labors had literally borne fruit over a hundred thousand square miles of territory, at the close of a warm day, after traveling twenty miles, he entered the house of a settler in Allen County, Indiana, and was, as usual, warmly welcomed. He declined to eat with the family, but accepted some bread and milk, which he partook of sitting on the door-step and gazing on the setting sun. Later in the evening he delivered his "news right fresh from heaven" by reading the Beatitudes. Declining other accommodation, he slept, as usual, on the floor, and in the early morning he was found with his features all aglow with a supernal light, and his body so near death that his tongue refused its office. The physician, who was hastily summoned, pronounced him dying, but added that he had never seen a man in so placid a state at the approach of death. At seventy-two years of age, forty-six of which had been devoted to his self-imposed mission, he ripened into death as naturally and beautifully as the seeds of his own planting had grown into fibre and bud and blossom and the matured fruit.

Part Two

Boosters and Knockers

I

TALL TALK

1. Making a Noise in Language

THE language of the ring-tailed roarer—and without his language he was like Samson without his hair—was tall talk. Tall talk may be defined as the art of making a noise in language. As such, it is characterized by grandiloquence, boasting, and exaggeration. At its best it is a kind of poetry. At its worst it is bombast and buncombe. For the most part, however, it is comic in effect or intention, insofar as exaggeration is a source of humor or as tall talk has been associated with the local-color sketches, yarns, and tall tales of the old Southwest. "Froth and specks" of the "fermentation processes" of language (as that tall-talking poet, Whitman, described slang), tall talk is the slang of the frontier movement, when windy bragging and laughing at bragging were at their height.

Tall talk is not only "frontier" in spirit; it is also national and regional. Since "broad exaggeration" has been identified with American humor and through it with the character of the people and the physical features of the country, tall talk has come to be considered a part of our national heritage, along with tall tales and tall heroes. During the growth of nationalism and the "new nation" after the War of 1812, "rankness and protestantism in speech" accompanied the release of political and industrial energies in this country. Robert Kempt, the British compiler of *The American Joe Miller*, wrote in 1865 of his American cousins: "Their ordinary speech is hyperbole, or tall talk. They never go out shooting unless with the long bow."

Regional characteristics are clearly stamped upon tall talk. In the United States what has been called the "dividing line of loquacity" runs East and West as well as North and South.

It corresponds roughly to the Mason and Dixon Line and the Mississippi or Missouri River. The tradition of good talk and talkativeness has been at home South by West. Here country frolics and public gatherings—parties, picnics, barbeques, camp and political meetings, muster and court days—have invited talk—folk talk, man talk, back talk—and encouraged yarn-swapping and stump-speech eloquence. Such backwoods eloquence is "expansive eloquence," in contrast to the "reluctant" Yankee cracker-box philosopher brand.

It must not be thought, however, that tall talk was illiterate. In its "bundle of crooked and stupendous" words and phrases it possessed many of the features of a "literary dialect."

"Gentle reader," admonishes the anonymous author of *Sketches and Eccentricities of Col. David Crockett, of West Tennessee*, in a prefatory statement belied by "A Vote for Crockett," "I can promise you, in no part of this volume, the wild rhodomontades of 'Bushfield'; nor can I regale you with the still more delicate repast of a constant repetition of the terms *'bodyaciously,' 'tetotaciously,' 'obflisticated,'* &c. Though I have had much intercourse with the West, I have never met with a man who used such terms unless they were alluded to, as merely occupying a space in some printed work. They have, however, thus been made to enter, as a component part, into the character of every backwoodsman. . . ."

Like most literary dialects, tall talk was spread on thick by its practitioners. The picturesque, grotesque tropes and expletives attributed to backwoodsmen and boatmen in fiction, for all their allusions to everyday objects and activities of the time and place, constitute a species of literary folklore. Basic to this "strong language" is, of course, what John Russell Bartlett (in his *Dictionary of Americanisms*, 1848), refers to as the fondness of Americans, especially in the South and West, for "intensive and extravagant epithets"—awful, powerful, monstrous, dreadful, mighty, almighty, all-fired. Tall talk was "strong language" constantly striving to outdo itself. Thus Bartlett defines *teetotaciously* as "A strange Western term, meaning a little more than teetotally, if such a thing be possible." By means of strained blends and coinages, coupled with far-fetched comparisons and extravagant conceits—as shaggy and rambunctious as the backwoodsmen who were supposed to utter them—tall talk went the whole hog.

2. "An Entire Zoölogical Institute"

Tall talk also had its mythology, in which animal allusions figure prominently. These point to a hunting and trapping existence and to love of sports of "turf and field," such as produced the hunting and sporting yarns that filled William T. Porter's virile journal of oral and anecdotal humor, *The Spirit of the Times* (1831–1861). Like the woods, the Crockett almanacs were full of bear, catamount, beaver, panther, moose, wolf, raccoon, possum, turkey, etc. Of the word *screamer* ("a bouncing fellow or girl"), Bartlett notes: "This, like the word roarer, is one of the many terms transferred from animals to men by the hunters of the West." It is not too fantastic to see in this transfer of names as in nicknames, a totemic transfer of traits, reflected in the application to humans of such terms as hoss (old hoss), colt (a pretty severe colt), coon (a right smart coon, a gone coon), varmint, critter.

Strong Language

I. Fanciful, Facetious, and Factitious
Intensifying Words
(From the Specimens in Part One)

absquatulate, v. (cf. *abscond* and *squat*), to depart, run away

anngelliferous, a. angelic

bodaciously, *bodyaciously*, adv. (cf. *bold* and *audacious*; or, possibly "an absurd exaggeration of bodily") wholly, completely (Southern dialect; "bodaciously tired," "bodaciously ruint")

boliterated, p. p. see exfluncted

exfluncted, *exfluncticated*, *exflunctificated*, *explunctified*, *explunctificated*, p. p. (cf. *flunkt*, *flunked*, overcome, outdone) exhausted, crushed, demolished, beaten thoroughly

obflisticated, *obflusticated*, *obfusticated*, p. p. obfuscated, bewildered, confused, put out of the way

ramsquaddled, *rumsquaddled*, p. p. see *exfluncted*

ring-tailed roarer or *squealer*, n. a stentorian braggart (Thornton)

ripstaver, n. a first-rate person or thing (Thornton); a dashing fellow (Bartlett)

screamer, n. a bouncing fellow or girl (Bartlett)

slantindicular, adv. in a slanting direction

tarnal, tarnacious, a. eternal, a Yankee form of swearing (Thornton)

tetotal, teetotal, a. total

tetotaciously, teetotaciously, adv. totally

wolfish, wolfy, a. savage

II. FIGURATIVE EXPRESSIONS

I[1]

Shut pan, and sing dumb, or I'll throw you into the drink.

Hold your tongue, you beauty, or you shall smell brimstone through a nail hole.

I wish I may run on a sawyer if I didn't.

I'll be choked with a saw-log if I do.

See if I don't row you up Salt River before you are many days older.

I wouldn't risk a huckleberry to a persimmon that we don't every soul get treed and sink to the bottom like gone suckers.

Drive him like a flash of lightning through a gooseberry-bush.

A mighty grist of rain.

I'll be shot.

Prayed like a horse.

He had turned the edge of a razor in attempting to cut through a fog.

I'll wool lightning out of you if you interrupt me.

He'll find I'm from the forks of Roaring River, and a bit of a screamer.

I told him I knew him as well as a squirrel knows a hickory-nut from an acorn.

I told him stories that were enough to set the Mississippi afire.

You do take the rag off the bush.

Poking his nose everywhere like a dog smelling out a trail.

You don't know a B from a Buffalo's foot.

II[2]

Hang me up for bar-meat, ef I don't push off without them.

Bile me fur a sea-horse, ef I wouldn't rather crawl into a nest o' wild-cats, heels foremost, than be cotched alone with you in the night-time.

Quicker nor a alligator can chew a puppy.
Choked to death like a catfish on a sandbank.
Harder nor climbin' a peeled saplin', heels uppard.

Animal Comparisons

I'm a hoss what never war rode.[3]

I can walk like an ox, run like a fox, swim like an eel . . . make love like a mad bull.[4]

I'm shaggy as a bear, wolfish about the head, active as a cougar, and can grin like a hyena, until the bark will curl off a gum log. There's a sprinkling of all sorts in me, from the lion down to the skunk; and before the war is over, you will pronounce me an entire zoological institute, or I miss a figure in my calculation.[5]

A man that comes to settle in these parts must be wide awake, and rip and tear away like a horse in a canebrake.

A man must begin with the eggshell on him, as the partridge learns to run, and get up before daylight many a year in and year out, before he can get to be worth much—I mean in the way of living in these parts.[6]

Ar'n't I the leaping trout of the waters?[7]

One said, "I am a man; I am a horse; I am a team. I can whip any man *in all Kentucky,* by G-d."

The other replied, "I am an alligator; half man, half horse; can whip any *on the Mississippi,* by G-d."

The first one again, "I am a man; have the best horse, best dog, best gun, and handsomest wife in all Kentucky, by G-d."

The other, "I am a Mississippi snapping turtle: have bear's claws, alligator's teeth, and the devil's tail; can whip *any man,* by G-d."[8]

II

THE SKY'S THE LIMIT

1. THE EAGLE SCREAMS

IN a wild country, it was good business for "wild men" to go about scaring people with strange noises and by "making terrible faces playfully." But as the hunter was displaced by the second and third orders of "back settlers," the squatter and the homesteader, the roarers and screamers were not only out-hollered but out-licked by a new type of boaster and tall talker. This was the boomer and booster, drunk not with his own powers but with the bigness of the country and the illusion of inexhaustible resources and opportunities.

Here history repeated itself. As the backwoodsman's antics and war-cries were partly in imitation of the Indian,[1] so the advocates of Western expansion and settlement borrowed from the backwoodsman the elbow-room motif. This had been given expression for all time by Daniel Boone when in 1799, at the age of 65, he was asked why he was leaving Kentucky for frontier Missouri: "Too many people! Too crowded! Too crowded! I want more elbow room!" The frontier also had a saying: "When you see the smoke of your neighbor's chimney, it's time to move."

"The backwoodsman," says the Crockett Almanac for 1838, "is a singular being, always moving westward like a buffalo before the tide of civilization. He does not want a neighbor nearer than ten miles; and when he cannot cut down a tree that will fall within ten rods of his log house, he thinks it is time to sell out his betterment and be off."

But to the expansionists and the promoters of free land and the West, elbow-room meant room for improvements, for free enterprise, and so for more neighbors—in terms of nothing less than a continent and manifest destiny.

With the movement for territorial expansion and free land,

the country entered upon one of the greatest advertising campaigns in history—the booming of the West. This was a campaign in which statesmen and orators joined with land and railroad companies, farmers' organizations, departments of agriculture, bureaus of immigration, boards of trade, and chambers of commerce. The theme of countless speeches, immigrant handbooks, emigrants' and railroad guides, state and regional guidebooks and gazetteers, state year books, rural almanacs, real estate directories, and government reports was "The sky's the limit," "Watch us grow," "We don't have to prove it—we admit it."

In style this propaganda rivalled the "expansive eloquence" of the ring-tailed roarer and the stump-speaker. Its flamboyant ballyhoo proved that, more than the protective coloration of the homespun hero playing the tough guy and the smart aleck, tall talk is the highfalutin style of all provincial Americans whose motto is "Braggin' saves advertisin'."

In the vanguard of Western expansion was another screamer, the American eagle. This "favorite fowl of orators" was derived from the American emblem in the Great Seal and in coinage—not, according to Franklin, the most appropriate emblem of America. But the bird suffers not so much from the "bad moral character"—"generally poor, and often very lousy" and a "rank coward"—ascribed to it by Franklin, as from sheer triteness.

From the apex of the Allegheny to the summit of Mount Hood, the bird of America has so often been made to take flight, that his shadow may be said to have worn a trail across the basin of the Mississippi. . . .[2]

The scream of the expansionist eagle is heard in the swelling peroration of Samuel C. Pomeroy's impassioned plea for the Homestead Bill, whose passage climaxed the ten-years' debate in Congress on the free land question. Both the "patriotic epidemic" and the spread-eagle oratory of expansionism are taken off in the mock-speech on the Oregon question by the comedian, Yankee Hill, whose peroration is in the tall-talking tradition of "Change the Name of Arkansas? Hell, No!"

2. The Wonder State

In his speech on the land policy of the United States, cited above, the Hon. Richard Yates expressed the hope that "we will not be governed by the narrow considerations of a sectional jealousy. . . . A railroad in Illinois, like a light-house on the seacoast, is the common property of the nation. . . . We have one country; our interests are one, our history is one; our destiny is the same—a glorious destiny of free and sovereign States to unexampled power and renown." But it was the destiny and the prerogative of free and sovereign states to claim, each in its own way, "unexampled power and renown."

State nicknames, which have become part of the folklore of American places, crystallized these local aspirations or pretensions to uniqueness and excellence: the Boomer's Paradise (Oklahoma), the Garden of the West (Illinois, Kansas), the Land of Heart's Desire, or the Land of Sunshine (New Mexico), the Land of Plenty (New Mexico, South Dakota), the Wonder State (Arkansas).[8]

As an instance of the willingness with which state governments took the lead in "telling the world of our wonderful possibilities," one may point to the concurrent resolution of the Arkansas Senate approving the nickname, "The Wonder State"—virtually an argument in favor of changing the name of Arkansas. The objection to the earlier nickname of "The Bear State" is typical of the desire of the self-conscious West to live down its frontier past, commemorated in such uncomplimentary terms as the Puke State (Missouri) and the Grasshopper State (Kansas).

The prince of state greeters and boosters was Robert Love Taylor (1850–1912), the "Fiddling Governor" of Tennessee and the apostle of "Love, Laughter, and Sunshine," who devoted his sky-painting talents as orator, editor, and writer chiefly to booming the South. His "village apocalypse quality" and "inventive, epic earnestness" have been praised by another village improver, Vachel Lindsay, in his poem, "Preface to Bob Taylor's Birthday." For all his Pollyanna optimism and mush-and-syrup sentiment, Taylor had something of the folk touch in his art of improvisation and a backwoodsy homeliness in his native figures and allusions. Above all, he had a big heart, which went out to all things big, such as Uncle Sam, Dixie, and Tennessee, or any state that exerted or felt the influence of the sunny South. Here is tall talk in the plug hat, swallow-tailed coat, and striped trousers of a "gladhanded" Uncle Sam.

The advertising pages of *Bob Taylor's Magazine*, a monthly addressed to "all Parts of the Prosperous South," were filled with the "come-on" invitations of Southwest railroad and land companies and "commercial clubs," for whose promotion

Taylor set the pace in his editorials and essays and, in October, 1906, gave the cue with the following query:

Have you a Board of Trade, or a Chamber of Commerce, or a Boosters' Club? . . . A Southern Town now without a live Board of Trade might as well disincorporate and go back into the woods.

One of the most elaborate of these advertisements rivalled Taylor's lush pen in depicting the farm lands of the Nueces River Valley as a paradise on earth worthy of Theodore Roosevelt's characterization of Texas as the "garden spot of the land."

3. God's Country

Besides manifest destiny, free land, and state pride, the West had another string to its bow—the long bow which it drew in order to live down its wild and woolly reputation and to attract settlers. This was the myth of a land flowing with milk and honey—part of the American dream of a promised land of plenty, opportunity, and "beginning," which had first attracted settlers from the Old World to the New and was now transferred to the fabulous, far-off West. To make its ardors outweigh its endurances, orators, promoters, and guidebook writers painted this unknown country in the rosy hues of fairyland.

The land of "nature's bounty" was "God's country," defined as "a special part of the United States or the country as a whole, viewed nostalgically as almost a paradise."[4] "God's country" was sometimes the country one was going to—perhaps always going to and never reaching, like the pot of gold at the end of the rainbow; and it was sometimes the place that one was going back to. Or perhaps it was only in the heart—not a place but a state of mind. To Boone in retrospect it was real enough—the Kentucky he had left behind him. " 'I have traveled,' he said in his old age, 'over many new countries in the great Mississippi Valley; I have critically examined their soils; their mineral wealth; their healthful climates; their manufacturing situations; and the commercial advantages given them by nature. I have discovered where these endowments were given most bountifully in many localities, singly and in groups, *but I have never found but one Kentucky—a spot of earth where nature seems to have concentrated all her bounties.*' "[5] For many a pioneer settler, however, who, while in quest of God's country, often had to ask: "Is this God's Country or not?"

The potency of this phrase was part of the "pioneer myth." This assumed that land, which should be as free as the air and sunshine, was a symbol of the inalienable rights of man; that all land was good land and all settlers were good farmers; that in its "green pastures" one should not want; that the land had certain imperishable values of its own from which one could derive, not only sustenance and profit, but also strength and courage; and that the pioneer, "inured to self-reliance" through hardship and discouragement, was a soldier of civilization and of God.

4. "WITHAL THERE IS AN EFFECT OF CLIMATE"

In a land of violent extremes and abrupt contrasts of weather and climate, the quest for health and happiness put a premium on optimum environment. Land advertisements boasted of such advantages as dry, bracing air; three hundred (or more) days of sunshine a year; and—negatively—no killing frosts, hail, blizzards, hot winds, heat waves, tornadoes, cyclones, whirlwinds, hurricanes, earthquakes, and similar afflictions. "Why Shovel Snow and Shiver?" was one rhetorical question. "No chills, no negroes, no saloons, no mosquitoes," went a sweeping statement from Arkansas.

The guidebooks were equally reassuring.

It is complained that the "wind blows." As it blows elsewhere, so it blows in Colorado—occasionally. Sometimes these winds are momentarily disagreeable, but they serve nature as one of her sanitary measures and their effect is refreshing and beneficial.[6]

Withal there is an effect of climate, and something of freedom caught from the outdoorness of life. Sunshine and green salads all the year will promote cheerfulness. Where there are no bitter winds, no sleet or hail, no blizzards to kill flocks and herds, no "cold snaps" to freeze poultry on the perch or waterpipes in the kitchen, it is not at all surprising that people laugh and are affected by the great world of sun and summer in which they dwell.[7]

Emigrant and Western songs fell in line with the chauvinism, utopianism, and arcadianism of the guidebooks, reflected in many a state song and poem of the "sweet singer" or boosting variety and many a popular song of nostalgia for this, that, or the other "wonder state."[8]

The boast of a climate "so healthy that people rarely die,

except from accident or old age," as in the Nueces River
Valley land advertisement, was a common one.[9] One of the
best of the stories on this theme is related by Barnum, as he
heard it from a sleight-of-hand artist named Henry Hawley.

Related to the stories of life-prolonging air are the stories of
air that restores life.

In East Texas it is the wind that revives corpses.

Truth of it is, Dad was dead, but when that coffin bust open
and that strong healthy plains wind hit him it just filled his lungs
full of good revivin air, and Dad nor no one else could stay dead.[10]

In Florida it is the sunshine, as on the occasion when the
corpse of a gangster had been imported from Chicago so that
a funeral could be staged by the local dealer in cemetery lots.

The coffin was taken to the graveside and the lid was opened
to give the bystanders a glimpse of the beautiful way the corpse
had been laid out, a masterpiece of the undertaker's art. As the
Florida sunshine hit the body, there was an immediate stir. The
gangster arose with a yell, feeling for his gun. The bystanders had
to kill him again before they could go on with the funeral.[11]

Variations on the theme are found in the stories of a dying
person being revived by the air expelled from a bicycle or
automobile tire, which had been pumped up in California or
Arizona, or of an incurable victim of tuberculosis being
healed by a single ray of Florida sunshine.[12]

Rival claims of salubrious climate are accompanied by
mutual recrimination in which state rivalry is keen. Thus
Florida papers cast aspersions on California as a "terrible
place, going rapidly to the bad with frost, storms, earthquakes,
and other calamities. California and other resort places re-
ciprocate."[13] To the older feud between Florida and California
has more recently been added the competition between California and the Rio Grande Valley.

But we have the healthiest climate in California. It is so healthy
we had to shoot a man in order to start a graveyard.

That's no comparison with our Valley climate for health. One
of our citizens went out to California, took sick and died there.
They shipped his remains back to the Valley, the friends of the
deceased were gathered around the corpse. When they opened the
casket he raised up, greeted his friends and walked off.[14]

Tacked on to Hawley's yarn is the tale of the "monstrous large gun," which "required one pound of powder and four pounds of shot to load it properly," and with which Hawley shot off four-and-a-half bushels of wild pigeons' feet and legs (without killing a single bird) when the flock rose off the ground just a half second ahead of his shot. The great number of pigeons and the large field of buckwheat which it was feared they would destroy reflect the abundance of crops and game associated with the marvels of climate and soil. Here brags about rich land and big crops shade off into yarns of varying degrees of exaggeration. The boosters' club gives way to the liars' club—with an occasional knock for the famine that often followed the feast or the bust that followed the boom.

In 1851 the Commissioner of Patents reported an "address delivered by A. Williams, Esq., at a meeting in San Francisco, for presenting the premium of a silver goblet, offered by Mr. C. A. Shelton for the best varieties of vegetables and grains." Among the prize products are an onion weighing 21 pounds, a turnip "which equalled exactly in size the top of a flour barrel," another weighing 100 pounds, a cabbage measuring 13 feet, six inches around, a beet weighing 63 pounds, and carrots three feet in length, weighing 40 pounds, not to mention a single potato, "larger than the size of an ordinary hat," of which twelve persons partook at a dinner in Stockton, "leaving at least the half untouched." Then the speaker added ironically:

And we have some still larger and taller specimens of other things nearer home, here in our own city, to which many who hear me will bear witness from experience, and which come to maturity *"monthly in advance"*—rents, the tallest kind of rents, put up higher than the pines, and sometimes harder to get around than red-wood![15]

5. LAUGHING IT OFF

Praise of the wonders and glories of the new country was offset by a healthy skepticism which viewed with alarm instead of pointing with pride. Hardship and failure gave rise to inverse exaggeration and defensive boasting—of the kind that proceeds from having too little rather than too much.

A common symbol of disillusionment was the returning emigrant or prospector admonishing the westward traveler to turn back. In the frontispiece of "Major Wilkey's" *Narrative*,[16] the fashionable young man in the smart chaise behind the spirited horse, proclaims: "I am going to Illinois!" whereas from the lips of the broken-down owner of a "broken down waggon!—a broken winded horse!—a broken hearted wife!— a broken legged dog! and, what is still more to be lamented, the irreparable broken constitutions of my three Fever and Ague sons, Jonathan, Jerry, and Joe!"—the reply emanates: "I have been!" A modern parallel is furnished by *The Grapes of Wrath*, in which the Joads, on their way to "where it's rich an' green," and they can get work and a "piece a growin' land with water," are laughed at by a ragged man who inquires:

"You folks all goin' to California, I bet." "I tol' you that," said Pa. "You didn' guess nothin'." The ragged man said slowly, "Me— I'm comin' back. I been there. . . . I'm goin' back to starve. I ruther starve all over at oncet."[17]

Disappointed victims of gold fever, who had been advised "not to be too sanguine of success," turned back with mottoes properly amended to express their disgust. "Busted, by thunder!" set the pattern in slogans for all settlers who did not have the "grit, grace, and gumption" necessary to tough it out in a tough country.

Disillusionment in turn was seasoned with stoical humor of the type known as "laughing it off," or smiling in the face of adversity. Grasshopper plagues were commemorated in the wagon inscription, "Hoppers et all but the wagonsheet," in the saying that the grasshoppers had eaten everything except the mortgage, and in the story of the grasshopper who ate the farmer's team of mules and then pitched the horseshoes for the wagon. In Nebraska one could stand by the side of a field and hear the grasshoppers threatening. "On the potato vines they would eat downward, and when they came to a potato bug would calmly kick it and go on their devastating way."[18]

On the Great Plains, it has been said, "If you ain't burned up by drought and winds hot as hell or frozen out by blizzards and hail storms, you're eat up by grasshoppers, speculators, and politicians."[19]—and, it might have been added, centipedes, snakes, bedbugs, fleas, and other pests that infested the primitive shelters of pioneer settlers.

—And Nothing but the Continent*

"MR. SPEAKER: When I take my eyes and throw them over the vast expanse of this expansive country: when I see how the yeast of freedom has caused it to rise in the scale of civilization and extension on every side; when I see it growing, swelling, roaring, like a spring-freshet—when I see all *this*, I cannot resist the idea, Sir, that the day will come when this great nation, like a young schoolboy, will burst its straps, and become entirely too big for its boots!

"Sir, we want *elbow-room*—the continent—the *whole* continent—and nothing *but* the continent! And we will *have* it! Then shall Uncle Sam, placing his hat upon the Canadas, rest his right arm on the Oregon and California coast, his left on the eastern sea-board, and whittle away the British power, while reposing his leg, like a freeman, upon Cape Horn! Sir, the day *will*—the day *must* come!"

Manifest Destiny**

MR. CHAIRMAN, the population of the Valley of the Mississippi already constitutes more than one third of the entire population of the Union. And, sir, the time is not distant when the seat of empire, the stronghold of numerical power, will be west of the Alleghanies. The handwriting is on the wall. It is *manifest destiny*, sir. It is written on the signs of the times in clear, fresh and unmistakable lines. . . .

. . . The same flag that flashes its stars to the sun on the banks of the Hudson and Potomac is hailed by millions of rejoicing freemen on the banks of the Mississippi and the Columbia.

. . . Within the last five years three new States have been added to the Union, and there is the territory at the head of the Missouri and the Arkansas, the Territories of Nebraska,

* ". . . 'specimen of eloquence' from an authentic speech made by General Buncombe, in the House of Representatives, in the days of 'Fifty-four Forty or Fight,'" *Knickerbocker Magazine*, XLVI (August, 1855), No. 2, p. 212. New York: Samuel Hueston.
** From "Speech of Hon. Richard Yates, of Illinois, on the Land Policy of the United States, and in Defense of the West," delivered in the House of Representatives, April 23, 1852.

New Mexico, Utah, and Oregon—and the vision of an ocean-bound Republic is now a reality. Sir, what a mighty theater for American enterprise! What a mighty course for the race of democratic liberty! . . .

It is already our boast as a nation, sir, that we enjoy more of liberty, a more universal diffusion of knowledge, and a more exalted national character than any nation on the globe. But the striking feature of the American character is its enterprise—an enterprise that knows no obstacles, counts no cost, fears no dangers, triumphs over all obstacles. . . .

Speech on the Oregon Question*

. . . YET the time is not far off, when the locomotive will be steaming its way to the Rocky Mountains, with a mighty big train of cars running after it. Yes, the whistle of the engine will echo through the South-west Pass, and sharply hint to the free people of that great territory the approach of hundreds and thousands tew, who are to be their neighbors. No, sir, the time is not far distant, when our commerce with China will equal that of all the world; when the Pacific Ocean will be crossed with as much ease as the Frog pond on Boston Common. Yes, Mr. Speaker, as my eloquent friend from the Hoosier State remarks, "Men of blood, and friends of General Washington, and that old hoss, General Jackson, I want your attention. *Lightnin'* has burst upon us; and Jupiter has poured out the ile of his wrath. Thunder has broke loose and slipped its cable, and is now rattling down the mighty Valley of the Mississippi, accompanied by the music of the alligator's horn-pipe. Citizens and fellers; on the bloody ground on which our fathers catawampously poured out their claret free as ile, to enrich the soil over which we now honor and watch with hyena eyes, let the catamount of the inner varmint loose and prepare the engines of vengeance, for the long looked-for day has come. The crocodile of the Mississippi has gone into his hole, and the sun that lit King David and his host across the Atlantic Ocean, looks down upon the scene, and drops a tear

* From "Speech on the Oregon Question," by Yankee Hill, in *Life and Recollections of Yankee Hill: together with Anecdotes and Incidents of His Travels,* edited by W. K. Northall, pp. 101–104. New York: Published for Mrs. Cordelia Hill, by W. F. Burgess. 1850.

to its memory." I am with you, and while the stars of Uncle Sam, and the stripes of his country, triumph and float in the breeze, whar, whar is the craven, low-lived, chicken-bred, toad-hoppin', red-mouthed mother's son of ye who will not raise the beacon-light of triumph, snouse the citadel of the aggressor, and press onward to liberty and glory? Wha-ah! Hurrah! where's the inimy?

The Wonder State*

WHEREAS, it is an admitted fact that the State of Arkansas excels all others in natural resources, its store of mineral wealth being practically inexhaustible, its vast forests supplying pine and hardwoods in quantities sufficient to place the state in the forefront, and its agricultural and horticultural prowess recognized not only in the United States, but in foreign countries as well, and

Whereas, the publicity campaign of the Arkansas Advancement Association has so indelibly stamped upon the mind of the world that Arkansas is "The Wonder State," and

Whereas, this title is so befitting, while the old one, "The Bear State" is a misnomer, and leads to a false impression, while "The Wonder State" is accurate and is deserving of special recognition:

Now, Therefore,

Be It Resolved by the Senate of the State of Arkansas, the House of Representatives Concurring:

That we accept the name, "The Wonder State," given us by this Patriotic association which has done much to acquaint the world with Arkansas and its wealth of resource, and we hereby specially proclaim that hereafter Arkansas shall be known and styled "The Wonder State."

---

* *Acts of Arkansas, 1923: General Acts and Joint and Concurrent Resolutions and Memorials and Proposed Constitutional Amendments of the Forty-fourth General Assembly of the State of Arkansas, Passed at the Session at the Capitol, in the City of Little Rock, Arkansas, Commencing on the 8th Day of January, 1923, and Ending on the 18th Day of March, 1923,* by authority (Democrat Printing and Lithographing Company, Little Rock, Arkansas, 1923), pp. 803–804. Cited in *American Nicknames; Their Origin and Significance,* by George Earlie Shankle, p. 19. Copyright, 1937, by George Earlie Shankle. New York: The H. W. Wilson Company.

In the Land of Dixie*

I LOVE to live in the land of Dixie, under the soft Southern skies, where summer pours out her flood of sunshine and showers, and the generous earth smiles with plenty. I love to live on Southern soil, where the cotton-fields wave their white banners of peace, and the wheat-fields wave back their banners of gold from the hills and valleys which were once drenched with the blood of heroes. I love to live where the mocking-birds flutter and sing in the shadowy coves, and bright waters ripple in eternal melody, by the graves where our heroes are buried. I love to breathe the Southern air, that comes filtered through jungles of roses, whispering the story of Southern deeds of bravery. I love to drink from Southern springs and Southern babbling brooks, which once cooled the lips of Lee and Jackson and Forrest and Gordon, and the worn and weary columns of brave men, who wore the gray. I love to live among Southern men and women, where every heart is as warm as the Southern sunshine, and every home is a temple of love and liberty.

I love to listen to the sweet old Southern melodies, which touch the soul and melt the heart and awaken to life ten thousand precious memories of the happy long ago, when the old-time darkeys used to laugh and sing, and when the old-time black "mammy" soothed the children to slumber with her lullabies. But, oh, the music that thrills me most is the melody that died away on the lips of many a Confederate soldier as he sank into the sleep that knows no waking—

"I'm glad I am in Dixie."

* Extract from "Address of Welcome by Governor Taylor to the Ex-Confederates, at Ex-Confederate Reunion, on Confederate Day, at Tennessee Centennial, June 24, 1897." From *Echoes, Centennial and other Notable Speeches, Lectures, and Stories,* by Governor Robt. L. Taylor, pp. 26–27. Copyright, 1899, by S. B. Williamson & Co. Nashville, Tennessee.

Nueces River Valley Paradise*

. . . Located on that middle plain between East Texas, where it rains too much, and the arid section of West Texas, where it does not rain enough; . . .

Where the constant sea breeze makes cool summers and warm winters without snow or hard freezes;

Where there are no blizzards, nor tornadoes, nor earthquakes, nor cyclones;

Where the flowers bloom ten months in the year;

Where the greatest variety of products can be grown;

Where the farmers and gardeners, whose seasons never end, eat home grown June vegetables in January, and bask in midwinter's balmy air and glorious sunshine;

Where the land yield is enormous, and the prices always remunerative;

Where something can be planted and harvested every month in the year;

Where the climate is so mild that the Northern farmer here saves practically all his fuel bills and three-fourths the cost of clothing his family in the North;

Where the country is advancing and property values rapidly increasing;

Where all stock, without any feed, fatten, winter and summer, on the native grasses and brush which equal any feed pen;

Where the same land yields the substantials of the temperate and the luxuries of the tropic zones;

Where the farmer does not have to work hard six months in the year to raise feed to keep his stock from dying during winter, as they do in the North and Northwest;

Where the winter does not consume what the summer produces, and there are markets for all produced;

Where two full crops of the same kind, three vegetable crops, or four mixed crops, can be raised from the same land in one year;

Where vegetation is so rapid that in two years the home is

---

* From an advertisement of C. F. Simmons, San Antonio, Texas, "How to Secure a River Farm and Home in Town for $120," in *Bob Taylor's Magazine*, November, 1906. Copyright, 1906, by the Taylor Publishing Company. Nashville, Tennessee.

surrounded by trees and shrubs which would require five years to develop in a colder climate;

Where there are no aristocrats and people do not have to work hard to have plenty and go in the best society;

Where ten acres, judiciously planted in fruits, will soon make one independent, all varieties being wonderfully successful and profitable;

Where the natives work less and have more to show for what they do than in any country on earth;

Where peace, plenty and good will prevail to such an extent that the people sleep with their doors and windows open the year around, without danger of molestation;

Where it is so healthy that people rarely die, except from accident or old age; . . .

Going to God's Country*

WE WERE going to God's country. Eighteen hundred and 90. With a husle and busle to get things ready. With five litel childern and the oldest only 10 years old. And geting food and clothing for a long journey. We could do that job very well for we did not realise what we were geting into. We had some cousens that had gone 2 years before to the Indian Territory way down on what was called the Fleet Wood Farms in the Chicksaw Nation. Its part of Oklahoma now. And that was where we were going. (P. 11.)

It was prety hard to part with some of our things. We didn't have much but we had worked hard for everything we had. You had to work hard in that rocky country in Missouri. I was glad to be leaving it. We were going to God's Country. (Pp. 12–13.)

TOUGHF MISSOURI

Old Missouri was after all a prety toughf place. I hated to leave it though for it was all I knew. But we were going to God's Country. We were going to a new land and get rich. Then we could have a real home of our own. But we didn't know what was ahead of us. (P. 41.)

---

* From *Going to God's Country*, by Martha L. Smith, with an introduction by Dr. Clara E. Krefting. Copyright, 1941, by the Christopher Publishing House. Boston.

A PRARIE FIRE

In 1892 the prarie grass was most as high as our covered wagons. One day by some means a fire got started. We never knew how but any way it was exsiting. You could see the blaze leap. It looked like it was fifty feet in the air. We had burned a very small patch around our house. Perhaps one half an acer. We had just built us a shed for our teams and a chicken house for a cow corell. Our horses were all tied in the shed and the fire was coming so fast that we could not tell whether we would have time to get them out or what to do. It looked like our horses and our milk cows and our famly too would go up in the flames. We did manage to get the teams and harness out of the shed and close to the house. But the fire was geting very close. Just about half mile away I should judge.

We were so frightent. The litel childern crying and screaming and the horses snorting and I was praying and working too. We had a well that we had dug just in front of the house. We had to draw the water by hand with a bucket and I was drawing water so as we might try to save our house and childern. The fire was geting pretty close and we could see jack rabits, prarie dogs, prarie chickens, cyotes, all kinds of birds and antilopes, runing in front of the fire. While we were watching the animels and birds I had every available thing full of water that I had drawn from the well. We could hear the fire roaring and see the flames leaping. We were all covered with the burning grass. We put the six litel childern all in the house and fastened the door and the one window.

While we were standing in front of the hut watching the fire I just hapend to turn my head to get some of the burned grass out of my eyes and I thought that I could see some moving objects coming from the north. I wiped my eyes again and looked. Then I said to my husband, "Look, there is something coming from the north." He wiped his eyes and looked. It looked like a herd of stampeded catle. And if it was that, we were goners for they were coming toward us. We watched for a moment but it was smokey and so much burned grass flying in the air, for the fire was coming from the south west and was blowing very hard, we couldn't see. All that we could do was to stand there and wait.

There we were, we thought, between two fires. We could plainly see the fire coming from the south west and my husband said if it was a stampeded herd of catle that we were in for something. I ask him if we hadnt beter go in the house with the childern and he said that I might but that he would watch. But I never did go in, for just about that time I wiped my eyes again and I could see that it wasnt catle. But we couldn't make out just what it was. It looked like men the best we could see through all that smoke. We just stood and looked and I told my husband perhaps it was Indians on the war path. He said it might be but he did not think so. But I do believe he thought it was Indians for he turned white. So white that I could see he was scerd. And so was I. The fire coming one way and the Indians or stampeded catle the other.

We just stood there most petrified for a few seconds and then I could see that it was men. But what kind of men. Cow boys or Indians? But all at once one man whiped ahead of the rest and then I felt like it was cow boys. And shure enoughf he just came chargen up. I felt some relief but I was shakin so I could hardly stand on my feet and so was my husband. The six litel childern in the house got over being scerd and were just playing. When we opened the door they looked so surprised to see so many cow boys. They never said a word but just looked so amased.

Cow Boys Save the Day

Then the boys said that Roof Benton had sent them for he could see the fire and thought we might be in danger and some of his catle might too. All the water I had drawd out of the well was used for when the cow boys got there they got off their horses, droped their briedl reins, went to the shed, gathered up all the old feed sacks and two of them picked up the water and walked out to the edge of the high grass. Then they all wet the feed sacks and began to set the grass a fire but they did not tell us what they were going to do. We soon found out. They were back firing.

We Buy Some Texas Land

We heard of good land that was selling around Vernon, Texas, so we decided that we would go to Texas and see. We thought that we were in God's Country now and might take a chance on something. We went to Geary and took the train to Texas. Of course we were met by a lot of real estate men. They drove us all over the country. . . . But anyway we bought seven hunderd and forty acers. We just paid five hunderd dolars down. . . . We had paid ten dolars per acer.

And that was quite a lot of money. We let a man have the place to sow wheat but it did not make very much. So then did some of the Geary people laugh and say that we were crazy. We didn't say very much for we began to think that maby we had made a mistake.

Pay day came around and we had to pay five hunderd dolars and the interest so that was over one thousand dolars gone. And no crop. We didn't say much to our neighbors about it. Some of them felt sory and some of them were tickled. It didn't weary me for I knew that we had been in so many tight places before and had all ways come out all right and I felt that we would this time. And we did.

That fall we got a telegram from the same man that we bought from saying that we could get fifteen dolars per acer. So we talked it over and sent him a telegram saying, "Twenty dolars an acer and no less." The next day here came a telegram saying, "Sold. Deeds will follow." Was we ever hapy.

But since then that land was worth lots of money for there was big produsing oil wells all over the seven hunderd acers. So you see one never knows what to do. But we made good for we cleard four thousand dolars. We thought that was prety good and we bought another farm close to us with what we made. We thought that was the easiest money we had ever made. And only one thousand dolars invested for eight months. And then we wonderd if maybe Texas wasnt God's Country. (Pp. 170–172.)

HUNTING AGAIN

So now we were all set for another search for God's Country. For another wild goose chase. And this time it was Oregon. My father was there and I had a sister there too and they had been writing what a wonderful country it was. They wrote that "Oregon is really God's Country." We had been in search of God's Country ever since we left Missouri so we decided we would taken another chance. We decided that it was—on to Oregon. (P. 173.)

A TREK ACROSS COUNTRY

That was nineteen and eight. And there were seven childern and H. H. and myself. Two of the boys were in college, one was about twelve, three litel girls and the baby boy, Harley. He was born in nineteen and seven, the money panic year and the year Oklahoma became a State.

It was a husel around to get off but this time we were going on the train and not in the coverd wagons. I thought it would be much beter. And of course it was. We were only five days on the train. But believe me it was some job even then with all those litel folks. It was a big trek across the country. Easy though. For it was made by train.

We landed in Salem Oregon about the midle of June. It was so difernt but it was a lovly country. Somehow I did not like it. But we thought that we would try it.

We had to have some place to live and we could not find anything to rent that was fit to live in so we began to look for something to buy. (Pp. 174–175.)

We Look Back toward Oklahoma

It was geting fall now and we began to think of going back to our old stomping ground. We did not like it in Oregon. It was a very good place but just wasnt what we thought it would be.

I was geting discouraged hunting for God's Country. I knew there must be such a place. But where? We decided that maybe Oklahoma wasn't so bad. Any way we decided to go back. (P. 179.)

We Find God's Country

We found just about every kind of person in every part of the country we lived. We worked, made friends, helped out where we could and usually found that others were willing to help us when we had our troubles. We were comencing to wonder if there was a certain place that was God's Country. Or if God's Country was everywhere? Or if God wasnt in the country—then in what?

H. H. and I did a lot of thinking and a litel talking. We had been living out on the farm in Woodward County for three years when H. H. had a stroke of paralysis. We moved back to Enid so we could be near good doctors. He lived for two years. Then my beloved died. We had spent 48 years together hunting for God's Country. Before he died we learned something. Something teribly important.

We learned that God's Country isnt in the country. It is in the mind. As we looked back we knew that all the time we was hunting for God's Country we had it. We worked hard. We was loyal. Honest. We was happy. For 48 years we lived together in God's Country. (Pp. 185–186.)

Beautiful and Healthful Iowa

I[20]

IOWA is noted for the glory and beauty of its autumns. That gorgeous season denominated "Indian Summer" cannot be described, and in Iowa it is peculiarly charming. Day after day, for weeks, the sun is veiled in a hazy splendor, while the forests are tinged with the most gorgeous hues, imparting to all nature something of the enchantments of fairyland. Almost imperceptibly, these golden days merge into winter, which holds its stern reign without the disagreeable changes experienced in other climes, until spring ushers in another season of life and beauty. And so the seasons pass, year after year, in our beautiful and healthful Iowa.

II[21]

Our climate is one of the most delightful in nature. Our spring usually commences in March, and by the middle of April the prairies are green with mild, beautiful weather. In May, all the face of nature is covered with flowers and the foliage of the prairies bends before the breeze like the waves of an enchanted lake, whilst the whole atmosphere is scented with the breath of flowers. At all seasons of the year, a gentle breeze is fanning the prairies, and a day is never so sultry but that a cooling breath comes to moderate the melting temperature.

A Home on the Range*

Oh, give me a home where the buf—fa—lo roam, Where the deer and the an—te—lope

---

* From *Cowboy Songs and Other Frontier Ballads*, collected by John A. Lomax and Alan Lomax, Revised and Enlarged, pp. 424–426. Copyright, 1910, 1916, 1938, by The Macmillan Company. Copyright, 1938, by John A. Lomax.

play; Where sel—dom is heard a dis—cour—ag—ing word And the skies are not cloud—y all day

Refrain

Home, home on the range, Where the deer and the an—te—lope play, Where sel—dom is heard a dis—cour—ag—ing word And the skies are not cloud—y all day

Where the air is so pure, the zephyrs so free,
The breezes so balmy and light,
That I would not exchange my home on the range
For all the cities so bright.

The red men was pressed from this part of the West,
He's likely no more to return
To the banks of Red River where seldom if ever
Their flickering campfires burn.

How often at night when the heavens are bright
With the light of the glittering stars,
Have I stood here amazed and asked as I gazed
If their glory exceeds that of ours.

Oh, I love these wild flowers in this dear land of ours;
The curlew I love to hear scream;
And I love the white rocks and the antelope flocks
That graze on the mountain-tops green.

Oh, give me a land where the bright diamond sand
Flows leisurely down the stream;
Where the graceful white swan goes gliding along
Like a maid in a heavenly dream.

> Then I would not exchange my home on the range,
> Where the deer and the antelope play;
> Where seldom is heard a discouraging word
> And the skies are not cloudy all day.

The First California Booster Story*

THE wear and tear of this covered-wagon life on the plains discourages many, although (who can doubt it?) we are journeying to a land unexcelled in all the world—even if there isn't a single nugget of gold within its boundary lines! This is illustrated by the yarn of a man who had lived in California, until he had reached the interesting age of 250 years. In most countries a man that old would be pretty feeble and decrepit, but not in California—Oh no! In fact such were the exhilarating, life-giving, and youth-preserving qualities of that climate that our hero at 250 was in the perfect enjoyment of his health and every faculty of mind and body. But he had become tired of life. The perpetual responsibility of managing a large fortune made him long for a new state of existence, unencumbered with this world's cares, passions, and strifes. Yet, notwithstanding his desire—for which he daily and hourly prayed to his maker—health and vigor typical of residents of California clung persistently to him. He could not shake them off. At times he contemplated suicide; but the holy padres (to whom he confessed his thoughts) admonished him that that was damnation; being a devout Christian, he would not disobey their injunction. A lay friend, however, no doubt the heir to his estate, with whom he daily consulted on this subject, at last advised him to a course which, he thought, would produce the desired result. It was to make his will and then travel into a foreign country. This suggestion was pleasing to our California patriarch in search of death, and he immediately adopted it. He visited a foreign land; and very soon, in accordance with his plan and his wishes, he fell sick and died. In his last will and testament, however, he required his heir and executor, upon pain of disinheritance, to transport his remains to his own beloved country and there entomb them. This requisition was

* From *Forty-Niners, the Chronicle of the California Trail,* by Archer Butler Hulbert, pp. 20–21. Copyright, 1931, by Archer Butler Hulbert. Boston: Little, Brown & Company.

faithfully complied with. His body was interred with much be-candled pomp and ceremony in his own California, and prayers were duly rehearsed in all the churches for the rest of his soul. He was happy, it was supposed, in Heaven, where, for a long series of years, he had prayed to be; and his heir was happy that he was there. But who can safely mock Providence? Being brought back and interred in Californian soil, with the health-breathing, youth-preserving, Californian zephyrs rustling over his grave, the energies of life were immediately restored to his inanimate corpse! Herculean strength was imparted to his frame and, bursting the prison-walls of death, he appeared before his chapfallen heir reinvested with all the vigor and beauty of early manhood! He submitted to his fate with Christian resignation and determined bravely to live his appointed time.[22]

The Abundant and Luxuriant Produce of Illinois*

. . . "PURE air—sweet water—*healthy climate*—(mark that, fellow traveler)—fertile and easy cultivation of the prairies—extensive and self-sown wheat fields!"—and, what was wonderful indeed, always free and accessible to innumerable droves of well-fatted wild Hogs! ripe for the slaughter, and so exceedingly kind and accommodating to Maine emigrants, as to approach their barn-yards once a week (not to be *fed*, but lo) to be *butchered!* Indeed, there was nothing of that country's produce which the "Squire" did not most extravagantly boast, the Fever and Ague excepted, about which he was as mum as a toad-fish! although the whole country so abounded therewith, that had seven-eighths been *barrelled* and *exported* to other parts of the world, there would have remained enough in all conscience, to have set half New England into the *shivers!*

---

* From *Western Emigration, Narrative of a Tour to, & One Year's Residence in "Edensburgh,"* (Illinois), by Major Walter Wilkey, An Honest Yoeman of Mooseboro', State of Maine . . . , pp. 6–7. New York: G. Claiborne, and Others, Publishers, 1839. Reprinted by William Abbatt, 1914, being Extra No. 28 of *The Magazine of History with Notes and Queries.*

The Elephant

I[23]

AMONG thousands of returning emigrants we passed one jovial party with a huge charcoal sketch of an elephant upon their wagon cover labeled: "What we saw at Pike's Peak."

II[24]

. . . Here we begin to meet people who are turning back, discouraged. They had seen enough of "the Elephant." No one seems able to explain that expression—which is the commonest heard along the California Trail. "I suppose," said Meek, "that it comes from circus talk, like if you went to the circus folks'll ask: 'Well, did you see the Elephant?'—meaning in general, Did you go where you set out for? Did you see what you went to see? Did you see the thing you started on through to the end?" As applied to our case it means undergoing the hardships and privations of the California trip, and getting there. You hear the phrase used variously of these quitters that are heading back for Independence as: "They've seen too much of the Elephant," or "The Elephant's tracks got too close." In rare instances the continent is referred to as "the Elephant," and the continental divide ahead of us (South Pass) as the top of the Elephant's back.[25]

Busted*

I

"PIKE'S PEAK OR BUST"[26]

AMONG the most significant mottoes we have seen upon any of the wagons going out to the mines, was upon that of an Illinoisan, about three weeks ago, inscribed in flowing letters of red chalk, though not in the most approved style of art— "Pike's Peak or bust." The indefatigable and energetic sucker, returned the other day upon a gaunt and starving mule, that

---

* From *Colorado Gold Rush*, Contemporary Letters and Reports 1858–1859, edited by LeRoy R. Hafen, p. 319. The Southwest Historical Series, edited by LeRoy R. Hafen, X. Copyright, 1941, by the Arthur H. Clark Company. Glendale, California.

looked as if he had climbed the Peak. He was asked why he didn't go through, "Wal," he said, "he'd got clean on beyond Kearny, and—he busted, so he just rubbed out 'Pike's Peak or bust,' and turned back."

II

WAGON INSCRIPTIONS—EMPHATIC[27]

We have been somewhat amused in noticing the inscriptions and devices on the wagon covers of the Pike's Peak emigrants. One went through a day or two since, with a large elephant painted over the whole cover. Another had a rude attempt at a pike, with a pyramid to represent the Peak. But the most unequivocal inscription yet, we noticed on the wagon cover of a returned emigrant on Saturday. It reads: "Oh Yes! Pike's Peak in H—l and D—n nation!" We think the man owning that wagon must be of the opinion that he has been badly humbugged, and he thus emphatically expressed himself.

Disgusted*

THE legend "Pike's Peak or Bust" began to appear on wagon covers. Others had "Ho for the gold fields of Kansas" painted on them. Still others, the names of places from which they hailed, or the owners' names, or sometimes even a verse of Scripture. I noticed that the men who meant business mostly had no time for signs, and that the more romantic a man was the more he painted his wagon cover.

... It wasn't long before we began to see the word "Busted" scrawled under the "Pike's Peak or Bust" legend. Then the rush got as thick coming as going. ...

... D. C. Oakes came east to get a saw mill outfit, and was almost lynched going back again when a group of busted boomers who had read his book discovered his identity. ...

... Again we came across that legend, "Pike's Peak or Bust," this time with "Busted, by Thunder." It was said that some of our returning pilgrims were so passionately exercised that they dug Major Oakes' grave every time they camped.

---

* From *Three Frontiers; Memories, and a Portrait of Henry Littleton Pitzer, as Recorded by his Son, Robert Claiborne Pitzer*, pp. 78, 79, 83–84. Copyright, 1938, by Robert Claiborne Pitzer, Muscatine, Iowa: The Prairie Press.

A Grasshopper Was Seen*

WHEN the hoppers were thickest the air was full of them and the ground literally covered with them. Mr. Hoisington, then editor of the *Register*, greatly amused the people by placing this unique sentence at the head of a leading news column: "A grasshopper was seen on the court-house steps." This patient man brushed the pests out of his eyes, and off his nose, but with true Kansas grit and editorial dignity absolutely ignored their presence so far as any further remarks were concerned in that copy of the paper.

"Oklahoma Rain"**

IT WAS reported that dust had been found in the vault at the bank, that a banana crate used as a wastepaper basket by the local editor was full and running over with dust. One man claimed that gravel had come through his windowpane and wakened him during the night. Another, finding his car stalled by the grit in the engine, opened the door and shot ground squirrels overhead which were tunneling upward for air! A local paper reported finding gold nuggets in the street which had been blown from the mines in New Mexico. The county farm agent advised his clients that it would be unnecessary to rotate crops in the future, since the wind was rotating soils. One of the natives proposed a test for wind velocity: "Fasten one end of a logchain to the top of a fencepost. If the wind does not blow the chain straight out from the post, the breeze is moderate. You have a calm day."

Allergy in its various forms became so common that, it was said, even the snakes had learned to sneeze; in the night you could tell when a duster was coming by the sneezing of the rattlesnakes on the prairie. Everyone jestingly referred to a dust storm as an "Oklahoma rain." A man caught some huge bullfrogs, so he said, and put them in his watertank to multi-

* From *A Kansas Farm, or The Promised Land*, by Fannie McCormick, pp. 75–76. Copyright, 1891, by Fannie McCormick. New York: John B. Alden, Publisher.
** From *Short Grass Country*, by Stanley Vestal, pp. 205–206, 208. *American Folkways*, edited by Erskine Caldwell. Copyright, 1941, by Stanley Vestal. New York: Duell, Sloan & Pearce.

ply; but, he said, the poor things all drowned immediately. It hadn't rained for so long that they had never had a chance to learn to swim.

A housewife claimed that she scoured her pans by holding them up to a keyhole. The sand coming through in a stream polished them better than she could by the usual method. One old lady, on hearing a man compare the climate to that of hell, put her chin up and declared that if the good Lord sent *her* to hell, he'd have to give her a constitution to stand it.

They laughed about the Black Snow which covered their fields. One farmer said he was going to leave Texas and move to Kansas to pay taxes—"There's where my farm is now."

Another said he could not keep up with his farm, which had taken a trip north. "But next week she'll be back," he said. "I can plow then."

One leather-faced dry farmer said, "I hope it'll rain before the kids grow up. They ain't never seen none." . . .

Those who left the Plains generally did so unwillingly, and, in the midst of their disaster, with a joke on their lips: "Well, the wind blew the dirt away. But we haven't lost everything. We still got the mortgage!"

Dakota Land*

Air: After "Beulah Land."

We've reached the land of desert sweet,
Where nothing grows for man to eat.
The wind it blows with feverish heat
Across the plains so hard to beat.

Chorus:

> O Dakota land, sweet Dakota land,
> As on thy fiery soil I stand,
> I look across the plains
> And wonder why it never rains,
> Till Gabriel blows his trumpet sound
> And says the rain's just gone around.

We've reached the land of hills and stones
Where all is strewn with buffalo bones.

---

* From *The American Songbag*, by Carl Sandburg, p. 280. Copyright, 1927, by Harcourt, Brace & Company. New York. As "Nebraska Land" this is sung to "Maryland, My Maryland" or "Sweet Genevieve."

O buffalo bones, bleached buffalo bones,
I seem to hear your sighs and moans.

We have no wheat, we have no oats,
We have no corn to feed our shoats;
Our chickens are so very poor
They beg for crumbs outside the door.

Our horses are of bronco race;
Starvation stares them in the face.
We do not live, we only stay;
We are too poor to get away.

III

LOCAL CRACKS AND SLAMS

1. Names and Nicknames

In all times and places popular tradition embraces terms, phrases, sayings, allusions, rhymes, songs, and jokes that poke fun at a particular locality or group.[1] In America geographical and cultural diversity intensifies rather than modifies the spirit of clannishness, provincialism, and rivalry which motivates local gibes. Minority and sectional conflicts and the mobility of the population are contributing factors. The restlessness of travel and internal migration makes local differences stand out in sharp relief and heightens the power of observation and the sense of the incongruous. Corresponding to "local color" in fiction, the humor of local characters and customs is an integral part of our folklore.

From another point of view, local taunts and insults are inspired by reaction against the excessive optimism and confidence of boasting and boosting. This boosting in reverse has already been noted in mock brags and orations, inverse brags, and "laughing it off." Mockery and skepticism also break out in open scoffs and jeers, pricking the inflated self-opinion of places. Exaggeration is the weapon as well as the object of attack.

The thrusts and shots of deflating sarcasm are also related to the national habit of "knocking" or faultfinding. The fact that knocking is as much at home in America as boosting may be attributed to the see-saw of American life, with its ups and downs of feasts and famines, booms and busts— "always up in the clouds or down in the dumps." More than the opposite of boosting, however, knocking is the spirit of social criticism and protest at work on the inequalities and contradictions of "individual competitive aggressiveness." When accompanied by wit and humor, knocking is relieved of rancor and in the guise of panning or razzing becomes not only good fun but an effective form of debunking.

In the matter of name-calling nicknames go even further and call a spade a shovel. Slang names of the states and their inhabitants popular during the last century were mostly uncomplimentary. One of the harshest of these is Puke, for a Missourian. "Early Californians christened as 'Pukes' the immigrants from Missouri, declaring that they had been vomited forth from that prolific State."[2] Collections of these sportive and slighting sobriquets illustrate not only local pride and prejudice but also the fondness for "intensive and extravagant epithets" noted by Bartlett and the "perennial rankness and protestantism" in speech which Whitman identified with slang.

A simple form of local witticism is nomenclature. Out of a realistic sense of humor and the apt phrase, frontier communities assumed disreputable, hard-sounding names, with a rough-and-ready appropriateness and facetious raciness. Bret Harte has capitalized and popularized such places as Roaring Camp, Poker Flat, Red Gulch, One Horse Gulch, Rough and Ready.

In these hardy, improvised names, born out of the moment's humor—good or bad—, the American expressed the same irreverence and impudence as in the "barbaric yawp" of tall talk and boasting. "The appetite of the people of These States," wrote Whitman in *An American Primer*, "is for unhemmed latitude, coarseness, directness, live epithets, expletives, words of opprobrium, resistance. . . . Words of Names of Places are strong, copious, unruly, in the repertoire for American pens and tongues."

Such names, far from being confined to the West, had been anticipated in the East, where they have entered into mountain speech and thence into mountain fiction. John Fox, Jr.'s readers are familiar with the grotesque or whimsical sound and the native salt and savor of Hell fer Sartain, Cutshin, Frying Pan, Kingdom Come, Troublesome, Lonesome.

2. POOR COUNTRY

A common butt of ridicule is "poor country," whose lack of fertility and productiveness has given rise to almost as many jests as rich land has to brags.[3] In the East, especially the Southeast, "poor country" is apt to be exhausted or impoverished land, eroded and inefficiently farmed.

The typical "poor country" of the West is dry country. In the geography books of the last century the Great American Desert extended as far east as the Mississippi Valley, but as more and more of the land was put under cultivation or grazing, the desert was pushed farther and farther west. Recently, as a result of overgrazing and plowing under of the grassland, the desert—this time man-made—has moved east again, in what, since the dust storms of May, 1933, has become known as the Dust Bowl.

At their best, however, the Great Plains are semi-arid or sub-humid. The formula has thus been stated by Walter Prescott Webb: "east of the Mississippi civilization stood on three legs—land, water, and timber: west of the Mississippi not one but two of these legs were withdrawn—water and timber—and civilization was left on one leg—land."[4]

In this land where "You can see farther and see less than anywhere else on earth" and "Between Amarillo and the North Pole there is nothing to stop the wind but a barbed wire fence," many a jest and saying speak of too much wind and too little water.

Although applicable to and diffused over the entire Plains area, "dry country" jests become attached to individual states. Thus the genial "hymn of hate" describing the "hell" of the arid Southwest is known variously as "Hell in Texas," "The Birth of New Mexico," and "Arizona." Similarly, "Dakota Land," "Kansas Land," and "Nebraska Land" (cited above) are essentially the same song about another "land of little rain." In other cases a song, in spite of many parallels, is more or less definitely associated with a single state. This is true of "In Kansas," whose prototype is "Over There" and which is akin to songs like "The Cows Fly High" and "The Eagles They Fly High."

In the hill country of New England and the South a related type of local jest has grown up around the humors of hillside cultivation.[5]

3. "—WHO WOULD SOONER BE FUNNY THAN ACCURATE"

According to the author of *The Truth about Arkansas* (1895), "Probably about no other State are there so many misconceptions and so many inaccurate ideas as about Arkansas. . . . For this we may credit the class of writers who would sooner be funny than accurate. The chronicler of the wanderings of that noted personage, 'The Arkansas Traveler,' for example, may be said to have cost the State millions of dollars. . . . In spite of all that the State has suffered at the hands of traducers and thoughtless writers, it is undergoing a wonderful development."[6]

As a form of criticism or propaganda, local satire may be a power for good as well as for evil. Beyond its uses for mere entertainment, in the hands of journalists and politicians the humorous treatment of localities has had a serious purpose. Its range of possibilities is indicated by two widely differing examples—the *Salome Sun* and *Duluth!* In the former the local sage and wit assumes the mask of naïveté and the rustic, drawling accents of the "cracker-box philosopher." In the latter a leading Congressional humorist summons all the resources of polished wit, learning, and eloquence in an elaborate burlesque as felicitous as it is devastating. Both have their springs in the native humor of local allusion and popular jest.

In what is perhaps the most humorous speech ever delivered in Congress—*Duluth!*, by J. Proctor Knott, of Kentucky—, which proved to be a boomerang, the author unwittingly turned out to be a booster in the guise of a knocker. The reason was his curiously mistaken notion (based on ignorance of Minnesota geography and history) that Duluth rather than its rival Superior would profit from the proposed St. Croix & Bayfield Railroad grant. Turning the full force of his ridicule on Duluth, he caused the defeat of the bill—which was precisely what Duluth wanted. As an unexpected result of the speech, however, Duluth was flooded with inquiries concerning the location and price of lots; a grateful real estate dealer sent Knott some handsome photographs of the city and an invitation to accept its hospitality (which he did in 1890); the speech was reprinted by local boosters; and in 1895 the

village of Proctorknott (now a part of Duluth) was named for
him. Thus not only the speech itself, which is mined out of
the lore of boosting and knocking, but the ironic sequel, which
was a good joke on Knott, constitutes an amusing chapter in
the history of American humor and "floating literature."[7]

Proceeding on the theory that "every knock's a boost," Dick
Wick Hall (1877–1926), of Salome (rhymes with "home"),
Arizona (population, 100), put the town and himself on the
map by playing the role of Salome's "best friend and severest
critic." Homesteading, ranching, and mining had given him
an intimate knowledge of the region. As postmaster, garage
owner, and editor and publisher of a one-man, single-sheet
mimeographed newspaper, the Salome *Sun* (issued monthly
beginning in January, 1921), he combined civic responsibility
and business with literature. His puns, whoppers, and wisecracks, often in rhymed prose, are in the "Bingville Bugle"
tradition of the comic country newspaper. His frog who had
never learned to swim is straight out of American folklore.
And his small town stuff—overtly good fun and covertly
agitation for improved roads—sums up a whole phase of
American life and humor, best described by the sign on his
"Laughing Gas" filling station: "Smile—You Don't Have to
Stay Here but We Do."[8]

The classic of American humorous folklore is *The Arkansas
Traveler* (1840). Local in origin and allusion, it belongs to
the older and larger tradition of the saucy, riddling dialog, or
cross questions and crooked answers, between a traveler and
a crotchety innkeeper.[9] The wit and humor of the dialog are
largely elementary—a mixture of puns, paradoxes, insults,
involving misunderstanding, the matching of wits, the naïveté
of the rustic, the discomfiture of the stranger, and the
solecisms of dialect. In style it is characterized by the humor
of understatement, more typically identified with Yankee
laconic wit or "reluctant eloquence," as opposed to the
"expansive eloquence" of the backwoods.[10] Here the grudging
response of the Squatter is associated with the stubborn
cantankerousness of the native, due in part to suspicion and
dislike of strangers (which in the Crockett almanacs inspired
pugilistic encounters, including those of the purely verbal
order) and in part to the low standard of living of the "unfit
of the frontier," with its shiftless wantlessness and attendant
ills of malaria, hookworm, and pellagra. Certainly the piece,
for all its broadness, is far from a caricature; and the spoofing
of the well-groomed Traveler on his milk-white horse (as

pictured in the famous painting of the same name by Edward Payson Washbourne, 1858) derives an added social interest and significance from its realism as well as an extra satirical fillip from the outwitting of the socially superior by the socially inferior.

The Arkansas Traveler has other backwoods connotations. In the love of music that unites the Traveler and the Squatter when the former supplies the "Turn of the Tune" (also pictured by Washbourne in the companion painting of that name) is reflected the popularity of the fiddle as a socializing agent, following the frontier. Again, the character of the Squatter may be a reflection of the dislike and contempt which the yeomanry has felt for the "poor white," as signified in such derogatory nicknames as poor white trash, no 'count, po' buckra, peckerwood, mean whites, low downers, sand-hillers, pineywoods tackies, hill-billies, dirt-eaters, clay-eaters.[11] Something, too, of the conservative's distrust of the pioneer and "coonskin" democracy enters into the treatment of backwoods hospitality, which is here taken off as somewhat less spontaneous and generous than usually represented in backwoods sketches and travel accounts.

The dialog is not only a piece of folk humor; it is also a popular entertainment. Essentially a folk drama, it is known to have been acted out by wagoners in at least one tavern bar-room, at Salem, Ohio,[12] and has inspired a play, *Kit, the Arkansas Traveler*, besides being used in plays like Paul Green's *Saturday Night*, for folklore color. As a recitation, with or without music, it has circulated in songbooks and jokebooks, to many of which it has given its name.[13] The tune itself (first printed in 1847)[14] rivals *Turkey in the Straw (Zip Coon)* as the liveliest and most popular of American fiddle tunes.

Apart from its local color interest, *The Arkansas Traveler* remains one of the most American of folklore themes, in both its symbolism—that of the backwoods, defined as a "state of society where rusticity reigns supreme"—and its form—that of a question-and-answer "frame" dialog which has attracted to itself a number of typically rural jokes.

No less vigorous, if more scurrilous, is that other Arkansas classic, *Change the Name of Arkansas? Hell, No!*, a mythical speech which takes off the fulminating rhetoric of backwoods legislators. Though the unprintable version smacks more of the smoking car than of the halls of state, it represents the less seemly side of tall talk, which in another version has been cleaned up with the aid of passages lifted from the raftsman talk in Mark Twain's *Life on the Mississippi.*

In the role of inquiring traveler American humorists have developed a type of humorous travelog, which has been made popular by jokebooks and has served as a vehicle for monologists and lecturers. Its origin may be traced, on the one hand, to serious and imaginary travel literature and, on the other, to the humorous travel or local color sketch of the almanac variety. It has developed mainly in two directions: the comic account of " 'scapes and scrapes" (represented in this book by *The Adventures of Big-Foot Wallace*) and the satiric commentary on local manners. Various "literary comedians" —William Tappan Thompson ("Major Jones"), Bill Nye, Artemus Ward, and Mark Twain—have worked this vein of local humor in one form or another.

On the popular or quasi-folk level it is almost pure vaudeville—rapid-fire, sure-fire stuff, interspersing wisecracks with gags and puns. Thomas W. Jackson's *On a Slow Train through Arkansaw* (1903) has had many imitators, including a dozen or so jokebooks on the same pattern by Jackson himself. On a more sophisticated level it has produced the "hick-baiting" and "Babbitt-baiting" "Americana" of the *American Mercury* type. The inquiring traveler, with his gibes at local fads, freaks, and follies, is one of the many incarnations of the "cracker-box philosopher," providing material for a comic social history of the U.S.A.

Mining Localities Peculiar to California*

Jim Crow Cañon	Ladies' Cañon	Shanghai Hill
Happy Valley	Dead Wood	Mad Cañon
Ground Hog's Glory	Last Chance	Plug-Head Gulch
Red Dog	Miller's Defeat	Shirt-tail Cañon
Hell's Delight	Gouge Eye	Guano Hill
Jackass Gulch	Greenhorn Cañon	Slap Jack Bar
Devil's Basin	Loafer Hill	Skunk Gulch
Bogus Thunder	Puke Ravine	Rattlesnake Bar

* From *Put's Golden Songster,* Containing the Largest and Most Popular Collection of California Songs Ever Published, by the Author of "Put's Original California Songster," pp. 63–64. Entered according to Act of Congress, in the year 1858, by John A. Stone, in the Clerk's Office of the District Court of the United States for the Northern District of California. San Francisco: D. E. Appleton & Co.

Quack Hill
Snow Point
Wild Cat Bar
Paradise
Nary Red
Dead Mule Cañon
Blue-Belly Ravine
Gas Hill
Dead Man's Bar
Wild Goose Flat
Sluice Fork
Ladies' Valley
Brandy Flat
Shinbone Peak
Graveyard Cañon
Gridiron Bar
Seven-up Ravine
Gospel Gulch
Hen-Roost Camp
Loafer's Retreat
Chicken-Thief Flat
Lousy Ravine
Humpback Slide
Hungry Camp
Lazy Man's Cañon
Swellhead Diggings

Coon Hollow
Murderer's Bar
Whiskey Bar
Pepper-Box Flat
Poor Man's Creek
Poverty Hill
Nigger Hill
Humbug Cañon
Greasers' Camp
Seventy-Six
Bloomer Hill
Christian Flat
Piety Hill
Grizzly Flat
Rough and Ready
Hog's Diggings
Rat Trap Slide
Ragtown
Brandy Gulch
Pike Hill
Sugar-Loaf Hill
Liberty Hill
Port Wine
Poker Flat
Love-Letter Camp
Mud Springs

Logtown
Cayote Hill
Skinflint
Git-up-and-git
Poodletown
American Hollow
Gopher Flat
Yankee Doodle
Gold Hill
Stud-Horse Cañon
Horsetown
Pancake Ravine
Bob Ridley Flat
Petticoat Slide
Centipede Hollow
One Eye
Chucklehead Diggings
Nutcake Camp
Push-Coach Hill
Mount Zion
Seven-by-nine Valley
Puppytown
Barefoot Diggings
Paint-Pot Hill

"Hasty and Grotesque"*

. . . AMONG the far-west newspapers, have been, or are, *The Fairplay* (Colorado) *Flume, The Solid Muldoon*, of Ouray, *The Tombstone Epitaph*, of Nevada, *The Jimplecute*, of Texas, and *The Bazoo*, of Missouri. Shirttail Bend, Whiskey Flat, Puppytown, Wild Yankee Ranch, Squaw Flat, Rawhide Ranch, Loafer's Ravine, Squitch Gulch, Toenail Lake, are a few of the names of places in Butte County, Cal.

Perhaps indeed no place or term gives more luxuriant illustrations of the fermentation processes I have mention'd, and their froth and specks, than our Mississippi and Pacific coast regions, at the present day. Hasty and grotesque as are some of the names, others are of an appropriateness and originality unsurpassable. . . . Hog-eye, Lick-skillet, Rake-pocket, and Steal-easy are the names of some Texas towns. . . .

* From "Slang in America," by Walt Whitman, *The North American Review*, CXLI (November, 1885), No. 348, p. 435. Copyright, 1885, by Allen Thorndike Rice. New York.

"Slops and Pairings of Names"*

. . . IN SHORT, Texas is one great, windy lunatic; or if you please, a bundle of crooked and stupendous phrases, tied together with a thong of rawhide.

But it is in geography that this gift gives forth its most amazing manifestations. We all have heard some of our exquisite American names, such as Last Chance, Sorrel Horse, Righteous Ridge, Scratch Gravel, Pinchtown, Marrow Bones, etc.; but now read these from Texas: Lick Skillet, Buck Snort, Nip and Tuck, Jimtown, Rake Pocket, Hog Eye, Fair Play, Seven League, Steal Easy, Possum Trot, Flat Heel, Frog Level, Short Pone, Gourd Neck, Shake Rag, Poverty Slant, Black Ankle, Jim Ned.

"Bizarre and Original Place Names" of Appalachia**

THE qualities of the raw backwoodsman are printed from untouched negatives in the names he has left upon the map. His literalness shows in Black Rock, Standing Stone, Sharp Top, Twenty Mile, Naked Place, The Pocket, Tumbling Creek, and in the endless designations taken from trees, plants, minerals, or animals noted on the spot. Incidents of his lonely life are signalized in Dusk Camp Run, Mad Sheep Mountain, Dog Slaughter Creek, Drowning Creek, Burnt Cabin Branch, Broken Leg, Raw Dough, Burnt Pone, Sandy Mush, and a hundred others. His contentious spirit blazes forth in Fighting Creek, Shooting Creek, Gouge-eye, Vengeance, Four Killer, and Disputanta.

*   *   *   *   *

A sardonic humor, sometimes smudged with "that touch of grossness in our English race," characterizes many of the backwoods place-names. In the mountains of Old Virginia

* From "South-Western Slang," by Socrates Hyacinth, *The Overland Monthly*, Devoted to the Development of the Country, Vol. III (August, 1869), No. 2, p. 125. Entered . . . 1869, by John H. Carmany. San Francisco: A. Roman & Company.
** From *Our Southern Highlanders*, by Horace Kephart, pp. 301, 302, 304. Copyright, 1913, by Outing Publishing Company, and 1922, by The Macmillan Company.

we have Dry Tripe settlement and Jerk 'em Tight. In West Virginia are Take in Creek, Get In Run, Seldom Seen Hollow, Odd, Buster Knob, Shabby Room, and Stretch Yer Neck. North Carolina has its Shoo Bird Mountain, Big Bugaboo Creek, Weary Hut, Frog Level, Shake a Rag, and the Chunky Gal. In eastern Tennessee are No Time settlement and No Business Knob, with creeks known as Big Soak, Suee, Go Forth, and How Come You. Georgia has produced Scataway, Too Nigh, Long Nose, Dug Down, Silly Cook, Turkey Trot, Broke Jug Creek, and Tear Breeches Ridge.

* * * * *

. . . Rip Shin Thicket, Dog-hobble Ridge, the Rough Arm, Bearwallow, Woolly Ridge, Roaring Fork, Huggins's Hell, the Devil's Race-path, his Den, his Courthouse, and other playgrounds of Old Nick—they, too, were well and fitly named.

"Circuitous Styles of Expression"*

. . . THE propensity to approach a meaning not directly and squarely, but by circuitous styles of expression, seems indeed a born quality of the common people everywhere, evidenced by nick-names, and the inveterate determination of the masses to bestow subtitles, sometimes ridiculous, sometimes very apt. . . . Among the rank and file, both armies, it was very general to speak of the different States they came from by their slang names. Those from Maine were called Foxes; New Hampshire, Granite Boys; Massachusetts, Bay Staters; Vermont, Green Mountain Boys; Rhode Island, Gun Flints; Connecticut, Wooden Nutmegs; New York, Knickerbockers; New Jersey, Clam Catchers; Pennsylvania, Logher Heads; Delaware, Muskrats; Maryland, Claw Thumpers; Virginia, Beagles; North Carolina, Tar Boilers; South Carolina, Weasels; Georgia, Buzzards; Louisiana, Creoles; Alabama, Lizzards; Kentucky, Corn Crackers; Ohio, Buckeyes; Michigan, Wolverines; Indiana, Hoosiers; Illinois, Suckers; Missouri, Pukes; Mississippi, Tad Poles; Florida, Fly up the Creeks; Wisconsin, Badgers; Iowa, Hawkeyes; Oregon, Hard Cases. . . .

* From "Slang in America," by Walt Whitman, *The North American Review*, Vol. CXLI (November, 1885), No. 348, p. 433. Copyright, 1885, by Allen Thorndike Rice. New York.

Illinois As It Was*

A SMART sprinkling of the inhabitants of Illinois are from New England, a heap from Kentucky, and the balance are John Bulls, Paddies, Pukes, Wolverines, Snags, Hoosiers, Griddle-greasers, Buckeyes, Corn-crackers, Pot-soppers, Hard Heads, Hawk Eyes, Rackensacks, Linsey-Woolseys, Greenhorns, Whigs, Conservatives, Canada Patriots, Loafers, Masons, Anti-Masons, Mormons, and some few from the Jarseys. The Loafers are perfectly peaceable; the Mormons and politicians wrathy, and fond of hunting, cock-fighting, and getting into trouble in order to get out again.

Hoosier**

HOOSIER. A nickname given at the West to a native of Indiana.

A correspondent of the Providence Journal, writing from Indiana, gives the following account of the origin of this term: "Throughout all the early Western settlements were men who rejoiced in their physical strength, and on numerous occasions, at log-rollings and house-raisings, demonstrated this to their entire satisfaction. They were styled by their fellow citizens, 'hushers,' from their primary capacity to still their opponents. It was a common term for a bully throughout the West. The boatmen of Indiana were formerly as rude and as primitive a set as could well belong to a civilized country, and they were often in the habit of displaying their pugilistic accomplishments upon the Levee at New Orleans. Upon a certain occasion there, one of these rustic professors of the 'noble art' adroitly and successfully practised the 'fancy' upon several individuals at one time. Being himself not a native of this Western world, in the exuberance of his exultation he sprang up, exclaiming, in foreign accent, 'I'm a hoosier, I'm a hoosier.' Some of the New Orleans papers reported the case, and afterwards transferred the corruption of the epithet 'husher'

---

* From "Olympia Pioneer," in the *Bangor Mercury* of 1845. Cited by Thornton, in *An American Glossary* (1912), Vol. II, p. 974.
** From *Dictionary of Americanisms* by John Russell Bartlett, pp. 180–181. New York: Bartlett and Welford, 1848.

(*hoosier*) to all the boatmen from Indiana, and from thence to all her citizens.

There was a long-haired *hoosier* from Indiana, a couple of smart-looking *suckers* from Illinois, a keen-eyed, leather-belted *badger* from Wisconsin; and who could refuse to drink with such a company—*Hoffman, Winter in the West*, p. 210.

The *hoosier* has all the attributes peculiar to the backwoodsmen of the West. . . . One of them visited the city [New Orleans] last week. As he jumped from his flat-boat on to the Levee, he was heard to remark that he "didn't see the reason of folks livin' in a heap this way, where they grew no corn and had no *bars* to kill."— *Pickings from the Picayune.*

Sucker*

SUCKER. A nickname applied throughout the West to a native of Illinois.

The origin of this term is as follows:

The Western prairies are, in many places, full of the holes made by the "crawfish," (a fresh water shell-fish similar in form to the lobster) which descends to the water beneath. In early times, when travellers wended their way over these immense plains, they very prudently provided themselves with a long hollow weed, and when thirsty, thrust it into these natural artesians, and thus easily supplied their longings. The crawfish-well generally contains pure water, and the manner in which the traveller drew forth the refreshing element gave him the name of *"Sucker."* —*Let. from Illinois, in Providence Journal.*

A correspondent of the New York Tribune, writing from Illinois, says:

We say to all friends of association, come West; to the land of *suckers* and liberal opinions.

* From *Dictionary of Americanisms*, by John Russell Bartlett, p. 343. New York: Bartlett and Welford, 1848.

A Poor Country

I[15]

The dogs, in a certain county in Maryland, are so poor, that they have to lean against the fence to bark. The kildees are so poor, that they have to let down the draw-bars to enable them to go into a field; and the pigs are so poor, that to prevent them from upsetting as they run down hill, they are compelled to suspend a lump of lead to their tails to balance them.

II[16]

An eastern editor, in alluding to a rival town, says, that it takes several of their pigs to pull up a blade of grass; that they are so poor, the foremost seizes the spear in his mouth, the balance having taken each other by the tail, when they give a pull, a strong pull, and a pull altogether, and if it breaks, the whole tumble to the ground for want of sufficient strength to support themselves. It must take three or four such pigs to make a shadow.

Hill-Country Wonders*

WEST VIRGINIA is a hill-country State, and this has produced a type of farm surprising to newcomers within its borders. Planted fields seem to hang precariously on steep hillsides. The visitor is apt to be told by a native, quite earnestly, that the corn is sown by standing on one hillside with a gun and firing it into the opposite hillside. Pumpkins and squash, as soon as they begin to grow, have to be tethered to the corn-stalks to hold them till harvest time. Cultivation on these slopes is so difficult that the native son at times will say with a perfectly straight face that he has to roughlock his harrow to get it down off the hill.

In the steep grazing country, it is told without even the

---

* From *Hill-Country Wonders*, by C. S. Barnett, in *American Stuff; An Anthology of Prose & Verse by Members of the Federal Writers' Project*, with *Sixteen Prints by the Federal Art Project*, pp. 53–54. Copyright, 1937, by the Guild's Committee for Federal Writers' Publications, Inc. New York: The Viking Press.

suggestion of a smile that a breed of cattle has been developed with legs shorter on one side so they can graze around the hill without discomfort. The only herd of goats in the district had to be equipped with telephone linemen's climbers before they could get to pasture.

One man with an apple orchard on a steep hill just behind his house is said to have nothing to do when he harvests his crop except to open the gate to the orchard, shake the trees, and the apples roll right into his cellar.

A farmer with a cornfield on top of a high hill is reported to shuck out his corn and toss it down a natural chute of rock, so that when it gets to the bottom, all he has to do is to separate the corncobs from the shelled corn, put the corn in the bin for the winter, and stack up the corncobs in a little outhouse in case the mail-order catalogue should be used up.

There is also some extremely hardscrabble country in West Virginia. A visitor in Webster Springs, having had supper at the hotel, went out for a smoke and a little walk. Zip! A cat ran past. He watched it in surprise. Zip! Zip! Two more cats ran by in the same direction. Within about fifteen minutes he saw twenty-seven cats, all running in the same direction. "Where are all those cats going?" he asked a native. "Aw, don't pay no attention to that," the man replied. "They do it every day. It's seventeen miles down to the junction and that's the only place around here where they can find any dirt."

There is one place in the State where the country is so rough that the people have no teeth. The reason for this is said to be that level land is so scarce that cabin chimneys always open out close under the slope of the hills, and when beans are cooked in the fireplace, gravel from the hills runs down into the chimney and mixes with the beans, and the people wear out their teeth chewing on them. In this area folks always watch up the chimney to see the cows come home.

Some of the valleys are very narrow. The razorback hog is thought to have got his start in these narrow valleys: if he got too fat, he just naturally stuck between the walls of the valleys and had to get thin again before he could amble along. And there are valleys so narrow that the dogs wag their tails up and down. In fact, some valleys are so narrow that it is said you have to lie down and look up to see out; but one is so extremely narrow that the moonshine has to be wheeled out on a wheelbarrow early every morning, and the daylight wheeled in.

Dry Country*

... OF COURSE it gets dry out there, they say, so dry sometimes that the cattle starve down and climb through the holes in the chicken wire, and hide among the chickens, and that's annoying ... and they say that you're a tenderfoot until you can taste the difference between Texas, Oklahoma, Colorado, Kansas, and the Dakotas.

A drop of water hit a man, and they had to throw two buckets of dirt in his face to bring him to. . . . We keep track of the wind by hanging a log chain on a post. If it stands out straight, that's a breeze, but when it gets to whipping around, and links snap off, look out; it's likely to be windy by sundown.

What They Say on the Plains**

"DOES the wind blow this way here all the time?" asked the ranch visitor in the West.

"No Mister," answered the cowboy; "it'll maybe blow this way for a week or ten days, and then it'll take a change and blow like hell for a while."

*   *   *   *   *

"This," said the newcomer to the Plains, "would be a fine country if we just had water."

"Yes," answered the man whose wagon tongue pointed east, "so would hell."

"In this country," said the cowboy, "we climb for water and dig for wood."[17]

"No woman should live in this country who cannot climb a windmill or shoot a gun."

"On the plains," said another, "the wind draws the water and the cows cut the wood."

---

* From *Behold Our Land*, by Russell Lord, pp. 2, 211. Copyright, 1938, by Russell Lord. Boston: Houghton, Mifflin Company.
** From *The Great Plains*, by Walter Prescott Webb, pp. 22, 320. Copyright, 1931, by Walter Prescott Webb. Boston: Ginn and Company.

From One Extreme to Another*

A GAUNT westerner, fed up on dry farming in the arid Southwest, decided to migrate to a place of eternal rain. Upon being asked why, he drawled:

"I'm tard uv sweatin' dust, that's WHY. Out here the only rains are dust storms. Buzzards hev to wear goggles an' fly back'ards to keep from chokin' to death, an' grasshoppers carry haversacks to keep from starvin'. The only fish to be ketched in dry lakes are dried herring an' blind robin, an' my mouth is allers so DRY, the only way I kin whistle to my dog is by ringin' a bell."

A traveller from the wet delta region of Arkansas, attracted by the reports of a land where rain was a novelty, decided to go to the Southwest for relief. When asked why, he replied:

"This dang Delty's too wet for ME. Why, here the onliest time the sun ever shines is when it rains. Even the pores uv ma hide air sproutin' WATER CRESS. But I could stand ma ole houn' dawg havin' crawdads 'stid uv fleas; fer water bugs to take the place uv flies; fer the chickens to grow web footed an' their aigs to hatch out turtles. Why I just laffed at the bullfrogs croakin' on the haid uv ma bed; at the pollywogs in the drinkin' water; an' I even stood it without too much cussin' when all the young'uns tookd down with water rash an' the ole woman got water-on-the-knee. But, when I started ketchin' CATFISH in the settin' room MOUSE TRAP, I figgered 'twuz time to MOVE!"

Hell in Texas**

Oh, the Dev-il in Hell they say he was chained, And there for a thous——and years he re——mained; He

---

* From *Tall Tales*, Compiled by Jim Blakley, p. 12. Copyright, 1936, by Eldridge Entertainment House, Inc. Franklin, Ohio, and Denver, Colorado.
** From "Hell in Texas," by George E. Hastings, *Southwestern Lore*, Publications of the Texas Folk-Lore Society, Number IX, edited by J. Frank Dobie, pp. 178–180. Copyright, 1931, by the The Texas Folk-Lore Society. Dallas: The Southwest Press.

nei—ther com—plained nor did he groan, But de-
cid—ed he'd start up a hell of his own, Where
he could tor—ment the souls of men With—out
be—ing shut in a pris—on pen, So he
asked the Lord if He had an—y sand Left
o—ver from mak—ing this great land.

The Lord He said, "Yes, I have plenty on hand,
But it's away down south on the Rio Grande,
And, to tell you the truth, the stuff is so poor
I doubt if 'twill do for hell any more."
The Devil went down and looked over the truck,
And he said if it came as a gift he was stuck,
For when he'd examined it carefully and well
He decided the place was too dry for a hell.

But the Lord just to get the stuff off His hands
He promised the Devil He'd water the land,
For He had some old water that was of no use,
A regular bog hole that stunk like the deuce.
So the grant it was made and the deed it was given;
The Lord He returned to His place up in heaven.
The Devil soon saw he had everything needed
To make up a hell and so he proceeded.

He scattered tarantulas over the roads,
Put thorns on the cactus and horns on the toads,
He sprinkled the sands with millions of ants
So the man that sits down must wear soles on his pants.
He lengthened the horns of the Texas steer,
And added an inch to the jack rabbit's ear;
He put water puppies[18] in all the lakes,
And under the rocks he put rattlesnakes.

He hung thorns and brambles on all of the trees,
He mixed up the dust with jiggers and fleas;

The rattlesnake bites you, the scorpion stings,
The mosquito delights you by buzzing his wings.
The heat in the summer's a hundred and ten,
Too hot for the Devil and too hot for men;
And all who remained in that climate soon bore
Cuts, bites, stings, and scratches, and blisters galore.

He quickened the buck of the bronco steed,
And poisoned the feet of the centipede;
The wild boar roams in the black chaparral;
It's a hell of a place that we've got for a hell.
He planted red pepper beside of the brooks;
The Mexicans use them in all that they cook.
Just dine with a Greaser and then you will shout,
"I've hell on the inside as well as the out!"

In Kansas*

Oh, they chaw tobacco thin
    In Kansas.
They chaw tobacco thin
    In Kansas.
They chaw tobacco thin
And they spit it on their chin
And they lap it up agin
    In Kansas.

Oh, they churn the butter well
    In Kansas.
They churn the butter well
    In Kansas.
They churn the butter well
And the buttermilk they sell
And they get as lean as hell
    In Kansas.

Oh, the potatoes they grow small
    In Kansas.
Potatoes they grow small
    In Kansas.
Oh, potatoes they grow small

* From *Nebraska Folklore* (Book Three), Written and Compiled by Workers of the Writers' Program, Work Projects Administration in the State of Nebraska, pp. 11–12. Copyright, 1941, by the State Superintendent of Public Instruction. Lincoln: Woodruff Printing Company. For one tune see *Ballads and Songs Collected by the Missouri Folk-Lore Society*, by H. M. Belden (1940), p. 429.

And they dig 'em in the fall
And they eat 'em hides and all
   In Kansas.

Oh, they say that drink's a sin
   In Kansas.
They say that drink's a sin
   In Kansas.
They say that drink's a sin
So they guzzle all they kin,
And they throw it up agin
   In Kansas.

Come all who want to roam
   To Kansas.
Come all who want to roam
   To Kansas.
Come all who want to roam
And seek yourself a home
And be happy with your doom
   In Kansas.

Salome—"Where She Danced"*

I

MANY tourists and easterners ask about the past, present and future history of Salome—so here is it. Salome is the principal stopping point on the Santa Fe Railroad and the International Auto & Air Route, between Phoenix and Los Angeles —which means that when you are not in the auto you ought to be in the air—and Salome put the air in Arizona.

The train stops here twice each day—when it goes from Phoenix and when it comes back from Los Angeles. Some folks have wondered why it comes back from Los Angeles but the engineer's wife has the asthma and lives in Phoenix— so he comes back. The train stops here because Salome has the only good water for a long ways—and the engine has to have water. The train goes through here becuz it can't get through the Granite Wash Mountains without going right through Salome—otherwise some of the natives might not know what a train looks like.

---

* From *Salome Sun*, Vol. 1, Nos. 2 and 4, February and April, 1921. Dick Wick Hall, Editor and Miner. Salome, Arizona.

Some sweet day someone with a trained and talcum powdered tongue and an unlimited vocabulary of alluring and entrancing adjectives will attempt to describe the wonders and beauties of Salome. Meantime, it is a good place to live, if you like it—and a good place to die, if you don't.

Salome is not as large as Los Angeles, but larger than Phoenix used to be—and a much better town than either of them to live in—if you like them small and quiet—not dead, but sleeping.

Twenty years ago there was no one here but me—and now there's folks a living as far as you can see. On some nights when the Tourists are thick and the section men all in town and a good game going at Blarney Castle, as many as 75 or 90 people have been counted here—which is a big increase from nothing in twenty years.

It is a characteristic of the country, however, as one cow man who now has over a thousand head of cattle is said to have come here riding a blind mule and driving one red steer. It really would be fine cattle country if we had more grass & water.

Almost everything grows well here. Squint Eye Johnson built a barn last year and on account of the high price of lumber cut four big cottonwood posts and set them in the ground for the corners, nailing boards on to complete the barn. It rained soon after and the corner posts started to grow—and it kept Squint Eye busy all summer nailing on more boards at the bottom to keep the cows from getting out—and now he has a two story barn and uses the top story for a hen house. Squint Eye says one more wet year and he will have to buy an aeroplane to feed his chickens.

Melons don't do very well here becuz the vines grow so fast they wear the melons out dragging them around the ground—and in dry years we sometimes have to plant onions in between the rows of potatoes and then scratch the onions to make the potatoes eyes water enough to irrigate the rest of the garden—and the kids sure do hate to scratch the onions on moonlight nights.

Salome has the purest water and the clearest air in the whole world—including Texas. Don't mix Salome with Yuma, where the bad soldier lived, and when he died—well, he sent for his blankets and overcoat. Yes, it was through the streets of Yuma that the coyote chased the jack rabbit—and they were both walking—and it wasn't more than three figures in the shade at midnight either. Just warm.

II

Stop when you get to Salome—where she danced and fill your tires with that soft Salome air—it rides easier and is used to dodging bumps—use our laughing gas—a free smile with every quart—we laugh becuz we like to live here—we have to and you don't—you just keep on riding by and buy asking which road and dodging bumps and chucks coming and going—we wonder where—and why becuz we've been here a long time—a l-o-n-g time trying to save something for a rainy day—Rockefeller and Henry Ford used to get all the money before we started.

But we haven't saved anything—and it hasn't rained—there's frogs here seven years old that haven't learned to swim yet—so why should we worry about rainy days? We thank you—and if you have to come this way again why—stop and say hello! Maybe Salome will dance again or the frog might learn to swim by that time. Adios!

Duluth!*

... YEARS ago, when I first heard that there was somewhere in the vast *terra incognita*, somewhere in the bleak regions of the great North-west, a stream of water known to the nomadic inhabitants of the neighborhood as the river St. Croix, I became satisfied that the construction of a railroad from that raging torrent to some point in the civilized world was essential to the happiness and prosperity of the American people, if not absolutely indispensable to the perpetuity of republican institutions on this continent. [Great laughter.] I felt instinctively that the boundless resources of that prolific

---

* From *Duluth!* Speech of Hon. J. Proctor Knott, of Kentucky, delivered in the House of Representatives, on the St. Croix and Superior Land Grant, January 27, 1871.

region of sand and pine-shrubbery would never be fully developed without a railroad constructed and equipped at the expense of the Government, and perhaps not then. [Laughter.] I had an abiding presentiment that, some day or other, the people of this whole country, irrespective of party affiliations, regardless of sectional prejudices, and "without distinction of race, color, or previous condition of servitude," would rise in their majesty and demand an outlet for the enormous agricultural productions of those vast and fertile pine-barrens, drained in the rainy season by the surging waters of the turbid St. Croix. [Great laughter.]

* * * * *

If gentlemen will examine it, they will find Duluth not only in the centre of the map, but represented in the centre of a series of concentric circles one hundred miles apart, and some of them as much as four thousand miles in diameter, embracing alike in their tremendous sweep the fragrant savannas of the sunlit South and the eternal solitudes of snow that mantle the ice-bound North. [Laughter.] How these circles were produced is perhaps one of those primordial mysteries that the most skilful paleologist will never be able to explain. [Renewed laughter.] But the fact is, sir, Duluth is pre-eminently a central place, for I am told by gentlemen who have been so reckless of their own personal safety as to venture away into those awful regions where Duluth is supposed to be, that it is so exactly in the centre of the visible universe that the sky comes down at precisely the same distance all around it. [Roars of laughter.]

I find by reference to this map that Duluth is situated somewhere near the western end of Lake Superior, but as there is no dot or other mark indicating its exact location I am unable to say whether it is actually confined to any particular spot, or whether "it is just lying around there loose." [Renewed laughter.] I really cannot tell whether it is one of those ethereal creations of intellectual frostwork, more intangible than the rose-tinted clouds of a summer sunset; one of those airy exhalations of the speculator's brain, which I am told are ever flitting in the form of towns and cities along those lines of railroad, built with Government subsidies, luring the unwary settler as the mirage of the desert lures the famishing traveler on, and ever on, until it fades away in the darkening horizon, or whether it is a real, *bona fide,* substantial city, all "staked off," with the lots marked with their owners' names, like that proud commercial metropolis recently discovered on the desirable shores of San Domingo. [Laughter.] But, however that may be, I am satisfied Duluth is there, or thereabout, for I see it stated here on this map that it is exactly thirty-nine hundred and ninety miles from Liverpool [laughter]; though I have no doubt, for the sake of convenience, it will be moved back ten miles, so as to make the distance an even four thousand. [Renewed laughter.]

Then, sir, there is the climate of Duluth, unquestionably the most salubrious and delightful to be found anywhere on the Lord's earth. Now, I have always been under the impression, as I presume other gentlemen have, that in the region around Lake Superior it was cold enough for at least nine months in the year to freeze the smoke-stack off a locomotive. [Great laughter.] But I see it represented on this map that Duluth is situated exactly half way between the latitudes of Paris and Venice, so that gentlemen who have inhaled the exhilarating airs of the one or basked in the golden sunlight of the other may see at a glance that Duluth must be a place of untold delights [laughter], a terrestrial paradise, fanned by the balmy zephyrs of an eternal spring, clothed in the gorgeous sheen of ever-blooming flowers, and vocal with the silvery melody of nature's choicest songsters.

Look at it, sir [pointing to the map], do not you see from these broad, brown lines drawn around this immense territory that the enterprising inhabitants of Duluth intend some day to inclose it all in one vast corral, so that its commerce will be bound to go there whether it would or not? [Great laughter.] And here, sir [still pointing to the map], I find within a convenient distance the Piegan Indians, which, of all the many accessories to the glory of Duluth, I consider by far the most inestimable. For, sir, I have been told that when the small-pox breaks out among the women and children of that famous tribe, as it sometimes does, they afford the finest subjects in the world for the strategical experiments of any enterprising military hero who desires to improve himself in the noble art of war [laughter]; especially for any valiant lieutenant general whose

> "Trenchant blade, Toledo trusty,
> For want of fighting has grown rusty,
> And eats into itself for lack
> Of somebody to hew and hack."

[Great laughter.]

The Arkansas Traveler*

A LOST and bewildered Arkansas Traveler approaches the cabin of a Squatter, about forty years ago, in search of lodgings, and the following dialogue ensues:

DIALOGUE

Traveler.—Halloo, stranger.

Squatter.—Hello yourself.

T.—Can I get to stay all night with you?

S.—No, sir, you can't git to—

T.—Have you any spirits here?

S.—Lots uv 'em; Sal seen one last night by that ar ole hollar gum, and it nearly skeered her to death.

T.—You mistake my meaning; have you any liquor?

S.—Had some yesterday, but Ole Bose he got in and lapped all uv it out'n the pot.

T.—You don't understand; I don't mean pot liquor. I'm wet and cold and want some whisky. Have you got any?

S.—Oh, yes—I drunk the last this mornin.

T.—I'm hungry; havn't had a thing since morning; can't you give me something to eat?

S.—Hain't a durned thing in the house. Not a mouffull uv meat, nor a dust uv meal here.

T.—Well, can't you give my horse something?

S.—Got nothin' to feed him on.

T.—How far is it to the next house?

S.—Stranger! I don't know, I've never been thar.

T.—Well, do you know who lives here?

S.—Yes sir!

T.—As I'm so bold, then, what might your name be?

S.—It might be Dick, and it might be Tom; but it lacks right smart uv it.

T.—Sir! will you tell me where this road goes to?

S.—It's never gone any whar since I've lived here; it's always thar when I git up in the mornin'.

T.—Well, how far is it to where it forks?

---

* From *The Arkansas Traveler*, B. S. Alford, Photographer, Little Rock, Arkansas. Entered according to Act of Congress, in the Year 1876, by B. S. ALFORD, LITTLE ROCK, ARK., in the Office of the Librarian of Congress, Washington, D. C.

S.—It don't fork at all; but it splits up like the devil.

T.—As I'm not likely to get to any other house to night, can't you let me sleep in yours; and I'll tie my horse to a tree, and do without anything to eat or drink?

S.—My house leaks. Thar's only one dry spot in it, and me and Sal sleeps on it. And that thar tree is the ole woman's persimmon; you can't tie to it, 'caze she don't want 'em shuk off. She 'lows to make beer out'n um.

T.—Why don't you finish covering your house and stop the leaks?

S.—It's been rainin' all day.

T.—Well, why don't you do it in dry weather?

S.—It don't leak then.

T.—As there seems to be nothing alive about your place but children, how do you do here anyhow?

S.—Putty well, I thank you, how do you do yourself?

T.—I mean what do you do for a living here?

S.—Keep tavern and sell whisky.

T.—Well, I told you I wanted some whisky.

S.—Stranger, I bought a bar'l more'n a week ago. You see, me and Sal went shars. After we got it here, we only had a bit betweenst us, and Sal she didn't want to use hern fust, nor me mine. You see I had a spiggin in one eend, and she in tother. So she takes a drink out'n my eend, and pays me the bit for it; then I'd take un out'n hern, and give her the bit. Well, we's getting long fust-rate, till Dick, durned skulking skunk, he born a hole on the bottom to such at, and the next time I went to buy a drink, they wont none thar.

T.—I'm sorry your whisky's all gone; but, my friend, why don't you play the balance of that tune?

S.—It's got no balance to it.

T.—I mean you don't play the whole of it.

S.—Stranger, can you play the fiddul?

T.—Yes, a little, sometimes.

S.—You don't look like a fiddlur, but ef you think you can play any more onto that thar tune, you kin just try it.

(The traveler takes the fiddle and plays the whole of it.)

THE TURN OF THE TUNE.

S.—Stranger, tuck a half a duzen cheers and sot down. Sal, stir yourself round like a six-horse team in a mud hole. Go round in the hollar whar I killed that buck this mornin', cut off some of the best pieces, and fotch it and cook it for me and this gentleman, d'rectly. Raise up the board under the head of the bed, and get the ole black jug I hid from Dick, and gin us some whisky; I know thar's some left yit. Til, drive ole Bose out'n the bread-tray, then climb up in the loft, and git the rag that's got the sugar tied in it. Dick, carry the gentleman's hoss round under the shead, give him some fodder and corn; much as he kin eat.

Til.—Dad, they ain't knives enuff for to sot the table.

S.—Whar's big butch, little butch, ole case, cob-handle, granny's knife, and the one I handled yesterday! That's nuff to sot any gentleman's table, outer you've lost um. Durn me, stranger, ef you can't stay as long as you please, and I'll give you plenty to eat and to drink. Will you have coffey for supper?

T.—Yes, sir.

S.—I'll be hanged if you do, tho', we don't have nothin' that way here, but Grub Hyson,[19] and I reckon it's mighty good with sweetnin'. Play away, stranger, you kin sleep on the dry spot to-night.

T.—(After about two hours' fiddling.) My friend, can't you tell me about the road I'm to travel to-morrow?

S.—To-morrow! Stranger, you won't git out'n these diggins for six weeks. But when it gits so you kin start, you see that big sloo over thar? Well, you have to git crost that, then you take the road up the bank, and in about a mile you'll come to a two-acre-and-a-half corn-patch. The corn's mityly in the weeds, but you needn't mind that: jist ride on. About a mile and a half or two miles from thar, you'll cum to the damdest swamp you ever struck in all your travels; it's boggy enouff to mire a saddle-blanket. Thar's a fust rate road about six feet under thar.

T.—How am I to get at it?

S.—You can't git at it nary time, till the weather stiffens down sum. Well, about a mile beyant, you come to a place whar thar's no roads. You kin take the right hand ef you want to; you'll foller it a mile or so, and you'll find its run out; you'll then have to come back and try the left; when you git about two miles on that, you may know you're wrong, fur they ain't any road thar. You'll then think you're mity lucky ef you kin find the way back to my house, whar you kin cum and play on thata'r tune as long as you please.

"Change the Name of Arkansas? Hell, No!"*

I

MR. SPEAKER, You blue-bellied rascal! I have for the last thirty minutes been trying to get your attention, and each time I have caught your eye, you have wormed, twisted and squirmed like a dog with a flea in his hide, damn you!

Gentlemen, you may tear down the honored pictures from the halls of the United States Senate, desecrate the grave of George Washington, haul down the Stars and Stripes, curse the Goddess of Liberty, and knock down the tomb of U. S. Grant, but your crime would in no wise compare in enormity with what you propose to do when you would change the name of Arkansas! Change the name of Arkansas—hell-fire, no!

Compare the lily of the valley to the gorgeous sunrise; the discordant croak of the bull-frog to the melodious tones of a nightingale; the classic strains of Mozart to the bray of a Mexican mule; the puny arm of a Peruvian prince to the muscles of a Roman gladiator—but never change the name of Arkansas. Hell, no!

II[20]

Change the name of Arkansas! Hell, no! stand back and give him room according to his strength. Blood's his natural drink! and the wails of the dying is music to his ears! Cast your eyes on the gentleman, and lay low and hold your breath, for he's 'bout to turn himself loose! He's the bloodiest son of a wild-cat that lives, who would change the name of Arkansas!

---

* From *Folklore of Romantic Arkansas*, by Fred W. Allsopp, Volume II, pp. 87–90. Copyright, 1931, by the Grolier Society.

Hold him down to earth, for he is a child of sin! Don't attempt to look at him with your naked eye, gentlemen; use smoked glass. The man who would change the name of Arkansaw, by gosh, would use the meridians of longitude and the parallels of latitude for a seine, and drag the Atlantic ocean for whales! He would scratch himself awake with the lightning, and purr himself asleep with the thunder! When he's cold, he would "bile" the Gulf of Mexico and bathe in it! When he's hot, he would fan himself with an equinoctial storm! When he's thirsty, he would reach up and suck a cloud dry like a sponge! When he's hungry, famine follows in his wake! You may put your hand on the sun's face, and make it night on the earth; bite a piece out of the moon, and hurry the seasons; shake yourself and rumble the mountains; but, sir, you will never change the name of Arkansaw!

The man who would change the name of Arkansaw, would massacre isolated communities as a pastime. He would destroy nationalities as a serious business! He would use the boundless vastness of the Great American Desert for his private grave-yard! He would attempt to extract sunshine from cucumbers! Hide the stars in a nail-keg, put the sky to soak in a gourd, hang the Arkansas River on a clothesline; unbuckle the belly-band of Time, and turn the sun and moon out to pasture; but you will never change the name of Arkansaw! The world will again pause and wonder at the audacity of the lop-eared, lantern-jawed, half-breed, half-born, whiskey-soaked hyena who has proposed to change the name of Arkansaw! He's just starting to climb the political banister, and wants to knock the hay-seed out of his hair, pull the splinters out of his feet, and push on and up to the governorship. *But change the name of Arkansaw, hell, no!*

Part Three

🦋

Jesters

I

PRANKS AND TRICKS

1. From Gibes to Sells

THE lore of "sells" (which, as Peck indicates, are only a step removed from sales) centers in the Yankee peddler. As the "American Autolycus," the Yankee has been the peddler not only of wares but also of wit and wisdom—"Yankee notions" in the intellectual sense—to the nation. In fact, as cracker-box philosopher, he has become a national type, from Seba Smith to Will Rogers, much as Cousin Jonathan has become Brother Jonathan or Uncle Sam.

During the last century the feud between the backwoodsman and the Yankee peddler, who sold the other things he didn't want, assumed the proportions of a comic contest of wits. As a butt of ridicule and the victim of counterplots, the Yankee was penalized for his superior sagacity. "You might as well try to hold a greased eel as a live Yankee." For Yankee trickiness or slickness the name Sam Slick has become proverbial. The original clockmaker of that name (who has had many namesakes) was the creation of a Nova Scotia judge, T. C. Haliburton, and was in reality half Yankee or down-easter and half ring-tailed roarer, by a curious blend of rival traits.[1] Perhaps a truer embodiment of the Yankee spirit of sharpness of wit and trade was P. T. Barnum, of whom one of his friends said: "If he was shipwrecked and thrown on a desert island, he would try to sell maps of the island to the inhabitants."[2]

Back of the similar libels of sheepherders are the feuds between cowmen and sheepmen and, within the ranks of the latter, between herders and shearers, old hands and new, and bosses and men.

2. PRACTICAL JOKES

In popular tradition the spirit of mischief and roguery has been embodied in trickster heroes of varying degrees of innocence and malice—Robin Goodfellow, Tyl Eulenspiegel, Reynard the Fox, and Brer Rabbit. It has also inspired the countless pranks and tricks that are part of the folkways and folk humor of everyday life, from the wild-goose chases and ridiculous deceptions of April Fool's Day[3] to what Governor Bob Taylor calls the "eternal war between the barefooted boy and the whole civilized world."

The apotheosis of the "bad boy" in American humor is Peck's Bad Boy.[4] George W. Peck saw no contradiction between the vagaries of the Bad Boy—"wide awake, full of vinegar"—and success in life, and in fact admitted the possibility of a correlation between toughness and smartness. The charm of the Bad Boy, as distinguished from such plaguy brats as the Katzenjammer Kids, lies not so much in pure deviltry as in ingenuity and gumption, the horse sense in his horseplay taking the form of sly, shrewd digs at grown-up frauds and shenanigans.

A modern, sophisticated, feminine counterpart of Peck's Bad Boy is Little Audrey (as she is generally known), whose rôle is that of a spectator at life's little tragedies rather than a perpetrator of mischief. The catastrophes, however, are in the nature of ironic tricks or pranks of fate; and Little Audrey has a trick of her own, that of just laughing and laughing, followed by an I-knew-it-all-the-time observation involving a pun or a surprise.

In backwoods, frontier, and small-town America practical jokes (ranging from the low comedy of badger fights and snipe hunts to pure orneriness) are similarly both a pastime and a means of getting along by hook or by crook. Together with fighting, drunkenness, blackguarding, boasting, and savage sports, horseplay and fool stunts afford relief from monotony, loneliness, and strain; an outlet for surplus energy and animal spirits; and an opportunity for exhibitionism. Western humorists have used the practical joke as a form of democratic attack on pretense and affectation. To realists and satirists village japes and monkeyshines are an expression of the sadistic or moronic in American life.[5]

The practicalness of a "practical joke" is said to consist in the fact that something is done rather than said. Such a joke differs from a mere gibe in that the butt of the joke is also its victim. Functionally, a practical joke is intended to take advantage of ignorance, in the person of the newcomer or the green hand, and as such is related, on the one hand, to the dislike of strangers, and, on the other, to the exploitation of the weak. From the point of view of the victim, practical jokes exemplify the gullibility of human nature.

Even verbal jests may partake of the nature of a practical joke when a whopper or a riddle ends with a "sell," which pulls the leg of the victim or leaves him holding the sack.

"There I was out in that prairie, not a tree or a bush in a thousand miles, and a bald-faced bull took after me. I run about fifty feet and climbed up a tall tree."

"Why you —— liar, you said there was no trees or bushes in a thousand miles."

"There had to be one—just had to be one."[6]

Or the narrator gets himself cornered by hostile Indians or wild animals in order to elicit a query as to what happened to him and to permit the solemn announcement: "Why—then them damn redskins killed me," or "They got me."

Riddles often conceal a surprise which is akin to a sell. Lincoln liked to ask: " 'If three pigeons sit on a fence and you shoot and kill one of them, how many will be left?' . . . The answer was, 'Two, of course.' To which Lincoln responded, 'No, there won't, for the other two will fly away.' "[7]

Here, too, belong children's riddling tricks and catches, such as "Just like me," "I'm a gold lock," "Adam and Eve and Pinchme,"[8] and arithmetical jokes like Barnum's.

In almost every occupation, part of the education or initiation of the new hand consists in sending him on fool's errands, usually in search of a mythical or impossible object, such as a left-handed monkey wrench, a bottle stretcher, a four-foot yard stick, or a sky-hook, or in otherwise exposing his ignorance ridiculously and perhaps painfully.

The youngest fellow on the works always had to take the "rawhiding," but I soon learned to hold my own. I was hired to work on "macaroni" farms, sent to buy "striped paint," but was not as bad as the fellow who looked all day in a mud puddle for a frog, because they needed it on the railroad.[9]

Greenhorns and tenderfeet are pranked by falsifying narratives and dialogs (often acted out in a little byplay) as well as by practical jokes. These recitals usually involve animals surrounded by mystery and terror, such as inhabit Paul Bunyan's woods. Yarns of "fearsome critters" have the double purpose of taking in the newcomer and entertaining the old-timers, and so belong to the kingdom of lies as well as of pranks. Sometimes the hazing narratives take the form of circular stories, or "long-winded tales that ingeniously held the listener's interest, but eventually disclosed that they had no point, making this disclosure sometimes by reverting to the starting-place and reiterating word for word."[10] In national parks and on Western ranches the hazing of "dudes" and tenderfeet has produced many classics among sells.

Besides "breaking in" new hands, practical jokes also serve the purpose of getting even with enemies or getting rid of intruders. Where the element of revenge is present, the idea is to give "trick for trick." Where the presence of the victim is unwelcome, the aim is to frighten him away. In any case, as in love or war, all is what Davy Crockett calls "fairation" when one is dealing with a rival.

3. A Pretty Cute Little Stunt

The ruses of trade and swindling are more practical than practical jokes in that they are a means to an end—the end being gain—rather than an end in themselves. At the same time, many swindling dodges, such as selling a greenhorn gold bricks, the Brooklyn Bridge, Grant's Tomb, or the Woolworth Building, are hoaxes. The hoax differs from the ordinary prank in that it is played for greater stakes and before a larger audience. As a "deliberately concocted untruth, made to masquerade as truth,"[11] the hoax differs also from true superstition or myth as deliberate falsification differs from erroneous observation or false inference. Yet in their fictitious build-up, hoaxes involve mythical elements and are "folklore in the making." In between the more elaborate hoaxes, like Barnum's Mermaid, which belong to history and journalism rather than to folklore, and the myth-making stunts involving freaks and monsters, such as sea serpents, petrified men, and "fearsome critters" of the hodag type, are the hoaxing, cheating tricks akin to practical jokes—the pretty cute little stunts by which one outsmarts a customer in a trade, whether it be selling or swapping.

A Yankee Pedlar*

YES! I have laughed this morning, and that heartily, but I fear I shall scarce be able to amuse you at second-hand with what depends altogether on certain *un-writable* turns of countenance and manner. The hero of the occasion was an old pedlar, who came jogging along in his hearse-shaped cart, soon after breakfast, and before this dripping humour beset the weather. He stopped his cart on seeing several men at work, and it was not long before the laughter of the men, who usually pursue their business in solemn silence, drew my attention. The aspect of the pedlar secured it, for he was a personification of Momus. His face was very red, and of a most grotesque turn, and his nutcracker nose and chin were like nobody but Punch. His grey eyes twinkled through a pair of mock spectacles made of a strip of tin twisted into the requisite form and placed far down his nose, so that he was obliged to throw his head back in order to look through them. When I went to the window, he was enumerating the contents of his covered cart with a bewildering rapidity, but as soon as he observed me, he stopped short, pulled off the remains of an old straw hat, and made a very low bow in the style of Sir Pertinax, who thought the world was to be won by "booing."

"My dear beautiful lady," said he, "could I sell you anything this morning? I sell things for nothing, and I've got most everything you ever heard tell on. Here's fashionable calicoes,"—holding up a piece of bright scarlet,—"splendid French work collars and capes,"—and here he displayed some hideous things, the flowers on which were distinctly traceable from where I stood,—"elegant milk pans, and Harrison skimmers, and *ne plus ultry* dippers! patent pills, cure anything you like—ague bitters—Shaker yarbs—essences, winter green, peppermint, lobely—tapes, pins, needles, hooks and eyes—broaches and brasslets—smelling bottles—castor ile—corn-plaster—mustard—garding seeds—silver spoons—pocket combs—tea pots—green tea—saleratus—tracts, songbooks—thimbles—babies' whistles—copybooks, slates, playin' cards—puddin' sticks—butter-prints—baskets—wooden bowls—"

"Any wooden nutmegs, daddy?" said one of the men.

---

* From *The Americans at Home;* or, Byeways, Backwoods, and Prairies, edited by the Author of "Sam Slick" (T. C. Haliburton), Vol. II, pp. 212–215. London: Hurst and Blackett, Publishers. 1854.

"No, but as I come past I see your father a turnin' some out o' that piece o' lignum vitae you got him last week," said the pedlar quietly; then turning again to the window—"Can I suit you today, ma'am? I've all sorts o' notions—powder and shot, (but I s'pose you do all your shootin' at home), but may be your old man goes a gunnin'—I shan't offer you lucifers, for ladies with sich eyes never buys matches,—but you can't ask me for any thing I haven't got, I guess."

While I was considering my wants, one of the men must try a fall with this professed wit.

"Any goose-yokes, mister?" said he.

"I'm afraid I've sold the last, sir; there is so many wanted in this section of the country. But I'll take your measure, and fetch you a supply next time I come along." This of course produced a laugh.

"Well! I want a pair o' boots, any how," said the prostrate hero, rallying, to show that he was not discomforted. "These here old ones o' mine lets in gravel, but won't let it out again. If you've got any to fit me, I'll look at 'em." And thus saying he stretched out a leg of curious wire-drawn appearance. "Any to fit, old boss?"

"Fit you like a whistle, sir," said the pedlar, fumbling among his wares, and at length drawing forth a pair of *candle moulds*, much to the amusement of the bystanders.

The rain which had begun to fall now cut short our conference. I bought a few trifles, and the pedlar received his pay with a bow which was almost a salaam. Mounting his blue hearse, he drove off in triumph, not minding the rain, from which he was completely sheltered by a screen of boughs fitted in the sides of his wagon, and meeting over his head,— a protection against sun and rain which I much admired.

A Sheep Herder from Yale*

REED & CASHION and other sheepmen come down here into Happy Valley every spring to lamb and shear—the sheep, I mean, not Reed & Cashion or the sheepmen; also to eat up all of Mrs. Peck's cow feed and help out some of the poor people around Wenden, the side track 5 miles up the line from Salome, the Mining Metropolis.

Algernon McGoogle—"Hotfoot Mac" they called him at

* From *Salome Sun*, Vol. 3, No. 2, February, 1922. Dick Wick Hall, Editor and Miner. Salome, Arizona.

Yale, on account of his sprinting ability—also came out here this spring, on account of his health, having exercised too much in his BVD's while training to beat the 100 yard record, and taken a bad cold, which settled on his lungs, so the doctors ordered Arizona and outdoor life for Mac. Mac had lived all his life in the city and Happy Valley, Arizona was a new experience to him.

Mac landed in Happy Valley soon after the sheep—and he has been after them most of the time since, he says. Reed was short of herders and Mac was short of cash, and Scotch by descent, so Mac was soon hired to herd a band of about 2,000 ba ba's. It is customary to herd the sheep around the desert among the greasewood and sage brush during the day, bringing them back to the corrals at night on account of the coyotes.

Mac was started out the first morning with his band and instructed to wander along slowly towards a little butte several miles away, letting the sheep feed as they went along, and to start back towards camp so as to get in before dark. "Try and get them back here by five o'clock," Reed called to him as he left, "and don't let any of the lambs get away from the band," he added jokingly, as there were no lambs in the band and the ewes were not due to lamb for several weeks yet.

The sheep and Mac soon disappeared in the brush and nothing more was thought of them until supper time came and no sign of Mac or the sheep. Reed commenced to worry, about the sheep, and about seven o'clock was about to start out looking for them when Mac at last came driving them up through the brush into the corral and, after shutting them in, came up to the chuck tent, streaked with dust and perspiration and, from all appearances, tired out. Before Reed could say anything, Mac burst out:

"Boss," he said, "I'm through. They thought back east that I was a foot racer, but I'm not. Almost any sheep herder that can herd that band for a week and not lose those lambs can beat all the world's records. I didn't lose any today and I ran every one of those damn lambs back into the band every time they tried to get away, but one day is enough for me. I'm all in, but they are all there. Go and count them up and then give me my time. I'm done."

Reed, knowing that there were no lambs in the band and that none of the ewes could have lambed yet, went down to the corral to investigate and, off, in one corner, huddled up by themselves, he counted 47 jackrabbits and 16 cottontails.

The Adventures of Little Audrey*

LITTLE AUDREY is a folk-lore character about whom thousands
of nonsensical short tales—during the past five or six years—
have been told. Sometimes Little Audrey parades as Little
Emma or Little Gertrude, but she usually is recognizable by
a catch phrase—"she just laughed and laughed." The amusing
incident is typically a catastrophe. Little Audrey sees the humor
in any situation. . . .

Little Audrey and her papa were out riding one day in their
new streamlined car. Papa was proud of the car, and he was
giving it the gas; he wanted to see how much it would make.
All of a sudden the road turned, but papa did not; he went
straight on and into the lake. Little Audrey saw what was
going to happen, and she just laughed and laughed. She knew
all of the time that their car had floating power.

Once upon a time all the children in Little Audrey's
neighborhood were taking lessons. It was the proper thing to
do; if you did not take lessons, you simply were not in the
social swim. So Little Audrey cried and cried, 'cause she was
not taking lessons.

After a while her mama said, "Little Audrey, if you will
just stop that bawling, I'll let you take lessons." That made
Little Audrey awful happy; so she sat down to think about
what kind of lessons she would take. Well, after a long time
she decided to take parachute lessons. So Little Audrey
practiced and practiced, and after a while it was time to give
her recital; you know if you take lessons you just have to give
recitals.

Well, people came from far and near to see Little Audrey
parachute jump. She went way up high in the airplane and
got ready to jump. She looked down and saw all those people
watching her, and then she jumped out. On her way down
she just laughed and laughed, 'cause she knew she was going
to fool those people; she didn't have on her parachute.

Once upon a time Little Audrey got lost on a desert island.
Along came a big bunch of black cannibals and kidnapped her.
They tied her up to a tree and started their pot to boiling.

* By Cornelia Chambers. From *Straight Texas*, Publications of the Texas
Folk-Lore Society, Number XIII, 1937, edited by J. Frank Dobie and Mody
C. Boatright, pp. 106–110. Copyright, 1937, by the Texas Folk-Lore Society.
Austin.

Little Audrey knew they were going to make stew out of her; so she looked around at those lean, hungry cannibals and counted them. There were nineteen. Little Audrey just laughed and laughed, 'cause she knew she was not big enough to make enough stew to go around.

A Most Original Wager

THE CAPE COD SAILOR AND THE GANNINIPPER*

A CAPE COD sailor laid a wager, that he would lie down naked in the salt meadow a quarter of an hour, and submit to the utmost fury of the moschetoes for that term without once wincing. Accordingly the wager was staked; he lay down in one of the calm hot evenings of August, on the side of a marsh where the moschetoes were flying about by millions. Thirteen minutes and a half he lay in this situation, without shrinking, and put the whole host of the winged little fiends at defiance. One of the company, fearing at last that the fellow would win the wager, stept aside, and put the small end of a walking stick into the fire, with which he returned, and slily applied it to the man's naked back; he could hold out no longer, but shrunk from the touch with some violence, taking it for the bite of a large fly. "You have lost the wager," said one of the company. "I have lost it surely," said he, "but if it had not been for that d—d ganninipper I should have won it!" [A ganninipper is a large green fly, abounding in pine woods, of a very keen sting, peculiarly painful and venomous.]

A Snipe Hunt**

ONE of our most popular forms of amusement was playing practical jokes on each other, and some of them were of a pretty rough character. I remember one joke we played on Rector, a jolly and useful member of the troop, albeit so deaf one had to yell at him to make him hear. The boys called him "Reck." He was fond of natural history, and was never so delighted as when he captured a curious insect, or shot a rare

---

* From *Jack's Kit; or, Saturday Night in the Forecastle*, by An Old Salt, p. 156. New York: Bunce & Brother.
** From *A Texas Ranger*, by N. A. Jennings, foreword by J. Frank Dobie, pp. 185–189. Copyright, 1930, by Southwest Press. Dallas, Texas.

bird, or killed a fine specimen of a snake. One day, one of the boys asked Reck if he'd ever gone "sniping."

"Shooting snipe?" said Reck. "Lots of times."

"No, no," said the Ranger, "not shooting them; catching them in a bag. I thought nearly everyone knew about 'sniping.' "

"Never heard of it," said Reck. "How can anyone catch snipe in a bag?"

"Oh, it's simple enough when you know how," explained the other. "A party of half a dozen or more men start out about sundown and go to some marshy place, near a river, where the snipe are apt to be at night. They take a bag—an old gunny-sack is best—and some candles with them. They select a likely spot and, when it is quite dark, one of the party holds the mouth of the bag open and places a lighted candle in front of it, on the ground. The others go off and make a big circle, which they gradually narrow as they approach the one who is holding the bag. They beat the chaparral and make all the noise they can as they get near to him, and they frighten all the snipe and start them running toward him, too. The snipe are attracted by the light from the candle and, as they get close to it, are blinded by its rays. They run straight into the mouth of the open sack. It's great sport, and I know a place, about three miles from here, where the snipe are as thick as hops. Let's get up a party to go after them to-night."

Reck was delighted with the idea and a party of nine snipe-hunters was quickly made up. Strangely enough, all of the men except Reck had often been on sniping expeditions and knew all about them. I was in the secret and formed one of the party.

We started soon after sundown and went up the river, led by the Ranger who proposed the sport. He took us, by winding, roundabout paths, to a swampy piece of ground where we sank to our ankles at every step. The place was swarming with mosquitoes. When we reached what we agreed was a favorable spot, we stopped and had an animated discussion as to who should hold the sack. We all wanted to hold it apparently, because it was so much more fun to bag the snipe than to go tramping around in the brush, beating up the birds. Finally someone said that it took more skill to beat up the snipe than it did to hold the sack and, as Reck was green at the work, perhaps it would be better to let him have the coveted part. The rest agreed to this as a fair solution of the question and two candles were lighted and stuck in the marshy ground, while Reck squatted down and held the mouth of the sack open behind them. It took both his hands to hold the sack properly, and when we left him the mosquitoes were singing in high glee about his head.

And so we came away from him. To beat up the snipe? Oh, no; to get by the nearest way out of that mosquito-infested marsh and back to camp. We reached there shortly, and the boys howled with wicked delight as we drew graphic pictures of poor Reck holding on with both hands to that sack, while every mosquito in the swamp within sight of the candles made a bee line for the spot.

Reck came into camp about midnight. He got lost in hunting it and came near having to pass the night in the brush. He brought the sack with him and went straight to where the man who had invited him to go "sniping" lay asleep. He woke him up and all near him with a wild warwhoop.

"Hello, Reck!" exclaimed the practical joker, as he sat up; "did you get any snipe?"

"You bet your boots I did!" cried Reck, as he suddenly shook the contents of his sack all over the joker. "Look at all those fine fellows."

The man gave a yell and scrambled to his feet. Reck had shaken about two quarts of big black ants all over him, and he knew from experience that ants in Texas bite like fiends. Reck had stumbled over an ant-hill in wandering back to camp and gathered a lot of them into his sack, so as to get even with the sniping party. He did it very effectually, for the ants spread in all directions and made things decidedly uncomfortable for us the rest of the night. That was the last "sniping" party we ever had in the Rangers, but it was far from being the last practical joke played. . . .

Swallowing an Oyster Alive

A STORY OF ILLINOIS—BY A MISSOURIAN*

AT A late hour, the other night, the door of an oyster house in our city was thrust open, and in stalked a hero from the Sucker state. He was quite six feet high, spare, somewhat

* From *The Big Bear of Arkansas, and Other Sketches*, Illustrative of Characters and Incidents in the South and South-West, edited by William T. Porter, pp. 80–86. Entered, according to Act of Congress, in the year 1845, by Carey & Hart, in the Clerk's Office of the District Court of the United States, of the Eastern District of Pennsylvania. Philadelphia.

stooped, with a hungry, anxious countenance, and his hands
pushed clear down to the bottom of his breeches pockets. His
outer covering was hard to define, but after surveying it
minutely, we came to the conclusion that his suit had been
made in his boyhood, of a dingy yellow linsey-woolsey, and
that, having sprouted up with astonishing rapidity, he had
been forced to piece it out with all colours, in order to keep
pace with his body. In spite of his exertions, however, he had
fallen in arrears about a foot of the necessary length, and
consequently, stuck that far through his inexpressibles. His
crop of hair was surmounted by the funniest little seal-skin cap
imaginable. After taking a position, he indulged in a long
stare at the man opening the *bivalves*, and slowly ejaculated—
"Isters?"

"Yes, sir," responded the attentive operator,—"and fine
ones they are, too."

"Well, I've heard of isters afore," says he, "but this is the
fust time I've seed 'm, and *pre-haps* I'll know what *thar* made
of afore I git out of town."

Having expressed this desperate intention, he cautiously
approached the plate and scrutinized the uncased shell-fish
with a gravity and interest which would have done honour to
the most illustrious searcher into the hidden mysteries of
nature. At length he began to soliloquize on the difficulty of
getting them out, and how queer they looked when out.

"I never seed any thin' hold on so—takes an amazin' site
of screwin, hoss, to get 'em out, and aint they slick and
slip'ry when they does come? Smooth as an eel! I've a good
mind to give that feller lodgin', jist to realize the effects, as
uncle Jess used to say about speckalation."

"Well, sir," was the reply, "down with two bits, and you
can have a dozen."

"Two bits!" exclaimed the Sucker, "now come, that's stickin'
it on rite strong, hoss, for *isters*. A dozen on 'em aint nothin'
to a chicken, and there's no gettin' more'n a picayune a piece
for *them*. I've only realized forty-five picayunes on my first
ventur' to St. Louis. I'll tell you what, I'll gin you two
chickens for a dozen, if you'll conclude to deal."

A wag, who was standing by indulging in a dozen, winked
to the attendant to shell out, and the offer was accepted.

"Now mind," repeated the Sucker, "all fair—two chickens
for a dozen—you're a witness, mister," turning at the same
time to the wag; "none of your tricks, for I've heard that your
city fellers are mity slip'ry coons."

The bargain being fairly understood, our Sucker squared himself for the onset; deliberately put off his seal-skin, tucked up his sleeves, and, fork in hand, awaited the appearance of No. 1. It came—he saw—and quickly it was bolted! A moment's dreadful pause ensued. The wag dropped his knife and fork with a look of mingled amazement and horror—something akin to Shakespeare's Hamlet on seeing his daddy's ghost—while he burst into the exclamation—

"Swallowed alive, as I'm a Christian!"

Our Sucker hero had opened his mouth with pleasure a moment before, but now it *stood* open. Fear—a horrid dread of he didn't know what—a consciousness that all wasn't right, and ignorant of the extent of the wrong—the uncertainty of the moment was terrible. Urged to desperation, he faltered out—

"What on earth's the row?"

"Did you swallow it alive?" inquired the wag.

"I swallowed it jest as he gin it to me!" shouted the Sucker.

"You're a dead man!" exclaimed his anxious friend, "the creature is alive, and will eat right through you," added he, in a most hopeless tone.

"Get a pizen pump and pump it out!" screamed the Sucker, in a frenzy, his eyes fairly starting from their sockets. "O gracious!—what 'ill I do?—It's got holds of my innards already, and I'm dead as a chicken!—do somethin' for me, do —don't let the infernal sea-toad eat me afore your eyes."

"Why don't you put some of this on it?" inquired the wag, pointing to a bottle of strong pepper-sauce.

The hint was enough—the Sucker, upon the instant, seized the bottle, and desperately wrenching out the cork, swallowed half the contents at a draught. He fairly squealed from its effects, and gasped and blowed, and pitched, and twisted, as if it were coursing through him with electric effect, while at the same time his eyes ran a stream of tears. At length becoming a little composed, his waggish adviser approached, almost bursting with suppressed laughter, and inquired,—

"How are you now old fellow—did you kill it?"

"Well, I did, hoss'—ugh, ugh o-o-o my inards. If that *ister* critter's dyin' agonies didn't stir a 'ruption in me equal to a small arthquake, then 'taint no use sayin' it—it squirmed like a sarpent, when that killin' stuff touched it; hu' "—and here with a countenance made up of suppressed agony and present determination, he paused to give force to his words, and slowly and deliberately remarked, "If you git two chickens from me for that live animal, I'm d—d!" and seizing his seal-skin he vanished.

Concerning Bald-Headed Whizzers*

TYPICAL adjunct to life in the hell-roarin' days of the Argonauts when camps reeked gold and the humors of men were raw as new-plowed prairie land, was that effervescent phenomenon known as the Whizzer.

The Whizzer was the high ace in the deck of life as it was dealt over gravel bar and auriferous stream bank. Individuals and towns reaped fame by it. A successful Whizzer not only crowned its originator and perpetrator with glory, but shed an enviable light upon the entire community that witnessed— or suffered—its execution. Whizzers of superlative merit have been embalmed in the memories of very old men who still sun themselves in the ghost towns of gold and who can be led, with much chuckling, to recount them. In a few rare volumes of reminiscences long out of print you'll find samples of this long extinct genus pinned like gorgeous butterflies to the pages.

A noteworthy swindle, a practical joke, a brilliant hoax: these were the magic components of which the Whizzer was made. They were of two classes, the plain and the bald-headed. A bald-headed Whizzer was one so adroitly built upon a human foible or frailty, so carefully exploited by its author as to bring a whole community into the arena of mocking laughter. The distinction between the two varieties was comparative; the gage, you might say, of genius.

One of the earliest Whizzers of the gold diggin's to gain immortality was that one perpetrated by a genius whose name comes down as Pike Sellers—undoubtedly one of the Wild Missouri hellions generically lumped as "Pikes," in the vocabulary of the mines. This Pike had an imagination and a devilishly sly humor which would qualify him to-day for one of our highly specialized lines of salesmanship.

It was in the spring of '50 when word of the incredible richness of Downie's Flat, away up near the headwaters of

---

* From *The Hell-Roarin' Forty-Niners*, by Robert Welles Ritchie, pp. 233–237. Copyright, 1928, by J. H. Sears & Co., Incorporated. New York.

Yuba's north fork, swept downstream and set a crowd of wild-eyed boomers hurrying thither. Original discoverers of Downie's Flat were digging a pound of gold a day to the man out of crevices under the rim rock with the point of a butcher knife. Major Downie himself had sifted downstream to Bullard's Bar with $3000 in nuggets, result of three days' work! So rumor exploded.

When the first of the rush commenced to lower themselves hand over hand down the precipitous wall of the gorge to Downie's camp on the forks of white water they were not very cordially received by the ten or a dozen original discoverers who'd spent a hard winter there. It was, in fact, quite true that Downie and his associates had been hitting raw gold out of the bank with butcher knives and iron spoons over several months; and they did not welcome a division of riches.

Then it was that Pike Sellers had his inspiration.

He was working away at the soft dirt of the stream bank one day when he saw one of the boomers, pack on back, crawling precariously down trail. Pike, unseen himself, scrambled up out of the stream bed and commenced furiously prying with his long knife at the bark slabs on a jack-pine. Just as the stranger came up one of the rough shags of bark became loosened. Pike pushed two fingers behind it and withdrew a fat gold nugget.

Eyes of the stranger popped. Pike tackled another bark slab without so much as a glance over shoulder at the fascinated onlooker. By a simple trick of legerdemain that hunk yielded a second alluring gold pebble.

"My Gawd!"—from the tenderfoot. "I hearn ye was diggin' the yaller stuff outa cracks in the rocks, but I didn't know she grew on trees."

"Gits lodged thar when th' tree's pushing up through th' soil," indifferently from Pike. "Most of th' nuggets is up higher, but too dam'd much trouble to shin up th' trees. Me, I'm jist satisfied to peck round nigh th' ground."

Under the believing eyes of the newcomer Pike found a couple more nuggets. Then the former whipped out his bowie-knife and started to work on a near-by jack-pine.

"Hold on thar!" commandingly from the Sellers person. "Yo're on my claim. Rule in this camp ev'ry fella's entitled to ten gold bearin' pines; that thar one belongs to me."

The boomer wanted to know in an excited whine where he could stake himself to a tree. Reluctantly Pike Sellers abandoned his work to stride through the forest to where a jack-pine of smaller growth reared.

"Like I said, she's richest nigh th' top. Ye can climb this one 'thout a ladder iffen yo're so minded." Pike showed a commendable interest in seeing the newcomer make his first strike of jack-pine gold. The latter dropped his pack and, bowie in teeth, commenced to shin up the rough trunk.

"Higher up's better," bawled Pike when his protege had come to the first limbs. "Nothin' but flake gold low down mostly."

Up went the avid tenderfoot, before his eyes the vision of a man prying nuggets from beneath tree bark. Pike let him risk his neck until the luckless light-wit was fifty or sixty feet from the ground.

"That's a likely 'nough place to begin on. Only be mighty keerful not to drop any nuggets. I kain't be held responsible fer losses like that."

The searcher after tree gold began to attack the bark with his bowie knife. Pike Sellers sifted back to the stream bed to bring an audience for the farce comedy he had staged. Thereafter "jack-pine gold" became a synonym through all the Northern Mines.

Pike Sellers reaped enduring fame as the father of a Whizzer.

A Voice from Shiloh*

ANSWERING questions in rapid succession at the close of a New York banquet, Mark Twain said:

"In writing, it is usually stronger and more dramatic to have a man speak for himself than to have someone else relate a thing about him."

Billy Boynton, whom I had introduced to Mark Twain a few moments before, interrupted, "Suppose a man dies. Is it stronger to have the man himself say that he has died?"

Mark Twain smiled affably. "Sometimes," he answered. "Take the case of Major Patterson, down in Missouri, when a squatter had moved in on some of the extensive lands he laid claim to. Deciding to use the frightening method to get the squatter off, the major donned a mask one dark night,

---

* From *Mark Twain and I*, by Opie Read, p. 3. Copyright, 1940, by the Reilly & Lee Co. Chicago.

mounted an enormous black horse, rode to the squatter's door, called him out, and asked for a bucket of water. The major had also availed himself of a contrivance used by the Ku Klux Klan, a large leather bag on his chest and stomach, buttoned securely under his coat.

"When the squatter had brought the water the major raised the three-gallon bucket, slowly poured its contents into the bag through an opening at his throat, turned to the astonished squatter and said, 'Ah-h-h——That's the first drink of water I've had since I was killed at the battle of Shiloh!'

"The squatter disappeared from that part of the country," concluded Mark Twain. "And I think you will agree that when the major spoke for himself, the effect was stronger than otherwise."

Yankee Notions*

I

"WHAT is the price of razor-strops?" inquired my grandfather of a peddler, whose wagon, loaded with Yankee notions, stood in front of our store.

"A dollar each for Pomeroy's strops," responded the itinerant merchant.

"A dollar apiece!" exclaimed my grandfather. "They'll be sold for half the money before the year is out."

"If one of Pomeroy's strops is sold for fifty cents within a year, I'll make you a present of one," replied the peddler.

"I'll purchase one on those conditions. Now, Ben, I call you to witness the contract," said my grandfather, addressing himself to Esquire Hoyt.

"All right," responded Ben.

"Yes," said the peddler, "I'll do as I say, and there's no backout to me."

My grandfather took the strop, and put it in his side coatpocket. Presently drawing it out, and turning to Esquire Hoyt, he said, "Ben, I don't much like this strop now I have bought it. How much will you give for it?"

* From *Struggles and Triumphs: or, The Life of P. T. Barnum*, Written by Himself, edited, with an introduction, by George S. Bryan, Vol. I, pp. 19–20, 48–50. Copyright, 1927, by Alfred A. Knopf, Inc. New York and London.

"Well, I guess, seeing it's you, I'll give fifty cents," drawled the Squire, with a wicked twinkle in his eye, which said that the strop and the peddler were both incontinently sold.

"You can take it. I guess I'll get along with my old one a spell longer," said my grandfather, giving the peddler a knowing look.

The strop changed hands, and the peddler exclaimed, "I acknowledge, gentlemen. What's to pay?"

"Treat the company, and confess you are taken in, or else give me a strop," replied my grandfather.

"I never will confess nor treat," said the peddler, "but I'll give you a strop for your wit"; and suiting the action to the word, he handed a second strop to his customer. A hearty laugh ensued, in which the peddler joined.

"Some pretty sharp fellows here in Bethel," said a bystander, addressing the peddler.

"Tolerable, but nothing to brag of," replied the peddler. "I have made seventy-five cents by the operation."

"How is that?" was the inquiry.

"I have received a dollar for two strops which cost me only twelve and a half cents each," replied the peddler; "but having heard of the cute tricks of the Bethel chaps, I thought I would look out for them and fix my prices accordingly. I generally sell these strops at twenty-five cents each, but, gentlemen, if you want any more at fifty cents apiece, I shall be happy to supply your whole village."

Our neighbors laughed out of the other side of their mouths, but no more strops were purchased.

II

Dr. Carrington, Esquire James Clarke, and other well-known jokers of Danbury, were the authors of many anecdotes which I heard in my younger days. The doctor kept a country store. A small farmer coming to trade with him one day, asked him if he took cheese in exchange for goods. "Certainly," was the reply. The farmer brought in a large bag and emptied out eleven very small cheeses. "Only eleven!" said the doctor counting them. "I can't do any thing with them."

"Why not?" asked the farmer.

"There is not a full set—there should be twelve," responded the doctor.

"A full set of what?" inquired the farmer.

"Button molds, of course," was the reply.

Fortunately the farmer was of a humorous turn and took the joke in good part.

"Tin peddlers," as they were called, were abundant in those days. They travelled through the country in covered wagons, filled with tin ware and small Yankee notions of almost every description, including jewelry, dry goods, pins, needles, etc., etc. They were a sharp set of men, always ready for a trade whether cash or barter, and as they generally were destitute of moral principle, whoever dealt with them was pretty sure to be cheated. Dr. Carrington had frequently traded with them, and had just as frequently been shaved. He at last declared he would never again have any business transaction with that kind of people.

One day a peddler drove up to the doctor's store, and jumping from his wagon went in and told him he wished to barter some goods with him.

The doctor declined trading, quietly remarking that he had been shaved enough by tin peddlers, and would have nothing more to do with them.

"It is very hard to proscribe an entire class because some of its members happen to be dishonest," said the wary peddler, "and I insist on your giving me a trial. I am travelling all through the country, and can get rid of any of your unsaleable goods. So, to give you a fair chance, I will sell you any thing I have in my wagon at my lowest wholesale price, and will take in exchange any thing you please to pay me from your store at the retail price."

"Your offer seems a fair one," said the doctor, "and I will look over your goods."

He proceeded to the wagon, and seeing nothing that he wanted except a lot of whetstones, of which the peddler had a large quantity, he inquired the price.

"My wholesale price of whetstones is $3 per dozen," replied the peddler.

"Well, I will take a gross of them," said the doctor.

The twelve dozen whetstones were brought in, counted out, and carefully placed upon a shelf behind the counter.

"Now," said the peddler, "you owe me $36, for which I am to take such goods as you please at the retail price. Come, doctor, what are you going to pay me in?"

"In whetstones at fifty cents each, which will take just six dozen," replied the doctor gravely, at the same time commencing to count back one half of his purchase.

The peddler looked astonished for a moment, and then bursting into what is termed "a horse laugh," he exclaimed, "Took in, by hokey! Here, doctor, take this dollar for your trouble (handing him the money); give me back my truck, and I'll acknowledge for ever that you are too sharp for a tin peddler!"

The doctor accepted the proposed compromise, and was never troubled by that peddler again.

The Sky Foogle*

THERE was a printer named Dan Shriner who lived in Chillicothe in the early nineties. His chief claim to fame was for his invention of the "sky foogle." The "sky foogle," according to Shriner, was a ferocious animal that had never before been seen or captured. Shriner hired a hall, charged the eager crowd admission for a glimpse of the "terror." When the good Chillicotheans were assembled, there was a fearful rattling of chains, some horrible cries off stage and Shriner, torn and dishevelled, burst upon the scene crying, "Run for your lives, the terrible 'sky foogle' has escaped." The audience ran. They forgot to ask for their money back on the way out. Nobody ever knew what became of Shriner, or, for that matter, of the "sky foogle."

The Glorious Whitewasher**

SATURDAY morning was come, and all the summer world was bright and fresh, and brimming with life. There was a song in every heart; and if the heart was young the music issued at the lips. There was cheer in every face and a spring in every step. The locust trees were in bloom and the fragrance of the blossoms filled the air. Cardiff Hill, beyond the village and above it, was green with vegetation, and it lay just far enough away to seem a Delectable Land, dreamy, reposeful, and inviting.

* From *Chillicothe and Ross County*, compiled and written by Federal Writers' Project of Ohio, Works Progress Administration, pp. 29–30. Copyright, 1938, by the Ross County Northwest Territory Committee.
** From *The Adventures of Tom Sawyer*, by Mark Twain, pp. 12–19. Copyright, 1875, 1899, and 1903, by Samuel L. Clemens, 1917, by Clara Gabrilowitsch, 1917, 1920, by Mark Twain Company. New York: Harper & Brothers.

Tom appeared on the sidewalk with a bucket of whitewash and a long-handled brush. He surveyed the fence, and all gladness left him and a deep melancholy settled down upon his spirit. Thirty yards of board fence nine feet high. Life to him seemed hollow, and existence but a burden. Sighing he dipped his brush and passed it along the topmost plank; repeated the operation; did it again; compared the insignificant whitewashed streak with the far-reaching continent of unwhitewashed fence, and sat down on a tree-box discouraged. Jim came skipping out at the gate with a tin pail, and singing "Buffalo Gals." Bringing water from the town pump had always been hateful work in Tom's eyes, before, but now it did not strike him so. He remembered that there was company at the pump. White, mulatto, and Negro boys and girls were always there waiting their turns, resting, trading playthings, quarreling, fighting, skylarking. And he remembered that although the pump was only a hundred and fifty yards off, Jim never got back with a bucket of water under an hour—and even then somebody generally had to go after him. Tom said:

"Say, Jim, I'll fetch the water if you'll whitewash some."

Jim shook his head and said:

"Can't, Mars Tom. Ole missis, she tole me I got to go an' git dis water an' not stop foolin' roun' wid anybody. She say she spec' Mars Tom gwine to ax me to whitewash, an' so she tole me go 'long an' 'tend to my own business—she 'lowed *she'd* 'tend to de whitewashin'."

"Oh, never you mind what she said, Jim. That's the way she always talks. Gimme the bucket—I won't be gone only a minute. *She* won't ever know."

"Oh, I dasn't, Mars Tom. Ole missis she'd take an' tar de head off'n me. 'Deed she would."

"*She!* She never licks anybody—whacks 'em over the head with her thimble—and who cares for that, I'd like to know. She talks awful, but talk don't hurt—anyways it don't if she don't cry. Jim, I'll give you a marvel. I'll give you a white alley!"

Jim began to waver.

"White alley, Jim! And it's a bully taw."

"My! Dat's a mighty gay marvel, *I* tell you! But Mars Tom, I's powerful 'fraid ole missis—"

"And besides, if you will I'll show you my sore toe."

Jim was only human—this attraction was too much for him. He put down his pail, took the white alley, and bent over the toe with absorbing interest while the bandage was being unwound. In another moment he was flying down the street with his pail and a tingling rear, Tom was whitewashing with vigor, and Aunt Polly was retiring from the field with a slipper in her hand and triumph in her eye.

But Tom's energy did not last. He began to think of the fun he had planned for this day, and his sorrows multiplied. Soon the free boys would come tripping along on all sorts of delicious expeditions, and they would make a world of fun of him for having to work—the very thought of it burnt him like fire. He got out his worldly wealth and examined it—bits of toys, marbles, and trash; enough to buy an exchange of *work*, maybe, but not half enough to buy so much as half an hour of pure freedom. So he returned his straitened means to his pocket, and gave up the idea of trying to buy the boys. At this dark and hopeless moment an inspiration burst upon him! Nothing less than a great, magnificent inspiration.

He took up his brush and went tranquilly to work. Ben Rogers hove in sight presently—the very boy, of all boys, whose ridicule he had been dreading. Ben's gait was the hop-skip-and-jump—proof enough that his heart was light and his anticipations high. He was eating an apple, and giving a long, melodious whoop, at intervals, followed by a deep-toned ding-dong-dong, ding-dong-dong, for he was personating a steamboat. As he drew near, he slackened speed, took the middle of the street, leaned far over to starboard and rounded to ponderously and with laborious pomp and circumstance—for he was personating the *Big Missouri*, and considered himself to be drawing nine feet of water. He was boat and captain and engine-bells combined, so he had to imagine himself standing on his own hurricane-deck giving the orders and executing them:

"Stop her, sir! Ting-a-ling-ling!" The headway ran almost out and he drew up slowly toward the sidewalk.

"Ship up to back! Ting-a-ling-ling!" His arms straightened and stiffened down his sides.

"Set her back on the stabboard! Ting-a-ling-ling! Chow! ch-chow-wow! Chow!" His right hand, meantime, describing stately circles—for it was representing a forty-foot wheel.

"Let her go back on the labboard! Ting-a-ling-ling! Chow-ch-chow-chow!" The left hand began to describe circles.

"Stop the stabboard! Ting-a-ling-ling! Stop the labboard! Come ahead on the stabboard! Stop her! Let your outside turn over slow! Ting-a-ling-ling! Chow-ow-ow! Get out that headline! *Lively* now! Come—out with your spring-line—what're you about there! Take a turn round that stump with the bight of it! Stand by that stage, now—let her go! Done with the engines, sir! Ting-a-ling-ling! *Sh't! sh't! sh't!*" (trying the gauge-cocks).

Tom went on whitewashing—paid no attention to the steamboat. Ben stared a moment and then said:

"Hi-*yi*! *You're* up a stump, ain't you!"

No answer. Tom surveyed his last touch with the eye of an artist, then he gave his brush another gentle sweep and surveyed the result, as before. Ben ranged up alongside of him. Tom's mouth watered for the apple, but he stuck to his work. Ben said.

"Hello, old chap, you got to work, hey?"

Tom wheeled suddenly and said:

"Why, it's you, Ben! I warn't noticing."

"Say—*I'm* going in a-swimming, *I* am. Don't you wish you could? But of course you'd druther *work*—wouldn't you? Course you would!" Tom contemplated the boy a bit, and said:

"What do you call work?"

"Why, ain't *that* work?"

Tom resumed his whitewashing, and answered carelessly:

"Well, maybe it is, and maybe it ain't. All I know, is, it suits Tom Sawyer."

"Oh come, now, you don't mean to let on that you *like* it?" The brush continued to move.

"Like it? Well, I don't see why I oughtn't to like it. Does a boy get a chance to whitewash a fence every day?"

That put the thing in a new light. Ben stopped nibbling his apple. Tom swept his brush daintily back and forth—stepped back to note the effect—added a touch here and there—criticized the effect again—Ben watching every move and getting more and more interested, more and more absorbed. Presently he said:

"Say, Tom, let *me* whitewash a little."

Tom considered, was about to consent; but he altered his mind:

"No—no—I reckon it wouldn't hardly do, Ben. You see, Aunt Polly's awful particular about this fence—right here on the street, you know—but if it was the back fence I wouldn't mind and *she* wouldn't. Yes, she's awful particular about this fence; it's got to be done very careful; I reckon there ain't one boy in a thousand, maybe two thousand, that can do it the way it's got to be done."

"No—is that so? Oh come, now—lemme just try. Only just a little—I'd let *you*, if you was me, Tom."

"Ben, I'd like to, honest injun; but Aunt Polly—well, Jim wanted to do it, but she wouldn't let him; Sid wanted to do it, and she wouldn't let Sid. Now don't you see how I'm fixed? If you was to tackle this fence and anything was to happen to it—"

"Oh, shucks, I'll be just as careful. Now lemme try. Say— I'll give you the core of my apple."

"Well, here— No, Ben, now don't. I'm afeard—"

"I'll give you *all* of it!"

Tom gave up the brush with reluctance in his face, but alacrity in his heart. And while the late steamer *Big Missouri* worked and sweated in the sun, the retired artist sat on a barrel in the shade close by, dangled his legs, munched his apple, and planned the slaughter of more innocents. There was no lack of material; boys happened along every little while; they came to jeer, but remained to whitewash. By the time Ben was fagged out, Tom had traded the next chance to Billy Fisher for a kite, in good repair; and when *he* played out, Johnny Miller bought in for a dead rat and a string to swing it with—and so on, and so on, hour after hour. And when the middle of the afternoon came, from being a poor poverty-stricken boy in the morning, Tom was literally rolling in wealth. He had besides the things before mentioned, twelve marbles, part of a jews'-harp, a piece of blue bottle-glass to look through, a spool cannon, a key that wouldn't unlock anything, a fragment of chalk, a glass stopper of a decanter, a tin soldier, a couple of tadpoles, six firecrackers, a kitten with only one eye, a brass door-knob, a dog-collar—but no dog—the handle of a knife, four pieces of orange-peel, and a dilapidated old window-sash.

He had had a nice, good, idle time all the while—plenty of company—and the fence had three coats of whitewash on it! If he hadn't run out of whitewash, he would have bankrupted every boy in the village.

II

HUMOROUS ANECDOTES
AND JESTS

1. VARIETIES OF THE AMERICAN ANECDOTE

THE anecdote may be defined as a story with a point or a point with a story, depending upon where the emphasis falls. Unlike the fable or parable, the anecdote is not allegorical and is generally based on an actual occurrence. Because the point of an anecdote is wise or witty rather than moral, it is close to the aphorism; and in its use to enliven or illustrate conversation and oratory, it resembles the allusion and the figure of speech. All these values are embodied in Lincoln's remark—an anecdote in epitome—on the lawyer's paper: "It's like the lazy preacher that used to write long sermons, and the explanation was, he got to writin' and was too lazy to stop."

Typically, the anecdote is associated with character and custom, being commonly used to illustrate a trait of an individual or a community. Thus we are familiar with anecdotes (etymologically, "unpublished" stories) of famous persons and of places. In the broad sense, however, the anecdote is any traditional narrative of a single incident and of a realistic and usually humorous character, which is intended to be believed. Although all anecdotes are not humorous, all jests involving a narrative situation, with some development and elaboration, may be classed as anecdotes.

The evolution of an anecdote from a mere joke is illustrated by two versions of "Ain't Lost." In its simplest form the gag is a comeback, as given by Carl Sandburg in *The People, Yes:* "Which way to the postoffice, boy?" "I don't know." "You don't know much, do you?" "No, but I ain't lost."

In general, three types of anecdotes may be distinguished: the anecdote based on a witty remark, or *jeu d'esprit*, such as

234

"Ain't Lost," involving repartee, quibbles, and quiddities; the anecdote of character; and the social or cultural anecdote, which involves a comment on a way of living. In the United States, all three types are given local coloring and significance in what may be called the local anecdote.

It is perhaps in the local anecdote of character (e.g., "The Grist Mill") that one may best see the American anecdote on its way to becoming a short story, in line with Bret Harte's theory that the American anecdote was the "parent of the American 'short story.' "

2. PRACTICAL STORY-TELLERS

On the one hand, story-telling is a pastime or a form of social intercourse, associated with leisure, gregariousness, and travel. On the other hand, it may have a practical application, enforcing a point and enlivening a discourse with a parable or example. Because wit and humor add an extra seasoning to the sauce of narrative, the humorous anecdote has always been effective for the purposes of homiletic or forensic illustration, as demonstrated by the popularity of collections of stories and jokes for speakers. Thus the medieval Latin collections of *exempla*, or illustrative stories for use in sermons, which drew upon the storehouses of classical legend, fable, and merry tales, served as a link between the folk literatures of ancient and modern times and as a forerunner of the jest-book.

In America the practical value of the humorous anecdote lies not so much in teaching a lesson as in making a point. Hence the wide use of the practical story in business and politics. The master of the story with a point was Lincoln, unique among story-tellers and presidents in his ability "to tell his stories, and by them to illustrate matters of great pith."

Lincoln touches the art of the humorous American anecdote at almost every point. In young manhood he discovered the secret that the Yankee peddler had learned before him and that traveling salesmen, storekeepers, lawyers, and politicians have always known—how to mix business and sociability by making a good story break down resistance, build up good will, clinch or bolster an argument, or simply pass the time of day. Whether his business was floating a flatboat or raft down the river, logging, clerking in a store, practising law, representing his district in the state legislature or Congress, or directing the destiny of his country in a great Civil War, he knew that the apt saying or anecdote, expressive of a principle or truth, constituted one of his greatest assets.[1]

From the prize story-teller of his community and its spokesman at all the neighborhood gatherings, he rose to be storyteller to the nation and the voice of the people. He is our only folk hero who is also a folk artist. Akin to Aesop and Poor Richard, he differs from our other great folk story-teller, Mark Twain, in that he was not a professional humorist, and from other "funny men" in Congress—Hardin, Corwin, Knott, and Cox—in that with him the anecdote rather than repartee or satire was the weapon. Drawing his homely incidents, allusions, figures, aphorisms, and idioms from backwoods experience, he differs from all the ordinary raconteurs who have used funny stories to garnish oratory or tickle an audience. At the same time, steeped in the lore of humor, he learned many of his tricks from the cracker-box philosophers and jesters before him, including Joe Miller. He raised the wisecrack to the level of scripture.

The practical anecdote also has its religious uses, as parables, to illustrate sermons, to point the meaning of true religion, or perhaps to satirize a rival sect.

3. RURAL JESTS

Both Lincoln and Crockett, in common with many of our popular humorists and comedians, had hayseed in their hair. Near the end of the last century the vogue of rural humor coincided with the vogue of rural and provincial drama, fiction, and poetry of the *Old Homestead, David Harum,* and James Whitcomb Riley stamp. The appeal of rural character and illiteracy in American literature is based on various motives and related to various movements in American life. The frontier, the democratic tradition of the common man, local color, and naturism, with their cults of the soil, the "homely pathetic," and the "native," have conspired to make the dry wit and the slow drawl of the countryman the most effective and characteristic expression of American independence, ingenuity, and irreverence. In rural humor, with its blend of Yankee shrewdness, backwoods eccentricity, and Western breeziness, the central trait is the contrast between apparent simplicity and underlying wit and wisdom or between pretended knowledge and actual ignorance, coupled in either case with gumption and nerve. The spectacle of rustic follies and blunders affords entertainment not only to the city-dweller, who is something of a hick-baiter, but also to the countryman ruminating on the odds and ends of his daily life. The best of rural jests are local anecdotes of character and custom. On the "make-it-yourself-or-do-without" level of culture, moreover, story-telling is one of the chief leisure-time activities and an integral part of fun-making.

4. NEGRO JESTS

The laughter of the Negro, like that of other minorities, is a solace and a source of courage; but it is on the attack rather than merely on the defensive, emphasizing the Brer Rabbit resourcefulness of a highly adaptive and infinitely patient folk. Negro jests strike a note of defiance rather than of protest, as is the case with Negro blues and folk rhymes. As High John de Conquer (the folk name for the marsh St. John's wort, whose root wards off evil, in the form of disease, hants, witches, nightmares, and the like), the "John" of slavery anecdotes is a symbol of the Negro's brier-patch-bred ability to land on his feet in the briers and "skip out des ez lively ez a cricket in de embers." Old John gets out of tight places and turns the joke on Old Massa, by dint of what Zora Neale Hurston calls "hitting a straight lick with a crooked stick." "Now, High John de Conquer, Old Massa couldn't get the best of *him*. That Old John was a case!" High John de Conquer's laughter is a secret laughter, with a subtle power like that of the root of the same name—the power to help Negroes "overcome things they feel that they could not beat otherwise."[2]

5. FOOLS AND BUNGLERS

On the credit side, the countryman is as commonsensical as he is unlearned; on the debit side, he is apt to be as nonsensical as he is simple. The humor of rustic ignorance and gullibility, with the stupid person being taken in by the clever one, is part of the larger humor of mistakes and misunderstandings. From ancient times men have laughed at "that droll stupidity which is the characteristic of noodles or simpletons" and which, as in the following drolleries, takes the form of Irish bulls, Gaulardisms, pedantry, making easy things hard, absentmindedness, imagining troubles, and literal following of directions.[3]

6. GAGS AND WISECRACKS

From the perennial humor of wit and nitwit emerge stock themes, such as the absent-minded man, Scotch and "so tight" jokes, the ugliest man, the meanest man, as well as certain vogues, such as slow train and Ford jokes and, among sayings, "knock knocks" and "You tell 'em" English. The ephemeral humor of gags and wisecracks—the temporal counterpart of local anecdotes and sayings—provides a laboratory for the study of the patterns, variations, and diffusion of popular material. The idiom is largely urban and sophisticated, since the principal means of transmission is by press, stage, film, and radio, but the mold is the folk mold of popular fantasy patterned by repetition.

Almost every form of wit and rhetorical device is employed in the wisecrack or "jocular smart remark": puns, malapropisms, boners, and other varieties of word play and humorous mistakes (She was so dumb she thought a subordinate clause was one of Santa's offspring; He is a big needle and thread man from So-and-So; She is not my best girl—just necks best; Lettuce is a proposition); Wellerisms (As the pencil sharpener said, "Now to get down to the point"); Irish bulls and paradoxes (I couldn't commit suicide if my life depended on it; She would be cute if it wasn't for her face); extravagant impossibilities (Yours till elephants roost on rose bushes); nonsense (More fun than I've had since the day the cow catcher had a calf); exaggeration (She was so thin that she could fall through a flute and never strike a note); the fabulous or the tall tale (It was so cold the cows gave ice cream); *reductio ad absurdum* (If steamships sold for a nickel, I couldn't buy the echo of a whistle); *non sequitur* (Let's you and him fight until I get tired).

The use of the formula is basic to the wisecrack: so dumb, so tight, you tell 'em, they call, she was only, you don't have to, you may be. Certain formulae are identified with disparaging or insulting wisecracks, or "slams" (They call her a toe dancer because she dances on other people's toes; You don't have to hang from a tree to be a nut; You may be bread in old Kentucky but you're just a crumb around here).

The habit of wisecracking is related to the American trait of "laughing it off" and to the love of mottoes and slogans. Many trade slogans are nothing but wisecracks: We wash everything but the baby; You can whip our cream but you can't beat our milk; You furnish the girl, we furnish the rest; Look at your hat, everyone else does; Why kill your wife? Let us do the dirty work; You wreck 'em, we fix 'em.

The value of this floating linguistic material for both the poet and the social historian is evinced by the successful use of talk, jokes, and lingo made by Carl Sandburg in both *Abraham Lincoln, the Prairie Years* and *The People, Yes*.

Ain't Lost*

A FINE city man had a brand-new buggy and a prize-winning pair of trotters that he wished to try out. He drove along the country roads, speeding a little here and walking a little there, studying the good points and admiring the beauty of his new rig. He was so delighted with the prospect that he failed to notice the road. Later on he realized that he was lost, but he hoped by driving on to find his way, or at least to meet someone who could tell him how to get back to the city.

But it was a long lonesome road. For a long time he followed the windings, hoping every hilltop would bring him within sight of some dwelling. When it was almost dark he saw in front of him a cotton patch and a good-sized country boy chopping away in the rows. He reined his tired team near the fence and called out, "Hello, boy."

"Hello yourself," the boy replied, still wielding his hoe.

"Where does this road go to?"

"Hain't never seed it go nowhars. Hit allus stays right whar hit is," said the boy, still digging away.

"How far is it to the next town?"

"Don't know; never measured it," replied the boy.

Thoroughly disgusted, the man said with some heat, "You don't know anything. You are certainly the biggest fool I ever saw."

The boy looked a long time in the man's eyes; then he said with contempt, "I knows I don't know nothing. I knows I'se a fool. But I ain't lost."

---

* From "Anecdotes from the Brazos Bottoms," by A. W. Eddins, *Straight Texas*, Publications of the Texas Folk-Lore Society, Number XIII, 1937, edited by J. Frank Dobie and Mody C. Boatright, p. 94. Copyright, 1937, by the Texas Folk-Lore Society. Austin.

The Grist Mill*

THERE is no land on earth which has produced such quaint and curious characters as the great mountainous regions of the South, and yet no country has produced nobler or brainier men.

When I was a barefooted boy my grandfather's old grist mill was the Mecca of the mountaineers. They gathered there on rainy days to talk politics and religion, and to drink "mountain" dew and fight. Adam Wheezer was a tall, spindle-shanked old settler, as dark as an Indian, and he wore a broad, hungry grin that always grew broader at the sight of a fat sheep. The most prominent trait of Adam's character, next to his love of mutton, was his bravery. He stood in the mill one day with his empty sack under his arm, as usual, when Bert Lynch, the bully of the mountains, with an eye like a game rooster's, walked up to him and said: "Adam, you've bin a-slanderin' of me, an' I'm a-gwine to give you a thrashin'." He seized Adam by the throat and backed him under the meal spout. Adam opened his mouth to squall and it spouted meal like a whale. He made a surge for breath and liberty, and tossed Bert away like a feather. Then he shot out of the mill door like a rocket, leaving his old battered plug hat and one prong of his coat-tail in the hands of the enemy. He ran through the creek and knocked it dry as he went. He made a bee-line for my grandfather's house, a quarter of a mile away, on the hill. He burst into the sitting-room, covered with meal and panting like a bellowsed horse, frightening my grandmother almost into hysterics. The old lady screamed and shouted: "What in the world is the matter, Adam?" Adam replied: "That thar durned Bert Lynch is down yander a-tryin' to raise a fuss with me."

But every dog has his day. Brother Billy Patterson preached from the door of the mill on the following Sunday. It was his first sermon in that "neck of the woods" and he began his ministrations with a powerful discourse, hurling his anathemas against Satan and sin and every kind of wickedness. He denounced whisky. He branded the bully as a brute and a moral coward, and personated Bert, having witnessed his

---

* From "Visions and Dreams," in *Echoes, Centennial and other Notable Speeches, Lectures, and Stories,* by Governor Robt. L. Taylor, pp. 175–177. Copyright, 1899, by S. B. Williamson & Co. Nashville, Tennessee.

battle with Adam. This was too much for the champion. He resolved to "thrash" Brother Patterson, and in a few days they met at the mill. Bert squared himself and said: "Parson, you had your turn last Sunday; it's mine to-day. Pull off that broadcloth an' take your medicine. I'm a-gwine to suck the marrow out'n them ole bones o' yourn." The pious preacher pled for peace, but without avail. At last he said: "Then, if nothing but a fight will satisfy you, will you allow me to kneel down and say my prayers before we fight?" "Oh, yes, that's all right, Parson," said Bert, "but cut yer prayer short, for I'm a-gwine to give you a good sound thrashin'."

The preacher knelt and thus began to pray: "O Lord, thou knowest that when I killed Bill Cummins, and John Brown, and Jerry Smith, and Levi Bottles, that I did it in self defense. Thou knowest, O Lord, that when I cut the heart out of young Sliger, and strewed the ground with the brains of Paddy Miles, that it was forced upon me, and that I did it in great agony of soul. And now, O Lord, I am about to be forced to put in his coffin, this poor, miserable wretch, who has attacked me here to-day. O Lord, have mercy upon his soul, and take care of his helpless widow and orphans when he is gone!"

And he arose, whetting his knife on his shoe-sole, singing:

> "Hark, from the tomb a doleful sound,
>   Mine ears attend the cry."

But when he looked around, Bert was gone. There was nothing in sight but a little cloud of dust far up the road, following in the wake of the vanishing champion.

Weather Prophets*

It has been said that George B. Erath, the famous German pioneer and Indian fighter, was the author of the expression: "Nobody prophesies about Texas weather except newcomers and damn fools."

For many years this has been a favorite gag in Texas social life. It was one of the sells in the old saloon days, and the unfortunate tenderfoot who fell for it always had to set up the drinks to the crowd.

* From "Anecdotes from the Brazos Bottoms," by A. W. Eddins, *Straight Texas*, Publications of the Texas Folk-Lore Society, Number XIII, 1937, edited by J. Frank Dobie and Mody C. Boatright, pp. 88–89. Copyright, 1937, by the Texas Folk-Lore Society. Austin.

One dull, slow evening when things were at an absolute standstill in the saloon, a fresh young guy with a derby hat and store-bought clothes breezed into the place, walked up to the bar, and ordered a drink. The usual crowd of loafers looked on disapprovingly but said nothing. Leisurely finishing his drink and wiping his mouth with a bright silk handkerchief, the newcomer said, "Well, I believe it's going to rain."

The golden opportunity had arrived; the whole crowd was alert and watchful. Then the old nester, the leader in all the local wars of wits, said very fatherly, "My friend, did you know that there were only two kinds of people who prophesy about Texas weather?"

"Two kinds of people who prophesy on Texas weather?" mused the stranger. "That's very queer. Who are they?"

Then the old nester, with all the contempt and sarcasm in his power, sneered, "Newcomers and damn fools."

The crowd rose with a mighty shout and gathered around the newcomer shouting, "Haw, haw, haw." "He got you that time." "You are it." "He got you good." "Set um up. Set um up." "You owe the drinks to the house." "Come on, set um up."

The young fellow stood smiling at all their hurrah. He was not the least troubled about their demands for the drinks. When the hubbub had died down and they were all properly up against the bar, he said very calmly and slowly, "You say there are only two kinds of people who prophesy about Texas weather—newcomers and damn fools. You are right. Those are the only two kinds in Texas."

All Face*

ON A cold dreary day an Indian and a white man were making a journey together. The Indian had on no clothing except a blanket, while the white man was bundled up in all the clothes he possessed. The white man continued to complain about the cold and to wonder why the Indian was not freezing. He said to the Indian, "I don't understand it. With all my clothes I am about to freeze, and you, with only a thin blanket, do not seem to be cold at all."

---

* *Ibid.*, p. 90.

"Is your face cold?" asked the Indian.

"No, my face is not cold, but I'm just about to freeze everywhere else."

"Me all face," said the Indian.

The Laughing President*

RESPECTABLE friends, who cared about reputations as gentlemen and scholars, took it as a little queer, a little like "a country Jake," beneath dignity, that Lincoln should carry with him the book "Joe Miller's Jests," generally called Joe Miller's joke book. English puns, Irish bulls, Greek repartee, folk tales of Jews and Egyptians, brisk anecdotes, filled the book—more than a thousand, each with a serial number. No. 997 told of "the celebrated organist Abbe Vogler, once imitating a thunderstorm so well that for miles round all the milk turned sour." The Irishman was told of, who had been living in Scotland and was asked how he liked the country, replying, "I was sick all the time I was there, and if I had lived there till this time, I'd been dead a year ago." Lord Russell on the scaffold ready to have his head cut off, handed his watch to a bishop, with the remark, "Take this—it shows time; I am going into eternity and no longer need it." Another lord, owing many debts, was asked how he could sleep at night, and answered: "I sleep very well, but I wonder how my creditors can." A wounded officer on a bloody battlefield was howling with pain when another wounded officer near by called to him: "What do you make such a noise for? Do you think nobody is killed but yourself?"

Such was some of the foolery in the book that Lincoln occasionally took out of his carpetbag and read aloud to other lawyers. Some had the pith and poignancy of the grave-digger in the play of Hamlet, one joke reading: "An Irishman going to be hanged, begged that the rope might be tied under his arms instead of round his neck; for, said Pat, I am so remarkably ticklish in the throat, that if tied there, I will certainly kill myself with laughing." Or again Joke No. 506, reading: "Lieutenant Connolly, an Irishman in the service of

* From *Abraham Lincoln, The Prairie Years*, by Carl Sandburg, Vol. II, pp. 295-301, 312-313. Copyright, 1926, by Harcourt, Brace & Company, Inc. New York.

the United States, during the American war, chanced to take three Hessian prisoners himself, without any assistance; being asked by the commander-in-chief how he had taken them—'I surrounded them,' was the answer."

There were tales of the people. A traveler in Egypt said to a worker on the land: "I suppose you are quite happy now; the country looks like a garden and every village has its minaret." "God is great," replied the worker. "Our master gives with one hand and takes with two." Another traveler, reporting that he and his servant had made fifty wild Arabs run, said there was nothing surprising about it. "We ran and they ran after us." And again and again little tales of the people, the people. Into the street before Dean Swift's deanery came "a great rabble," waiting "to see the eclipse." And Dean Swift had the big bell rung, and a crier bawling: "O Yes, O Yes, all manner of persons here concerned take notice the eclipse be put off till tomorrow this time! so God save the King and his Reverence the dean." And the rabble went away, all but one Irishman who said he would stay because "the dean might change his mind and have the eclipse that day after all."

Thus Joe Miller's jests. They were a nourishing company to Lincoln. Once in a while he told a story that seemed to have been made over from Joe Miller and placed in Indiana. In his lighter moods his humors matched with the Rabelais definition, "a certain jollity of mind, pickled in the scorn of fortune."

He told of the long-legged boy "sparking" a farmer's daughter when the hostile father came in with a shotgun; the boy jumped through a window, and running across the cabbage patch scared up a rabbit; in about two leaps the boy caught up with the rabbit, kicked it high in the air, and grunted, "Git out of the road and let somebody run that knows how." He told of a Kentucky horse sale where a small boy was riding a fine horse to show off points, when a man whispered to the boy, "Look here, boy, hain't that horse got the splints?" and the boy answered: "Mister, I don't know what the splints is, but if it's good for him, he has got it; if it ain't good for him, he ain't got it."

Riding to Lewiston an old acquaintance, a weather-beaten farmer, spoke of going to law with his next neighbor. "Been a neighbor of yours for long?" "Nigh onto fifteen year." "Part of the time you get along all right, don't you?" "I reckon we do." "Well, see this horse of mine? I sometimes get out of patience with him. But I know his faults; he does fairly well as horses go; it might take me a long time to get used to some other horse's faults: for all horses have faults."

The instant dignity became bogus his eye caught it. He enjoyed such anecdotes as the one of a Brown County, Indiana, man who killed a neighbor's dog, and the proof of guilt was clear. The defendant's attorney cleared his throat and began a speech, "May it please the court, we are proud to live in a land where justice is administered to the king on the throne and the beggar on his dunghill." The squire then interrupted, "You may go ahead with your speech, but the case *are* decided."

Little folk tales and snatches of odd wisdom known to common people of the ancient kingdoms of the Persians and the Arabians, came to be known among the common people of the farming districts in Illinois, hitched up somehow to Abe Lincoln. When a story or saying had a certain color or smack, it would often be tagged as coming from Lincoln. He had said to a book agent, "For those who like that kind of a book, that's the kind of a book they'll like." He was the man walking along a dusty road when a stranger, driving a buggy came along. And he asked the stranger, "Will you be so good as to take my overcoat to town for me?" And the man in the buggy said he would. "But how will you get your overcoat back again?" "Oh, that's easy! I'm going to stay right inside of it." And of course, said some jokers, it was Abe Lincoln who first told a hotel waiter, "Say, if this is coffee, then please bring me some tea, but if this is tea, please bring me some coffee." And on Abe Lincoln was laid the remark, after tasting ice cream, "Say, waiter, I don't want to slander this hotel, but this here pudding's froze."

He had come out of a slushy snow into a courtroom to try a case and sat down to dry his feet at the stove. The words of the lawyer arguing against him came to his ears. All of a sudden he was out in the middle of the courtroom, one shoe off, calling: "Now, judge, that isn't fair. I'm not going to have this jury all fuddled up."

Did he not say when he met a man somewhat matching his own height, "Well, you're up some"—had they not seen how the clay of the earth clung to him? Before posing for a photographer, he stepped into a barber shop, saying, "I better get my hair slicked up." Then, sitting before the camera, he ran his fingers through his hair, caught himself, and said,

"Guess I've made a bird's nest of it again." It was he who agreed to make a horse trade, sight unseen, with a judge. First came the judge the next morning with a broken-down bone-rack of a horse; then came Lincoln carrying a wooden sawhorse on his shoulders, saying, "Well, judge, this is the first time I ever got the worst of it in a horse trade."

A walking, stalking library of stories he was. Some of them could have had musical accompaniments from barn-dance fiddles. The prize story tellers of one neighborhood and another had met him and they had competed. "That reminds me." "That's like the feller down at Goose Holler." And occasionally was one with a shine of many cross-lights in it. Lincoln told of a balloonist going up in New Orleans, sailing for hours, and dropping his parachute over a cotton field. The gang of Negroes picking cotton saw a man coming down from the sky in blue silk, in silver spangles, wearing golden slippers. They ran—all but one old timer who had the rheumatism and couldn't get away. He waited till the balloonist hit the ground and walked toward him. Then he mumbled: "Howdy, Massa Jesus. How's yo' Pa?"

Lincoln had stood with two umbrellas at an imaginary rat hole, impersonating Sam'l, the Quaker boy whose father wanted to stop the boy's using swear words. The two umbrellas were blacksmith tongs. Sam'l's father had said, "Now, Sam'l, thee will sit here until thee has a rat. If I hear thee swear, thee will sit here till thee has another." And Sam'l had sat there for hours, snipping the tongs a few times, but no rat caught. At last one came out from the rat hole, the whiskers peeping up, then the black nose, and the eyes blinking. And the two umbrella tongs snapped together in a flash. And Sam'l yelled, "By God, I have thee at last!" And Lincoln with a shaking, swaying frame let out a squeal and stood holding an imaginary wriggling rat between the two umbrellas. He had told this in Illinois towns during the debates with Douglas. And Robert R. Hitt, the phonographic reporter, said he forgot himself and politics and business and nearly believed there was a live squeaking rat caught between the two umbrellas. For a roomful of men in a hotel, Lincoln would perform this drama of Sam'l, Sam'l's father, and the rat, acting subtly the rôles of the earnest father, the obstreperous boy, and the furtive rat.

He picked up comedy, as he met it, and passed it on to others. In Cumberland County, one Dr. Hamburgher, a Democrat, forced his way to the front to reply to Lincoln's speech. As Hamburger worked into a frothy and threatening speech, a little man with a limp came over to Lincoln and said: "Don't mind *him*. I know *him;* I live here; I'll take care of *him*. Watch me." And he took the platform, and replying brought from Hamburger the cry, "That's a lie." To which the little man with the limp called out with high defiance, "Never mind, I'll take that from *you*—yes, I'll take anything from you, except your pills." At the mention of pills, the doctor snorted, "You scoundrel, you know I've quit practicing medicine." And the little man dropped down on the knee of his best leg, raised his hands toward the sky in thankfulness, and shouted, "Then, thank God! The country is safe."

Plato, the Kane County lawyer, had told him a story about a man who had beaten a dog to death and was in such a rage that he would go out of the house and again beat the dog to death. When Plato came one day to Lincoln's office in Springfield, Lincoln's greeting was, "Well, Plato, have you got that dog killed yet?"

A family in Indiana, according to Lincoln, picked dandelion tops or other leaves and boiled "greens" for dinner in the spring and early summer. Once after a mess of greens the whole family went out of commission. After that when they had greens a big helping would first be forked out for Zerah, a half-wit boy, as the family said: "Try it on Zerah. If he stands it, it won't hurt the rest of us." And a man had a horse that would balk and settle down on all four legs like a bird dog. He traded off the horse as good for hunting birds. As the horse crossed a creek he settled down in the middle of it like a bird dog and the man who had owned him called to the new rider: "Ride him! Ride him! He's as good for fish as he is for birds."

People looked at Lincoln, searching his face, thinking about his words and ways, ready to believe he was a Great Man. Then he would spill over with a joke or tell of some new horse-play of wit or humor in the next county. The barriers tumbled. He was again a strange friend, a neighbor, a friendly stranger, no far-off Great Man at all. "His face," Moncure D. Conway noted, "had a battered and bronzed look, without being hard." He fitted the measurements, "three parts sublime to one grotesque."

A crowd was bubbling with mirth in an Ohio town as a short friend stood alongside Lincoln to introduce him. Lincoln, pointing at himself, said, "This is the long of it," and putting an arm on the friend's shoulder, "and this is the short of it."

Joe Fifer, an eighteen-year-old corn husker, heard Lincoln at Bloomington after Swett made the opening address. "When Lincoln was starting to speak," Fifer noticed, "some men near me said Lincoln was no great shakes as a public speaker and Swett would make a better showing against Douglas. But when Lincoln got to going they listened; they stood still without moving out of their foot tracks. Lincoln looked out on a wall of faces still as if they had been made of stone."

The Springfield doctor, William Jayne, trying to fathom why Lincoln had carried the crowds with him usually in debating with Douglas, said: "Everybody thinks he is honest and believes what he says. If he was really a great man, or if people regarded him as a great man, he could not do half so much."

He was the man who had started a little circle of people to giggling one morning in Judge Davis's courtroom, and the judge sputtered out: "I am not going to stand this any longer, Mr. Lincoln. You're always disturbing this court with your tomfoolery." The fine was $5.00, for disorderly conduct. Lincoln sat with his hand over his mouth trying to keep his face straight. Later the judge called Lawrence Weldon to him and Weldon whispered into his ear what it was that Lincoln had told. Then the judge giggled. Getting his face straight, he announced, "The clerk may remit Mr. Lincoln's fine." The joke had to do with "taking up a subscription to buy Jim Wheeler a new pair of pants."

He could speak of So-and-So as "a quiet, orderly, faithful man." And he could hand a bottle to a baldheaded man he wished to get rid of, with the remarks: "Try this stuff for your hair. Keep it up. They say it will grow hair on a pumpkin. Come back in ten months and tell me how it works." When it was intimated to him that he was consulting too much with Judge Davis, he told of a New Hampshire judge who said: "The only time the chief judge ever consulted was at the close of a long day's session, when he turned and whispered, 'Don't your back ache?' " He liked to tell of the strict judge of whom it was said: "He would hang a man for blowing his nose in the street, but he would quash the indictment if it failed to specify which hand he blew it with."

When he presented Coles County relatives with a sad-faced photograph of himself, he said, "This is not a very good-looking picture, but it's the best that could be produced from the poor subject."

Baptist Chitlins, Methodist Chitlins*

THIS man had a tub on his head and with a musical voice was singing:—

> "Here's yer chitlins, fresh an' sweet,
>   Who'll jine de Union?
> Young hog's chitlins hard to beat,
>   Who'll jine de Union?
> Methodist chitlins, jest been biled,
>   Who'll jine de Union?
> Right fresh chitlins, dey ain't spiled,
>   Who'll jine de Union?
> Baptist chitlins by de pound,
>   Who'll jine de Union?
> As nice chitlins as ever was found,
>   Who'll jine de Union?

"Here's yer chitlins, out of good fat hog; jess as sweet chitlins as ever yer see. Dees chitlins will make your mouf water jess to look at 'em. Come an' see 'em."

At this juncture the man took the tub from his head, sat it down, to answer a woman who had challenged his right to call them "Baptist chitlins."

"Duz you mean to say dat dem is Baptiss chitlins?"

"Yes, mum, I means to say dat dey is real Baptist chitlins, an' nuffin' else."

"Did dey come out of a Baptiss hog?" inquired the woman.

"Yes, mum, dem chitlins come out of a Baptist hog."

"How duz you make dat out?"

"Well, yer see, dat hog was raised by Mr. Roberson, a hard-shell Baptist, de corn dat de hog was fatted on was also raised by Baptists, he was killed and dressed by Geemes Boone, an' you all know dat he's as big a Baptist as ever lived."

"Well," said the woman, as if perfectly satisfied, "lem-me have two poun's."

By the time the man had finished his explanation, and weighed out her lot, he was completely surrounded with

---

* From *My Southern Home: or, The South and its People*, by Wm. Wells Brown, M.D., pp. 172–175. Copyright, 1880, by Annie G. Brown. Boston: A. G. Brown & Co., Publishers.

women and men, nearly all of whom had their dishes to get the choice morsel in.

"Now," said a rather solid-looking man. "Now, I want some of de Meth-diss chitlins dat you's bin talking 'bout."

"Here dey is, ser."

"What," asked the purchaser, "you take 'em all out of de same tub?"

"Yes," quickly replied the vender.

"Can you tell 'em by lookin' at 'em?" inquired the chubby man.

"Yes, ser."

"How duz you tell 'em?"

"Well, ser, de Baptist chitlins has bin more in de water, you see, an' dey's a little whiter."

"But, how duz I know dat dey is Meth-diss?"

"Well, ser, dat hog was raised by Uncle Jake Bemis, one of de most shoutin' Methodist in de Zion connection. Well, you see, ser, de hog pen was right close to de house, an' dat hog was so knowin' dat when Uncle Jake went to prayers, ef dat hog was squealin' he'd stop. Why, ser, you could hardly get a grunt out of dat hog till Uncle Jake was dun his prayer. Now, ser, ef dat don't make him a Methodist hog, what will?"

"Weigh me out four pounds, ser."

"Here's your fresh chitlins, Baptist chitlins, Methodist chitlins, all good an' sweet."

And in an hour's time the peddler, with his empty tub upon his head, was making his way out of the street, singing,—

> "Methodist chitlins, Baptist chitlins,
>   Who'll jine de Union?"

Methodist Grasshopper and Baptist Possum*

DE METHODISS, my bruddren, is like de grasshopper—hoppin', all de time hoppin'—hop into heaven, hop out, hop into heaven, hop out. But, my bruddren, de Baptiss, when he get to heaven, *he's dar!* De Baptiss is like de 'possum. Hunter get after him, he climb de tree; he shake de limb, one foot gone; he shake de limb, anudder foot gone; but tink you, my brud-

* From *In the Brush; or Old-Time Social, Political, and Religious Life in the Southwest*, by Rev. Hamilton W. Pierson, pp. 267–268. Copyright, 1881, by D. Appleton and Co. New York.

dren, *'possum fall*? You know, my bruddren—you cotch too many—you know *'possum hang on by de tail*, and de berry debbil can't shake him off!

"De Reason Niggers Is Working So Hard"*

Dis is de way *dat* was.

God let down two bundles 'bout five miles down de road. So de white man and de nigger raced to see who would git there first. Well, de nigger out-run de white man and grabbed de biggest bundle. He was so skeered de white man would git it away from him he fell on top of de bundle and hollered back: "Oh, Ah got here first and dis biggest bundle is mine." De white man says: "All right, Ah'll take yo' leavings," and picked up de li'l tee-ninchy bundle layin' in de road. When he nigger opened up his bundle he found a pick and shovel and a hoe and a plow and chop-axe and then de white man opened up his bundle and found a writin'-pen and ink. So ever since then de nigger been out in de hot sun, usin' his tools and de white man been sittin' up figgerin', ought's a ought, figger's a figger; all for de white man, none for de nigger.

Why the Sister in Black Works Hardest**

Know how it happened? After God got thru makin' de world and de varmints and de folks, he made up a great big bundle and let it down in de middle of de road. It laid dere for thousands of years, then Ole Missus said to Ole Massa: "Go pick up dat box, Ah want to see whut's in it." Old Massa look at de box and it look so heavy dat he says to de nigger, "Go fetch me dat big ole box out dere in de road." De nigger been stumblin' over de box a long time so he tell his wife:

" 'Oman, go git dat box." So de nigger 'oman she runned to git de box. She says:

"Ah always lak to open up a big box 'cause there's nearly always something good in great big boxes." So she run and grabbed a-hold of de box and opened it up and it was full of hard work.

---

* From *Mules and Men,* by Zora Neale Hurston, p. 102. Copyright, 1935, by Zora Neale Hurston. Philadelphia and London: J. B. Lippincott Company.
** *Ibid.*, pp. 101–102.

Dat's de reason de sister in black works harder than anybody else in de world. De white man tells de nigger to work and he takes and tells his wife.

All Folks Was Born Black*

ALL folks was born black, an' dem what's turnt white, dey jest had more sense. Angel o' de Lord come down an' told de ontire bunch to meet on de fo'th Friday at de dark o' de moon an' wash deyselves in Jordan. He oxplained to 'em dat dey'd all turn white an' straighten de kinks outen deir hair. Angel kept preachin' an' preachin', but dem fool niggers didn't pay him no mind. Angel can't teach a nigger nothin'. When de fo'th Friday come a mighty little sprinklin' of 'em went down to de river an' commenced to scrub. Water was mighty low. 'Twarn't like Old Missip'——'scusin' de Lord's river—'twarn't no more'n a creek. You jest oughter seed dat crowd o' niggers settin' on de fence snickerin' at dem what went in washin'. Snickerin' an' throwin' slams. More niggers dan you ever see in Vicksburg on circus day.

Dem what went in de river kept scrubbin' and washin', special deir hair to git de kinks out. Old Aunt Grinny Granny— great-grandmammy of all dem niggers—she sot on a log all day long, eatin' cheese and crackers and lowratin' dem what was washin'. When fust dark come, she jumped up and clapped her hands: " 'Fore Gawd, dem niggers *is* gittin' white!" Grinny Granny jerked off her head handkercher an' went tumblin' down de bank to wash her hair, an' all dem fool niggers followed her. But de water was all used up, jest a tiny drap in de bottom, no more'n enough to moisten de palms o' deir hands and de soles o' deir feet. So dat's why a nigger is white in dem places.

---

* Recorded by Harris Dickson, Vicksburg, Mississippi. From "Phrases of the People," *American Stuff*, An Anthology of Prose & Verse by Members of the Federal Writers' Project, pp. 150–151. Copyright, 1937, by The Guilds' Committee for Federal Writers' Publications, Inc. The Viking Press. New York.

Two Plantation Tales*

I. ACCORDING TO HOW THE DROP FALLS

"Is I gwine tell you a tale right now?" said Uncle Remus, in response to a question by the little boy. "Well, I ain't right certain en sho' 'bout dat. It's 'cordin ter how de drap falls."

"Pshaw!" exclaimed the youngster, "I've heard you say that before. I don't know what you mean when you say it's according to how the drop falls."

"Ah-yi!" retorted Uncle Remus triumphantly, "den I'm a punkin ahead er yo' 'simmon, is I?"

"It's according to how the drop falls," rejoined the little boy, laughing.

"De way dat sayin' come 'bout," said Uncle Remus, "may be funny, but 't ain't no tale. It des happen so. Once time dey wuz a 'oman call on a neighbor 'oman des' fo' dinner-time. I dunner whedder de neighbor 'oman like dis mighty well, but she 'uz monst'us perlite all de same.

"She 'low, 'Come right in, en take off yo' things and make yo'se'f at home. You'll hatter skuzen my han's, kaze I'm makin' up dough. Fling yo' bonnet on de bed dar, en take a seat en be seated.'

"Well, de tudder 'oman, she sot dar en talk, en watch de neighbor 'oman mix dough fer de bread, en dey run'd on des like wimmin folks does. It seem like de neighbor 'oman got a bad col', en her eyes run water twel some un it crope down ter de een er her nose en hang dar. De tudder 'oman, she watch it, whiles dey er talkin'. De neighbor 'oman she work up de dough, en work it up, en talk. Sometimes she'd hol' her head fum over de tray en talk, en den ag'in she'd hol' it right spang over de dough, en shake 'er head en talk.

"Bimeby she 'low, 'Won't you stay ter dinner? I'll have dis bread done in two shakes uv a sheep's tail.'

"De tudder 'oman say, 'I can't tell you, ma'am; it's 'cordin' ter how de drap falls.'

"De tudder 'oman say, 'Dey ain't a cloud in de sky, so 't ain't gwine ter rain. You des ez well stay.'

* From *Uncle Remus and His Friends, Old Plantation Stories, Songs, and Ballads with Sketches of Negro Character*, by Joel Chandler Harris, pp. 147–153. Copyright, 1892, by Joel Chandler Harris. Boston and New York: Houghton, Mifflin and Company.

"De tudder 'oman 'low, 'I done tole you de trufe; hit's 'cordin' ter how de drap falls.'

"So, atter dat, when folks wan't right certain en sho' 'bout what dey gwine do, dey'd up en say 't wuz 'cordin' ter how de drap fall."

"Well, how did it fall, Uncle Remus—in the bread-tray, or on the table, or on the floor?" the little boy inquired.

"Lawsy, honey!" responded the old man, "ef I 'uz er tell you, I'd hatter dream it, en dreamin' ain't gwine do you er me any mo' good dan it done de nigger man what had de possum."

"I never heard of that," said the little boy.

"Oh, yes you is!" Uncle Remus asserted with some emphasis. "You been hearin' 'bout it off'n on sence you 'uz knee-high ter a duck, en you ain't much mo'n dat right now. No, suh! You des got de idee in yo' min' dat when I set down fer ter tell you sump'n hit's bleedz ter be a tale, en when yuther folks tells it 't ain't nothin' but talk. I ain't got no secret 'bout dish yer nigger man what had de possum, but I tell you right now, 'tain't no tale. Too many folks done been fool wid it.

II. THE MAN WHO HAD THE POSSUM

"Well, den, one time dey wuz a nigger man, en dish yer nigger man had a big fat possum en a half er peck er sweet 'taters. He tuck de possum en de taters home, en he lay um down,—de possum on one side de fireplace en de taters on tudder side. Den he get some wood and chips en make 'im a fier, en den he fotch out de skillet. He put de possum in dar, he did, en he put de taters in de ashes close by fer ter keep 'im comp'ny. Den he raked out some hot embers en sot de skillet on um, en he put on de skillet led, en piled some embers 'pon topper dat.

"He sot dar, he did, en wait fer de possum fer ter git done, en whiles he wuz a-waitin' he struck up a song. Maybe you done hear it 'fo' now, but dat ain't make no diffunce ter me, kaze when I git started dis away, I'm like de bull yearlin' gwine down de lane; dem what gits in de way gwine ter git run'd over —dey mos' sholy is!"

Uncle Remus leaned back in his chair, closed his eyes, and began to pat his foot. Then, after a little pause, he sang this fragment of a song:

"Virginny cut, chaw terbacker,
Nigger dance ter merlatter;
Hoe de corn, dig er tater,
Plant terbacker, 't is no matter.

"Mix de meal, fry de batter,
Nigger dance ter merlatter;
Warm de cake in er platter,
Fry um in de cooney fat.

"Grab er tater out de ash,
Nigger dance ter merlatter;
Possum meat dar in der platter,
Shoo! he make de nigger fatter."

Uncle Remus's voice was full of melody, and he sang the
song to a rollicking tune. The little boy was so much pleased
that he asked the old man to sing it again.

"Bless yo' soul, honey. If I git in a fa'r way er singin', de
niggers 'll all quit der work en crowd 'roun' here en jine in
wid me, en we'll have a reg'lar ole-timey camp-meetin' gwine
on here 'fo' you know it. I ain't got no time fer dat.

"Now, den, dish yer nigger man, what I been tellin' you
'bout, he got his taters in de ashes en his possum in de skillet,
en he sot dar en sing de song, en watch um all cook. Atter so
long a time dey got done, en he pull de taters out'n de embers,
en push de skillet 'way fum de fier. He 'low ter hisse'f, he
did, dat col' possum is better'n hot possum, dough bofe un um
is good nuff fer anybody. So he say he'll des let it set dar en
cool, en soak in de gravy. Den he say he b'lieve he'll do some
noddin', kaze den he'll dream he eatin' de possum, en den he'll
wake up en eat 'im sho nuff, en have de 'joyment er eatin' 'im
two times.

"Well, suh, dat des de way he done. He sot back in his
cheer, de nigger man did, en he nodded en nodded, en he
work his mouf des like he eatin' possum, en he grunt in his
sleep like he feelin' good. But whiles he settin' dar sleepin', a
nudder nigger man smell de possum, en he crope up ter de
door en peep in. He seed how de lan' lay en he slipped off his
shoes en stole in. He lif' up de led er de skillet, en dar wuz de
possum. He look on de side er de h'ath, en dar wuz de taters.
Now, den, when dat de case, what gwine ter happen? Possum, en tater, en hongry nigger! Well, suh, de fust news you
know, de possum wuz all bones, de taters wuz all peelin's, en

de nigger wuz mo' dan a nigger. He fix de bones in one little pile, en he fix de peelin's in anudder little pile, en den he tuck some er de possum gravy en rub it on de tudder nigger's mouf en han's, en den he went on 'bout his business.

" 'T wan't so mighty long atter dat 'fo' de noddin' nigger wake up. He open his eyes, he did, en stretch hisse'f, en look at de skillet en laugh.

"He 'low, 'You er dar, is you? Well, I'll tell you howdy now, en terreckly I'll tell you good-by!'

"He tuck de led off'n de skillet, en dey ain't no possum dar. He look 'roun' fer de taters, en dey ain't no taters dar. Dey ain't nothin' dar but a pile er bones en a pile er tater-peelin's. De nigger sot down in his cheer en went ter studyin'. He look at his han's, en he see possum grease on um. He lick out his tongue, en he tas'e possum gravy on his mouf. He shuck his head en study. He look at his han's: 'Possum been dar!' He lick his mouf: 'Possum been dar, too!' He rub his stomach: 'But I be bless ef any possum been here!' "

Way Down in Georgia*

ONCE upon a time, 'way down in Georgia, it wuz Sunday mawnin', an' de sun wuz hot. De folks in de big house didn' wake up, an' de crows, down in de cawn fiel', wuz a-pullin' up all de cawn. De ol' rooster see de crows a-pullin' up all de cawn an' he lifted up his voice an' say, "De crows a-pullin' up all de cawn! De crows a-pullin' up all de cawn! De crows a-pullin' up all de cawn!" [Imitation of a cock crowing.] An' de crows dey keep on sayin', "Cawn! Cawn! Cawn!" [Imitation of cawing.]

An' de sun keep a-gittin' hotter an' hotter, an' de folks in de big house didn' wake up, an' de crows kept on a-pullin' up de cawn. De ol' rooster he git more an' more excited an' lift up his voice a little higher an' say, "De crows a-pullin' up all de cawn! De crows a-pullin' up all de cawn! De crows a-pullin' up all de cawn!" An' de crows, way down in de fiel', keep on sayin', "Cawn! Cawn! Cawn!"

An' de sun keep a-gittin' hotter an' hotter, an' de folks in de big house didn' wake up, an' de crows keep on pullin' up de

* From *Negro Tales from West Virginia*, by John Harrington Cox, *The Journal of American Folklore*, Vol. XLVII (October-December, 1934), No. CLXXXVI, pp. 356–357. New York.

cawn. De ol' rooster he git more an' more excited an' lift his voice 'way up an' say, "De crows a-pullin' up all de cawn! De crows a-pullin' up all de cawn! De crows a-pullin' up all de cawn!" An' de crows, 'way down in de fiel', dey keep on a-sayin', "Cawn! Cawn! Cawn!"

By-m-by, de ol' turkey gobbler, a-settin' on de fence, he git excited, too. He flopped his wings er time er two, flew down inter de yahd, an' called as loud as he could, "Put! put! put! put! W'at de heck yer goin' ter do 'bout it? W'at de heck yer goin' ter do 'bout it? W'at de heck yer goin' ter do 'bout it?"

The Talking Mule*

OLE feller one time had uh mule. His name wuz Bill. Every mornin' de man go tuh ketch 'im he say, "Come round, Bill!"

So one mornin' he slept late, so he decided while he wuz drinkin' some coffee he'd send his son tuh ketch Ole Bill.

Told 'im say, "Go down dere, boy, and bring me dat mule up here."

Boy, he sich a fast Aleck, he grabbed de bridle and went on down tuh de lot tuh ketch Ole Bill.

He say, "Come round, Bill!"

De mule looked round at 'im. He told de mule, "Tain't no use you rollin' yo' eyes at *me*. Pa want yuh dis mawnin'. Come on round and stick yo' head in dis bridle."

Mule kept on lookin' at 'im and said, "Every mornin' it's 'Come round, Bill! Come round, Bill!' Don't hardly git no night rest befo' it's 'Come round, Bill!' "

De boy throwed down dat bridle and flew back tuh de house and told his Pa, "Dat mule is talkin'."

"Ah g'wan, boy, tellin' yo' lies! G'wan ketch dat mule."

"Naw suh, Pa, dat mule's done gone tuh talkin'. You hatta ketch dat mule yo' ownself. Ah ain't gwine."

Ole man looked at ole lady and say, "Se what uh lie dat boy is tellin'?"

So he gits out and goes on down after de mule hisself. When he got down dere he hollered, "Come round, Bill!"

Ole mule looked round and says, "Every mornin' it's come round, Bill!"

* From *Mules and Men*, by Zora Neale Hurston, pp. 217–218. Copyright, 1935, by Zora Neale Hurston. Philadelphia and London: J. B. Lippincott Company.

De old man had uh little fice dog useter foller 'im every-where he go, so he lit out wid de lil fice right behind 'im. So he told de ole lady, "De boy ain't told much of uh lie. Dat mule *is* talkin'. Ah never heered uh mule talk befo'."

Lil fice say, "Me neither."

De ole man got skeered agin. Right through de woods he went wid de fice right behind 'im. He nearly run hisself tuh death. He stopped and commenced blowin' and says, "Ah'm so tired Ah don't know whut tuh do."

Lil dog run and set down in front of 'im and went to hasslin'[4] and says, "Me too."

Dat man is runnin' yet.

Ole Massa and John
Who Wanted to Go to Heaven*

You know befo' surrender Ole Massa had a nigger name John and John always prayed every night befo' he went to bed and his prayer was for God to come git him and take him to Heaven right away. He didn't even want to take time to die. He wanted de Lawd to come git him just like he was—boot, sock and all. He'd git down on his knees and say: "O Lawd, it's once more and again yo' humble servant is knee-bent and body-bowed—my heart beneath my knees and my knees in some lonesome valley, crying for mercy while mercy kin be found. O Lawd, Ah'm astin' you in de humblest way I know how to be *so* pleased as to come in yo' fiery chariot and take me to yo' Heben and its immortal glory. Come Lawd, you know Ah have such a hard time. Ole Massa works me *so* hard, and don't gimme no time to rest. So come, Lawd, wid peace in one hand and pardon in de other and take me away from this sin-sorrowing world. Ah'm tired and Ah want to go home."

So one night Ole Massa passed by John's shack and heard him beggin' de Lawd to come git him in his fiery chariot and take him away; so he made up his mind to find out if John meant dat thing. So he goes on up to de big house and got hisself a bed sheet and come on back. He throwed de sheet over his head and knocked on de door.

* From *Mules and Men*, by Zora Neale Hurston, pp. 96–99. Copyright, 1935, by Zora Neale Hurston. Philadelphia and London: J. B. Lippincott Company.

John quit prayin' and ast: "Who dat?"

Ole Massa say: "It's me, John, de Lawd, done come wid my fiery chariot to take you away from this sin-sick world."

Right under de bed John had business. He told his wife: "Tell Him Ah ain't here, Liza."

At first Liza didn't say nothin' at all, but de Lawd kept right on callin' John: "Come on, John, and go to Heben wid me where you won't have to plough no mo' furrows and hoe no mo' corn. Come on, John."

Liza says: "John ain't here, Lawd, you hafta come back another time."

Lawd says: "Well, then Liza, you'll do."

Liza whispers and says: "John, come out from underneath dat bed and g'wan wid de Lawd. You been beggin' him to come git you. Now g'wan wid him."

John back under de bed not sayin' a mumblin' word. De Lawd out on de doorstep kept on callin'.

Liza says: "John, Ah thought you was so anxious to get to Heben. Come out and go on wid God."

John says: "Don't you hear him say 'You'll do'? Why don't you go wid him?"

"Ah ain't a goin' nowhere. Youse de one been whoopin' and hollerin' for him to come git you and if you don't come out from under dat bed Ah'm gointer tell God youse here."

Ole Massa makin' out he's God, says: "Come on, Liza, you'll do."

Liza says: "O, Lawd, John is right here underneath de bed."

"Come on John, and go to Heben wid me and its immortal glory."

John crept out from under de bed and went to de door and cracked it and when he seen all dat white standin' on de doorsteps he jumped back. He says: "O, Lawd, Ah can't go to Heben wid yo in yo' fiery chariot in dese old dirty britches; gimme time to put on my Sunday pants."

"All right, John, put on yo' Sunday pants."

John fooled around just as long as he could, changing them pants, but when he went back to de door, de big white glory was still standin' there. So he says agin: "O, Lawd, de Good Book says in Heben no filth is found and I got on dis dirty sweaty shirt. Ah can't go wid you in dis old nasty shirt. Gimme time to put on my Sunday shirt!"

"All right, John, go put on yo' Sunday shirt."

John took and fumbled around a long time changing his

shirt, and den he went back to de door, but Ole Massa was still on de doorstep. John didn't had nothin' else to change so he opened de door a little piece and says:

"O, Lawd, Ah'm ready to go to Heben wid you in yo' fiery chariot, but de radiance of yo' countenance is *so* bright, Ah can't come out by you. Stand back jus' a li'l way please."

Ole Massa stepped back a li'l bit.

John looked out agin and says: "O, Lawd, you know dat po' humble me is less than de dust beneath yo' shoe soles. And de radiance of yo' countenance is so bright Ah can't come out by you. Please, please, Lawd, in yo' tender mercy, stand back a li'l bit further."

Ole Massa stepped back a li'l bit mo'.

John looked out agin and he says: "O, Lawd, Heben is so high and wese so low; youse so great and Ah'm so weak and yo' strength is too much for us poor sufferin' sinners. So once mo' and agin yo' humber servant is knee-bent and body-bowed askin' you one mo' favor befo' Ah step into yo' fiery chariot to go to Heben wid you and wash in yo' glory—be so pleased in yo' tender mercy as to stand back jus' a li'l bit further."

Ole Massa stepped back a step or two mo' and out dat door John come like a streak of lightning. All across de punkin patch, thru de cotton over de pasture—John wid Ole Massa right behind him. By de time dey hit de cornfield John was way ahead of Ole Massa.

Back in de shack one of de children was cryin' and she ast Liza: "Mama, you reckon God's gointer ketch papa and carry him to Heben wid him?"

"Shet yo' mouf, talkin' foolishness!" Liza clashed at de chile. "You know de Lawd can't outrun yo' pappy—specially when he's barefooted at dat."

The Fortune Teller*

IN SLAVERY time dere was a colored man what was named John. He went along wid Ole Massa everywhere he went. He used to make out he could tell fortunes. One day him and his Ole Massa was goin' along and John said, "Ole Massa, Ah kin tell fortunes." Ole Massa made out he didn't pay him no attention. But when they got to de next man's plantation Ole

---

* *Ibid.*, pp. 111–112.

Massa told de landlord, "I have a nigger dat kin tell fortunes." So de other man said, "Dat nigger can't tell no fortunes. I bet my plantation and all my niggers against yours dat he can't tell no fortunes."

Ole Massa says: "I'll take yo' bet. I bet everything in de world I got on John 'cause he don't lie. If he say he can tell fortunes, he can tell 'em. Bet you my plantation and all my niggers against yours and throw in de wood lot extry."

So they called Notary Public and signed up de bet. Ole Massa straddled his horse and John got on his mule and they went on home.

John was in de misery all that night for he knowed he was gointer be de cause of Ole Massa losin' all he had.

Every mornin' John useter be up and have Ole Massa's saddle horse curried and saddled at de door when Ole Massa woke up. But *this* mornin' Ole Massa had to git John out of de bed.

John useter always ride side by side with Massa, but on de way over to de plantation where de bet was on, he rode way behind.

So de man on de plantation had went out and caught a coon and had a big old iron wash-pot turned down over it.

There was many persons there to hear John tell what was under de wash-pot.

Ole Massa brought John out and told him, say: "John, if you tell what's under dat wash-pot Ah'll make you independent, rich. If you don't, Ah'm goin' to kill you because you'll make me lose my plantation and every thing I got."

John walked 'round and 'round dat pot but he couldn't git de least inklin' of what was underneath it. Drops of sweat as big as yo' fist was rollin' off of John. At last he give up and said: "Well, you got de ole coon at last."

When John said that, Ole Massa jumped in de air and cracked his heels twice befo' he hit de ground. De man that was bettin' against Ole Massa fell to his knees wid de cold sweat pourin' off him. Ole Massa said: "John, you done won another plantation fo' me. That's a coon under that pot sho 'nuff."

So he give John a new suit of clothes and a saddle horse. And John quit tellin' fortunes after that.

The Bear Fight*

DEACON JONES an' he gal live in a section of de country wey dere been a heap er bears. An' one night he been guine to an experience meetin', an' dere been two roads, an' he gal say:

"Papa, le's we don't go through de woods road, kaze I seen a bear dere today."

An' de deacon say:

"I ain' care notin' 'bout no bear. I a Christian an' loves God an' God loves me, an' I puts my trust in Him. I loves God. God is good. I'm guine through dem woods."

An' de gal say:

"Papa, le's we don't make no mistakes. Le's we go 'round."

An' de deacon say:

"I'm guine through dem woods. I trust God. I puts my faith in God. God is good an' will pertec' me."

An' de gal say:

"I ain' trustin' all dat. I'm guine 'round."

An' de deacon say:

"Well, I'm guine through de woods. God is my pertecter."

An' he went through de woods, an' de gal went 'round.

An' when de deacon git half way through de woods, a bear jumped on him an' he had a terrible time fightin' wid dat bear. De bear tored mighty nigh all he clothes off, an' bit him up an' mighty nigh ruint him. But when he git loose, he made he way to de experience meetin'. An' when he git dere, dem niggers been tellin' 'bout dey experience wid God an' Jesus and de devil an' wid angels an' a passel er lies.

An' den dey spied Deacon Jones in de back er de congregation, an' dey call on him for his experience an' he say he ain' got nothin' to say. An' all dem brother an' all dem sister keep on hollerin' for him. An' atter while de deacon git up an' say:

"My brothers an' sisters, all I kin say is. God is good. God is good. I loves God. I sho' loves Him, an' I puts my faith in Him. God is good an' He'll help you in a lot er little things, but, my brothers an' sisters, good as God is, He ain' worth a damn in a bear fight."

---

* From *Nigger to Nigger*, by E. C. L. Adams, pp. 223–224. Copyright, 1928, by Charles Scribner's Sons. New York.

Story of a Cow*

Soon atter de negroes wus sot-free by Mr. Lincoln, two uv-um, by name uv Mose Smiff an Rastus Jones, cludes tuh buys a cow tuhgether, ez da lives on jinen places, an da goes ovah tuh a neighbor, an buys a cow fur $20.00 an each uv-um tuh pays $10.00 fur his haff.

Comin on back home, Mose say tuh Rastus: "Rastus, whut haff uv de cow you wants?" Rastus he say back: "I wants de front-en uv de cow." Mose say: "All right, I takes de hine-en fur mine." Few days later da goes ovah, pays fur de cow, an brings her back an turns her in Rastus' clover-patch, whar she main sevel days.

One mornin, Mose wife wake up an say: "Mose, aint you an Rastus Jones bought a cow tuther day?" He say: "Yes." She say: "Aint you done paid fur half de cow?" He say: "Yes." She say: "Whut haff uv de cow longs tuh you?" He says: "De hine-en uv de cow." She say: "Well era, ef de hine-en longs tuh you, how comes, yuh aint nuver looks atter yo-en, an melks de cow?" He say: "I hadnt thought uv dat." She say: "Now, you git-up an gits a bucket, an go ovah an melks dat cow, don't I gwina bus yo head wide-open wid a boad, nigger!"

Mose gits up an gits a bucket, an goes-ovah an says: "Rastus, aint me-en-you bought a cow tuther day?" He say: "Yes." Mose say: "Aint I done pay fur haff de cow, and tuck de hine-en?" He say: "Yes." Mose say: "Well era, I wants tuh melk my-en." Rastus say: "I been melkin de cow." Mose say: "De front en longs tuh you, an you tuh feeds de cow, an I tuh melks de cow!"

He Got the Possum**

Four of us went to Possom-hunting—Bill and John and Pete and I—all four of us niggers, and we didn't catch but one;

* From *Humorous Short Stories*, by Uncle Eaph (Jacob Thompson Johnson), pp. 35–36. Copyright, 1928, by Jacob T. Johnson. Atlanta, Ga.: Jacob T. Johnson Publishing Co.
** From *The Arkansaw Cracker Jack*, compiled by Taylor Beard, p. 17. Entered according to Act of Congress, in the year 1905, by the Rhodes & McClure Publishing Company, in the office of the Librarian of Congress, Washington, D. C. Chicago, Ill.

one possom, and we knew somebody would be without sweet potatoes and possom. So Bill said:

"I tell you what, we will all lay down and go to sleep, and the one that dreams the biggest dream will get the possom."

"All right," said we, and all laid down.

Bill dreamt that he was rich.

"Well, he got the possom."

"No, you forget, John was there, and he dreamt he was a millionaire."

"Oh, he got the possom."

"No, you forget, Pete was there; he dreamt he owned the whole round world."

"Well, that gives the possom to Pete."

"No, you forget that I was there yet."

"What did you dream?"

"I didn't go to sleep. I staid awake and got the possom myself. It is not the man that sleeps that gets the gravy, it's the man that stays awake."

The Three Dreams*

> Two Irishmen and a Hebrew one day
>   Went out for recreation.
> They took enough provisions along
>   To spend a week's vacation.
> One night they got lost in the woods;
>   The night was dark and lonely.
> At last the food they had gave out,
>   Except a piece of baloney.
> As one of them took up a knife,
>   I said, "It's no use of carving,
> For if we share this piece of baloney,
>   It won't keep us from starving."
> So I suggested we all go to sleep,
>   And so did Maloney.
> And the one that had the best of dreams
>   Wins the piece of baloney.
> The following morn we all got up,
>   It was quarter after seven.
> One of them said: "I had a dream,
>   I died and went to heaven;

* From The Journal of American Folk-Lore, Vol. XXXIV (July-September, 1921), No. CXXXIII, pp. 327–328.

St. Peter met me at the gate,
    Riding on a pony.
I guess that dream couldn't be beat,
    So that wins the piece of baloney."
The other one said: "I too had a dream;
    I died and went to heaven;
St. Peter met me at the gate,
    Stuck out his hand, and said, 'Hello, Maloney!'
I guess that dream couldn't be beat,
    So that wins the piece of baloney."
The Hebrew said: "It's true, my friend,
    That you were sleeping.
The reason why I know it is
    'Cause I was peeping.
I saw you both go up in heaven;
    And, believe me, I was lonely;
I thought you'd never come back again,
    So I got up and ate the baloney."

The Son Who Went to College*

A MAN and his wife had a boy and they thought so much of him that they sent him off to college. At de end of seven years, he schooled out and come home and de old man and his ma was real proud to have de only boy 'round there dat was book-learnt.

So de next mornin' after he come home, de ma was milkin' de cows and had one young cow dat had never been to de pail befo' and she used to kick every time anybody milked her.

She was actin' extry bad dat mornin' so de woman called her husband and ast him to come help her wid de cow. So he went out and tried to hold her, but she kept on rearin' and pitchin' and kickin' over de milk pail, so he said to his wife: "We don't need to strain wid dis cow. We got a son inside that's been to school for seben years and done learnt everything. He'll know jus' what to do wid a kickin' cow. Ah'll go call him."

So he called de boy and told him.

De boy come on out to de cow-lot and looked everything over. Den he said, "Mama cow-kickin' is all a matter of scien-

---

* From *Mules and Men*, by Zora Neale Hurston, pp. 163–164. Copyright, 1935, by Zora Neale Hurston. Philadelphia and London: J. B. Lippincott Company.

tific principle. You see before a cow can kick she has to hump herself up in the back. So all we need to do is to take the hump out the cow's back."

His paw said, "Son, Ah don't see how you gointer do dat. But 'course you been off to college and you know a heap mo' than me and yo' ma ever will know. Go 'head and take de hump outa de heifer. We'd be mighty much obliged."

De son put on his gold eyeglasses and studied de cow from head to foot. Then he said, "All we need to keep this animal from humping is a weight on her back."

"What kinda weight do she need, son?"

"Oh, any kind of a weight, jus' so it's heavy enough, papa," de son told him. "It's all in mathematics."

"Where we gointer git any weight lak dat, son?"

"Why don't you get up there, papa? You're just about the weight we need."

"Son, you been off to school a long time, and maybe you done forgot how hard it is for anybody to sit on a cow, and Ah'm gittin' old, you know."

"But, papa, I can fix that part, too. I'll tie your feet together under her belly so she can't throw you. You just get on up there."

"All right, son, if you say so, Ah'll git straddle of dis cow. You know more'n Ah do, Ah reckon."

So they tied de cow up short to a tree and de ole man got on by de hardest,[5] and de boy passed a rope under her belly and tied his papa on. De old lady tried to milk de cow but she was buckin' and rearin' so till de ole man felt he couldn't stand it no mo'. So he hollered to de boy, "Cut de rope, son, cut de rope! Ah want to git down."

Instead of de boy cuttin' loose his papa's feet he cut de rope dat had de cow tied to de tree and she lit out 'cross de wood wid de ole man's feet tied under de cow. Wasn't no way for him to git off.

De cow went bustin' on down de back-road wid de ole man till they met a sister he knowed. She was surprised to see de man on de cow, so she ast: "My lawd, Brother So-and-so, where you goin'?"

He tole her, "Only God and dis cow knows."

The Twist-Mouth Family*

THERE was once a father and a mother and several children, and all but one of them had their mouths twisted out of shape. The one whose mouth was not twisted was a son named John.

When John got to be a young man he was sent to college, and on the day he came home for his first vacation the family sat up late in the evening to hear him tell of all he had learned. But finally they prepared to go to bed, and the mother said, "Father, will you blow out the light?"

"Yes, I will," was his reply.

"Well, I wish you would," said she.

"Well, I will," he said.

So he blew, but his mouth was twisted, and he blew this way (the narrator shows how he did it—blowing upward), and he couldn't blow out the light.

Then he said, "Mother, will you blow out the light?"

"Yes, I will," was her reply.

"Well, I wish you would," said he.

"Well, I will," she said.

So she blew, but her mouth was twisted, and she blew this way (blowing downward) and she couldn't blow out the light.

Then she spoke to her daughter and said, "Mary, will you blow out the light?"

"Yes, I will," was Mary's reply.

"Well, I wish you would," said her mother.

"Well, I will," Mary said.

So Mary blew, but her mouth was twisted, and she blew this way (blowing out of the right corner of the mouth), and she couldn't blow out the light.

Then Mary spoke to one of her brothers and said, "Dick, will you blow out the light?"

"Yes, I will," was Dick's reply.

"Well, I wish you would," said Mary.

"Well, I will," Dick said.

So Dick blew, but his mouth was twisted, and he blew this

* By Clifton Johnson, Hadley, Mass. From *The Journal of American Folk-Lore*, Vol. XVIII (October–December, 1905), No. LXXI, pp. 322–323. Copyright, 1905, by the American Folk-Lore Society. Boston and New York: Houghton, Mifflin & Company.

way (blowing out of the left corner of the mouth), and he couldn't blow out the light.

Then Dick said, "John, will you blow out the light?"

"Yes, I will," was John's reply.

"Well, I wish you would," said Dick.

"Well, I will," John said.

So John blew, and his mouth was straight, and he blew this way (blowing straight), and he blew out the light.

The light was out and they were all glad that John had succeeded, and the father said, "What a blessed thing it is to have larnin'!"

Borrowing Trouble*

A FOLK-TALE common and often quoted by country people belonging to the States of New York and Ohio, in ridicule of those who unnecessarily "borrow trouble," is as follows:—

Once there was a girl. One day her mother came into the kitchen and found the girl sitting crying with all her heart. The mother said, "Why, what is the matter?" The girl replied, "Oh, I was thinking. And I thought how some day perhaps I might be married and how I might have a baby, and then I thought how one day when it would be asleep in its cradle the oven lid would fall on it and kill it," and she began to cry again.

A variant from Greenfield, Mass., which can be traced back fifty years, runs thus:—

A girl sat on a river bank crying. On being asked the cause of her grief, she replied, "Oh, I was thinking if I had a darter and my darter had a darter and she should fall into the warter, how dreadful it would be."

"Little Moron"**

THE little moron was nailing shingles on the house. Somebody noticed that he was throwing about half the nails away, and

---

* From "Borrowing Trouble," by Fanny D. Bergen, *The Journal of American Folk-Lore*, Vol. XI (January-March, 1898), No. XL, pp. 55–59. Copyright, 1898, by the American Folk-Lore Society.
** From "'Little Moron' Stories," by Ernest W. Baughman, *Hoosier Folklore Bulletin*, edited by Herbert Halpert, Vol. II (June, 1943), No. 1, pp. 17–18.

asked him why. "Because," said the little moron, "the heads are on the wrong ends." "Well, you dope," said the other, "those are for the other side of the house."

The little moron got up in the middle of the night to answer the telephone. "Is this one one one one?" says the voice. "No, this is eleven eleven." "You're sure it isn't one one one one?" "No, this is eleven eleven." "Well, wrong number. Sorry to have got you up in the middle of the night." "That's all right, mister. I had to get up to answer the telephone anyway."

Two little morons went hunting. The first one shot at a duck, and when it fell at his feet he felt bad that the little duck had died when he shot it. The other said, "Oh, don't feel so bad. The fall would have killed it anyway."

Little moron was painting the house when another one came up and said, "Got a good hold on that brush?" "Yep." "Well, if you are sure you got a good hold on that brush I'll borrow your ladder for a second." "O.K. but don't keep it long. The handle of this paint brush is kind of slippery."

Little moron's wife sent him down town after a bucket of ice. He came back with a pail of water. "I got this for half price because it was melted."

Little moron took two slices of bread and went down and sat on the street corner waiting for the traffic jam. A big truck came along and gave him a jar.

Why did the little moron go to the lumber yard?—To look for his draft board.

Then there was the little moron who broke his leg when he threw his cigarette butt down the manhole and tried to step on it.

And the one who took his nose apart to see what made it run.

Little moron tried to light his cigarette. He struck the first match on the seat of his pants, but it wouldn't light. He tried another. It wouldn't light. The third one finally lit. He lit his cigarette, carefully blew the match out and put it in his vest pocket. "What for did you put that match in your vest pocket." "That's a good match. I'll use it again."

Two little morons were in jail. They were trying to find a way out. "I know. I'll shine the flash light up to that window, you crawl up the beam and open that window." The other little moron objected. "Nothing doing. I'd get halfway up the beam and you'd turn the light off."

Absence of Mind*

I

A MAN, thinking he was at home, one evening lately, lay down on the common, and put his boots outside the gate to be blacked in the morning. Another person, after getting home one rainy night, put his umbrella in the bed, and leaned up in the corner himself.

II

We have just heard of a truly distressing instance of absence of mind, of which, we understand, our venerable friend, and contemporary, Mr. Bot Smith, was the victim. The other evening he proceeded bed-ward, as usual, and, in a fit of absence of mind, put the candle into the bed, *and blew himself out!*

III

The last "modern instance" recorded in the Yankee papers, is that of a Vermont waggoner going to market, who lifted his horse into the waggon, and tacked himself to the traces. The veracious chronicler adds, the waggoner did not discover his error until he endeavored to neigh!

T'other day a man in Baltimore, intending to wind up his watch, through a sudden attack of absence of mind, wound up himself. . . .

The *Nashville Observer* informs us of the following case of absence of mind, which took place in the person of an old lady, who, after stirring the fire with her knitting needle, proceeded to knit with the poker, and did not discover her error till she commenced scratching her head with it.

A woman in Ohio put her baby into the washing-tub, and its dirty frock and petticoat into the cradle, and set her little boy to rock it. She did not discover her mistake until the baby cried out when she pinned its left leg to the line, as she hung it out in the yard to dry.

We learn from the *Nashville Banner*, that a land-agent down there, by name Hiram S. Botts, having to ride out in

---

* From *Yankee Notions; or The American Joe Miller*, by Sam Slick, Junr., pp. 20, 28, 33, 39. London: Ball, Arnold & Co. Edinburgh: Fraser and Crawford. Glasgow: John Robertson. 1889.

great haste one day last week, actually clapped the saddle upon his own back instead of his mare's, and never found out the mistake till he was quite fatigued with vainly trying to get upon himself.

IV

A highly respectable inhabitant of the city of New York lately died under very remarkable circumstances. He was subject to fits of extreme absence of mind from childhood, and one night, upon retiring to bed, having carefully tucked his pantaloons under the bed-clothes, he threw himself over the back of a chair, and expired from the severe cold he experienced during the night.

Big Talk

I. COLOR[6]

THEN Gold spoke up and said, "Now, lemme tell one. Ah know one about a man as black as Gene."

"Whut you always crackin' me for?" Gene wanted to know. "Ah ain't a bit blacker than you."

"Oh, yes you is, Gene. Youse a whole heap blacker than Ah is."

"Aw, go head on, Gold. Youse blacker than me. You jus' look my color cause youse fat. If you wasn't no fatter than me you'd be so black till lightnin' bugs would follow you at twelve o'clock in de day, thinkin' it's midnight."

"Dat's a lie, youse blacker than Ah ever dared to be. Youse lam' black. Youse so black till they have to throw a sheet over yo' head so de sun kin rise every mornin'. Ah know yo' ma cried when she seen *you*."

"Well, anyhow, Gold, youse blacker than me. If Ah was as fat as you Ah'd be a yaller man."

"Youse a liar. Youse as yaller as you ever gointer git. When a person is poor he look bright and de fatter you git de darker you look."

"Is dat yo' excuse for being so black, Gold?"

II. AN UGLY MAN[7]

"Hey, Jim, where the swamp boss? He ain't got here yet."

"He's ill—sick in the bed Ah hope, but Ah bet he'll git here yet."

"Aw, he ain't sick. Ah bet you a fat man he ain't," Joe said.

"How come?" somebody asked him and Joe answered:

"Man, he's too ugly. If a spell of sickness ever tried to slip up on him, he'd skeer it into a three weeks' spasm."

Blue Baby[8] stuck in his oar and said: "He ain't so ugly. Ye all jus' ain't seen no real ugly man. Ah seen a man so ugly till he could get behind a jimpson weed and hatch monkeys."

Everybody laughed and moved closer together. Then Officer Richardson said: "Ah seen a man so ugly till they had to spread a sheet over his head at night so sleep could slip up on him."

They laughed some more, then Clifford Ulmer said:

"Ah'm goin' to talk with my mouth wide open. Those men y'all been talkin' 'bout wasn't ugly at all. Those was pretty men. Ah knowed one so ugly till you could throw him in the Mississippi river and skim ugly for six months."

"Give Cliff de little dog," Jim Allen said. "He done tole the biggest lie."

"He ain't lyin'," Joe Martin tole them. "Ah knowed dat same man. He didn't die—he jus' uglied away."

Slow Train*

TALK about your slow trains through Arkansaw and your snail specials over the Rockies, but I struck a train in Indiana that was sure enough slow. I got on it to go up the state about seventy-five miles. The thing ran so slow that I went to the conductor and said, "Look here, if you don't ginger the gait of this thing up a little, I'll get out and walk." He flared up and said, "Who's the boss of this train?" I said, "I suppose you are." He said, "Then dry up." I said, "Whose dead body have you on board?" He said, "Nobody's; why?" I said, "Because you're running so slow I thought maybe you were bossing a funeral procession." That made him still madder, and we hooked up. We jumped out on the right-o'-way, and the train running at full speed, and had a fight, and I knocked the breath out of him and ran down to a pond and got my hat full of water and poured it in his face and brought him to, and we both caught the hind end of the train as it came by—and it wasn't a long train either.

---

* From I Blew in from Arkansaw, A Trip of Fun through Hoosierdom, by Geo. D. Beason, pp. 48–49. Copyright, 1908, by Geo. D. Beason. Chicago: Geo. D. Beason, Publisher.

But the walloping I gave the conductor didn't make the thing go any faster. A fellow standing on the side of the track held up a knife and hollered, "Got a frog-sticker yer want to swap?" I lit out and looked his knife over, swapped with him and skinned him too bad to talk about, and caught the hind end of the train again as it came by. I went to the conductor next day and apologized for banging him up. He said, "Oh, that's all right. The only thing I regret is, I lost my cap back where we had the fight." I said, "I'll go back and get it." He said, "Don't put yourself to any trouble." I said, "It won't be any trouble." I went back and got his cap and caught up with the train at the next station.

I was on the slow outfit so long that I wore out one of the cushion seats, and had train sores. You may think I'm over-drawing it, but I'm not, when I tell you that a fellow took down with typhoid fever on the thing just after I got on, and when I got off at the end of my journey, he was sound and well, and he had a long siege of it, too.

Umpire Bait, and Jollys for Pitchers and Batters*

THAT base isn't made for a shelter, get into the open.

My kindergarten was the Polo Ground bleachers.

The first spiral staircase was built after the design of my fast curve.

Every time I swing the bat they have to give the ball a hydraulic treatment to coax it back into shape.

He couldn't hit a bunch of bananas with a bass fiddle.

Every time that Umps starts talking his tongue gets twisted around his eye tooth and he can't see what he's saying.

Data boy smoke, hit him on the head, you can't hurt him there.

Long fly to the pitcher, that's his noise.

Like a gate the way he swings.

Let him hit, let him hit, I got it.

He hasn't any more on that ball than September Morn wears.

Shut the gate, Nanny is wandering.

* From *Choice Slang*, by High Jinks Junior [Harold Poe Swartwood], pp. 74–75. Copyright, 1915, by The Coronodo Company.

He hasn't got a thing today, but a grin and a belt buckle.

On the hill with nothing but a glove and a prayer.

You're not so rotten, kid, in about forty years you'll be a ball player.

This fellow is made to order for you, get up there and sting one.

Let's pick him to pieces, piece by piece, and see what makes him tick.

Take him out, get the hook, the hook.

He never touched me, Umps, I'll leave it to you.

If rags were ribbon, you'd be silk.

Look out, you fellows on the bench, this bloat at bat is liable to spike you.

Come on, Smoke, old boy, give him the spitter.

That ball was so low it would have to reach up to touch bottom.

Put on your chains, Umps, you're skidding.

Cancel that rave, Umps.

A cozy corner in the nuttery for yours.

Back to the oven, you aren't done yet.

Is this a union of some kind? Does everybody strike?

Come on fellows, keep working. We gotta beat ten men, but one of them is blind.

I Should Worry———*

LIKE a ball and get bounced.

Like a button and get the hook.

Like a chandelier and get lit up every night.

Like dice and get shaken.

Like an elephant and carry my trunk.

Like a fresh clam and get the lemon.

Like a fireman and lose my hose.

Like glue and stick around.

Like a hat and order a colored band.

Like a lump of butter and get strong.

Like the ocean and get fresh like the lakes.

Like a patrol wagon and do in a pinch.

Like a peanut and get roasted.

Like a peninsula and stretch out to see.

Like a pin cushion and get all stuck up.

* *Ibid.*, pp. 105–106.

Like a piano stool and go for a spin.
Like a plumber and get all around the joints.
Like a railroad track and get some new ties.
Like a raisin and go on a bun.
Like a rolling pin and gather the dough.
Like a smokestack and get all puffed up.
Like a tree and get trimmed.
Like a washboard and get full of wrinkles.
Like a window washer and feel a pain.

"You Tell 'Em" English*

You tell 'em, mail carrier,
You're a man of letters!

You tell 'em,
My tongue's in my shoe!

You tell 'em, powder puff,
My lips stick.

You tell 'em, parcel post,
I can't express it.

You tell 'em, pony,
I'm a little horse.

You tell 'em, corsets,
You've been around women longer than I have.

You tell 'em, salad,
I'm dressing.

You tell 'em, Sahara,
You've got the sand.

You tell 'em, pieface,
You've got the crust.

You say it, goldfish,
You've been around the globe.

---

* From *Stuff That Travels*, by William G. Bradshaw, pp. 37, 51. Copyright,
1921, by William G. Bradshaw. Saratoga Springs, New York.

You tell 'em, victrola,
You've got the record.

You tell 'em, coffee,
You've got the grounds.

You tell 'em, little stream,
You've been through the mill.

You tell 'em, toothache,
You've got the nerve.

She Was Only a Daughter*

SHE was only a professor's daughter, but she learned her lesson.

She was only a fireman's daughter, but she sure did go to blazes.

She was only the tailor's daughter, but she pressed well.

She was only a photographer's daughter, but she delivered the goods.

She was only an electrician's daughter, but she had good connections.

She was only a blacksmith's daughter, but she knew how to forge ahead.

She was only a milkman's daughter, but she was the cream of the crop.

She was only a convict's daughter, but she knew all the bars.

She was only the parson's daughter, but she had her following.

She was only an acrobat's daughter, but she never turned over.

She was only a convict's daughter, but she knew when to faint.

She was only a florist's daughter, but she potted all the pansies.

She was only a dairyman's daughter, but what a calf.

She was only a woodcutter's daughter, but she hadn't been axed.

She was only a barber's daughter, but what a mug she had.

She was only a surgeon's daughter, but oh what a cut-up.

* From *Laughter for the Millions*, The Drollest Wit, The Funniest Gags, The Gayest Laughs, The Merriest Humor, The Greatest Hilarity, edited by Louis Shomer, p. 117. Copyright, 1938, by Louis Shomer. New York: Louellen Publishing Co.

Knock Knock, Who's There?*

CHESTER. Chester who? Chester song at twilight.

Cecil. Cecil who? Cecil have music wherever she goes.

Hoffman. Hoffman who? I'll hoffman I'll puff an' I'll blow yer house in.

Gretta. Gretta who? Gretta long little doggie—gretta long.

Gwen. Gwen who? Gwen an' out the winda. Gwen an' out the winda.

Shixa. Shixa who? Shixa one—half dozen of another.

Argo. Argo who? Argo chase yerself.

Hiram. Hiram who? Hiram I doin' hey hey.

Morris. Morris who? Morris Saturday—next day's Sunday.

Marcella. Marcella who? Marcella's fulla water.

Major. Major who? Major answer the door didn't I?

Thermos. Thermos who? Thermos be some one wait-ting who feels the way I do.

Arthur. Arthur who? Arthur any more at home like you?

Agatha. Agatha who? Agatha feeling you're foolin'.

Mortimer. Mortimer who? Mortimer pitied than scorned.

Akron. Akron who? Akron give you anything but love baby.

Alby. Alby who? Alby glad when you're dead you rascal you.

Hassan. Hassan who? Hassan a body here seen Kelly?

Irving. Irving who? Irving a good time wisha were here.

Upton. Upton who? Just upton and downtown.

Dick. Dick who? Dick 'em up—I'm tongue-tied.

Bob. Bob who? Bob ba black sheep hevya eny wool?

Cigarette. Cicarette who? Cigarette life if ya don't weaken.

Domino. Domino who? Domino thing if ya ain't got that swing.

Fletcher. Fletcher who? Fletcher self go—relax an' fletcher self go.

Wendy. Wendy who? Wendy moon comes over the mountain.

Sonia. Sonia who? Sonia shanty in ol' shanty town.

Igloo. Igloo who? Igloo through here—the music goes down an' round.

---

* From *Knock Knock*, Featuring Enoch Knox, by Bob Dunn. Copyright, 1936, by Whitman Publishing Co. Racine, Wisconsin. Published by Dell Publishing Company, Inc. New York.

Caesar. Caesar who? Caesar jolly good fellow, caesar jolly good fellow.

Ennui. Ennui who? I'm a dreamer, ennui all?

Thistle. Thistle who? Thistle be a lesson to me.

Tex. Tex who? Tex us to pull a good one, don't it?

Pettygil. Pettygil who? Pettygil is like a melody.

Edsall. Edsall who? Edsall there is—there is no more.

Phrases of the People*

PUT yo' brains in a jaybird's head an' he'd fly backwards.

Jump down your throat an' gallup your insides out.

Yessuh, my little boy he's tol'able honest for his age.

Dat road got littler an' littler til it jest run up a tree.

Been ponderin' so hard I ain't had time to think.

Got de hookworm hustle.

Mouth's so wide ef 'twarn't for his ears de top of his head would be an island.

Steppin' high like a rooster in deep mud.

When dat preacher leaves my house I steps out in de backyard an' counts my chickens.

*   *   *   *   *

I give him thunder an' lightning stewed down to a fine pizen.

Dat white cussed me from de birth o' Saul an' Silas to de death o' de devil, an' called me ev'ything 'cept a child o' God.

Cunnel, dat nigger sprinkled dis here peedee root an' love powders over me, an' dat's what fust injuced me to commit love.

So lazy yo' vittles don't taste good.

Water's so low dat de garfishes is gittin' freckle-faced.

Got tuk down drunk.

A fool's tongue is long enough to cut his throat.

Money thinks I'm dead.

You ain't got enough sense to deliver a chaw of tobacco in a spittoon.

The bosom of his trousers.

*   *   *   *   *

* From "Phrases of the People," recorded by Harris Dickson, Vicksburg, Mississippi, in *American Stuff*, An Anthology of Prose & Verse by Members of the Federal Writers' Project, pp. 149–152. Copyright, 1937, by The Guilds' Committee for Federal Writers' Publications, Inc. The Viking Press. New York.

Make your face look like a dime's wuth o' dog meat.

Jaybird jabber. [Gabble of women.]

Ef you wants to see how much folks is goin' to miss you, jest stick yo' finger in de pond den pull it out an' look at de hole.

Cavortin' like a fat pony in high oats.

Make a straight coattail. [Scared man running.]

Grinnin' like a baked 'possum.

Lean hound for a long race and a poor man for chillun.

So hongry my belly think's my throat's cut.

Cluttered with trouble.

Dat nigger ain't skeered o' work; he'll lie down beside de biggest kind o' job an' go to sleep.

* * * * *

Enjoyin' poor health.

Swamp's so dry dere's four million bullfrogs ain't never learned how to swim.

Dat ooman's nine years older'n God.

A mighty miration. [Make a to-do.]

De devil gits up when de sun goes down, an' comes to plow his field.

Life is short an' full o' blisters.

Wish I was at home sick in bed.

"How is you today?" "Po'ly, thank God!"

Heap o' stir an' no biskits.

Busy as a bumblebee in a bucket of tar.

Don't remember yo' name, but I knows yo' favor.

Why don't you put sugar in yo' shoes to coax yo' breeches down?

Rather tell a lie on credit dan de truth for cash.

Yo' head's a-blossomin' fer de grave.

Overspoke myself.

Got d' runnin' off at de mouth.

Honest farmer puts straight wood on de outside his load.

On dat day seven women shall take hold of one man.

Dey 'scused me wrongful. [False charge of crime.]

A dunghill gentleman.

Beat him into doll rags.

It's agin nature and can't be did.

Afterclaps can go to the devil.

In a turkey dream.

Handful o' the dockyments. [Playing cards.]

Wake, snakes, day's a-breakin'.

Busted to flinderjigs.
See him deep in hell as a pigeon can fly in a week.
Rich as mud.
A dog will cry if you beat him with a bone.
Tread in my footsteps ef you can spraddle far enough.
Full of wrath and cabbage.
Manhood distended his hide.
Whip you from the point of a dagger to the anchor of a
ship.

The Proverbs of a People

I[9]

A code arrives; language; lingo; slang;
behold the proverbs of a people, a nation:
Give 'em the works. Fix it, there's always
a way. Be hard boiled. The good die young.

Be a square shooter. Be good; if you can't
be good be careful. When they put you in
that six foot bungalow, that wooden kimono,
you're through and that's that.

The higher they go the farther they drop.
The fewer the sooner. Tell 'em. Tell 'em.
Make 'em listen. They got to listen when
they know who you are. Don't let 'em know
what you got on your hip. Hit 'em where
they ain't. It's good for whatever ails
you and if nothing ails you it's good for
that. Where was you raised—in a barn?

They're a lot of muckers, tin horns; show
those slobs where they get off at. Tell 'em
you're going to open a keg of nails. Beat 'em
to a fare-thee-well. Hand 'em the razz-berries.
Clean 'em and then give 'em car-fare home.
Maybe all you'll get from 'em you can put in
your ear, anyhow.

They got a fat nerve to try to tie a can
on you. Send 'em to the cleaners. Put the
kibosh on 'em so they'll never come back.
You don't seem to know four out of five
have pyorrhea in Peoria.

Your head ain't screwed on wrong, I trust.
Use your noodle, your nut, your think tank,
your skypiece. God meant for you to use it.
If they offer to let you in on the ground
floor take the elevator.
Put up a sign: Don't worry; it won't last;
nothing does. Put up a sign: In God we
trust, all others pay cash. Put up a sign:
Be brief, we have our living to make. Put
up a sign: Keep off the grass.

Aye, behold the proverbs of a people:
The big word is Service.
Service—first, last and always.
Business is business.
What you don't know won't hurt you.
Courtesy pays.
Fair enough.
The voice with a smile.
Say it with flowers.
Let one hand wash the other.
The customer is always right.
Who's your boy friend?
Who's your girl friend?
O very well.
God reigns and the government at Washington lives.
Let it go at that.
There are lies, damn lies and statistics.
Figures don't lie but liars can figure.
There's more truth than poetry in that.
You don't know the half of it, dearie.
It's the roving bee that gathers the honey.
A big man is a big man whether he's a president or a prizefighter.
Name your poison.
Take a little interest.
Look the part.
It pays to look well.
Be yourself.
Speak softly and carry a big stick.
War is hell.
Honesty is the best policy.
It's all in the way you look at it.
Get the money—honestly if you can.
It's hell to be poor.
Well, money isn't everything.
Well, life is what you make it.
Speed and curves—what more do you want?
I'd rather fly than eat.
There must be pioneers and some of them get killed.

The grass is longer in the backyard.
Give me enough Swedes and snuff and I'll build a railroad to hell.
How much did he leave? All of it.
Can you unscramble eggs?
Early to bed and early to rise and you never meet any prominent
    people.
Let's go. Watch our smoke. Excuse our dust.
Keep your shirt on.

II

Come on, superstition, and get my goat.[10]
I got mascots.
The stars of my birthday favor me.
The numbers from one to ten are with me.
I was born under a lucky star and nothing can stop me.
The moon was a waxing moon and not a waning moon when I was
    born.
Every card in the deck and both of the seven-eleven bones are
    with me.
So you hear them tell it and they mean if it works it's good and
    if it don't it costs nothing.
How to win love, how to win games, the spells and conjurations
    are named for fever, burns, convulsions, snakebite, milksick,
    balking horses, rheumatism, warts.
"Tie the heart of a bat with a red silk string to your right arm and
    you will win every game at which you play."
If your right foot itches you will soon start on a journey, if it's
    your left foot you will go where you are not wanted.
If you sing before breakfast you will cry before night, if you
    sneeze before breakfast you will see your true love before
    Saturday night.
Lightning in the north means rain, lightning in the south means
    dry weather.
Frost three months after the first katydid is heard. Three white
    frosts and then a rain.

Even a lousy cur has his lucky days.
Sweep dirt out of the door after night and
    you sweep yourself out of a home.
Shake the tablecloth out of doors after sunset
    and you will never marry.
The first to drive a hearse is the next to die.
Kill cats, dogs or frogs and you die in rags.
Point at a shooting star or even speak of it and
    you lose your next wish.

Better born lucky than rich.
Marry in May, repent always.
May is the month to marry bad wives.

The son of the white hen brings luck.
So does a horse with four white feet.

He planted gravel and up came potatoes.
When a bitch litters pigs that is luck.
The lucky fellow gets eggs from his rooster
and his hen eggs have two yolks.
Luck for the few, death for the many.

What have you above the ears?[11]
Or are you dead from the neck up?
If you don't look out for yourself nobody else will.
What counts most is what you got under your own hat.
Your best friend is yourself.
Every man for himself and the devil take the hindmost.
I'm the only one of my friends I can count on.
I'm not in the business for my health.
I'm a lone wolf; I work by myself.
I'm for me, myself and company.
Who said you could work this side of the street?

The rich own the land and the poor own the water.[12]
The rich get richer and the poor get children.
The rich have baby napkins, and the poor have diapers.
The big houses have small families and the small
houses big families.
Why did Death take the poor man's cow and the rich
man's child?

The mazuma, the jack, the shekels, the kale,[13]
The velvet, the you-know-what,
The what-it-takes, a roll, a wad,
Bring it home, boy.
Bring home the bacon.
Start on a shoestring if you have to.
Then get your first million.
The second million is always easier than the first.
And if you get more of them round iron men than you can use
you can always throw them at the birds: it's been done.
Now take some men, everything they touch turns into money:
they know how the land lays: they can smell where the
dollars grow.
Money withers if you don't know how to nurse it along: money
flies away if you don't know where to put it.
The first question is, Where do we raise the money, where is the
cash coming from?
A little horse sense helps: an idea and horse sense take you far:
if you got a scheme ask yourself, Will it work?
And let me put one bug in your ear: inside information helps:
how many fortunes came from a tip, from being on the

ground first, from hearing a piece of news, from fast riding, early buying, quick selling, or plain dumb luck?

Yes, get Lady Luck with you and you're made: some fortunes were tumbled into and the tumblers at first said, Who would have believed it? and later, I knew just how to do it.

Yes, Lady Luck counts: before you're born pick the right papa and mama and the news-reel boys will be on the premises early for a shot of you with your big toe in your mouth.

The cauliflower is a cabbage with a college education.[14]
All she needs for housekeeping is a can opener.
    They'll fly high if you give them wings.
Put all your eggs in one basket and watch that basket.
Everybody talks about the weather and nobody does anything about it.
The auk flies backward so as to see where it's been.
    Handle with care women and glass.
    Women and linen look best by candlelight.
One hair of a women draws more than a team of horses.
Blessed are they who expect nothing for they shall not be disappointed.
You can send a boy to college but you can't make him think.
The time to sell is when you have a customer.
Sell the buffalo hide after you have killed the buffalo.
The more you fill a barrel the more it weighs unless you fill it with holes.
A pound of iron or a pound of feathers weighs the same.
Those in fear they may cast pearls before swine are often lacking in pearls.
May you live to eat the hen that scratches over your grave.
He seems to think he's the frog's tonsils but he looks to me like a plugged nickel.
If you don't like the coat bring back the vest and I'll give you a pair of pants.
The coat and the pants do the work but the vest gets the gravy.
"You are singing an invitation to summer," said the teacher, "you are not defying it to come."

> Where you been so long?[15]
> What good wind blew you in?
> Snow again, kid, I didn't get your drift.
> Everything now is either swell or lousy.
> "It won't be long now," was answered,
> "The worst is yet to come."

> Why repeat? I heard you the first time.[16]
> You can lead a horse to water, if you've
>   got the horse.
> The rooster and the horse agreed not to
>   step on each other's feet.

The caterpillar is a worm in a raccoon coat going for a college education.

The cockroach is always wrong when it argues with the chicken.

If I hadn't done it Monday somebody else would have done it Tuesday.

Money is like manure—good only when spread around.

You're such a first-class liar I'll take a chance with you.

A short horse is soon curried.

A still pig drinks the swill.

Small potatoes and few in a hill.

A fat man on a bony horse: "I feed myself —others feed the horse."

No peace on earth with the women, no life anywhere without them.

Some men dress quick, others take as much time as a woman.

"You're a liar." "Surely not if you say so."

He tried to walk on both sides of the street at once.

He tried to tear the middle of the street in two.

"When is a man intoxicated?" "When he tries to kiss the bartender good-night."

"He says he'll kick me the next time we meet. What'll I do?" "Sit down."

He's as handy as that bird they call the elephant.

Now that's settled and out of the way what are you going to do next?

"From here on," said the driver at an imaginary line near the foothills of the Ozarks, "the hills don't get any higher but the hollers get deeper and deeper."

So slick he was his feet slipped out from under him.

The ground flew up and hit him in the face.

Trade it for a dog, drown the dog, and you'll be rid of both of them.

There'll be many a dry eye at his funeral.

"Which way to the post-office, boy?" "I don't know." "You don't know much, do you?" "No, but I ain't lost."

They have Irish bulls timeworn and mossgrown:[17]
You are to be hanged and I hope it will prove a warning to you.
I took so much medicine I was sick a long time after I got well.

I can never get these boots on till I have worn them for a while.
One of us must kill the other—let it be me. We were boys together
    —at least I was.
If all the world were blind what a melancholy sight it would be.
This will last forever and afterward be sold for old iron.
They would cut us into mince-meat and throw our bleeding heads
    on the table to stare us in the face.
On the dim and faroff shore of the future we can see the footprint
    of an unseen hand.
We pursue the shadow, the bubble bursts, and leaves in our hands
    only ashes.

> "Ah there tootsie woosie," has its day
>   till the good old summertime has gone
>   with the kit and caboodle of its day
>   into the second-hand bins, the rummage sales,
>   and another whim emerges in, "Okay toots!"

You can't come back to a home unless it was a[18]
    home you went away from.
Between hay and grass neither one nor the other.
Can't you be useful as well as ornamental?
Why don't you go roll a peanut around the corner?
    When did they let you out?
The mules went to ask horns and came back without ears.
When you get hold of a good thing freeze onto it.
    Nothing to do and all day to do it in.
So dumb he spent his last dollar buying a pocketbook to put it in.
    A little more sandpaper and this will be smooth.
Write on one side of the paper and both sides of the subject.
Swear to it on a stack of Bibles and they wouldn't believe you.
    Be not a baker if your head be of butter.
Yesterday? It's a nickel thrown on a Salvation Army drum.
How could I let go when it was all I could do to hold on?
Thousands drink themselves to death before one dies of thirst.
    He didn't have much till he married a hunk of tin.
    There's always a nut on every family tree.
    The mosquitoes organized and drove me out of bed.
We'll fight till hell freezes over and then write on the ice, "Come
    on, you bastards."

> "Is it far to the next town?"[19]
>   asked the Arkansas traveller
>   who was given the comfort:
>   "It seems farther than it is
>   but you'll find it ain't."

> Six feet six was Davy Tipton
> and he had the proportions

as kingpin Mississippi River pilot
nearly filling the pilothouse
as he took the wheel with a laugh:
"Big rivers ought to have big men."

"A long, tall man won't always make a good fireman," said the
Santa Fe[20] engineer to a couple of other rails deadheading
back. "Out of a dozen wants to be firemen you can pick 'em.
Take one of these weakly fellers he'll do his best but he's all
gone time you get nine miles. Take a short, stout feller, low
down so he can get at his coal, and he'll beat one of those
tall fellers has to stoop. But if a tall feller's got long arms he
can do wonders. I knowed one engineer used to say he had a
fireman he never saw him throw a shovel of coal on the fire
—his arms was so long he just reached and laid the coal on!"

He can turn around on a dime.
He has an automobile thirst and a wheelbarrow income.
I don't know where I'm going but I'm on my way.
I'll knock you so high in the air you'll starve coming down.
A bonanza is a hole in the ground owned by a champion liar.
All you get from him you can put in your eye.
He tried to get a bird in the hand and two in the bush but what he
got was a horse of another color.
If the government tried to pay me for what I don't know there
wouldn't be enough money in all the mints to pay me.
You can't tell him anything because he thinks he knows more now
than he gets paid for.
It's a slow burg—I spent a couple of weeks there one day.
He bit off more than he could chew.
Don't take a mouthful bigger than your mouth.
Let's take it apart to see how it ticks.
If we had a little ham we could have some ham and eggs if we
had some eggs.
He always takes off his hat when he mentions his own name.
What's the matter with him? The big I, always the big I.
"Why didn't you zigzag your car and miss him?" "He was zigzag-
ging himself and outguessed me."
"Are you guilty or not guilty?" "What else have you?"
"Are you guilty or not guilty?" "I stands mute."

Part Four

*

Liars

I

YARNS AND TALL TALES

1. The Art of Casual Narrative: The Yarn

A YARN is a long, rambling, extravagant tale, with that quality of deliberate casualness and improvisation which stamps the "humorous story," in Mark Twain's view, as the distinctive development of story-telling in America.

The humorous story may be spun out to great length, and may wander around as much as it pleases, and arrive nowhere in particular; but the comic and witty stories must be brief and end with a point.

In Mark Twain's distinction between the comic or witty story and the humorous story is implied the difference between the anecdote and the yarn—a difference in form, style, and structure, based on a difference in purpose. Since the purpose of the anecdote as a wise or witty story is to make or illustrate a point, its business is to get to the point as quickly as possible (but not too quickly) and to make it clear and unmistakable. To that end the anecdote is bright and snappy, as brisk in movement as it is sharp in point. Since the purpose of the yarn is to create an effect of the odd, grotesque, or whimsical and to accumulate a certain kind of detail in order to produce that effect, the yarn takes its time, building up a good case for itself and delaying the ending or let-down, which is frequently an anti-climax.

The difference is essentially one of timing. The anecdote is closer to the short story, and the yarn to the sketch or tale in tempo. Whereas the former moves directly toward its goal, with, as the short-story text-books put it, the greatest economy of means that is consistent with the utmost emphasis, the latter is leisurely, even to the point of being long-winded, and profuse to the point of diffuseness. The prolixity of the yarn is an oral quality, reflecting the relaxed mood of men who sit around and swap stories. While the anecdote suggests the give-and-take of conversational repartee, the yarn tends toward the monolog and garrulousness, with all the repetitions and digressions of monopolizing talk. In print the yarn becomes a mock-oral tale, imitating the slow drawl and sprawling ease of spoken, spontaneous narrative.

The enormous popularity of the mock-oral yarn which was the vehicle of backwoods and frontier humorists in the thirties is due as much to the naturalness and informality of the medium as to the genuineness of its humor. The humble art of humble life, the yarn presupposes leisure and loquacity. It was something both the teller and the listener could sink their teeth into. Though it may have lost its appeal for a generation used to a snappier lore, it still has the freshness that marked the discovery made by its first literary practitioners—the discovery that "something old in talking might look new in writing."[1]

As in the case of "The Celebrated Jumping Frog of Calaveras County," the same story may be told as an anecdote or as a yarn. Based on a bit of mining-camp lore of the gold rush days, Mark Twain's version is a perfect example of oral, vernacular humorous story-telling.

2. STRETCHING FACTS: THE TALL TALE

A special, and to some the most distinctive, type of yarn is the tall tale. "Exuberant combinations of fact with outrageous fiction," in Walter Blair's definition, tall tales originate when the delicate balance between truth and untruth is turned in favor of the latter. "Some of the incidents I know to be true," writes the narrator of "The Wind," "—just enough truth in them to make good story material and to incite the imagination to try to improve on actual happenings."

This improving on actual happenings rather than outright lying is the distinguishing feature of the tall tale, which carries it beyond the mere incongruity or absurdity of the yarn and saves it from the whole-cloth invention of the ordinary whopper. The tall tale has a twofold relation to fact. On the one hand, as in the tall tales which were the chief stock-in-trade of Southern and Western humorists of the 1830's and 1840's, the eccentric or outlandish traits of backwoods and frontier life are singled out for realistic portrayal, the object being to create a "cumulative effect of the grotesque, romantic, or humorous." On the other hand, as in the later development of the genre, the prevailing interest is in the freaks of nature and in establishing a circumstantial basis for sub-human or superhuman marvels. In either case, the incongruity proceeds partly from the contrast between fact and fancy and is enhanced by enclosing the story in a realistic framework and employing the traditional device of the frame-tale, or group of stories within a story. This tendency of tall tales to grow and move in cycles also leads to their attraction about a central figure or hero of the Paul Bunyan variety.

Old-timers' reminiscences seem to make the best tall tales, all things considered, because the tricks of memory and distance come to the aid of the imagination in improving on actual happenings, while the exaggerations themselves are mellowed by time and immunized against criticism by the venerability that belongs to the narrator's years. Personal reminiscences gain further credence from the fact that they are the first-hand accounts of eye-witnesses or participants, backed up by the expressed or implied guarantee of "I saw or heard (if not actually did) these things myself." Sometimes the narrator employs the device of quoting an informant, named or unnamed, "long since dead" or lost track of, or of drawing upon travels (his own or some one else's) to report the wonders of distant places beyond checking up on. Credibility is also established by liberal use of local color and circumstantial detail.

In spite of the pretense of verisimilitude, which smacks of a hoax, the tall tale deals frankly with marvels, with the remarkable or prodigious, as the epithet signifies. As J. Frank Dobie points out, the tall-tale teller does not expect to be believed, except by the uninitiated. His task is essentially that of the poet; namely, to heighten fact and deal in illusions by creating a mood and an atmosphere favorable to the "willing suspension of disbelief that constitutes poetic faith." In "The Wind," for example, to the usual embellishments of garrulous elaboration and digression, the narrator adds the poetry of odd comparisons and conceits, akin to the hyperbole of tall talk. In these tales the wind itself, "pesky" and "cavortin'," takes on some of the attributes of poetic personification, playing pranks and performing miracles like any mythical hero.

The use of freaks of nature for tall tale material is associated not only with the experience of old-timers and travelers in their capacity as historians of the primitive type of a Herodotus or as naturalists of the credulous order of a Pliny but also with the American habit of boosting (as in stories of healthful climate and fertile soil) or boasting (as in brags of hunting and fishing) and with the pioneer trait of "laughing it off," or making light of misfortunes. Next to rural brags and gags, the most fertile source of tall tales is industry and remarkable inventions, an expression of the mechanical genius of Americans which has flowered in folklore ranging from Yankee contraptions like the bone-picking machine to the large-scale contrivances of Paul Bunyan. The bone-picking machine is of the same breed as the automatic feeder in Chaplin's *Modern Times*.

"I've got a new machine," said a Yankee pedlar, "for picking bones out of fish. Now, I tell you, it's a leetle bit the darndest thing you ever did see. All you have to do is to set it on a table and turn a crank, and the fish flies right down your throat and the bones right under the grate. Well, there was a country greenhorn got hold of it the other day, and he turned the crank the wrong way; and, I tell you, the way the bones flew down his throat was awful. Why, it stuck that fellow so full of bones, that he could not get his shirt off for a whole week!"[2]

3. TALL TALES OF OCCUPATIONS

In a sense, most yarns of cowboys, miners, lumberjacks, farmers may be considered occupational—the sense, namely, of involving experiences encountered in the course of making a living. A true occupational tale, however, is told by as well as about workers and gives the feel of the job—something of how the work is done and how the workers feel about it. Although frequently incorporating sayings, jokes, and anecdotes that go the rounds, occupational tall tales are traditional tales which fall midway between the more esoteric or technical lore of the group and popular jokes and stories. They are to be distinguished also from the stories of practical jokes in which new hands are sent in search of impossible objects and from the legendary cycles of the Paul Bunyan type, into which these occupational tall tales may grow.

Like the best tall tales, occupational tall tales have a strong realistic and sociological coloring, even to a note of social criticism and protest. Although boastful, in the ring-tailed roarer tradition, they temper their brags with humorous complaints of hard work and bad conditions and with satire at the expense of bosses and fellow-workers. The spirit of an ironic Joe Hill hovers over a fable like "Crumbs," which has passed beyond the stage of glorification of the timber beast to the militant stage of Wobbly unrest.

At the same time occupational tall tales tell us much of the inside story of craftsmanship and industry and what happens when machine labor displaces hand labor and when one kind of tool is outmoded by another. Technological changes and differences give rise to feuds and contests, involving deeds of prodigious strength or skill. Rivalries take such subtle forms as the feud between cable-tool drillers and rotary workers in the oil fields or such obvious forms as the feud between old and new hands. Resentment against the machine and nostalgia for the good old days also creep in as normal reactions of displaced hand workers.

The language of the tales is colored by occupations, both in the use of technical terms and trade slang and in the sprinkling of all talk of men who work with their hands. In spite of the fact that freaks of machinery have replaced freaks of nature as subjects of these tall tales, there is a distinct hangover of the frontier-hero tradition of strong men and tough customers—hell-raisers or star performers. "I'm a man as is work-brickle," says the Demon Bricksetter from Williamson County. "I'm a man as can't say quit. When I lay a-holt, I'm like a turtle and I don't let loose till it thunders. I'm from Williamson County, and maybe you've heerd of the men they raise down there where the screech owls roost with the chickens."

The Celebrated Jumping Frog
of Calaveras County*

There was a feller here once by the name of *Jim* Smiley, in the winter of '49—or may be it was the spring of '50—I don't recollect exactly, somehow, though what makes me think it was one or the other is because I remember the big flume wasn't finished when he first came to the camp; but any way, he was the curiosest man about always betting on anything that turned up you ever see, if he could get anybody to bet on the

* From *The Celebrated Jumping Frog of Calaveras County, and Other Sketches*, by Mark Twain, edited by John Paul, pp. 7–19. New York: C. H. Webb, Publisher. 1867.

other side; and if he couldn't, he'd change sides. Any way that suited the other man would suit him—any way just so's he got a bet, *he* was satisfied. But still he was lucky, uncommon lucky; he most always come out winner. He was always ready and laying for a chance; there couldn't be no solit'ry thing mentioned but that feller'd offer to bet on it, and take any side you please, as I was just telling you. If there was a horse-race, you'd find him flush, or you'd find him busted at the end of it; if there was a dog-fight, he'd bet on it; if there was a cat-fight, he'd bet on it; if there was a chicken-fight, he'd bet on it; why, if there was two birds setting on a fence, he would bet you which one would fly first; or if there was a camp-meeting, he would be there reg'lar to bet on Parson Walker, which he judged to be the best exhorter about here, and so he was too, and a good man. If he even seen a straddle-bug start to go anywheres, he would bet you how long it would take him to get wherever he was going to, and if you took him up, he would foller that straddle-bug to Mexico but what he would find out where he was bound for and how long he was on the road. Lots of the boys here has seen that Smiley, and can tell you about him. Why, it never made no difference to *him*—he would bet on *any* thing—the dangdest feller. Parson Walker's wife laid very sick once, for a good while, and it seemed as if they warn't going to save her; but one morning he come in, and Smiley asked how she was, and he said she was considerable better—thank the Lord for his inf'nit mercy—and coming on so smart that with the blessing of Prov'dence she'd get well yet; and Smiley, before he thought, says, "Well, I'll risk two-and-a-half she don't anyway."

Thish-yer Smiley had a mare—the boys called her the fifteen-minute nag, but that was only in fun, you know, because of course she was faster than that—and he used to win money on that horse, for all she was so slow and always had the asthma, or the distemper, or the consumption, or something of that kind. They used to give her two or three hundred yards' start, and then pass her under way; but always at the fag-end of the race she'd get excited and desperate-like, and come cavorting and straddling up, and scattering her legs around limber, sometimes in the air, and sometimes out to one side amongst the fences, and kicking up m-o-r-e dust and raising m-o-r-e racket with her coughing and sneezing and blowing her nose—and always fetch up at the stand just about a neck ahead, as near as you could cipher it down.

And he had a little small bull-pup, that to look at him you'd

think he wa'n't worth a cent but to set around and look or-
nery and lay for a chance to steal something. But as soon as
money was up on him he was a different dog; his under-
jaw'd begin to stick out like the fo'castle of a steamboat, and
his teeth would uncover and shine savage like the furnaces.
And a dog might tackle him and bully-rag him, and bite him,
and throw him over his shoulder two or three times, and
Andrew Jackson—which was the name of the pup—Andrew
Jackson would never let on but what *he* was satisfied, and
hadn't expected nothing else—and the bets being doubled and
doubled on the other side all the time, till the money was all
up; and then all of a sudden he would grab that other dog
jest by the j'int of his hind leg and freeze to it—not chaw,
you understand, but only jest grip and hang on till they
throwed up the sponge, if it was a year. Smiley always come
out winner on that pup, till he harnessed a dog once that
didn't have no hind legs, because they'd been sawed off by a
circular saw, and when the thing had gone along far enough,
and the money was all up, and he come to make a snatch for
his pet holt, he saw in a minute how he'd been imposed on,
and how the other dog had him in the door, so to speak, and
he 'peared surprised, and then he looked sorter discour-
aged-like, and didn't try no more to win the fight, and so he
got shucked out bad. He give Smiley a look, as much as to
say his heart was broke, and it was *his* fault, for putting up a
dog that hadn't no hind legs for him to take holt of, which
was his main dependence in a fight, and then he limped off a
piece and laid down and died. It was a good pup, was that
Andrew Jackson, and would have made a name for hisself if
he'd lived, for the stuff was in him and he had genius—I know
it, because he hadn't had no opportunities to speak of, and
it don't stand to reason that a dog could much such a fight
as he could under them circumstances if he hadn't had no
talent. It always makes me feel sorry when I think of that
last fight of his'n, and the way it turned out.

Well, thish-yer Smiley had rat-tarriers, and chicken cocks,
and tom-cats and all them kind of things, till you couldn't
rest, and you couldn't fetch nothing for him to bet on but he'd
match you. He ketched a frog one day, and took him home,
and said he calk'lated to edercate him; and so he never done
nothing for three months but set in his back yard and learn
that frog to jump. And you bet you he *did* learn him, too.
He'd give him a little punch behind, and the next minute

you'd see that frog whirling in the air like a doughnut—see him turn one summerset, or maybe a couple, if he got a good start, and come down flat-footed and all right, like a cat. He got him up so in the matter of ketching flies, and kept him in practice so constant, that he'd nail a fly every time as far as he could see them. Smiley said all a frog wanted was education, and he could do 'most anything—and I believe him. Why, I've seen him set Dan'l Webster down here on this floor—Dan'l Webster was the name of the frog—and sing out, "Flies, Dan'l, flies!" and quicker'n you could wink he'd spring straight up and snake a fly off'n the counter there, and flop down on the floor ag'in as solid as a gob of mud, and fall to scratching the side of his head with his hind foot as indifferent as if he hadn't no idea he'd been doin' any more'n any frog might do. You never see a frog so modest and straightfor'ard as he was, for all he was so gifted. And when it come to fair and square jumping on a dead level, he could get over more ground at one straddle than any animal of his breed you ever see. Jumping on a dead level was his strong suit, you understand; and when it come to that, Smiley would ante up money on him as long as he had a red. Smiley was monstrous proud of his frog, and well he might be, for fellers that had traveled and been everywheres, all said he laid over any frog that ever *they* see.

Well, Smiley kept the beast in a little lattice box, and he used to fetch him down town sometimes and lay for a bet. One day a feller—a stranger in the camp, he was—come across him with his box, and says:

"What might it be that you've got in the box?"

And Smiley says, sorter indifferent-like, "It might be a parrot, or it might be a canary, maybe, but it ain't—it's only just a frog."

And the feller took it, and looked at it careful, and turned it round this way and that, and says, "H'm—so 'tis. Well, what's *he* good for?"

"Well," Smiley says, easy and careless, "he's good enough for *one* thing, I should judge—he can outjump any frog in Calaveras county."

The feller took the box again, and took another long, particular look, and give it back to Smiley, and says, very deliberate, "Well," he says, "I don't see no p'ints about that frog that's any better'n any other frog."

"Maybe you don't," Smiley says. "Maybe you understand

frogs and maybe you don't understand 'em; maybe you've had experience, and maybe you ain't only a amature, as it were. Anyways, I've got *my* opinion and I'll risk forty dollars that he can outjump any frog in Calaveras county."

And the feller studied a minute, and then says, kinder sad like, "Well, I'm only a stranger here, and I ain't got no frog; but if I had a frog, I'd bet you."

And then Smiley says, "That's all right—that's all right—if you'll hold my box a minute, I'll go and get you a frog." And so the feller took the box, and put up his forty dollars along with Smiley's and set down to wait.

So he set there a good while thinking and thinking to himself, and then he got the frog out and prized his mouth open and took a teaspoon and filled him full of quail shot—filled him pretty near up to his chin—and set him on the floor. Smiley he went to the swamp and slopped around in the mud for a long time, and finally he ketched a frog, and fetched him in, and give him to this feller, and says:

"Now, if you're ready, set him alongside of Dan'l's, with his fore-paws just even with Dan'l's, and I'll give the word." Then he says, "One—two—three—jump!" and him and the feller touched up the frogs from behind, and the new frog hopped off, but Dan'l give a heave, and hysted up his shoulders—so—like a Frenchman, but it wa'n't no use—he couldn't budge; he was planted as solid as an anvil, and he couldn't no more stir than if he was anchored out. Smiley was a good deal surprised, and he was disgusted too, but he didn't have no idea what the matter was, of course.

The feller took the money and started away; and when he was going out at the door, he sorter jerked his thumb over his shoulders—this way—at Dan'l, and says again, very deliberate, "Well, *I* don't see no p'ints about that frog that's any better'n any other frog."

Smiley he stood scratching his head and looking down at Dan'l a long time, and at last he says, "I do wonder what in the nation that frog throw'd off for—I wonder if there ain't something the matter with him—he 'pears to look mighty baggy, somehow." And he ketched Dan'l by the nap of the neck, and lifted him up, and says, "Why, blame my cats, if he don't weigh five pound!" and turned him upside down and he belched out a double handful of shot. And then he see how it was, and he was the maddest man—he set the frog down and took out after that feller, but he never ketched him.

The Saga of Little Ab Yancey*

WINDY BILL HATFIELD was the best talker in the entire Holler when he got started, and it wasn't very hard to get him started, either. One day I asked Windy if he had ever known any real honest-to-God bad men in the Ozark country. "Wal now, lemme see," he drawled. "Them James brothers—Jesse slept in our house a many a time—was bad 'nough in some ways, an' th' Younger boys warn't exactly whut you might call sody-squirts, neither. Some o' th' Dalton gang come through hyar oncet in a while, too, an' so did Cherokee Bill an' Henry Starr an' that Doolin feller whut kilt all them folks over t' Southwest City."

But these men, as I pointed out, were merely hard-working bank-robbers, while I wanted to hear about genuine despera-does, light-hearted gunfighters such as Billy the Kid. Windy had never heard of the Kid, but he got my meaning all right, and immediately bethought himself of one Abner Yancey, who had terrorized these wilds in the eighties. "Yes sir," he said, "I reckon Leetle Ab was 'bout th' fightin'est feller whut ever showed up in th' Holler. He'd fight a circle-saw, an' turn it hisse'f! He drinked a right smart o' licker, an' played cyards for money, an' run atter th' womenfolks, an' kilt three-four fellers whut crowded him too fur. But me an' him allus got 'long fine—they warn't no rale meanness in him.

"Hit puts me in mind o' whut Lew Merriwether said, th' time they was a-tryin' Ab for killin' a feller over t' Durgenville. Th' prosecutin' attorney was a newcomer, an' he heerd how Lew an' Ab had fit two-three years back, so he got Lew up on th' stand t' testify whut a bad character Ab was. Atter th' jury heerd all 'bout th' fraction th' lawyer he says: 'Now, Mister Merriwether, you think Ab Yancey is a mighty dangerous man, don't ye?' Lew he studied a-while an' then he says: 'Naw, I wouldn't go so fur as t' say that.' Th' 'torney he hollers out: 'Whut? This hyar defendant shot you twicet an' battered your head all up an' run you plumb home an' set your house afire—an' you figger he ain't dangerous?' Lew he jest grinned kinder foolish-like an' says: 'Wal sir, I wouldn't

* By Vance Randolph. From *Folk-Say IV, The Land Is Ours*, edited by B. A. Botkin, pp. 235–238. Copyright, 1932, by B. A. Botkin. Norman: The University of Oklahoma Press.

want t' call nobody out'n their name,' says he. Th' pore lawyer was turrible sot back. 'Lord Gawd, Mister Merriwether,' says he, 'whut kind of a man *is* this hyar Yancey, then?' Lew he scratched his head a minute an' then he says: 'Wal Jedge, I reckon Ab is jest a feller whut it won't do t' monkey with, nohow!'

"Ab was a right comical leetle cuss, too—allus a-doin' somethin' t' make folks laugh. I 'member th' time him an' Batty Ross was 'rested for fightin', an' ol' Squire Perkins he fined 'em five dollars apiece. Batty was a turrible big feller, an' he'd ketched Ab drunk an' beat him purty nigh t' death, but Ab he spoke right up in court jest th' same. 'Hell fire, Jedge,' says he, 'hit ain't right t' fine that poor leetle scallywag— ever'body knows he couldn't do no fightin'. Hit was *me* whut done th' fightin', Jedge, an' I shore aim t' pay th' hull damage myse'f!'—an' with that he slapped out a ten-spot on th' counter. Batty he jest stood thar plumb flabbergasted, an' even ol' Squire Perkins had t' chuckle a leetle.

"He was purty cagey in his young days, an' had a name for tom-cattin' round atter th' married women. Hit shore did git him into a heap o' trouble, too, but seems like he allus wiggled out'n it some way. One time Ab had snuck in t' visit one o' th' neighbor women—I ain't a-callin' no names, mind ye—an' while he was in thar they heerd somebody open th' gate. Th' heifer she says, 'Oh Gawd, that's my ol' man, shore!' an' Ab he says, 'Wal, whut'd I better do?' She was that skeered she couldn't say nothin', but Ab he run quick an' hid in th' scaldin'-bar'l. Purty soon hyar come a feller in, but it warn't her husband nohow. Hit was Big Jim Applegate, an' he run up t' th' woman an' begin a-huggin' an' a-kissin' an' a-lallygaggin' an' all like that. Ab he jest set thar still as a mouse. He couldn't see nothin', but he shore heerd a plenty. Purty soon th' gate slammed ag'in, an' this time it *was* her ol' man shore 'nough. Big Jim he put on his hat an' coat mighty quick, an' when th' feller walked in he says, 'Howdy, neighbor! I jest come over t' borry your scaldin'-bar'l—we-uns is aimin' t' butcher t'morrer.' Th' feller didn't like the looks o' things none too good, but he jest says, 'Wal Jim, thar it is, over thar in th' corner.'

"When Big Jim picked th' dang thing up he tuck note it was all-fired heavy, but figgered this hyar warn't no time t' argufy 'bout th' heft of a scaldin'-bar'l, nohow. So he jest hustled off down th' road with it, an' he never did stop till he was plumb out o' sight. 'My Gawd,' says he, when he finally

got whar he could set her down an' rest hisse'f a minute, 'I
shore did git out o' that mess mighty slick!' 'Bout that time
Leetle Ab he pushed th' led off'n th' bar'l an' crope out. 'You
shore did, Jim,' says he, 'an' I didn't do so *turrible* bad
myse'f!' "

It seemed to me that this tale was reminiscent of something
I had read in Boccaccio, or some other old writer. I intimated as much to Windy Bill, too, but on learning that Boccaccio had lived in Europe several hundred years ago he
scouted my theory in no measured terms. "Ab Yancey," he
said impressively, "was borned an' raised right up thar on
Greasy Creek. He never went nowhar outside th' county, an'
he shore didn't have no truck with no furriners. How could
this hyar Bo-whut-do-ye-call-him feller of knowed whut Ab
done hyar in Poot Holler? Hit's plumb redic'lous, Doc—
sometimes I think you ain't jest right in your head!"

No satisfactory reply to this sort of logic occurred to me
at the moment, so I dropped the matter of origins rather
precipitately, and pressed Bill for more information about
Yancey's exploits. Most of them were commonplace enough
—Ab's fights and frolics and sprees and adulteries had not
differed very much from those of any other mountain bravo.
When I asked for the particulars of his death Bill said shortly
that he died from drinking too much popskull whisky, but
admitted later on that it was no ordinary case of alcoholic
poisoning.

"Wal, ye see, Ab got t' drinkin' in th' tavern an' I don't
mind tellin' you he drinked jest a leetle more'n he'd orter.
Atter while he got t' talkin' kinder wild, a-makin' out like he
figgered on killin' somebody afore sun-up. So finally me an'
Bob Nowlin jest jumped onto him all of a suddent an' tuck
his gun away, an' then we put him t' bed on a pile o' gunny-
sacks. . . . When he come t' hisse'f next mornin' Ab begun t'
holler whar was his gun at? An' then he says how come me all
skun up like this, an' my clothes all tore? Frank Pease he was
a-tendin' bar that mornin', an' he seen how Ab didn't remember nothin' whut happened last night. So he says, 'Wal Ab, we
all drinked a leetle too much, an' you got t' fightin' with a
couple o' furriners from th' Injun Territory, an' they jest
knocked you plumb senseless,' says he. Frank he didn't mean
no harm—he was jest tryin' t' fix it so's Ab wouldn't hold
nothin' ag'in me an' Bob Nowlin. So then he give Ab his gun
back from under th' counter, an' Ab he jest clicked th' loadin'-
gate an' stuck it in his britches same as allus. Hit was one o'

these hyar ol' single-action thumb-busters, an' he allus carried it thataway with th' gate stuck out for a hook onto his belt, so's it wouldn't slip down his pants-leg. . . . Ab warn't a-feelin' peart 'nough t' eat no breakfast but he tuck three-four good snorts o' licker an' went a-rampin' off down th' road. An' that's th' last time I ever seen Ab Yancey till they fetched th' corpse back home in th' wagon.

"But th' way I heerd it next mornin', Ab jest walked on down by th' creek, an' purty soon he perked up a leetle—he was a-whistlin' when he passed Ol' Man Joslyn's place, any-how. He met up with two strangers down by th' ford, an' they howdied him civil as anybody. But Ab he figgered it was maybe these hyar fellers whut got th' best of him last night. 'Whar-bouts do you-uns live at?' he ast 'em, an' when they says they been a-workin' over in th' Nation he out with his six-shooter. 'Wade out in th' creek, Gawd damn ye!' he hollers t' th' biggest 'un. 'Git down on your knees, an' drink water like a cow!' an' th' feller done it. But t'other 'un he jest stood thar, an' when Ab started in a-cussin' *him* he jest pulled out his pistol an' shot Ab right squar' in th' belly! Ab snapped his thumb buster four times, an' he'd of kilt both of 'em shore, only his gun warn't loaded. Me an' Bob Nowlin had done tuck th' hulls out'n it that night, an' pore Ab was so fuddled he never noticed 'em bein' gone, an' Frank Pease he never thought t' tell him.

"Some o' Ab's kinfolks was mighty high ag'in them fellers from th' Nation, but I never could make out t' blame 'em much myse'f. Whut'd you do, if you was a-walkin' 'long 'tendin' t' your own business, an' some feller tuck t' pullin' out guns an' a-carryin' on like whut Ab done? Ol' Joe Yancey allus helt it ag'in Frank Pease—said he hadn't orter of give Ab no empty gun thataway—an' Ab's woman she 'lowed me an' Bob Nowlin didn't have no business a-takin' th' ca'tridges out like we done. . . . But I allus figgered it was drinkin' bad whisky whut kilt Ab Yancey. Hit stands t' reason, if Ab hadn't of got drunk we wouldn't never of snatched his gun off'n him thataway, or tuck th' hulls out'n it. An' if he'd kept sober he'd of knowed whut happened, an' Frank wouldn't never told him that big windy 'bout fellers from th' Nation, neither. An' more'n that, if his head had been a-workin' he'd of loaded his gun an' kilt both them fellers easy, an' ever'thing would of been all right. . . . We-uns give him a high-tone buryin' as was ever saw in these parts, an' he's got th' biggest grave-rock in th' hull dang country. Hit ain't no more'n right, neither, 'cause Ab was one o' th' best-liked fellers ever lived in th' Holler."

A Texas Norther*

LAWRENCE CHRISTOPHER CRISS, an old Texas guide and buffalo-hunter, is responsible for the following tale of a "norther." Criss vouched for the absolute truth of it, and even offered to take me to the spot where it happened and show me the ashes of the camp-fire to prove it.

"It was along in the winter of '69 that I was out huntin' buffalo with a little hunch-back we called Twisted Charley," said Criss, telling me the yarn one night, sitting by a camp-fire near El Paso, Texas. "We were up in the Panhandle, and dead oodles of buffalo grazed around us. We had run across a herd in the afternoon, and killed nineteen between us. Twisted Charley and I were skinnin' them, and were takin' off the hides of four or five when the worst norther I ever remembered struck us.

"We piled all the wood we could find on the fire, but we couldn't begin to keep warm, and when night come on it got colder, and colder, and colder, till the coffee, boilin' in the coffee-pot on the fire, had a skim of ice on it that we had to break before we could pour the coffee out.

"Well, a bright idea struck me, and I took one of the green buffalo-hides and wrapped myself up in it, and in a minute I was as warm and comfortable as a man could wish to be anywhere. You know there's nothin' warmer than a buffalo-hide, and this one was extra thick. Charley saw what I had done, and he went and got a hide, too, and wrapped himself up in it. We were not long in fallin' asleep after that, and I was peacefully dreamin' about skinnin' Jacarilla Apache buck Injuns to make moccasins out of, when, all of a sudden, I was woke up by the most awful howlin' I ever heard.

"I was sure the Injuns were down on us, and I jumped up and grabbed my rifle in a hurry. Then I saw it was Twisted Charley who was doing the yellin'. I went over to where he lay, wrapped up in the green buffalo-hide, and I gave him a kick to wake him up, for I thought, of course, he had a nightmare.

* From *A Texas Ranger*, by N. A. Jennings, foreword by J. Frank Dobie, pp. 17-21. Copyright, 1930, by Southwest Press. Dallas, Texas.

" 'Help me out, help me out!' he yelled.

" 'What's the matter with you?' I asked.

" 'Don't you see I'm froze up in this hide and can't get out?' he howled.

"I took hold of the hide and tried to unroll it, but it was froze 'round him as hard as boiler-iron. He was warm enough, for he had wrapped himself in it with the hairy side next to him, but he wanted to get out bad.

" 'I can't unwrap that hide any way,' I said, after I'd made a trial at it.

" 'Cut it open,' said Twisted Charley.

"I took my skinning-knife and tried to cut it, but the hide was so hard it turned the knife-edge.

" 'I'll have to give it up,' I said, at last.

" 'What?' yelled Charley. 'Man, I can't stay in this hide forever.'

" 'You won't have to,' I says; 'this norther'll blow itself out in three days, and then you'll thaw out naturally.'

" 'Thaw me out at the fire,' said Charley.

"That seemed reasonable, and I rolled him over by the fire and began toastin' first one side and then the other. I thought I'd never get him out; but after awhile, when the hide was actually roasted, I managed to unroll it enough for him to get out. He sat up by the fire the rest of the night, swearin'. He was a beautiful swearer, and the air moderated a whole lot while he was sittin' there inventin' new oaths and lettin' 'em out."

Mirages*

ONE evening in the early fall of 1891, while on a round-up in the West Pasture, we got through supper early and had an hour or two to sit around the fire before we crawled into our "hot-rolls." One of the first northers of the season had blown up the day before, and the air was so crisp that evening that the fire felt good. The boys kept adding cow chips, and the coals glowed red but never blazed much. Some of the punchers sprawled full length on the ground, some leaned back against

---

* From *Rollie Burns or An Account of the Ranching Industry on the South Plains,* by W. C. Holden, pp. 171–176. Copyright, 1932, by W. C. Holden. Dallas, Texas: The Southwest Press.

their saddles, and some sat on their heels and smoked cigarettes.

We got to talking about mirages. To cow-punchers who knew nothing of scientific explanations, there was something mysterious about mirages. All the boys who had been on the Plains very long had seen freakish things happen. I had observed cattle which looked twenty-five feet tall, grazing near a mirage, and a man riding a horse that appeared forty feet tall. All kinds of peculiar things have happened in a mirage. Men have traveled miles towards a most realistic lake only to find it was not there. At a time when there were no houses, fences or trees within forty miles, one frequently saw such things only a few miles away. Newcomers on the Plains, unaccustomed to the peculiarities of mirages, sometimes thought of them as good or bad omens.

I told the boys about a mirage I saw during the spring of 1890. Estacado was twenty-two miles from the I O A headquarters and over a considerable ridge. The region immediately around Estacado was much more rolling than land commonly is in the vicinity of Crosby County. Approaching from the south, one could not see the town until he was in four or five miles of the place. One clear, frosty morning I stepped out into the back yard and saw Estacado elevated just above the horizon. Every house was visible. I could have counted the panes of glass in the west and south sides of the courthouse. I could see horses tied to the hitching posts in front of the stores and blacksmith shop, and people walking about the place. It seemed to me that, with the aid of field glasses, I would have been able to recognize the faces of the individuals.

In the late fall of 1890 I witnessed another illusion equally strange. Our rounding-up outfit was camped about eight miles from the Yellow House Canyon, practically due south of Buffalo Springs. The morning was chilly, still and frosty. When I got up between daylight and sunrise, the cook called to me, "Boss, I thought we camped several miles from the Canyon last night."

"We did."

"Look, we are right on the edge of it this morning."

I looked, and I never beheld a more perfect mirage. It was so realistic it would have fooled an old-timer. There was the bottom of the Canyon just below us, water running along the creek, a few hackberry trees along the edges of the water course, and cattle grazing along the sides of the Canyon. I saw familiar landmarks in the creek, trees and rocks. It seemed that I could have thrown a rock into the center of the Canyon. If I had not known that we were eight miles from the rim of the Canyon and over a slight rise, I would have sworn we were on the very edge.

"Last spring," said T Bar Dick, "while I was 'reping' for our outfit over on the Syndicate range, I heard an old punch tell about a mirage he had seen about fourteen years before when he was a buffalo hunter. His camp was beside a lake in one of the wide, shallow basins on the Plains. He got lost from camp and rode several days looking for it. There was plenty of water in the lakes and buffaloes everywhere; so he was in no danger in that respect, but he had to get back to camp eventually. Each morning he would get his bearings the best he could when the sun came up, and ride all day eyeing the horizon in every direction for the lost camp. One morning after riding a couple of hours, he looked back and saw an unusual mirage behind him. There were buffaloes, wild horses, antelopes, and wolves moving about without touching the earth. The reality of the scene impressed him so much he stopped to study it awhile. Directly he recognized his camp beside the lake. There were his wagon, piles of buffalo hides, and his horses grazing not far away. He knew enough about mirages to know that this was a reflected image of his camp. He took his bearing and headed back toward the mirage. The illusion soon vanished, but he kept the direction. He rode hard all day, and just before sun-down he topped a ridge, and there was his camp. That morning when he saw the mirage he must have been thirty or forty miles away."

None of us who had been on the Plains for a season or more doubted the story. "Shorty" Anderson had been stretched by the fire listening with rapt attention. Shorty always had a mischievous twinkle in his eye, and when he was up to something the twinkle became downright devilish.

"Speaking of buffaloes," he said, "I was out on the Plains once before any cowmen had ever ventured on top of the Caprock. I don't suppose there was a tree, or a post, or a man in fifty miles. I rode up on a ridge once and saw a big buffalo bull grazing near a lake. He didn't see me, and I rode back quickly and circled around to get on the wind side. I had only my Colt .45, and my horse was afraid of buffaloes. I thought my only chance was to leave my horse over the ridge and stalk the bull on foot. I figured that if everything worked just right I stood a chance to get within pistol range. I got up within thirty yards before the big brute sighted me. He looked at me a moment and couldn't decide whether to run at me or from me. In either case, I decided I had better let him have it. I banged away at him, and didn't hit where I aimed. The first shot caused him to turn towards me. I let him have five more shots, but you can't kill a buffalo with a .45 unless you hit him right behind his shoulder blade. If he had been in doubt about what to do beforehand, he didn't have any doubts after I put six lumps of lead under his hide. He gave a wild bellow and took after me. My horse was a mile away, and somehow I didn't get started in that direction. The bull gained on me for a little bit; he was snorting and blowing and it seemed like I could feel his breath. But after the first hundred yards I began to hold my own."

Shorty stopped suddenly as if that was the end of the story, but "Red" Wheeler couldn't leave him in that predicament.

"What did you do next?" asked Red.

"I climbed a tree."

"But you said there was not a tree in fifty miles."

"Well, you see, it was this way. It happened that one of those mirages like the boss has been telling about was right in front of me. There was a big hackberry tree growing by a water hole. Well, I climbed that mirage tree."

The Wind*

I

WELL—yes, the wind does get up and blow out here in West Texas sometimes. Most generally it comes from wherever it happens to be, but the real good hard winds out here come from the north or from the south unless, as happens every once in a while, it gets to goin whirligig fashion, and when that happens you might say that things do move.

But that reminds me of the time I was workin with a watermelon seedin crew here about twenty year ago last summer. Or have I ever told you this story before? Well, you see, we had begun seedin melons along right just after sun-up, and there was just a nice gentle little breeze a-blowin, almost seemed like the answer to a maiden's prayer. But along about

---

* By Frank Neff and William Henry. From *Folk-Say, A Regional Miscellany: 1930*, edited by B. A. Botkin, pp. 48–60. Copyright, 1930, by B. A. Botkin. Norman: University of Oklahoma Press.

noon the sun commenced glarin down on us hotter and hotter
and pretty soon we begin to see little whirligigs of wind
scuddin around here, there, and yonder over the purairie
pickin up little patches of dry grass and whippin up sand
sky-high until it begun to look like the whole damn purairie
was all afire. Of course, what looked like smoke rings was
only sand, but it was real enough to make a tenderfoot start
a backfire and get a fireguard ready.

I'm tellin you, 'i gosh, I never did see so many of them little
twisters all a-goin at one and the same time as I did that day,
and then all at once the funniest thing happened.

It seems as though the wind had just been pickin up speed
and about this time it decided to set in for some real straight
blowin. Well, 'bout one o'clock, when the sun had switched
over to the west side of things, here she come from the west
like a ball out of hell. Not a cloud anywheres but just a good
old west wind eastbound tryin to get acrost Texas immediately
if not sooner. Talk about speed now. There was a couple of
greyhounds chasin a rabbit in the next field and they just
about had him caught when he raised his ears and the wind
caught him and blew him clear out of sight 'fore the hounds
ever missed him.

I never was exactly sure till that day why there won't nothin
grow on these here purairies except buffalo grass. But I realize now that any other kind that was to try to grow would be
blowed plumb away 'fore it'd even have time to turn green
or take root. And nothin else'd have the nerve to crawl right
out from under the sand and keep right on a-growin regardless of whether it rained last week or last year.

Well—to get back to this here particular wind, which I
just don't rightly understand. Here we was seedin watermelons at one o'clock in the afternoon and the wind just
blowin hell's bells out of the west. By two o'clock the wind
had got so much harder that everything was a-leanin east and
we had to put the seeds eight inches in the ground to keep
them from blowin out. Well—the wind kept gettin harder
and harder until at three o'clock the sun was *actually standin
still*. 'I gosh, mister, I hope to tell you it was. Yes, sir, I believe that there old Bible story 'bout Joshuer makin the sun
and moon both stand still now. The only reason the moon
didn't stand still that day was because it hadn't come up in
time to meet this here wind.

Well—we just kept right on a-seedin watermelons and a-watchin that there damn sun a-standin still, and it stood there and stood there until we finally all agreed that it was at least three hours late goin down. And you never saw a sicklier-lookin thing anywhere than that poor old sun. The damn thing kept a-tryin to go down and tryin but it just was stuck up there and couldn't budge. It even stayed around till the stars come out and began to look around sorta surprised-like.

Then the wind finally begun to let up and the dog star come up and chased the sun away off over a hill, and then it got too dark to seed any more melons so we quit and went on home to supper. But I never yet seen just a plain straight old wind like that one was.

II

Wind? Wind? Did you ever see the wind blow? Stranger, I don't reckon you've lived in these here parts very long, have you? Let me tell you some of the things I've seen the wind do, right around in this particular community.

Man! I've seen the wind blow—by note and also by ear, you might say.

Just now I remember me of the time when it hadn't rained in these here regions for all of one summer—and a good part of the next one. The landscape had got so dry that there was rabbit tracks and gopher trails and coyote runs marked out in every direction like a college surveyor was a-tryin to set grade stakes for a new paper railroad that was to run from the North Pole to Nowhere—if only enough suckers could be induced to put their money into its watered stock so as it could loosen up a bit and get to runnin.

Well sir—'i gosh, this time that I'm a-thinkin about nobody but a tenderfoot would even dream that it would ever rain again. And as I was a-walkin along one side of my homestead and a-wonderin if there was enough buffalo grass to carry the stock through another winter, I looked away off to'ds the west, and as sure as shootin there was a little cloud a-peepin up over the west state line, and it just wasn't a mite bigger than a man's hand.

I just heaved another sigh and give up hopin for rain right then. But I want to tell you what happened. As I was a-moseyin along to'ds the shack the wind begins to blow. No, you ain't got it right—it did not come from the little cloud I'd just seen hidin on the rim of the world. No, sir, that wind was a-comin from the contrariwise direction, and man! how it did blow! But just before I got to the shack I looked back, a kinda helpless look to see what'd happen to the little cloud when that wind hit her.

You wouldn't expect anything but that the poor little cloud would be blown helter-skelter every which way from hell to breakfast. But it had just kinda rose up, and that heavy wind had missed her, and the little cloud was a-gettin bigger and was a-sailin along and was a-gettin bigger and bigger and a-comin nearer and nearer. But it still wasn't anything to think twice about.

And mister, right there was where I made my big mistake. And it come anigh ruinin all the rest of my life, and it did make a considerable dent in my future fortunes.

The contrary wind blowed stronger and stronger, and the little cloud puffed up and got blacker and blacker and bigger and then some; and she just come sailin on into our country. By that time the ground wind, seein it couldn't make no headway buckin the oncomin cloud—'i gosh, if it didn't turn right around and blow along with the cloud too. And by this time that little old cloud was as big as all out-o-doors and a-gettin blacker every minute.

Fust off henhouses and hog sheds seemed like they just give one look to'ds the black cloud rushin onto them, and then scairt-like they looked like they just flapped up into the sky, and off they all went. There was a regular whirlpool of boards and shingles gyratin round and round and up and off cross country.

It didn't seem like it lasted more'n a minute—and then there was some of the curiousest sights. One shingle had hit a tree, and the little end of it had hit the tree fust, and it was still a perfectly good shingle but stuck into the tree until no one could pull it out any way. Two boards had come together, crisscross, and one was driv' just exactly halfway through the other, and they was left a-sittin up on the ground like a letter X. My windmill wheel was blown away a slat at a time, and more'n a mile away I found them slats a-stickin in the ground in the shape of the letter S, and the top ends were all feathered out like some one had started to make toothpicks and didn't get done with the job. Where the storm crossed my field and the stalks of last year's crop was standin, it just took and wrapped every one of them stalks right down near the ground and round and round. Every one of my hens was blowed a mile or more out onto the purairie, and when I went out to look for them they had not a feather of any kind left on them, but the wind had done blowed them feathers so hard that they had hit my hogs, and one side of each hog was stickin full of chicken feathers, and they didn't seem hurt a bit.

The last look I had at the sky, before I took to my cave, was to see my settin hens' nests and my home brew go up together. And the sheriff found some good eggnog all blown into jugs and corked up regular way over into the next county, and there was talk of turning me in to the revenooers.

Yes sir—the wind sure did blow out here that day.

Big Frank*

TIME was when a man had no trouble at all following the wheat harvest from Texas to the Dakotas and making a few dollars. That was when all wheat was cut with a binder, shocked, stacked sometimes, and then threshed. Farmers needed many hands during the harvesting season. Now combine machines that cut and thresh the grain in one operation are becoming more common every year. Farmers need fewer and fewer hands. One of the migratory hands that used to come up through this part of Nebraska was Frank McDarmit —Big Frank, we called him. He was a bundle-slinger if ever there was one.

The first time I had dealings with Big Frank, he took a hundred dollars from me easy as nothing. I had just finished cutting fifty acres of wheat that I wanted shocked right away. I was afraid a rainy spell of weather might come along and spoil some of the grain. That was the finest field of wheat I ever raised; the bundles lay scattered three-deep over every inch of stubble. I hired Big Frank in the morning and told him I'd go to town and fetch some other shockers to help him.

Big Frank looked over the field, spat some tobacco juice, and said, "I don't need any help. I can shock that field myself and be finished by sundown."

* By Rudolph Umland. From the Manuscripts of the Federal Writers' Project of the Works Progress Administration for the State of Nebraska.

"You're crazy," I said.

"Maybe I am," he said, "but I can still shock that field myself and be finished by sundown."

"Man, you can't."

"I can."

I looked at him and wondered what institution he'd escaped from.

"I'll bet you fifty dollars I can," he said.

"I'll bet a hundred you can't."

Big Frank spat on his hands, pulled on his gloves, and went to work. I never saw a bundle-slinger move so fast before. In less than an hour, I knew I was going to lose that bet.

Big Frank could shock wheat faster than any two binders could kick out the bundles. He could set up a shock thirty feet away by just tossing the bundles where they belonged. Sometimes he'd pick up eight or ten bundles at once, set them down, and have as pretty a shock as you ever saw. No matter how hard a windstorm blew, Big Frank's shocks kept standing. He could hurl a bundle into the ground so deep that nobody could pull it up. He frequently did this out of pure orneriness to make the threshers cuss when they were gathering the bundles.

He was a one, that Big Frank! He never hired out as a shocker by the day. He always demanded pay by the acre. He wouldn't work in a field where there were other shockers; they got in his way. Why, damn it, he wouldn't even start shocking in a field where the grain wasn't all cut; he'd catch up with the binder in no time and then have to wait.

When Big Frank blew into a community, other hands moved on. They knew there wouldn't be much work left for them. All the farmers wanted to hire Big Frank. He was such a handy man to have around. The women-folk liked him too; that's why there are so many youngsters named Frank in this part of the country. Big Frank had only one bad fault. Summer after summer he made the ensilage spoil in silos. It took the farmers several years before they discovered that Big Frank was to blame for this. Old Sam Bates, my neighbor, rose early one morning and found Big Frank sound asleep at the foot of his silo with a straw in his mouth that had some brown juice on it. Old Sam shook him and shook him but he couldn't get him wakened. Then he sniffed the straw. Corn juice! Big Frank had been boring small holes in the bottom of the silo and sucking out the juice from the ensilage. When he finally woke from his stupor, he was as shamefaced as a schoolboy caught in a bad act. But the next night he did the same thing. He couldn't be broke of the habit. Old Sam Bates was mad at first, then he became curious. After tasting the juice himself, he didn't blame Big Frank any more. In fact he slept at the foot of silos himself. That was during prohibition and fermented corn juice tasted mighty good. All the silos in the neighborhood soon had little holes bored in them.

The first years Big Frank came here, he used to move north as soon as the wheat was all in shock. Then one year he stayed to help thresh. It was a sight to see him load a rack. He heaved entire shocks into the rack and in only a few minutes had bundles piled so high that you had to crane your neck to see the top of the load. Sam Bates and I ran the rig. Old Sam kept the engine running at full speed while I squirted oil in all the cracks and crannies of the separator so the contraption wouldn't take fire. It took only two throws for Big Frank to have his rack unloaded but the separator would still be choking and sputtering and spitting out straw and chaff from that load when Big Frank would be returning with his next. The other bundle-haulers quit as soon as they found that Big Frank didn't need any help. He could haul bundles a mile and keep engine and separator going at full speed all the while himself. He was a bundle-slinger, that fellow!

Sam Bates, Big Frank and I made up a three-man threshing outfit. We went from farm to farm and threshed all the wheat in the county that summer. Our little separator kept twenty wagons busy hauling away the threshed grain to granaries and elevators. The next year we bought a larger separator and kept thirty wagons busy. We threshed out seven Nebraska counties that year and two in South Dakota. Big Frank became better and better all the time. He pitched bundles so fast that our separator couldn't keep up with him. Old Sam and I got our heads together and agreed that something had to be done. We'd have to get a still larger separator. The next year we bought the largest separator on the market. It was a beauty! You probably won't believe me when I tell you, but we kept fifty wagons busy that year hauling away the threshed grain. We threshed out nineteen Nebraska counties and fifteen more in the Dakotas. Big Frank had to work hard to keep up with the separator but he always remained in good humor. As long as there was a silo somewhere near, Big Frank was contented. He would curl up beside it at night, suck corn juice, and get a good sleep. We never threshed in a county that didn't have at least half-a-dozen silos.

The Sissy from the Hardscrabble County Rock Quarries*

THE men that work in the rock quarries of Hardscrabble County are so tough they crack great big rocks just by spitting on them. The farther you go west in the county the tougher the men get, and the rock quarries are right on the western boundary line. When they set off a blast, those bullies are right out there with ten-year-old white oaks in their hands batting those big boulders around, or else they're playing catch without any gloves.

When they get constipated in the rock quarry camp they never use anything but blasting powder, and they whip their children with barb wire until the kids get to be ten years old and then they thresh their parents.

Strangers almost never travel into the rock quarry country, because no man, woman, beast or child that dared to try it ever returned to tell about it no more than any soul ever fetched back a report from hell.

When the quarrymen leave their camp, everybody but invalids, little children, and cripples take to the hills till danger's past. It's lucky that they usually come in a drove, and you can see their dust for miles away and hear their fearsome blackguarding and whooping for a good hour and a half before they strike the city limits.

Gentlemen, it's no lie nor fairy tale when I tell you that those Hardscrabble County quarrymen are enough to plague a saint. They use them in the farm villages to scare little children and make them behave, but the grownups are even scareder than the young ones.

One day a lone wolf got right into town before anybody knew he was on the way. He came riding two snapping, snarling panthers, straddling them with a foot on each, and he was lashing them into a lather with a whip made of three six-foot rattlesnakes knotted together.

This fellow was a sight to behold, and everybody knew in a minute that he was a quarryman. He stood a good eight feet without tiptoeing, and not enough fat on him to grease

* By Jack Conroy. From "Chicago Industrial Folklore." Manuscripts of the Federal Writers' Project of the Works Progress Administration for the State of Illinois.

a one-egg skillet. That man was muscled like a draft mule, and he moved around like a bolt of lightning on its holiday.

First thing off he went to the shoe store and bought him a pair of brogans. Then he got a nickel's worth of stout roofing nails from the hardware store and asked for the loan of a hammer. He drove these roofing nails right through the soles and heels of the shoes and put the shoes back on his feet. He wore a size fifteen, broad last.

"That's the way I like it," he said. "It gives you a good grip and all you got to do when your foot itches is to wiggle it around a little.

"I want to get prettied up a little," the quarryman said, and went into the barber shop. The barber took the edge off his shears when he tried to cut his hair.

"Ain't you got no tinsmiths in this town?" asked the quarryman. "Get a pair of tinsnips, extra large. And fetch a blowtorch from the plumber's. I ain't had a decent shave for a month of Sundays."

He dropped in the Blue Moon Saloon then and asked for a good stiff drink, talking as polite as chips. The bartender planked down a bottle of his strongest brand of fortyrod. Some of it sloshed over and ate a spot of varnish off the bar the size of a five-dollar bill. The quarryman lost his temper then, and snorted and fumed fit to kill.

"None of that bellywash for me! I'd as soon have a pinky, sticky ice cream sody with a cherry on it."

"What sort of a charge do you crave, stranger?" asked the bartender, his false choppers almost shaking out of his mouth.

"Gimme a prussic acid cocktail with a little sulphuric for a chaser," ordered the quarryman, "and see that you don't go diluting it with no carbolic, neither. What are you, anyway? One of them temperance cranks? You must think I'm a plumb teetotaler!"

The bartender dashed out the back way and hotfooted it to the drug store and got the stuff for the drinks. The quarryman got in a little better humor then, and began passing the time away by spitting on the floor and burning holes right through to the ground underneath.

"Not bad!" he said. "A little weak. Only trouble with this tipple is that it's hell on underwear. Every time you break wind it burns a hole in them."

"I guess you aim to get back to the quarries before nightfall, don't you, stranger?" said the bartender, hoping to God it was so.

"No, no!" answered the quarryman, shaking his head kind of sad. "I don't reckon I'll ever go back."

He grabbed a can of tomatoes off the shelf behind the bar and gulped it down without chewing it open.

"Don't it lay heavy on your stomach, stranger?" asked the bartender, terribly put out that the quarryman wasn't leaving that night.

"Not long," answered the quarryman. "I soon digest the can from around the tomatoes. It's easy. A doorknob is harder, but I can do it easy as pie when I set my head to it."

"You aim to make your home in our little Magic City?" asked the bartender, still hoping he had heard wrong.

"Hell's fire and damnation no, man!" said the quarryman, so riled he bit a foot long chunk out of the mahogany bar and spat it right in the bartender's face. "I wouldn't live here for love nor money. I wouldn't be caught dead here."

"Well, then," said the bartender, getting a little bolder, "why did you leave the quarries?"

"Aw, I didn't *want* to," answered the quarryman. "I had to."

"You had to? Why? Get in a fight or some kind of trouble there?"

"A fight? Are you plumb stark, staring looney, man? Whoever heard of a man getting into trouble over fighting in the Hardscrabble County rock quarries?"

"Why did you have to leave then?"

"Well," said the quarryman, looking like a sheepkilling dog. "They chased me out because they said I was a sissy."

The Boomer Fireman's Fast Sooner Hound*

A BOOMER fireman is never long for any one road. Last year he may have worked for the Frisco, and this year he's heaving black diamonds for the Katy or the Wabash. He travels light and travels far and doesn't let any grass grow under his feet when they get to itching for the greener pastures on the next road or the next division or maybe to hell and gone on the other side of the mountains. He doesn't need furniture

* *Ibid.*

and he doesn't need many clothes, and God knows he doesn't need a family or a dog.

When the Boomer pulled into the roadmaster's office looking for a job, there was that sooner hound of his loping after him. That hound would sooner run than eat and he'd sooner eat than fight or do something useful like catching a rabbit. Not that a rabbit would have any chance if the sooner really wanted to nail him, but that crazy hound dog didn't like to do anything but run and he was the fastest thing on four legs.

"I might use you," said the roadmaster. "Can you get a boarding place for the dog?"

"Oh, he goes along with me," said the Boomer. "I raised him from a pup just like a mother or father and he ain't never spent a night or a day or even an hour far away from me. He'd cry like his poor heart would break and raise such a ruckus nobody couldn't sleep, eat or hear themselves think for miles about."

"Well, I don't see how that would work out," said the roadmaster. "It's against the rules of the road to allow a passenger in the cab, man or beast, or in the caboose and I aim to put you on a freight run so you can't ship him by express. Besides, he'd get the idea you wasn't nowhere about and pester folks out of their wits with his yipping and yowling. You look like a man that could keep a boiler popping off on an uphill grade, but I just don't see how we could work it if the hound won't listen to reason while you're on your runs."

"Why, he ain't no trouble," said the Boomer. "He just runs alongside, and when I'm on a freight run he chases around a little in the fields to pass the time away."

> "That may be so, I do not know;
>   It sounds so awful queer.
> I don't dispute your word at all,
>   But don't spread that bull in here,"

sang the roadmaster.

"He'll do it without half trying," said the Boomer. "It's a little bit tiresome on him having to travel at such a slow gait, but that sooner would do anything to stay close by me, he loves me that much."

"Go spread that on the grass to make it green," said the roadmaster.

"I'll lay my first paycheck against a fin[3] that he'll be fresh as a daisy and his tongue behind his teeth when we pull into the junction. He'll run around the station a hundred times or so to limber up."

"It's a bet," said the roadmaster.

On the first run the sooner moved in what was a slow walk for him. He kept looking up into the cab where the Boomer was shoveling in the coal.

"He looks worried," said the Boomer. "He thinks the hog law[4] is going to catch us, we're making such bad time."

The roadmaster was so sore at losing the bet that he transferred the Boomer to a local passenger run and doubled the stakes. The sooner speeded up to a slow trot, but he had to kill a lot of time, at that, not to get too far ahead of the engine.

Then the roadmaster got mad enough to bite off a drawbar. People got to watching the sooner trotting alongside the train and began thinking it must be a mighty slow road. Passengers might just as well walk; they'd get there just as fast. And if you shipped a yearling calf to market, it'd be a bologna bull before it reached the stockyards. Of course, the trains were keeping up their schedules the same as usual, but that's the way it looked to people who saw a no-good mangy sooner hound beating all the trains without his tongue hanging out an inch or letting out the least little pant.

It was giving the road a black eye, all right. The roadmaster would have fired the Boomer and told him to hit the grit with his sooner and never come back again, but he was stubborn from the word go and hated worse than anything to own up he was licked.

"I'll fix that sooner," said the roadmaster. "I'll slap the Boomer into the cab of the Cannon Ball, and if anything on four legs can keep up with the fastest thing on wheels I'd admire to see it. That sooner'll be left so far behind it'll take nine dollars to send him a post card."

The word got around that the sooner was going to try to keep up with the Cannon Ball. Farmers left off plowing, hitched up, and drove to the right of way to see the sight. It was like a circus day or the county fair. The schools all dismissed the pupils, and not a factory could keep enough men to make a wheel turn.

The roadmaster got right in the cab so that the Boomer couldn't soldier on the job to let the sooner keep up. A clear track for a hundred miles was ordered for the Cannon Ball, and all the switches were spiked down till after that streak of lightning had passed. It took three men to see the Cannon

Ball on that run: one to say, "There she comes," one to say, "There she is," and another to say, "There she goes." You couldn't see a thing for steam, cinders and smoke, and the rails sang like a violin for a half hour after she'd passed into the next county.

Every valve was popping off and the wheels three feet in the air above the roadbed. The Boomer was so sure the sooner would keep up that he didn't stint the elbow grease; he wore the hinges off the fire door and fifteen pounds of him melted and ran right down into his shoes. He had his shovel whetted to a nub.

The roadmaster stuck his head out of the cab window, and —whosh!—off went his hat and almost his head. The suction like to have jerked his arms from their sockets as he nailed a-hold of the window seat.

It was all he could do to see, and gravel pinged against his goggles like hailstones, but he let out a whoop of joy.

"THE SOONER! THE SOONER!" he yelled. "He's gone! He's gone for true! Ain't *nowhere* in sight!"

"I can't understand that," hollered the Boomer. "He ain't *never* laid down on me yet. It just ain't like him to lay down on me. Leave me take a peek."

He dropped his shovel and poked out his head. Then he whooped even louder than the roadmaster had.

"He's true blue as they come!" the Boomer yelled. "Got the interests of the company at heart, too. He's still with us."

"Where do you get that stuff?" asked the roadmaster. "I don't see him nowhere. I can't see hide nor hair of him."

"We're going so fast half the journal boxes are on fire and melting the axles like hot butter," said the Boomer. "The sooner's running up and down the train hoisting a leg above the boxes. He's doing his level best to put out some of the fires. That dog is true blue as they come and he's the fastest thing on four legs, but he's only using three of them now."

Slappy Hooper, World's Biggest, Fastest, and Bestest Sign Painter*

SLAPPY HOOPER wasn't big because he was six foot nine and wide between the eyes, no more than he weighed three hun-

---

* By Jack Conroy. From "Chicago Industrial Folklore." Manuscripts of the Federal Writers' Project of the Works Progress Administration for the State of Illinois.

dred pounds without his cap on or his bucket in one hand and his brush in the other. It was just that there wasn't no job any too big for Slappy, and he never wanted a helper to mess around with. . . .

He used to get jobs of lettering advertising on the sky, and it didn't fade away in a minute like smoke that pours out of a plane and gets torn to pieces by the wind before you can hardly spell out what it says. It was all pretty and fancy colors, too; any shade a man's heart could wish for, and it'd stay right there for days if the weather was fair. Of course, birds would fly through it, and when it'd rain the colors would all run together and when the clouds rolled by, there'd be what folks got to calling a rainbow. It really was nothing but Slappy Hooper's sky-writing all jumbled together. It seems that no man, woman, child or beast, alive or dead, was ever able to invent waterproof sky paint. If it could have been done, Slappy would have done it.

His biggest job was for the Union Pacific Railroad, and stretched from one end of the line to the other. The only way you could read it all was to get on a through train and look out of the window and up at the sky all the time. Everybody got stiff necks, of course, so Slappy had the bright idea of getting Sloan's Liniment to pay him for a big sign right at the end of the Union Pacific sign.

Nobody ever did understand how Slappy managed to do the sky painting. He'd have been a chump to tell anybody. He always used to say when people asked him: "That's for me to know and you to find out," or, "If I told you that, you'd know as much as I do."

The only thing people was sure of was that he used sky hooks to hold up the scaffold. He used a long scaffold instead of the bosun's chair he used when he was painting smokestacks or church steeples. When he started in to fasten his skyhooks, he'd rent a thousand acre field and rope it off with barbed wire charged with electricity. He never let a living soul inside, but you could hear booming sounds like war times and some folks figured he was firing his skyhooks out of a cannon and that they fastened on a cloud or some place too high for mortal eyes to see or mortal minds to know about. Anyways, after a while—if you took a spy glass—you could see Slappy's long scaffold raising up, up, up in the air and Slappy about as big as a spider squatting on it.

But that played out, somehow. It wasn't that people didn't like his skypainting any more, but the airplanes got to buzzing around as thick as flies around a molasses barrel and they was always fouling or cutting Slappy's lines, and he was always afraid one would run smack into him and dump over his scaffold and spill his paint if nothing worse. Besides, he said, if advertisers was dumb enough to let a farting airplane take the place of an artist, the more he'd fool them, and it wasn't no skin off his behind. He could always wrangle three squares a day and a pad at night by putting signs on windows for shopkeepers if he had to. If I can stay off public works, I'll be satisfied, he thought to himself.

So Slappy said to hell with the *big jobs*. I'll just start painting smaller signs, but I'll make them so *real* and true to life that I can still be the fastest and bestest sign painter in the world, if I ain't the biggest any more. It's pure foolishness for a man to match himself against an airplane at making *big* signs.

He knew he could do it with one hand tied behind and both eyes punched out. Some sign painters couldn't dot the letter "i" without a pounce to go by. It was enough to make a dog laugh to see some poor scissorsbills wrastling around with a pounce, covered all over with chalk wet by sweat until they looked like a plaster of Paris statue.

Then, like as not, they'd get a pounce too small for the wall or billboard they was working on. When it was all on there was a lot of blank space left over. The boss'd yell: "Well, well, Bright Eyes! Guess the only thing to do is fetch a letter stretcher!" If the pounce happened to be too big, it was every bit as bad. "A fine job, Michael Angelo," the boss'd holler, "except you'll have to mix the paint with alum so's it'll shrink enough that we can squeeze it in with a crowbar."

One of Slappy's first jobs after he took to billboard painting was a picture of a loaf of bread for a bakery. It would make you hungry just to look at it. That was the trouble. The birds began to flying on it to peck at it, and either they'd break their bills and starve to death because they didn't have anything left to peck with, or they'd just sit there perched on the top of the billboard trying to figure out what was the matter until they'd just keel over. Some of them'd break their necks when they dashed against the loaf, and others'd try to light on it and slip and break their necks on the ground. Either way, it was death on birds. The humane societies complained so much and so hard that Slappy had to paint the loaf out, and just leave the lettering.

He didn't like this a bit, though, because, as he often said, any monkey who can stand on his hind legs and hold anything in his fingers can make letters. The loaf of bread business sort of gave Slappy a black eye. People was afraid to hire him.

Finally the Jimdandy Hot Blast Stove and Range Company hired him to do a sign for their newest model, showing a fire going good inside, the jacket cherry red, and heat pouring off in ever which direction. In some ways it was the best job Slappy ever done. The dandelions and weeds popped right out of the ground on the little plot between the billboard and the sidewalk, and in middle January of the coldest winter ever recorded by the Weather Bureau.

It was when the bums started making the place a hangout that the citizens and storekeepers of the neighborhood put in a kick. The hoboes drove a nail into the billboard so they could hang kettles and cans against the side of the heater and boiled their shave or boilup[5] water. They pestered everybody in the neighborhood for meat and vegetables to make mulligan stews. They found it more comfortable on the ground than in any flophouse in the city, so they slept there, too. They ganged up on the sidewalk so that you couldn't push through, even to deliver the United States mails. Mothers was afraid to send their little children to school or to the grocery store.

The company decided to hire a special watchman to shoo hoboes away, but this was a terrible expense. Not only that, but the watchman would get drowsy from the warmth, and no sooner did he let out a snore than the bums would come creeping back like old home week. Finally, the Company got the idea of having Slappy make the stove a lot hotter to drive the bums clean away.

So he did. He changed the stove from a cherry red to a white hot, and made the heat waves a lot thicker.

This drove the bums across the street, but it also blistered the paint off all the automobiles parked at the curb. Then one day the frame building across the way began to smoke and then to blaze. The insurance company told the Jimdandy Hot Blast Stove and Range Company to jerk that billboard down and be quick about it, or they'd go to law.

Slappy says now he feels like locking up his keister[6] and throwing away the key. They don't want big sign painting and they don't want true-to-life sign painting, and he has to do one or the other or both or nothing at all.

II

FROM THE LIARS' BENCH

1. "Exaggerative Invention": The Lying Tale

As a product of the untrammeled imagination, lying tales, whoppers, big windies, or big lies are a further specialization of the yarn and tall tale in the direction of the fabulous and mythical. Outside the realm of both probability and possibility, the world of lies is the world of supermen who perform miracles midway between nonsense and magic and who inhabit a land of giant vegetables and delightfully preposterous canny or composite creatures. Although more nearly akin to fairyland, this otherworld bears a faint resemblance and direct relation to the earthly paradise of Western guidebooks and land advertisements, out of whose boasts of marvels of climate and soil many whoppers have sprung.

In a land of vast distances and vast natural resources, where topographical features and human enterprises alike are on a grand scale, the line between fact and fantasy is hard to draw. Especially is this true in the "enchanted" Southwest, amidst flat, shining expanses of plain and desert, where the atmosphere, light, and distance play queer tricks with one's vision and imagination, making for mirage and legend.

The rabbits have somehow gotten the body of the hare and the ears of the ass; the frogs, the body of the toad, the horns of the stag-beetle, and the tail of the lizard; the trees fall up-hill, and the lightning comes out of the ground.[1]

Equally intense and dramatic is the history of the Southwest, with its kaleidoscope of land-openings, migrations, and industrial developments, centering in the kingdoms of cattle and oil, cotton and citrous fruit. Landscape and history thus combine to keep one in a state of restless excitement and stimulation, in which it is easy to confuse illusion with reality, and a highly sharpened dramatic sense causes travelers and old-timers to feed their own and others' love of marvels, relating not what they have seen but what they think they have seen and what their listeners want to hear.

A similar enchantment is bred by the mountains and valleys of the South and the West. Among the concealments and surprises of winding creek trails, mysterious woods, and misty hollows, the marvelous hunters and fishermen of Appalachia and Ozarkia keep alive the name or tradition and the fictions of Davy Crockett and Baron Munchausen. Amidst the less intimate and more frigid wonders of the Rockies and the coastal range, where "streams run uphill and Nature appears to lie some herself," scouts, trappers, hunters, and explorers like Jim Bridger, Jim Beckwourth, Joe Meek, and Black Harris acquired a reputation as spectacular windjammers.[2]

2. COMPETITIVE LYING: THE LIARS' CLUB

Since whoppers are based on extravagant claims, artistic lying, like artistic boasting, thrives on competition. And once the element of competition or contest is introduced, the artistic lie gives rise to the burlesque lie, as the artistic boast gives rise to the burlesque boast. The whopper then becomes a monstrous take-off, a lie to end all lies.

As a convenient device for lying contests, the tradition of the Liars' Bench has sprung up in rural America. Generally, this is a purely figurative expression for a mythical gathering of story-tellers in any setting, from courthouse steps or square, country store, barber shop, or bar-room to campfire or bunkhouse. In some cases, however, the bench is an actual one rather than a mere symbol.[3] Thus in Indiana:

In Nashville, county seat of Brown County, the bench stands beneath the locust trees on the courthouse lawn. It is an old wooden seat with iron legs, and a single arm, and has occupied the same position winter and summer for a number of years. Its seating capacity is limited to six. Here the Brown County story-tellers swap yarns.

There is an unwritten law that when this bench is full and other tale-tellers come to join those seated there, the one at the foot—the end without the arm—is pushed off to make room for the new recruits. Efforts are sometimes made to dislodge the man at the head, but the iron arm blocks this move and as a result one of the middle men is pushed out when the grand shove begins. It is to this comfortable loafing place that Nashville women come whenever they cannot find their husbands nearer home.

Gentryville has always had its loafing place since the days when the Gentry boys, Baldwin the blacksmith, Abe Lincoln, and Dennis Hanks used to congregate around Jones' store. But it was not until 1894 that a definite place was established where a man might go and be sure of an audience any time of day. A large heavy bridge plank was wedged between two locust trees near the entrance to one of the crossroad stores. The plank was thick and long, and with a brace in the center gave enough room for a number of men and boys who kept the bench full throughout the day and far into the night. As fast as one would leave some other would take his place.[4]

In response to the same urge for competitive lying and an audience, Liars' Clubs have also arisen, ranging from such hoaxes as the Sazerac Lying Club to regular organizations like the Tall Story Club of Lowell Thomas, the Burlington, Wisconsin, Liars' Club ("Originators and Promoters of the National Liars' Contest"), and the Goofy Liars' Club of Decatur, Illinois ("Organizers and Promoters of International Liars' Contest"). The Sazerac Lying Club was the creation of Fred H. Hart, born of a dearth of "local" copy to fill the columns of the *Reese River Reveille*, an Austin, Nevada, daily, of which he became editor in 1873.[5] The Tall Story Club grew out of a flood of fan-mail mosquito stories following a *Literary Digest* radio news commentary in which Lowell Thomas had cited the fact that the Arctic tundras rather than the tropics breed the biggest and worst mosquitoes.[6] The Burlington Liars' Club, like the Sazerac Lying Club, grew out of a newspaper hoax:

Back in 1929 a Burlington newspaper reporter wrote a story to the effect that these "old timers" got together each New Year's day at the police station, and lied for the championship of the city. He told a brother reporter of his plan, and the story was "sprung" just before New Year's.

They considered the story a good local joke, and after it had appeared in their respective newspapers, forgot about it. However, city editors, with an eye for interesting features, "put it on the wire," and the following December the Associated Press and other news agencies began phoning Burlington to find out if the city's annual contest would be repeated. By this time one of the reporters had left Burlington, but the other one, feeling it would be a shame to miss an opportunity to hornswoggle the public, concocted a story and sent it on its way. Letters began to trickle in from the four corners of the country commenting on the "contest." They furnished the inspiration for a real contest instead of a phoney one, national in scope, and the Burlington Liars' Club was formed to carry it on.[7]

The themes of whoppers are the perennial ones of weather, climate, soil, pests, monsters, hunting, fishing, marksmanship, in any extreme or excess that constitutes an asset or a liability, or both. On the asset side, stories of fertile land are perhaps the most common. From nearly all states comes a chorus of brags of giant vegetables—turnip, pumpkin, beet, potato, cucumber, corn—harking back to old world stories of the great cabbage and the pot that matched it, with disaster following in the trail of phenomenally large or rapid growth. On the liability side, stories of grasshoppers and potato bugs vie with those of mosquitoes as most destructive of crops or most annoying to mankind. Side by side with traditional whoppers are the individual inventions of professional humorists and literary men. Through all this lavish, contagious, and expansive mendacity runs a strain of elaborate hoaxing and jesting that belongs to the humor of exaggeration and deception but more often borders on pure nonsense or fantasy.

Nonsense and fantasy reach their height in the freakish behavior of animals and the lore of mythical monsters. Harking back to the "unnatural natural history" and bestiaries of ancient and medieval times, the most fearsome of these fabulous creatures are those that haunt the big woods, from Maine to Vancouver Island, where, as part of the lore of the lumberjack, they have been attracted into the Paul Bunyan cycle.

———————◆———————

Black Harris and the Putrified Forest*

" 'Twas about 'calf-time,' maybe a little later, and not a hundred year ago, by a long chalk, that the biggest kind of rendezvous was held 'to' Independence, a mighty handsome little location away up on Old Missoura. A pretty smart lot of boys was camp'd thar, about a quarter from the town, and

———————

* From *Life in the Far West*, by George Frederic Ruxton, pp. 14–18. New York: Harper & Brothers, 1849.

the way the whisky flowed that time was 'some' now, *I* can tell you. . . .

"Surely Black Harris was thar; and the darndest liar was Black Harris—for lies tumbled out of his mouth like boudins out of a bufler's stomach. He was the child as saw the putrified forest in the Black Hills. Black Harris come in from Laramie; he'd been trapping three year an' more on Platte and the 'other side'; and, when he got into Liberty, he fixed himself right off like a Saint Louiy dandy. Well, he sat to dinner one day in the tavern, and a lady says to him:—

" 'Well, Mister Harris, I hear you're a great travler.'

" 'Travler, marm,' says Black Harris, 'this niggur's no travler; I ar' a trapper, marm, a mountain-man, wagh!'

" 'Well, Mister Harris, trappers are great travlers, and you goes over a sight of ground in your perishinations, I'll be bound to say.'

" 'A sight, marm, this coon's gone over, if that's the way your 'stick floats.' I've trapped beaver on Platte and Arkansas, and away up on Missoura and Yaller Stone; I've trapped on Columbia, on Lewis Fork, and Green River; I've trapped, marm, on Grand River and the Heely (Gila). I've fout the 'Blackfoot' (and d—d bad Injuns they ar); I've raised the hair[8] of more *than one* Apach, and made a Rapaho 'come' afore now; I've trapped in heav'n, in airth, and h—; and scalp my old head, marm, but I've seen a putrified forest.'

" 'La, Mister Harris, a what?'

" 'A putrified forest, marm, as sure as my rifle's got hind-sights, and *she* shoots center. I was out on the Black Hills, Bill Sublette knows the time—the year it rained fire—and every body knows when that was. If thar wasn't cold doins about that time, this child wouldn't say so. The snow was about fifty foot deep, and the bufler lay dead on the ground like bees after a beein'; not whar we was tho', for *thar* was no bufler, and no meat, and me and my band had been livin' on our moccasins (leastwise the parflesh[9]) for six weeks; and poor doins that feedin' is, marm, as you'll never know. One day we crossed a 'cañon' and over a 'divide,' and got into a peraira, whar was green grass, and green trees, and green leaves on the trees, and birds singing in the green leaves, and this in Febrary, wagh! Our animals was like to die when they see the green grass, and we all sung out, 'hurraw for summer doins.'

" 'Hyar goes for meat,' says I, and I jest ups old Ginger at one of them singing birds, and down come the crittur elegant; its darned head spinning away from the body, but never stops singing, and when I takes up the meat, I finds it stone, wagh! 'Hyar's damp powder and no fire to dry it,' I says, quite skeared.

" 'Fire be dogged,' says old Rube. 'Hyar's a hos as 'll make fire come'; and with that he takes his ax and lets drive at a cotton wood. Schr-u-k—goes the ax agin the tree, and out comes a bit of the blade as big as my hand. We looks at the animals, and thar they stood shaking over the grass, which I'm dog-gone if it wasn't stone, too. Young Sublette comes up, and he'd been clerking down to the fort on Platte, so he know'd something. He looks and looks, and scrapes the trees with his butcher knife, and snaps the grass like pipe stems, and breaks the leaves a-snappin' like Californy shells.

" 'What's all this, boy?' I asks.

" 'Putrefactions,' says he, looking smart, 'putrefactions, or I'm a niggur.'

" 'La, Mister Harris,' says the lady, 'putrefactions! why, did the leaves, and the trees, and the grass smell badly?'

" 'Smell badly, marm!' says Black Harris, 'would a skunk stink if he was froze to stone? No, marm, this child didn't know what putrefaction was, and young Sublette's varsion wouldn't "shine" no how, so I chips a piece out of a tree and puts it in my trap-sack, and carries it in safe to Laramie. Well, old Captain Stewart (a clever man was that, though he was an Englishman), he comes along next spring, and a Dutch doctor chap was along too. I shows him the piece I chipped out of the tree, and he called it a putrefaction too; and so, marm, if that wasn't a putrefied peraira, what was it? For this hos doesn't know, and *he* knows "fat cow" from "poor bull," anyhow.' . . ."

Mushmouth Charlie's Lecture on the Petrified Forest*

Away out yonder in Arizony where it ain't rained since Noah and it's so dry you have to prime yourself to spit thar's a wonderful forest whar the trees is a-growin' jest the same as they did centuries and centuries ago, but a-a-ll pewtrified,

---

* From *The Hurricane's Children*, Tales from Your Neck o' the Woods, by Carl Carmer, p. 58. Copyright, 1937, by Carl Carmer. Farrar & Rinehart, Inc. New York. Toronto.

ladies and gentlemen, a-a-ll pewtrified. And the roots of them thar trees is a-growin' way down in the ground—a-spreadin' out and a-takin' holt on the dirt jest the same as they did centuries and centuries ago—but a-a-ll pewtrified, ladies and gentlemen, a-a-ll pewtrified; and the branches of them thar trees is a-growin' full of twigs and leaves and birds' nests jest the same as they did centuries and centuries ago. And flyin' around in them thar branches and through the pewtrified air is a number of pine hens, sandhill cranes, white-necked ravens, and yellow-headed blackbirds, all a-singin' their beautiful songs just as they did centuries and centuries ago, but a-a-ll pewtrified, ladies and gentlemen, a-a-ll pewtrified.

Now when I give a lecture on Arizony up to Boston last week and told this interestin' scientific fact, some unbelievin' miscreant sings out, "What about the law of gravitation?" and I sings right back at him, "Seems to me anybody with the sense of a coyote'd know that way out there in Arizony this here now law of gravitation hain't worked for centuries and centuries but is like everythin' else aout there—a-a-ll pewtrified, ladies and gentlemen, completely pewtrified.

The Wild Texan Tells Some Big Stories*

FROM Richmond I went on to Lexington, where my relatives lived. They were all glad to see me, and did all they could to make my time pass pleasantly while I was with them; though I could see very plainly that they all looked upon me as a sort of half-civilized savage that never could be entirely tamed; and perhaps they were right. I had lived too long the free and independent life of a ranger, to be contented a great while with the steady habits and humdrum existence of the people of the "Old States." I longed for the excitement of the chase, an Indian foray, a buffalo-hunt, or a bear-fight. However, everything for a time was new and strange to me, and I enjoyed myself as much as I could have expected.

A few weeks after my arrival I went to a "fandango" that was given for my especial benefit. There was a great crowd there, and everybody was anxious to see the "Wild Texan,"

* From *The Adventures of Big-Foot Wallace, the Texas Ranger and Hunter*, by John C. Duval, 274–281. Entered, according to Act of Congress, in the year 1870, by J. W. Burke & Co., in the Clerk's Office of the District Court of the United States for the Southern District of Georgia. Philadelphia: Claxton, Remsen & Haffelfinger. Macon, Ga.: J. W. Burke & Co.

as they called me. I was the "lion" of the evening, particularly with the young ladies, who never tired of asking me questions about Mexico, Texas, the Indians, prairies, etc. I at first answered truly all the questions they asked me; but when I found they evidently doubted some of the stories I told them which were facts, I branched out and gave them some "whoppers," which they swallowed down without "gagging." For instance, one young woman wanted to know how many wild horses I had ever seen in a drove. I told her perhaps thirty or forty thousand.

"Oh! now! Mr. Wallace," said she, "don't try to make game of me in that way. Forty thousand horses in one drove! well, I declare you are a second 'Munchausen'!"

"Well, then," said I, "maybe you won't believe me when I tell you there is a sort of spider in Texas as big as a peck measure, the bite of which can only be cured by music."

"Oh, yes," she answered, "I believe that's all so, for I have read about them in a book."

Among other "whoppers," I told her there was "varmint" in Texas, called the "Santa Fé," that was still worse than the tarantula, for the best brass band in the country couldn't cure their sting; that the creature had a hundred legs and a sting on every one of them, besides two large stings in its forked tail, and fangs as big as a rattlesnake's. When they sting you with their legs alone, you might possibly live an hour; when with all their stings, perhaps fifteen or twenty minutes; but when they sting and bite you at the same time, you first turn blue, then yellow, and then a beautiful bottle-green, when your hair all fell out and your finger nails dropped off, and you were as dead as a door-nail in five minutes, spite of all the doctors in America.

"Oh! my! Mr. Wallace," said she, "how have you managed to live so long in that horrible country?"

"Why, you see," said I, "with my tarantula boots made of alligator-skin, and my centipede hunting-shirt made of tanned rattlesnakes' hides, I have escaped pretty well; but these don't protect you against the stinging scorpions, 'cow-killers,' and scaly-back chinches, that crawl about at night when you are asleep! The only way to keep them at a distance is to 'chaw' tobacco and drink whisky, and that is the reason the Temperance Society never flourished much in Texas."

"Oh!" said she, "what a horrible country that must be, where people have to be stung to death, or 'chaw' tobacco and drink whisky! I don't know which is the worst."

"Well," said I, "the people out there don't seem to mind it much; they get used to it after a while; in fact, they seem rather to like it, for they chaw tobacco and drink whisky even in the winter-time, when the 'cow-killers' and stinging-lizards are all frozen up!"

I had been introduced to one young woman by the name of Matilda, who was as pretty as a pink! Her teeth were as white as an alligator's, and her eyes were as bright as two mesquite coals, and her mouth looked like a little gash cut in a juicy peach. She was a "deadener," I tell you, and a regular "knee-weakener," in the bargain; and I wanted to have a little talk with her the worst in the world; but somehow I felt a little afraid to venture. After a little while, however, she came up to me of her own accord, and began to ask me a great many questions about Texas and the Indians, wild horses, and the prairies, etc. Among other things, she asked me if young women were in great demand in Texas.

"I should think they were," said I. "The day the first young woman came into our settlement there were fourteen Spanish horses badly foundered on sedge-grass, by the young men who flocked in to see her, from forty miles around; and the next morning she had seventeen offers of marriage before breakfast! The young woman was a little confused by so many applications at once, and before she could make up her mind which one to take, one of the 'rancheros' watched his chance, and the first time she walked out he caught her up behind him on his horse, rode off full speed to San Patricio, drew his six-shooter on the padre, and forced him to marry them on the spot. This saved the young woman all further trouble on the subject, and they are now living happily together on one of the finest cattle ranches in the County of Karnes."

"Oh! I declare," said Miss Matilda, "that is delightful! How romantic to be run off with in that way by a handsome young 'ranchero.' I think, Mr. Wallace, I shall have to go to Texas."

"You might do worse," said I; "and besides, you would stand a chance of being run away with by some great Comanche or Tonkawa chief; with a bow and quiver on his back and eagle's feathers on his head, and nothing else to speak of in the way of clothes."

Miss Matilda didn't seem to hear that last part of my speech, for she jumped up and clapped her little hands: "Oh," said she, "wouldn't that be fine? To gallop over the flowery prairies, free as the wind, from morning till night, and listen to the feathered songsters pouring forth their untaught melodies from every grove and shady dell! Oh, it would be splendid, Mr. Wallace!"

"Yes," said I, "it would. One of the handsomest young women in our settlement was carried off, three or four years ago, by 'He-che-puck-sa-sa,' the 'Bellowing Bull,' and when I went on a visit to his tribe, not long ago, she was the favorite wife and head squaw of the wigwam, and had brass rings enough on her arms and legs to have made a pair of 'dog-irons,' if they had been melted up, besides one in her nose as big as the palm of my hand."

"Why! how many wives did the Mormon have?" asked Miss Matilda, looking a little down in the mouth.

"Oh! I can't say exactly," I answered; "I only saw six; but he had another wigwam at the village below. But," said I, "Miss Matilda, after riding over the flowery prairies all day, and listening to the coyotes howling in every grove and dell, where will you *put up* at night; and how will you manage to get along without hot rolls for breakfast, and baked custard for dinner?"

"Oh," said she, "I don't care for them; I can do very well without them; all I want is a nice cup of coffee in the morning, and a biscuit or a slice of toast, and a little fresh butter, or a few fresh-laid eggs; and for dinner a few vegetables and wild fruits, and now and then a nice beefsteak or a saddle of venison roasted before the fire!"

"Yes," says I, "that's all reasonable enough, and you could get them, I suppose, at any time; but you see, the Indians don't cook their meat."

"The cannibals!" exclaimed Miss Matilda; "they certainly don't eat it raw, do they?"

"Yes," said I, "as a general thing; only sometimes, when a fellow feels a little squeamish, he fastens a beef or mule steak under his saddle, and after riding and jolting on it all day, he finds it nicely 'done' when he stops at night; and it's a very convenient way of cooking, too, especially when a fellow is in a hurry (which the Indians always are, for they are always after somebody, or else somebody is after them); and besides, they say it is the best thing in the world for a sore-back horse!"

"Oh! dear," said Miss Matilda, "I don't believe I'll go to Texas, after all; for if I do, I must put up with a 'ranchero' —they don't eat their meat raw, do they?"

"No," said I, "except when they are out on the plains, and can't find buffalo-chips enough to cook it with."

"Oh! tell me, Mr. Wallace," said she, "did you ever see a 'mirage' on the plains?"

"A mirage?" said I, rather taken aback, for I hadn't the least idea what she meant, unless it was a drove of mustangs or a herd of buffalo; "why, certainly, I have seen a thousand of 'em."

"I didn't think they were so common," said she.

"Oh, yes," I answered; "the last one I saw was just back of Santa Fé, and it stampeded when we got in about a quarter of a mile of it; and such a dust as was kicked up you never saw, for there hadn't been a drop of rain in six months."

"Well, I declare!" said Miss Matilda; "I always heard that the mirage would disappear as you approached it, but I never heard of one kicking up a dust before."

"No," said I; "they don't in other countries, where the ground is kept wet by constant rain; but in Texas, you see, it is different."

Some Liars of the Old West*

SPEAKIN' of liars, the Old West could put in its claim for more of 'em than any other land under the sun. The mountains and plains seemed to stimulate man's imagination. A man in the States might have been a liar in a small way, but when he comes west he soon takes lessons from the prairies, where ranges a hundred miles away seem within touchin' distance, streams run uphill and Nature appears to lie some herself.

These men weren't vicious liars. It was love of romance, lack of reading matter, and the wish to be entertainin' that makes 'em stretch facts and invent yarns. . . .

Once up in Yogo, Bill Cameron pointed out Old Man Babcock an' another old-timer, Patrick, sayin', "There's three of the biggest liars in the world."

"Who's the third?" inquired a bystander.

"Patrick's one, an' old Bab's the other two," says Cameron. This Babcock one night is telling about getting jumped by

* From *Trails Plowed Under*, by Charles M. Russell, pp. 191–194. Copyright, 1927, by Doubleday, Page & Company. Garden City, New York.

50 hostile Sioux, a war party, that's giving him a close run. The bullets an' arrows are tearin' the dirt all around, when he hits the mouth of a deep canyon. He thinks he's safe, but after ridin' up it a way, discovers it's a box gulch, with walls straight up from 600 to 1,000 feet. His only get-away's where he come in, an' the Indians are already whippin' their ponies into it.

Right here old Bab rares back in his chair, closes his eyes, an' starts fondlin' his whiskers. This seems to be the end of the story, when one of the listeners asks:

"What happened then?"

Old Bab, with his eyes still closed, takin' a fresh chew, whispered: "They killed me, b' God!"

The upper Missouri River steamboats, they used to say, would run on a light dew, an' certainly they used to get by where there was mighty little water. X. Beidler an' his friend, Major Reed, are traveling by boat to Fort Benton. One night they drink more than they should. X. is awakened in the morning by the cries of Reed. On entering his stateroom, X. finds Reed begging for water, as he's dying of thirst.

X. steps to the bedside, and takin' his friend's hand, says: "I'm sorry, Major, I can't do anything for you. That damned pilot got drunk, too, last night, and we're eight miles up a dry coulee!"

"Some say rattlers ain't pizen," said Buckskin Williams, an old freighter, "but I know different. I'm pullin' out of Milk River one day with 14, when I notice my line hoss swing out an' every hoss on the near side crowds the chain. My near wheel hoss, that I'm ridin', rares up an' straddles the tongue. It's then I see what the trouble is—a big rattler has struck, misses my hoss an' hits the tongue. The tongue starts to swell up. I have to chop it off to save the wagon, an' I'm damn quick doin' it, too!"

A traveling man in White Sulphur Springs makes a bet of drinks for the town with Coates, a saloon keeper, that Coates can't find a man that will hold up his hand and take his oath that he has seen 100,000 buffalo at one sight. When the bet's decided, it's agreed to ring the triangle at the hotel, which will call the town to their drinks.

Many old-timers said they had seen that many buffalo, but refused to swear to it, and it looked like Coates would lose his bet until Milt Crowthers showed up. When a smile of confidence spread over Coates' face as he introduces Crowthers to the drummer.

"Mr. Crowthers," said the traveling man, "how many antelope have you seen at one time?"

Crowthers straightens up and looks wise, like he's turning back over the pages of the past. "Two hundred thousand," says he.

"How many elk?" asks the traveling man.

"Somethin' over a million," replies Crowthers.

"Mr. Crowthers, how many buffalo will you hold up your hand and swear you have seen at one sight?"

Crowthers holds up his hand. "As near as I can figure," says he, "about three million billion."

This is where Coates starts for the triangle, but the traveling man halts him, saying, "Where were you when you saw these buffalo, Mr. Crowthers?"

"I was a boy travelin' with a wagon train," replies Crowthers. "We was south of the Platte when we was forced to corral our wagons to keep our stock from bein' stampeded by buffalo. For five days an' nights 50 men kep' their guns hot killin' buffalo to keep 'em off the wagons. The sixth day the herd spread, givin' us time to yoke up an' cross the Platte, an' it's a damn good thing we did."

"Why?" asks the traveling man.

"Well," says Crowthers, "we no more than hit the high country north of the Platte, than lookin' back, here comes the main herd!"

Stories Told around the Camp Fire*

BUFFALO BILL, Pawnee Bill, and Three Dollar Bill were out scouting in Colorado, on the hunt of a war party of Cheyenne and Arapahoe Indians that were said to have captured a Mormon emigrant who was going from St. Joseph, Mo., to Salt Lake City. All at once the three Bills stopped and sniffed the air to see if they could locate their camp.

* From *Bill Jones of Paradise Valley, Oklahoma*. His Life and Adventures for Over Forty Years in The Great Southwest. He was a Pioneer in the Days of the Buffalo, The Wild Indian, The Oklahoma Boomer, The Cowboy and The Outlaw, by John J. Callison, pp. 115–118, 119–123. Copyright, 1914, by J. J. Callison. Kingfisher, Oklahoma.

"There it is," said Buffalo Bill, "just in the edge of that clump of timber, and it is just ten miles to their camp."

"Yes," said Pawnee Bill, "and they are in the center of the clump. That makes them ten miles and a half from here."

"No," said Three Dollar Bill. "They are on the farther side of the clump, and that makes them eleven miles away, and there are three hundred of the braves. Do you think we had better wait until night before we attempt to rescue the Mormons?"

"Yes," said Buffalo Bill. "We will wait until just before the moon comes up. Then we will slip in and rescue them, and by the time we can get those emigrants together the moon will be up, so we can be off about ten."

That night the three Bills slipped into the Indian camp and had no trouble in locating the Mormons. Buffalo Bill put the seventeen women on his pony and started for Ft. Hays, Kansas. Pawnee Bill gathered up the fifty-one kids, put them on his pony and started after Buffalo Bill. Three Dollar Bill was to trail along behind and keep a lookout for the Indians, in case they should attempt to recapture them. That old Mormon was so tickled over his capture that he just stayed in the Indian camp, and was captured three years later by some cowboys and hanged for stealing horses.

The Razorback*

COARSELY and variously colored, long-snouted, long-tailed, long-bodied, long-legged, long-tusked, even long in his squeal, the razorback of Texas and the South became the theme for a whole cycle of folk jokes and yarns. Modern pipeliners swear that their mythological hero, Paul Bunyan, laid his famous line through Arkansas by driving ahead of him a herd of razorbacks that rooted the ditch for the pipe. The story goes, too, that in early days an Eastern tenderfoot who had recently arrived in South Texas became very much interested in the native hogs. After learning how the settlers had to scour the country for hours sometimes before catching one of their hogs and then had to carry its dirty carcass for miles before getting home to butcher it, he exclaimed:

"All this must take an awful lot of trouble and time!"

* From *A Vaquero of the Brush Country*, by J. Frank Dobie, pp. 35–38. Copyright, 1929, by the Southwest Press. Dallas.

"Yes," replied a settler, "it does take time, but, hell, what's time to a hog—and besides we have lots of fun."

The Tennessee version of the story—as told by the fertile anecdoter, L. L. Click of Austin—goes better. A mountaineer was holding a razorback shoat in his arms and lifting him up so that he could "graze" on ripe persimmons still hanging on the tree. A stranger came along.

"You may get that hog fat after a while," he said to the mountaineer, "but it's going to take a mighty long time."

"Huh," replied the mountaineer, "what's time to a derned hawg?"

There was a time when Texans and citizens of other Southern states were not a bit ashamed of their respective varieties of razorbacks. One time, so one story goes, a real estate agent was showing a stranger some land in the Trinity River bottoms. The stranger saw what he took to be highwater marks far up on the trunks of the various trees and he called attention to these evidences of overflow.

"Oh, no, no," the agent corrected the prospective buyer, "them's not highwater marks at all. That's jest where our hawgs rubbed their backs. Let me tell you, man, this land grows the tallest hawgs in America."

A. L. Steele, of Lovington, New Mexico, who was born in Grimes County, Texas, 1841, tells another anecdote of the patriotic zeal with which some frontiersmen supported the razorback.

"Right after the close of the Civil War," says Mr. Steele, "I was in Natchez, Mississippi, with a herd of steers, from Navarro County. After we got them sold, Wash Little, who was with me, began to tank up on red-eye and to brag on Texas hogs. A Mississippian began glorifying the Mississippi variety, and in order to prevent a possible killing I had to take Wash across the river and stay all night in Vidalia."

Arkansas had zealous—and logical—advocates also, as a story recorded by Dallas T. Herndon in his *Centennial History of Arkansas* will illustrate. "Some swine breeders from other states brought their best specimens of fine stock—Chester White, Poland China, etc—to a county fair in Arkansas. The local farmers exhibited their hogs, which still retained many of the points of the true razorback, and, to the surprise of the owners of the thoroughbreds, the native hogs won every prize. After the awards had been made, one of the importers approached one of the judges and said:

"'We are not offended with your action in giving the prizes

to your neighbors, but we feel confident that our hogs are superior in many respects to those you have favored, and just for information I would like to ask upon what points you judges based your decision.'

" 'Well, stranger,' replied the judge, 'there's no doubt that your hogs could be fattened easier and made to weigh more, but the trouble is they can't run fast enough.'

" 'Can't run fast enough?' exclaimed the swine breeder. 'This is the first time I ever heard of speed being a good qualification in a hog. Why should a hog be able to run fast?'

" 'The niggers, sir, the niggers,' replied the judge. 'Your hogs would be all right for meat, but the niggers could steal them too easily. With our hogs they would have more trouble in catching them. Do you get the point?'

"The exhibitor evidently got the point, as the conversation ended and he took his fine hogs back home, having learned a lesson in swine breeding that he had previously overlooked."

Uncle Davy Lane*

I must not forget, in these random sketches, my old friend and neighbor, Uncle Davy Lane. Some men make an early and decided impression upon you—features, actions, habits, all the entire man, real and artificial. "Uncle Davy" was that kind of man.

I will mention a few things that make me remember him. His looks were peculiar. He was tall, dark, and rough-skinned; lymphatic, dull, and don't-care-looking in his whole physiognomy. He had lazy looks and movements. Nothing could move him out of a slow, horse-mill gait but snakes, of which "creeturs he was monstrous 'fraid." The reader shall soon have abundant evidence of the truth of this admission in his numerous and rapid flights from "sarpunts."

Uncle Davy was a gunsmith, and, as an evidence of the fact, he carried about with him the last gun he ever made. His gun, a rifle, was characteristic of its maker and owner— rough and unfinished outside, but good within. It was put in an old worm-eaten half-stock which he had picked up somewhere, and the barrel had never been dressed nor ground outside. He would visit a neighbor early in the morning, sit

* From *Fisher's River (North Carolina) Scenes and Characters*, by "Skitt" [H. E. Taliaferro], pp. 50–58, 63–74, 79–93. New York: Harper & Bros. 1859.

down with his rifle across his knees, in "too great a hurry" to
set it aside, would stay all day, would lay it by only at meals,
which he seldom refused, but "never was a-hongry."

He had a great fund of long-winded stories and incidents,
mostly manufactured by himself—some few he had "hearn"
—and would bore you or edify you, as it might turn out, from
sun to sun, interspersing them now and then with a dull,
guttural, lazy laugh.

He became quite a proverb in the line of big story-telling.
True, he had many obstinate competitors, but he distanced
them all farther than he did the numerous snakes that "run
arter him." He had given his ambitious competitors fair
warning thus:

"Ef any on 'um beats me, I'll sell out my deadnin' and
hustle off to other deadnin's."

In sheer justice to Uncle Davy, however, and with pleasure
I record the fact, that he reformed his life, became a
Christian, I hope, as well as a Baptist, and died a penitent
man.

As stated, he was never known to get out of a snail's gallop
only when in contact with snakes; and the reader shall now
have, in Uncle Davy's own style, an account of his flight
from a coachwhip snake.

I. The Chase

"I had a hog claim over beyant Moor's Fork, and I concluded I'd take old Bucksmasher (his rifle), and go inter the
big huckleberry patch, on Round Hill, in sarch for 'um. Off
I trolloped, and toddled about for some time, but couldn't
find head nur tail uv 'um. But while I was moseyin' about, I
cum right chug upon one uv the biggest, longest, outdacious-
est coachwhip snakes I uver laid my peepers on. He rared
right straight up, like a May-pole, licked out his tarnacious
tongue, and good as said, 'Here's at you, sir. What bizness
have you on my grit?' Now I'd hearn folks say ef you'd
look a vinimus animil right plump in the eyes he wouldn't
hurt you. Now I tried it good, just like I were trying to look
through a millstone. But, bless you, honey! he had no more
respect fur a man's face and eyes than he had fur a huckleberry, sure's gun's iron. So I seed clearly that I'd have to try
my trotters.

"I dashed down old Bucksmasher, and jumped 'bout ten

steps the fust leap, and on I went wusser nur an old buck fur 'bout a quarter, and turned my noggin round to look fur the critter. Jehu Nimshi! thar he were right dab at my heels, head up, tongue out, and red as a nail-rod, and his eyes like two balls uv fire, red as chain lightnin'. I 'creased my verlocity, jumped logs twenty foot high, clarin' thick bushes, and bush-heaps, deep gullies, and branches. Again I looked back, thinkin' I had sartinly left it a long gap behind. And what do you think? By jingo! he'd hardly begun to run—jist gittin' his hand in. So I jist put flatly down again faster than uver. 'T wasn't long afore I run out'n my shot-bag, I went so fast, then out'n my shirt, then out'n my britches—luther britches at that—then away went my drawers. Thus I run clean out'n all my linnen a half a mile afore I got home; and, thinks I, surely the tarnul sarpunt are distanced now.

"But what do you think now? Nebuchadnezzar! thar he were, fresh as a mounting buck jist scared up. I soon seen that wouldn't do, so I jumped about thirty-five foot, screamed like a wildcat, and 'creased my verlocity at a monstrous rate. Jist then I begun to feel my skin split, and, thinks I, it's no use to run out'n my skin, like I have out'n my linnen, as huming skin are scarce, so I tuck in a leetle.

"But by this time I'd run clean beyant my house, right smack through my yard, scaring Molly and the childering, dogs, cats, chickens—uvrything—half to death. But, you see, I got shet uv my inimy, the sarpunt, fur it had respect fur my house, ef it hadn't fur my face and eyes in the woods. I puffed, and blowed, and sweated 'bout half an hour afore I had wind to tell Molly and the childering what were the matter.

"Poor old Bucksmasher staid several days in the woods afore I could have the pluck to go arter him."

II. RIDE IN THE PEACH-TREE

"Now when I got my shot-bag off uv the moon, I lost no time, which I'd lost a great deal arter that old buck, as jist norated. I moseyed home in a hurry, straightened old Buck-smasher, and piked off to Skull Camp, to smash up a few old bucks on that grit. Soon as I landed I seen 'bout a dozen old bucks and one old doe. I planted myself, fur they was comin' right smack to'ads me, and I waited tell they got in shootin' range, as it were. I knowed ef I smashed Mrs. Doe fust I'd be right apt to smash all the Mr. Bucks. That's the way with all creation—the males allers a-traipsin' arter the females.

"So I lammed away at her, fotched her to the yeth, and the bucks scampered off. Agin I got loadened up they come back to the doe, smellin' round, and I blazed away again, and tripped up the heels uv one uv 'um. They'd run off a little ways uvry time, but again I'd load up thar'd allers be one ready to be smashed, and I jist kep' smashin' away tell there were but one left, and he were a whopper.

"I felt in my shot-bag, and, pox take the luck! there warn't a bullit in it—nothin' but a peach-stone. I crammed it down, thort I'd salute him with that, and blazed away, aimin' to hit him right behind the wethers, and, by golly! ef he didn't slap down his tail and outrun creation, and give it two in the game. I run up, out with my butcher-knife, stuck uvry one on 'um afore you could cry 'cavy. And sich a pile on 'um, all lyin' cross and pile, you nuver seen in yer borned days.

"I moseyed home in a turkey-trot, got Jim and Sanders and the little waggin, went arter 'um, and, I tell you, we had nice livin' fur a fortnight. Some o' the old bucks would a cut four inches clare fat on the rump. Molly didn't hev to use any hog fat nur fry no bacon with 'um. We sopped both sides uv ur bread, and greased ur mouths from ear to ear. It made the childering as sassy as it does a sea-board feller when he gits his belly full uv herrin'. Thar was skins plenty to make me and all the boys britches, and to buy ammernition to keep old Bucksmasher a-talkin' fur a long time, fur he's a mighty gabby old critter to varmunts uv uvry kind, well as to old bucks, he is.

"Arter makin' a desput smash among old bucks uvry whar else fur three very long years, I thort I'd try my luck in Skull Camp agin. I took plenty uv ammernition with me this time —didn't care about shootin' peach-stones any more out'n old Bucksmasher—and piked off full tilt.

"Soon as I got on good hunting yeth, I seen right by the side uv a clift uv rocks (I were on the upper side uv the clift) a fine young peach-tree, full uv master plum peaches. I were monstrous hongry and dry, and thanked my stars fur the good luck. I sot down old Bucksmasher, stepped from the top uv the clift inter the peach-tree—nuver looked down to see whar it were growin'—jerked out old Butch, and went to eatin' riproarin' fashion.

"I hadn't gulluped down more'n fifty master peaches afore, by golly! the tree started off, with me in it, faster nur you uver seen a scared wolf run. When it had run a mile ur so, I looked down to see what it mout mean. And what do you think? True as preachin', the peach-tree was growin' out'n an old buck, right behind his shoulders.

"I thort my time had come, for on he moseyed over logs, rocks, clifts, and all sorts o' things, and me up in the tree. He went so fast, he did, that he split the wind, and made it roar in my head like a harricane. I tried to pray, but soon found I had no breath to spar in that way fur he went so orful fast that my wind was sometimes clean gone. He run in that fashion fur fifteen mile, gin out, stopped to rest, when I got out'n my fast-runnin' stage mighty soon, and glad o' the chance.

"I left him pantin' away like he were mighty short o' wind, returned thanks fur once, tuck my foot in my hand, and walked all the way back to old Bucksmasher. I seen more old bucks on my way than I uver seen in the same length uv time in all my borned days. They knowed jist as well as I did that I had nothin' to smash 'um with. Thar they was a-kickin' up thar heels and snortin' at me fur fifteen long miles—miles measured with a 'coon-skin, and the tail throwed in fur good measure, fur sure. It were a mighty trial, but I grinned and endured it. I piked on and landed at the place whar I started in my peach-tree stage, found old Bucksmasher, shouldered him, and moseyed fur home, with my feathers cut, fur I'd made a water haul that time, fur sure and sartin."

"To—be—shore, Mr. Lane?" said old Mr. Wilmoth, a good, credulous old man; "ef I didn't know you to be a man of truth, I couldn't believe you. How do you think that peach-tree come up in the back of that deer?"

"Bless you, man! it was from the peach-stone I shot in his back, as jist norated—nothin' plainer."

They Have Yarns*

> They have yarns
> Of a skyscraper so tall they had to put hinges
> On the two top stories so to let the moon go by,
> Of one corn crop in Missouri when the roots
> Went so deep and drew off so much water
> The Mississippi riverbed that year was dry,
> Of pancakes so thin they had only one side,

* From *The People, Yes*, by Carl Sandburg, pp. 88–93. Copyright, 1936, by Harcourt, Brace & Company, Inc.

Of "a fog so thick we shingled the barn and six feet out on the fog,"

Of Pecos Pete straddling a cyclone in Texas and riding it to the west coast where "it rained out under him,"

Of the man who drove a swarm of bees across the Rocky Mountains and the Desert "and didn't lose a bee,"

Of a mountain railroad curve where the engineer in his cab can touch the caboose and spit in the conductor's eye,

Of the boy who climbed a cornstalk growing so fast he would have starved to death if they hadn't shot biscuits up to him,

Of the old man's whiskers: "When the wind was with him his whiskers arrived a day before he did,"

Of the hen laying a square egg and cackling "Ouch!" and of hens laying eggs with the dates printed on them,

Of the ship captain's shadow: it froze to the deck one cold winter night,

Of mutineers on that same ship put to chipping rust with rubber hammers,

Of the sheep counter who was fast and accurate: "I just count their feet and divide by four."

Of the man so tall he must climb a ladder to shave himself,

Of the runt so teeny-weeny it takes two men and a boy to see him,

Of mosquitoes: one can kill a dog, two of them a man,

Of a cyclone that sucked cookstoves out of the kitchen, up the chimney flue, and on to the next town,

Of the same cyclone picking up wagon-tracks in Nebraska and dropping them over in the Dakotas,

Of the hook-and-eye snake unlocking itself into forty pieces, each piece two inches long, then in nine seconds flat snapping itself together again,

Of the watch swallowed by the cow—when they butchered her a year later the watch was running and had the correct time,

Of horned snakes, hoop snakes that roll themselves where they want to go, and rattlesnakes carrying bells instead of rattles on their tails,

Of the herd of cattle in California getting lost in a giant redwood tree that had hollowed out,

Of the man who killed a snake by putting its tail in its mouth so it swallowed itself,

Of railroad trains whizzing along so fast they reach the station before the whistle,

Of pigs so thin the farmer had to tie knots in their tails to keep them from crawling through the cracks in their pens,

Of Paul Bunyan's big blue ox, Babe, measuring between the eyes forty-two ax-handles and a plug of Star tobacco exactly,

Of John Henry's hammer and the curve of its swing and his singing of it as "a rainbow round my shoulder."

A Trip Down East*

WHEN I'M AT HOME I stops in Chuckahokee digging in the state of Indiana. We raised a mighty crop of wheat this year, I reckon upon nigh four thousand bushels, and a sprinklin of corn, oats, potatoes and garden sass. You could hear the earth groan all round our settlement, the crops were so heavy, and that's what gives rise to the stories about the earthquakes. It was near enough to make a young earthquake to hear the corn grow as it did, and as to the potatoes, I'll be skinned alive, if ever I saw any thing like it. Why, any one of them warm nights, you just go out into a little patch of fifty acres, close to the house, and hold your ear down, you could hear the young potatoes quarrelling, and the old ones grumbling at them because they didn't lay along and stop crowding. I calculate you didn't raise such crops in these parts. Why one day one of our squash vines chased a drove of hogs better than half a mile, and they ran and squealed as if the old boy was after them. One little pig stubbed his toe and fell down and never was heard of afterwards.

"According to Nature"**

"SUCH timber, and such bottom land, why you can't preserve any thing natural you plant in it unless you pick it young, things thar will grow out of shape so quick. I once planted in those diggins a few potatoes and beets: they took a fine start, and after that an ox team couldn't have kept them from growing. About that time I went off to old Kentuck on bisiness, and did not hear from them things in three months, when I accidentally stumbled on a fellow who had stopped at my place, with an idea of buying me out. 'How did you like things?' said I. 'Pretty well,' said he; 'the cabin is convenient, and the timber land is good; but that bottom land ain't worth the first red cent.' 'Why?' said I. ' 'Cause it's full of cedar stumps and Indian mounds,' said he, *and it can't be cleared.*'

---

* From *Mince Pie for the Million.* Philadelphia and New York: Turner & Fisher. 1846.
** From "The Big Bear of Arkansas," by T. B. Thorpe. Originally published in *The Spirit of the Times,* 1841; reprinted in *The Big Bear of Arkansas and Other Sketches, Illustrative of Characters and Incidents in the South and South-West,* edited by William T. Porter, Philadelphia, 1845, and *The Hive of the Bee Hunter,* by T. B. Thorpe. New York. 1854.

'Lord,' said I, 'them ar "cedar stumps" is beets, and them ar "Indian mounds" ar tater hills.' As I expected, the crop was overgrown and useless: the sile is too rich, *and planting in Arkansas is dangerous*. I had a good-sized sow killed in that same bottom land. The old thief stole an ear of corn, and took it down where she slept at night to eat. Well, she left a grain or two on the ground, and lay down on them: before morning the corn shot up, and the percussion killed her dead. I don't plant any more: natur intended Arkansaw for a hunting ground, and I go according to natur."

"Nothing to What I Have Seen"*

EARLY in the forenoon Dr. Binninger, Tom Fenton, Jim Hart, the retired miner, and Fraser, the Canadian, came up and began inspecting the crops.

"Oh, this is very well; very well, indeed, for Jersey," said Dr. Binninger, at last, as they sat on the fence by the cornfield, after their labors, smoking; "but nothing to what I have seen. In Gastley County, Missouri, I once saw the corn growing to such an unprecedented height, and the stalks so exceptionally vigorous, that nearly every farmer stacked up, for winter firewood, great heaps of cornstalks, cut up into cordwood length by power saws run by threshing engines. One man, Barney Gregory, took advantage of the season to win a fortune by preparing cornstalks for use as telegraph poles. . . ."

"What is one man's meat is another man's poison," said Fenton. "Fine growing weather, similar to that which made Gregory's fortune in Missouri, has come near ruining those of the Western Nebraska farmers who raised pumpkins. Just as, by all ordinary rules, the crop should have been ready to house, a mysterious rot began to destroy the great green globes glowing to yellow in the sun. An examination by the chemists of the State Agricultural College, showed that the trouble was due to the too rapid growth of the vines, which dragged the pumpkins about after them, all over the fields, until the pumpkins' lower cuticle, being worn out by the abrasion, they succumbed easily to rot in the bruised portion. Should another such year come, the farmers will avoid a like

* From *The Book of Lies*, by John Langdon Heaton, pp. 143–146. Copyright, 1896, by John Langdon Heaton. New York: The Morse Company.

catastrophe by providing each pumpkin with a straw-lined nest, or a little truck with casters.

"A good illustration of nature's bounty happened some time ago in Doniphan County, Kansas," continued Fenton. "A seven-year-old daughter of James Steele was sent, in the middle of the forenoon, to carry a jug of switchel to the men, who were at work near the middle of one of those vast Kansas cornfields. The corn was about up to little Annie's shoulders as she started, but as she went along it rose and rose before her eyes, shooting out of the soil under the magic influence of the sun and the abundant moisture. Almost crazed with fear, she hastened on, but before she could reach the men, the stalks were waving above her head. The men were threatened in a like manner, but by mounting a little fellow on a big man's shoulders, to act as a lookout, they managed to get out, when they promptly borrowed a dog, to follow little Annie's trail. It was not until late in the afternoon that they reached her, where she lay, having cried herself to sleep, with the tear-stains streaking her plump cheeks."

"The soil of some of the Southern California counties is so rich as to become an actual detriment to the farmer," observed Eckels. "In San Bernardino County, a farmer, named Jones, has been forced entirely to abandon the culture of corn, because the stalks, under the influence of the genial sun, mild air, and mellow soil, shoot up into the air so fast that they draw their roots after them; when, of course, the plant dies as a rule. Cases have been known, however, where cornstalks thus uprooted, and lifted into the air, have survived for some time upon the climate alone."

"Why," said Dr. Binninger, "we used to have the same trouble in Kentucky, but it was solved long ago by burying a heavy stone under each cornstalk, and wiring the stalk down to it. I have known the price of stone to treble in one season in consequence of the purely agricultural demand."

Idaho Potatoes*

IN THE Snake River Valley lives an old-timer who is known as Old Jim. Old Jim comes to town now and then and boasts

* From *Idaho Lore*, prepared by the Federal Writers' Project of the Work Projects Administration, Vardis Fisher, State Director, American Guide Series p. 139. Copyright, 1939, by George H. Curtis, Secretary of State for the State of Idaho. Caldwell, Idaho: The Caxton Printers, Ltd.

of the fertility of his land, but complains that he is unable to market the stuff. He grew pumpkins, but they were so large he could not get them on to a wagon, and then ventured into potatoes. When, two years ago, a CCC camp was established nearby, Old Jim was approached by a man who wanted to buy a hundred pounds of spuds. "Only a hundred pounds?" he asked, scratching his pate. "No, I can't do it. I wouldn't cut a spud in two for no one."

"Dat Ain't No Lie"*

WILL HOUSE SAID, "Ah know a lie on a black gnat. Me and my buddy Joe Wiley was ramshackin' Georgy over when we come to a loggin' camp. So bein' out of work we ast for a job. So de man puts us on and give us some oxes to drive. Ah had a six-yoke team and Joe was drivin' a twelve-yoke team. As we was comin' thru de woods we heard somethin' hummin' and we didn't know what it was. So we got hungry and went in a place to eat and when we come out a gnat had done et up de six-yoke team and de twelve-yoke team, and was sittin' up on de wagon pickin' his teeth wid a ox-horn and cryin' for somethin' to eat."

"Yeah," put in Joe Wiley, "we seen a man tie his cow and calf out to pasture and a mosquito come along and et up de cow and was ringin' de bell for de calf."

"Dat wasn't no full-grown mosquito at dat," said Eugene Oliver. "Ah was travellin' in Texas and laid down and went to sleep. De skeeters bit me so hard till Ah seen a ole iron wash-pot, so Ah crawled under it and turned it down over me good so de skeeters couldn't git to me. But you know dem skeeters bored right thru dat iron pot. So I up wid a hatchet and bradded their bills into de pot. So they flew on off 'cross Galveston bay wid de wash-pot on their bills."

"Look," said Black Baby, "on de Indian River we went to bed and heard de mosquitoes singin' like bull alligators. So we got under four blankets. Shucks! dat wasn't nothin'. Dem mosquitoes just screwed off dem short bills, reached back in they hip-pocket and took out they long bills and screwed 'em on and come right on through dem blankets and got us."

* From *Mules and Men*, by Zora Neale Hurston, pp. 132–137, 149–151. Copyright, 1935, by Zora Neale Hurston. Philadelphia and London: J. B. Lippincott Company.

Remarkable Tenacity of Life*

A FEW evenings since, in the "private crib" of one of our exchanges, there was a learned dissertation, subject, "Bedbugs, and their Remarkable Tenacity of Life." One asserted of his own knowledge that they could be boiled, and then come to life. Some had soaked them for hours in turpentine without any fatal consequences. Old Hanks, who had been listening as an outsider, here gave in his experience in corroboration of the facts. Says he, "Some years ago I took a bedbug to an iron-foundry, and dropping it into a ladle where the melted iron was, had it run into a skillet. Well, my old woman used that skillet pretty constant for the last six years, and here the other day it broke all to smash; and what do you think, gentlemen, that 'ere insect just walked out of his hole, where he'd been layin' like a frog in a rock, and made tracks for his old roost upstairs! But," added he, by way of parenthesis, "he looked mighty pale."

Grasshoppers**

THERE are lots of people who remember the summer, fall, and winter of 1874; hot winds, grasshoppers and government aid. First, came the hot winds. They were like a furnace, and would blister the hands and face like fire. We had to get into the house and shut the windows and doors to keep cool. A few days later came the grasshoppers, and they were a hungry bunch of tramps. They got everything that was green, and ate a good many things that were not green. They ate up forty rods of stone fence in thirty-seven and a half minutes by the watch. They destroyed more stone fences that fall than all the boys, dogs, and rabbits put together. The green-headed horseflies were pretty bad that fall, and they made it hot for the stock. We had a pet cow, and in order to keep the flies

---

* From *The American Joe Miller*, A Collection of Yankee Wit and Humor, compiled by Robert Kempt, pp. 8–9. London: Adams and Francis. 1865.
** From *Bill Jones of Paradise Valley, Oklahoma*, His Life and Adventures for Over Forty Years in The Great Southwest. He Was a Pioneer in the Days of the Buffalo, The Wild Indian, The Oklahoma Boomer, The Cowboy and The Outlaw, by John J. Callison, pp. 25–26. Copyright, 1914, by J. J. Callison. Kingfisher, Oklahoma.

from eating her, we covered her with some green paint that we had left over, after painting the house. The hoppers came along, ate up the cow, paint and all.

The hoppers would hold up the children on their way to school and take their lunches away from them. After the grasshoppers had eaten everything, we turned in and ate the grasshoppers. One old fellow said he used to live with the digger Indians in Idaho, and they considered a grasshopper equal to or better than oysters, crawdads, clams, chili, or chop suey. So we all learned to eat grasshoppers, and I can say from experience that they were fine; but I do not want to live long enough to eat them three times a day again. After that we had grasshoppers for about six weeks and had them cooked and served in every way that could be thought of.

The Sway-Back Horse*

THE chickens were digging at their oil sacks and the colts were racing along the pasture fence, tails erect like banners. A very sway-backed old gelding had hung his head over the fence and was asking dumbly to be let into the barn.

"Ol' cuss!" said Mike O'Day. "He knows it's gonna rain pitchforks an' he wants in the barn, though he won't be gittin' no grain of a Sunday when he ain't workin'."

The old man and the old horse had the same air of weariness and lost energy. The driving sand had taken the shine from the horse's coat, and the sun had faded the man's eyes and his overalls to a gray blue.

Mike walked over to the gate and scratched the old horse under the chin. "Me an' you's gittin' along, ain't we?" he said. "Ain't 'lopin' around the pasture fence with our tails in the air."

"Mister O'Day," said the Gunn boy shrilly, "whut makes that horse's back bent like it's bent?"

"Well," Mike said, "you see it was like this. One day when we was livin' up in Kansas this critter got out into the green corn an' filled hisself up with roastin' ears, which he allays was a fool about roastin' ears. An when he was so blamed

---

* From *The Codder*, by William Cunningham, *Folk-Say IV: The Land Is Ours*, edited by B. A. Botkin, pp. 210–211. Copyright, 1932, by B. A. Botkin. Norman: University of Oklahoma Press.

full that he was about to bust he come up to the water trough to git hisself a drink. It was a hot day an' he was thirsty, an' he allays was careless about the way he *stood*."

Mike paused for his audience to get the full significance of this fact.

"The way he stood, with his hind feet too far from his front feet. You know, a critter has to be careful to keep his hind feet a certain distance behind his front feet, an' likewise to keep his front feet the same distance in front of his hind feet. If he don't he'll stretch hisself.

"Well, this ol' cuss come up to the trough full of green roastin' ears an' he started to drinkin'. An' he musta drunk a tubful, an' all the time his hind feet was too far behind, an' his front feet too far in front.

"Well, I seen him jist as he was finishin', an' I seen how he was standin', an' I yells at him, but it was too late. All that weight in his belly had bent him like that, an' he won't never straighten out."

Shriveled, pasty-faced, toothless old Walt Harper had just enough wit to share in the codding. "Couldn't ya lay 'im on 'is back, Mike, an' git a pole er somepin' an' bend 'im back?" he asked. "Couldn't ya straighten 'im out, like? Kinda git 'im on 'is back an' bend 'im like he otta be?" He was overcome by mirth at his own joke. Baring his gums to the heavens, he leaned far back and filled his lungs with the dusty air. Then he doubled up, emitting a series of gasps and whoops, slapped one knee after the other and marched about in a circle, apparently at the point of choking to death.

The senior Gunn grinned. His boy was being codded, but it was part of the Western code that the young and tender should be taught the great verities by generous untruths. The dull red glow that filled the spaces between the boy's freckles showed that he was learning. The boy was bright, no doubt of that, like his mother, who could read and write.

Mike's expression did not change. "No," he said, "I seen that tried with a sway-back horse oncet when I was a boy on the ranch. They got the critter straight all right, but after that his back was so limber that it'd bend in any direction. Finally one day he tried to kick another horse, an' you know, he kicked hisself plumb in two, he was that weak in the back. I never seen a critter look so surprised, when his hind end come off. We felt awful sorry for him, because he'd been a good horse in his day, an' allays pushed in the collar. We shot 'is front end, an' burried him in the same hole."

At that instant a whirlwind was born in the barnyard. A fog of blinding, stinging sand rose up and the three men and the boy ducked their heads and clasped hands over their hats.

When it was gone, they sputtered and rubbed their eyes and brushed their sleeves. "Damn!" said Mike. "That shore come of a sudden. You know, I seen a whirlwind come up like that oncet in Kansas when a bunch of us was standin' on the porch of the general store. An' you know, Ike Marlow who was runnin' the store had hung a sack of meal up on the porch fer advertisin', an' that blamed whirlwind blew the sack off an' left the meal hangin' there."

Pulling Teeth*

OUR Doctor in Demijohnville was an old man and had seen hard times in his day, especially in pulling teeth. He says that when the country was new and thinly settled, teeth came out much harder than they do in these days. A nail and hammer were indispensable in reforming out a grinder, and sometimes they would not start then; but the worst case that he knew, was a long-sided fellow by the name of Barney, who sent for him on Sunday. On applying the hammer and nail to Barney's tooth, it was found impossible to loosen it by the ordinary means, he cut away the gum around it, and fastened on a stout line made of cat gut. Then having tied Barney's heels to a ring bolt in the barn floor, he called on the inmates of the house to assist him in pulling. Barney's wife took hold of the Doctor's coat tail, and the rest ranged themselves in a regular line; but they could not start the tooth, although they pulled so hard that the patient could scarcely keep on his feet. Several foot passengers were called on to assist; and now they gave "a long pull, and a strong pull, and a pull altogether"; but the tooth remained firm, although they could hear poor Barney's neck snap, so violent was the strain; but twelve o'clock arrived, and the good people begun to bundle home from meeting. As they went by, they were called upon to hitch on, until the line of pulling men and women extended over the hill, and several lads at the tail, were even compelled to stand in the swamp. These benevolent individuals then

---

* From *The Crockett Almanac, 1841*, p. 19. Entered According to the Act of Congress, in the year 1840, by Turner & Fisher, in the Clerk's Office of the District Court of the United States, in and for the Eastern District of Pennsylvania. Boston: Published by J. Fisher.

begun to pull—in a moment Barney was hauled off his feet, and hung horizontally in the air like a man on the rack. He cried, "stop"; but it was too late, for the whole line of operators suddenly fell backward, and tumbled over each other; when it was supposed the tooth had come out; but, on looking, it was discovered that Barney's head had come off, near the shoulders. The Doctor examined the tooth, and found that the roots went down through the whole length of his body, and were clinched on the bottom of his foot.

Just Set*

IN THE old days, we didn't have no automobiles and paved roads and all sich fancy likes. We didn't even have no trails and bridges. One time I 'member my wife was sick and I had to go Orofino for to bring a doctor. But when I got to the river I couldn't figger out how to cross. I decided to jump but when I was about three-fourths across I seen I wouldn't make it so I come back to think some more. Then I had to put my mind to it. There was a big tree on the edge of the river, so I hooked my lasso on a limb and got back and run for it, using the lasso to give me a swing across. That was good thinkun, but not everybody woulda 'membered the lasso would bring him right back agin if he wasn't durned keerful. Me, I cut the lasso when I was half way across. I tell you, I don't know what some of them-there modern squirts woulda done in a case like that. Just set on the bank, I guess.

John Hance, Darby, and the Grand Cañon**

"I WAS ridin' on the rim just below here, one day, when Darby come round an uprooted pine and stepped right up on top of a she-grizzly as big as a buffalo—and you ought to seen him pull his freight! Stop him? Why, man, the Day o' Judgment wouldn't have stopped that hoss! I tried to haul him to one side into my wood-trail; but he just naturally *helled* straight

* From *Idaho Lore*, prepared by the Federal Writers' Project of the Work Projects Administration, Vardis Fisher, State Director, American Guide Series, p. 135. Copyright, 1939, by George H. Curtis, Secretary of State for the State of Idaho. Caldwell, Idaho: The Caxton Printers, Ltd.

** From *Mesa, Cañon and Pueblo*, by Charles F. Lummis, p. 43. Copyright, 1925, by The Century Co. New York and London.

for the rim, and before I could fall off, there we was way out
in the sky, pretty near half-way across the cañon! I give him
the rowels and the quirt, sort o' hoping he could reach the
other bank; but it wasn't in him; and we went down like a
rock—down and down and d-o-w-n—plumb to the bottom.
Pore old Darby! I never *will* get another hoss like him!"

"But how about you, John? Why weren't you killed, too?"

"Huh! Too smart! You see Darby fell about sixty-five
hundred feet; but just before he lit, I jumped off—so *I* only
fell about twenty feet!"

"Good Shootin' "*

A MAN had a wife and a whole passle of young 'uns, and they
didn't have nothin' to eat.

He told his ole lady, "Well, Ah got a load of ammunition
in my gun, so Ah'm gointer go out in de woods and see what
Ah kin bring back for us to eat."

His wife said: "That's right, go see can't you kill us something—if 'tain't nothin' but a squirrel."

He went on huntin' wid his gun. It was one of dese muzzle-
loads. He knowed he didn't have but one load of ammunition
so he was very careful not to stumble and let his gun go off
by accident.

He had done walked more'n three miles from home and he
ain't saw anything to shoot at. He got worried. Then all of
a sudden he spied some wild turkeys settin' up in a tree on
a limb. He started to shoot at 'em, when he looked over in
de pond and seen a passle of wild ducks; and down at de
edge of de pond he saw a great big deer. He heard some
noise behind him and he looked 'round and seen some
partiges.

He wanted all of 'em and he didn't know how he could get
'em. So he stood and he thought and he thought. Then he
decided what to do.

He took aim, but he didn't shoot at de turkeys. He shot
de limb de turkeys was setting on and de ball split dat limb
and let all dem turkeys' feets dropped right down thru de
crack and de split limb shet up on 'em and helt 'em right
dere. De ball went on over and fell into de pond and kilt all

* From *Mules and Men*, by Zora Neale Hurston, pp. 151–153. Copyright,
1935, by Zora Neale Hurston. Philadelphia and London: J. B. Lippincott
Company.

dem ducks. De gun had too heavy a charge in her, so it bust and de barrel flew over and kilt dat deer. De stock kicked de man in de breast and he fell backwards and smothered all dem partiges.

Well, he drug his deer up under de tree and get his ducks out de pond and piled them up wid de turkeys and so forth. He seen he couldn't tote all dat game so he went on home to get his mule and wagon.

Soon as he come in de gate his wife said:

"Where is de game you was gointer bring back? You musta lost yo' gun, you ain't got it."

He told his wife, "Ah wears de longest pants in dis house. You leave me tend to my business and you mind yours. Jus' you put on de pot and be ready. Plenty rations is comin'."

He took his team on back in de woods wid him and loaded up de wagon. He wouldn't git up on de wagon hisself because he figgered his mule had enough to pull without him.

Just as he got his game all loaded on de wagon, it commenced to rain but he walked on beside of the mule pattin' him and tellin' him to "come up," till they got home.

When he got home his wife says: "De pot is boilin'. Where is de game you tole me about?"

He looked back and seen his wagon wasn't behind de mule where it ought to have been. Far as he could see—nothin' but them leather traces, but no wagon.

Then he knowed de rain had done made dem traces stretch, and de wagon hadn't moved from where he loaded it.

So he told his wife, "De game will be here. Don't you worry." So he just took de mule out and stabled him and wrapped dem traces 'round de gate post and went on in de house.

De next day it was dry and de sun was hot and it shrunk up dem traces, and about twelve o'clock they brought dat wagon home, "Cluck-cluck, cluck-cluck," right on up to de gate.

Shooting Match*

I LEARNED that an old-fashioned shooting match was to be pulled off out at a country store, and I wended my way

* From *I Blew in from Arkansaw*, A Trip of Fun through Hoosierdom, by Geo. D. Beason, pp. 50–53. Copyright, 1908, by Geo. D. Beason. Chicago: Geo. D. Beason, Publisher.

thither. I was told that two of the biggest liars of that section would be there, and I would hear something worth while.

When I arrived the contestants were lined up ready to go to shooting. Most of them were long, lean, hungry-looking specimens with guns to match. It was agreed that each contestant could use his own fowling-piece, and fire three shots for the prize, which was a caddy of chewing tobacco. I stood and watched them shoot and saw the winner, an eagle-eyed fellow from back in the brush where the timber grows tall, receive the prize. He opened up the tobacco and told all present to help themselves.

The crowd took seats on dry goods boxes around the front of the store, went for the tobacco, spit red and started the ball to rolling. The lying was what I went to hear, and I heard it. A dry-talking fellow told about a marksman he knew once who could shave a squirrel's nose at the top of the tallest tree on the Wabash. Bill Sikes, one of the notorious liars present, said, "That's nothing."

"What's nothing?"

"Why, that squirrel nose shaving. I knew a marksman by the name of Buck Mabre who could sure enough shoot. Did any of you ever hear of him?"

All present shook their heads.

"Well, Mabre was the slickest fellow with a gun I ever saw. He could shoot a cigar out of your mouth, burst marbles, cut a rooster's comb off, shoot through a gimlet hole, hit a knitting needle every crack ten steps, spat a target in the same place fifty times hand running, kill quail on the wing with a rifle, and—"

"And what?"

"Why, Buck Mabre could actually shoot so fast and so true that he could shoot away twenty-five cartridges and you would think he had shot but once, and when you looked to see where he hit, you would find but one hole."

Rube Allen, the other notorious liar present, said, "That's shooting, but I knew a fellow by the name of Bob Neely who could lift your man clear out of his boots. Did any of you know him?"

Nobody present had ever heard of him.

"Bob was a clipper. He made his living by his superior marksmanship. You could see him shoot, and if you had any money about your clothes, you would offer to give him the last cent you had. You couldn't help it. He mesmerized you with his fine shooting."

"How did he do it?"

"By the way he made his bullets whiz. He would put up a series of India rubber targets off about fifty yards, and by shooting at them and making his bullets bounce back at different angles and whiz, he could play any tune he ever heard. I've stood and heard him play Yankee Doodle, Dixie, Turkey in the Straw, and many other tunes. He had a red bullet he shot. He would shoot and the red ball would hit a target and bounce right back into his rifle barrel, and he was so quick that he could slap in a fresh charge of powder before the ball bounced back every time. The ball passed to and fro so rapidly that it looked like a red clothes line."

"But where did the mesmerizing come in?"

"Well, just before he closed a performance he would make his bullets whiz in such a way that he said it went like the Siren's singing, and his audience would become so charmed, or mesmerized, that it would do just anything he said. He would take up a collection and those present would try to chip in every cent they had. He wouldn't accept a contribution of more than a dollar."

Cougar Tamers*

YUP, we usta have quite a bit of trouble with cougars and we wuz pretty keerful to have a gun with us when we ambled out. One time though, I plumb forgot my gun and I had a narrow squeak with one of them-there varmints. 'Twas over to that place I usta have in the valley. I goes out after supper to bring the cows home and I was right dog-eared busy when I happened to look up. There was a cougar comun down the hill after me, and me without a gun. I had to think right smart about it. When the varmint got up to me with wide open mouth I just reached in and grabbed his tail and turned him wrong side out quickern a flash. Of course, he was headed in the wrong direction then, and so doggone surprised that he went lickety-split right back up the hill and out of sight.

---

* From *Idaho Lore*, prepared by the Federal Writers' Project of the Work Projects Administration, Vardis Fisher, State Director, American Guide Series, p. 121. Copyright, 1939, by George H. Curtis, Secretary of State for the State of Idaho. Caldwell, Idaho: The Caxton Printers, Ltd.

Big as an Idaho Potato*

YES, I'n tell you about wolves. My partner and me, we went up in the Sawtooths and got two elk and was headun home when we looked around and seen eleven wolves after us. We cut a elk loose and they et that. In another mile we give them the other elk and they et that. Then we left our horses and run for it, and they came up and et the horses. I said to my partner that I would rest and shoot a wolf and then run while he was restun and then he could shoot one. So we did. I shot one and the wolves pounced on it while I was runnin; and then my partner, he shot one. Well, we kept that up till we had shot ten of them. Then my partner yelled, "God a-mighty, Jim, look!" I looked behind me and there right on our tails was the biggest wolf anybody ever laid eyes on. He was as big as a house. And then I remembered he'd have to be that big, seeing as how he'd et two elk, two horses, and ten wolves.

They Make Excellent Pets**

WHEN I was just a wee lad I wanted to be a cowboy and it was then that I found out what a swell friend a rattlesnake could be. I was riding through a pass one day when I saw a rattler pinned under a stone: dismounting, I made ready to kill him, but changed my mind. Didn't seem fair. So I pushed the rock off and went home. As I went along I kept hearing funny noises behind me and looked back and saw it was that silly snake. It came right to my cabin and I opened some canned milk; and that snake drank it all, and you could just see the gratitude in his eyes. He stayed around and got so friendly he slept under my bed.

One night I was sleeping soundly when a bang awakened me. I could hear someone panting and struggling, so I grabbed my gun and said, "Hands up! If you move it wouldn't surprise me if I shot something!" A loud voice yelled, "For God's sake, take this damned thing off of me!" I lit a

---

* *Ibid.*, p. 126.
** *Ibid.*, p. 116.
By Mrs. Jennie E. Schmelzel. Coeur d'Alene.

candle. There, sprawled on the floor, was a guy who had sneaked in to steal my gold dust. But my rattler had wrapped himself around the man's leg and the leg of the table—and had his tail through the keyhole, rattling for the sheriff!

A Family Pet*

ACME SULPHIDE came in from his prospect on Caribou creek, bringing a big cougar to Larry Frazee's taxidermist shop. "Want him skun out and made into a rug?" asked Larry.

"No sir. Stuff him as is. I wouldn't think of walkun on Petronius."

"Why not? Just a cougar, ain't he?"

"Not by your tin horn. He's an institution, that's what he is. When he was just a kitten I ketched him by the mine shaft. Him and Pluto, they was great friends until Petronius growed up. Then one evening when I comes back, my Pluto was gone and Petronius wouldn't eat his supper. I was plumb mad, but I figgered Pluto was gettun old and wasn't so much account nohow. Then, by gum, I missed Mary, the goat. When I missed the last of the chickens and Petronius showed up with feathers in his whiskers, I made up my mind to shoot him. But I got to thinkun how that goat could butt, and the hens wasn't layun anyhow. So I let it go. But I shoulda bumped him then.

"Lydie, she's my old woman—or she was. Partner of my joys and sorrows for forty years. One evening when I gets back she was gone. No sign of her anywhere exceptun one shoe. And Petronius didn't want no supper agin. That got me mad, danged if it didn't, and I went for my gun to blast the varmint. Then I got to thinkun. Lydie wasn't much for looks and besides, she was about to leave me. She was all for hittun the trail, so I puts my gun up."

"Then what happened?"

"Well, last night he jumped me on the trail and took a big hunk right out of me. That was too danged much. So mount him up pretty. He repersents my whole family."

---

* Ibid., p. 117.

The Fence That Moved*

ONE night in camp two boys, Ira and Tom, got in rather late. Some of the boys already in camp after having retired to the bunkhouse asked the late comers what they had been doing that day.

Tom sez: "You tell 'em, Iry, 'cause I'm too tired."

Iry sez: "Well, it ain't much to tell, ceptin' that we saved the boss lots of time and money today. He set us out to fence in a section pasture. When we got over there, there wasn't enough fence posts and in going up a draw I smelt a terrible smell and asked Tom what it might be. He said he didn't think, he knowed already what it was. It was a snake den, and the snakes were crawlin' out to get the sunshine. I sed to him, 'There ain't much sunshine, for it's cold today.' "

"Well," sez he, "mebbe they come out yesterday to warm themselves when it was good and warm and stayed out too late last night and got froze to death."

"Shore enough, when we got up to this snake den there was somewhere between five and ten thousand rattlesnakes all the way from six to fourteen feet long, lying stretched out and froze stiff. I sez to Tom, 'Right here's where we get our fence posts,' so we just throwed a rope around a bundle of 'em and drag 'em to where we was goin' to fence the 'trap' and I'd hold the pointed end of the snake with the rattles on it into the ground, and while Tom'd sit on his horse he'd hammer on the blunt end, that is the end his head's on, with a six pound sledge hammer, and drove him in the ground. We got through by about eleven o'clock, and thinkin' we was through so quick that the boss wouldn't care if we laid down and took a nap. Which we did, an' in the meantime the sun come shinin' out and the boss thought he'd ride over to see how we was gettin' along and caught us sleepin'. I told him he needn't to git mad because we had saved him a lot of time and money but I wouldn't tell him just how we done it. I told him to come and go with me and I would show him. Well, sir, I'll be dadgoned if he didn't show his appreciation by tellin' me an' Tom to come on down to the bunkhouse and go to sleep, bein' as how we was in such need of sleep and come to the office in the morning and get our money."

* From *Cowboy Lore*, by Jules Verne Allen, pp. 29–31. Copyright, 1933, by the Naylor Printing Company. San Antonio, Texas.

One of the boys sed: "Why, Iry, why did he want to fire you, you savin' him all that money expense of cutting fence posts like you did?"

Iry sed: "Oh hell, when that sun commenced to shinin' them damned snakes thawed out and carried off two miles of good barbed wire."

Tall Tales of the Mines*

I worked in the Enterprise mine when it was only a drift many years ago. The vein didn't have much surface on to it and when I throwed a fall, the damn toppin' caved in on me—sand, slate, coal 'n' all. I shook it off all right, but when I cleared me eyes I found meself face to face with a buck which had pretty two-pointed antlers. "I guess we're into it, butty," says I to meself, "and so let's make the best of things." Well, sir, the buck he gave a snort and started to run off. I caught him by the tail and lifted meself on to his back. Then I took hold of his antlers. Bucky ran from one breast to another and then into the gangway, and from the gangway he hopped out of the mine to the surface, and with one leap he bounded up to the top of the mountain. From there he looked down to the cave-in and turned his head as if to ask me if I wanted to get down into the mine again. With one leap he was inside the mine again with me holding on to his antlers. Once again he leaped from breast to breast, into the gangway and up to the top of the mountain and down into the mine again. He repeated this a third time after which, wantin' to put an end to the nonsense, I slashed his throat with me big toenail and he bled to death.

*   *   *   *   *

Two miners made a bet over their beer to see who knew of a deeper shaft.

"I went into a colliery engine house onc't," said one, "and found the h'isting engineer asleep at the lever. Seein' as the engine was at top speed I quick woke him up. The engineer looked at his watch with half an eye open and yawned, 'I got three hours' sleep yet; she won't land on my shift.'"

---

* From *Minstrels of the Mine Patch*, Songs and Stories of the Anthracite Industry, by George Korson, pp. 72–73. Copyright, 1938, by the University of Pennsylvania Press. Philadelphia.

"Ugh," grunted the other. "That ain't much of a shaft. I went to a mine for a job onc't. It was Wednesday, as I recall. I asked the topman where I could find the boss and he told me the boss had just stepped on the cage at the bottom and if I came back Saturday night I could catch him as he landed."

Yarns of the Sea*

I. THE FLYING SPOUSE

ALL "eddicated seafarin' men" have heard of the ship built from designs of a Cornishman, the frigate that scraped off Dover Cliff, trying to wedge through the Channel. Young sailors went into the shrouds of her and came down with long white beards on them; and one of her discarded jackstays, sunk into the London mud, made "Piccalilly Circus."

The New Peninsula built such a ship under direction of Asey Shiverick. She was so tall that sailors took their wives when they went up to furl the toproyals. Later they sent down their grandsons to report that orders had been filled.

The Dover Cliff was a thornberry scratch compared with what befell Cape Cod when the *Flying Spouse*, as she was christened, tried to turn around in the Bay. She could not make it, could not come "nigh to it," so Asey sawed off her flying jib boom at the cap. That took three years. Still she could not make it, so he sawed off her Dolphin striker and her whisker boom. That took five years. Still she could not make it, so he sawed off her jib boom and her bowsprit. Hard sawing and Sunday-work, that took him ten years. Then he put her helm down hard and swung her till her nose knocked, whacking Billingsgate Island, plunging it under water. After that, Asey thought: how about taking her out stern first? So he cleared her neatly, but by that time the good meadows of Billingsgate, all owned by ministers, had disappeared in the Bay. The pirates up by Wellfleet had buried their gold on Billingsgate Island, and they lost a "deal of treasure."

Asey's ship was rigged with sheets so heavy that no gang could haul them. A team of mules was put aboard, and with this and that, so many mules were required to work ship that no room was left in the hold for cargo. She was nothing but

* From *The Narrow Land*, by Elizabeth Reynard, pp. 247–251, 255–259. Copyright, 1934, by Elizabeth Reynard. Boston: Houghton Mifflin Company.

a fancyman's dream. Yet Asey was so proud of her that he bet Captain Obed Paine of Eastham that the *Flying Spouse* could sail to Ireland, there and back in six days and rest upon the seventh. Obed took Asey up, and went along to see fair play. The mules hauled anchor on a Monday.

For all her size the *Flying Spouse* was no faster than the wind blows, so Obed was sure that Asey could never get her to Ireland and return in a matter of six days. What he forgot when he made his reckonings, was that her bow, when her stern was three days out, would be wedged tight into Queenstown Harbour and likely to get stuck there.

"You're a right smart sailorman, Asey," said Obed, when the ship reached Ireland, Wednesday night, "but how're y' goint' pull 'er out an' swing 'er aroun', Asey?"

Captain Shiverick grinned. "God save King George!" he yelled, jumping on the fore deck. "God save England! Horray for Parlyment!"

The Irish were that mad they pushed the prow of the *Flying Spouse* so hard out of Queenstown Harbour that she shot backward across the Atlantic into the Clay Pounds. Broke them up with a blow from her counter, scarred them, cracked them; all in strips they are, grooved by her stern timbers.

II. THE SAUCER-BACK HALIBUT

Whiskery as a "porkypine," tanned to the colour of an old leather boot, Jereboam Thacher of Provincetown, longshore fisherman, looked old enough to have fished in the flood. One leg, missing from the knee-joint, was pieced out with the loom of an oar.

"How did I lose my leg?" asked he. "It's a tale that would turn your hair gray. I don't often tell about it, for folks won't believe me. Haint nobody left these days that kin remember what the fishin was like when I was a young feller. But I'm tellin you life was different when a man could walk alongshore with a pitchfork and load up an oxcart with squiteague, and when the cod schooled right in to the rocks and laid there for days. In them times the lobsters used to crawl in on the marshes and bed down for the winter as soon as the weather cooled up, and men dug em out by the bushel along in Januwary—Febuwary.

" 'Twas a halibut took my leg off, although the critter didn't mean no harm. Used to be a lot of em around inshore in them days, big fellers, shaped like a sole or a flounder, broad, with both eyes on one side of their heads; spotted light and dark brown on the back and dead white underneath. Only place they git em now is well offshore, but in them days they used to run right in to the beach. And they run from twenty-five pound weight up to, waal, no man ever knew how big the biggest one was. They get em now that run to three-four hundred pound.

"There was bigger ones than that when I was young.

"A halibut is a bottom fish, but there's times when they come up. They'll skitter acrost-water, jump out clean, and then there's times when they'll lay almost awash, with their sides and fins curled up like a saucer. Jest lay there. What for? The Lord only knows.

"Waal, this day, I had run off-shore into the bay, haulin lobsterpots, doin a little hand-linin and managin to git a hundred er two pounds of lobsters and bout as many fish. I was runnin right along under sail in my smack-boat, makin good time before a light southerly that was blowin, and glad of it, too, because the fog was makin. I must have been three mile from land when all to oncst I fetched up solid. Pretty nigh capsized. Figgered 'twas a piece of driftin wreck, and I went forrad to shove clear and look for damage, but it waant a wreck at all. It looked like bottom, but no bottom that I ever seen before. Besides, there was forty foot of water there.

"I got clear, put her on the other tack and stood off, wonderin about it. I run on for mebbe twenty minutes, then tacked inshore and bingo! I was aground agen! Bout six times I hit before I fin'lly tuk in that there was somethin between me and home. What it was I couldn't tell, but it was there. And then, jest as I was pushin off the last time, I noticed a flurry some fathoms ahead of me, and I see somethin big break water, a oval brown thing that opened and shet. It was a head, but, Godfreys, what a head! I could see two eyes, twice the length of a whaleboat oar apart. Lookin around they was.

"Bimeby I reelized what the eyes belonged to. A halibut! Layin awash. And I had been sailin acrost his saucer-back for nigh on an hour!

"Things didn't look too good to me, but I waant real worried. How to git clear, that was the question. Fin'lly I figgered that I'd run on to his fin agen, climb out, stand on it, and hang onto my boat, which might be lightened enough to ride over. I trimmed aft my sheet and headed for where I knew his side laid. I miscalkerlated some, and hit it before expected, hit it hardish, too. Then I passed the slack of my halliards round me, and jumped over the bow. Something hit my knee, and I never felt sech pain before. I crawled over the gunnel, more dead than alive, saw that my leg was bleedin bad, and wound a line tight around it. Then I took an oar, and dizzy with pain, I tried to shove the boat over. As she moved ahead, and went clear, I saw what had done the damage:

"I had struck that fish solid and started up a couple of scales. There they laid, four foot acrost, standin half on edge, sharp as a meat-axe, hard as flint. I had stumbled onto the edge of one, and later, when some of the bunch picked me up, they found that my leg was so nigh cut off that they had to finish the job."

III. JACK TAFFRIL AND TOM STAYSIL

Back in the Seventeen Hundreds lived two ancient sailormen, Jack Taffril who sailed on the *Mary Ann*, Tom Staysil who sailed on the *Nancy*. Whenever they made the home port, the old salts met in Sandwich Tavern, and after a round or two of rum they swapped the "logs" of their voyages. Whatever the waves or the whales or the mate had done to Jack Taffril, the waves and the whales and the "murderish mate" had done Tom Staysil one better.

Once Jack came home from sea and told how porpoises followed ship till a sailor spilled a pail of red paint over the side. All the porpoises ate that paint. All of them turned red.

But that same voyage Tom Staysil, given a bottle of rum by the mate and suspicioning that it was poison, poured the firewater over the taffrail. A shark alongside opened his mouth and received a dose of grog. Was that shark happy? Was that shark faithful? It followed the *Nancy* around the Horn, and west to the Island of Tahiti.

Now at Tahiti sailors go ashore "to get their eddication," and when Tom no longer appeared, leaning over the ship's rail to pour out a share of his rum, the Faithful Shark "took to worritin'." Likewise the shark grew thirsty, so he slowly cruised around the shoreline looking for his old friend, Tom. By and by he found him, sitting on a sea-cliff singing tunes to a Yoo-hoo Lady decked out in floral ornaments and playing on a twang-stringer. The shark stuck his snout over the cliff, opened his mouth, and bared his teeth like a long white row of tombstones.

Tom picked the twang-stringer off the Yoo-hoo and cast it

down the shark's throat, where it sunk athwartships and stuck in the gullet. Every time the shark swallowed, his palate swept across the cords of that Yoo-hoo love-fiddle. Thereafter the Faithful Shark made music wherever he went.

On the next voyage, Jack Taffril was capsized from a stove-in boat. He landed on a whale's back and held to the driven harpoon. With perilous speed he rode the whale, above seas and below seas, till the great mammal bled, weakened, drifted. No. 2 boat rescued Jack.

That was the year in which Tom Staysil took an oar in a whaleboat out to strike a Killer! The plunging brute came under the keel and smashed the boat to driftwood. Tom, still clinging to an oar, was taken between gaping jaws; swallowed by the whale. Once inside, Tom struck his flint, looked around and thought about Jonah. He tickled the ribs of the Killer for a time but the whale would not cough up. Then Tom drew out his knife and thrust it in the Killer's heart. Two hours later, while the pious seaman was reading his pocket Bible by whale-oil taper, the mammal sighed, floated on the ocean, and Tom climbed aloft.

He peered out through a picket-fence of white whale's teeth. A full gale beat the waves skyward. Icebergs clung to the Killer's whiskers. Glaciers floated on the sea. Tom went below where the weather was warmer, cut a hole in the stern of the whale, stuck his oar through; then he sculled and he sculled, till he sculled that Killer to Fairhaven.

A year later Jack Taffril was captured by the cannibals. Stripped, trussed, ready for the kettle, he decided to die like a Christian. He raised his voice in a psalm:

> "And I shall be like to ye tree
>   Implanted by ye rivers,
> That in my season yield my fruits
>   Unlike ye leaf that withers."

Jack sang valiantly. The cannibals rejoiced. They appeased their hunger with missionary-men, and the chief kept Jack beside him to sing during council-meetings. Jack married a cannibal lady and lived like a king till the captain of the *Mary Ann*, needing an able seaman, paid for him with ransom.

Part Five

Folk Tales and Legends

I

ANIMAL TALES

NEXT to hero tales and tall tales, animal tales are perhaps the most congenial to American folk story-tellers and their audiences. Animal tales proper, as distinct from mere tales about animals, are those in which animal characters talk and act like human beings. Originating in the primitive's sense of kinship with animals, animal tales have lent themselves to the purposes of allegory, satire, and children's "bedtime" stories. The fact that the best-known of our animal tales, the Uncle Remus stories, survive on the nursery level is another illustration of the "downward process" of tradition (also seen in games), by which children retain what was once the property of adults.

Historically, the social rôle of the Negro slave as story-teller to his master's children accounts for the large proportion of African survivals in Negro animal tales as compared with the predominance of white traits in other parts of his lore. At the same time, a good many of the plantation stereotypes linger in the nostalgic versions of Negro folk stories and story-tellers by Joel Chandler Harris, Louise Clarke Pyrnelle, and Virginia Frazer Boyle.

Although Harris discounted the literary value of the "old darkey's poor little stories" and the art of his own retelling, his renditions of "fantasies as uncouth as the original man ever conceived of" are perhaps more properly literature than folklore More scientific, if what Harris would term more "painful" in their dialect, are the Gullah versions of Mrs. A. M. H. Christensen, Ambrose E. Gonzales, and Charles C. Jones, Jr. But whether quaint or stark, Negro animal tales project the "compensatory dreams of the subject races and serf-populations, expressed both in folk-tale and folk-ballad, [which] delight in the victory of the weak over the strong

368

and in the triumph of brains over brute strength."[1] The way in which the Negro, more peculiarly than any other minority group, has made this symbolism his own and a vehicle for his philosophy, constitutes one of his most important contributions to folk literature and wisdom.

The Wonderful Tar-Baby Story

I. How Mr. Fox Caught Mr. Rabbit*

"Didn't the fox *never* catch the rabbit, Uncle Remus?" asked the little boy next evening.

"He came mighty nigh it, honey, sho's you born—Brer Fox did. One day atter Brer Rabbit fool 'im wid dat calamus root, Brer Fox went ter wuk en got 'im some tar, en mix it wid some turkentime, en fix up a contrapshun wat he call a Tar-Baby, en he tuck dish yer Tar-Baby en he sot 'er in de big road, en den he lay off in de bushes fer to see wat de news wuz gwineter be. En he didn't hatter wait long, nudder, kaze bimeby here come Brer Rabbit pacin' down de road—lippity-clippity, clippity-lippity—dez ez sassy ez a jay-bird. Brer Fox, he lay low. Brer Rabbit come prancin' 'long twel he spy de Tar-Baby, en den he fotch up on his behime legs like he wuz 'stonished. De Tar-Baby, she sot dar, she did, en Brer Fox, he lay low.

" 'Mawnin'!' sez Brer Rabbit, sezee—'nice wedder dis mawnin',' sezee.

"Tar-Baby ain't sayin' nothin', en Brer Fox, he lay low.

" 'How duz yo' sym'tums seem ter segashuate?' sez Brer Rabbit, sezee.

"Brer Fox, he wink his eye slow, en lay low, en de Tar-Baby, she ain't sayin' nothin'.

" 'How you come on, den? Is you deaf?' sez Brer Rabbit, sezee. 'Kaze if you is, I kin holler louder,' sezee.

"Tar-Baby stay still, en Brer Fox, he lay low.

* From *Uncle Remus, His Songs and His Sayings*, by Joel Chandler Harris, pp. 7–11. Copyright, 1880, 1895, by D. Appleton and Company, and 1908, 1921, by Esther La Rose Harris. New York and London: D. Appleton-Century Company.

" 'Youer stuck up, dat's w'at you is,' says Brer Rabbit, sezee, 'en I'm gwineter kyore you, dat's w'at I'm a gwineter do,' sezee.

"Brer Fox, he sorter chuckle in his stummuck, he did, but Tar-Baby ain't sayin' nothin'.

" 'I'm gwineter larn you howter talk ter 'spectubble fokes ef hit's de las' ac,' sez Brer Rabbit, sezee. 'Ef you don't take off dat hat en tell me howdy, I'm gwineter bus' you wide open,' sezee.

"Tar-Baby stay still, en Brer Fox, he lay low.

"Brer Rabbit keep on axin' 'im, en de Tar-Baby, she keep on sayin' nothin', twel present'y Brer Rabbit draw back wid his fis', he did, en blip he tuck 'er side er de head. Right dar's whar he broke his merlasses jug. His fis' stuck, en he can't pull loose. De tar hilt 'im. But Tar-Baby, she stay still, en Brer Fox, he lay low.

" 'Ef you don't lemme loose, I'll knock you agin,' sez Brer Rabbit, sezee, en wid dat he fotch 'er a wipe wid de udder han', en dat stuck, Tar-Baby, she ain't sayin' nothin', en Brer Fox, he lay low.

" 'Tu'n me loose, fo' I kick de natal stuffin' outen ou,' sez Brer Rabbit, sezee, but de Tar-Baby, she ain't sayin' nothin'. She des hilt on, en den Brer Rabbit lose de use er his feet in de same way. Brer Fox, he lay low. Den Brer Rabbit squall out dat ef de Tar-Baby don't tu'n 'im loose he butt 'er cranksided. En den he butted, en his head got stuck. Den Brer Fox, he sa'ntered fort', lookin' des ez innercent ez one er yo' mammy's mockin'-birds.

" 'Howdy, Brer Rabbit,' sez Brer Fox, sezee. 'You look sorter stuck up dis mawnin',' sezee, en den he rolled on de groun', en laughed twel he couldn't laugh no mo'. 'I speck you'll take dinner wid me dis time, Brer Rabbit. I done laid in some calamus root, en I ain't gwineter take no skuse,' sez Brer Fox, sezee."

Here Uncle Remus paused, and drew a two-pound yam out of the ashes.

"Did the fox eat the rabbit?" asked the little boy to whom the story had been told.

"Dat's all de fur de tale goes," replied the old man. "He mout, en den agin he moutent. Some say Jedge B'ar come 'long en loosed 'im—some say he didn't. I hear Miss Sally callin'. You better run 'long."

II. How Mr. Rabbit Was too Sharp for Mr. Fox*

"Uncle Remus," said the little boy one evening, when he had found the old man with little or nothing to do, "did the fox kill and eat the rabbit when he caught him with the Tar-Baby?"

"Law, honey, ain't I tell you 'bout dat?" replied the old darkey, chuckling slyly. "I 'clar ter grashus I ought er tole you dat, but old man Nod wuz ridin' on my eyelids twel a leetle mo'n I'd a disremember'd my own name, en den on to dat here come yo' mammy hollerin' atter you.

"W'at I tell you w'en I fus' begin? I tole you Brer Rabbit wuz a monstus soon creetur; leas'ways dat's w'at I laid out fer ter tell you. Well, den, honey, don't you go en make no udder calkalashuns, kaze in dem days Brer Rabbit en his fambly wuz at de head er de gang w'en enny racket wuz on han', en dar dey stayed. 'Fo' you begins fer ter wipe yo' eyes 'bout Brer Rabbit, you wait en see whar'bouts Brer Rabbit gwineter fetch up at. But dat's needer yer ner dar.

"W'en Brer Fox fine Brer Rabbit mixt up wid de Tar-Baby, he feel mighty good, en he roll on de groun' en laff. Bimeby he up'n say, sezee:

"'Well, I speck I got you dis time, Brer Rabbit,' sezee; 'maybe I ain't, but I speck I is. You been runnin' roun' here sassin' atter me a mighty long time, but I speck you done come ter de een' er de row. You bin cuttin' up yo' capers en bouncin' 'roun' in dis neighborhood ontwel you come ter b'leeve yo'se'f de boss er de whole gang. En den youer allers some'rs whar you got no bizness,' sez Brer Fox, sezee. 'Who ax you fer ter come en strike up a 'quaintance wid dish yer Tar-Baby? En who stuck you up dar whar you iz? Nobody in de roun' worril. You des tuck en jam yo'se'f on dat Tar-Baby widout waitin' fer enny invite,' sez Brer Fox, sezee, 'en dar you is, en dar you'll stay twel I fixes up a bresh-pile and fires her up, kaze I'm gwineter bobbycue you dis day, sho,' sez Brer Fox, sezee.

"Den Brer Rabbit talk mighty 'umble.

"'I don't keer w'at you do wid me, Brer Fox,' sezee, 'so you don't fling me in dat brier-patch. Roas' me, Brer Fox,' sezee, 'but don't fling me in dat brier-patch,' sezee.

"'Hit's so much trouble fer ter kindle a fier,' sez Brer Fox, sezee, 'dat I speck I'll hatter hang you,' sezee.

---

* *Ibid.*, pp. 16–19.

" 'Hang me des ez high ez you please, Brer Fox,' sez Brer Rabbit, sezee, 'but do fer de Lord's sake don't fling me in that brier-patch,' sezee.

" 'I ain't got no string,' sez Brer Fox, sezee, 'en now I speck I'll hatter drown you,' sezee.

" 'Drown me des ez deep ez you please, Brer Fox,' sez Brer Rabbit, sezee, 'but do don't fling me in dat brier-patch,' sezee.

" 'Dey ain't no water nigh,' sez Brer Fox, sezee, 'en now I speck I'll hatter skin you,' sezee.

" 'Skin me, Brer Fox,' sez Brer Rabbit, sezee, 'snatch out my eyeballs, t'ar out my years by de roots, en cut off my legs,' sezee, 'but do please, Brer Fox, don't fling me in dat brier-patch,' sezee.

"Co'se Brer Fox wanter hurt Brer Rabbit bad ez he kin, so he cotch 'im by de behime legs en slung 'im right in de middle er de brier-patch. Dar wuz a considerbul flutter whar Brer Rabbit struck de bushes, en Brer Fox sorter hang 'roun' fer ter see w'at wuz gwineter happen. Bimeby he hear somebody call 'im, en way up de hill he see Brer Rabbit settin' cross-legged on a chinkapin log koamin' de pitch outen his har wid a chip. Den Brer Fox know dat he bin swop off mighty bad. Brer Rabbit wuz bleedzed fer ter fling back some er his sass, en he holler out:

" 'Bred en bawn in a brier-patch, Brer Fox—bred en bawn in a brier-patch!' en wid dat he skip out des ez lively ez a cricket in de embers."

Sheer Crops*

BR'ER BEAR en Br'er Rabbit dey wuz farmers. Br'er Bear he has acres en acres uf good bottom land, en Br'er Rabbit has des' er small sandy-land farm. Br'er Bear wuz allus er "raisin' Cain" wid his neighbors, but Br'er Rabbit was er most engenerally raisin' chillun.

Arter while Br'er Rabbit's boys 'gun to git grown, en Br'er Rabbit 'lows he's gwine to have to git more land if he makes buckle en tongue meet.

So he goes ober to Br'er Bear's house, he did, en he say, sez

* From "Brazos Bottom Philosophy," by A. W. Eddins, *Southwestern Lore*, Publications of the Texas Folk-Lore Society, Number IX, 1931, edited by J. Frank Dobie, pp. 153–156. Copyright, 1931, by the Texas Folk-Lore Society. Dallas: The Southwest Press.

he, "Morning, Br'er Bear. I craves ter rent yer bottom field nex' ye'r."

Br'er Bear he hum en he haw, en den he sez, "I don't spec I kin 'commodate yer, Br'er Rabbit, but I moughten consider hit, bein's hit is you."

"How does you rent yer land, Br'er Bear?"

"I kin onliest rent by der sheers."

"What is yer sheer, Br'er Bear?"

"Well," said Br'er Bear, "I takes der top of de crop fer my sheer, en you takes de rest fer yo' sheer."

Br'er Rabbit thinks erbout it rale hard, en he sez, "All right, Br'er Bear, I took it; we goes ter plowin' ober dare nex' week."

Den Br'er Bear goes back in der house des' er-laughin'. He sho is tickled ez to how he hez done put one by ole Br'er Rabbit dat time.

Well, 'long in May Br'er Rabbit done sont his oldest son to tell Br'er Bear to come down to de field to see erbout dat are sheer crop. Br'er Bear he comes er-pacin' down to de field en Br'er Rabbit wuz er-leanin' on de fence.

"Mo'nin', Br'er Bear. See what er fine crop we hez got. You is to hab de tops fer yer sheer. Whare is you gwine to put 'em? I wants ter git 'em off so I kin dig my 'taters."

Br'er Bear wuz sho hot. But he done made dat trade wid Br'er Rabbit, en he had to stick to hit. So he went off all huffed up, en didn't even tell Br'er Rabbit what to do wid de vines. But Br'er Rabbit perceeded to dig his 'taters.

'Long in de fall Br'er Rabbit 'lows he's gwine to see Br'er Bear ergin en try to rent der bottom field. So he goes down to Br'er Bear's house en after passin' de time of day en other pleasant sociabilities, he sez, sez he, "Br'er Bear, how erbout rentin' der bottom field nex' year? Is yer gwine ter rent hit to me ergin?"

Br'er Bear say, he did, "You cheat me out uf my eyes las' year, Br'er Rabbit. I don't think I kin let yer hab it dis ye'r."

Den Br'er Rabbit scratch his head er long time, en he say, "Oh, now, Br'er Bear, you know I ain't cheated yer. Yer just cheat yerself. Yer made de trade yerself en I done tuck yer at yer word. Yer sed yer wanted der tops fer yer sheer, en I gib um ter you, didn't I? Now you des' think hit all ober ergin en see if you can't make er new deal fer yerself."

Den Br'er Bear said, "Well, I rents to you only on dese perditions: dat yer hab all de tops fer yer sheer en I hab all de rest fer my sheer."

Br'er Rabbit he twis' en he turn en he sez, "All right, Br'er Bear, I'se got ter hab more land fer my boys. I'll tuck hit. We go to plowin' in dare right away."

Den Br'er Bear he amble back into de house. He wuz shore he'd made er good trade dat time.

Way 'long in nex' June Br'er Rabbit done sont his boy down to Br'er Bear's house ergin, to tell him to come down ter de field ter see erbout his rent. When he got dare, Br'er Rabbit say, he did:

"Mo'nin', Br'er Bear. See what er fine crap we hez got? I specks hit will make forty bushels to der acre. I'se gwine ter put my oats on der market. What duz yer want me ter do wid yer straw?"

Br'er Bear sho wuz mad, but hit wa'n't no use. He done saw whar Br'er Rabbit had 'im. So he lies low en 'lows to hisself how he's gwine to git eben wid Br'er Rabbit yit. So he smile en say, "Oh, der crop is all right, Br'er Rabbit. Jes' stack my straw enywheres eround dare. Dat's all right."

Den Br'er Bear smile en he say, "What erbout nex' year, Br'er Rabbit? Is you cravin' ter rent dis field ergin?"

"I ain't er doin' nothin' else but wantin' ter rent hit, Br'er Bear," said Br'er Rabbit.

"All right, all right, you kin rent her ergin. But dis time I'se gwine ter hab der tops fer my sheer, en I'se gwine ter hab de bottoms fer my sheer too."

Br'er Rabbit wuz stumped. He didn't know what ter do nex'. But he finally managed to ask, "Br'er Bear, ef yer gits der tops en der bottoms fer yer share, what will I git fer my sheer?"

Den old Br'er Bear laff en say, "Well, you would git de middles."

Br'er Rabbit he worry en he fret, he plead en he argy, but hit does no good.

Br'er Bear sez, "Take hit er leave hit," en jes' stands pat.

Br'er Rabbit took hit.

Way 'long nex' summer ole Br'er Bear 'cided he would go down to der bottom field en see erbout dat dare sheer crop he had wid Br'er Rabbit. While he wuz er-passin' through de woods on his way, he sez to himself, he did:

"De fust year I rents to de ole Rabbit, I makes de tops my sheer, en ole Rabbit planted 'taters; so I gits nothin' but vines. Den I rents ergin, en der Rabbit is to hab de tops, en I de bottoms, en ole Rabbit plants oats; so I gits nothin' but straw. But I sho is got dat ole Rabbit dis time. I gits both de tops en de bottoms, en de ole Rabbit gits only de middles. I'se bound ter git 'im dis time."

Jes' den de old Bear come ter de field. He stopped. He look at hit. He shet up his fist. He cuss en he say, "Dat derned little scoundrel! He done went en planted dat fiel' in corn."

How Sandy Got His Meat—A Negro Tale from the Brazos Bottoms*

BRER RABBIT an Brer Coon wuz fishermuns. Brer Rabbit fished fur fish an Brer Coon fished fur f-r-o-g-s.

Arter while de frogs all got so wile Brer Coon couldent ketch em, an he hadn't hab no meat to his house an de chilluns wuz hongry and de ole oman beat em ober de haid wid de broom.

Brer Coon felt mighty bad 'an he went off down de rode wid he haid down wundering what he gwine do. Des den ole Brer Rabbit wuz er skippin down de rode an he seed Brer Coon wuz worried an throwed up his years an say-ed:

"Mornin, Brer Coon."

"Mornin, Brer Rabbit."

"How is yer copperrosity segashuatin, Brer Coon?"

"Porely, Brer Rabbit, porely. De frogs haz all got so wile I caint ketch em an I aint got no meat to my house an de ole oman is mad an de chilluns hongry. Brer Rabbit, I'se got to hab help. Sumthin' haz got to be dun."

Old Brer Rabbit looked away crost de ruver long time; den he scratch his year wid his hind foot, an say:

"I'll tole ye whut we do, Brer Coon. We'll git eber one of dem frogs. You go down on de san bar an lie down an play des lack you wuz d-a-i-d. Don't yer mobe. Be jes as still, jest lack you wuz d-a-i-d."

Ole Brer Coon mosied on down to de ruver. De frogs hear-ed em er comin an de ole big frog say-ed:

"Yer better look er roun. Yer better look er roun. Yer better look er roun."

Nother ole frog say-ed:

"Knee deep, knee deep, knee deep."

An "ker-chug" all de frogs went in de water.

---

* By A. W. Eddins. From *Publications of the Folk-Lore Society of Texas, No. I*, edited by Stith Thompson, pp. 47–79. Copyright, 1916, by the Folk-Lore Society of Texas. Austin.

But Ole Brer Coon lide down on de san an stretched out jest lack he wuz d-a-i-d. De flies got all ober em, but he never moobe. De sun shine hot, but he never moobe; he lie still jest lack he wuz d-a-i-d.

Directly Ole Brer Rabbit cum er runnin tru de woods an out on de san bar an put his years up high an hollered out:

"Hay, de Ole Coon is d-a-i-d."

De ole big frog out in de ruver say-ed:

"I don't bleve it, I don't bleve it, I don't bleve it."

An all de littul frogs roun de edge say-ed:

"I don't bleve it, I don't bleve it, I don't bleve it."

But de ole coon play jes lack he's d-a-i-d an all de frogs cum up out of de ruver an set er roun whare de ole coon lay.

Jes den Brer Rabbit wink his eye an say-ed:

"I'll tell you what I'de do, Brer Frogs. I'de berry Ole Sandy, berry em so deep he never could scratch out."

Den all de frogs gun to dig out de san, dig out de san from under de ole coon. When dey had dug er great deep hole wid de ole coon in de middle of it, de frogs all got tired an de ole frog say-ed:

"Deep er nough,—deep er nough,—deep er nough."

An all de littul frogs say-ed:

"Deep er nough,—deep er nough,—deep er nough."

Ole Brer Rabbit was er takin er littul nap in der sun, an he woke up an say-ed:

"Kin you jump out?"

De ole big frog look up to de top of de hole an say-ed:

"Yes I kin. Yes I kin. Yes I kin."

An de littul frogs say-ed:

"Yes I kin. Yes I kin. Yes I kin."

Ole Brer Rabbit tole em:

"Dig it deeper."

Den all de frogs went to wuk an dug er great deep hole way down inside de san wid Ole Brer Coon right in de middle jest lack he wuz d-a-i-d. De frogs wuz er gittin putty tired an de ole big frog sung out loud:

"Dep er nough. Deep er nough. Deep er nough."

An all de littul frogs sung out too:—

"Deep er nough. Deep er nough. Deep er nough."

An Ole Brer Rabbit woke up er gin an exed em:—

"Kin yer jump out?"

"I bleve I kin. I bleve I kin. I bleve I kin."

Ole Brer Rabbit look down in de hole agin an say-ed:—

"Dig dat hole deeper."

Den all de frogs gin to wuk throwin out san, throwin out san, clear till most sun down and dey had er great deep hole way, way down in de san, wid de ole coon layin right in de middle. De frogs wuz plum clean tired out and de ole big frog say-ed:—

"Deep er nough. Deep er nough. Deep er nough."

An all de littul frogs say-ed:—

"Deep er nough. Deep er nough. Deep er nough."

Ole Brer Rabbit peeped down in de hole agin an say:—

"Kin yer jump out?"

An de ole frog say:—

"No I cain't. No I cain't. No I cain't."

An all de littul frogs say:—

"No I cain't. No I cain't. No I cain't."

Den Ole Brer Rabbit jump up right quick an holler out:—

"RISE UP SANDY AN GIT YOUR MEAT."

An Brer Coon had meat fer sepper dat nite.

Brer Dog and Brer Rabbit*

I

How Brer Dog Lost His Beautiful Voice

JOE WILEY said, " 'Tain't nothin' cute as a rabbit. When they come cuter than him, they got to have 'cute indigestion." He cleared his throat and continued:

Dat's de reason de dog is mad wid de rabbit now—'cause he fooled de dog.

You know they useter call on de same girl. De rabbit useter g'wan up to de house and cross his legs on de porch and court de girl. Brer Dog, he'd come in de gate wid his banjo under his arm.

"Good evenin', Miss Saphronie."

"My compliments, Brer Dog, come have a chair on de pe-azza."

"No thank you ma'am, Miss Saphronie. B'lieve Ah'll set out here under de Chinabery tree."

So he'd set out dere and pick de banjo and sing all 'bout:

---

* From *Mules and Men*, by Zora Neale Hurston, pp. 145–148. Copyright, 1935, by Zora Neale Hurston. Philadelphia and London: J. B. Lippincott Company.

If Miss Fronie was a gal of mine
She wouldn't do nothin' but starch and iron.

So de girl wouldn't pay no mind to Brer Rabbit at all. She'd be listenin' to Brer Dog sing. Every time he'd stop she'd holler out dere to him, "Won't you favor us wid another piece, Brer Dog? Ah sho do love singin' especially when they got a good voice and picks de banjo at de same time."

Brer Rabbit saw he wasn't makin' no time wid Miss Saphronie so he waylaid Brer Dog down in de piney woods one day and says:

"Brer Dog, you sho is got a mellow voice. You can sing. Wisht Ah could sing like dat, den maybe Miss Fronie would pay me some mind."

"Gawan, Brer Rabbit, you makin' great 'miration at nothin'. Ah can whoop a little, but Ah really do wish Ah could sing enough to suit Miss Fronie."

"Well, dat's de very point Ah'm comin' out on. Ah know a way to make yo' voice sweeter."

"How? Brer Rabbit, how?"

"Ah knows a way."

"Hurry up and tell me, Brer Rabbit. Don't keep me waitin' like dis. Make haste."

"Ah got to see inside yo' throat first. Lemme see dat and Ah can tell you exactly what to do so you can sing more better."

Brer Dog stretched his mouth wide open and the rabbit peered way down inside. Brer Dog had his mouth latched back to de last notch and his eyes shut. So Brer Rabbit pulled out his razor and split Brer Dog's tongue and tore out across de mountain wid de dog right in behind him. Him and him! Brer Rabbit had done ruint Brer Dog's voice, but he ain't had time to stop at Miss Fronie's nor nowhere else 'cause dat dog is so mad he won't give him time.

II

WHAT THE RABBIT LEARNED

De dog is sho hot after him. Run dem doggone rabbits so that they sent word to de dogs dat they want peace. So they had a convention. De rabbit took de floor and said they was tired of runnin', and dodgin' all de time, and they asted de dogs to please leave rabbits alone and run somethin' else. So de dogs put it to a vote and 'greed to leave off runnin' rabbits.

So after de big meetin' Brer Dog invites de rabbit over to his house to have dinner wid him.

He started on thru de woods wid Brer Dog but every now and then he'd stop and scratch his ear and listen. He stop right in his tracks. Dog say:

"Aw, come on Brer Rabbit, you too suscautious. Come on."

Kept dat up till they come to de branch just 'fore they got to Brer Dog's house. Just as Brer Rabbit started to step out on de foot-log, he heard some dogs barkin' way down de creek. He heard de old hound say, "How o-l-d is he?" and the young dogs answer him: "Twenty-one or two, twenty-one or two!" So Brer Rabbit say, "Excuse me, but Ah don't reckon Ah better go home wid you today, Brer Dog."

"Ah, come on, Brer Rabbit, you always gitten scared for nothin'. Come on."

"Ah hear dogs barkin', Brer Dog."

"Naw, you don't, Brer Rabbit."

"Yes, Ah do. Ah know, dat's dogs barkin'."

"S'posin' it is, it don't make no difference. Ain't we done held a convention and passed a law dogs run no mo' rabbits? Don't pay no 'tention to every li'l bit of barkin' you hear."

Rabbit scratch his ear and say,

"Yeah, but all de dogs ain't been to no convention, and anyhow some of dese fool dogs ain't got no better sense than to run all over dat law and break it up. De rabbits didn't go to school much and he didn't learn but three letter, and that's trust no mistake. Run every time de bush shake."

So he raced on home without breakin' another breath wid de dog.

"Dat's right," cut in Larkins White. "De Rabbits run from everything. They held a meetin' and decided. They say, 'Le's all go drown ourselves 'cause ain't nothin' skeered of us.' So it was agreed.

"They all started to de water in a body fast as time could wheel and roll. When they was crossin' de marsh jus' befo' they got to de sea, a frog hollered, 'Quit it, quit it!' So they say, 'Somethin' is 'fraid of us, so we won't drown ourselves.' So they all turnt 'round and went home."

Buh Tukrey Buzzud and de Rain*

BUH TUKREY BUZZARD, him yent hab no sense no how. You watch um.

Wen de rain duh po down, eh set on de fench an eh squinch up isself. Eh draw in eh neck, an eh try fur hide eh head, an eh look dat pittyful you rale sorry for um. Eh duh half cry, an eh say to isself: "Nummine, wen dis rain ober me guine buil house right off. Me yent guine leh dis rain lick me dis way no mo."

Wen de rain done gone, an de win blow, an de sun shine, wuh Buh Tukrey Buzzud do? Eh set on de top er de dead pine tree way de sun kin wam um, an eh tretch out eh wing, an eh tun roun an roun so de win kin dry eh fedder, an eh laugh to isself, an eh say: "Dis rain done ober. Eh yent guine rain no mo. No use fur me fuh buil house now." Caless man dis like Buh Tukrey Buzzud.

Compair Lapin and Mr. Turkey**

EVERY evening when Compair Lapin returned from his work he passed through a yard where there was a large turkey sleeping on its perch, and like all other turkeys that one also had its head under its wing to sleep.

Every evening Compair Lapin stopped to look at the turkey, and he asked himself what it had done with its head. Finally, one evening, he was so curious that he stopped underneath the perch, and said: "Good evening, Mr. Turkey."

"Good evening," said the turkey, without raising its head.

"Do you have a head, Mr. Turkey?"

"Yes, I have a head."

"Where is it?"

"My head is here."

Compair Lapin looked in vain, but he could not see Mr. Turkey's head. As he saw that the turkey did not want to talk to him or show him where was its head, he went to his

---

* From *Negro Myths from the Georgia Coast, Told in the Vernacular*, by Charles C. Jones, Jr., p. 4. Copyright, 1888, by Charles C. Jones, Jr. Boston and New York: Houghton, Mifflin & Company.
** From *Louisiana Folk-Tales*, in French Dialect and English Translation, collected and edited by Alcée Fortier, Memoirs of the American Folk-Lore Society, Volume II, p. 25. Copyright, 1895, by the American Folk-Lore Society. Boston and New York: Houghton, Mifflin & Company.

house and said to his sister: "Do you know that to go to sleep turkeys take off their heads? Well, I believe I shall do the same thing, because it is less trouble to sleep without a head, and one can speak without a head, for the turkey spoke to me."

Before his sister had the time to tell him anything, he took an axe and cut off his head. His sister tried in every way possible to stick it on again, but could not do so, as her brother had killed himself.

Compair Bouki and the Monkeys*

COMPAIR BOUKI put fire under his kettle, and when the water was very hot he began to beat his drum and to cry out:

> Sam-bombel! Sam-bombel tam!
> Sam-bombel! Sam-bombel dam!

The monkeys heard and said: "What? Bouki has something good to eat, let us go," and they ran up to Bouki and sang: "Molési cherguinet, chourvan! Chéguillé, chourvan!" Compair Bouki then said to the monkeys: "I shall enter into the kettle, and when I say 'I am cooked,' you must take me out." He jumped into the kettle, and the monkeys pulled him out as soon as he said "I am cooked."

The monkeys, in their turn, jumped into the kettle, and cried out, immediately on touching the water, "We are cooked." Bouki, however, took his big blanket, and covering the kettle, said: "If you were cooked you could not say so." One little monkey alone escaped, and Bouki ate all the others. Some time after this Compair Bouki was hungry again, and he called the monkeys:

> Sam-bombel! Sam-bombel tam!
> Sam-bombel! Sam-bombel dam!

When the monkeys came, he jumped into the kettle again and said: "I am cooked, I am cooked." The monkeys, however, which had been warned by the little monkey which had escaped the first time, did not pull Bouki out, but said: "If you were cooked you could not say so."

---

* *Ibid.*, pp. 25, 27.

II

NURSERY TALES

STORY-TELLING for children has kept alive not only folk tales but also the art of oral narration. For young and old alike the fairy tale is the most appealing of folk tale types. This is the story of the trials and ultimate success of an imaginary hero or heroine, involving elements of the supernatural or the marvelous. The nature of the fairy tale, as compared with other folk-tale types, is that it is told not to be believed but to be enjoyed and admired or wondered at. For, unlike the lying tale, which deceives, the fairy tale or wonder tale may inculcate a certain imaginative wisdom and even instruction. It is imaginatively true in the way that dreams are true—a projection of subconscious desires and a survival of primitive patterns of experience and faith. The appeal of the fairy tale lies not only in the ingeniousness of the incidents but also in its beauty of form and style. Here stock motifs, episodes, and plots play an important part. The effectiveness of repetition and especially cumulative iteration as a device of oral narration is demonstrated by its wide use in both fairy tales and ballads. Above all, the atmosphere of the fairy tale, as of the ballad, weaves a spell of far away and long ago and diffuses a light that never was on land or sea.

The most effective American folk tales employ homely vernacular or dialect and other oral devices. Certain tales, like "Tailypo" (which may be traced to the "Teeny-Tiny" of English fairy tales), depend almost entirely upon the voice for their effect. Mark Twain gave this technique an amusing twist in his platform recital of a variant of "The Golden Arm." This is the tale in which the husband has stolen the coppers from the eyelids of his dead wife and is haunted by her ghost, which repeatedly appears wailing, "Who's got my money? I want my money." After working up his audience to an excruciating pitch, Mark Twain remained silent for a couple of seconds and, slowly advancing, with appropriate gestures, suddenly stamped and yelled "Boo!"[1]

——————◆——————

The Talking Eggs*

THERE was once a lady who had two daughters; they were called Rose and Blanche. Rose was bad, and Blanche was good; but the mother liked Rose better, although she was bad, because she was her very picture. She would compel Blanche to do all the work, while Rose was seated in her rocking-chair. One day she sent Blanche to the well to get some water in a bucket. When Blanche arrived at the well, she saw an old woman, who said to her: "Pray, my little one, give me some water; I am very thirsty." "Yes, aunt," said Blanche, "here is some water"; and Blanche rinsed her bucket, and gave her good fresh water to drink. "Thank you, my child, you are a good girl; God will bless you."

A few days after, the mother was so bad to Blanche that she ran away into the woods. She cried, and knew not where to go, because she was afraid to return home. She saw the same old woman, who was walking in front of her. "Ah! my child, why are you crying? What hurts you?" "Ah, aunt, mamma has beaten me, and I am afraid to return to the cabin." "Well, my child, come with me; I will give you supper and a bed; but you must promise me not to laugh at anything which you will see." She took Blanche's hand, and they began to walk in the wood. As they advanced, the bushes of thorns opened before them, and closed behind their backs. A little further on, Blanche saw two axes, which were fighting; she found that very strange, but she said nothing. They walked further, and behold! it was two arms which were fighting; a little further, two legs; at last, she saw two heads which were fighting, and which said: "Blanche, good morning, my child; God will help you." At last they arrived at the cabin of the old woman, who said to Blanche: "Make some fire, my child, to cook the supper"; and she sat down near the fireplace, and

* From *Louisiana Folk-Tales*, in French Dialect and English translation, collected and edited by Alcée Fortier, Memoirs of the American Folk-Lore Society, Volume II, pp. 117–119. Copyright, 1895, by the American Folk-Lore Society. Boston and New York: Houghton, Mifflin & Company.

took off her head. She placed it on her knees, and began to louse herself. Blanche found that very strange; she was afraid, but she said nothing. The old woman put back her head in its place and gave Blanche a large bone to put on the fire for their supper. Blanche put the bone in the pot. Lo! in a moment the pot was full of good meat.

She gave Blanche a grain of rice to pound with the pestle, and thereupon the mortar became full of rice. After they had taken their supper, the old woman said to Blanche: "Pray, my child, scratch my back." Blanche scratched her back, but her hand was all cut, because the old woman's back was covered with broken glass. When she saw that Blanche's hand was bleeding, she only blew on it, and the hand was cured.

When Blanche got up the next morning, the old woman said to her: "You must go home now, but as you are a good girl I want to make you a present of the talking eggs. Go to the chicken-house; all the eggs which say 'Take me,' you must take them; all those which will say 'Do not take me,' you must not take. When you will be on the road, throw the eggs behind your back to break them."

As Blanche walked, she broke the eggs. Many pretty things came out of those eggs. It was now diamonds, now gold, a beautiful carriage, beautiful dresses. When she arrived at her mother's, she had so many fine things that the house was full of them. Therefore her mother was very glad to see her. The next day, she said to Rose: "You must go to the woods to look for this same old woman; you must have fine dresses like Blanche."

Rose went to the woods, and she met the old woman, who told her to come to her cabin; but when she saw the axes, the arms, the legs, the heads, fighting, and the old woman taking off her head to louse herself, she began to laugh and to ridicule everything she saw. Therefore the old woman said: "Ah! my child, you are not a good girl; God will punish you."

The next day she said to Rose: "I don't want to send you back with nothing; go to the chicken-house, and take the eggs which say 'Take me.' "

Rose went to the chicken-house. All the eggs began to say: "Take me," "Don't take me"; "Take me," "Don't take me." Rose was so bad that she said: "Ah, yes, you say 'Don't take me,' but you are precisely those I want." She took all the eggs which said "Don't take me," and she went away with them.

As she walked, she broke the eggs, and there came out a

quantity of snakes, toads, frogs, which began to run after her. There were even a quantity of whips, which whipped her. Rose ran and shrieked. She arrived at her mother's so tired that she was not able to speak. When her mother saw all the beasts and the whips which were chasing her, she was so angry that she sent her away like a dog, and told her to go live in the woods.

The Singing Bones*

ONCE upon a time there lived a man and a woman who had twenty-five children. They were very poor; the man was good, the woman was bad. Every day when the husband returned from his work the wife served his dinner, but always meat without bones.

"How is it that this meat has no bones?"

"Because bones are heavy, and meat is cheaper without bones. They give more for the money."

The husband ate, and said nothing.

"How is it you don't eat meat?"

"You forget that I have no teeth. How do you expect me to eat meat without teeth?"

"That is true," said the husband, and he said nothing more, because he was afraid to grieve his wife, who was as wicked as she was ugly.

When one has twenty-five children one cannot think of them all the time, and one does not see if one or two are missing. One day, after his dinner, the husband asked for his children. When they were by him he counted them, and found only fifteen. He asked his wife where were the ten others. She answered that they were at their grandmother's, and every day she would send one more for them to get a change of air. That was true, every day there was one that was missing.

One day the husband was at the threshold of his house, in front of a large stone which was there. He was thinking of his children, and he wanted to go and get them at their grandmother's, when he heard voices that were saying:

> Our mother killed us,
> Our father ate us.
> We are not in a coffin,
> We are not in the cemetery.

* *Ibid.*, p. 61.

At first he did not understand what that meant, but he raised the stone, and saw a great quantity of bones, which began to sing again. He then understood that it was the bones of his children, whom his wife had killed, and whom he had eaten. Then he was so angry that he killed his wife; buried his children's bones in the cemetery, and stayed alone at his house. From that time he never ate meat, because he believed it would always be his children that he would eat.

Tailypo*

ONCE upon a time, way down in de big woods ob Tennessee, dey lived a man all by hisself. His house didn't hab but one room in it, an' dat room was his pahlor, his settin' room, his bedroom, his dinin' room, an' his kitchen, too. In one end ob de room was a great, big, open fiahplace, an' dat's wha' de man cooked an' et his suppah. An' one night atter he had cooked an' et his suppah, dey crep' in troo de cracks ob de logs de curiestes creetur dat you ebber did see, an' it had a *great, big, long tail.*

Jis' as soon as dat man see dat varmint, he reached fur his hatchet, an' wid one lick, he cut dat thing's tail off. De creetur crep' out troo de cracks ob de logs an' run away, an' de man, fool like, he took an' cooked dat tail, he did, an' et it. Den he went ter bed, an' atter a while, he went ter sleep.

He hadn't been 'sleep berry long, till he waked up, an' heerd sumpin' climbin' up de side ob his cabin. It sounded jis' like a cat, an' he could heer it *scratch, scratch, scratch,* an' by-an'-by, he heerd it say, "*Tailypo, tailypo; all I want's my tailypo.*"

Now dis yeer man had t'ree dogs: one wuz called Uno, an' one wuz called Ino, an' de udder one wuz called Cumptico-Calico. An' when he heerd dat thing he called his dawgs, *huh! huh! huh!* an' dem dawgs cum bilin' out from under de floo', an' dey chased dat thing way down in de big woods. An' de man went back ter bed an' went ter sleep.

Well, way long in de middle ob de night, he waked up an' he heerd sumpin' right above his cabin doo', tryin' ter git in. He listened, an' he could heer it *scratch, scratch, scratch,* an'

* From *Negro Tales from West Virginia,* by John Harrington Cox, *The Journal of American Folk-Lore,* Vol. XLVII (October-December, 1934), No. CLXXXVI, pp. 341–342. New York.

den he heerd it say, "*Tailypo, tailypo; all I want's my tailypo.*" An' he sot up in bed and called his dawgs, *huh! huh! huh!* an' dem dawgs cum bustin' round de corner ob de house an' dey cotched up wid dat thing at de gate an' dey jis' tore de whole fence down, tryin' ter git at it. An' dat time, dey chased it way down in de big swamp. An' de man went back ter bed agin an' went ter sleep.

Way long toward mornin' he waked up, an he heerd sumpin' down in de big swamp. He listened, an' he heerd it say, "*You know, I know; all I want's my tailypo.*" An' dat man sot up in bed an' called his dawgs, *huh! huh! huh!* an' you know dat time dem dawgs didn' cum. Dat thing had carried 'em way off down in de big swamp an' killed 'em, or los' 'em. An' de man went back ter bed an' went ter sleep agin.

Well, jis' befo' daylight, he waked up an' he heerd sumpin' in his room, an' it sounded like a cat, climbin' up de civers at de foot ob his bed. He listened an' he could heer it *scratch, scratch, scratch*, an' he looked ober de foot ob his bed an' he saw two little pinted ears, an' in a minute, he saw two big, roun', fiery eyes lookin' at him. He wanted to call his dawgs, but he too skeered ter holler. Dat thing kep' creepin' up until by-an'-by it wuz right on top ob dat man, an' den it said in a low voice, "*Tailypo, tailypo; all I want's my tailypo.*" An' all at once dat man got his voice an' he said, "*I hain't got yo' tailypo.*" And dat thing said, "*Yes you has,*" an' it jumped on dat man an' scratched him all to pieces. An' sum folks say he got his tailypo.

Now dey ain't nothin' lef' ob dat man's cabin way down in de big woods ob Tennessee, 'ceptin' the chimbley, an' folks w'at lib in de big valley say dat when de moon shines bright an' de win' blows down de valley you can heer sumpin' say, "Tailypo . . . ," an' den, die away in de distance.

Wiley and the Hairy Man*

WILEY'S pappy was a bad man and no-count. He stole watermelons in the dark of the moon, slept while the weeds grew higher than the cotton, robbed a corpse laid out for burying, and, worse than that, killed three martins and never even chunked at a crow. So everybody thought that when Wiley's

* By Donnell Van de Voort. From the Manuscripts of the Federal Writers' Project of the Works Progress Administration for the State of Alabama.

pappy died he'd never cross Jordan because the Hairy Man would be there waiting for him. That must have been the way it happened, because they never found him after he fell off the ferry boat at Holly's where the river is quicker than anywhere else. They looked for him a long way down river and in the still pools between the sand-banks, but they never found pappy. And they heard a big man laughing across the river, and everybody said, "That's the Hairy Man." So they stopped looking.

"Wiley," his mammy told him, "the Hairy Man's done got yo' pappy and he's go' get you 'f you don't look out."

"Yas'm," he said, "I'll look out. I'll take my hound-dogs ev'rywhere I go. The Hairy Man can't stand no hound-dog."

Wiley knew that because his mammy had told him. She knew because she was from the swamps by the Tombigbee and knew conjure. They don't know conjure on the Alabama like they do on the Tombigbee.

One day Wiley took his axe and went down in the swamp to cut some poles for a hen-roost and his hounds went with him. But they took out after a shoat and ran it so far off Wiley couldn't even hear them yelp.

"Well," he said, "I hope the Hairy Man ain't nowhere round here now."

He picked up his axe to start cutting poles, but he looked up and there came the Hairy Man through the trees grinning. He was sure ugly and his grin didn't help much. He was hairy all over. His eyes burned like fire and spit drooled all over his big teeth.

"Don't look at me like that," said Wiley, but the Hairy Man kept coming and grinning, so Wiley threw down his axe and climbed up a big bay tree. He saw the Hairy Man didn't have feet like a man but like a cow, and Wiley never had seen a cow up a bay tree.

"What for you done climb up there?" the Hairy Man asked Wiley when he got to the bottom of the tree.

Wiley climbed nearly to the top of the tree and looked down. Then he climbed plumb to the top.

"How come you climbin' trees?" the Hairy Man said.

"My mammy done tole me to stay 'way from you. What you got in that big croaker-sack?"

"I ain't got nothing yet."

"Gwan 'way from here," said Wiley, hoping the tree would grow some more.

"Ha," said the Hairy Man and picked up Wiley's axe. He

swung it stout and the chips flew. Wiley grabbed the tree close, rubbed his belly on it and hollered, "Fly, chips, fly, back in yo' same old place."

The chips flew and the Hairy Man cussed and damned. Then he swung the axe and Wiley knew he'd have to holler fast. They went to it tooth and toe-nail then, Wiley hollering and the Hairy Man chopping. He hollered till he was hoarse and he saw the Hairy Man was gaining on him.

"I'll come down part t'way," he said, " 'f you'll make this bay tree twicet as big around."

"I ain't studyin' you," said the Hairy Man, swinging the axe.

"I bet you cain't," said Wiley.

"I ain't go' try," said the Hairy Man.

Then they went to it again, Wiley hollering and the Hairy Man chopping. Wiley had about yelled himself out when he heard his hound-dogs yelping way off.

"Hyeaaah, dog. Hyeaaah," he hollered. "Fly, chips, fly, back in yo' same old place."

"You ain't got no dogs. I sent that shoat to draw 'em off."

"Hyeaaah, dog," hollered Wiley, and they both heard the hound-dogs yelping and coming jam-up. The Hairy Man looked worried.

"Come on down," he said, "and I'll teach you conjure."

"I can learn all the conjure I wants from my mammy."

The Hairy Man cussed some more, but he threw the axe down and balled the jack off through the swamp.

When Wiley got home he told his mammy that the Hairy Man had most got him, but his dogs ran him off.

"Did he have his sack?"

"Yas'm."

"Nex' time he come after you, don't you climb no bay tree."

"I ain't," said Wiley. "They ain't big enough around."

"Don't climb no kind o' tree. Jes stay on the ground and say, 'Hello, Hairy Man.' You hear me, Wiley?"

"No'm."

"He ain't go' hurt you, chile. You can put the Hairy Man in the dirt when I tell you how to do him."

"I puts him in the dirt and he puts me in that croaker-sack. I ain't puttin' no Hairy Man in the dirt."

"You jes do like I say. You say, 'Hello, Hairy Man.' He says, 'Hello, Wiley.' You say, 'Hairy Man, I done heard you 'bout the best conjureman 'round here.' 'I reckon I am.' You say, 'I bet you cain't turn yo'self into no gee-raff.' You keep tellin' him he cain't and he will. Then you say, 'I bet you cain't turn yo'self into no alligator.' And he will. Then you say, 'Anybody can turn theyself into somep'n big as a man, but I bet you cain't turn yo'self into no 'possum.' Then he will, and you grab him and throw him in the sack."

"It don't sound jes right somehow," said Wiley, "but I will." So he tied up his dogs so they wouldn't scare away the Hairy Man, and went down to the swamp again. He hadn't been there long when he looked up and there came the Hairy Man grinning through the trees, hairy all over and his big teeth showing more than ever. He knew Wiley came off without his hound-dogs. Wiley nearly climbed a tree when he saw the croaker-sack, but he didn't.

"Hello, Hairy Man," he said.

"Hello, Wiley." He took the sack off his shoulder and started opening it up.

"Hairy Man, I done heard you 'bout the best conjure man round here."

"I reckon I is."

"I bet you cain't turn yo'self into no gee-raff."

"Shux, that ain't no trouble," said the Hairy Man.

"I bet you cain't do it."

So the Hairy Man twisted round and turned himself into a gee-raff.

"I bet you cain't turn yo'self into no alligator," said Wiley.

The gee-raff twisted around and turned into an alligator, all the time watching Wiley to see he didn't try to run.

"Anybody can turn theyself into somep'n big as a man," said Wiley, "but I bet you cain't turn yo-self into no 'possum."

The alligator twisted around and turned into a 'possum, and Wiley grabbed it and threw it in the sack.

Wiley tied the sack up as tight as he could and then he threw it in the river. He went home through the swamp and he looked up and there came the Hairy Man grinning through the trees.

"I turn myself into the wind and blew out. Wiley, I'm go' set right here till you get hongry and fall out of that bay tree. You want me to learn you some more conjure."

Wiley studied a while. He studied about the Hairy Man and he studied about his hound-dogs tied up most a mile away.

"Well," he said, "you done some pretty smart tricks. But I bet you cain't make things disappear and go where nobody knows."

"Huh, that's what I'm good at. Look at that old bird-nest on the limb. Now look. It's done gone."

"How I know it was there in the fus' place? I bet you cain't make somep'n I know is there disappear."

"Ha ha," said the Hairy Man. "Look at yo' shirt."

Wiley looked down and his shirt was gone, but he didn't care, because that was just what he wanted the Hairy Man to do.

"That was jes a plain old shirt," he said. "But this rope I got tied round my breeches been conjured. I bet you cain't make it disappear."

"Huh, I can make all the rope in this county disappear."

"Ha ha ha," said Wiley.

The Hairy Man looked mad and threw his chest way out. He opened his mouth wide and hollered loud.

"From now on all the rope in this county has done disappeared."

Wiley reared back holding his breeches with one hand and a tree-limb with the other.

"Hyeaaah, dog," he hollered loud enough to be heard more than a mile off.

When Wiley and his dogs got back home his mammy asked him did he put the Hairy Man in the sack.

"Yes'm, but he done turned himself into the wind and blew right through that old croaker-sack."

"That *is* bad," said his mammy. "But you done fool him twicet. 'F you fool him again he'll leave you alone. He'll be mighty hard to fool the third time."

"We gotta study up a way to fool him, mammy."

"I'll study up a way tereckly," she said, and sat down by the fire and held her chin between her hands and studied real hard. But Wiley wasn't studying anything except how to keep the Hairy Man away. He took his hound-dogs out and tied one at the back door and one at the front door. Then he crossed a broom and an axe-handle over the window and built a fire in the fire-place. Feeling a lot safer, he sat down and helped his mammy study. After a little while his mammy said, "Wiley, you go down to the pen and get that little suckin' pig away from that old sow."

Wiley went down and snatched the sucking pig through the rails and left the sow grunting and heaving in the pen. He took the pig back to his mammy and she put it in his bed.

"Now, Wiley," she said, "you go on up to the loft and hide."

So he did. Before long he heard the wind howling and the trees shaking, and then his dogs started growling. He looked out through a knot-hole in the planks and saw the dog at the front door looking down toward the swamps, with his hair standing up and his lips drawn back in a snarl. Then an animal as big as a mule with horns on its head ran out of the swamp past the house. The dog jerked and jumped, but he couldn't get loose. Then an animal bigger than a great big dog with a long nose and big teeth ran out of the swamp and growled at the cabin. This time the dog broke loose and took after the big animal, who ran back down into the swamp. Wiley looked out another chink at the back end of the loft just in time to see his other dog jerk loose and take out after an animal, which might have been a 'possum, but wasn't.

"Law-dee," said Wiley. "The Hairy Man is coming here sho'."

He didn't have long to wait, because soon enough he heard something with feet like a cow scrambling around on the roof. He knew it was the Hairy Man, because he heard him damn and swear when he touched the hot chimney. The Hairy Man jumped off the roof when he found out there was a fire in the fire-place and came up and knocked on the front door as big as you please.

"Mammy," he hollered, "I done come after yo' baby."

"You ain't go' get him," mammy hollered back.

"Give him here or I'll bite you. I'm blue-gummed and I'll pizen you sho'."

"I'm right blue-gummed myself," mammy sang out.

"Give him here or I'll set yo' house on fire with lightnin'."

"I got plenty of sweet-milk to put it out with."

"Give him here or I'll dry up yo' spring, make yo' cow go dry and send a million boll-weevils out of the ground to eat up yo' cotton."

"Hairy Man, you wouldn't do all that. That's mighty mean."

"I'm a mighty mean man. I ain't never seen a man as mean as I am."

" 'F I give you my baby will you go on way from here and leave everything else alone."

"I swear that's jes what I'll do," said the Hairy Man, so mammy opened the door and let him in.

"He's over there in that bed," she said.

The Hairy Man came in grinning like he was meaner than he said. He walked over to the bed and snatched the covers back.

"Hey," he hollered, "there ain't nothin' in this bed but a old suckin' pig."

"I ain't said what kind of a baby I was givin' you, and that suckin' pig sho' belonged to me 'fo' I gave it to you."

The Hairy Man raged and yelled. He stomped all over the house gnashing his teeth. Then he grabbed up the pig and tore out through the swamp, knocking down trees right and left. The next morning the swamp had a wide path like a cyclone had cut through it, with trees torn loose at the roots and lying on the ground. When the Hairy Man was gone Wiley came down from the loft.

"Is he done gone, mammy?"

"Yes, chile. That old Hairy Man cain't ever hurt you again. We done fool him three times."

Wiley went over to the safe and got out his pappy's jug of shinny that had been lying there since the old man fell in the river.

"Mammy," he said, "I'm goin' to get hog-drunk and chicken-wild."

"You ain't the only one, chile. Ain't it nice yo' pappy was so no-count he had to keep shinny in the house?"

III

WITCH TALES

STORIES of witches survive long after people have ceased to believe in witchcraft or take it seriously. The cult itself, allied to the black art, may linger in remnants of spells and charms or counter-charms, as in conjure or hoodoo, becoming mixed with beliefs in hants and spirits generally. But present-day witch tales, like ghost and devil tales, are told either to thrill or to amuse.

On the eerie and blood-chilling side is the favorite motif of the witch prevented from reëntering her skin. This is based on the "slip-skin" belief that a skinless person is invisible and that witches slip off their skin after midnight in order to perform their nefarious deeds unseen. In "De Witch-'ooman an' de Spinnin'-Wheel" this motif is combined with that of the witch-wife. The shape-shifting witch-woman may be discovered by a mutilated hand or foot or other part of the body, according to the notion that wounds inflicted on the animal shape persist in the human form.

On the prankish side, witches are tricksters who make a nuisance of themselves in all the ways known to playfully malevolent spirits. Their pranks range from milk-stealing to riding a person in his sleep. In one of the best of American legends of the supernatural, "The Bell Witch of Tennessee and Mississippi," the hag or disembodied spirit is both revenant and hobgoblin, combining the destructive persecution of the vampire with the obstreperous annoyance of the poltergeist or noisy ghost.

De Witch-'ooman an' de Spinnin'-Wheel*

THE WITCH PREVENTED FROM REËNTERING HER SKIN: A TALE FROM LOUISIANA.

ONE time dey wuz a man whar rid up at night ter a cabin in de eedge o' de swamp. He wuz dat hongry an' ti'd dat he say ter hissef: "Ef I kin git a hunk o' co'n-pone and a slice o' bakin', I doan kur what I pays!" On dat here come a yaller-'ooman spankin' out'n de cabin. She wuz spry on her foot ez a catbird, an' her eyes wuz sof' an' shiny. She ax de man fer ter light an' come in de cabin, an' git some supper. An' Lawd! how he mouf do water when he cotch a glimpst er de skillet on de coals! He luk it so well dat he stay; an' he sot eroun' in dat cabin outwel he git so fat dat de grease fa'r run out'n he jaws when he look up at de sun. De yaller-'ooman she spen' her time cookin' fer him, an' waitin' on him wi' so much oberly, dat at las' de man, he up an' marry dat yaller-'ooman.

At fus' dey git erlong tollable well, but a'ter erwhile he gin ter notice dat sump'n curus 'bout dat yaller-'ooman. She ain' never in de cabin when he wake up in de night time! So, he mek up his min' fer ter spy on her. He lay down one night

* By Mrs. M. E. M. Davis, New Orleans, La. From *The Journal of American Folk-Lore*, Vol. XVIII (July-September, 1905), No. LXX, pp. 251–252. Copyright, 1905, by the American Folk-Lore Society. Boston and New York: Houghton, Mifflin & Company.

on de fo' pos' bed in de cornder, 'ten luk he sleep. De yaller-'ooman watch him out'n de een o' her eye, an' when she hear him gin a sno' (caze *cose* he 'ten luk he sno') she jump up an' pat a juba in de middle o' de flo'. Den she reach down a big gridi'on fum de wall, an' rake out some coals, an' haul de big spinnin'-wheel close ter de ha'th. Den, she sot herself down on dat gridi'on, an' soon ez it wuz red-hot she 'gin ter spin her skin off'n her body on de spinnin'-wheel. "Tu'n an' spin, come off skin, tu'n an' spin, come off skin." An' fo' de Lawd, de skin come off'n dat witch-'ooman's body, berginning at de top o' her head, ez slick es de shush come off de ear o' corn. An' when it wuz fa'r off, dan she wuz a gret big yaller cat. Den, she tuk her skin an' chuck it onder de bed. "Lay dar, skin," she say, "wi' dat fool nigger sno'in' in de bed, ontwel I come back. I gwine ter ha' some fum, I is."

Wi' dat she jump out'n de winder an' lope off. Soon ez she wuz gone de man, he jump out'n de bed an' tuk out skin an' fill it plum full o' salt an' pepper, un' th'ow it back onder de bed. Den he crope out an' watch thro' de key-hole ontwel de witch-'ooman come home. She laugh whilse she wuz rakin' out de skin fum onder de bed, an' shakin' herse'f inter it. But when she feel de salt an' pepper, she laugh on de yether side her mouf. She moan an' groan so you kin hear her a mile! But she ain' able ter git out'n dat skin, an' de man watch her thoo de key-hole twel she fall down an' die on de flo'.

Aunt Sally Hillock's Witch Story*

UNCLE PHIL was a great deer hunter, and he had two favorite short-eared hounds, old Salty and young Jerry. One day in the fall of the year they had been hunting with rare luck in the Little Valley which lies between the two ridges of the Bald Eagle Mountains north of Nippenose Valley, and when night came on he went into his cabin on the side of the mountain, grallocked and hung up three stags, built a big fire, ate supper and lay down in his bunk by the wall, his dogs resting on the ground close beside him. In a short time a handsome heath hen entered the shack—there was no door on the hinges—and sat down on the hearth with one side of

* From *Two Pennsylvania Mountain Legends*, collected by Henry W. Shoe-maker, pp. 13–15, Publications of The Pennsylvania Folk-Lore Society, Volume I, Number 4. Published by The Reading Eagle Press, Reading, Pa. 1928.

her to the fire. She was not long in that position when she began to swell. After a while she rose and turned the side under her to the fire, and if she swelled before, she now swelled seven times bigger. At last she became an old woman, in a brownish grey cloak, and her toppy was a tall, pointed hat with a broad brim, which almost concealed her peaked brown face. She walked over to the bunk and stood before Uncle Phil, who had been wide awake all the time. As soon as the hounds noted her nearness to their master they assumed an angry attitude and sprang at her fiercely. "Tell your dogs to lie down," demanded the old woman. "I cannot make them mind," answered Uncle Phil. She pulled a white hair from her head and gave it to the hunter, who noticed that after he took it in his hand it became jet black. "Tie them up with that," she said.

He pretended to be fastening them with her hair, but he put one of the hairs from his beard, which was equally black, on them instead. As soon as the hag thought the dogs were tied she reached into the bunk and laid hold of Uncle Phil. The dogs sprang again to seize her. "Tighten my hair," she now said. "Slacken *my* hair," replied the hunter. At last the dogs broke loose and caught hold of the old cotton-head. She loosened her hold on Uncle Phil, and bolted for the open door, the dogs close at her heels. The hounds followed her until they drove her over the side of the bench which sloped down just in front of the cabin. It was very steep and rocky, and when they reached the creek which flowed in the bottom of the valley, the fight was resumed in earnest and lasted a good long time. But at length the battle came to an end. The dogs returned to their master, much bedraggled and torn, while the old woman staggered down the hollow toward the head of Kearns' Run, saying, "If the young hound's tush had been in the old hound's mouth, or the old hound's wit in the young hound's head, I would never have escaped them."

Next day Uncle Phil went home, and when he arrived at his log-cabin on the river bluff he met his wife, Aunt Minerva, going in a hurry to a neighbor lady's house, whose daughter, dark Cathlin Drago, was in great pain, and to all appearance, at the point of death. He prevailed on Aunty to first return home and give him a snack, as he was hungry; then they both went together to the double log house of the sick girl, which was the most pretentious dwelling in the whole of the Fair Play Men's Country. When the girl, who was very beautiful and had been greatly beloved by Uncle Phil, though he feared to declare himself to such quality—she was the late Col. Michael Q. Drago's only child—saw him coming with his wife, she ordered the Indian servants in the house to shut and bar the doors. They did as she told them, while she lay on her face, watching through the window lights. But as soon as Uncle Phil and Aunt Minerva came near enough and saw the unfriendly conduct, they curled and picked up a pur-line and drove in one of the doors. When they entered they went straight to the bed where the beautiful black-haired girl lay on her face, her faultlessly lovely features pinched in dreadful agony.

Stung with curiosity, Uncle Phil threw the kivers back as far as the girl's knees. A terrible sight was now revealed to them. The girl's buttocks were torn off and her hips and thighs horribly lacerated by the hounds' fangs. Uncle Phil understood the cause, and bent over to whisper something in dark Cathlin's ear, for he knew that it was she who was with him the previous night at his shanty in the shape of an old woman and had been attacked by his hounds when they chased her from his bunk. Aunt Minerva, who had been jealous of this lovely girl for a long time, had her fears verified by her husband's concern, and quickly drew her dirk and stabbed the girl in the small of the back, and she died the death of a hechs.

Uncle Phil was raving mad and left that night in his canoe to 'list under Colonel Loudon at Fort Augusta. But in the army he could not shake off the memory that he was the cause of dark Cathlin's death, especially since he knew that after all she had returned his love and had visited him at his hunting shanty in the Little Valley in the form of a hechs.

Andres Hironimus, his messmate, had the Black Book, or Hechsen-hammer, so he lifted it one night and struck out for the mountains. He arrived at the Little Valley with the book and tried to raise dark Cathlin's spook by pow-wowing. But she would not return, so he went to his home, thinking that he would have better luck among scenes where she had been last in life, or at her grave. But he could not bring her ghost and he hated his wife more than ever for having murdered her as a hechs. He was quarreling every day with Aunt Minerva and was in constant fear of arrest for deserting from his regiment, and even his father, who was an Ensign in the Rangers, sent word from the front that unless he reported for duty at once he would come home on leave and shoot him down like a penny dog.

One dark night, after pow-wowing for several hours without success over dark Cathlin Drago's grave in Spook Hollow, a neighbor saw Uncle Phil walking up the hill in the direction of Cable's Woods with a stout rope tied around his waist. Climbing the tallest oak—it is still standing—he fastened the rope around his neck and to the stoutest branch, and leaped off. That night there was a terrible storm, such as usually follows a suicide, but after it was over they found Uncle Phil's body with a smile on his dead face.

Witches and Witch-Masters*

SO LONG as the loafers in Bib Tarkey's blacksmith shop discussed crops and politics I paid them scant attention, but when the talk turned to witchcraft I pricked up my ears at once. The old-timers spoke tolerantly of modern disbelief. "Wal," said old Lem Whatley, "I reckon maybe thar *ain't* many witches a-runnin' loose nowadays, but in my day an' time th' woods was full of 'em. My pappy follered gunsmithin' mostly, but he was a witch-master too, an' he shore kilt a many un when we lived up thar on Flat Crick.

"I mind th' time somebody witched our hawgs, so's when I went out t' slop 'em they never come t' th' trough—jest lent back on their tails an' squole. An' th' cow never give no milk, neither, for seven days a-runnin'. Pap he figured it mought be ol' Gram French, whut laid up in a rock-house t'other side o' th' Narrers.

"Funny thing about Gram was, she allus had plenty o' cream an' butter in th' spring-house, but nobody ever seen her do no milkin'. Wal, Pap he snuck over an' bushed up back o' her place, an' peeked in th' winder ever' chanst he got. Finally he seen Gram hang a ol' dirty dishrag on th' potrack an' start in a-squeezin' milk out'n it—she squoze out four big gourdfuls whilst he set thar a-watchin' her, with his eyes a-buggin' out like a tromped-on toadfrog. An' now he knowed how come ol' Muley never give down no milk for seven days a-runnin'.

"When Pap got home he looked mi-ighty solemn. Th' first thing he done was t' git down his ol' silver-mounted witch-rifle,

---

* By Vance Randolph. From *Folk-Say, A Regional Miscellany:1931*, edited by B. A. Botkin, pp. 86–93. Copyright, 1931, by B. A. Botkin. Norman: University of Oklahoma Press.

an' th' next thing he done was t' melt up th' dollar an' mold hisse'f a silver bullet. Next mornin' he tuck him a burnt stick an' drawed a pitcher o' ol' Gram French on a peeled sycamore. Hit didn't look much like Gram, but he written her name on it good an' big, so's not t' resk no boggle. Soon's he got th' hull thing drawed an' wrote t' suit him, back he come an' picked up th' ol' witch-killer.

"I was jest a teen-age boy then, an' I got kinder skeerylike, but Pap he'd kilt a lot o' witches in his time, an' he jest stood thar stiddy as a rock. *Bang*, says th' ol' witch-rifle, an' when we run up t' th' pitcher we seen whar th' silver bullet plunked her right squar' in th' middle. We-uns begun t' feel a heap better then, I tell you! An' thet same day, mind you, ol' Gram French fell off'n th' bluff an' kilt herse'f—busted plumb wide open like a rotten apple! Ol' Muley give down lashin's o' milk thet night, too, an' we never had no more trouble with our hawgs, neither."

The blacksmith had stopped his work to listen to old man Whatley's tale, and appeared to be particularly impressed by its happy conclusion. "Witches," he said with feeling, "is for them ol' fellers whut knows how t' handle 'em, like your paw, Lem. Hit's plumb resky for a common ord'nary evr' day feller t' fool with 'em. One o' them Pea Ridge witch-hunters come dang near killin' me one time. . . . Hit was th' year o' th' big freshet, an' th' Bradford boys had lost most ever'thing. They warn't very bright, nohow, an' 'pears like they was loonier'n usual thet fall.

"When their ol' cow died hit jest about wiped out th' Bradford family. It was holler-horn kilt her, I reckon, but Poly Bradford he figgered she was witched. So he went an' got him a silver spoon somers an' loaded up a ol' scatter-gun they had. Then he ambled out in th' flat-woods an' raked up a big circle o' leaves an' bresh—musta been purty nigh sixty foot acrost, I reckon. 'Long 'bout midnight he set them 'ar bresh afire, an' then he hid out in back of a big cedar stump t' wait for th' witch.

"Wal sir, it jest happened I was a-comin' home 'crost th' flats thet night—I'd been over a-settin' up t' th' Widder Lane's biggest gal Iny—an' I seen this hyar big fire-ring. I'd orter o' knowed better, but my head was all gaumed up with sparkin', an' I never oncet thought o' witches. Anyhow, I rid right into thet 'ar ring, an' th' next thing I knowed hyar come Poly a-prancin' out, 'ith th' ol' gun a-p'intin' fa'r an' squar' at my stummick! 'Bib Tarkey!' he hollers out, 'who'd ever a' thunk *you* was a witch! Wal, anyhow, I got ye now, an' I got a silver bullet in this hyar gun, an' I'm obleeged for t' kill ye!'

"My Gawd, boys, I thought I was a goner shore, an' th' bar'l o' thet ol' musket looked big as a stovepipe. I lent backwards jest as Poly made his fire, an' th' bullet ploughed a big lane right through my whiskers. Th' horse jumped an' throwed me, too, an' hyar was thet fool Poly right on top o' me, a-swingin' at my head with th' butt o' his gun.

"I dodged him ag'in, though, an' finally I got my thumb in his eye an' wrassled him down. I was purty dang mad by this time, an' I jest churned his head up an' down, an' beat him dang nigh t' death. 'Go on an' kill me, Bib,' says he, 'you've done kilt th' critters, an' me an' Lizzie'll starve t' death this Winter anyhow'—an' with thet he begun t' beller like a calf. 'I ain't no witch, you pore ignor'nt, misbegotten eediot,' I says, 'I been over t' Widder Lane's an' I rid into this hyar witch-ring unthoughted-like, 'fore I rightly knowed whar I was at.' Poly he kept on a-grumblin', but he was plumb docile now, so I let him up, an' wiped th' blood off'n his face. 'An' th' next time your danged ol' cow gits witched,' I says, 'you go tell ol' Pap Whatley, an' let him tend to it. You jest leave witches t' th' witch-masters,' says I, 'an' don't you never do no more cunjurin' roun' hyar of a night. Hit's too dang resky-like for th' neighbors.' "

With this Tarkey returned to his blacksmithing, but Charley Howard was moved to rehearse the exploits of his cousin Tom, who had wrestled mightily with the powers of darkness in the Eighties. "Hit all happened way back yander afore me an' my wife was married, an' th' first I heerd of it was one day Tom he come over an' told us how their cow was a-comin' home jest plumb stripped, an' Gran'paw Langley was a-follerin' th' critter round all day t' see who was a-milkin' her. Wal sir, he snuck an' he watched, an' finally he seen two big ol' swamp-rabbits a-suckin' her! Sich a thing was never saw nor heerd tell of afore, I reckon, but Gran'paw he up with th' ol' shotgun an' made his fire jest as them two rabbits was a-hoppin' off together. Th' ol' gun was loaded heavy with turkey-shot, an' they warn't more'n thirty foot off, but danged if he didn't clean miss 'em! Right then an' thar th' ol' man seen how things was, an' he come a-runnin' up t' th' house a-hollerin', 'Witches! Witches!' with his eyes a-buggin' out bigger'n duck-aigs.

"Wal sir, Tom he shucked right out an' dug up th' corner post whar th' money was vaulted, an' they melted up a dollar. Gran'paw he run th' bullets hisse'f, a-shakin' like a white-oak leaf in a Christmas wind, an' Mary she loaded up th' ol' rifle-gun afore th' ball was cold scarcely. Tom got a soon start in th' mornin', an' we was all a-settin' on th' stake-an'-rider when he kilt th' ol' she-rabbit—th' buck run off afore he could git th' gun charged. . . . An' then 'bout four o'clock come th' news thet somebody had went an' kilt ol' Miz' Ricketts over in Hell Holler—shot her plumb through th' heart. Doc he never did find th' bullet, but ever'body knowed how it was, all right."

The subject must certainly be exhausted now, I thought, but another hillman, a stranger to me, had something to contribute to the symposium. "Speakin' o' witches," he said, after helping himself to a big drink of corn from the fruit-jar provided by Whatley, "puts me in mind of a 'sperience Buck Peters had one time when we was berry-pickin' down on Bug Scuffle. Buck was th' loud-talkin'est, drinkin'est, fightin'est feller ever come t' them parts. He'd fight a circle-saw an' turn it hisse'f, an' he warn't skeered o' nothin' in this world or th' next 'un, neither. Thar was a ol' tore-down shanty in back o' Lum Hobart's grocery whar witches had been a-usin' round, an' one day some o' th' boys bannered Buck t' sleep in thar all night. Buck he says if they git him a jug o' right good drinkin' likker he'll sleep anywhar, an' if any witches come round *him* a-lookin' for trouble they'll shore git a lavish of it. Wal, Lum says he'd furnish th' jug hisse'f, pervidin' Buck was still alive come mornin', an' they set thar a-drinkin' an' a-jowerin' an' a-spewin' ambeer over each an' ever', till finally Buck he loaded up with whiskey an' went into th' ol' shanty an' shet th' door. I tuck notice he packed in a-plenty o' candles, too—reckon he warn't a-hankerin' t' fight no witches in th' dark.

"Buck he set thar a long time, a-studyin' 'bout witches an' hants an' th' like o' thet, when all of a suddint up jumps th' Gawd-awfullest big she-cat ever saw in Arkansas, a-yowlin' an' spittin' like a Injun with his tail-feathers afire! Buck he was feelin' kinder mean an' narvish-like anyhow, so he drawed his ol' horse-pistol an' pulls back th' rooster. Lucky for him he done it, too, for jest a ha'r later th' varmint jumped right squar' at him. Th' ol' gun roared like a Christmas anvil, an' one o' th' cat's hind feet was blowed plumb off. Somers a woman hollers out, 'Oh my Gawd!' an' Buck allus swore he seen a woman's bare foot, all shot up an' bloody, a-wigglin' round on th' table. But jest then th' candle went out. Buck he went out too, right through th' winder, an' never stopped a-runnin' till he got plumb home. I never did blame him none, myse'f. Gawda' mighty! Sich doin's as thet 'ar 'd skeer anybody! . . . Purty soon hyar come a feller name Burdick a-ridin' in for t' git Doc Holton—says his ol' woman has done shot her foot off accidental-like. She up an' bled t' death, though, spite of all Doc could do. They do say she died a-yowlin' an' a-spittin' like a cat. . . ."

At the end of the stranger's story I tore myself away, and repaired to the log residence of Uncle Bill Hatfield and his wife, who provided me with bed and board. After supper I broached the general subject of witchcraft and demonology to Uncle Bill, remarking that I myself gave no credence to such idle superstitions as appeared to obtain in this benighted region.

"I ain't superstitious, neither," said Uncle Bill mildly, "but a lot o' things whut some folks *call* superstitions is jest as true as Gawd's own gospel. An' as for witches, it ain't no manner o' use t' tell me thar ain't none, 'cause I know better. Why, I've been rode by 'em myse'f, many th' time!

"I war jest a-dozin' off one night, in th' ol' cabin way back in up on Leetle Piney, when in come th' purtiest gal I ever seen, with a bran'-new bridle in her hand. She fetched a whoop an' jumped plumb astraddle o' my back, an' th' first thing I knowed she had thet 'ar bridle onto me, with th' big cold bit a-cuttin' into my gooms! An' th' *next* thing I knowed she turned me into a flea-bit gray pony, an' we was a-tearin' down th' road hell-bent for 'lection, with th' spurs a-sockin' into my hams at ever' jump.

"Up hills an' down hollers an' 'crost branches an' through berry-patches we went, till we met up with some furriners a-packin' big sacks full o' money—bankrobbers, I reckon they was, or somethin'. Th' witch-woman she lit down then, an' holp them fellers, an' danged if they didn't pile all them big pokes on my back! Hit was all gold money, 'peared like, an' it shore was heavy. Purty soon we come t' a big cave in under a clift, an' she tied me up t' a white oak-saplin', whilst they all tuck th' money inside for t'hide it, I reckon. Atter while th' furriners come out, a-talkin' an' a-laughin' 'mongst theirse'fs, an' purty soon she come out too, an' rid me back home ag'in.

"Wal, th' next night she come an' rid me some more, an' we met up with th' same fellers, an' they drug in another turrible big load o' money. . . . An' th' next night th' same an' more of it, an' the next night, too—hit seemed like thar warn't no end t' th' money we-uns toted into thet 'ar cave-hole. Ever' mornin' I'd wake up plumb tuckered out an' brier-scratched; my head was full o' cockleburrs constant, an' my mouth a-tastin' like a cat had done littered in it.

"I never said nothin' t' th' ol' woman 'bout this hyar witch-ridin' an' all, but I shore done a heap o' studyin' over it. I spent a lot o' time a-lookin' for thet 'ar cave, too, but I couldn't make out t' find it noways, so one mornin' I hobbled off down t' ol' Pap Jennin's shanty an' told him th' hull story. Pap he was a witch-master from who laid th' chunk, an' I knowed in reason he'd tell me whut I better do. Th' ol' man he jest pondered awhile, a-shakin' of his head kinder juberous, an' then he says: 'Wal, Bill, I reckon you-all better mark thet 'ar cave so we kin find it easy. When you git it marked I'll jest lay for this hyar witch-woman an' kill her with a silver bullet. Then we-uns 'll git th' gold-money, o' course.'

"The next night, when she hitched me outside th' cave, I jest drapped as many drappin's as I could, an' started in for t' chaw me a good big blaze on th' white-oak saplin', like Pap told me. I chawed an' I chawed. All of a suddint come a hell of a noise an' a big flash o' light, an' then I heerd a lot o' hollerin'—my ol' woman was a-doin' th' hollerin'. . . . Quick as a wink I seen I was home ag'in, an' it seemed like"—and here Uncle Bill stole a furtive glance at his wife, who sat stolidly smoking by the fireplace—"hit seemed like I'd went an' benastied th' bed-blankets bad, an' dang near bit th' ol' woman's laig off!"

The unexpected conclusion of the story "sot me back right smart," and the whole shanty shook with Bill's uproarious laughter. Uncle Bill is one of the very few old-time Ozarkers whom I have heard speak lightly of these matters. They sometimes assert their unbelief, but they don't joke about it. . . . Aunt Lavina told me later that deep down in his heart Bill still believes in witchcraft, but refuses to admit it to any but his most intimate friends nowadays. And so it is with others of his generation.

The Bell Witch of Tennessee and Mississippi*

BACK in the days before the War there lived somewhere in old North Carolina a man by the name of John Bell. Bell was a

* By Arthur Palmer Hudson and Pete Kyle McCarter. From *The Journal of American Folk-Lore*, Vol. XLVII (January-March, 1934), No. CLXXXIII, pp. 45–63.

planter and was well-fixed. He had a good-sized plantation and a dozen niggers of field-hand age, and mules and cows and hogs a-plenty. His family was made up of his wife, a daughter thirteen or fourteen years old they say was mighty pretty, and two or three young-uns that don't figure much in this story. Until he hired him an overseer, Bell got along fine.

The overseer was a Simon Legree sort of fellow, always at sixes and sevens with other folks, and especially with the niggers. He didn't even mind jawing with his boss. They say Mr. Bell was half a mind to fire the scoundrel and hire another one. But he tended to his business. He had a way with the women-folks. Some say he had an eye open for Mary, the daughter. And Mrs. Bell stood up for him. So he stayed on for a good while, and the longer he stayed the uppiter he got. Whenever he and Bell had a row—and their rows got bigger and bitterer—the overseer went out and blacksnaked three or four niggers, for they were the only critters in the shape of man that he could abuse without a come-back. He was the worst kind of a bully, and a man of high temper, in fact, a regular overseer of the kind you hear about in Yankee stories.

Mr. Bell had a tall temper too, and the men did not spend a lot of time patting each other on the back and bragging about each other's good points. A stand-up fight was bound to come off.

It did. Some say it was about the way the overseer had beat up one of the niggers. Some say it was about something Mr. Bell heard and saw from behind a cotton-house one day when Mary rode through the field where the overseer was working a gang of niggers. Bell went away blowing smoke from his pistol barrel, and mumbling something about white trash. The overseer didn't go away at all.

Of course Bell was brought into court, but he plead self-defense, and the jury let him off. He went home, hired another overseer, and allowed that everything was settled. But the truth was that everything was now plumb unsettled.

That year and the next and the next the crops on the Bell place were an out-and-out failure: bumblebee cotton and scraggly tobacco and nubbin corn. His mules died of colic or some strange disease like it. His cows and hogs got sick of something the horse-doctor couldn't cure. He had to sell his niggers one by one, all except an old woman. Finally he went broke. He got what he could for his land—lock, stock, and barrel—and moved with his family to Tennessee. They say that where he settled down the town of Bell, Tennessee, was named for him. Anyway, he bought him a house and a patch of land near the home of old Andy Jackson, who had knocked off from being President and was living in a big house called the Hermitage.

Not long after the move to Tennessee, strange things began to happen in the Bell home. The children got into the habit of tumbling, or being tumbled, out of bed at least once a week, and of waking up every morning with every stitch of the bed-clothes snatched off and their hair all tangled and mussed up. Now for young-uns to tumble out of bed and to wake up in the morning with their heads uncombed is a mighty strange thing, and the Bells realized it. The children couldn't explain this carrying-on, for they were always asleep till they hit the floor; and it was a peculiar fact that they were never tumbled out while awake.

The old nigger woman told them it was the ha'nt of the overseer Mr. Bell had killed that was pestering the children. She was as superstitious as any other nigger, and she said she had always felt jubous about what the ha'nt of a man like the overseer would do. But she had spunk, and one day she allowed she would find out whether she was right by spending the night under the young-uns' bed. In the middle of the night Mr. and Mrs. Bell were fetched out of their bed by a squall like a pant'er's. When they lit a lamp and ran into the room, they found the old nigger woman sprawled in the middle of the floor, dripping cold sweat like an ash-hopper, her face gray-blue as sugar-cane peeling, and her eyes like saucers in a dish-pan. She was stiff-jointed and tongue-tied. When they got her sitting up and her tongue loosened, she screeched: "Hit's him! Hit's him! Fo' Gawd, hit's him! Hit peenched me all over, stuck pins in me, snatched de keenks outen ma haiuh, an' whup me, Lawd Gawd, how hit whup me, whup me limber and whup me stiff, whup me jes' lack *him*. Ain't gwine back dauh no mo', ain't gwine back dauh no mo'."

The Bells were so scared they told some of the neighbors. Old Andy Jackson heard about it and decided to ride over. He didn't take any stock in ha'nts, and as he rode through the gate he spoke his mind out loud about tarnation fools that believed nigger tales about them. He hadn't got the words out of his mouth before something whaled him over the head and skipped his hat twenty or thirty yards back down the road. Old Andy didn't say any more. He motioned his nigger boy to hand him his hat, and he went away from there.

It seems like the Witch could get hungry like folks, and was satisfied with folks' grub. But it had to be the best. One day the old nigger woman came tearing into the front room where Mrs. Bell was quilting and said the Witch was back in the kitchen drinking up all the sweet milk.

Mrs. Bell was scared and said the old woman was lying.

"Come see fo' yo'se'f, missus. Come see fo' yo'se'f. Ah was back dauh a-mixin' up de biscuit, an' Ah retched ovah to git a cup o' miu'k, an' fo' Gawd, de cup was in de middle o' de auh, an' de miu'k was a-runnin' rat outen hit—an' hit wa'n't gwine nowheah, missus—hit wa'n't gwine nowheah. Jes' run outen de cup, an' den Ah couldn't see hit no mo'."

"You're just seeing things," said Mrs. Bell.

"Jes' whut Ah ain' doin'—ain' seein' de miu'k. Go on back in de kitchen efen you don' believe hit. Go on back dauh an' look fo' yo'se'f. . . . No, ma'am, Ah hain' gwine back in dat place. No, ma'am, dat ha'nt kin guzzle an' bile up all de miu'k de cows evah give 'fo' Ah raise mah finger to stop hit."

Mrs. Bell went back into the kitchen and looked. There was a cup there that had had milk in it, and the milk was gone, sure as shootin'. She was now as scared as the old nigger woman, and sent right away for her husband to come out of the field.

They couldn't figure out how a ghost could drink milk, or what becomes of the milk if he does. Does the milk dry up into the ghost of itself? If not, where does it go when the ghost swallows it? Ghosts can't be seen. At least, this one couldn't. They could see through where it was. If they could see through it, why couldn't they see the milk as plain when it was inside the ghost as when it was outside? The old nigger woman said the milk was running out of the cup, but it "wa'n't gwine nowheah." An old Holy Roller preacher from down in Tallahatchie bottom who rode over to talk about it argued that if the old woman's tale was so milk must be of a higher class than folks. When it turns into the soul of itself, it leaves nothing behind; but folks leave behind a corpse that must be covered up with dirt right away. Folks argued about it on front galleries in the summer time and around the fire in winter—but they didn't argue about it on the Bells' front gallery or by the Bells' fire. And the preachers preached about it at camp meetings.

But the Witch didn't let up on the Bells' grub. No one ever saw it; but lots of times some member of the family would see something to eat dive out of the cupboard or pop out of the safe. The Witch's favorite was cream, and he got to skimming it from every pan in the spring-house. The Bells were never able to get any butter from the churning.

Mr. Bell might have stood for having his young-uns' rest disturbed and his old nigger woman all tore up this way, but he couldn't stand for letting the ghost eat him out of house and home. So he called the family together and allowed he would move again—this time to Mississippi, where land was rich and cheap. Mrs. Bell raised up.

"Pa," said she, "it seems like to me we have been gettin' along tolerable well here. I don't see any use moving away. What would be to keep the Witch from following us down there?"

"Nothing in the world," spoke up a hide-bottomed chair from a corner of the room. "I'll follow you wherever you go," the Chair went on. "And I'll tell you what: if you stay on here, I won't bother you much; but if you go traipsing off to Mississippi—well, you'll wish you hadn't."

Mr. Bell was scared and bothered, but he studied a while and screwed up his courage enough to ask the Witch why he couldn't live where he pleased. But there was no answer. He asked some more questions. But the Chair had lapsed into the habit of silence that chairs have.

Mary, Mr. Bell's daughter, was now old enough to argue with the old folks about things. She was pretty as a spotted puppy, they say, and had lots of spunk and took after her pa. She sided with him. Girls always like to be moving. So when the family got over its scare about the Chair they argued back and forth. But finally Mrs. Bell and what they remembered about the Witch got the upper hand. Mr. Bell and Mary gave up the idea of moving to Mississippi—for a while anyway.

And for a while the Witch eased up on them. It even did some good turns. One day Mr. Bell was talking of visiting a family across the creek where he had heard everybody was sick. "I have just come from there," said a Voice from the eight-day clock, and went on to tell how well everybody was and what everybody was doing. Later Mr. Bell met up with a member of the family and learned that everything the Witch said was so.

Maybe because she had taken side with him in the argument about going to Mississippi, the Witch was partial to Mrs. Bell. The old nigger woman said the ha'nt sided with her because she had stood up for the overseer when Mr. Bell wanted to fire him in North Carolina.

One Christmas time the family was invited to a taffy-pulling. Mrs. Bell was sick and couldn't go. They talked about whether they ought to go off and leave their mammy feeling poorly. Mr. Bell was invited too, and they needed him to do the driving; so Mary and the children begged him to take them. Mrs. Bell told them to go ahead, she didn't need them and could make out all right. So they all piled into the wagon and started.

But before they got far one of the wagon wheels flew off and let the axle down into the road with a bump. It looked like a common accident, and the old man climbed down and put the wheel back on the axle and stuck the linchpin in. He looked at all the other linchpins and saw they were on all right. Before long another wheel flew off. They looked on the ground for the linchpin but couldn't find it there. Mr. Bell whittled a new one, and when he went to put the wheel back on he found the old one in place. He fixed the wheel and drove off again, telling all of the children to watch all of the wheels. Soon they saw something like a streak of moonshine dart around the wagon, and all four wheels flew off, and the wagon dropped kersplash into a mud-hole. They put them back on, turned round, and drove back home, going quiet and easy, like sitting on eggs.

When they got there, they found their mammy sitting up by the Christmas tree eating a plate of fresh strawberries, and feeling lots better.

Other pranks were laid to the Witch. Often when the old man and the boys would go to the stable to catch the horses and mules for the day's plowing or a trip to town, the critters would back their ears and rare and kick and stomp like hornets or yellow-jackets were after them. Some morning they would be puny as chickens with the pip, and caked with sweat and mud, and their manes and tails tangled in witch-locks. The neighbors said that off and on they met an unbridled and bare-backed horse, and the horse would stop, and something on his back that they couldn't see would talk to them—but not long—they had business the other way.

Maybe because Mary had sided with her pa against her mammy and the Witch, the Witch was harder on her after the argument than anybody else. She would wake up in the middle of the night, screaming and crying that something cold and heavy had been sitting on her breast, sucking her breath and pressing the life out of her.

One time she was getting ready to go to a play-party. Some

of the young sprouts were waiting for her in the front room. While she was combing her long, black hair, it suddenly was full of cuckleburs. She tugged and pulled and broke the comb to untangle it, and when she couldn't, she leaned on the bureau and cried.

"I put them in your hair," said the Witch from the looking-glass. "You've got no business going to the party. Stay here with me. I can say sweet things to you."

She screamed, and the young fellows rushed in the room, and when she told them about the Voice they shot at the glass with their pistols. But the glass didn't break. And the Witch caught every bullet and pitched it into their vest pockets and laughed. So they called it a draw and went out of there. And Mary stayed at home.

Mary was now mighty near grown. She had turned out to be a beautiful woman. She had lots of beaux. But whenever one of them screwed himself up to the point of popping the question he always found that the words stuck in his throat and his face and ears burned. For young fellows these were strange signs. But it was always that way. And none of them seemed to be able to ask Mary the question. They laid it on the Witch, and finally quit hitching their horses to the Bell fence.

All but one. His name was Gardner. He was a catch for any girl, smart as a briar, good-looking, easy-going and open-hearted, and the owner of rich bottom land, a passel of niggers, and a home as big as the courthouse, with columns as tall and white. He got all wrapped up in Mary, and they say Mary was leaning to him.

The way of the Witch with him was different, more business-like. Maybe it was because the Witch realized this was the man Mary was setting her heart on. One night when Gardner was walking up the row of cedars in the Bell yard to see Mary, something he couldn't see reached out from a big cedar and touched him on the shoulder, and a voice said, "Wait a minute." Gardner was afraid to wait, but he was more afraid to run. So he waited.

"You might as well understand, here and now, that you are not going to have Mary Bell."

"Why not?" Gardner asked.

"You might have guessed from all that's happened round here. I'm in love with her myself. It's going to be hard to get her consent, and it may be harder to get the old man's. But she's not going to marry you. I'll see to that. If you open your mouth about it to-night, you'll be dead as a door-nail before morning."

Gardner studied a while and said, "If you'd only come out like a man."

The cedar tree stepped out and snatched his hat off and stomped it.

"Well, I reckon I'll have to lay off for a while," says Gardner. "But I do love her, and I'd go to the end of the world for. . . ."

"Well, you don't have to go that far, and it wouldn't do you any good if you did, and if you love her the only way you can keep her out of hell is to get out yourself. If you keep on hanging round here, I'll make it hell for you. Now this is how far you go. Pack up your traps and get out of the country, hide and hair. Go any place you think the Bells won't hear tell of you—and go before breakfast. If you slip out quiet without raising any rookus I'll never pester you again. What's more, on the day you get married I'll give you a pair of new boots you'll be proud of all your life."

Gardner couldn't see why the Witch's promise of a pair of wedding boots was in the same class as the threat of death before breakfast, but he didn't split hairs, and he didn't argue any more. He picked up his hat, sneaked back to his horse, and rode off.

He never said or wrote a thing to the Bells about what had happened, part because he was scared, but more because he was ashamed of being scared. He left the neighborhood before sunup and moved to the western part of the state. He got somebody else to sell out for him. They say the town of Gardner, where he settled, was named after him when he got old and respected.

After he had been there a while he fell in love with a girl and got engaged to her. And they say that when he was dressing for the wedding he couldn't find his boots. He looked high and low, every place a pair of boots was liable to be and lots of places where they couldn't possibly be, but no boots could he find. He was about to give up and go to his wedding in his sock feet, when a Voice told him to crawl out from under the bed and look in the bed. And there between the sheets he found a pair of shiny new boots. He put them on and went his way rejoicing and thinking of how well a ghost kept his word, and wondering if the boots would ever wear out and if they were like the Seven-League boots he had read about in old McGuffey.

But they looked like natural boots. He told some of his friends how he had got them. They thought he was a liar. But they had to own up they were wrong. One day Gardner's house-boy made a mistake and carried them instead of another pair to a cobbler. The cobbler said they were in perfect shape, that they were not made by mortal hands, and that the soles were sewed on in a way that no man or man-made machine could have stitched them. And there is a lady in this neighborhood who has seen the boots.

While Gardner's mind was getting mossed over about Mary, Mr. Bell decided again to move to Mississippi. It looked like his move from North Carolina was jumping from the frying pan into the fire, but he figured maybe the skillet wouldn't be any hotter. Gardner's break-up with Mary and Mary not marrying hung heavy on his mind. Mrs. Bell raised up again, telling him about rolling stones. And the Witch horned in. By this time the family got used to the Witch and would talk free with him, but respectful. Every time the question came up there was a row between Mr. Bell and Mary on one side and Mrs. Bell and the Witch on the other. The old nigger woman told Mr. Bell the ha'nt didn't want him to move because he was afraid of witch hunters in Mississippi. She said there were powerful ones down there.

And so one winter after the crops had petered out on him again, he sold his place dirt cheap. But the old nigger woman told him to wait till spring to start. She said Easter was early that year and there would be plenty of time to pitch a crop. Good Friday would be a good day to leave, she said, for the ha'nt would have to go back to his grave and stay three days under the ground and would be puny-like several days more. While he was in good working order he could be in two or three places at once and be in any of them in the bat of an eye, but then he would have to lie low, and that would give them plenty of start. So Mr. Bell early on Good Friday stacked his furniture and duds in a couple of wagons, climbed into the front one with Mary, put the old nigger woman and his biggest boy into the hind one, and told Mrs. Bell, "Git in with old Patsy if you're a-comin', and don't forgit the young-uns."

And that was the way the Bell family came to Mississippi. Mr. Bell bought him a little place in Panola County, ten miles east of Batesville on the Oxford road. He was all ready to begin life over again without supernatural interference.

But the Witch made a quick come-back, not before the

family got there, but before they moved into their new home.

When Mr. Bell first got to Batesville, or Panola as they called it then, he left the family there and went out to look at the land he aimed to buy. When he got a place that suited him, he went back to town for his family and stuff. There was some sort of hitch, and the wagons did not get started till late in the evening. As the wagons moved slowly out of town, dark clouds began to roll up in the south and west, and before they had gone three miles the storm broke. Dark came on earlier than usual, for the clouds hid the sun. The rain beat down on the wagon covers. Every now and then the lightning flashes lit up the swaying trees on each side of the road, the draggle-tailed horses, and the road itself,—a long, muddy creek,—and then it was dark as a stack of black cats. The folks all stopped talking. There was nothing to listen to but the beating rain and the thunder and the suck of the horses' feet and the wheels in the mud.

All at once the hind wagon, with the family in it slid to the side of the road and sunk into the mud up to the bed. Mr. Bell saw it in a lightning flash and came back. It couldn't be moved; the horses had no foothold, and the wheels were in too deep. The fix they were in wasn't dangerous, but it was mighty uncomfortable.

And then the Witch took a hand.

"If you'll go back to your wagon and stop your cussin'," said the empty dark beside the wagon, "I'll get you out. Hump it back to your wagon now—light a shuck!"

Mr. Bell waded back and crawled in.

And then the horses and the wagon and the furniture and the family and the dog under the wagon and the calf tied behind and everything else but the mud on the wheels riz up about eight feet high and floated down the road till they were just behind the front wagon, and then they settled down easy and went on home without any trouble.

The family got settled down in their two-story double-loghouse amongst the cedars on the Oxford road.

A few nights later, the Witch spoke up from one of the andirons and told Mr. and Mrs. Bell he was in love with Mary. He said he wanted to marry her. Mr. Bell was shocked and surprised. He explained, respectful but emphatic like, that he could never dream of letting a daughter of his marry a ghost, not even so noble a ghost like the one he was talking with.

"I got a claim on you, John Bell," said the Witch. "I got

a claim on you and yours. I got a claim." And his voice was deep and hollowlike.

This was a point Mr. Bell maybe didn't want to hear any more about. So he said, "Have you spoken to Mary?"

"No, not spoken."

"Well, how do you know she would have you?"

"I don't. But I haven't got any reason to believe she wouldn't love me. She's never seen me. She doesn't know whether she would or not. Maybe she would consider it an honor to be married to a ghost. Not many girls are, you know. Why, it would make her famous."

"I don't want any daughter of mine getting famous that way. And besides, what if you were to have children? What in the world do you reckon they'd be like? Like you or her? Maybe half good human meat and bone, and the other half sight unseen. Or maybe they'd be the vanishin' kind and goin' round here and raisin' hell invisible. Do you think I want a passel of soap-suds young-uns floatin' round here and poppin' up into puffs of wind every time I p'inted to the stovewood pile or sprouts on a ditch bank? Not on your life. I reckon plain flesh and blood's good enough for Mary."

"But, John Bell, I love Mary. And remember. Remember."

"So do I, and that's why I'm not a-goin' to let you marry her. Why, when she got old and hard-favored I reckon you'd quit her for some young hussy. You could do it easy enough. Mary'd have a hard time keepin' up with a stack of wind and a voice, and I'd have a hard time trackin' down and shootin' a low-down, no-count dust devil. When Mary marries, she marries a man that's solid and alive in body."

"I gather, John Bell, that you're opposed to me courting your daughter. But she's the one to say, and I'm going to talk to her about it. You'll be my father-in-law yet, or you'll be a-mourning, a-mourning."

"But what kind of wedding would it be like?" Mrs. Bell put in. "Think of it. Mary standing in front of the preacher and the preacher saying, 'Do you take this woman?' to a vase of flowers. And the ring floating down to Mary from the hanging-lamp maybe, or rising up from under a bench. I won't stand for it. I've stood for a lot of things, and you can't say I haven't been a friend to you. But I won't stand for Mary being a laughing-stock and disgrace to the family."

"If we're a-goin' to add to this family," Mr. Bell took up, "we're a-goin' to be able to see what we're addin'. I don't even know what shape you've got, if any."

"Oh, I can give you some idea what shape I have. I'll let you shake hands with me. But you must promise not to squeeze. We're very delicate, especially when we touch folks. Here, hold out your hand, and I'll put mine in it."

Mr. Bell held out his hand, felt something, and grabbed it. It was, he said later, the hand of a new-born baby—soft and crinkly and warm and just about the size of a new-born baby's hand.

"How big are you all over?" he asked.

"I can't tell you that."

"Well, there's one other thing I want to know. How do you get into this house any time you want to when every window and door is locked and barred? Do you ooze through the walls?"

"No. It's a lot easier than that. If you'll watch the corner of the ceiling up there, you'll see."

And all the rest of his life Mr. Bell swore to trustworthy witnesses that he saw the corner of the ceiling raised a good three feet and then let down again—all without the slightest racket.

"Do you mean to tell me that anything with a hand like that can h'ist the top off of the house that a-way?"

"Sure," came the answer. "But—about Mary. I'm going to talk to her right off."

"Don't," said Mr. Bell. "Do you want to drive her crazy?"

But the meeting was over, for there was no answer. And the fire had died down, and the andiron looked glum.

The story is kind of skimpy here. Nobody seems to know what the Witch said to Mary or what Mary said to the Witch.

But the family noticed next day that she was drooping and wasn't minding what was going on around her. For days she wandered about the house and up and down the yard under the gloomy old cedars, like somebody sleep-walking. And the color left her face, and deep in her wide-open black eyes was a far-away look, like she was trying to see something that ought to be but wasn't there. Every day she got up later and went to bed earlier.

And finally there came a day when she didn't get up at all. In the evening a screech-owl hollered in a cedar right by the gallery.

That night her fever was high, and by midnight she was

raving. "We've put off. seein' a doctor too long," said Mrs. Bell.

"The roads like they are, it'll take me two hours goin' and him and me two hours comin'," said Mr. Bell. "It'll be might' nigh daylight before we get back. But I reckon you're right, and I'll go as quick as I can saddle a horse."

"No use," said a Voice. "All the doctors and medicines in the world won't cure her. But if you want one, I'll get him, and get him a lot quicker than you can."

The doctor got there just as the old eight-day clock struck one. "I heard somebody hollering at my window about midnight, telling me to come out here right away. When I got to the door, nobody was there; but I thought I'd better come anyway." He was a young doctor just starting out. "Say, what kind of road overseer and gang do you fellows have out this way? Last time I came over this road, about Christmas, it was the the worst I ever saw. Why, I picked up a Stetson hat in the middle of a mud-hole near the four-mile board, and by George there was a man under it. 'You're in the middle of a bad fix, old man,' I said. 'Hell,' he said, 'that ain't nothin' to the fix this mule's in under me.' I had to lift up my feet half the way to keep them from dragging in the mud by the horse's belly. But to-night my horse skimmed over it in an hour. Well, who's sick out here?"

"It's her mind and nerves," he told them after he had questioned them and examined Mary. "I won't conceal from you, she's in pretty bad shape. And medicine won't do her any good. You've just got to be gentle and careful with her. Humor her and be patient with her. I'll give her something to put her to sleep when she gets like this. Watch her close and don't let her get lonesome. She's young and strong and ought to come round in time."

But she never did. For a month she lay there on the bed, looking at nothing and yet straining to see something. Something too far off. At night her pa and ma took turns sitting up. They didn't want the neighbors in. They called the doctor back a few times, but he shook his head and said he couldn't do any more. So they would watch and wait, wanting to do something, but helpless.

One night her ma was sitting there, holding Mary's hand and stroking the dark hair back from her forehead. Suddenly Mary pushed her mother away and sat up and looked across the foot of the bed, as if somebody was standing there.

"Mamma," she whispered, "Mamma . . . I see him . . . at last. . . . And I think . . . I think . . . I'm going . . . to love him."

And she died with the only expression of happiness they had seen on her face in months.

Some folks have tried to explain Mary's strange death. A few say the Witch tortured her continually and kept her in such constant terror that her mind was affected. Others have heard that a school teacher ventriloquist that was jealous of Gardner played tricks on her and the family, and then when she wouldn't have him tormented and frightened her to death. Some believe she was in love with the overseer from the first, and then when he was killed she was in love with the Witch and didn't want to live because she knew she would never be happy with him until she too became a ghost.

But she died, just the same. And they say that on the day of the funeral, when the coffin was carried from the house to a wagon a great black bird flew down from the sky and hung in the air just above the wagon. And around its neck was a bell that tolled in the mournfullest tone ever heard by the ear of man. And when the funeral procession began to move, the great bird floated just in front of it all the way to the graveyard and circled round and round the grave during the burial, the bell tolling all the while. And when the mound was rounded up, the bird swung high up in the air and flew away to the west and finally became just a little speck above the treetops and disappeared. But long after it was gone the mourning notes of the bell floated back to those who stood and watched.

The Leeds Devil*

WITHIN recent times the Leeds Devil has ramped about the New Jersey pine region, between Freehold and Cape May, though it should have been "laid" many years ago. Its coming portends evil, for it appears before wars, fires, and great calamities.

Albeit a sober Quaker in appearance, Mother Leeds, of Burlington, New Jersey, was strongly suspected of witchcraft;

* From *American Myths and Legends*, by Charles M. Skinner, Vol. I, pp. 240–243. Copyright, 1903, by J. B. Lippincott Company. Philadelphia & London.

and suspicion became certainty when, in 1735, a child was born to her. The old women who had assembled on that occasion, as they always do assemble wherever there is death or birth or marriage, reported that while it was like other human creatures at first, the child changed, under their very eyes. It began to lose its likeness to other babes, and grew long and brown; it presently took the shape of a dragon, with a snake-like body, a horse's head, a pig's feet, and a bat's wings. This dreadful being increased in strength as it gained in size, until it exceeded the bulk and might of a grown man, when it fell on the assemblage, beating all the members of the party, even its own mother, with its long, forked, leathery tail. This despite being wreaked, it arose through the chimney and vanished, its harsh cries mingling with the clamor of a storm that was raging out-of-doors.

That night several children disappeared: the dragon had eaten them. For several years thereafter it was glimpsed in the woods at nightfall, and it would wing its way heavily from farm to farm, though it seldom did much mischief after its first escape into the world. To sour the milk by breathing on it, to dry the cows, and to sear the corn were its usual errands. On a still night the farmers could follow its course, as they did with trembling, by the howling of dogs, the hoots of owls, and the squawks of poultry. It sometimes appeared on the coast, generally when a wreck impended, and was seen in the company of the spectres that haunt the shore: the golden-haired woman in white, the black-muzzled pirate, and the robber, whose head being cut off at Barnegat by Captain Kidd, stumps about the sands without it, guarding a treasure buried near. When it needed a change of diet the Leeds Devil would breathe upon the cedar swamps, and straightway the fish would die in the pools and creeks, their bodies, whitened and decayed by the poison, floating about in such numbers as to threaten illness to all the neighborhood. In 1740 the service of a clergyman was secured, who, by reason of his piety and exemplary life, had dominion over many of the fiends that plagued New Jersey, and had even prevailed in his congregation against applejack, which some declared to be a worse fiend than any other, if, indeed, it did not create some of those others. With candle, book, and bell the good man banned the creature for a hundred years, and, truly, the herds and henneries were not molested in all that time. The Leeds Devil had become a dim tradition when, in 1840, it burst its cerements, if such had been put about it; or, at all events, it broke through the clergyman's commandments, and went whiffling among the pines again, eating sheep and other animals, and making clutches at children that dared to sport about their dooryards in the twilight. From time to time it reappeared, its last raid occurring at Vincentown and Burr-ville in 1899, but it is said that its life has nearly run its course, and with the advent of the new century many worshipful commoners of Jersey dismissed, for good and all, the fear of this monster from their minds.

IV

GHOST TALES

"REAL" ghost stories or accounts of individual experiences with hants and legends of haunted houses and other places belong to psychic research and local history rather than to folklore. To have fun with ghosts, as with witches, the story-teller must not take them too seriously. Fair game for such a story-teller are persons who accept a dare or a bet to spend the night in a haunted house, especially those who boast that they are not afraid of ghosts. Here practical jokes are a great temptation.

"The Half-Clad Ghost" is an amusing take-off on the ghost who returns for a missing object, already seen in "Tailypo," a theme which is treated with gruesome effect in "Cap'n Santos' Leg."

Four Black Cats and More*

ONE TIME I was on trip in South Ca'lina and I got out of money, and it was in the fall of the year. And it was raining and very cool on my tramp, too. So I begin to hunt a place

---

* From *Cold Blue Moon, Black Ulysses Afar Off*, by Howard W. Odum, pp. 19–28. Copyright, 1931, by Howard W. Odum. Indianapolis: The Bobbs-Merrill Company, Publishers.

to rest for the night. And on the roadside I come to big white house. And so I goes up to this house and knocks on door. And a man come to the door. And I explain to him my condition. I told him I were a long ways from home, and I wanted to know if he would let me stay for the night in dog-house or barn or sumpin'.

So the man look at me and says he had house up on the hill an' I could stay there for the night. He told me I would find wood to make fire and bed to sleep in but no one was livin' there now. So now I felt satisfied. So I thanks him and tells him good night and off I goes up to that house on the hill.

I opens the door and goes in. Everything looks well and fine. So I strikes match and lit lamp. And also makes fire in fireplace. And I set down an' begin to dry and rest with ease, ease, my Lawd, settin' in the Kingdom jes' like John. Until all at once I heard some one say up-stairs, "I'm comin' down, I'm comin' down."

And just 'bout that time I look and there he was dress all in white between me an' the door, yes sir, Lawd, Lawd, between me an' the door. So out the window I had business.

I run 'bout seven miles down road and I met a preacher and he halt me and I stop. He said, "Young man, where are you going in such hurry?" I told him if he had seen what I seen he would be in a hurry too. So I explain to him what I had seen.

So he said, "My Brother, it is nothing to that."

I told him, "You don't tell me!"

So he says, "Listen, my friend, I'll prove that you are wrong."

I asks him, "How?"

He says then, "I'll go with you to the house." So then I asks him who was going to be with us an' he said the good Lord.

So off we went, I and he side by side. We kep' walkin', an' after so long time we come to the house. The light was still lit and fire was in fine shape. So he opens door and walks in. So I raises window and he sets down and opens his Bible an' begins to read. So I heard a voice sayin', "I'm comin' down, I'm comin' down." So there he was again. The preacher look at me and I look at him an' he look at me. So 'bout that time out the window I goes again, preacher in behind me. So after little ways we were side by side, 'cause he sho' wus runnin' for the Lord. So after we had run 'bout ten miles I asks old preacher if good Lord is with us now.

And preacher, he says, "Well, if He is, I be-dam' if He ain't traveling some!"

* * * * *

Well, that ain't no preacher ghost story at all. I heard tell 'bout preacher was offered so much money would he stay in ha'nted house all night. So he goes an' takes Bible an' sets down important like an' opens up Bible an' begins to read. 'Bout that time first ghost comes sneakin' in like hot air or maybe like cold breeze an' wet, look lak man only ain't got no head, 'scusin' if he have head ain't got no body, else if he have body ain't got no arms. So he says to preacher, "Is you gonna stay here till Whalem-Balem comes?"

Ole man so skeered he don't say nothin'. So nex' ghost come in he look lak mule, maybe old gray mule only he ain't got no head neither, 'scusin' if he got long-eared head, ain't got no body. So he says to preacher, "Is you gonna stay here till Whalem-Balem comes?"

Still the old man so skeered he don't know whut to do; thinks maybe he better be goin', neither can he move. So 'bout that time, third ghost comes in, look lak cat, only biggest cat anybody ever seen, got red eyes lak fire and spittin' and mewin' like red-hot stove or sumpin'. So he meows, "Is you gonna stay here till Whalem-Balem comes?"

'Bout that time old preacher ain't got no voice an' feel mighty sick at his stomach and decided maybe he better make him little coffee and fry some meat. So he does. 'Bout time he be ready to drink his hot flambotia strong, fo'th ghost comes in, look lak dog, only got big tushes lak boar. So he reaches down an' et up all meat an' lap up all coffee. He then snaps up at preacher with tushes all showin' an' like impudent snarl, maybe snappin' teeth together like wolf, "Is you gonna stay here till Whalem-Balem comes?"

So old preacher hollers, "Hell, no, I'm done gone."

* * * * *

Well, I got better ghost story 'bout preacher an' cat, 'scusin' got so many don't know which ones to tell. Can't count 'em, so many take me till to-morrow night to name 'em. Wus one old preacher boastin' 'bout he ain't skeered of no ghosts. So sisters say, "You don't say. Ain't he brave man?" So they tells him 'bout big house ain't nobody never stayed all night in it since war.

So he goes over to house with Bible, gits down on his knees an' prays Lawd to keep him lak he kep' Daniel in lion's den. Jes' 'bout that time little bitty black kitty rubs 'gainst his leg. So he says, "Amen, Lawd, Amen." So he gits up an' sets down in cheer an' begins readin' Bible an' reaches down to rub kitten. Can't tech it. Howsomever, he sees it settin' down nex' to him.

So he goes on readin' till hears sumpin' else an' looks down. Settin' side of first kitten is 'nother black kitten little bigger, lookin' up at him an' lickin' his lips. So he tries to rub this kitten neither can he tech it.

'Bout that time 'nother black cat little bigger than other two wus settin' down side of other kittens. Howsomever, that ain't all cats he's gonna see. So 'nother one 'bout big as wildcat slips in, look lak he be laughin' at preacher. So 'bout that time one come in 'bout big as dog, then 'nother one 'bout big as calf. So preacher looks out of window an' up-stairs an' still cats keep comin', more an' bigger an' blacker. Then all black cats start meowin' and screamin' till old man jes' natchelly near 'bout skeered to death. Nobody never heard the like since they been born; little cats meowin', big cats growlin', screamin' and spittin', Lawd, Lawd, look like Jedgment day. Old man must 'a' fainted an' yelled, till somebody come by. Said they found Bible leaves layin' all over flo' and old man's hands all scratched up. So they took old man on home; thought he woke up groanin' an' singin'.

> Oh, Lord, I feel like feather in the air,
> Oh, Lord, feel like I never prayed a prayer.

* * * * *

Well, I heard 'bout black-cat ghost myself. One time fellow wus road hustlin' down that lonesome road. So when night ketches him he seen house. So he asks man to let him stay all night. "No," he says, "I got mo' chillun than I can bed, but there's house up 'bout mile nobody can stay in."

So he asks him why, an' he says it's ha'nted. "That ain't nothin'," fellow tells him, "I ain't skeered o' no ha'nts."

So he goes up 'bout dark, gits a lot o' light'ood an' wood, and built him big fire, roasted some 'taters, got box to set on, an' sholy wus feelin' lucky, 'cause started rainin' 'bout that time. So he dozed off to sleep. Long 'bout twelve o'clock wus woke up by sound, so he gits up lookin' fer ghost; got light'ood stick an' looks all through house. Eve'ything wus quiet an' wus nothin' he could see, so he says, "Well, this is fine." So thought he would pile down on flo' in front of fire an' go to sleep. So down he sot to pull off his old shoes. So he sot there bakin' his feet an' must 'a' nodded off 'cause all of sudden he felt wus company in room. So he looked an' do' wus shet, window wus shet, but still he look 'roun' and seen turr'blest thing he ever seen. Thing looked at him, he looked at thing, settin' right on end of box. Sholy wus settin' up, jes' bones, no skin, jes' bones, knees stickin' out an' techin' his leg. Oh, Lawd, creepin' feelin' all over fellow; wus shakin' so till thing jes' rattled self again an' grin at him.

So all of sudden this ghost turned into big black cat. 'Bout that time it ups an' says, "Seem like ain't nobody here but me an' you to-night." So this fellow says, "If I can jes' stand up little bit, won't be nobody here but you." So fellow gives mighty holler an' left through window an' run an' run, gettin' mo' skeerder ever' minute he run, till he jus' drop down in road. So big hollow voice meows at his elbow, "Sholy wus some race." Race, hell, that cat didn't know nuthin' 'bout race an' runnin'. Nex' time fellow didn't run, good God, he flew an' bu'st in white man's house what sent him up to old house. So this man says, "Hell, nigger, you skeered me 'bout to death; but whut you got on yo' neck?" So fellow look an' had brung whole blamed winder-sash clean all way from other house. So white man asks him if he wus going back after his shoes. Fellow tells him guess they can stay up there wid 'bout one hundred mo' pairs he seen settin' by fire.

Cap'n Santos' Leg*

"You fellers wouldn't remember old Cap'n John Santos— feller that had his leg et off by a shark on the Western Banks. But I can remember him, back when I was a boy, and how proud he was of the new juryleg they rigged him up with. It was a sight, I tell you, to watch him dance a *chamarita* with

* From *Cape Cod Pilot*, by Jeremiah Digges, with Editorial and Research Assistance of the Members of the Federal Writers' Project, pp. 234–236. American Guide Series, Federal Writers' Project, Works Progress Administration for the State of Massachusetts. Sponsored by Poor Richard Associates. Copyright, 1937, by Poor Richard Associates. Modern Pilgrim Press and the Viking Press. Provincetown and New York.

that leg and not nick the floor once. Carried around furniture polish just like the doctor carries iodine, in case of a cut or scratch, and one time he copper-bottomed her to make sure the worms wouldn't get to him before his time.

"Well, you know once a man is chawed on by a shark, he's shark-jonahed for the rest of his life. Some day a shark's going to get the rest of that feller, if he keeps on going to sea. And Cap'n John kept on.

"The Cap'n's trawler, the *Hetty K*, was ten mile from the Race when the Portland Gale struck. That was November 27. On the 28th she come crippling round the Point under bare poles with two foot of harbor water over her lee rail. The crew said Cap'n John was washed overboard, along with two other men.

"The bodies of the other two drifted ashore; the Cap'n wasn't never found. But a couple of days after, Joe Barcia picked up the old man's wooden leg off the beach. He took it home to Mary Santos, the widow.

"Married thirty years, them two. When Joe Barcia brought back the leg, Mary took it into the house. She petted it and talked to it.

"Nothing more come of it till the night of November 26, a year later. That night, Mary said, she set up in bed, and there, standing straight as two yards of pump-water on his one leg, was old Cap'n John. He hopped over alongside the bed and canted over. Then he whispered to her.

" 'Barometer's falling, Mary,' he says, 'and the wind's no'theast. We're in for thick weather, and I'll want my store leg to keep me steady when she strikes.' He pinched her cheek, and Mary let out a yell. When she looked again, the Cap'n was gone.

"Next morning, Mary said, she had a little red spot on her cheek. And before she turned in that night, she took the skipper's leg out of the spice-cupboard and left it laid out for him in a corner near the fireplace.

"That night a breeze of wind come up, and in a couple of hours it turned into a living gale—from the no'theast. The willer tree outside howled like the yo-ho bird of every dead sailor in hell come there to roost. All of a sudden Mary hears a thump-thump-thump across the floor, down below, and then the door shut to. She stayed in bed.

"Next morning she went to look if the Cap'n's leg was still there. It was, but when she picked it up, it was wet.

"Well, it'd rained bad enough to come in by the chimney. But it gallied her so, the sight of that leg, with the water on it, that she got sick. She called in Doc Atwood. When he got through sounding, and didn't find nothing sprung, Doc said something was eating on her. Then she told him the whole story.

"When he'd went over the leg, he looked hard at the widow.

" 'You say you left it by the fireplace all night and rain come in on it?' he asks. Then he sets the leg down, comes over to the widow, and tells her straight out. 'Mrs. Santos,' he says, 'I'm going to ask you to have one of the men take this thing out to sea, and weight it with netleads, and heave it overboard. I'm a doctor,' he says, 'and I don't listen to stories. But Mrs. Santos,' he says, 'I put my tongue to that wood. *It don't rain salt water!*' "

The Death Waltz[*]

YEARS ago, when all beyond the Missouri was a waste, the military post at Fort Union, New Mexico, was the only spot for miles around where any of the graces of social life could be discovered. Among the ladies at the post was a certain gay young woman, the sister-in-law of a captain, who enjoyed the variety and spice of adventure to be found there, and enjoyed, too, the homage that the young officers paid to her, for women who could be loved or liked were not many in that wild country. A young lieutenant proved especially susceptible to her charms, and devoted himself to her in the hope that he should ultimately win her hand. His experience with the world was not large enough to enable him to distinguish between the womanly woman and the coquette.

One day messengers came dashing into the fort with news of an Apache outbreak, and a detachment was ordered out to chase and punish the marauding Indians. The lieutenant was put in command of the expedition, but before starting he confided his love to the young woman, who not only acknowledged that she returned his affection, but promised that if the fortune of war deprived him of life she would never marry another. As he bade her good-by he was heard to say, "That is well. Nobody else shall have you. I will come back and make my claim."

In a few days the detachment came back, but the lieutenant was missing. It was noticed that the bride-elect grieved but little for him, and nobody was surprised when she announced her intention of marrying a young man from the East. The wedding day arrived. All was gayety at the post, and in the evening the mess-room was decorated for a ball. As the dance was in full swing a door flew open with a bang, letting in a draught of air that made the candles burn dim, and a strange cry, unlike that of any human creature, sounded through the house. All eyes turned to the door. In it stood the swollen body of a dead man dressed in the stained uniform of an officer. The temple was marked by a hatchet-gash, the scalp was gone, the eyes were wide open and burned with a terrible light.

Walking to the bride the body drew her from the arms of her husband, who, like the rest of the company, stood as in a trance, without the power of motion, and clasping her to its bosom began a waltz. The musicians, who afterward declared that they did not know what they were doing, struck up a demoniac dance, and the couple spun around and around, the woman growing paler and paler, until at last the fallen jaw and staring eyes showed that life was also extinct in her. The dead man allowed her to sink to the floor, stood over her for a moment, wrung his hands as he sounded his fearful cry again, then vanished through the door. A few days after, a troop of soldiers who had been to the scene of the Apache encounter returned with the body of the lieutenant.

The Half-Clad Ghost*

"I KNEW a' ole man once that alluz wo' two paiah o' draw's. But when he died his wife didn' lay out but one but paiah foh 'im. Well, after de fune'l, he kep' a-comin' back an' a-comin' back. Evah night he'd come right in dat front do' o' her house. So she moved from dat place, but he jes' kep' a-comin'

* From "Dyin' Easy," by Martha Emmons, *Tone the Bell Easy*, Publications of the Texas Folk-Lore Society, edited by J. Frank Dobie, Number X, p. 59. Copyright, 1932, by the Texas Folk-Lore Society. Austin.

jes de same. She moved fo' o' five times, an' he jes' kep' on a-comin' back evah night o' de worl'. Finely she talked to some o' her frien's. They asked 'er why she don' talk to 'im. She say 'cause she scared to. But they say foh 'er to say, 'What in de name o' de Lawd do you want?' So dat night he come ag'in.

"This time she walk' right up an' met 'im an' say, 'What in de name o' de Lawd do you want?'

"He looked at 'er right study foh a long time, but she nevah move, an' she jes' stan' theah; an' finely he say, 'Honey, gimme 'nother paiah o' draw's, please.'

"She say, 'Aw right, I'll give 'em to you'; an' from dat day to this he nevah has come back no mo', she say. An' dat's de way it is: When you ask 'em what in de name o' de Lawd they want, an' then tell 'em you'll give it to 'em, they'll go 'way an' leave you alone."

V

DEVIL TALES

PEOPLE who traffic with the Devil for their own gain or pleasure generally end up by disappearing in smoke or turning into a jack-o-lantern or an African monkey. Sometimes the poor Devil is the victim, duped or discomfited by superior brain or brawn. Slightly less familiar are the Devil's musical exploits. He not only loves singing but is a master of the violin, of which instrument of evil he is reputedly the inventor. By the same token he can give mastery of the violin, bartering infernal skill for the pupil's soul. These legends are related to the larger belief in the supernatural origin of musical skill and individual songs (e.g. the fiddle tune, "The Devil's Dream").[1]

Big Sixteen and the Devil*

IT WAS slavery time, Zora, when Big Sixteen was a man. They called 'im Sixteen 'cause dat was de number of de shoe he wore. He was big and strong and Ole Massa looked to him to do everything.

One day Ole Massa said, "Big Sixteen, Ah b'lieve Ah want you to move dem sills Ah had hewed out down in de swamp."

"I yassuh, Massa."

Big Sixteen went down in de swamp and picked up dem 12×12's and brought 'em on up to de house and stack 'em. No one man ain't never toted a 12×12 befo' nor since.

So Ole Massa said one day, "Go fetch in de mules. Ah want to look 'em over."

Big Sixteen went on down to de pasture and caught dem mules by de bridle but they was contrary and balky and he tore de bridles to pieces pullin' on 'em, so he picked one of 'em up under each arm and brought 'em up to Ole Massa.

He says, "Big Sixteen, if you kin tote a pair of balky mules, you kin do anything. You kin ketch de Devil."

"Yassuh, Ah kin, if you git me a nine-pound hammer and a pick and shovel!"

Ole Massa got Sixteen de things he ast for and tole 'im to go ahead and bring him de Devil.

Big Sixteen went out in front of de house and went to diggin'. He was diggin' nearly a month befo' he got where he wanted. Then he took his hammer and went and knocked on de Devil's door. Devil answered de door hisself.

"Who dat out dere?"

"It's Big Sixteen."

"What you want?"

"Wanta have a word wid you for a minute."

Soon as de Devil poked his head out de door, Sixteen lammed him over de head wid dat hammer and picked 'im up and carried 'im back to Ole Massa.

Ole Massa looked at de dead Devil and hollered, "Take dat ugly thing 'way from here, quick! Ah didn't think you'd ketch de Devil sho 'nuff."

---

* From *Mules and Men*, by Zora Neale Hurston, pp. 207–208. Copyright, 1935, by Zora Neale Hurston. Philadelphia and London: J. B. Lippincott Company.

So Sixteen picked up de Devil and throwed 'im back down de hole.

'Way after while, Big Sixteen died and went up to Heben. But Peter looked at him and tole 'im to g'wan 'way from dere. He was too powerful. He might git outa order and there wouldn't be nobody to handle 'im. But he had to go somewhere so he went on to hell.

Soon as he got to de gate de Devil's children was playin' in de yard and they seen 'im and run to de house, says, "Mama, mama! Dat man's out dere dat kilt papa!"

So she called 'im in de house and shet de door. When Sixteen got dere she handed 'im a li'l piece of fire and said, "You ain't comin' in here. Here, take dis hot coal and g'wan off and start you a hell uh yo' own."

So when you see a Jack O'Lantern in de woods at night you know it's Big Sixteen wid his piece of fire lookin' for a place to go.

Samson and Satan*

SATAN said to Samson, "They tell me that you are the strongest man in the world." Samson says, "Yes, I s'pose I am. Let us to-day try our strength." Satan said to Samson, "I will fus' try de hammer dat knock upon anvil." Samson says to Satan, "T'row dat hammer up, see how high you can t'row it." He t'rowed it seventy-five miles. Samson says, "Why, Satan, have you another hammer?" He says, "Why, yes!" He says, "What's the name of that hammer?"—"De one dat we wel's ahn (weld iron) with." He says, "How high can you t'row dat one?"— "Oh," he says, "'bout a hundred miles."—"Oh," he says, "you can't t'row at all. I t'ought you was a man." He says, "Now, Satan, you stan' back! you ahn't a man at all." Samson steps an' takes up de anvil an' looks up ter de skies, an' said, "Michael an' Rafeel an' all de holy angils," he says, "stan' back, because here comes de anvil!" An' when he swing de anvil twice, Satan said to Samson, he said, "Don' do that! Save heaven an' de hos'." He said, "If you knock 'em outer existence, what shall we do fe livin'?"

---

* From "Folk-Tales Collected at Miami, Fla.," by Elsie Clews Parsons, *The Journal of American Folk-Lore*, Vol. XXX (April-June, 1917), No. CXVI, p. 223. Copyright, 1917, by the American Folk-Lore Society. New York.

The Devil and Tom Walker*

A FEW miles from Boston in Massachusetts, there is a deep inlet, winding several miles into the interior of the country from Charles Bay, and terminating in a thickly-wooded swamp or morass. On one side of this inlet is a beautiful dark grove; on the opposite side the land rises abruptly from the water's edge into a high ridge, on which grow a few scattered oaks of great age and immense size. Under one of these gigantic trees, according to old stories, there was a great amount of treasure buried by Kidd the pirate. The inlet allowed a facility to bring the money in a boat secretly and at night to the very foot of the hill; the elevation of the place permitted a good look-out to be kept that no one was at hand; while the remarkable trees formed good landmarks by which the place might easily be found again. The old stories add, moreover, that the devil presided at the hiding of the money, and took it under his guardianship; but this it is well known he always does with buried treasure, particularly when it has been ill-gotten. Be that as it may, Kidd never returned to recover his wealth; being shortly after seized at Boston, sent out to England, and there hanged for a pirate.

About the year 1727, just at the time that earthquakes were prevalent in New-England, and shook many tall sinners down upon their knees, there lived near this place a meagre, miserly fellow, of the name of Tom Walker. He had a wife as miserly as himself; they were so miserly that they even conspired to cheat each other. Whatever the woman could lay hands on, she hid away; a hen could not cackle but she was on the alert to secure the new-laid egg. Her husband was continually prying about to detect her secret hoards, and many and fierce were the conflicts that took place about what ought to have been common property. They lived in a forlorn-looking house that stood alone, and had an air of starvation. A few straggling savin-trees, emblems of sterility, grew near it; no smoke ever curled from its chimney; no traveler stopped at its door. A miserable horse, whose ribs were as articulate as the bars of a gridiron, stalked about a field, where a thin carpet of moss, scarcely covering the ragged beds of puddingstone,

* From *Tales of a Traveller*, by Geoffrey Crayon, Gent.,[n] pp. 376–392. Entered . . . , 1849, by Washington Irving. The Works of Washington Irving, New Edition, Revised, Volume VII. New York: George P. Putnam.

tantalized and balked his hunger; and sometimes he would lean his head over the fence, look piteously at the passer-by, and seem to petition deliverance from this land of famine.

The house and its inmates had altogether a bad name. Tom's wife was a tall termagant, fierce of temper, loud of tongue, and strong of arm. Her voice was often heard in wordy warfare with her husband; and his face sometimes showed signs that their conflicts were not confined to words. No one ventured, however, to interfere between them. The lonely wayfarer shrunk within himself at the horrid clamor and clapper-clawing; eyed the den of discord askance; and hurried on his way, rejoicing, if a bachelor, in his celibacy.

One day that Tom Walker had been to a distant part of the neighborhood, he took what he considered a short cut homeward, through the swamp. Like most short cuts, it was an ill-chosen route. The swamp was thickly grown with great gloomy pines and hemlocks, some of them ninety feet high, which made it dark at noonday, and a retreat for all the owls of the neighborhood. It was full of pits and quagmires, partly covered with weeds and mosses, where the green surface often betrayed the traveller into a gulf of black, smothering mud: there were also dark and stagnant pools, the abodes of the tadpole, the bull-frog, and the water-snake; where the trunks of pines and hemlocks lay half-drowned, half-rotting, looking like alligators sleeping in the mire.

Tom had long been picking his way cautiously through this treacherous forest; stepping from tuft to tuft of rushes and roots, which afforded precarious footholds among deep sloughs; or pacing carefully, like a cat, along the prostrate trunks of trees; startled now and then by the sudden screaming of the bittern, or the quacking of a wild duck, rising on the wing from some solitary pool. At length he arrived at a piece of firm ground, which ran out like a peninsula into the deep bosom of the swamp. It had been one of the strongholds of the Indians during their wars with the first colonists. Here they had thrown up a kind of fort, which they had looked upon as almost impregnable, and had used as a place of refuge for their squaws and children. Nothing remained of the old Indian fort but a few embankments, gradually sinking to the level of the surrounding earth, and already overgrown in part by oaks and other forest trees, the foliage of which formed a contrast to the dark pines and hemlocks of the swamp.

It was late in the dusk of evening when Tom Walker

reached the old fort, and he paused there awhile to rest himself. Any one but he would have felt unwilling to linger in this lonely, melancholy place, for the common people had a bad opinion of it, from the stories handed down from the time of the Indian wars; when it was asserted that the savages held incantations here, and made sacrifices to the evil spirit.

Tom Walker, however, was not a man to be troubled with any fears of the kind. He reposed himself for some time on the trunk of a fallen hemlock, listening to the boding cry of the tree toad, and delving with his walking staff into a mound of black mould at his feet. As he turned up the soil unconsciously, his staff struck against something hard. He raked it out of the vegetable mould, and lo! a cloven skull, with an Indian tomahawk buried deep in it, lay before him. The rust on the weapon showed the time that had elapsed since this death-blow had been given. It was a dreary memento of the fierce struggle that had taken place in this last foothold of the Indian warriors.

"Humph!" said Tom Walker, as he gave it a kick to shake the dirt from it.

"Let that skull alone!" said a gruff voice. Tom lifted up his eyes, and beheld a great black man seated directly opposite him, on the stump of a tree. He was exceedingly surprised, having neither heard nor seen any one approach; and he was still more perplexed on observing, as well as the gathering gloom would permit, that the stranger was neither negro nor Indian. It is true he was dressed in a rude half-Indian garb, and had a red belt or sash swathed round his body; but his face was neither black nor copper-color, but swarthy and dingy, and begrimed with soot, as if he had been accustomed to toil among fires and forges. He had a shock of coarse black hair, that stood out from his head in all directions, and bore an axe on his shoulder.

He scowled for a moment at Tom with a pair of great red eyes.

"What are you doing on my grounds?" said the black man, with a hoarse growling voice.

"Your grounds!" said Tom with a sneer, "no more your grounds than mine; they belong to Deacon Peabody."

"Deacon Peabody be d—d," said the stranger, "as I flatter myself he will be, if he does not look more to his own sins and less to those of his neighbors. Look yonder, and see how Deacon Peabody is faring."

Tom looked in the direction that the stranger pointed, and

beheld one of the great trees, fair and flourishing without, but rotten at the core, and saw that it had been nearly hewn through, so that the first high wind was likely to blow it down. On the bark of the tree was scored the name of Deacon Peabody, an eminent man, who had waxed wealthy by driving shrewd bargains with the Indians. He now looked round, and found most of the tall trees marked with the name of some great man of the colony, and all more or less scored by the axe. The one on which he had been seated, and which had evidently just been hewn down, bore the name of Crowninshield; and he recollected a mighty rich man of that name, who made a vulgar display of wealth, which it was whispered he had acquired by buccaneering.

"He's just ready for burning!" said the black man, with a growl of triumph. "You see I am likely to have a good stock of firewood for winter."

"But what right have you," said Tom, "to cut down Deacon Peabody's timber?"

"The right of a prior claim," said the other. "This woodland belonged to me long before one of your white-faced race put foot upon the soil."

"And pray, who are you, if I may be so bold?" said Tom.

"Oh, I go by various names. I am the wild huntsman in some countries; the black miner in others. In this neighborhood I am known by the name of the black woodsman. I am he to whom the red men consecrated this spot, and in honor of whom they now and then roasted a white man, by way of sweet-smelling sacrifice. Since the red men have been exterminated by you white savages, I amuse myself by presiding at the persecutions of Quakers and Anabaptists; I am the great patron and prompter of slave-dealers, and the grand-master of the Salem witches."

"The upshot of all which is, that, if I mistake not," said Tom, sturdily, "you are he commonly called Old Scratch."

"The same, at your service!" replied the black man, with a half-civil nod.

Such was the opening of this interview, according to the old story; though it has almost too familiar an air to be credited. One would think that to meet with such a singular personage, in this wild, lonely place, would have shaken any man's nerves; but Tom was a hard-minded fellow, not easily daunted, and he had lived so long with a termagant wife, that he did not even fear the devil.

It is said that after this commencement they had a long

and earnest conversation together, as Tom returned homeward. The black man told him of great sums of money buried by Kidd the pirate, under the oak-trees on the high ridge, not far from the morass. All these were under his command, and protected by his power, so that none could find them but such as propitiated his favor. These he offered to place within Tom Walker's reach, having conceived an especial kindness for him; but they were to be had only on certain conditions. What these conditions were may easily be surmised, though Tom never disclosed them publicly. They must have been very hard, for he required time to think of them, and he was not a man to stick at trifles where money was in view. When they had reached the edge of the swamp, the stranger paused—"What proof have I that all you have been telling me is true?" said Tom. "There is my signature," said the black man, pressing his finger on Tom's forehead. So saying, he turned off among the thickets of the swamp, and seemed, as Tom said, to go down, down, down, into the earth, until nothing but his head and shoulders could be seen, and so on, until he totally disappeared.

When Tom reached home, he found the black print of a finger, burnt, as it were, into his forehead, which nothing could obliterate.

The first news his wife had to tell him was the sudden death of Absalom Crowninshield, the rich buccaneer. It was announced in the papers with the usual flourish, that "A great man had fallen in Israel."

Tom recollected the tree which his black friend had just hewn down, and which was ready for burning. "Let the freebooter roast," said Tom, "who cares!" He now felt convinced that all he had heard and seen was no illusion.

He was not prone to let his wife into his confidence; but as this was an uneasy secret, he willingly shared it with her. All her avarice was awakened at the mention of hidden gold, and she urged her husband to comply with the black man's terms, and secure what would make them wealthy for life. However Tom might have felt disposed to sell himself to the Devil, he was determined not to do so to oblige his wife; so he flatly refused, out of the mere spirit of contradiction. Many and bitter were the quarrels they had on the subject, but the more she talked, the more resolute was Tom not to be damned to please her.

At length she determined to drive the bargain on her own account, and if she succeeded, to keep all the gain to herself.

Being of the same fearless temper as her husband, she set off for the old Indian fort towards the close of a summer's day. She was many hours absent. When she came back, she was reserved and sullen in her replies. She spoke something of a black man, whom she had met about twilight at the root of a tall tree. He was sulky, however, and would not come to terms: she was to go again with a propitiatory offering, but what it was she forbore to say.

The next evening she set off again for the swamp, with her apron heavily laden. Tom waited and waited for her, but in vain; midnight came, but she did not make her appearance: morning, noon, night returned, but still she did not come. Tom now grew uneasy for her safety, especially as he found she had carried off in her apron the silver teapot and spoons, and every portable article of value. Another night elapsed, another morning came; but no wife. In a word, she was never heard of more.

What was her real fate nobody knows, in consequence of so many pretending to know. It is one of those facts which have become confounded by a variety of historians. Some asserted that she lost her way among the tangled mazes of the swamp, and sank into some pit or slough; others, more uncharitable, hinted that she had eloped with the household booty, and made off to some other province; while others surmised that the tempter had decoyed her into a dismal quagmire, on the top of which her hat was found lying. In confirmation of this, it was said a great black man, with an axe on his shoulder, was seen late that very evening coming out of the swamp, carrying a bundle tied in a check apron, with an air of surly triumph.

The most current and probable story, however, observes, that Tom Walker grew so anxious about the fate of his wife and his property, that he set out at length to seek them both at the Indian fort. During a long summer's afternoon he searched about the gloomy place, but no wife was to be seen. He called her name repeatedly, but she was nowhere to be heard. The bittern alone responded to his voice, as he flew screaming by; or the bull-frog croaked dolefully from a neighborhood pool. At length, it is said, just in the brown hour of twilight, when the owls began to hoot, and the bats to flit about, his attention was attracted by the clamor of carrion crows hovering about a cypress-tree. He looked up, and beheld a bundle tied in a check apron, and hanging in the branches of the tree, with a great vulture perched hard by, as if keeping watch upon it. He leaped with joy; for he recognized his wife's apron, and supposed it to contain the household valuables.

"Let us get hold of the property," said he, consolingly to himself, "and we will endeavor to do without the woman."

As he scrambled up the tree, the vulture spread its wide wings, and sailed off screaming into the deep shadows of the forest. Tom seized the check apron, but woful sight! found nothing but a heart and liver tied up in it!

Such, according to the most authentic old story, was all that was to be found of Tom's wife. She had probably attempted to deal with the black man as she had been accustomed to deal with her husband; but though a female scold is generally considered a match for the devil, yet in this instance she appears to have had the worst of it. She must have died game, however; for it is said Tom noticed many prints of cloven feet deeply stamped about the tree, and found handfuls of hair, that looked as if they had been plucked from the coarse black shock of the woodman. Tom knew his wife's prowess by experience. He shrugged his shoulders, as he looked at the signs of a fierce clapper-clawing. "Egad," said he to himself, "Old Scratch must have had a tough time of it!"

Tom consoled himself for the loss of his property, with the loss of his wife, for he was a man of fortitude. He even felt something like gratitude towards the black woodman, who, he considered, had done him a kindness. He sought, therefore, to cultivate a further acquaintance with him, but for some time without success; the old black-legs played shy, for whatever people may think, he is not always to be had for calling for: he knows how to play his cards when pretty sure of his game.

At length, it is said, when delay had whetted Tom's eagerness to the quick, and prepared him to agree to any thing rather than not gain the promised treasure, he met the black man one evening in his usual woodman's dress, with his axe on his shoulder, sauntering along the swamp, and humming a tune. He affected to receive Tom's advances with great indifference, made brief replies, and went on humming his tune.

By degrees, however, Tom brought him to business, and they began to haggle about the terms on which the former was to have the pirate's treasure. There was one condition which need not be mentioned, being generally understood in all cases where the devil grants favors; but there were others about which, though of less importance, he was inflexibly obstinate. He insisted that the money found through his means should be employed in his service. He proposed, therefore, that Tom should employ in it the black traffick; that is to say, that he should fit out a slave-ship. This, however, Tom resolutely refused: he was bad enough in all conscience; but the devil himself could not tempt him to turn slave-trader.

Finding Tom so squeamish on this point, he did not insist upon it, but proposed, instead, that he should turn usurer; the devil being extremely anxious for the increase of usurers, looking upon them as his peculiar people.

To this no objections were made, for it was just to Tom's taste.

"You shall open a broker's shop in Boston next month," said the black man.

"I'll do it to-morrow, if you wish," said Tom Walker.

"You shall lend money at two per cent a month."

"Egad, I'll charge four!" replied Tom Walker.

"You shall extort bonds, foreclose mortgages, drive the merchant to bankruptcy—"

"I'll drive him to the d—l," cried Tom Walker.

"You are the usurer for my money!" said the black-legs with delight. "When will you want the rhino?"

"This very night."

"Done!" said the devil.

"Done!" said Tom Walker.—So they shook hands and struck a bargain.

A few days' time saw Tom Walker seated behind his desk in a counting-house in Boston.

His reputation for a ready-moneyed man, who would lend money out for a good consideration, soon spread abroad. Everybody remembers the time of Governor Belcher, when money was particularly scarce. It was a time of paper credit. The country had been deluged with government bills; the famous Land Bank had been established; there had been a rage for speculating; the people had run mad with schemes for new settlements; for building cities in the wilderness; land-jobbers went about with maps of grants, and townships, and Eldorados, lying nobody knew where, but which everybody was ready to purchase. In a word, the great speculating fever which breaks out every now and then in the country, had raged to an alarming degree, and everybody was dreaming of making sudden fortunes from nothing. As usual the fever had subsided; the dream had gone off, and the imaginary fortunes with it; the patients were left in doleful plight, and the whole country resounded with the consequent cry of "hard times."

At this propitious time of public distress did Tom Walker set up as usurer in Boston. His door was soon thronged by customers. The needy and adventurous; the gambling speculator; the dreaming land-jobber; the thriftless tradesman; the merchant with cracked credit; in short, every one driven to raise money by desperate means and desperate sacrifices, hurried to Tom Walker.

Thus Tom was the universal friend of the needy, and acted like a "friend in need"; that is to say, he always exacted good pay and good security. In proportion to the distress of the applicant was the hardness of his terms. He accumulated bonds and mortgages; gradually squeezed his customers closer and closer: and sent them at length, dry as a sponge, from his door.

In this way he made money hand over hand; became a rich and mighty man, and exalted his cocked hat upon 'Change. He built himself, as usual, a vast house, out of ostentation; but left the greater part of it unfinished and unfurnished, out of parsimony. He even set up a carriage in the fulness of his vainglory, though he nearly starved the horses which drew it; and as the ungreased wheels groaned and screeched on the axle-trees, you would have thought you heard the souls of the poor debtors he was squeezing.

As Tom waxed old, however, he grew thoughtful. Having secured the good things of this world, he began to feel anxious about those of the next. He thought with regret on the bargain he had made with his black friend, and set his wits to work to cheat him out of the conditions. He became, therefore, all of a sudden, a violent church-goer. He prayed loudly and strenuously, as if heaven were to be taken by force of lungs. Indeed, one might always tell when he had sinned most during the week, by the clamor of his Sunday devotion. The quiet Christians who had been modestly and steadfastly travelling Zionward, were struck with self-reproach at seeing themselves so suddenly outstripped in their career by this new-made convert. Tom was as rigid in religious as in money matters; he was a stern supervisor and censurer of his neighbors, and seemed to think every sin entered up to their account became a credit on his own side of the page. He even talked of the expediency of reviving the persecution of Quakers and Anabaptists. In a word, Tom's zeal became as notorious as his riches.

Still, in spite of all this strenuous attention to forms, Tom had a lurking dread that the devil, after all, would have his due. That he might not be taken unawares, therefore, it is said he always carried a small Bible in his coat-pocket. He had also a great folio Bible on his counting-house desk, and would frequently be found reading it when people called on business; on such occasions he would lay his green spectacles in the book, to mark the place, while he turned round to drive some usurious bargain.

Some say that Tom grew a little crack-brained in his old days, and that fancying his end approaching, he had his horse new shod, saddled and bridled, and buried with his feet uppermost; because he supposed that at the last day the world would be turned upside down; in which case he should find his horse standing ready for mounting, and he was determined at the worst to give his old friend a run for it. This, however, is probably a mere old wives' fable. If he really did take such a precaution, it was totally superfluous; at least so says the authentic old legend, which closes his story in the following manner.

One hot summer afternoon in the dog-days, just as a terrible black thundergust was coming up, Tom sat in his counting-house in his white linen cap and India silk morning-gown. He was on the point of foreclosing a mortgage, by which he would complete the ruin of an unlucky land speculator for whom he had professed the greatest friendship. The poor land-jobber begged him to grant a few months' indulgence. Tom had grown testy and irritated and refused another day.

"My family will be ruined and brought upon the parish," said the land-jobber. "Charity begins at home," replied Tom; "I must take care of myself in these hard times."

"You have made so much money out of me," said the speculator.

Tom lost his patience and his piety—"The devil take me," said he, "if I have made a farthing!"

Just then there were three loud knocks at the street door. He stepped out to see who was there. A black man was holding a black horse, which neighed and stamped with impatience.

"Tom, you're come for," said the black fellow, gruffly. Tom shrunk back, but too late. He had left his little Bible at the bottom of his coat-pocket, and his big Bible on the desk buried under the mortgage he was about to foreclose: never was sinner taken more unawares. The black man whisked him like a child into the saddle, gave the horse the lash, and away he galloped, with Tom on his back, in the midst of the thunderstorm. The clerks stuck their pens behind their ears, and stared after him from the windows. Away went Tom Walker, dashing down the streets; his white cap bobbing up and down; his morning-gown fluttering in the wind, and his steed striking fire out of the pavement at every bound. When the clerks turned to look for the black man he had disappeared.

Tom Walker never returned to foreclose the mortgage. A countryman who lived on the border of the swamp, reported that in the height of the thundergust he had heard a great clattering of hoofs and a howling along the road, and running to the window caught sight of a figure, such as I have described, on a horse that galloped like mad across the fields, over the hills and down into the black hemlock swamp towards the old Indian fort; and that shortly after a thunderbolt falling in that direction seemed to set the whole forest in a blaze.

The good people of Boston shook their heads and shrugged their shoulders, but had been so much accustomed to witches and goblins and tricks of the devil, in all kind of shapes from the first settlement of the colony, that they were not so much horror-struck as might have been expected. Trustees were appointed to take charge of Tom's effects. There was nothing, however, to administer upon. On searching his coffers all his bonds and mortgages were found reduced to cinders. In place of gold and silver his iron chest was filled with chips and shavings; two skeletons lay in his stable instead of his half-starved horses, and the very next day his great house took fire and was burnt to the ground.

Such was the end of Tom Walker and his ill-gotten wealth. Let all griping money-brokers lay this story to heart. The truth of it is not to be doubted. The very hole under the oak-trees, whence he dug Kidd's money, is to be seen to this day; and the neighboring swamp and old Indian fort are often haunted in stormy nights by a figure on horseback, in morning-gown and white cap, which is doubtless the troubled spirit of the usurer. In fact, the story has resolved itself into a proverb, and is the origin of that popular saying, so prevalent throughout New England, of "The Devil and Tom Walker."

Why Spuyten Duyvil Is So Named*

THE tide-water creek that forms the upper boundary of Manhattan Island is known to dwellers in tenements round about as "Spittin' Divvle." The proper name of it is Spuyten Duyvil, and this, in turn, is the compression of a celebrated boast by Anthony Van Corlaer. This redoubtable gentleman, famous for fat, long wind, and long whiskers, was trumpeter for the garrison at New Amsterdam, which his countrymen had just bought for twenty-four dollars, and he sounded the brass so sturdily that in the fight between the Dutch and Indians at the Dey Street peach orchard his blasts struck more terror into the red men's hearts than did the matchlocks of his comrades. William the Testy vowed that Anthony and his trumpet were garrison enough for all Manhattan Island, for he argued that no regiment of Yankees would approach near enough to be struck with lasting deafness, as must have happened if they came when Anthony was awake.

Peter Stuyvesant—Peter the Headstrong—showed his appreciation of Anthony's worth by making him his esquire, and when he got news of an English expedition on its way to seize his unoffending colony, he at once ordered Anthony to rouse the villages along the Hudson with a trumpet call to war. The esquire took a hurried leave of six or eight ladies, each of whom delighted to believe that his affections were lavished on her alone, and bravely started northward, his trumpet hanging on one side, a stone bottle, much heavier, depending from the other. It was a stormy evening when he arrived at the upper end of the island, and there was no ferryman in sight, so, after fuming up and down the shore, he swallowed a mighty draught of Dutch courage,—for he was as accomplished a performer on the horn as on the trumpet,—and swore with ornate and voluminous oaths that he would

---

* From *Myths and Legends of Our Own Land*, by Charles M. Skinner, Vol. I, pp. 51–52. Copyright, 1896, by J. B. Lippincott Company. Philadelphia and London.

swim the stream "in spite of the devil" [Eu spuyt den Duyvil].

He plunged in, and had gone half-way across when the Evil One, not to be spited, appeared as a huge moss-bunker, vomiting boiling water and lashing a fiery tail. This dreadful fish seized Anthony by the leg; but the trumpeter was game, for, raising his instrument to his lips, he exhaled his last breath through it in a defiant blast that rang through the woods for miles and made the devil himself let go for a moment. Then he was dragged below, his nose shining through the water more and more faintly, until, at last, all sight of him was lost. The failure of his mission resulted in the downfall of the Dutch in America, for, soon after, the English won a bloodless victory, and St. George's cross flaunted from the ramparts where Anthony had so often saluted the setting sun. But it was years, even then, before he was hushed, for in stormy weather it was claimed that the shrill of his trumpet could be heard near the creek that he had named, sounding above the deeper roar of the blast.

VI

QUEER TALES

GHOSTLY and devilish adventures like those of Peter Rugg and Dowsabel Casselman and curious relations between people and animals as in the stories of "The Lobo Girl of Devil's River" and "Gretchen and the White Steed" carry over from folk tales to local legends. Many of the latter are adaptations of migratory legends. Thus "Peter Rugg, the Missing Man" is a landlubber version of the Flying Dutchman, and "The Lobo Girl of Devil's River" relates to the world-wide legend of wolf-children.

Approaching fiction in the individuality of their characterization and setting, tales like these stand out above the lovers'-leap type of local legend; and yet for all their bizarreness they do not, like many a literary treatment of legend, smell of the lamp. Recalling the saga (e.g., Dick Whittington) type of folk tale, they lend enchantment to history. Defoe might have written of Peter Rugg; Irving, of Dowsabel Casselman; and Frank Stockton, of the Lobo Girl.

———————

Peter Rugg, the Missing Man*

(From Jonathan Dunwell of New York to Mr. Herman Krauff)

SIR,—Agreeably to my promise, I now relate to you all the particulars of the lost man and child which I have been able to collect. It is entirely owing to the humane interest you seemed to take in the report that I have pursued the inquiry to the following result.

You may remember that business called me to Boston in the summer of 1820. I sailed in the packet to Providence; and when I arrived there, I learned that every seat in the stage was engaged. I was thus obliged either to wait a few hours, or accept a seat with the driver, who civilly offered me that accommodation. Accordingly I took my seat by his side, and soon found him intelligent and communicative. When we had travelled about ten miles, the horses suddenly threw their ears on their necks as flat as a hare's. Said the driver, "Have you a surtout with you?"

"No," said I; "why do you ask?"

"You will want one soon," said he. "Do you observe the ears of all the horses?"

"Yes"; and was just about to ask the reason.

"They see the storm-breeder, and we shall see him soon."

At this moment there was not a cloud visible in the firmament; soon after a small speck appeared in the road.

"There," said my companion, "comes the storm-breeder; he always leaves a Scotch mist behind him. By many a wet jacket do I remember him. I suppose the poor fellow suffers much himself—much more than is known to the world."

Presently a man with a child beside him, with a large black horse and a weather-beaten chair, once built for a chaise-

———————

* By William Austin. From *A Book of New England Legends and Folk Lore in Prose and Poetry*, by Samuel Adams Drake, pp. 90–105. Copyright, 1883, by Samuel Adams Drake. Boston: Roberts Brothers.

body, passed in great haste, apparently at the rate of twelve miles an hour. He seemed to grasp the reins of his horse with firmness, and appeared to anticipate his speed. He seemed dejected, and looked anxiously at the passengers, particularly at the stage-driver and myself. In a moment after he passed us, the horses' ears were up, and bent themselves forward so that they nearly met.

"Who is that man?" said I; "he seems in great trouble."

"Nobody knows who he is; but his person and the child are familiar to me. I have met him more than a hundred times, and have been so often asked the way to Boston by that man, even when he was travelling directly from that town, that of late I have refused any communication with him; and that is the reason he gave me such a fixed look."

"But does he never stop anywhere?"

"I have never known him to stop anywhere longer than to inquire the way to Boston. And let him be where he may, he will tell you he cannot stay a moment, for he must reach Boston that night."

We were now ascending a high hill in Walpole; and as we had a fair view of the heavens, I was rather disposed to jeer the driver for thinking of his surtout, as not a cloud as big as a marble could be discerned.

"Do you look," said he, "in the direction whence the man came; that is the place to look. The storm never meets him, it follows him."

We presently approached another hill; and when at the height the driver pointed out in an eastern direction a little black speck about as big as a hat,—"There," said he, "is the seed storm; we may possibly reach Polley's before it reaches us, but the wanderer and his child will go to Providence through rain, thunder, and lightning."

And now the horses, as though taught by instinct, hastened with increased speed. The little black cloud came on rolling over the turnpike, and doubled and trebled itself in all directions. The appearance of this cloud attracted the notice of all the passengers; for after it had spread itself to a great bulk, it suddenly became more limited in circumference, grew more compact, dark, and consolidated. And now the successive flashes of chain lightning caused the whole cloud to appear like a sort of irregular network, and displayed a thousand fantastic images. The driver bespoke my attention to a re-markable configuration in the cloud; he said every flash of lightning near its centre discovered to him distinctly the form of a man sitting in an open carriage drawn by a black horse. But in truth I saw no such thing. The man's fancy was doubtless at fault. It is a very common thing for the imagination to paint for the senses, both in the visible and invisible world.

In the mean time the distant thunder gave notice of a shower at hand; and just as we reached Polley's tavern the rain poured down in torrents. It was soon over, the cloud passing in the direction of the turnpike toward Providence. In a few moments after, a respectable-looking man in a chaise stopped at the door. The man and child in the chair having excited some little sympathy among the passengers, the gentleman was asked if he had observed them. He said he had met them; that the man seemed bewildered, and inquired the way to Boston; that he was driving at great speed, as though he expected to outstrip the tempest; that the moment he had passed him, a thunder-clap broke directly over the man's head, and seemed to envelop both man and child, horse and carriage. "I stopped," said the gentleman, "supposing the lightning had struck him; but the horse only seemed to loom up and increase his speed; and as well as I could judge, he traveled just as fast as the thunder-cloud."

While this man was speaking, a pedlar with a cart of tin merchandise came up all dripping; and on being questioned, he said he had met that man and carriage, within a fortnight, in four different States; that at each time he had inquired the way to Boston, and that a thunder-shower, like the present, had each time deluged his wagon and his wares, setting his tinpots, etc., afloat, so that he had determined to get marine insurance done for the future. But that which excited his surprise most was the strange conduct of his horse; for that long before he could distinguish the man in the chair, his own horse stood still in the road, and flung back his ears. "In short," said the pedlar, "I wish never to see that man and horse again; they do not look to me as though they belonged to this world."

This was all I could learn at that time; and the occurrence soon after would have become with me "like one of those things which had never happened," had I not, as I stood recently on the doorstep of Bennett's Hotel in Hartford, heard a man say, "There goes Peter Rugg and his child! He looks wet and weary, and farther from Boston than ever." I was satisfied it was the same man I had seen more than three years before; for whoever has once seen Peter Rugg can never after be deceived as to his identity.

"Peter Rugg!" said I; "and who is Peter Rugg?"

"That," said the stranger, "is more than any one can tell exactly. He is a famous traveller, held in light esteem by all inn-holders, for he never stops to eat, drink, or sleep. I wonder why the Government does not employ him to carry the mail."

"Ay," said a bystander; "that is a thought bright only on one side. How long would it take in that case to send a letter to Boston?—for Peter has already, to my knowledge, been more than twenty years traveling to that place."

"But," said I, "does the man never stop anywhere? Does he never converse with any one? I saw the same man more than three years since near Providence, and I heard a strange story about him. Pray, sir, give me some account of this man."

"Sir," said the stranger, "those who know the most respecting that man say the least. I have heard it asserted that Heaven sometimes sets a mark on a man either for judgment or a trial. Under which Peter Rugg now labors, I cannot say; therefore I am rather inclined to pity than to judge."

"You speak like a humane man," said I; "and if you have known him so long, I pray you will give me some account of him. Has his appearance much altered in that time?"

"Why, yes; he looks as though he never ate, drank, or slept; and his child looks older than himself; and he looks like time broken off from eternity, and anxious to gain a resting-place."

"And how does his horse look?" said I.

"As for his horse, he looks fatter and gayer, and shows more animation and courage, than he did twenty years ago. The last time Rugg spoke to me he inquired how far it was to Boston. I told him just one hundred miles.

" 'Why,' said he, 'how can you deceive me so? It is cruel to mislead a traveller. I have lost my way; pray direct me the nearest way to Boston.'

"I repeated, it was one hundred miles.

" 'How can you say so?' said he; 'I was told last evening it was but fifty, and I have travelled all night.'

" 'But,' said I, 'you are now travelling from Boston. You must turn back.'

" 'Alas!' said he, 'it is all turn back! Boston shifts with the wind, and plays all around the compass. One man tells me it is to the east, another to the west; and the guide-posts, too, they all point the wrong way.'

" 'But will you not stop and rest?' said I; 'you seem wet and weary.'

" 'Yes,' said he; 'it has been foul weather since I left home.'

" 'Stop, then, and refresh yourself.'

" 'I must not stop; I must reach home to-night, if possible; though I think you must be mistaken in the distance to Boston.'

"He then gave the reins to his horse, which he restrained with difficulty, and disappeared in a moment. A few days afterward I met the man a little this side of Claremont, winding around the hills in Unity, at the rate, I believe, of twelve miles an hour."

"Is Peter Rugg his real name, or has he accidently gained that name?"

"I know not, but presume he will not deny his name; you can ask him—for see, he has turned his horse, and is passing this way."

In a moment a dark-colored, high-spirited horse approached, and would have passed without stopping; but I had resolved to speak to Peter Rugg, or whoever the man might be. Accordingly I stepped into the street, and as the horse approached, I made a feint of stopping him. The man immediately reined in his horse. "Sir," said I, "may I be so bold as to inquire if you are not Mr. Rugg?—for I think I have seen you before."

"My name is Peter Rugg," said he: "I have unfortunately lost my way. I am wet and weary, and will take it kindly of you to direct me to Boston."

"You live in Boston, do you?—and in what street?"

"In Middle Street."

"When did you leave Boston?"

"I cannot tell precisely; it seems a considerable time."

"But how did you and your child become so wet? It has not rained here to-day."

"It has just rained a heavy shower up the river. But I shall not reach Boston to-night if I tarry. Would you advise me to take the old road, or the turnpike?"

"Why, the old road is one hundred and seventeen miles, and the turnpike is ninety-seven."

"How can you say so? You impose on me! It is wrong to trifle with a traveller. You know it is but forty miles from Newburyport to Boston."

"But this is not Newburyport; this is Hartford."

"Do not deceive me, sir. Is not this town Newburyport, and the river that I have been following the Merrimac?"

"No, sir; this is Hartford, and the river the Connecticut."

He wrung his hands and looked incredulous.

"Have the rivers, too, changed their courses, as the cities have changed places? But see! the clouds are gathering in the south, and we shall have a rainy night. Ah, that fatal oath!"

He would tarry no longer. His impatient horse leaped off, his hind flanks rising like wings; he seemed to devour all before him, and to scorn all behind.

I had now, as I thought, discovered a clew to the history of Peter Rugg, and I determined, the next time my business called me to Boston, to make a further inquiry. Soon after, I was enabled to collect the following particulars from Mrs. Croft, an aged lady in Middle Street, who has resided in Boston during the last twenty years. Her narration is this:

The last summer, a person, just at twilight, stopped at the door of the late Mrs. Rugg. Mrs. Croft, on coming to the door, perceived a stranger, with a child by his side, in an old weather-beaten carriage, with a black horse. The stranger asked for Mrs. Rugg, and was informed that Mrs. Rugg had died in a good old age more than twenty years before that time.

The stranger replied, "How can you deceive me so? Do ask Mrs. Rugg to step to the door."

"Sir, I assure you Mrs. Rugg has not lived here these nineteen years; no one lives here but myself, and my name is Betsey Croft."

The stranger paused, and looked up and down the street, and said: "Though the painting is rather faded, this looks like my house."

"Yes," said the child; "that is the stone before the door that I used to sit on to eat my bread and milk."

"But," said the stranger, "it seems to be on the wrong side of the street. Indeed everything here seems to be misplaced. The streets are all changed, the people are all changed, the town seems changed; and, what is strangest of all, Catherine Rugg has deserted her husband and child. Pray," continued the stranger, "has John Foy come home from sea? He went a long voyage; he is my kinsman. If I could see him, he could give me some account of Mrs. Rugg."

"Sir," said Mrs. Croft, "I never heard of John Foy. Where did he live?"

"Just above here, in Orange Tree Lane."

"There is no such place in this neighborhood."

"What do you tell me? Are the streets gone? Orange Tree

Lane is at the head of Hanover Street, near Pemberton's Hill."

"There is no such lane now."

"Madam! you cannot be serious. But you doubtless know my brother, William Rugg. He lives in Royal Exchange Lane, near King Street."

"I know of no such lane, and I am sure there is no such street as King Street is this town."

"No such street as King Street! Why, woman, you mock me! You may as well tell me there is no King George! However, madam, you see I am wet and weary; I must find a resting-place. I will go to Hart's tavern, near the market."

"Which market, sir?—for you seem perplexed; we have several markets."

"You know there is but one market,—near the Town dock."

"Oh, the old market; but no such person has kept there these twenty years."

Here the stranger seemed disconcerted, and uttered to himself quite audibly: "Strange mistake! How much this looks like the town of Boston! It certainly has a great resemblance to it; but I perceive my mistake now. Some other Mrs. Rugg, some other Middle Street."

"Then," said he, "madam, can you direct me to Boston?"

"Why, this is Boston, the city of Boston. I know of no other Boston."

"City of Boston it may be; but it is not the Boston where I live. I recollect now, I came over a bridge instead of a ferry. Pray what bridge is that I just came over?"

"It is Charles River Bridge."

"I perceive my mistake; there is a ferry between Boston and Charlestown; there is no bridge. Ah, I perceive my mistake. If I were in Boston my horse would carry me directly to my own door. But my horse shows by his impatience that he is in a strange place. Absurd, that I should have mistaken this place for the old town of Boston! It is a much finer city than the town of Boston. It has been built long since Boston. I fancy it must lie at a distance from this city, as the good woman seems ignorant of it."

At these words his horse began to chafe and strike the pavement with his fore-feet. The stranger seemed a little bewildered, and said, "No home to-night"; and giving the reins to his horse, passed up the street, and I saw no more of him.

It was evident that the generation to which Peter Rugg belonged had passed away.

This was all the account of Peter Rugg I could obtain from Mrs. Croft; but she directed me to an elderly man, Mr. James Felt, who lived near her, and who had kept a record of the principal occurrences for the last fifty years. At my request she sent for him; and after I had related to him the object of my inquiry, Mr. Felt told me he had known Rugg in his youth; that his disappearance had caused some surprise; but as it sometimes happens that men run away, sometimes to be rid of others, and sometimes to be rid of themselves; and Rugg took his child with him, and his own horse and chair; and as it did not appear that any creditors made a stir,—the occurrence soon mingled itself in the stream of oblivion, and Rugg and his child, horse and chair, were soon forgotten.

"It is true," said Mr. Felt, "sundry stories grew out of Rugg's affair,—whether true or false I cannot tell; but stranger things have happened in my day, without even a newspaper notice."

"Sir," said I, "Peter Rugg is now living; I have lately seen Peter Rugg and his child, horse, and chair. Therefore I pray you to relate to me all you know or ever heard of him."

"Why, my friend," said James Felt, "that Peter Rugg is now a living man, I will not deny; but that you have seen Peter Rugg and his child is impossible, if you mean a small child; for Jenny Rugg, if living, must be at least—let me see —Boston Massacre, 1770—Jenny Rugg was about ten years old. Why, sir, Jenny Rugg, if living, must be more than sixty years of age. That Peter Rugg is living, is highly probable, as he was only ten years older than myself, and I was only eighty last March; and I am as likely to live twenty years longer as any man."

Here I perceived that Mr. Felt was in his dotage; and I despaired of gaining any intelligence from him on which I could depend.

I took my leave of Mrs. Croft, and I proceeded to my lodgings at the Marlborough Hotel.

If Peter Rugg, thought I, has been travelling since the Boston Massacre, there is no reason why he should not travel to the end of time. If the present generation know little of him, the next will know less; and Peter and his child will have no hold on this world.

In the course of the evening I related by adventure in Middle Street.

"Ha!" said one of the company, smiling, "do you really think you have seen Peter Rugg? I have heard my grandfather speak of him as though he seriously believed his own story."

"Sir," said I, "pray let us compare your grandfather's story of Mr. Rugg with my own."

"Peter Rugg, sir, if my grandfather was worthy of credit, once lived in Middle Street, in this city. He was a man in comfortable circumstances, had a wife and one daughter, and was generally esteemed for his sober life and manners. But, unhappily, his temper at times was altogether ungovernable; and then his language was terrible. In these fits of passion, if a door stood in his way, he would never do less than kick a panel through. He would sometimes throw his heels over his head and come down on his feet, uttering oaths in a circle; and thus in a rage he was the first who performed a somerset, and did what others have since learned to do for merriment and money. Once Rugg was seen to bite a tenpenny nail in halves. In those days everybody, both men and boys, wore wigs; and Peter, at these moments of violent passion, would become so profane that his wig would rise up from his head. Some said it was on account of his terrible language; others accounted for it in a more philosophical way, and said it was caused by the expansion of his scalp,—as violent passion, we know, will swell the veins and expand the head. While these fits were on him Rugg had no respect for heaven or earth. Except this infirmity, all agreed that Rugg was a good sort of man; for when his fits were over, nobody was so ready to commend a placid temper as Peter.

"It was late in autumn, one morning, that Rugg, in his own chair, with a fine large bay horse, took his daughter and proceeded to Concord. On his return a violent storm overtook him. At dark he stopped in Menotomy, now West Cambridge, at the door of a Mr. Cutter, a friend of his, who urged him to tarry the night. On Rugg's declining to stop, Mr. Cutter urged him vehemently. 'Why, Mr. Rugg,' said Cutter, 'the storm is overwhelming you: the night is exceeding dark: your little daughter will perish: you are in an open chair, and the tempest is increasing.' 'Let the storm increase,' said Rugg, with a fearful oath; 'I will see home to-night, in spite of the last tempest, or may I never see home!' At these words he gave his whip to his high-spirited horse, and disappeared in a moment. But Peter Rugg did not reach home that night, or the next; nor, when he became a missing man, could he ever be traced beyond Mr. Cutter's in Menotomy.

"For a long time after, on every dark and stormy night, the wife of Peter Rugg would fancy she heard the crack of a whip, and the fleet tread of a horse, and the rattling of a carriage passing her door. The neighbors, too, heard the same noises; and some said they knew it was Rugg's horse, the tread on the pavement was perfectly familiar to them. This occurred so repeatedly, that at length the neighbors watched with lanterns, and saw the real Peter Rugg, with his own horse and chair, and child sitting beside him, pass directly before his own door, his head turned toward his house, and himself making every effort to stop his horse, but in vain.

"The next day the friends of Mrs. Rugg exerted themselves to find her husband and child. They inquired at every public-house and stable in town; but it did not appear that Rugg made any stay in Boston. No one, after Rugg had passed his own door, could give any account of him; though it was asserted by some that the clatter of Rugg's horse and carriage over the pavements shook the houses on both sides of the streets. And this is credible, if indeed Rugg's horse and carriage did pass on that night. For at this day, in many of the streets, a loaded truck or team in passing will shake the houses like an earthquake. However, Rugg's neighbors never afterward watched; some of them treated it all as a delusion, and thought no more of it. Others, of a different opinion, shook their heads and said nothing.

"Thus Rugg and his child, horse and chair, were soon forgotten, and probably many in the neighborhood never heard a word on the subject.

"There was, indeed, a rumor that Rugg afterward was seen in Connecticut, between Suffield and Hartford, passing through the country with head-long speed. This gave occasion to Rugg's friends to make further inquiry. But the more they inquired, the more they were baffled. If they heard of Rugg one day in Connecticut, the next day they heard of him winding round the hills in New Hampshire; and soon after, a man in a chair with a small child, exactly answering the description of Peter Rugg, would be seen in Rhode Island inquiring the way to Boston.

"But that which chiefly gave a color of mystery to the story of Peter Rugg was the affair at Charlestown Bridge. The toll-gatherer asserted that sometimes on the darkest and most stormy nights, when no object could be discerned, about the time Rugg was missing, a horse and wheel carriage, with a noise equal to a troop, would at midnight, in utter contempt of the rates of toll, pass over the bridge. This occurred so frequently, that the toll-gatherer resolved to attempt a discovery. Soon after, at the usual time, apparently the same horse and carriage approached the bridge from Charlestown Square. The toll-gatherer, prepared, took his stand as near the middle of the bridge as he dared, with a large three-legged stool in his hand. As the appearance passed, he threw the stool at the horse, but heard nothing, except the noise of the stool skipping across the bridge. The toll-gatherer, on the next day, asserted that the stool went directly through the body of the horse; and he persisted in that belief ever after. Whether Rugg, or whoever the person was, ever passed the bridge again, the toll-gatherer would never tell; and when questioned, seemed anxious to waive the subject. And thus Peter Rugg and his child, horse and carriage, remain a mystery to this day."

This, sir, is all that I could learn of Peter Rugg in Boston.

The Right Hand of Robber Lewis*

IT WAS on a fine Monday morning in the early fall of 1820, and wash day. An old-time copper kettle on a spider was boiling water by the kitchen door of the tavern, which was on the side of the building on which was painted on the plastered wall the white horse of colossal proportions which gave the old inn its name. Rosanna Casselman, the innkeeper's bustling wife, was at work over the tubs on the side porch, and her young daughter Dowsabel was carrying buckets of water from the well to replenish the kettle. The girl, who was of amazing loveliness, was standing by the well box, and while the long pole with chain attached was dipped into the watery depths to replenish "the old oaken bucket," a horseman approached on the road which led from the south. The autumnal sun was clearing away the fogs and mist as he drew rein at the horse-trough which received the overflow from the fountain's copious source. The stranger was a young man of possibly

---

* From *Two Pennsylvania Mountain Legends*, collected by Henry W. Shoe-maker, pp. 2–11, Publications of The Pennsylvania Folk-Lore Society, Volume I, Number 4. Published by The Reading Eagle Press, Reading, Pa. 1928.

thirty years of age, wearing a broad-brimmed black felt hat, in which was stuck the wing feather of a golden eagle, and pulled down over his eyes, almost hiding his regular features, and his handsome dark side-whiskers; he wore a cloak, or "Cardinal," as they were called in those days, which was loosened at the collar, as the exercise and growing warmth of the day had made it a trifle uncomfortable. He was mounted on a superb black horse, an entire, called Pulverhorn, said to be a son of old Topgallant, by a fugitive union with a Cumberland horse doctor's mare; the same Topgallant known as the "iron horse" which later won the great race against Whalebone at Baltimore, in three mile heats, when in his twenty-fourth year. Hiram Woodruff, the greatest of horse trainers, said of him: "His like was never seen before or since." Touching the brim of his hat, the rider asked the girl if she could hand him a can of water from the well, while his horse quenched his thirst at the trough, which was hewed from a solid log of original white pine. The girl looked at him boldly, and deciding to be polite, as she liked his appearance, she, after balancing the filled bucket on the coping of the well, ran to the waterbench on the porch to get a cup. Returning in a minute with a gourd, she filled it to the brim with the sparkling water, and handed it over the paling fence to the thirsty horseman, smiling at him in her pleasantest manner. This is how she impressed the stranger, who was a hardened citizen of the world, and a connoisseur of the fair sex.

Dowsabel Casselman was a Pennsylvania mountain beauty, typical of her medley of Continental ancestors, all except in the coloring, for her cropped curly hair, instead of being of raven blackness, was of coppery gold. It is strange that out of every thousand of the dark mountain girls of Pennsylvania there will be one or two red heads, and these will be of rarest loveliness. Her eyes, however, were dark, a hazel or amber, though her skin was fair, transparently white as alabaster. She was a little above the average height, smoothly and gracefully built, with a wonderful pair of legs, as her skirts, worn above the knees in the style of the Indian girls of those days, generously disclosed. Pleased with his reception, and promising to return shortly for a stay at the hotel, the handsome stranger resumed his way in the direction of Berlin, and Brunerstown, now called Somerset. Dowsabel, fascinated, daydreamed watching after him, until her mother brought her back to earth by incessantly shouting, "Bring that water instanter, or I'll put a tin ear on you, you dulless slommach, standing out there grinning at that laddy-buck like a Cheshire cat." Several days later Dowsabel was again at the well drawing a bucket of water to fill the big pint Stiegel glasses which were placed on the table at dinner time, when outside the fence she noticed the small figure of an old, old man, whose head hardly came above the top of the horse-trough. The aged stranger wore a broad-brimmed soft black hat, adorned with an eagle's plume, and pulled down over his eyes, barely revealing his fine high nose and full blue eyes; the rest of his face was hidden by a huge beard, yellowish white and curly, which hung several inches below his waist. Naturally short, his big head seemed top-heavy even for his sturdy body to support, and seemed to rest on one of his shoulders. He wore a ragged great-coat that had once been brown. In one hand he carried a blackthorn cane with a branch curling around it like a grapevine, and in the other hand a small charcoal brazier, which he used partly to warm himself in the cold sheds and outbuildings where he generally slept, and partly to heat glue, for he was a traveling furniture-mender by occupation. Tipping his crumpled hat with old world politeness, he said: "Milady, would you be so kind as to fetch me a can so that I may have a drink of your good water." The handsome girl gazed at him a moment, contempt appearing in her flawless features, and, at length, replied in cutting tones: "Who do you think I am, old codger, to get your kind a cup; besides, I haven't got one, and if you're dry, the trough's in front of you."

The hardened old wayfarer was taken aback, but replied with spirit: "Young missy, if I was your lover, you would not have spoken that way to me, and would have broken your neck to get me a drink." The girl's pale face colored a little as she replied: "I have no lover, and you can see for yourself there is no cup." "Stuff and nonsense, Carrots," said the old man, as he turned to walk away, "you have had a dozen lovers already, and a thirteenth is on the way, and when he is finished you will be ready to lead an ape in hell. Au revoir, for I am sure that we will probably meet again a couple of times."

Dowsabel said nothing more, but filled her bucket and carried it to the house, for again her mother had her "dander up." "You goosesap," she shouted, "I've a notion to give you the worst ferricadouzer of your young life, shilly-shallying out there with that old chuckle-head." But the old man's remarks made an ugly impression on the girl's mind, and she was silent and moody the rest of the day.

Several days went by again, and the handsome stranger returned from Somerset and made a stay of nearly a week at the tavern, ostensibly to condition his horse, which he said had a "sidebone." While the steed rested the young man was tireless in pressing his suit with the lovely Dowsabel. It was an easy conquest, as he had the youth, the good looks, the smooth ways of the big world, which were the attributes that girls of Dowsabel's type most admired. When he went away the beautiful girl was in tears and begged him to return soon. "Quit your blubbering, kid, I'll be back soon enough," he said, as he mounted Pulverhorn and rode away.

Several weeks elapsed, and the stranger was at the White Horse again for a longer stay. This time he was put in the great east room, which commanded a glorious view from its long windows, the room that William Makepeace Thackery occupied on his second American tour, when he sat on the broad window sill and wrote his name with a diamond on one of the small "lights" of home-made glass, and penned his immortal descriptions of Pennsylvania mountain scenery. He was laying his plans carefully for the coup that he had been planning ever since he first set eyes on the incomparably lovely girl at the well earlier in the autumn. He soon found out that she wasn't happy at home. He slept in the next room, and could hear her mother punishing her almost every night, and her cries of agony and outraged pride.

When he at last told her that he was leaving and might not return for a long time, if at all, Dowsabel again begged tearfully to be taken along. The stranger knew that his time had come, and in the chance meetings they had in the hallways, on the porch, in the yard, and in the harness room at the barn, gradually made clear to her who and what he was. He told her that while his real name was David Pevreferry, he was known on the roads as "Young Lewis," so much were his deeds and characteristics like the famous "David Lewis, the Robber," who had died a few months before in Bellefonte jail, having been mortally wounded by a sheriff's posse on the Driftwood Branch of Sinnemahoning, and buried in the jail yard of said prison on the night of July 13, 1820.

"I will take you along if you'll stop your didoes and can prove to me that you have the guts to stay with a dabster like myself." Dowsabel protested that there was no test or ordeal she would not undergo to prove her worthiness and fitness to be the companion of a man of the highroads, and be like Dally Sanry, the loveliest friend of David Lewis. "From the first time I laid eyes on you I would have put on boy's clothing and followed you to the ends of the earth," she protested over and over again. Then he explained to her that to prove this fitness she must secure for him what he most wanted, David Lewis' right hand, to be cut off the corpse which was now resting in the grave in the jail yard at Bellefonte.

It was a well-founded tradition on the roads in Europe, as well as in Pennsylvania and Maryland, that anyone possessing the right hand of a successful marauder, done to death for his crimes, exercised a spell over those he came in contact with, was able to put entire households to sleep and ransack premises at his leisure, and have nothing to fear in the way of annoyance, interference, apprehension or arrest. At the time of the wholesale hanging of highwaymen at Harper's Ferry in 1816, the only man who escaped had the right hand of an Indian murderer in his pocket, and thus equipped his horse could outrun any posse of pursuers on the road. But how was the hand to be secured from its grave inside the jail yard, with Dowsabel on the outside and guiltless of any offense making her eligible to be inside? "Young Lewis" then stated that as a prerequisite of her worthiness to be a second Dally Sanry she must help him decamp with her father's hooded gig, which was the old taverner's holiday and Battalion Day pride, also his best brass-mounted harness, and with these they would drive to the vicinity of Bellefonte, as far as Earlysburg. Then she must walk to Bellefonte, and put up at the Benner House, and wait there until bills announcing rewards for her capture as a runaway were posted at the hotel and she was recognized and taken up. These he would have printed at Lewistown while she was on her way to Bellefonte, and see that they were on view in every public house and every conspicuous post and pillar in the "village of the belles."

Dowsabel heard the plot with keen interest and could scarcely repress screaming with enthusiasm. On a dark night during the equinoctial rains "Young Lewis" drugged the girl's parents by putting the parings of finger nails in their wine, and made his departure with the gig and harness, driving off behind his black horse through a back lane to a point a mile down the Pike, where, under a clump of old white pines,

Dowsabel awaited him, filled with loving excitement. She had slipped out of the house earlier in the evening and was not missed. The plucky steed, which had once been a lead horse in a stage-coach, was fit for the long drive ahead of him, carrying them at a break-neck pace through the muddy roads, on and on without stopping, over a succession of mountain ranges in the direction of Earlysburg. There were no telegraphs or other rapid means of communication, and only a few weekly newspapers in the back country in those days and news traveled slowly. By the time that John Caspar Peter Casselman recovered from his surprise and went to Brunerstown to advertise the loss of daughter, covered gig, brass-mounted harness and best whip with stock of mountain ash (to ward off highwaymen or evil eye), the wonderful-looking, copper-haired Dowsabel was comfortably ensconced at the spacious old Benner House at Bellefonte. There she was the object of admiration and consternation of the village sheiks who frequented the hostelry. Meanwhile the pseudo Lewis, Jr. had gotten bills struck off at Lewistown, which read approximately:

$100 REWARD IN GOLD COIN

Disappeared from "The White Horse," in Somerset County, Pa., on night of September 14, 1820, girl answering name of Dowsabel Urckart Casselman: She is aged eighteen years coming November 19, will weigh 120 lbs., 5:5½ inches tall, red gold hair worn Indian style, jasper eyes, white complexion, wore white linsey woolsey jersey, dark green velvet skirt, black cotton stockings, low-cut shoes. All are asked to take her up on sight and communicate with Col. J. C. P. Casselman, Wellersburg, Pa.

Coming to the hotel at dinner time, "Lewis" tacked the bill below the face of the grandfather clock in the lobby, unobserved by anyone. He had arranged with the trusting belle that if she should be seized by too zealous claimants for the reward and hurried in the direction of Brunerstown without the formality of consigning her to jail, he would adopt desperate measures and waylay and rescue her at the rock once frequented by the genuine David Lewis, on top of the Seven Brothers (this rock was blasted away only a few months ago by State Highway engineers while reconstructing the Earlysburg-Milroy road), and he whispered to her that it might even be said that "she had been captured and carried off by Robber Lewis' ghost." But it was most likely that she would first be put in jail and her family notified, and kept there until they arrived to divide the rewards among those who gave information, the sheriff and jailers.

But the hardest ordeal of all was that she must exhume the right arm of Lewis, break the hand off at the wrist, and climb to freedom over the twenty-foot jail wall. If she couldn't scale the wall, the stranger would have to wait until she started for Brunerstown with her captors, when he would waylay and capture her in the place and manner previously stated. The landlord at the Benner House quickly recognized the girl described on the bill so mysteriously tacked up on the clock as his guest. The broadside was worded in a way to arouse most anyone's cupidity, and, despite her tears and protests, the beautiful Dowsabel was marched off to the gloomy precincts of Bellefonte jail. There were several graves of unfortunates in the central court-yard of the jail, and the rows of "cells" looked out on this enclosure. Some of the cells intended for robbers or hardened criminals were equipped with a grille of iron bars, over which doors were closed at night, while the rest were like boxstalls at a race track with oaken panelled doors and no gratings. There were small barred windows at the backs of all the cells. Young Lewis had given the girl a tiny saw to sever the bars, which she kept in the corsage of her dress, as, not being accused of any crime except truancy, she was not likely to be searched before her committal. She was not put in a cell, but in one of the "stalls" with an oaken door, and heavy lock and key. The approximate location of Lewis' grave had been explained to her by the stranger, but Dowsabel quickly verified it from her fellow-inmates of the jail. But there was another complication. A big dog, part wolf, which today would be called a "German police dog," had the run of the jailyard at night. "Lewis, Jr." had given the girl some pills to put to sleep the little penny dog at the White Horse (called Wasser, which meant that no hechs could ever take hold of him) the night of their joint escape, in reality nux vomica, which killed the poor little faithful watcher despite his mystic name. She had some of this poison left to use on the magnificent half-wild beast of the Seven Mountains. But Dietz, the wolf-dog, took an uncanny fancy to her, and as she was allowed the freedom of the jailyard, he attached himself to her like a shadow.

It was arranged that she should make her getaway on the second night, but before she was locked in her "box" for the night, the dog became so friendly that Nick Pankaloss, the old Greek from Aaronsburg, who acted as warder, allowed the animal to sleep by her spool bed. There were only three other prisoners in the jail at the time, all decrepit old men, "in" for variations of the more or less technical charge of vagrancy and beneath the dignity of the dog to guard. One of them happened to be Gaston Ythorrotz, the old furniture-mender whose request for a cup of water at the White Horse she had so insolently refused, but he chose not to notice her, and she pretended that she had never seen him before. However, his presence again made her nervous and melancholy. At eight o'clock on the appointed night a game of French ruff was in progress in the sheriff's parlor facing the main street, participated in by the high sheriff himself, his deputy, the turnkey and the old Greek, who, in his way, was a regular levanter, or card sharper. Dowsabel, inspired by great love, which gave her added strength to return to the man of her choice, and anxiety to be away from the old furniture-mender, cleverly broke off the old, rusty lock, and with the big dog licking at her hands, calmly walked out into the jail-yard. The other cell doors were shut tight, and none could see her even if there had been any light. It had been arranged that she was to be arrested during the dark of the moon, and this was a dreary night, cold, and a few snowdrops drifting about. There was a pick and shovel standing against the stone wall in a corner of the yard, and Dowsabel was soon at work digging open David Lewis' grave in the half-frozen ground.

The erstwhile robber chief had been buried three feet deep, but the quicklime had already gotten in its work. The darkness saved the girl from a gruesome sight, but she soon had a grip on the crumbling right arm, and dragged it forth, deftly twisting off the hand at the wrist, which caused such an odor of lime to arise that her eyes smarted. She covered the body again with the lime and clay, while Dietz lay beside her, flopping his tail against the hard ground as if to register satisfaction. Then, almost before the dog could realize what she was doing, the girl walked to the door of the warden's house, through the hall, and out into the street, holding all the while the ghastly but precious relic of David Lewis, which would forever keep her lover out of the toils of the law and make his horse show his heels to the fleetest of his foes, and which acted as a charm to her.

At the end of the steep road which leads out of town below the present site of the Academy, "Lewis, Jr.," was waiting with the covered gig and the black horse resplendent in the brass-mounted harness. And they made a second getaway into the night, into a snowstorm which came out of the east and grew in velocity as they sped down Penn's Valley and almost engulfed them when the reached the Narrows.

After Dowsabel had gone, the wolf-dog began to run about and howl dismally, but he was given to such spells of melancholy restlessness. Besides, the jailers were too intent on French ruff and too much under the influence of "shrub" to recall that Dietz had been locked up with the girl. In the morning Dowsabel's "box" was found open; the $200 golden bird had flown. Snow had mercifully covered Lewis' rifled grave, and there were no signs but that it was still inviolate. None of the prisoners could have seen her escape, and they were not questioned. Five days later, before the hue and cry was scarcely beyond the borders of Centre County—in fact, the local authorities did not want the news to spread, in the hopes that they might recapture the fair jail-breaker and save the rewards for themselves—a hooded gig, drawn by a great black horse, drew up in front of the old stone tavern on the edge of Millerstown. Until the day before "Young Lewis" and Dowsabel had been only a few miles outside of Centre County, quietly "stowed away" in a resort frequented by counterfeiters and gamblers, near the easterly outlet of the dark, wooded narrows between Motz's Bank, now known as Woodward and Hartley Hall, now called Hartleton in the shadow of Jones Mountain. The pattern of David Lewis ordered the girl, who was joyously glad to comply with his slightest wish, to go in the hotel to see if accommodations were to be had. As she hurried into the kitchen, the only room where there was any light, she noticed an old man seated on one of the courting blocks in the inglenook. When he saw her, he rose up, waving his heavy blackthorn staff and pointing at her, his eyes ablaze with surprise and rage. It was Gaston Ythorrotz, the old furniture-mender. "Bloody murder," he shouted, "here's that young huzzy that made the getaway from Bellefonte jail; there's reward of $100 in gold from her people in Somerset County, and $100 more gold from Centre County. Boys, oh, boys, take her up quick!"

His cries literally "brought the whole house to the kitchen," to use an old expression. Dowsabel turned to escape, but the old man was already at the door blocking the way with his cane. There she was caught red-headed; she didn't have a chance. In fact, her screams for assistance only served as a warning to "Young Lewis," knight of the road, outside in the covered gig, who fancied that his new-found possession of the grisly right hand of David Lewis was quickly beginning to prove his lucky talisman. He laid the long whip with its stock of "quicken tree" over the black horse's flank, and was gone like a spectre into the night, leaving his sweetie and slave in hostile hands, a prisoner for cash rewards.

Soon the sturdy Dutch landlord and his boys, acting under the old furniture-mender's instructions, tied her hand and foot. "She's cute as a pet fox, and quick as chain lightning," he said. They tossed her on a sofa in an alcove in a cold, empty room to await the morning. After she was placed in that helpless position like a sack of buckwheat, and the captors made ready to leave the room, the old man came close to her, holding aloft his old brazier, like a lantern, saying: "Now, my beauty, the tables have turned. When I saw you in Bellefonte jail I thought to myself, 'I will say nothing, my time is the third time we meet,' and I let you get away as neat as any hechs could have done it. Now I say, 'I am the law, the law of retribution.'"

After a further consultation with the landlord it was suggested that with $200 in gold at stake, a gigantic sum in those poverty stricken days, when the whole country was "flat" from the effects of the War of 1812–1815, someone should watch her all night, lest "Young Lewis" return and stage another "Bellefonte jail delivery." "That dressy off-scouring will not come back for her," said the old furniture-mender, "I've known him and his kind too well for more than fifty years. Yet I'll watch this tricky minx only too gladly, but I don't think she is overly anxious to go home." Then he drew a huge flint-lock pistol from his belt under his long coat, which he brandished in a menacing fashion. "All right, daddy, go at it, we know we're leaving her in good hands," said the landlord, as he left the room. The old man drew a deer horn stool out of the hall, and slouched down on it in a corner, with the smouldering brazier at his feet.

For a time he sat there, pistol in his lap, gazing at the gagged and helpless damsel in all the misery of her ignominious position. As soon as they were alone together, Dowsabel never allowed her dark Levantine eyes off his face, seeking to cast her glamor over him, as they say in the mountains. Gradually, under the effect of her dazzling beauty, as revealed to him by the red glow of the brazier, the old man began to review his past life, the man he might have been before the weight of human misery and injustice had borne him down, and he became less determined. Women had ill-used him in many lands, in war and in peace, and he had no kindly feeling for any of them except the one who gave him birth, yet he had never taken a mean advantage of any of them. Dowsabel's coppery beauty tantalized him as no other woman's had, cold as she was to him.

Looking at her with his squinty, bloodshot eyes that had beheld from afar many pulchritudinous women, he fancied that she must be fully as beautiful as that red-headed Dutch girl of Bruges, in honor of whom Duke Philip of Burgundy instituted the Order of the Golden Fleece. At last he whispered to her: "I am so very sorry that I let you into this mess, but my heart rebelled at the way you treated me at the 'White Horse.' " Dowsabel did not answer; it was as if she had known what was coming, the usual tribute to the power of her matchless loveliness. Rising up from the stool, the old man fumbled in his belt, under his long coat, drawing forth from its shabby sheath a schlor, or Gipsy dagger, made out of a single piece of steel, and sharp and glistening as a misericorde. With it he cut the gag, and the ropes which bound her lovely wrists and ankles. "Go," he continued, "I don't care where, back home to your mother, who'll whallop the lights out of you, to your lover, who'll deceive the heart out of you, or to lead an ape in hell, it's all the same to me."

Dowsabel straightened herself up, and on tiptoes vanished from the room, uttering not a word, partly because she was naturally wayward and partly as she knew that her real days of suffering were close in front of her. The old man put his schlor back in sheath, his pistol in his belt, settled down on the stool, and began warming his hands at the almost extinguished flame of his rusty brazier. As he gazed at the empty couch his brooding thoughts began to picture, while his great head nodded, an ideal kingdom of life where the obstacles of age, poverty and physical imperfection were but a state of mind that vanished, and he had but to fix his fancy on a person for his love to be requited. But those moments of sublime introspection were as near to human happiness as he would ever reach in his long span of earthly existence. Just before the tall clock in a corner of the kitchen, which had painted on the dial that strange Biscayan proverb, "Every hour wounds, the last one kills," struck three, and the Creeley roosters had begun to crow, he pulled himself together and slipped out a side door, fading into the fog which precedes the dawn along the Juniata. When, half an hour later, the landlord and his family came downstairs, they felt as if the previous evening's happenings had been some fantastic dream.

The Lobo Girl of Devil's River*

IN THE fall of 1830 John Dent and Will Marlo went in partners to trap fur along the headwaters of Chickamauga River in Georgia. Pelts were plentiful, and they got along harmoniously enough until the spring of 1833, when they fell out over a division of the winter's catch.

A woman was at the bottom of the quarrel. She was Mollie Pertul, daughter of a mountaineer. While trapping in the vicinity of the Pertul cabin, John Dent had fallen in love with her and the two had engaged to be married. In forming their partnership the two trappers had agreed to sell jointly all pelts they took and to divide the money equally. Through two seasons this agreement they had carried out, but now Dent insisted on taking half the hides and disposing of them in his own way. He had a notion that he could get more money, to start married life on, by selling his fur separately.

After a bitter quarrel the division was made as Dent wanted it. Immediately almost, Marlo began telling around that he had been cheated. The quarrel went on for about two weeks; then there was a fight in which Dent stabbed Marlo to death. Public opinion was against him, and there was nothing for him to do but skip the country. Before leaving, however, he managed to see his love and tell her that he was going to locate a place in which they could live together and that he would return and steal her away.

Months passed by and people began to lose interest in the matter. During all this time, presumably, Mollie Pertul heard nothing from her murderer lover. Then a little after sundown on April 13, 1834—just a year to the day after Marlo was stabbed—the mountaineer girl went to the cow lot to milk as was her daily custom. After she had been absent from the house an unusually long time, her parents decided to investigate and see if anything had gone wrong. They found

* By L. D. Bertillion. From *Straight Texas*, Publications of the Texas Folk-Lore Society, Number XIII, edited by J. Frank Dobie and Mody C. Boatright, pp. 79–85. Copyright, 1937, by the Texas Folk-Lore Society.

the cows unmilked and in the empty milk pail a Bowie knife with dried blood caked about the hilt. It had a staghorn handle of peculiar design that made it easily identified, next day, as the knife with which Dent had killed Marlo.

In the darkness of the night the parents called and searched for Mollie, but in vain. As soon as daylight showed, a few mountaineers who had been summoned began looking for sign. They struck the tracks of a man and woman leading to the Chickamauga River. There they found in the bank a freshly driven stob to which, apparently, a small canoe had recently been moored. Mollie Pertul was gone without a word of explanation and without a moment's preparation. All she took with her were the clothes on her back.

Six months passed. Then old Mrs. Pertul received a letter postmarked Galveston, Texas. It read:

"Dear Mother,
"The Devil has a river in Texas that is all his own and it is made only for those who are grown.

"Yours with love—
Mollie."

In those days the people of Georgia were not familiar with the streams of Texas and their names. Indeed, very few people in Texas itself knew anything about Devil's River, far to the west of San Antonio, the outpost of all settlements, its inhabitants almost exclusively Spanish-speaking. Mrs. Pertul and her husband and neighbors merely considered that somewhere in Texas Dent had to himself a river on which to trap. They knew that Dent was a devil all right, though maybe they were a little surprised at Mollie's admitting it.

Now, one of the little known chapters in Texas history is of a small colony of English people who in 1834 settled on Devil's River, calling their settlement Dolores. It was short-lived. Indians killed most of the settlers. A few of them drifted into Mexico. The remainder, fourteen adults and three children, in attempting to get back east were attacked at Espantosa Lake, near what is now Carrizo Springs. After killing them all, the Comanches threw their bodies and the carts in which they were traveling into the lake. That is why to this day Mexicans consider the lake haunted, the name Espantosa meaning "frightful."

Dent and his bride had joined this English colony. Devil's River had plenty of beaver; so did the Rio Grande both above and below where Devil's River empties into it. We may be sure that Dent did not live in the group of Englishmen, but, like the lone wolf he was, off to one side. He, no doubt, had an agreement with the Indians. A considerable ride westward two or three Mexican families, more Indianized than anything else, raised a few goats on the Pecos Canyon.

About noon one day in May of the year 1835, a rider on a reeling horse drew up at one of these goat ranches. He told the Mexican *ranchero* and his wife that he was camped where Dry Creek runs into Devil's River. He said that his wife was giving birth to a baby and that they must have help. The Mexican woman agreed to go with her husband, who at once began saddling the horses. Meantime, one of those black electricity-charged clouds for which that part of the country is noted was coming up. A bolt of lightning struck the messenger dead.

This delayed the Mexicans considerably in getting off. From the description of his camp site given by the dead man the *ranchero* knew how to reach it, but night came on before he and his wife got over the divide to Devil's River. They did not find the camp until next morning. There, under an open brush arbor lay the woman dead, alone. Indications pointed to the fact that she had died while giving birth to a child. Yet no child was visible. No child could be found. No trace of it was evident anywhere. Tracks thick around the brush arbor made the *ranchero* suspect that lobo wolves had devoured the infant.

In the scantily furnished brush cabin the Mexicans found a letter, which they took along to show the first person they might encounter who could read English. This letter, as it later developed, had been written by Mollie Pertul Dent to her mother in Georgia several weeks before her death. It served to identify her and her husband. Thus their romance ended.

Ten years passed. A wagon road that had been laid out across the new Republic of Texas to El Paso went by San Felipe Springs (now Del Rio), where there were a few Mexicans, and on across Devil's River, only twelve miles beyond, and then across the Pecos. Occasionally armed travelers passed over the road. In the year 1845 a boy living at San Felipe Springs reported that he had seen a pack of lobo wolves attacking a herd of goats and with them a creature, long hair half covering its features, that looked like a naked girl. Some passing Americans who heard the story quizzed him. But they seemed more interested in getting his description of what a naked girl looked like than in getting information about the strange creature he reported. The story was ridiculed, but it spread back among the settlements.

Not more than a year after this a Mexican woman at San Felipe declared she had seen two big lobos and a naked girl devouring a freshly killed goat. She got close to them, she said, before they saw her. Then they all three ran. The naked girl ran at first on all-fours, but then rose up and ran on two feet, keeping in company with the wolves. The woman was positive of what she had seen. The few people in the Devil's River country began to keep a sharp lookout for the girl. They recalled the disappearance of the dead Mollie Dent's infant amid lobo tracks. Men of the camp told how female wolves carried their cubs by the scruff of the neck without injuring them. Perhaps, they said, some lobo wolf in whom the mother instinct was strong had carried the new-born to her den and raised it. Indians reported having noted in sandy places along the river barefoot tracks, sometimes accompanied by hand prints.

A hunt was organized to capture the Lobo, or Wolf, Girl of the Devil's River, as she had now come to be called. It was made up mostly of wild-riding Mexican vaqueros. These people had doubtless never heard anything of the story of the wolf-suckled Romulus and Remus who founded Rome or of wolf-nursed children in India like Kipling's Mowgli, but far out on this isolated, stark border they had been confronted with unmistakable evidence of a human being reared by and running wild with lobo wolves.

On the third day of the hunt two of the riders jumped the girl near a side canyon. She was with a big lobo that cut off from her when she dodged into a crevice. Here the vaqueros cornered her. She cowered at first like a rabbit. Then she spat and hissed like a wildcat. She fought too, clawing and biting. While the vaqueros were tying her she began to belch forth pitiful, frightful, unearthly sounds described as resembling both the scream of a woman and the howl of a lobo but being neither. As she was howling forth this awful scream, a monster he-wolf, presumably the one from whom she had become separated, suddenly appeared rushing at her captors. The fact that one of them saw it coming before it got close enough to use its powerful jaws probably saved their lives. He shot it dead with a pistol. At that the wild girl sank into a silent faint.

The captured creature was now securely tied and could be examined more carefully. She was excessively hairy, but breasts of beautiful curvature and other features showed that she was a normally formed human female. Her hands and arms were muscled in an extraordinary manner but not ill proportioned.

Having revived from her faint, she was placed on a horse and carried to the nearest ranch. There she was unbound and turned loose in an isolated room for the night. With gestures of kindness she was offered a covering for her body, food and water, but no eagle of the free air, no lion of the deep jungle, ever showed more distrust and fear of its captors than she. She backed into the darkest corner, and there she was left alone. The door to the room was closed. The only other opening was a little window across which a board had been nailed.

The ranch was but a two-roomed hovel, alone amid the desert wilderness. By dark four or five men were gathered at it, and now the wild and frantic being fastened up in the room began voicing forth the terrifying screamish howls. Through the log walls of many vents they carried far on the night air. Soon they were answered by the long drawn out, deep howls of lobos beyond. Lobos seemed to answer from all sides, and their dismal and far-carrying voices brought answers from farther and farther away. All the lobos of the western world seemed to be gathering. Rancheros who all their lives had heard lobos howl had never heard anything like this, either from such a number of wolves now assembling or in the sullen, doom-like quality of the long, deep howling. Nearer and more compactly the horde gathered. Now they would howl all in unison, a bass-throated chorus of ferocity and darkness and lost hopes such as no musician of the world ever dreamed of. Then they would be silent as if waiting for some answer, and the wild girl in the dark room there would answer back with her unearthly howling scream, a voice neither of woman nor of beast.

After a time the great pack made a rush for the corrals, attacking goats, milk cows and the saddle horses. The noises made by these domestic animals, especially the screams and neighs of the plunging kicking horses, brought the men to the rescue. Ordinarily no man at all familiar with lobo wolves would fear one. Now these rancheros kept together, shooting in the darkness and yelling as they advanced. The wolves retreated.

Meantime, in the pandemonium, the Lobo Girl somehow wrenched the cross plank from the window and got out. It was supposed that she immediately rejoined the wolves. Hardly another howl was heard that night, and the next day not a track of the girl could be found. For a long time the sight of a wolf in that particular region was very rare.

Nothing more was heard of the Wolf Girl of Devil's River for six years. Meantime, gold had been discovered in California and travel westward had greatly increased. Along in 1852 an exploring party of frontiersmen hunting a route to El Paso that would be better watered than the Chihuahua Trail, as the road used was called, rode down to the Rio Grande at a sharp bend far above the mouth of Devil's River.

They were almost upon the water before they saw it or could be seen from its edge. There, sitting on a sand bar, two young wolf whelps tugging at her full breasts, they at close range caught clear sight of a naked young woman. In an instant she was upon her feet, a whelp under each arm, dashing into the breaks at a rate no horse could follow. The creature could have been no other than the wild Lobo Girl of Devil's River.

So far as is known she was never glimpsed by man after this, though perhaps some of the old-time Apaches might have had a tale to tell could they have been asked. What the fate of the Lobo Girl—or woman—was, nobody probably will ever know. During the war of extermination that has been waged on lobos, the most predatory of animals that stockmen of America have known, in the border country, a wolf has occasionally been found with a marked human resemblance, and for many years now "human-faced" wolves, so called, have been considered the final culmination of a Georgia murder and elopement. If man can bear the "mark of the beast," why may not beast bear the mark of the man? Speaking only for myself, I will say that despite the fact that over a century has passed since the beginning of the incidents just related, yet during the past forty years I have in the western country met more than one wolf face strongly marked with human characteristics.

Gretchen and the White Steed*

ALWAYS in the narratives of the soil the Pacing White Mustang is a generous, beneficent animal. Black Devil was the fighter, the slayer, and any report accusing the White Steed of manslaughter may be set down to the confused memories of people who had heard of the black murderer. A tale that illustrates the White Sultan's benignity and intelligence came to me from the late J. O. Dyer, of Galveston. He heard it in the seventies from an old woman who as a girl, about 1848, was among German colonists locating homes in Texas. Her name was Gretchen.

As the story goes, her family, in company with some other German immigrants, was moving up the Guadalupe River to locate on a wide spread of the valley. They traveled in wagons, single file. The family in the last wagon, Gretchen's family, had a very gentle old gray mare that followed along without rope or halter, stopping every once in a while to grab a mouthful of particularly lush grass. She was stupid and lazy and her ears flopped, but she was faithful. On her back she carried two big sacks of corn meal so arranged that they made a kind of platform.

The wagon was running over with such things as German settlers carried—beds and bedding, pots and pans, a heavy chest of drawers, a few pot plants, and a great many children. Gretchen, eight or nine years old, was the liveliest of these. One day she told her father that she wanted to get out and ride the old gray mare. He could see no harm in this; in fact, her absence might lessen the constant hubbub. So he lifted Gretchen up on the platform of corn meal sacks and tied her there with a rope in such a way that she would be comfortable and could not fall off. The old mare hardly batted an eye, and with Gretchen on her back continued as usual to walk and pick grass along behind the wagon.

That afternoon, however, one wheel of the wagon was wrenched in a buffalo wallow, and a halt had to be made for repairs. Gretchen was asleep at the time, firmly tied on her pillion of corn meal. She did not know when the old gray mare grazed out of sight down a mesquite draw. Her father

* From "The White Steed of the Prairies," *Tales of the Mustang*, by J. Frank Dobie, pp. 58–64. Copyright, 1936, by J. Frank Dobie. Dallas: The Book Club of Texas.

was busy with the wheel; her mother, like the old woman who lived in a shoe, had so many children that she did not know what to do; and so neither of them noticed. It was only after the wagon was repaired and the other children were counted into it and the train started on, that little Gretchen was missed. Then the old gray mare could not be found. None of the German men, so new to the frontier, could follow her tracks in the maze of mustang tracks they now discovered. They struck camp to search. Night came and no little Gretchen; the next day came and passed and no little Gretchen. Then on the morning of the third day the old gray mare brought her in, and this is the explanation the little girl gave.

After dozing she knew not how long, she awoke with a start. The lazy old mare was lumbering along in a gallop after a prancing, neighing, pacing white horse with cream-colored mane and tail. She tried to stop the old mare, but she had neither bridle nor halter. She tried to jump off, but she was tied on and the knots of the rope were beyond her reach.

After they had trotted and galloped until nearly sundown, the white horse all the time pacing ahead "like a rocking chair," they came to a large bunch of mares. These were, though Gretchen then knew nothing of such matters, the White Steed's *manada*. They came out full of curiosity to greet their new sister, and they were very cordial in their greeting. Here I will say that no human beings can be more cordial towards each other than horses. I have seen a pair of horses that had been separated from each other and then allowed to get together again, rub each other's noses, caress each other's necks, nip each other fondly with their teeth, nicker, and otherwise show the most sincere affection and delightful cordiality in the world.

The wild mares seemed not to notice little Gretchen at all. They were so cordial in their nosings of the old gray mare that soon their muzzles were touching the meal sacks. Probably the sacking was salty; certainly some of the meal had sifted through so that it could be tasted. The mares tasted it. No matter if it was the first taste of corn they had ever had, they liked it.

They began to nip at the meal sacks so eagerly that they nipped Gretchen's bare legs. She screamed. She expected to be chewed up right away, even if the mares meant no harm. But at her screams the Pacing White Stallion was with one bound beside her. He was as considerate as he was intelligent. He drove the wild mares off. Then he chewed in two the ropes that bound Gretchen, took her gently by the collar of her dress, as a cat takes one of her kittens, and set her down upon the ground.

It was about dark now and the coyotes were beginning to howl. Little Gretchen howled too, but there was no danger. After a while she made a kind of nest in some tall fragrant grass near a mesquite bush and, having cried a while, fell asleep.

When she awoke, the sun was high and not a horse was within sight. She was hungry. She went down to a waterhole that she saw close by and drank water for breakfast. She had heard that a person lost on the prairies had better stay in one place until he "found himself" or until someone found him. She had no hope of finding herself, but she did hope that her papa would come. She remained near the waterhole.

Noon came and still no horse or person appeared within sight. Gretchen was hungrier than ever. It was the spring of the year, and she gathered some of the red agrito berries (called also wild currants) growing near, but the thorny leaves pricked her fingers so severely that she quit before she had eaten enough of them to satisfy her hunger. Evening fell and she was still alone. She gathered some sheep sorrel down in the bottom of the draw and drank some more water. Darkness came, the stars came out, the coyotes set up their lonely howling. Little Gretchen lay down in her nest again, and again cried herself to sleep.

When she awoke the next morning, there standing over her, sound asleep, ears flopped down and lower lip hanging shapeless like a bag of curd, was the old gray mare. Gretchen was as glad as the redbird singing over her head. She jumped up and, as soon as she had washed her face, ran to the mare and tried to get on her. But the old mare was too tall. Then Gretchen grasped her by the mane and tried to lead her to a log that lay near at hand. If she could get the old mare beside it, she could use it as a stepping block. But the stupid old mare would not budge. After vainly pulling, coaxing, and jumping about for a long time, Gretchen began to wail.

She was leaning against the shoulder of the old mare sobbing, when she heard swift hoofbeats, rhythmic and racking. She looked up and saw coming out of the bushes the beautiful White Steed. The sunshine was on his whiteness. He came arching his neck and pacing with all the fire of a mustang emperor, but there was something about him that prevented Gretchen from being in the least frightened. On the contrary, she stretched her arms towards him and gave a childish "oh" of welcome. He paced right up to where she stood, gently grasped the collar of her dress and the scruff of her neck in his teeth and lifted her upon the mare. Then he must have told the old gray mare to go home. At least she went—went with Gretchen but no corn meal.

Home was the camp by the buffalo wallow where the wagon had broken down. Gretchen's parents were so happy at having her restored to them that they did not mind the loss of the meal. After she had told her adventures, she showed the nipped places on her legs.

In after years she told the story many, many times. When she was an old woman and some of her grandchildren seemed doubtful of the facts, she would in a pet pull down her cotton stockings and show the small, faint scars on her legs where the wild mares had nipped her. Then the grandchildren would have to believe her. Coincidentally, almost at the very time little Gretchen's family was moving towards a homestead, the German scientist Ferdinand Roemer, in July, 1846, noted —as he soon thereafter set down in his *Texas*—between San Marcos and the Colorado River "a magnificent white stallion speeding away at the head of a herd of mustangs."

Part Six

❦

Songs and Rhymes

I

PLAY RHYMES AND CATCH COLLOQUIES

ONE of the most fascinating fields for the student of beliefs and customs as these enter into the vernacular poetry of folk rhymes is the jingles and doggerels of childhood. The persistence and diffusion of such rhymes in infinite variety and yet in much the same form all over the world offers conclusive evidence of the twin aspects of tradition, especially the tradition of children—its inventiveness and its conservatism.

Like popular jests and sayings in general, play rhymes and catches have their local and contemporary sources or applications, illustrating the principle that "The happiness of a witticism or of a taunt hangs on its relationship at some sort of angle to the customs and notions prevalent in a country."[1] The 1944 version of the old counting-out rhyme has it, in Washington, D. C.:

> Eenie, meenie, minie, mo,
> Catch a Jap by the toe.
> If he hollers, make him say:
> "I surrender, U. S. A."

In 1938, in the shadow of war and hunger, New York City children jingled this ironic bit of nonsense reminiscent of Old Dan Tucker:

> Haile Selassie was a kind old man,
> He lit the match to the frying pan.
> When all the people tasted the beef,
> They all trucked off to the home relief.

These "waifs and strays of folklore," remnants of ancient charms and rituals, are both trivia and curiosa, eloquent with nostalgia for the side-walks and back-yards of one's play-time. Recited or chanted as a rhymed or rhythmic accompaniment to rope-skipping or ball-bouncing, as a formula for counting out, as a nominy or set speech, as a taunt, quip, or crank, they have social and poetic interest apart from their game or pastime usage.

New England Rhymes for Counting Out*

THERE ARE VARIOUS WAYS in which children decide who shall begin in a game, or, as the phrase is, be "it." When this position is an advantage, it is often determined by the simple process of "speaking first." So far as can be determined when all are shouting at once, the first speaker is then entitled to the best place. Otherwise it is the practice to draw straws, the shortest gaining; to "toss up" a coin, "heads or tails"; or to choose between the two hands, one of which holds a pebble.

The most interesting way of decision, however, is by employing the rhymes for "counting out." A child tells off with his finger one word of the rhyme for each of the group, and he on whom the last word falls is "out." This process of exclusion is continued until one only is left, who has the usually unpleasant duty of leading in the sport. All European nations possess such rhymes, and apply them in a like manner. These have the common peculiarity of having very little sense, being often mere jargons of unmeaning sounds. This does not prevent them from being very ancient. People of advanced years often wonder to find their grandchildren using the same formulas, without the change of a word. The identity between American and English usage establishes the currency of some such for three centuries, since they must have been in common use at the time of the settlement of this country.

> Onery, uery, ickory, Ann,
> Filisy, folasy, Nicholas John,
> Queevy, quavy, Irish Mary,
> Stingalum, stangalum, buck.
> —*New England*.

* From *Games and Songs of American Children*, collected and compared by William Wells Newell, pp. 194–203. New and Enlarged Edition. Copyright, 1893, 1903, by Harper & Brothers. New York and London.

Onery, uery, ickory, a,
Hallibone, crackabone, ninery-lay,
Whisko, bango, poker my stick,
Mejoliky one leg!
  —*Scituate, Mass.* (about 1800).

One's all, zuzall, titterall, tann,
Bobtailed vinegar, little Paul ran,
Harum scarum, merchant marum,
Nigger, turnpike, toll-house, out.
   —*Salem, Mass.*

Onery, uery, ickery, see,
Huckabone, crackabone, tillibonee;
Ram pang, muski dan,
Striddledum, straddledum, twenty-one.
   —*Connecticut.*

Eny, meny, mony, my,
Tusca, leina, bona, stry,
Kay bell, broken well,
We, wo, wack.
  —*Massachusetts.*

Eny, meny, mony, mine,
Hasdy, pasky, daily, ine,
Agy, dagy, walk.
   —*Connecticut.*

Ena, mena, mona, my,
Panalona, bona, stry,
Ee wee, fowl's neck,
Hallibone, crackabone, ten and eleven,
O-u-t spells out.

Intery, mintery, cutery corn,
Apple-seed and apple-thorn,
Wire, briar, limber lock,
Five mice in a flock;
Catch him Jack,
Hold him Tom,
Blow the bellows,
Old man out.
   —*Massachusetts.*

Ikkamy, dukkamy, alligar, mole,
Dick slew alligar slum,
Hukka pukka, Peter's gum,
Francis.
   —*Massachusetts.*

Tricks and Catches*

BOY: Now you say, "Just like me," every time I stop, and I'll tell you a story.

FRIEND: All right.

BOY: I went up one flight of stairs.

FRIEND: Just like me.

BOY: I went up two flights of stairs.

FRIEND: Just like me.

BOY: I went up three flights of stairs.

FRIEND: Just like me.

BOY: I went up four flights of stairs.

FRIEND: Just like me.

BOY: I went into a little room.

FRIEND: Just like me.

BOY: I looked out of a window.

FRIEND: Just like me.

BOY: And I saw a monkey.

FRIEND: Just like me.

BOY: Oh, ho, ho, ho! Just like *you!*

The friend collapses, and seeks another boy whom he can try the same on. The boy who knows the catch turns the tables by going through everything right but his final sentence. That he changes to "Just like *you!* Ha, ha, ha! You didn't get me that time!"

There are various rough tricks that have their outbreaks and periods of infliction among school-boys just like measles or whooping-cough. One of these is the making another fellow "walk Spanish." You catch him by the collar and the slack of his pants behind, and make him step along on the tips of his toes. The walker feels very awkward and helpless, and the other fellows are very much amused by his manner. This performance is also called "The Shirt-tail Run."

ANCIENT JOKE

FIRST PERSON: Did you ever notice that when you get up in the morning it is always your left foot that you dress last?

SECOND PERSON: No; and I don't believe it is, either.

---

* From *What They Say in New England*, A Book of Signs, Sayings, and Superstitions, collected by Clifton Johnson, pp. 167–173. Copyright, 1896, by Lee and Shepard. Boston.

FIRST PERSON: Well whichever foot you dress first, the other must be the *left* one, mustn't it?

When this point has been made, it is proper that the company should laugh.

A CHICKEN QUESTION

BOY TO COMPANION: Which would you rather have, a rooster or a pullet?

If boy number two says "a rooster," boy number one goes behind him, and gives him a hoist with his knee.

If he says "a pullet," number one pulls number two's nose. Number one considers himself very smart in either case.

A PRESENT

BOY: Don't you want me to give you a little red box?
COMPANION: Yes.

The boy then gives the other a box on the ear.

THE MONKEY AT SCHOOL

FIRST CHILD: Do you want to see a monkey?
SECOND CHILD: Yes.

Then number one holds up a mirror before number two, or goes outside and holds a dark shawl up against the window-pane for number two to look into.

A FOREIGN LANGUAGE

HOG LATIN: "Igry knowgry somegry thinggry yougry don't-gry knowgry."
TRANSLATION: "I know something you don't know."

A conversation carried on in this language between two children is as blind to their uninitiated mates as real Latin. How the speakers can make anything out of such outlandish grunting talk is a great puzzle. But children find it even more difficult than grown people to keep a secret, and this accomplishment is not long in becoming a common possession.

Catches and Riddles*

Twenty-nine and one?
> Thirty.
Your face is dirty.

April's gone, summer's come;
You're a fool and I'm none.

Red-headed sinner,
Come down to your dinner.

Red-headed fox,
Stole your mother's pigeon-box.

Over latch, under latch,
It takes good kisses to make a match.

Where was little Moses when the light went out,
What was he adoing and what was he about?

I climbed up the apple tree
And all the apples fell on me.
Make a pudding, make a pie.
Did you ever tell a lie?
Yes, you did, you know you did,
You stole your mother's teapot lid.

Rhymes and Jingles**

WHEN about to run a race or engage in a jumping-match, this rhyme is appropriate:—

One to begin
Two to show,
Three to make ready,
And four to go.

---

* From "Games of Washington Children," by W. H. Babcock, *The American Anthropologist*, Vol. I (July, 1888), No. 3, p. 271. Washington, D.C.: Judd & Detweiler, Printers.
** From *What They Say in New England*, A Book of Signs, Sayings, and Superstitions, collected by Clifton Johnson, pp. 174-197. Copyright, 1896, by Lee and Shepard. Boston.

At the end of the race the one who came in last sometimes consoles himself by calling out:—

> First's the worst,
> Second's the same,
> Last's the best of all the game.

> QUESTION: What's your name?
> ANSWER: Pudden tame;
>   Ask me again
>   And I'll tell you the same.

Some of the boys give a much ruder answer to this question in these words:—

> John Brown,
> Ask me again and I'll knock you down.

Second form:—

> QUESTION: What's your name?
> ANSWER: Pudden tame.
> QUESTION: What's your natur'?
> ANSWER: Pudden tater.
> QUESTION: What's your will?
> ANSWER: Pudden swill.

> Crowing hens and jumping sheep
> Are the worst property a farmer can keep.

Boys often say it in this way:—

> Whistling girls and crowing hens
> Always come to some bad ends.

Another version is:—

> Whistling girls and blatting sheep
> Are the worst property a farmer can keep.

The girl's response to this innuendo is, "That is not right. It's like this:—

> Whistling girls and merino sheep
> Are the *best* property a farmer can keep."

When a boy gets mad at another he will sometimes call out derisively:—

> Paady Whacker, chew tobacker,
> If he dies, it is no matter.

In the following, two children stand and take told of hands, and swing their arms from side to side in time to the rhythm of the verse they repeat. With the final words, hands still clasped, they turn the arms on one side over their heads and at the same time turn around themselves. The verse runs as follows:—

> Wash your mother's dishes,
> Hang 'em on the bushes.
> When the bushes begin to crack,
> Hang 'em on the nigger's back.
> When the nigger begins to run,
> Shoot him with a leather gun.

In a game of tag, it is the proper thing to shout out to the one in chase:—

> Fire on the mountain,
> Fire on the sea,
> You can't catch me.

A variation:—

> Fire on the mountain
> Run, boys, run;
> The cat's in the cream-pot,
> Run, girls, run!

Rhyme addressed to a person who has red hair:—

> Redny, redny, fire on top,
> All the rednys come flipperty flop.

When you are getting ready to jump, swing your arms and say this:—

> One, two, three,
> The bumble bee,

> The rooster crows,
> And away he goes.

> Lazy folks work the best
> When the sun is in the west.

One person says to another:—

> Adam and Eve and Pinchme
> Went out for a swim;
> Adam and Eve got drowned,
> Who was saved?

The second person answers, "Pinchme."
Number one responds by giving number two a pinch.

Old rhyme:—

> Said Aaron to Moses,
> "Let's cut off our noses,"
> Says Moses to Aaron,
> "It's the fashion to wear 'em."

A boy ties another's stockings together, and then hollers as
loud as he can:—

> "Charlo beef,
> The beef was tough,
> Poor little Charley
> Couldn't get enough."

The name in the third line is changed to suit the case in
hand.

This stocking-tying is usually done by a boy's friends while
he is in swimming, and the jokers try to tie such a knot that
the owner can only untie it by using his teeth. The appropriate time to say the poetry is when the boy begins to work with
his teeth on the knot.

If a boy has a friend named Joseph, he can entertain him
by the following rhyme:—

> Joe, Joe,
> Broke his toe
> Riding on a buffalo.

If the friend's name is Frank, the following will suit:—

> Frank, Frank,
> Turned the crank,
> His mother come out and gave him a spank,
> And knocked him over the sandbank.

If his name is Bert the following is appropriate:—

> Bert, Bert, tore his shirt
> Riding on a lump of dirt.

If his name is Samuel, he will very likely be interested in this:—

> Sam, Sam,
> The dirty man,
> Washed his face in a frying-pan,
> Combed his hair with the back of a chair,
> And danced with the toothache in the air.

Something like the above ditty is appropriate for a boy named John. The accepted way to repeat the jingle is as follows:—

> My son John is a nice old man,
> Washed his face in a frying-pan,
> Combed his hair with a wagon-wheel,
> And died with the toothache in his heel.

Take the baby's foot in your hand, wiggle the toes one after the other, beginning with the big one, and recite:—

> This little pig says, "I go steal wheat";
> This little pig says, "Where'll you get it?"
> This little pig says, "In father's barn";
> This little pig says, "I go tell";
> And this little pig says, "Quee, quee, quee!"

A variation of this story is the following:—

> This little pig goes to market,
> This little pig stays home,
> This little pig has plenty to eat,
> This little pig has none,

This little pig says, "Wee, wee, wee!"
all the way home.

A verse for a small boy:—

Fishy, fishy, in the brook,
Papa catch him with a hook,
Mama fry him in a pan,
Georgy eat him fast's he can.

The last line sometimes ends, "Like a man."

The last two lines may also be changed to read:—

Mama fry him in the spider,
Georgie eat him like a tiger.

The boy's name can be varied to suit the speaker.

A political couplet shouted by schoolboys:—

Republican rats, take off your hats,
And make way for the Democrats.

A jingle to say when churning:—

Come, butter, come,
Peter's at the gate,
Waiting for a patty cake.

This used to be said as a charm to make the butter come quickly.

When you have the baby in your lap, you can amuse it by saying:—

"Pat a cake, pat a cake, baker's man."
"So I will, master, as fast as I can."
"Roll it, roll it, roll it,
Prick it, prick it, prick it,
Toss it up in the oven and bake it."

You at the same time take the baby's hands in yours, and pat them together to suit the two first lines, rub them against each other to suit the third, take one finger and dig it into the palm of the other hand to suit the fourth, and toss both hands up, and the baby too if you choose, to suit the final line. Then, if the baby is anything like the babies used to be, it will crow and be very happy.

Here is a variation of the same theme:—

> Pat a cake, pat a cake, baker's man,
> Pat it and pat it as fast as you can,
> Pat it and prick it, and mark it with B,
> And toss it in the oven for baby and me.

This is acted out in the same way, and the letter B is marked with a finger on the child's palm. B, of course, stands for baby.

Jog the baby up and down on your knees, and says:—

> Trot, trot to Boston,
> To buy a loaf of bread.
> Trot, trot, home again,
> The old trot's dead.

Trot the baby on your knee, and say:—

> Seesaw, Jack in the hedge,
> Which is the way to London Bridge?

When you have the baby in your arms and are rocking it to sleep, say:—

> Bye baby hunting,
> Papa's gone a-hunting;
> Mother's gone to milk the cow;
> Sister's gone—*I* don't know how;
> Brother's gone to get a skin
> To wrap the baby bunting in.

Two children sit opposite each other with their palms on their knees. They say this rhyme together, and clap each other's hands in time to the metre:—

> Bean porridge hot,
> Bean porridge cold,
> Bean porridge's best
> When nine days old.

In the English version, it is pease porridge or pease pudding, but New Englanders are not acquainted with those dishes.

The child's hands in the following are put palm down on the table. Go over the fingers one word to each to the end of the incantation. The finger that has the final word is turned under. Go over the remaining nine with the same lingo, and turn under the one that comes last. Repeat the process till all are turned under.

> Intra, mintra, cut-ra corn,
> Apple-seed and apple-thorn,
> Wire, brier, limber lock,
> Six geese in a flock,
> Sit and sing by the spring
> O-u-t, out; up on yonder hill
> There sits old Father Wells;
> He has jewels, he has rings,
> He has many pretty things,
> Whip-jack, two nails, blow the bellows
>   out, old man.

THE WEEK

> Wash on Monday,
> Iron on Tuesday,
> Bake on Wednesday,
> Brew on Thursday,
> Churn on Friday,
> Mend on Saturday,
> Go to meeting on Sunday.

A girl will sometimes make the following remarks to the new moon. I have never heard that the revelation was made to her that she prayed for—at any rate, not by the moon.

> New moon, new moon, pray tell to me
> Who my true lover is to be.—
> The color of his hair,
> The clothes he will wear,
> And the day he'll be wedded to me.

If before April first one boy tries to fool another, boy number two squelches the would-be fooler by saying:—

> April fool's a-coming,
> And you're the biggest fool a-running.

If the attempt is made after April first, he says:—

> April fool is past,
> And you're the biggest fool at last.

A rhyme that does service for both occasions is this:—

> Up the ladder, and down the tree,
> You're a bigger fool than me.

A Jingle for the Baby's Feet

> Shoe the old horse, shoe the old mare,
> Drive a nail here, and drive a nail there;
> But let the little nobby colt go bare.

At picnics you will sometimes hear the children say:—

> Lemonade,
> Made in the shade,
> Stirred with a spade,
> By an old maid.

Here is one way to amuse a child. Clasp your hands with the fingers turned inward, and repeat the following ditty, which you illustrate by changing the position of your fingers and hands:—

> Here's a meeting-house, there's the steeple,
> Look inside and see all the people.
> Here's the singers going up-stairs,
> And here's the minister saying his prayers.

To make the steeple, elevate your forefingers with the tips joined. To suit the second line open your hands a little, and wiggle the ends of your clasped fingers. Illustrate the singers going up-stairs by making the fingers of your right hand walk up those of your left. Lastly, clinch your hands, put one fist on top of the other, and that is the minister.

A Finger Poem

> Five little rabbits went out to walk;
> They liked to boast as well as talk.
> The first one said, "I hear a gun!"
> The second one said, "I will not run!"
> Two little ones said, "Let's sit in the shade."
> The big one said, "I'm not afraid!"
> Bang, Bang! went a gun,
> And the five little rabbits run.

The child holds up one of its hands while it repeats these lines. The fingers are the five rabbits. With his other hand he takes hold of each finger in turn as he speaks of the rabbit it represents. "The first one" is the thumb. "The second one" is the forefinger. "The two little ones" are the two final fingers. "The big one" is the middle finger.

A SCHOOLBOY JINGLE

"Fire, fire!"
　Said Mrs. McGuire.
"Where, where?"
　Said Mrs. Ware.
"Down town!"
　Said Mrs. Brown.
"Oh, Lord save us!"
　Said Mrs. Davis.

Pin Lore*

See a pin and pick it up,
All that day you will have luck;
See a pin and let it lay,
You'll have bad luck all that day.

Needles and pins!
Needles and pins!
When a man's married
His trouble begins.

Rope-Skipping Rhymes**

Cinderella dressed in yellow
Went uptown to meet her fellow.
How many kisses did he give her?
　(Count until there is a miss.)

---

* From "Pin Lore," by Charles G. Leland, *The Journal of American Folk-Lore*, Vol. IV (April–June, 1891), No. XIII, p. 174. Copyright, 1891, by the American Folk-Lore Society. Boston and New York: Houghton, Mifflin & Company.

** From "Rope-Skipping, Counting-Out, and Other Rhymes of Children," by Paul G. Brewster, *Southern Folklore Quarterly*, Vol. III (September, 1939), No. 3, pp. 173–178. Gainesville: University of Florida.

Johnny over the ocean,
Johnny over the sea,
Johnny broke a teacup
And blamed it on me.

I told Ma,
Ma told Pa;
Johnny got a lickin',
Hee, hee, haw!
Salt, vinegar,
Mustard, pepper!
(Gradual increase of speed.)

Standing on the corner
Chewing bubble gum,
Along came a beggar
And asked me for some.

O you dirty beggar,
O you dirty bum!
Ain't you ashamed
To ask me for gum?

I love coffee,
I love tea;
How many boys
Are stuck on me?
(Count until there is a miss.)

Down in the valley
Where the green grass grows
There sat *(girl's name)*
Sweet as a rose.
She sang, she sang,
She sang so sweet;
Along came *(boy's name)*
And kissed her cheek.
How many kisses did he give her?
   (Count until there is a miss.)

Ice cream soda, lemonade pop;
Tell me the initials of your sweetheart.
(Call letters of the alphabet until there is a miss.)

Johnny gave me apples,
Johnny gave me pears,
Johnny gave me fifteen cents
And kissed me on the stairs.

I'd rather wash the dishes,
I'd rather scrub the floor,
I'd rather kiss a nigger boy
Behind the kitchen door.

Red, white, and yellow,
Went downtown to meet my fellow:
How many kisses did he give me?
(Count until there is a miss.)

Rooms for rent,
Inquire within;
When I move out,
Let —— move in.
(Used for "calling in.")

Charlie Chaplin sat on a fence
Trying to make a dollar out of fifteen cents.

Charlie Chaplin went to France
To teach the ladies how to dance;
First a heel and then a toe,
A skip and a hop and away you go!

Old lady, old lady, touch the ground;
Old lady, old lady, turn around;
Old lady, old lady, point your shoe;
Old lady, old lady, 23 skidoo!

Miss, miss, little Miss, miss;
When she misses, she misses like this.

Last night and the night before
Twenty-four robbers came to my door,
And this is what they said:
"Buster, Buster, hands on head;
Buster, Buster, go to bed;
Buster, Buster, if you don't,
I'm afraid they'll find you dead."

Apples, peaches, creamery butter,
Here's the name of my true lover.
(Call letters of the alphabet.)

I went uptown to see Miss Brown;
She gave me a nickel and I bought a pickle;
The pickle was sour, so I bought a flower;
The flower was red, so I bought a thread;
The thread was thin, so I bought a pin;

[The pin was sharp, so I bought a harp;]
And on this harp I played;
I love coffee, I love tea;
How many boys are stuck on me?
      (Count until there is a miss.)

> One, two, buckle my shoe;
> Three, four, shut the door;
> Five, six, pick up sticks;
> Seven, eight, shut the gate;
> Nine, ten, begin again.

Teacher, teacher, don't whip me;
Whip that nigger behind that tree;
He stole peaches, I stole none;
Put him in the calaboose just for fun,

> Johnny over the ocean,
> Johnny over the sea;
> If you can catch Johnny
> You can catch me.

> Johnny over the ocean,
> Johnny over the sea;
> You may catch Johnny,
> But you can't catch me.

Sidewalk Rhymes of New York*

One, two, three a-lair-y, I spied Mis-sus Sa-ry,
Sit-ting on a bum-ble-air-y, Just like a choc-late fair-y

> Roses are red,
> Violets are blue,
> I like pecans,
> Nuts to you.

> Roses are red,
> Violets are blue,

* From "Songs of Innocence," by Dorothy Mills and Morris Bishop, *The New Yorker*, Vol. XIII (November 13, 1937), No. 39, pp. 32–42. Copyright, 1937, by the F-R Publishing Corporation. New York City. Tunes transcribed by Charles Seeger.

Elephants are fat
And so are you.

Roses are red,
Violets are blue,
If I had your mug,
I'd join the zoo.

Roses are red,
Violets are blue,
Everybody stinks
And so do you.

Roses are red,
Violets are blue,
I use Lifebuoy.
Why don't you?

Looie, pooie,
You're full of hooey.

Oh, Mar—gue—rite! go wash your feet. The
Board of Health is a——cross the street.

Eight and eight are sixteen,
Stick your nose in kerosene,
Wipe it off with ice cream.

Tonight, tonight,
The pillow fight,
Tomorrow's the end of school,
Break the dishes, break the chairs,
Trip the teachers on the stairs.

My mother, your mother, hanging out the clothes,
My mother gave your mother a punch in the nose.
What color did it turn?
Red, yellow, blue, green, violet, orange, etc.

Your mother, my mother, live across the way;
Every night they have a fight,
And this is what they say:
"Your old man is a dirty old man,
'Cause he washes his face in the frying pan,

He combs his hair
With the leg of a chair;
Your old man is a dirty old man."

I should worry, I should care,
I should marry a millionaire;
He should die, I should cry,
I should marry another guy.

I had a little brother,
His name was Tiny Tim;
I put him in the bathtub
To teach him how to swim.
He drank up all the water,
He ate up all the soap;
He died last night
With a bubble in his throat.

Mother, Mother, I am sick;
Send for the doctor, quick, quick, quick.
Doctor, Doctor, shall I die?
Yes, my darling, do not cry.
How many coaches shall I have?
Ten, twenty, thirty, etc.
(Till the skipper misses.)

Silence in the courtroom!
The judge wants to spit.

Jesus, lover of my soul,
Lead me to the sugar bowl.
If the sugar bowl is empty,
Lead me to my mamma's pantry.

Up the river,
Down the lake;
The teacher's got
The bellyache.

Hot roasted peanuts,
Tell the teacher she's nuts;
If she asks you what's your name,
Tell the teacher she's a pain.

Mary's mad,
And I am glad,
And I know what will please her:
A bottle of wine

To make her shine,
And a sweet little boy to squeeze her.

If you don't like my apples,
Then don't shake my tree;
I'm not after your boy friend,
He's after me.

When you get married,
And your husband gets cross,
Just pick up the broom
And ask who's boss.

May your life be strewn with roses,
And your children have pug noses.

First comes love,
Then comes marriage;
Then comes Edith
With a baby carriage.

Buck, buck, you lousy muck,
How many fists have I got up,
One, two, or none?

Minnie and a minnie and a ha, ha, ha,
Kissed her fellow in a trolley car;
I told Ma, Ma told Pa,
Minnie got a licking and a ha, ha, ha.

Cinderella, dressed in yellow,
Gone downtown to buy an umbrella;
On the way she met her fellow.
How many kisses did she receive?
Five, ten, fifteen, twenty, etc.

I won't go to Macy's any more, more, more,
There's a big fat policeman at the door, door, door,
He grab me by the collar and he make me pay a dollar,
So I won't go to Macy's any more, more, more.

Ivory soap,
See it float
Down the river
Like a boat.

Roll, roll, Tootsie Roll,
Roll, marble, in the hole.

Floor to let,
Inquire within;
Lady put out
For drinking gin.
If she promises to drink no more,
Here's the key to her back door.

When Buster Brown was one,
He used to suck his thumb,
Thumb me over, thumb me over,
A, B, C.
When Buster Brown was two,
He used to buckle his shoe,
Shoe me over, shoe me over,
A, B, C, etc.

Happy Hooligan, number nine,
Hung his breeches on the line;
When the line began to swing,
Happy Hooligan began to sing:
"On the mountain stands a lady,
Who she is I do not know;
All she wants is gold and silver,
And a nice young man with whom to go."
Come in, my sister ——,
Go out, my sister ——.

Toots and Casper went to town,
Tootsie bought an evening gown,
Casper bought a pair of shoes,
Buttercup bought the *Daily News.*
How many pages did he read?
Five, ten, fifteen, twenty, etc.

Annie bolanny,
Tillie annie, go sanny,
Tee-legged, tie-legged,
Bow-legged Annie.

I asked my mother for fifty cents
To see the elephant jump the fence;
He jumped so high,
He reached the sky,
And never came back till the Fourth of July.

Yellow-belly, yellow-belly, come and take a swim;
Yes, by golly, when the tide comes in.

II

SINGING AND
PLAY-PARTY GAMES

In the field of the game and dance, two distinctive American developments from British sources are the square dance, quadrille, or cotillion (as distinguished from the English contra-dance or longways dance, which still persists in New England) and the play-party.

In the United States the term square dance has come to stand for old-time set dancing generally, whether of the square, longways, or circle formation. Although the guitar and the banjo are used to accompany the fiddle at dances, as well as to accompany the folk singer, the fiddle is the American folk musical instrument par excellence. Its portability and adaptability made it the musical voice of backwoods and frontier America and the country fiddler one of the most picturesque of pioneer folk characters. Another minstrel type is the square-dance caller or prompter, who, in a mixture of rhythmic prose and doggerel made up of "calls" interspersed with patter, intones and (in the Northeast and Southwest) sings or half-sings the directions.

Because of religious prejudice against dancing and especially the fiddle, as the instrument of the devil, the young people of rural America developed the play-party as an alternative form of amusement, which substituted singing for instrumental accompaniment. A cross between dancing and the traditional singing games of children, the play-party retains the best features of both. To the courtship and other dramatic devices of the game, such as choosing and stealing partners, the play-party adds certain square dance movements and figures, in which, however, partners are swung by the hands instead of by the waist. The leader combines the functions of caller and floor-manager; and like the caller he is something of a folk-poet, with the gift of improvisation.

A comparison of play-party games and singing games shows the former returning to the grown-up level from which the latter were originally descended. Whether or not singing games reflect, in their form and content, the traditional formations and formulae of ancient pagan ceremonials, they represent the survival, on the childhood level, of the rounds, reels, and carols of adults of an earlier day. In the process of "downward transmission," singing games have acquired many childish features, such as the "pleasures of motion" and "playing at work." Play-party games, on the other hand, have come of age, and make the most of realistic and satiric comment on the personalities of the players and incidents of the "swinging play" as well as on the customs, characters, objects, activities, and backgrounds of rural and frontier America.

These changes also illustrate the process of modernization and localization. Thus in an Oklahoma version of "Hog Drovers" (originally an Irish game played at wakes) cowboys and oil-drillers are among the rejected occupations. One of the largest collections of allusive stanzas, many of them interchangeable with other play-party songs, such as "Cindy" and "Liza Jane," has been attracted to "Old Joe Clark," which is a vigorously and fabulously vulgar comic epic of cards, chickens, courting, chains, coons, coon dogs, and other critters.

There She Stands, a Lovely Creature*

THIS pretty song has been recited to us by informants of the most cultivated class, and, on the other hand, we have seen it played as a round by the very "Arabs of the street," in words identically the same. It is an old English song, which has been fitted for a ring-game by the composition of an additional verse, to allow the selection of a partner.

* From *Games and Songs of American Children*, collected and compared by William Wells Newell, pp. 55–56. Copyright, 1883, 1903, by Harper & Brothers. New York and London.

"There she stands, a love—ly crea—ture,
Who she is, I do not know;
I have caught her for her beau—ty,
Let her an—swer, yes or no."

"Madam, I have gold and silver,
    Lady, I have houses and lands,
Lady, I have ships on the ocean,
    All I have is at thy command."

"What care I for your gold and silver,
    What care I for your houses and lands,
What care I for your ships on the ocean—
    All I want is a nice young man."

                        New York.

Do, Do, Pity My Case*

Do, do, pit—y my case, In some la—dy's
gar—den; My clothes to wash when I get home,
In some la—dy's gar——den.

Do, do, pity my case,
    In some lady's garden;
My clothes to iron when I get home,
    In some lady's garden.

And so on, the performers lamenting the duty which lies upon
them of scrubbing their floors, baking their bread, etc.

                        Louisiana.

---

* *Ibid.,* p. 87.

This pretty dance, with its idiomatic English, which comes to us from the extreme South, is obviously not modern. The chorus refers, not to the place of the labor, but to the locality of the dance: it may have been originally *in my lady's garden.* Our informant remembers the game as danced by Negro children, their scanty garments flying as the ring spun about the trunk of some large tree; but (though the naïve appeal to pity may seem characteristic of Southern indolence) this is evidently no Negro song.

Hunt the Squirrel (Itisket, Itasket)*

A RING of players is formed, about the outside of which circles a child who carries a knotted handkerchief, with which he finally taps another on the shoulder, and starts to run around the ring. The child touched must pick up the handkerchief, and run in the opposite direction from the first. The two players, when they meet, must curtsey three times. The toucher endeavors to secure the other's place in the ring, failing which, he must begin again. As he goes about the circle, he recites the words:

> Hunt the squirrel through the wood,
> I lost him, I found him;
> I have a little dog at home,
> He won't bite you,
> He won't bite you,
> And he *will* bite you.
>
> *Cambridge, Mass.*

In Philadelphia, a corresponding rhyme begins:

> I carried water in my glove,
> I sent a letter to my love.

A variation from New York:

I tis—ket, I tas—ket, A green and yel—low bas—ket. I
sent a let—ter to my love, And on the way I dropped it.

---

* *Ibid.*, pp. 168–169.

The name of the game in England is "Drop-glove."

Another and apparently older way of playing "Hunt the Squirrel" is a game in which the child touched follows the toucher until he has caught him, pursuing him both in and out of the ring, being obliged to enter and leave the circle at the same point as the latter.

A kissing-game, in which the player who makes the circuit taps another on the shoulder, and then takes flight, while the person touched is entitled to a kiss if he can capture the fugitive before the latter has made the tour of the circle and gained the vacant place, is a favorite among the "Pennsylvania Dutch," under the name of "Hen-slauch" (Hand-slag), that is, striking with the hand. The game is there called "Ring," and has inspired certain verses of Harbach, the nearest approach to a poet which that unimaginative race has produced.

In a similar game, formerly played in Massachusetts, the leader of the game touches one of the party on the shoulder, and asks, "Have you seen my sheep?" The first replies, "How was it dressed?" The toucher now describes the costume of some player, who, as soon as he recognizes the description of himself, must take flight, and endeavor to regain his place in safety.

Walking on the Green Grass*

This dance, belonging to young men and women as well as to children, is described by the recorder as follows:

The men select their partners as if for a dance, and, thus paired, promenade as in a school procession, singing the first verse, "Walking on the green grass." The procession then resolves itself into a ring, youths and maidens alternating, all singing: "And now we form a round ring." During the singing of this stanza the ring has kept moving. It is next broken into two lines, one of maidens, the other of youths, facing each other as for a reel. The song is resumed with the words, "And now the king upon the green," and each of the actions described in the verse is performed by the couple at the head of the lines. Having thus called out, saluted, and swung his partner, the man begins with the second woman, and thence

---

* *Ibid.*, pp. 227–229.

Walk-ing on the green grass, Walk-ing side by side,

Walk-ing with a pret-ty girl, She shall be my bride. And

now we form a round ring, The girls are by our sides;

Danc-ing with the pret-ty girls Who shall be our brides. And

now the king up-on the green, Shall choose a girl to be his queen; Shall

lead her out his bride to be, And kiss her one, two, three.

Now take her by the hand, this queen, And

swing her round and round the green. Oh, now we'll go a —

round the ring, And ev'—ry one we'll swing.

Oh, swing the king and swing the queen, Oh,

swing the king and swing the queen, Oh, swing 'em round and

round the green, Oh, swing 'em round the green.

down the line, swinging each of the women dancers in turn, the example being followed by his partner with the men, the song continuing, "Oh, now we'll go around the ring, and every one we'll swing." These words are sung over and over, if necessary, until all the dancers have been swung. Thereupon the king and queen take their places at the foot of the lines, and

become the subjects of another couple, song and action beginning with the verse, "And now the king upon the green," etc.
After all the couples have played at royalty, the promenade is
resumed, and the game begun again, generally with change of
partners.

This song is unrecorded in Great Britain; but its antiquity
and status as a portion of a dance of which "Tread the Green
Grass" is also a fragment seem to me sufficiently attested by
correspondence with the third verse of the following rhyme,
given by Mrs. Gomme:

> Here we come up the green grass,
>   Green grass, green grass,
> Here we come up the green grass,
>   Dusty, dusty, day.
>
> Fair maid, pretty maid,
>   Give your hand to me,
> I'll show you a blackbird,
>   A blackbird on the tree.
>
> We'll all go roving,
>   Roving side by side;
> I'll take my fairest ——,
>   I'll take her for a bride.

Sugar-Lump*

Mr. Babcock supplies a rude rhyme, obviously the reduction
of this pretty dance [Walking on the Levy]. The play begins,
"Bounce around, my sugar-lump," and proceeds, "Lower the
window," "Hoist the window," "Don't miss a window," the
player accosted being always addressed as "sugar-lump." The
game seems to continue until a window is missed.

"Sugar-lump" is British also, but I have not elsewhere
noticed as term of endearment "cinnamon," which occurs in a
Florida dance resembling the "Virginia Reel." The first man
leads his partner to the foot of the ladies' line, himself proceeds to the top of the men's line, and turns each lady, as his
partner does each man, the couple themselves turning after
each of the others, to the melody:

---

* *Ibid.*, p. 231.

All up and down, my hon-ey, All up and down we go. That la-dy's a-rock-in' her sug-ar lump, That la-dy's a-rock-in' her sug-ar lump, That la-dy's a-rock-in' her sug-ar lump, O, turn, cin-na-mon, turn.

Swine-Herders (Hog Drovers)*

"Hog- dri— vers, hog-dri—vers, hog- dri—vers we air, A- cour—tin' yer-dar-ter so sweet and fair, And kin we git lodg——in' here, O here And kin we git lodg——in' here?"

"Now this is my darter that sets by my side,
And no hog-driver can get 'er fer a bride;
And you kain't git lodgin' here, O here—
And you k ain't git lodgin' here."

"Yer darter is pretty, yer ugly yerself,
So we'll travel on further and seek better wealth,
And we don't want lodgin' here, O here—
And we don't want lodgin' here."

"Now this is my darter that sets by my side,
And Mr. —— kin git 'er fer a bride,
And he kin git lodgin' here, O here—
And he kin git lodgin' here."

* *Ibid.*, pp. 232–233.

Come un-der, come un-der, My hon-ey, my love, my heart's a-bove, Come
un—der, come un—der, Be——low ,Gal—i—lee.

> We've caught you as a prisoner,
>   My honey, my love, my heart's above—
> We've caught you as a prisoner,
>   Below Galilee.
>
> Then hug 'er neat, and kiss 'er sweet,
>   My honey, my love, my heart's above—
> Then hug 'er nice, and kiss 'er twice,
>   Below Galilee.

* * * * *

From the communication of the recorder is given the following account of the manner of playing: A man, generally an older man, and a girl sit side by side on two chairs in the middle of a room, so placed as to face in opposite directions; another man and a girl walk around hand in hand, and sing, "Naow this is my darter," etc. The "Hog-drivers" retort with the second verse, after which the father sings the third verse, in which he names as partner of his daughter any man whom the girl selects. The latter and her chosen swain then join hands and withdraw, another girl sits beside the father, and the performance is repeated until all players are paired. Then the last girl and the father stand up, and by joining hands make a bridge; they sing, "Come under," etc., while the other couples pass through. On a second attempt at passage, the first couple is captured by the father and his companion, who sing, "We've caught you as a prisoner," etc. The imprisoned man kisses his partner twice, the two are released, and the game continues with another couple. In the Hickory Gap region, some twenty miles from Asheville, the game is popular with old and young. These mountaineers consider dancing immoral, but gather from far and wide whenever a "fuss" is on foot.

In regard to the music, the recorder remarks that none of the intervals are absolutely correct, and that the impression made on the hearer curiously resembles that caused by songs of North American Indians. The intervals could be accurately reproduced only by a violin, but in singing the effect may be gained by flatting the crossed intervals.

In the mountains the game would be designated as "comic," such appellation being bestowed on any song which cannot be termed "sacred."

North Carolina Mountains (near Asheville, N. C.).

Sailing at High Tide*

Sail-ing in the boat when the tide runs high,

Sail-ing in the boat when the tide runs high,

Sail-ing in the boat when the tide runs high,

Wait-ing for the pret-ty girl to come by'm by.

Here she comes so fresh and fair, Sky—blue

eyes and curl-y hair, Ros-y in cheek, dim-ple in her

chin, Say, young men, but you can't come in.

Rose in the garden for you, young man,   [*twice*]
Rose in the garden, get it if you can,
But take care and don't choose a frost-bitten one.

Choose your partner, stay till day,   [*thrice*]
Never mind what the old folks say.

Old folks say 'tis the very best way,   [*thrice*]
To court all night and sleep all day.
                              Ashford, Conn. (1865).

* *Ibid.*, pp. 238–239.

The recorder[1] remarks concerning this game and others from the same neighborhood that they were played as late as the year 1870, at the so-called "Evening Party." About midnight were served refreshments, and the singing and dancing kept up until about four o'clock in the morning, when the young men huddled about the door, and as the girls came out each offered his arm to the maid of his choice, with the words, "Can I see you home?" After which they separated, and went in the dark, often across fields, to their scattered homes, perhaps two miles away. At the door of the fair one there was always a final hug and kiss. Of flirting there was not much; when a girl had acquired the name of "liking the boys" (which meant receiving questionable attentions from more than one) she herself, and the young men who would "wait on her," were considered as of doubtful character, and likely no more to be accepted as escorts by those on whom no reproach rested.

Weevily Wheat*

It's step her to your weev-ly wheat, It's step her to your bar-ley, It's step her to your weev-ly wheat, To bake a cake for Char-ley.

Chorus:
> O Charley he's a fine young man,
> O Charley he's a dandy,
> He loves to hug and kiss the girls,
> And feed 'em on good candy.

The higher up the cherry tree,
The riper grow the cherries,
The more you hug and kiss the girls,
The sooner they will marry.

Over the river to water the sheep,
To measure up the barley,

* From *The American Songbag*, by Carl Sandburg, p. 161. Copyright, 1927, by Harcourt, Brace & Company, Inc. New York.

Over the river to water the sheep,
To bake a cake for Charley.

My pretty little Pink, I suppose you think,
I care but little about you,
But I'll let you know before you go
I cannot do without you.

Old Joe Clark*

Old Joe Clark, the preacher's son,
    He preached all over the plain.
The highest text he ever took
    Was high, low, Jack an' the game.

Chorus:
    Round an' around, Old Joe Clark,
        Round an' around we're gone.
    Round an' around, Old Joe Clark,
        An' a by-by, Lucy Long.

Old Joe Clark he had a dog,
    As blind as he could be.
Ran a redbug round a stump,
    And a coon up a holler tree.

* From *The American Play-Party Song, With a Collection of Oklahoma Texts and Tunes*, by B. A. Botkin, pp. 272–285. Copyright, 1937, by B. A. Botkin. The University Studies of the University of Nebraska, Volume XXXVII, Nos. 1–4. Lincoln, Nebraska.

If you see that girl of mine,
    Tell her if you please
Whenever she goes to roll that dough
    To roll up her dirty sleeves.

If you see that girl of mine,
    Tell her if you can
Whenever she goes to roll that dough
    To wash her dirty hands.

III

BALLADS AND SONGS

FOLK song should properly be regarded as an activity, a functional activity of the group singing or playing for self-gratification or for power, to attain the ends of social adjustment and human freedom, by lightening labor, filling leisure, recording events, voicing praise or protest. Certain "traditionalist" folk-song authorities like Cecil J. Sharp tend to stress the "heritage" rather than the "participation" aspects of folk song and the passive rather than the active rôle of the folk singer, making him out to be a carrier of national culture, who sings to "forget himself and everything that reminds him of his everyday life" and thus, by escaping into an "imaginary world," to "enter into [his] racial inheritance."[1] The "functionalists," on the other hand, such as Alan Lomax, stress the rôle of folk song in America as "an expression of its democratic, interracial, international character, as a function of its inchoate and turbulent many-sided development." According to this view, people not only sing songs in their own way but make their own songs as they begin to "examine their problems self-consciously and comment on them with an objective vigor and irony."[2] Taking issue with Sharp, John and Alan Lomax fling down this challenge:

The American singer has been concerned with themes close to his everyday experience, with the emotions of ordinary men and women who were fighting for freedom and for a living in a violent new world.[3]

Accepting the latter interpretation, one comes to regard the difference between folk singers and art singers as not so much the difference between not having and having an audience as a difference in the relationship between the singer and his audience. In the case of folk singing, like folk story-telling, there is no sharp differentiation between performer and auditor. The rôles are interchangeable, and both participate in the performance as a shared experience, drawing upon the common stock of ideas and expressions and communicating chiefly by symbols, or signs which "bind value to value and man to man by bonds of common meaning and shared emotion."

Every folk song, of course, has an author; but his authorship is conceived in terms of the proverb's wit of one and wisdom of the many, and he is eventually forgotten as his song enters into the public domain. The folk singer, as truly as the professional singer, is an artist in his own right; but he is a people's artist, who sings from the heart and to the hearts of the people and whose distinguishing mark is a sense of the proper balance between remembering and inventing, between pattern and variation. In him the art of improvisation has been raised to high art. This is a matter not of "ad libbing" but of fitting new words to old tunes and old texts to changing circumstances. It is participation made spontaneous. It is rhythmic and poetic freedom akin to the freedom of interpolation and variation that belongs to the blues and jazz and the impromptu steps of the square dance.

The folk basis of the blues and jazz in Negro blues, work songs, hollers, and reels points to the existence of an urban as well as a rural folk music and to the fact that folk music is not a pure but a hybrid activity, which is a fusion of "folk," "art," and "popular" idioms and tastes. This very quality of mixed style and of a certain complex, plastic simplicity and collective individuality, rather than any other single trait, may be the hallmark of folk song as of all folk art. The exploitation of folk music for the purposes of commercial entertainment has resulted in cheapening and slicking up the product by means of hokum and "corn." But there is good "corn" as well as bad "corn," and even "hillbilly" has its place in the hierarchy of American folk styles.

The same mixed or hybrid character applies to types of folk song, and requires that we do not distinguish too sharply between them. For instance, the ballad, or story-telling song, has its lyric elements, as the folk-lyric has its narrative or dramatic elements. Although ballads are not something that we read in the newspapers, they deal with the same situations that make the headlines—wars, crimes, disasters, love tragedies, family feuds, and passion and violence generally. Just as ballad singers and hawkers of broadside ballads once performed a journalistic function, so spectacular and sensational events, such as wrecks, storms, floods, fires, and executions, still bring in their train the crude minstrelsy of local bards. Here the line between fact and fantasy, the timely and the timeless, is a shifting one. History passes into legend and legend into history.

In the same way written and unwritten tradition, the academic and the commercial, mingle in the creation and diffusion of ballads and folk songs. In addition to broadsides, songsters, manuscript collections, and scrapbooks, the stage, traveling troupes of singers, medicine and minstrel shows, camp and political meetings, and the like have served to keep folk songs alive and afloat. To-day the phonograph, the radio, the folk song archive, and the folk festival tend to perform the same function in folk song survival or revival. But for all these external aids folk song is still distinguished from popular and art song by the predominance of word-of-mouth transmission.

Perhaps the best example of the transitional, evolving nature of folk song as the product of an interim or backward stage of culture or society is afforded by Negro folk song—slave songs, spirituals, work songs, reels, and blues. With the displacement of hand by machine labor, work songs of the choral type, such as shanties, field songs, chopping songs, steel-driving songs, etc., tend to disappear. The last refuge of gang or group-hand-labor songs in the United States has been the Southern prison, which until recently provided a "pocket" for primitive labor conditions that have passed out of existence elsewhere. Cultural isolation, as in the Southern mountains, has also fostered the survival of traditional ballads and social songs. With the exception of sea shanties and cowboy songs, our white occupational songs, including lumberjack, canaller, and miners' songs, are social songs to accompany leisure rather than work, or songs of protest, akin to the "hard times" songs of the pioneer, or (more recently) industrial union songs.

Almost every phase or period of American life has left its record in the form of folk songs that describe, reflect, or evoke the time and the place, their conditions, customs, and characters. In this sense American folk song provides material for a social and cultural history of the United States which comes as near as anything we have to being a folk or people's history —a history of, by, and for the people, in which for the first time the people speak and are allowed to tell their own story, in their own way.

BALLADS

Bonny Barbara Allen*

If was up—on a high, high hill, Two maid—ens chose their dwell—ing, And one was known both far and wide, Was known as Bar——bra Al—len.

'Twas in the merry month of May,
All the flowers blooming,
A young man on his deathbed lay
For the love of Barb'ra Allen.

He sent a servant unto her
In the town where she was dwelling.
"Come, Miss, O Miss to my master dying
If your name be Barb'ra Allen!"

Slowly, slowly she got up,
And to his bedside going,

* From *American Anthology of Old-World Ballads*, compiled and edited by Reed Smith, settings by Hilton Rufty, pp. 32–34. Copyright, 1937, by J. Fischer & Bro. New York.

She drew the curtain to one side
And said, "Young man you're dying."

He stretched one pale hand to her
As though he would to touch her.
She hopped and skipped across the floor.
"Young man," says, "I won't have you."

"Remember, 'member in the town,
'Twas in the tavern drinking,
You drank a health to the ladies all
But you slighted Barb'ra Allen."

He turned his face toward the wall,
His back upon his darling.
"I know I shall see you no more,
So goodbye, Barb'ra Allen."

As she was going to her home,
She heard the church bell tolling.
She looked to the east and looked to the west,
And saw the corpse a-coming.

"O hand me down that corpse of clay
That I may look upon it.
I might have saved that young man's life,
If I had done my duty.

"O mother, mother, make my bed;
O make it long and narrow.
Sweet William died for me today,
I shall die for him tomorrow."

Sweet William died on a Saturday night,
And Barb'ra Allen on a Sunday.
The old lady died for the love of them both,
She died on Easter morning.

Sweet William was buried in one graveyard,
Barb'ra Allen in another;
A rose grew on Sweet William's grave
And a brier on Barb'ra Allen's.

They grew and they grew to the steeple top,
And there they grew no higher;
And there they tied in a true-lover knot,
The rose clung 'round the brier.

The Hangsman's Tree*

"Slack your rope, hangs-a-man, O slack it for a while; . I think I see my fa—ther com-ing, Rid—ing man-y a mile. O fa—ther have you brought me gold? Or have you paid my fee? Or have you come to see me hang-ing On the gal-lows tree?" "I have not brought you gold; I have not paid your fee; But I have come to see you hang-ing On the gal-lows tree."

"Slack your rope, hangsaman,
O slack it for a while;
I think I see my mother[4] coming," etc.

"Slack your rope, hangsaman,
O slack it for a while;
I think I see my true love coming," etc.
"Yes, I have brought you gold;
Yes, I have paid your fee;
Nor have I come to see you hanging
On the gallows tree."

---

* *Ibid.*, pp. 37–38.

On Springfield Mountain*

On Spring-field moun-tain there did dwell A hand-some
youth, was known full well, Lieu—ten—ant
Mer—rill's on-ly son, A like-ly youth, near twen-ty-one.

On Friday morning he did go
Down to the meadows for to mow.
He mowed, he mowed all around the field
With a poisonous serpent at his heel.

When he received his deathly wound
He laid his scythe down on the ground.
For to return was his intent,
Calling aloud, long as he went.

His calls were heard both far and near
But no friend to him did appear.
They thought he did some workman call.
Alas, poor man, alone did fall!

Day being past, night coming on,
The father went to seek his son,
And there he found his only son
Cold as a stone, dead on the ground.

He took him up and he carried him home
And on the way did lament and mourn,
Saying, "I heard but did not come,
And now I'm left alone to mourn."

In the month of August, the twenty-first,
When this sad accident was done.
May this a warning be to all,
To be prepared when God shall call.

---

* *Ibid.*, pp. 15–16.

SONGS OF SAILORMEN AND RIVERMEN

Blow, Ye Winds*

'Tis ad—ver—tised in Bos——ton, New York and Buf—fa—lo, Five hun—dred brave A—mer—i—cans, a—whal—ing for to go, sing—ing,

Chorus

Blow, ye winds in the morn—ing, And blow, ye winds, high—o! Clear a—way your run—ning gear, And blow, ye winds, high——o!

They send you to New Bedford, that famous whaling port,
And give you to some land-sharks to board and fit you out.

They send you to a boarding-house, there for a time to dwell;
The thieves they there are thicker than the other side of hell!

They tell you of the clipper-ships a-going in and out,
And say you'll take five hundred sperm before you're six months
out.

It's now we're out to sea, my boys, the wind comes on to blow;
One half the watch is sick on deck, the other half below.

But as for the provisions, we don't get half enough;
A little piece of stinking beef and a blamed small bag of duff.

* From *Songs of American Sailormen*, by Joanna C. Colcord, pp. 191–192.
Copyright, 1938, by W. W. Norton & Company. New York.

Now comes that damned old compass, it will grieve your heart
full sore.
For theirs is two-and-thirty points and we have forty-four.

Next comes the running rigging, which you're all supposed to
know;
'Tis "Lay aloft, you son-of-a-gun, or overboard you go!"

The cooper's at the vise-bench, a-making iron poles,
And the mate's upon the main hatch a-cursing all our souls.

The Skipper's on the quarter-deck a-squinting at the sails,
When up aloft the lookout sights a school of whales.

"Now clear away the boats, my boys, and after him we'll travel,
But if you get too near his fluke, he'll kick you to the devil!"

Now we have got him turned up, we tow him alongside;
We over with our blubber-hooks and rob him of his hide.

Now the boat-steerer overside the tackle overhauls,
The Skipper's in the main-chains, so loudly he does bawl!

Next comes the stowing down, my boys; 'twill take both night and
day.
And you'll all have fifty cents apiece on the hundred and ninetieth
lay.

Now we are bound into Tonbas, that blasted whaling port,
And if you run away, my boys, you surely will get caught.

Now we are bound into Tuckoona, full more in their power,
Where the skippers can buy the Consul up for half a barrel of
flour!

But now that our old ship is full and we don't give a damn,
We'll bend on all our stu'nsails and sail for Yankee land.

When we get home, our ship made fast, and we get through our
sailing,
A winding glass around we'll pass and damn this blubber whaling!

Greenland Fishery*

'Twas in eigh-teen hun-dred and fif-ty-three And of June the thir—teenth day, That our gal—lant ship her an—chor weighed, And for Green—land bore a——way, brave boys, And for Green——land bore a——way.

The lookout in the crosstrees stood,
With his spyglass in his hand.
"There's a whale, there's a whale, there's a whalefish," he cried,
"And she blows at every span, brave boys,
And she blows at every span."

The captain stood on the quarter-deck,
And a fine little man was he.
"Overhaul! Overhaul! Let your davit-tackles fall,
And launch your boats for sea, brave boys,
And launch your boats for sea."

Now the boats were launched and the men aboard,
And the whale was in full view;
Resolv-ed was each seaman bold
To steer where the whalefish blew, brave boys,
To steer where the whalefish blew.

We struck that whale, the line paid out,
But she gave a flourish with her tail;
The boat capsized and four men were drowned,
And we never caught that whale, brave boys,
And we never caught that whale.

"To lose the whale," our captain said,
"It grieves my heart full sore;

---

* *Ibid.*, pp. 151–152.

But oh! to lose four gallant men,
It grieves me ten times more, brave boys,
It grieves me ten times more."

"The winter star doth now appear,
So, boys, we'll anchor weigh;
It's time to leave this cold country,
And homeward bear away, brave boys,
And homeward bear away."

Oh, Greenland is a dreadful place,
A land that's never green,
Where there's ice and snow, and the whalefishes blow,
And the daylight's seldom seen, brave boys,
And the daylight's seldom seen.

Stormalong*

Old Stormy he is dead and gone,
Oh, poor old Stormy's dead and gone.

We'll dig his grave with a silver spade, *(twice)*

And lower him down with a golden chain. *(twice)*

I wish I was old Stormy's son;
I'd build me a ship of a thousand ton.

I'd sail this wide world round and round;
With plenty of money I'd be found.

I'd fill her up with New England rum,
And all my shellbacks they'd have some.

Oh, Stormy's dead and gone to rest;
Of all the sailors he was the best.

* *Ibid.,* pp. 88–89.

Raftsman Jim and His Songs*

IT WAS NOT ALWAYS hymnody of a kind to edify the youthful mind, but I am bound to say that, when there were children about, the raftsmen, if they happened to be sufficiently sober, would put some restraint upon both their language and their lyric offerings. They had a singular and absorbing passion for music—crude music, but still something approaching melody. Most rafts carried fiddlers as conscientiously as they carried cooks.

A few of the old songs and their tunes still run in my memory. Those that provided a chorus or an opportunity to dance a few steps between the stanzas were the favorites. "One-Eyed Riley" went like this:

He was prime fav'-rite out our way, The
wo-men folks all loved him dear-ly; He taught the par-sons
how to pray, An' he got their tin, or pret—ty near-ly.
He's the man they speak of high-ly! W—a—h—hoop! [Spoken]
Chorus
Rid—dle, lid—dle, link—tum! One—eyed Ri—ley!

The music now goes on without stopping, the air is repeated, and they dance out the measure until they come to the chorus:

> W-a-h-hoop!!
> Riddle, liddle, linktum!—[*pause*]
> One-eyed Riley!

When "tum" is reached, all the boot-soles must slap the floor together. Then the dancers remain rigid until the refrain, which they deliver with roaring enthusiasm, "One-eyed Riley!"

* From *A-Rafting on the Mississip'*, by Charles Edward Russell, pp. 205–219. Copyright, 1928, by Charles Edward Russell. New York and London: The Century Co.

"The Big Maquoketa," flowerage of an undiscovered river laureate, was sung to an alteration of an air once a favorite in the politest circles.

"Raftsman Jim" was a narrative of somewhat dubious adventures of a youth that embodied the ideals of gallantry and daring supposed to typify the calling. The air was pilfered. I can recall a few stanzas. One went thus:

As in the other instance, the air was repeated after a stanza, when everybody danced, ending with four slapping steps sounding in unison and the roaring of the refrain:

Dandy, handy Raftsman Jim!

But at all times the standard favorite was "Buffalo Gals."
I have been told that this song originated on the old Erie
Canal and landed early on the Mississippi in the keel-boat
days, before the advent of steam. If so, it is the eldest of these
lyrics, and certainly it had the widest vogue. From Pembina
to New Orleans men sang it and danced to it; taken by its
lively refrain and the pleasant alternations in its recurrent
phrasing.

If the words had been twice as boshy—a thing that would
not be in nature—that refrain would still have carried them.
I offer the text with a sense of humiliation; and yet I have
found this song on old Broadway programs as having been
sung to audiences that ought to have known better, and there
is evidence that East and West it was the darling of its times.

I ask'd her would she have some talk,
   Have some talk,
   Have some talk,
As she stood close to me. [*Chorus*]

I ask'd her would she have some dance,
   Have some dance,
   Have some dance.
I thought that I might get a chance
To shake a foot with her. [*Chorus*]

I'd like to make that gal my wife,
    Gal my wife,
    Gal my wife.
I'd be happy all my life
If I had her by me. [Chorus]

* * * * *

LUMBERJACK SONGS

The Bigler's Crew*

Come all my boys and listen, a song i'll sing to you. It's all about the Big-ler and of her jol-ly crew. In Mil-wau-kee last Oc-to-ber I chanced to get a sight In the schoo-ner called the Big-ler be-long-ing to De-troit.

Chorus

Watch her, catch her, jump up on her ju-ber-ju. Give her the sheet and let her slide, The boys will push her through. You ought to seen us howl-ing, the winds were blow-ing free, On our pas-sage down to Buf-fa-lo from Mil-wau-kee.

* From *Ballads and Songs of the Shanty-Boy*, collected and edited by Franz Rickaby, pp. 168–172. Copyright, 1926, by Harvard University Press. Cambridge.

It was on a Sunday morning about the hour of ten,
The Robert Emmet towed us out into Lake Michigan;
We set sail where she left us in the middle of the fleet,
And the wind being from the south'ard, oh, we had to give her
     sheet.

Then the wind chopped round to the sou'-sou'west and blew both
     fresh and strong,
But softly through Lake Michigan the Bigler she rolled on,
And far beyond her foaming bow the dashing waves did fling.
With every inch of canvas set, her course was wing and wing.

But the wind it came ahead before we reached the Manitous.
Three dollars and a half a day just suited the Bigler's crew.
From there unto the Beavers we steered her full and by,
And we kept her to the wind, my boys, as close as she would lie.

Through Skillagalee and Wabble Shanks, the entrance to the
     Straits,
We might have passed the big fleet there if they'd hove to and
     wait;
But we drove them on before us, the nicest you ever saw,
Out into Lake Huron from the Straits of Mackinaw.

We made Presque Isle Light, and then we boomed away,
The wind it being fair, for the Isle of Thunder Bay.
But when the wind it shifted, we hauled her on her starboard tack,
With a good lookout ahead for the Light of the Point Aubarques.

We made the Light and kept in sight of Michigan North Shore,
A-booming for the river as we'd ofttimes done before.
When right abreast Port Huron Light, our small anchor we let go
And the Sweepstakes came alongside and took the Bigler in tow.

The Sweepstakes took eight in tow and all of us fore and aft,
She towed us down to Lake St. Clare and stuck us on the flats.
She parted the Hunter's tow-line in trying to give relief,
And stem and stern went the Bigler into the boat called Maple
     Leaf.

The Sweepstakes then she towed us outside the River Light,
Lake Erie for to roam and the blustering winds to fight.
The wind being from the south'ard, we paddled our own canoe,
With her nose pointed for the Dummy she's hell bent for Buffalo.

We made the Oh and passed Long Point, the wind was blowing
     free,
We howled along the Canada shore, Port Colborne on our lee.
What is it that looms up ahead, so well known as we draw near?
For like a blazing star shone the light on Buffalo Pier.

And now we are safely landed in Buffalo Creek at last,
And under Riggs' elevator the Bigler she's made fast.
And in some lager beer saloon we'll let the bottle pass,
For we are jolly shipmates and we'll drink a social glass.

Gerry's Rocks*

Come all ye true born shan-ty-boys, Who-ev-er that ye be, I would have you pay at-ten-tion and lis-ten un-to me, Con-cern-ing a young shan-ty-boy, so tall, gen-teel and brave, 'Twas on a jam on Ger-ry's Rocks he met a wa-try grave.

It happened on a Sunday morn as you shall quickly hear.
Our logs were piled up mountain high, there being no one to keep
   them clear.
Our boss he cried, "Turn out, brave boys. Your hearts are void
   of fear.
We'll break that Jam on Gerry's Rocks, and for Agonstown we'll
   steer."

Some of them were willing enough, but others they hung back.
'Twas for to work on Sabbath they did not think 'twas right.
But six of our brave Canadian boys did volunteer to go
And break the jam on Gerry's Rocks with their foreman, young
   Monroe.

They had not rolled off many logs when the boss to them did say,
"I'd have you be on your guard, brave boys. That jam will soon
   give way."
But scarce the warning had he spoke when the jam did break and
   go,
And it carried away these six brave youths and their foreman,
   young Monroe.

* *Ibid.*, pp. 11–14.

When the rest of the shanty-boys these sad tidings came to hear,
To search for their dead comrades to the river they did steer.
One of these a headless body found, to their sad grief and woe,
Lay cut and mangled on the beach the head of young Monroe.

They took him from the water and smoothed down his raven hair.
There was one fair form amongst them, her cries would rend the air.
There was one fair form amongst them, a maid from Saginaw town.
Her sighs and cries would rend the skies for her lover that was drowned.

They buried him quite decently, being on the seventh of May.
Come all the rest of you shanty-boys, for your dead comrade pray.
'Tis engraved on a little hemlock tree that at his head doth grow,
The name, the date, and the drowning of this hero, young Monroe.

Miss Clara was a noble girl, likewise the raftsman's friend.
Her mother was a widow woman lived at the river's bend.
The wages of her own true love the boss to her did pay,
And a liberal subscription she received from the shanty-boys next day.

Miss Clara did not long survive her great misery and grief.
In less than three months afterwards death came to her relief.
In less than three months afterwards she was called to go,
And her last request was granted—to be laid by young Monroe.

Come all the rest of ye shanty-men who would like to go and see,
On a little mound by the river's bank there stands a hemlock tree.
The shanty-boys cut the woods all around. These lovers they lie low.
Here lies Miss Clara Dennison and her shanty-boy, Monroe.

The Little Brown Bulls*

Not a thing on the riv-er Mc——Clus——key did fear When

he drew the stick o'er the big spot—ted steers. They were

* *Ibid.,* pp. 65–68.

young, quick, and sound, girt-ing eight foot and three. Says Mc-
Clus-key the Scotch-man, "They're the lad—dies for me."
Chorus
Der——ry down, down, down der-ry down.

Bull Gordon, the Yankee, on skidding was full,
As he cried "Whoa-*hush*" to the little brown bulls.
Short-legged and soggy, girt six foot and nine.
Says McCluskey the Scotchman, "Too light for our pine."

It's three to the thousand our contract did call.
Our hauling was good and the timber was tall.
McCluskey he swore he'd make the day full
And skid two to one of the little brown bulls.

"Oh no," says Bull Gordon; "that you cannot do,
Though it's well do we know you've the pets of the crew.
And mark you, my boy, you would have your hands full,
If you skid one more log than the little brown bulls."

The day was appointed and soon it drew nigh,
For twenty-five dollars their fortunes to try.
Both eager and anxious that morning were found,
And scalers and judges appeared on the ground.

With a whoop and a yell came McCluskey in view,
With the big spotted steers, the pets of the crew,
Both chewing their cuds—"O boys, keep your jaws full,
For you easily can beat them, the little brown bulls."

Then out came Bull Gordon with a pipe in his jaw,
The little brown bulls with their cuds in their mouths;
And little we think, when we seen them come down,
That a hundred and forty could they jerk around.

Then up spoke McCluskey: "Come stripped to the skin.
We'll dig them a hole and tumble them in.
We'll learn the d—d Yankee to face the bold Scot.
We'll mix them a dose and feed it red hot."

Said Gordon to Stebbin, with blood in his eye,
"Today we must conquer McCluskey or die."
Then up spoke bold Kennebec, "Boy, never fear,
For you ne'er shall be beat by the big spotted steers."

The sun had gone down when the foreman did say,
"Turn out, boys, turn out; you've enough for the day.
We have scaled them and counted, each man to his team,
And it's well do we know now which one kicks the beam."

After supper was over McCluskey appeared
With the belt ready made for the big spotted steers.
To form it he'd torn up his best mackinaw.
He was bound he'd conduct it according to law.

Then up spoke the scaler, "Hold on, you, a while.
The big spotted steers are behind just one mile.
For you have a hundred and ten and no more,
And Gordon has beat you by ten and a score."

The shanty did ring and McCluskey did swear.
He tore out by handfuls his long yellow hair.
Says he to Bull Gordon, "My colors I'll pull.
So here, take the belt for the little brown bulls."

Here's health to Bull Gordon and Kennebec John;
The biggest day's work on the river they done.
So fill up your glasses and fill them up full;
We'll drink to the health of the little brown bulls.

COWBOY SONGS

The Old Chisholm Trail*

Come a-long boys and lis-ten to my tale, I'll
tell you of my trou-bles on the old Chis-holm trail, Come a
ti yi yip—pee, come a ti yi yea, Come a
ti yi yip—pee, come a ti yi yea.

* From *American Songs for American Children*, [edited by Alan Lomax, Charles Seeger, and Ruth Crawford Seeger], pp. 8–9. Chicago: Music Educators National Conference. 1942.

Oh, a ten-dollar hoss and a forty-dollar saddle,
And I'm goin' to punchin' Texas cattle.

I wake in the mornin' afore daylight
And afore I sleep the moon shines bright.

It's cloudy in the west, a-lookin' like rain,
And my durned old slicker's in the wagon again.

No chaps, no slicker, and it's pourin' down rain,
And I swear, by gosh, I'll never night-herd again.

Feet in the stirrups and seat in the saddle,
I hung and rattled with them long-horn cattle.

The wind commenced to blow, and the rain began to fall,
Hit looked, by grab, like we was goin' to lose 'em all.

I don't give a darn if they never do stop;
I'll ride as long as an eight-day clock.

We rounded 'em up and put 'em on the cars,
And that was the last of the old Two Bars.

Oh, it's bacon and beans most every day,
I'd as soon be a-eatin' prairie hay.

I went to the boss to draw my roll,
He had it figgered out I was nine dollars in the hole.

Goin' back to town to draw my money,
Goin' back home to see my honey.

With my knees in the saddle and my seat in the sky,
I'll quit punchin' cows in the sweet by and by.

Git Along, Little Dogies*

As I was a-walk-ing one morn—ing for plea-sure, I
spied a young cow-punch-er rid—ing a—lone, His

---

* From *Singing Cowboy,* A Book of Western Songs, collected and edited
by Margaret Larkin, arranged for the piano by Helen Black, pp. 96–97.
Copyright, 1931, by Alfred A. Knopf, Inc. New York.

hat was throwed back and his spurs was a—jing—ling,
As he ap—proached me a — sing—ing this song.
Chorus
Whoop-ee ti yi yo, git a — long, lit—tle do—gies, Its
your mis—for—tune and none of my own, Whoop-ee
ti yi yo, git a — long, lit—tle do—gies, For you
know Wy—o—ming will be your new home.

Some fellows goes up the trail for pleasure,
But that's where they've got it most awfully wrong,
For you haven't an idea the trouble they give us,
As we go a-driving them dogies along.

Oh, you'll be soup for Uncle Sam's Injuns,
"It's beef, heap beef," I hear them cry.
Git along, git along, you lazy little mavericks,
You're going to be beef steers by and by.

The night's coming on, we'll hold them on the bedground,
These little dogies that roll on so slow.
Round up the herd and cut out the strays,
And roll the little dogies that never rolled before.

The Buffalo Skinners*

Come all you jol—ly cow-boys, and lis—ten to my song, There

---

* From Resettlement Song Sheets, [edited by Charles Seeger]. "Number 7 of a series of American songs to supplement popular collections." Washington, D. C.: Special Skills Division of the Resettlement Administration. [1936–1937.]

As sung by John A. Lomax.

are not man—y vers—es, it won't de—tain you long; Its con—
cern—ing some young fel—lows who did a—gree to go   And
spend one sum—mer pleas—ant—ly on the range of the buf—fa—lo.

It happened in Jacksboro, in the spring of seventy-three,
A man by the name of Crego came stepping up to me;
Says, "How do you do, young fellow, and how would you like to go
And spend one summer pleasantly on the range of the buffalo?"

"It's me being out of employment," this to Crego I did say,
"This going out on the buffalo range depends upon the pay;
But if you will pay good wages, and transportation too,
I think, sir, I will go with you to the range of the buffalo."

"Yes, I will pay good wages, give transportation too,
Provided you will go with me and stay the summer through;
But if you should grow homesick, come back to Jacksboro,
I won't pay transportation from the range of the buffalo."

It's now we've crossed Pease River, boys, our troubles have begun.
The first damned tail I went to rip, gosh! how I cut my thumb!
While skinning the damned old stinkers our lives wasn't a show,
For the Indians watched to pick us off while skinning the buffalo.

Our meat it was buffalo rump and iron wedge bread,
And all we had to sleep on was a buffalo robe for a bed;
The fleas and graybacks worked on us, oh, boys, it was not slow,
I'll tell you there's no worse hell on earth than the range of the
    buffalo.

The season being near over, old Crego he did say
The crowd had been extravagant, was in debt to him that day.
We coaxed him and we begged him, and still it was no go—
We left his damned old bones to bleach on the range of the
    buffalo.

Oh, it's now we've crossed Pease River and homeward we are
    bound,
No more in that hell-fired country shall ever we be found.
Go home to our wives and sweethearts, tell others not to go,
For God's forsaken the buffalo range and the damned old buffalo.

Rye Whisky*

I'll eat when I'm hun-gry, I'll drink when I'm dry; If the hard times don't kill me, I'll live till I die. *Refrain* Rye whis-ky, rye whis-ky, rye whis-ky, I cry, If you don't give me rye whis-ky, I sure-ly will die.

I'll tune up my fiddle, and I'll rosin my bow,
And make myself welcome wherever I go.

Beefsteak when I'm hungry, red liquor when I'm dry,
Greenbacks when I'm hard up, and religion when I die.

They say I drink whisky; my money's my own,
All them that don't like me can leave me alone.

Sometimes I drink whisky, sometimes I drink rum,
Sometimes I drink brandy, at other times none.

But if I get boozy, my whisky's my own,
And them that don't like me can leave me alone.

Jack o' diamonds, jack o' diamonds, I know you of old,
You've robbed my poor pockets of silver and gold.

Oh, whisky, you villain, you've been my downfall;
You've kicked me, you've cuffed me, but I love you for all.

If the ocean was whisky and I was a duck
I'd dive to the bottom and get one sweet suck.

But the ocean ain't whisky and I ain't a duck,
So we'll round up the cattle and then we'll get drunk.

Sweet milk when I'm hungry, rye whisky when I'm dry,
If a tree don't fall on me, I'll live till I die.

* From *Cowboy Songs and Other Frontier Ballads*, collected by John A. Lomax and Alan Lomax, Revised and Enlarged, pp. 163–165. Copyright, 1910, 1916, 1938, by The Macmillan Company. New York. Copyright, 1938, by John A. Lomax.

I'll buy my own whisky, I'll make my own stew;
If I get drunk, madam, it's nothing to you.

I'll drink my own whisky, I'll drink my own wine;
Some ten thousand bottles I've killed in my time.

I'll drink and I'll gamble, my money's my own,
And them that don't like me can leave me alone.

My foot in the stirrup, my bridle in my hand,
A-courting fair Mollie, to marry if I can.

My foot's in my stirrup, my bridle's in my hand;
I'm leaving sweet Mollie, the fairest in the land.

Her parents don't like me, they say I'm too poor;
They say I'm unworthy to enter her door.

I've no wife to quarrel, no babies to bawl;
The best way of living is no wife at all.

Way up on Clinch Mountain I wander alone;
I'm as drunk as the devil. Oh, let me alone.

You may boast of your knowledge, and brag of your sense,
'Twill all be forgotten a hundred years hence.

I Ride an Old Paint*

I ride an old paint, and I lead an old dam, I'm going to Mon-ta-na for to throw the hou-li-han. They feed in the cou-lees and wa-ter in the draw; Their tails are all mat-ted, and their backs are all raw. *Chorus* Git a-long, you. little do-gies, git a-long there slow, for the fi-ery and the snuf-fy are a-r'ar-ing to go!

* From *Singing Cowboy*, A Book of Western Songs, collected and edited by Margaret Larkin. Arranged for the piano by Helen Black, pp. 17-19. Copyright, 1931, by Alfred A. Knopf, Inc. New York City.

Old Bill Jones had two daughters and a song,
One went to Denver and the other went wrong.
His wife she died in a pool room fight,
But still he sings from morning till night.

Oh, when I die take my saddle from the wall,
Put it on my pony, lead him out of his stall,
Tie my bones to his back, turn our faces to the West,
And we'll ride the prairies that we love best.
Chorus:
   Ride around the little dogies, ride around 'em slow,
   For the fiery and the snuffy are a-r'aring to go!

The Cowboy's Lament*

As I walked out in the streets of La-re—do, As I walked out in la—re—do one day, I spied a poor cow—boy wrapped up in white lin—en, Wrapped up in white lin—en as cold as the clay.

"Oh beat the drum slowly and play the fife lowly,
Play the dead march as you carry me along;
Take me to the green valley, there lay the sod o'er me,
For I'm a young cowboy and I know I've done wrong.

"I see by your outfit that you are a cowboy"—
These words he did say as I boldly stepped by.
"Come sit down beside me and hear my sad story;
I am shot in the breast and I know I must die.

* From *Cowboy Songs and Other Frontier Ballads*, collected by John A. Lomax and Alan Lomax. Revised and Enlarged, pp. 417–420. Copyright, 1910, 1916, 1938, by The Macmillan Company. New York. Copyright, 1938, by John A. Lomax.

"Let sixteen gamblers came handle my coffin,
Let sixteen cowboys come sing me a song.
Take me to the graveyard and lay the sod o'er me,
For I'm a poor cowboy and I know I've done wrong.

"My friends and relations they live in the Nation,
They know not where their boy has gone.
He first came to Texas and hired to a ranchman
Oh, I'm a young cowboy and I know I've done wrong.

"It was once in the saddle I used to go dashing,
It was once in the saddle I used to go gay;
First to the dram-house and then to the card-house;
Got shot in the breast and I am dying today.

"Get six jolly cowboys to carry my coffin;
Get six pretty maidens to bear up my pall.
Put bunches of roses all over my coffin,
Put roses to deaden the sods as they fall.

"Then swing your rope slowly and rattle your spurs lowly,
And give a wild whoop as you carry me along;
And in the grave throw me and roll the sod o'er me
For I'm a young cowboy and I know I've done wrong.

"Oh, bury beside me my knife and six-shooter,
My spurs on my heel, my rifle by my side,
And over my coffin put a bottle of brandy
That the cowboys may drink as they carry me along.

"Go bring me a cup, a cup of cold water,
To cool my parched lips," the cowboy then said;
Before I returned his soul had departed,
And gone to the round-up—the cowboy was dead.

We beat the drum slowly and played the fife lowly,
And bitterly wept as we bore him along;
For we all loved our comrade, so brave, young, and handsome,
We all loved our comrade although he'd done wrong.

MINERS' SONGS

What Was Your Name in the States?*

Oh, what was your name in the States? Was it Thomp—son or John—son or Bates? Did you mur—der your wife And fly for your life? Say, what was your name in the States?

Sweet Betsy from Pike**

Oh, don't you re-mem-ber sweet Bet-sey from Pike, Who crossed the big moun-tains with her lov-er Ike, With two yoke of cat-tle, a large yel-low dog, A tall shang-hai roost-er and one spot-ted hog.

Chorus:
Singing tooral lal looral lal looral lal la,
Singing tooral lal looral lal looral lal la,
Sing tooral lal looral, sing tooral lal la,
Singing tooral lal looral lal looral lal la.

* From *The American Songbag*, by Carl Sandburg, p. 106. Copyright, 1927, by Harcourt, Brace & Company, Inc.
** From *Put's Golden Songster*, Containing the Largest and Most Popular Collection of California Songs Ever Published, by the Author of "Put's Original California Songster," pp. 50–52. Copyright, 1858, by John A. Stone. San Francisco: D. E. Appleton & Co.

One evening quite early they camped on the Platte,
'Twas near by the road on a green shady flat,
Where Betsey, sore-footed, lay down to repose—
With wonder Ike gazed on that Pike County rose.

Their wagon broke down with a terrible crash,
And out on the prairie rolled all kinds of trash;
A few little baby clothes done up with care—
'Twas rather suspicious, though all on the *square*.

The shanghai ran off, and their cattle all died;
That morning the last piece of bacon was fried;
Poor Ike was discouraged, and Betsey got mad,
The dog drooped his tail and looked wondrously sad.

They stopped at Salt Lake to inquire the way,
When Brigham declared that sweet Betsey should stay;
But Betsey got frightened and ran like a deer,
While Brigham stood pawing the ground like a steer.

They soon reached the desert, where Betsey gave out,
And down in the sand she lay rolling about;
While Ike, half distracted, looked on with surprise,
Saying, "Betsey, get up, you'll get sand in your eyes."

Sweet Betsey got up in a great deal of pain,
Declared she'd go back to Pike County again;
But Ike gave a sigh, and they fondly embraced,
And they travelled along with his arm round her waist.

They suddenly stopped on a very high hill,
With wonder looked down upon old Placerville;
Ike sighed when he said, and he cast his eyes down,
"Sweet Betsey, my darling, we've got to Hangtown."

Long Ike and sweet Betsey attended a dance;
Ike wore a pair of his Pike County pants;
Sweet Betsey was covered with ribbons and rings;
Say Ike, "You're an angel, but where are your wings?"

A miner said, "Betsey, will you dance with me?"
"I will that, old hoss, if you don't make too free;
But don't dance me hard; do you want to know why?
Dog on you! I'm chock full of strong alkali!"

This Pike County couple got married of course,
And Ike became jealous—obtained a divorce;
Sweet Betsey, well satisfied, said with a shout,
"Good-by, you big lummox, I'm glad you've backed out!"

Lousy Miner*

It's four long years since I reached this land, In search of gold a-mong the rocks and sand; And yet I'm poor when the truth is told. I'm a lous—y min— er, I'm a lous—y min—er in search of shin—ing gold.

I've lived on swine till I grunt and squeal,
No one can tell how my bowels feel,
With slapjacks a-swimming round in bacon grease.
I'm a lousy miner,
I'm a lousy miner; when will my troubles cease?

I was covered with lice coming on the boat,
I threw away my fancy swallow-tailed coat,
And now they crawl up and down my back;
I'm a lousy miner,
I'm a lousy miner, a pile is all I lack.

My sweetheart vowed she'd wait for me
Till I returned; but don't you see
She's married now, sure, so I'm told,
Left her lousy miner,
Left her lousy miner, in search of shining gold.

Oh, land of gold, you did me deceive,
And I intend in thee my bones to leave;
So farewell, home, now my friends grow cold,
I'm a lousy miner,
I'm a lousy miner in search of shining gold.

* From *The Gold Rush Song Book*, Comprising a Group of Twenty-Five Authentic Ballads as They Were Sung by the Men Who Dug for Gold in California during the Period of the Great Gold Rush of 1849, compiled by Eleanora Black and Sidney Robertson, pp. 24–25. Copyright, 1940, by the Colt Press. San Francisco, California.

Me Johnny Mitchell Man*

Oh, you know Joe Sil-o-vats-ky, Dat man my brud-der; Last night him come fer my shan-ty: John, I'm come un tell you fer, I'm tell you fer to-mor-ra,   Ev'—ninck dark like night; Lot-sa min-ers all, beeg un shmall, Gon-na have a shtrike.

Dunt be shcab-by fel-la, John, Dat's I'm tell you right." I'm say, "No sir, Joe, come out on shtrike, Me John-ny Mit-chell man."

Chorus

Vell, I dunt 'fraid fer not-tink, Dat's me nev-air shcare, Cam-in' shtrike to-mor-ra night? Dat's de biz-ness, I dunt care.

Right-a here I'm tell-a you,   Me no shcab-by fel-la, Me good un-ion cit-i-zen, Me John—ny Mit-chell man.

Vell, me belong fer union,
Me good citizen,
Seven, mebbe 'leven, year,
I'm vorkin' in beeg, beeg, 'merica;
I'm vorkin' fer de Black Heat',
Down in Lytle shaft,
In de Pine Hill shaft, Pine Knot shaft,

---

* From *Minstrels of the Mine Patch*, Song and Stories of the Anthracite Industry, by George Korson, pp. 234–236. Copyright, 1938, by the University of Pennsylvania Press, Philadelphia.

Un every place like dat.
Me got lotsa money,
Nine hoondret, mebbe ten,
Un shtrike kin come, like son-of-a-gun,
Me Johnny Mitchell man.

Ah, son-of-a-gun, Mr. Truesdale,
Dat's a bugger, Mr. Baer,
He dunt vantsa gib it ten per zent,
Cripes a'mighty dat's no fair.
I'm vorkin' in a gangway,
Vorkin' in a breast,
I'm loadin' coal every day,
By jeez, me nevair rest.
Me got lotsa money,
Nine hoondret, mebbe ten,
Un shtrike kin come, like son-of-a-gun,
Me Johnny Mitchell man.

Down, Down, Down*

"Down, Down, Down," another barroom ballad, relates the experiences of a miner reporting for work with a hangover. But it is more than the record of a tipsy worker's muddled thoughts. Rather is it a reflection of the anthracite miner's buffetings which gives it added significance.

With your kind at—ten-tion, a song I will trill, All ye who must toil with the pick and the drill, And sweat for your bread in that hole in Oak Hill, That goes down, down, down.

* *Ibid.*, pp. 38–41, 48–53.

When I was a boy says my daddy to me;
"Stay out of Oak Hill, take my warning," says he,
"Or with dust you'll be choked and a pauper you'll be,
Broken down, down, down."

But I went to Oak Hill and I asked for a job,
A mule for to drive or a gangway to rob.
The boss said, "Come out, Bill, and follow the mob
That goes down, down, down."

On the strength of the job and the tune of this rhyme,
I strolled into Tim's an' drank twenty-five shines;
Reported next morning, half dead but on time
To go down, down, down.

Says Pete McAvoy, "Here's Bill Keatin' the scamp."
Just back, Pete supposed, from a million-mile tramp.
Pete showed me the "windie" where I'd get a lamp
To go down, down, down.

The lamp man he squints through the window at me,
"What's your name? What's your age? What's your number?" says
   he
"Bill Keatin', I'm thirty, number twenty-three,
Mark that down, down, down."

With a frown of disfavor, my joke it was met,
For an argument plainly, the lamp man was set.
He told me that divil a damp would I get
To go down, down, down.

Says I, "Mr. Lamp Man, now don't l'ave us fight;
Can't ye see be me eyes I was boozin' all night?
Sure the mines will be dark and I'll have to have light
While I'm down, down, down."

With an old greasy apron, Jim polished his specks,
Declarin' the lamp house rules would be wrecked,
If he'd give out his lantherns 'thout gettin' brass checks
From us Clowns! Clowns! Clowns!

I found the supply clerk, of him I inquired
If he had any checks of the sort Jim desired.
He said: "Here's a check, if you lose it, you're fired,
Mark that down, down, down."

I had the precious lamp check that would pacify Jim,
Flip, into his window, I flung it to him
Sayin', "Now quit your grumbling, an' give me a glim
To go down, down, down."

A contraption Jim gave me, a hose on a box,
'Twas so heavy I thought it was loaded with rocks.
If a car jumped the track, you could use it for blocks
While you're down, down, down.

The box breaks the bones in the small of your back,
Wears the hide off your hips where it hangs be a strap;
Oh! the gawk that transported such lamps to the Gap
May go down, down, down.

When you ask for a lamp you commit an offense,
You'd imagine the lamp man stood all the expense;
While for lamps that won't light we pay sixty-five cents
While we're down, down, down.

We wait at Jim's window while winter winds stab,
While the lamp man unravels a lot of crank gab.
Did ye e'er meet a lamp man that wasn't a crab
In your rounds? Aren't they hounds?

Crabbed lamp lords, ye'll cringe for your cranks whin ye die,
For the way that ye bulldozed me butties and I;
Me and Tracy'll be twanging this ballad on high
While you're down, down, down.

Then into the office I sauntered to Boss Sam.
With a cheery "Good mornin'," says I, "here I am,
With booze in me bottle and beer in me can
To go down, down, down."

"Well, Billy, me bucko, how are you today?"
"Outside of a headache," says I, "I'm O.K.
I've been samplin' the soda in every café
In the town, town, town.

'Sam, where is my job at?" I wanted to know.
"Was it in the new drift?" Sam shook his head, no.
"When you hit the fifth lift you'll have one more to go,
So get down, down, down."

I asked Sam what tools would I need in the place.
"Very few," said the boss with a grin on his face.
"One seven-size scoop in a coop-stoopy space
Away down, down, down."

With a note from the boss to the shaft I made haste,
Saluted the top-man and in line took me place
Sayin' "Gi' me a cage, for I've no time to waste,
Let me down, down, down."

"All aboard for the bottom!" the top-man did yell,
We stepped on the cage, he ding-donged a bell;
Through that hole in Oak Hill, like a bat out o' hell
We went down, down, down.

In wet or dry weather that shaft always rains,
There's a trembling of timbers and clanking of chains.
Just off of a spree, it flip-flopped me few brains
Going down, down, down.

It happened that something was wrong with the pump;
The water was up—we struck a wet bump.
But the cage kept descending and into the sump
We went down, down, down.

I've been on the outside and inside before,
I fell into oceans and rivers galore,
But that dip in that deep dirty sump made me sore
Away down, down, down.

The fireboss he flagged me, fool questions to ask.
Was I married, or single and where I worked last.
Says I, "Lind me your pincil, me present and past
I'll write down, down, down."

Between the sump bath and headache I felt like a dope,
Going down in the gloom of the underground slope,
On a tricky man-truck and a rotten old rope,
Going down, down, down.

She was blocked from the dish to the knuckle with smoke,
The dust was so thick that I thought I would choke.
Says I to meself I guess here's where I croak
Away down, down, down.

Groped into the gangway they gave me a scoop,
The cut was just fired, muck heaped to the roof.
I stooped an' I scooped till me back looped-the-loop
Stoopin' down, down, down.

That first car we loaded held five tons I swore
And that Buck Mountain coal has the weight of iron ore.
We scooped seven cars but when they brought us one more
I laid down, down, down.

She was heaved on the bottom and cracked on the top
Ne'er a pole, ne'er a slab, ne'er a laggin', nor prop
Pretty soon I expect that Gap Mountain will drop
And come down, down, down.

That journey each morning it near breaks me heart;
The steps in the mule-way is ten feet apart;
You must watch your brogans, for if you get a start
You'll roll down, down, down.

The Oak Hill officials are foxy galoots,
With company-store tyrants they're all in cahoots;
With the gangways a river, you're bound to buy boots,
While you're down, down, down.

On pay days I rave; Rube Tracy oft swore,
In fact 'twas enough to make both of us sore,
When our wives drag our wages all out in the store
While we're down, down, down.

But yet I'm in right, for I'm on the ground floor,
In deep in the wet and in deep in the store;
If they sink Oak Hill shaft six or seven lifts more
I'll go down, down, down.

It's a most cruel fate, but continue we must,
Delvin' deep for black diamonds, beneath the earth's crust,
Moil for mush and molasses and eating coal dust
Away down, down, down.

All I drew for a year was a dollar or three,
Those company-store thieves made a pauper of me,
But for ballads like this, I'd have starved for a spree
In the town, town, town.

Toil, you put early-gray on my poor daddy's head,
While he slaved in Oak Hill to provide us with bread;
How I wish I had heeded the warning he plead:
"Don't go down, down, down."

Now my back is toil-bent, my feet work-worn, slow.
Soon the hair on my head will be white as the snow.
Then I fear I'll be shipped to the Pogie below—
Broken down, a pauperized clown.

SONGS OF THE FARMER

Young Man Who Wouldn't Hoe Corn*

I'll sing you a song and it's not ver-y long, It's a-
bout a young man who wouldn't hoe corn; The
rea — son why, I can't tell,
This young man was al — ways well.

He planted his corn in the month of June
And in July it was knee high;
First of September came a big frost
And all this young man's corn was lost.

He went to the fence and there peeped in,
The weeds and the grass came up to his chin;
The weeds and the grass they grew so high,
They caused this young man for to sigh.

So he went down to his neighbor's door,
Where he had often been before:
"Pretty little miss, will you marry me?
Pretty little miss, what do you say?"

"Here you are, a-wanting for to wed
And cannot make your own cornbread!
Single I am, single I'll remain,
A lazy man I'll not maintain.

"You go down to that pretty little widow
And I hope by heck that you don't get her."
She gave him the mitten, sure as you're born,
All because he wouldn't hoe corn.

---

* From Resettlement Song Sheets, [edited by Charles Seeger]. "Number 3
of a series of American Songs rarely found in popular collections." Washington, D. C.: Special Skills Division of the Resettlement Administration. [1936–
1937.]

Seven-Cent Cotton and Forty-Cent Meat*

Se—ven—cent cot—ton and for—ty—cent meat,
How in the world can a poor man eat? Flour up high and
cot—ton down low; How in the world can we
raise the dough? Clothes worn out, shoes run down,
Old slouch hat with a hole in the crown. Back near-ly bro-ken and
fing—ers all sore, Cot-ton gone down to rise no more.

Seven-cent cotton and eight-dollar pants,
Who in the world has got a chance?
We can't buy clothes and we can't buy meat;
Too much cotton and not enough to eat.
Can't help each other, what shall we do?
I can't explain it so it's up to you.
Seven-cent cotton and two-dollar hose,
Guess we'll have to do without any clothes.

Seven-cent cotton and forty-cent meat,
How in the world can a poor man eat?
Mules in the barn, no crops laid by,
Corn crib empty and the cow's gone dry.
Well water low, nearly out of sight,
Can't take a bath on Saturday night.
No use talking, any man is beat
With seven-cotton and forty-cent meat.

Seven-cent cotton and forty-cent meat,
How in the world can a poor man eat?

* As sung by the Almanac Singers. Transcribed by the Almanac Singers. Copyright 1929 by Triangle Music Publishing Co., Inc., under title 'Leven Cent Cotton (Forty Cent Meat), words and music by Bob Miller and Emma Dermer. Copyright assigned to Mayfair Music Corporation, New York. Used by permission.

Poor getting poorer all around here;
Kids coming regular every year.
Fatten our hogs, take 'em to town,
All we get is six cents a pound.
Very next day we have to buy it back,
Forty cents a pound in a paper sack.

We'll raise our cotton, we'll raise our meat.
We'll raise everything we eat.
We'll raise our chickens, pigs, and corn;
We'll make a living just as sure as you're born.
Farmers getting stronger every year,
Babies getting fatter all around here.
No use talking, Roosevelt's the man,
To show the world that the farmer can.

The Farmer Comes to Town*

When the far-mer comes to town, With his wag-on bro-ken down, Oh, the
far-mer is the man who feeds them all. If you'll
on-ly look and see, I am sure you will a-gree That the
Chorus
far-mer is the man who feeds them all. The
far-mer is the man, The far-mer is the man,
Lives on cred-it till the fall; Then they
take him by the hand And they lead him from the land, And the
mid—dle—man's the man who gets it all.

* From Resettlement Song Sheets, [edited by Charles Seeger]. "Number 1 in a series of American songs rarely found in popular collections." Washington, D. C.: Special Skills Division of the Resettlement Administration. [1936–1937.]

Chorus:
> The farmer is the man,
> The farmer is the man,
> Lives on credit till the fall;
> Then they take him by the hand
> And they lead him from the land,
> And the middleman's the man who gets it all.

When the lawyer hangs around,
While the butcher cuts a pound,
Oh, the farmer is the man who feeds them all.
And the preacher and the cook
Go a-strolling by the brook,
Oh, the farmer is the man who feeds them all.

Chorus:
> The farmer is the man,
> The farmer is the man,
> Lives on credit till the fall;
> With the int'rest rate so high,
> It's a wonder he don't die,
> For the mortgage man's the man who gets it all.

When the banker says he's broke,
And the merchant's up in smoke,
They forget that it's the farmer feeds them all.
It would put them to the test
If the farmer took a rest;
Then they'd know that it's the farmer feeds them all.

Chorus:
> The farmer is the man,
> The farmer is the man,
> Lives on credit till the fall;
> And his pants are wearing thin,
> His condition it's a sin;
> He's forgot that he's the man who feeds them all.

Wayfaring Stranger*

I'm just a poor way-far-ing stran-ger, a-trav'-ling

* *Ibid.* "Number 9 of a series of American songs to supplement popular collections."

through this world of woe; But there's no sick-ness, toil nor dan-ger in that bright world to which I go. I'm go-ing there to see my fa-ther, I'm go-ing there no more to roam, I'm just a-going o-ver Jor-dan, I'm just a-go-ing o-ver home

A

I'm just a poor wayfaring stranger, a-trav'ling through this world of woe;
But there's no sickness, toil nor danger in that bright world to which I go.
I'm going there to see my mother, I'm going there no more to roam,
I'm just a-going over Jordan, I'm just a-going over home.

B

The following modern verses from Virginia and Florida respectively have been received:

Our fathers dear fought for our liberty,
Across the ocean they did roam,
They suffered pain and many hardships,
For in this land to build a home.

We've lived here many generations,
And many dear ones here have died,
But still our lives are filled with trouble,
In vain a helping hand we've cried.

I'm just a poor and lonesome traveler,
Behind a mule that's powerful slow,
A-creaking on to debt and worry,
The only place that I can go.

My father lived and died a farmer,
A-reaping less than he did sow;
And now I travel in his footsteps,
A-knowing less than he did know.

HOBO AND JAILHOUSE SONGS

Hallelujah, Bum Again*

I

Oh, why don't I work like the other men do?
How the hell can I work when the skies are so blue?

Chorus:
　Hallelujah, I'm a bum!
　Hallelujah, bum again,
　Hallelujah! Bum a handout,
　Revive me again.

If I was to work and save all I earn,
I could buy me a bar and have whiskey to burn.

Oh, I love Jim Hill, he's an old friend of mine,
Up North I ride rattlers all over his line.

Oh, I ride box cars and I ride fast mails,
When it's cold in the winter I sleep in the jails.

I passed by a saloon and I hear someone snore,
And I found the bartender asleep on the floor.

I stayed there and drank till a fly-mug came in,
And he put me to sleep with a sap on the chin.

Next morning in court I was still in a haze,
When the judge looked at me, he said, "Thirty days!"

Some day a long train will run over my head,
And the sawbones will say, "Old One-Finger's dead!"

II

When spring—time does come, Oh, won't we have

---

* From *The Hobo's Hornbook*, A Repertory for a Gutter Jongleur, collected and annotated by George Milburn, pp. 97–101. Copyright, 1930, by George Milburn. New York: Ives Washburn.

fun! We'll all throw up our jobs And we'll
go on the bum. Hal—le—lu—jah, I'm a bum, Hal—le—
lu—jah, bum a—gain, Hal—le—lu—jah, give us a
hand—out To re—vive us a—gain.

Oh, springtime has come,
And I'm just out of jail,
Ain't got no money,
It all went for bail.

I went up to a house
And I knocked on the door.
A lady came out, says,
"You been here before!"

I went up to a house,
Asked for some bread;
A lady came out, says,
"The baker is dead."

I went up to a house,
Asked for a pair of pants;
A lady came out, says,
"I don't clothe no tramps!"

I went into a saloon,
And I bummed him for a drink;
He gave me a glass
And he showed me the sink.

Oh, I love my boss,
And my boss loves me;
That is the reason
I'm so hun-ga-ree!

"Why don't you go to work
Like all the other men do?"
"How the hell we going to work
When there ain't no work to do?"

The Big Rock Candy Mountains*

One ev'-ning as the sun went down And the jun-gle fire was burn-ing, Down the track came a ho-bo, ham-ming, And he said, "Boys, I'm not turn-ing. I'm head-ed for a land that's far a-way, Be-side the crys-tal foun-tains. I'll see you all this com-ing fall In the *Refrain* Big Rock Can-dy Moun-tains. In the Big Rock Can-dy Moun-tains, There's a land that's fair and bright, Where the hand-outs grow on bush-es And you sleep out ev'-ry night, Where the box-cars all are emp-ty And the sun shines ev'-ry day— Oh, the birds and the bees and the cig-a-ret trees, The rock-and-rye springs where the whang-dood-le sings, In the Big Rock Can-dy Moun-tains."

* Ibid., pp. 86–89.

"In the Big Rock Candy Mountains,
All the cops have wooden legs,
And the bulldogs all have rubber teeth,
And the hens lay softboiled eggs.
The farmers' trees are full of fruit,
And the barns are full of hay.
Oh, I'm bound to go where there ain't no snow,
Where the sleet don't fall and the wind don't blow,
In the Big Rock Candy Mountains.

"In the Big Rock Candy Mountains,
You never change your socks,
And the little streams of alkyhol
Come trickling down the rocks.
The shacks all have to tip their hats
And the railroad bulls are blind,
There's a lake of stew and of whisky, too,
You can paddle all around in a big canoe,
In the Big Rock Candy Mountains.

"In the Big Rock Candy Mountains,
The jails are made of tin,
And you can bust right out again
As soon as they put you in.
There ain't no shorthandled shovels,
No axes, saws or picks—
I'm a-going to stay where you sleep all day—
Oh, they boiled in oil the inventor of toil
In the Big Rock Candy Mountains.

"Oh, come with me, and we'll go see
The Big Rock Candy Mountains."

Pie in the Sky*

Long-haired preach-ers come out ev'-ry night, Try to
tell you what's wrong and what's right; But when

* *Ibid.*, pp. 83–85.

asked a-bout some-thing to eat, They will an-swer in ac-cents so

Chorus

sweet: You will eat bye and bye, In that

glo-ri-ous land a-bove the sky. Work and pray, live on

hay, You'll get pie in the sky when you die.

And the starvation army they play,
And they sing and they clap and they pray,
Till they get all your coin on the drum,
Then they'll tell you when you're on the bum:

Holy rollers and jumpers come out,
And they holler and jump and they shout,
But when eating time comes around they will say,
"You will eat on that glorious day."

Hard Times in Mount Holly Jail*

When you go to Mount Hol-ly, it's there where you're

set, Its whis-ky and to-bac-co you get damned a
Chorus

bit. And it's hard times in Mount Hol-ly

Jail, And it's hard times in Mount Hol-ly Jail.

Chorus:
And it's hard times in Mount Holly Jail,
And it's hard times in Mount Holly Jail.

* From "Ballads and Folk Songs from New Jersey," by Herbert Halpert,
The Journal of American Folk-Lore, Vol. 52, No. 203, pp. 67–68. Copyright, 1938, by The American Folk-Lore Society. New York.

Your hands and your feet chained down to the floor,
God damn their old souls why can't they do more.

Soup that you get is not very neat,
It's full some scraps and some damned dirty meat.

Fetched from the kitchen in an old slop pail,
And that's the way they serve you in Mount Holly Jail.

Oh lice! Oh lice! as big as young quails,
You can't help get lousy in Mount Holly Jail.

There is High Sheriff Townsell, I almost forgot,
He's greatest old loafer was in the whole lot.

If he was tried and had his just due,
He'd been sent to state's prison 'count burglaries too.

There's Billy Reeves I almost forgot,
He's the damndest old loafer was in the whole lot.

Your pockets he'll pick and your clothes he will sell,
Get drunk on your money at Townsell's hotel.

There is Mr. Pitcher, he's a very nice man,
If you ask him for a favor, he'll do it if he can.

That ain't all I'd have you to know,
Every Sunday morning we have Holy Joe.

There he will stand and the truth he will tell,
To save the poor prisoners from going to hell.

The Roving Gambler*

I am a rov-in' gam-bler, I gam-ble down in town; Where — ev-er I meet with a deck of cards I

---

* From Champion record, Number 45063 B ("Old Time Singin'"), sung with harmonica by Pie Plant Pete. Decca Records, Inc. New York. Transcribed by Peter Seeger.

lie my mon-ey down. I had not been in Wash-ing-ton

man-y more weeks than three, When I fell in love with a

pret-ty lit-tle girl and she fell in love with me.

She took me in her parlor, she cool me with her fan;
She whispered soft in her mother's ear, "I love this gambling man."
"O daughter, O dear daughter, why do you treat me so?
To leave your dear old mother and with a gambler go!"

"O mother, O dear mother, you know I love you well,
But the love I have for the gambling man no human tongue can
tell."
I've gambled down in Washington, I've gambled down in Spain,
I'm goin' down to Georgia to gamble my last game.

I hear the train a-comin', a-comin' around the curve,
A-whistlin' and a-blowin', and strainin' every nerve.
"O mother, my dear mother, I'll tell you if I can
If you ever see me comin' back it'll be with a gambling man."

MOUNTAIN SONGS

Rowan County Troubles*

Come on young men and la-dies, moth-ers and fa-thers

too, I'll re-late to you the his-try of the Row-an Coun-ty

crew, Con-cern-ing blood-y Row-an and her

* From *Ballad Makin' in the Mountains of Kentucky*, by Jean Thomas ("The Traipsin' Woman"), pp. 5–9. Copyright, 1939, by Henry Holt and Company, Inc. New York.

man-y hein-ous deeds. Now, friends, please give at-
ten-tion, re——mem-ber how it reads.

It was in the month of August upon election day,
John Martin he was wounded, they say by Johnny Day,
Martin could not believe it, he could not think it so;
He thought it was Floyd Tolliver that struck the fatal blow.

They shot and killed Sol Bradley, a sober innocent man,
He left his wife and loving children to do the best they can,
They wounded young Ad Sizemore; although his life was saved
He seemed to shun the grog shops since he stood so near the
    grave.

Martin did recover, some months had come and past,
In the town of Morehead those men both met at last;
Tolliver and a friend or two about the streets did walk,
He seemed to be uneasy and with no one wished to talk.

He walked in Judge Carey's grocery and stepped up to the bar,
But little did he think, dear friends, that he met the fatal hour;
The sting of death was near him, Martin rushed in at the door,
A few words passed between them concerning a row before.

The people soon were frightened, began to rush out of the room,
A ball from Martin's pistol laid Tolliver in the tomb.
His friends soon gathered round him, his wife to weep and wail;
Martin was arrested and soon confined in jail.

He was put in the jail of Rowan there to remain a while,
In the hands of law and justice to bravely stand his trial.
The people all talked of lynching him, at present though they
    failed,
The prisoner's friends soon moved him into the Winchester jail.

Some persons forged an order, their names I do not know,
The plan was soon agreed upon, for Martin they did go;
Martin seemed discouraged, he seemed to be in dread,
"They have sought a plan to kill me," to the jailer Martin said.

They put the handcuffs on him, his heart was in distress,
They hurried to the station, stepped on the night express.
Along the line she lumbered at her usual speed;
They were only two in numbers to commit the dreadful deed.

Martin was in the smoking car accompanied by his wife,
They did not want her present when they took her husband's life;
When they arrived at Farmers they had no time to lose,
A band approached the engineer and bid him not to move.

They stepped up to the prisoner with pistols in their hands,
In death he soon was sinking, he died in iron bands.
His wife soon heard the horrid sound; she was in another car,
She cried, "Oh Lord! they've killed him!" when she heard the
    pistol fire.

The death of these two men has caused great trouble in our land,
Caused men to leave their families and take the parting hand.
Retaliating, still at war they may never, never cease,
I would that I could only see my land once more in peace.

They killed the deputy sheriff, Baumgartner was his name,
They shot him from the bushes after taking deliberate aim;
The death of him was dreadful, it may never be forgot,
His body pierced and torn with thirty-three buckshot.

I compose this as a warning. Oh! beware, young men!
Your pistols may cause trouble, on this you may depend;
In the bottom of a whisky glass the lurking devils dwell,
It burns the breast of those who drink, it sends their souls to hell.

Crawdad*

Sit-tin' on the ice till my feet got cold, sug-ar-babe,

Sit-tin' on the ice till my feet got cold, sug-ar-babe,

Sit-tin' on the ice till my feet got cold, Watch-in' dat

craw-dad go to his hole, sug-ar-babe.

Crawdad, crawdad, you'd better dig deep, sugar-babe, *(twice)*
Crawdad, crawdad, you'd better dig deep,
For I'm a-goin' to ramble in my sleep, sugar-babe.

* *Ibid.,* pp. 245–246.

Sittin' on the ice till my feet got hot, sugar-babe, *(twice)*
Sittin' on the ice till my feet got hot,
Watchin' that crawdad rock and trot, sugar-babe.

Crawdad, crawdad, you'd better go to hole, sugar-babe, *(twice)*
Crawdad, crawdad, you'd better go to hole,
If I don't catch you, damn my soul, sugar-babe.

Sittin' on the ice till my feet got numb, sugar-babe, *(twice)*
Sittin' on the ice till my feet got numb,
Watchin' that crawdad back and come, sugar-babe.

Shoot your dice and roll 'em in the sand, sugar-babe, *(twice)*
Shoot your dice and roll 'em in the sand,
I ain't a-goin' to work for no damned man, sugar-babe.

Apple cider and cinnamon beer, sugar-babe, *(twice)*
Apple cider and cinnamon beer,
Cold hog's head and a nigger's ear, sugar-babe.

Sourwood Mountain*

She sits up with ole Si Hall,
Hey, diddledum dey.
Me and Jeff can't go there a-tall,

* From *30 and 1 Folksongs* (From the Southern Mountains), Compiled and Arranged by Bascom Lamar Lunsford and Lamar Stringfield, pp. 24–25. Copyright, 1929, by Carl Fischer, Inc. New York. International Copyright secured.

Hey, diddledum dey,
Hey, diddledum dey,
Hey, diddledum dey.
Me and Jeff can't go there a-tall,
Hey, diddledum dey.

Some-a these days before very long,
Hey, diddledum dey,
I'll get that gal and a-home I'll run,
Hey, diddledum dey,
Hey, diddledum dey,
Hey, diddledum dey.
I'll get that gal and a-home I'll run,
Hey, diddledum dey.

Cindy*

I wish I was an ap-ple, A hang-in' in the tree, And ev'-ry time my sweet-heart passed, She'd take a bite of me. She told me that she loved me, She called me su-gar plum, She threwed 'er arms a-round me— I thought my time had come.

Chorus

Git a-long home, Cin-dy, Cin-dy, Git a-long home, Cin-dy, Cin-dy, Git a-long home, Cin-dy, Cin-dy, I'll mar-ry you some time.

* *Ibid.*, pp. 42–43. Copyright, 1929, by Carl Fischer, Inc. New York. International Copyright secured.

She took me to the parlor,
She cooled me with her fan,
She swore that I's the purtiest thing
In the shape of mortal man.
Oh where did you git your liquor,
Oh where did you git your dram,
I got it from a nigger
Away down in Rockinham.

Cindy got religion,
She had it once before,
When she heard my old banjo
She 'uz the first un on the floor.
I wish I had a needle,
As fine as I could sew,
I'd sew the girls to my coat tail,
And down the road I'd go.

Careless Love*

It's on this rail-road bank I stand, It's
on this rail-road bank I stand, It's on this rail-road
bank I stand, All for the love of a rail-road man.
How I wish that train would come, How I wish that train would
come, How I wish that train would come, And
take me back where I come from. *Chorus* Love, oh, love, oh, care-less
love, Love, oh, love, oh, care-less love, Love, oh, love, oh,
care-less love, See what care-less love has done

* *Ibid.*, pp. 40–41. Copyright, 1929, by Carl Fischer, Inc. New York. International Copyright secured.

When my apron string will bow,
When my apron string will bow,
When my apron string will bow,
You'll pass my door an' say "hello."
But when my apron string won't pin,
When my apron string won't pin,
When my apron string won't pin,
You'll pass my door an' won't come in.

It's caused me to weep, it's caused me to mourn,
It's caused me to weep, it's caused me to mourn,
It's caused me to weep, it's caused me to mourn,
It's caused me to leave my happy home.
What do you reckon my mama'll say,
What do you reckon my mama'll say,
What do you reckon my mama'll say,
When she hears I've gone astray.

Down in the Valley*

Down in the val—ley, val—ley so low, Hang your head o—ver, hear the wind blow. Hear the wind blow, dear, hear the wind blow; Hang your head o—ver, hear the wind blow.

If you don't love me, love whom you please;
Throw your arms round me, give my heart ease.
Give my heart ease, dear, give my heart ease;
Throw your arms round me, give my heart ease.

Write me a letter, send it by mail;
And back it in care of Birmingham Jail.
Birmingham Jail, dear, Birmingham Jail,
And back it in care of Birmingham Jail.

---

* From Resettlement Song Sheets, [edited by Charles Seeger]. "Number 5 of a series of American songs to supplement popular collections." Washington, D. C.: Special.

Writing this letter, containing three lines,
Answer my question, "Will you be mine?"
Will you be mine, dear, will you be mine?
Answer my question, "Will you be mine?"

Go build me a castle, forty feet high,
So I can see her as she goes by.
As she goes by, dear, as she goes by,
So I can see her as she goes by.

Roses love sunshine, violets love dew;
Angels in heaven know I love you.
Know I love you, dear, know I love you,
Angels in heaven know I love you.

BLACK SONGS

I'm Gwine to Alabamy*

I'm gwine to A-la-ba-my, Oh..........
For to see my mam-my, Ah..........

She went from Ole Virginny, — Oh,
And I'm her pickaninny, — Ah.

She lives on the Tombigbee, — Oh,
I wish I had her wid me, — Ah.

Now I'm a good big nigger, — Oh,
I reckon I won't git bigger, — Ah.

But I'd like to see my mammy, — Oh,
Who lives in Alabamy, — Ah.

---

* From *Slave Songs of the United States*, by William Francis Allen, Charles Pickard Ware, Lucy McKim Garrison, p. 89. Copyright, 1867. Reprinted 1929. New York: Peter Smith.
 A very good specimen, so far as notes can give one, of the strange barbaric songs that one hears upon the Western steamboats.—W. F. A., C. P. W., L. McK. G.

Run, Nigger, Run!*

O some tell me that a nig—ger won't steal, But I've seen a nig—ger in my corn-field; O run, nig—ger, run, for the pa—trol will catch you, O run, nig—ger, run, for 'tis al—most day.

The Grey Goose**

Well, las' Mon—day morn—in', Lawd, Lawd, Lawd! Well, las' Mon—day morn—in', Lawd, Lawd, Lawd!

My daddy went a-hunting.

Well, he carried along his zulu.

Well, along come a grey goose.

Well, he throwed it to his shoulder.

Well, he reared his hammer 'way back.

Well, he pulled on his trigger.

Well, a-down he come windin'.

He was six weeks a-fallin'.

We was six weeks a-findin'.

And we put him on his wagon.

And we taken him to the white house.

---

* Ibid., p. 89.
** As sung by Alan Lomax. Transcribed by Charles Seeger. The design of the song is the African leader-chorus form, and this version is used on the Texas prison farms for hoeing—a whole gang moving forward together, their hoes flashing together in the sun, across an irrigation ditch, thus:
Well, *las'* Monday *morn*in',
Lawd, Lawd, *Lawd!*
—A. L.

He was six weeks a-pickin'.

Lordy, your wife and my wife.

Gonna give a feather-pickin'.

And we put him on to parboil.

He was six months a-parboil'.

And we put him on the table.

Now the forks couldn't stick him.

And the knife couldn't cut him.

And we throwed him in the hog-pen.

And he broke the belly's jawbone.

And we taken him to the sawmill.

And he broke the saw's teeth out.

And the last time I seen him.

Well, he's flyin' across the ocean.

With a long string o' goslin's.

And he's goin' "Quank quink-quank!"

Po' Laz'us (Poor Lazarus)*

---

* From *American Ballads and Folk Songs*, collected and compiled by John A. Lomax and Alan Lomax, pp. 91–93. Copyright, 1934, by The Macmillan Company. New York. Some of the verses of this ballad work song we have taken from *Negro Workaday Songs*. The rest of the words and the tune were recorded in Southern Prison camps.—J. A. L. and A. L.

Oh, bad man Laz'us done broke in de commissary winder,
Oh, bad man Laz'us done broke in de commissary winder.
He been paid off, Lawd, Lawd, he been paid off.

Oh, de deputy 'gin to wonder, where in de worl' he could fin' him.
Oh, de deputy 'gin to wonder, where in de worl' he could fin' him.
Well, I don' know, Lawd, Lawd, I jes' don' know.

Oh, dey foun' po' Laz'us way out between two mountains,
Oh, dey foun' po' Laz'us way out between two mountains,
An' dey blowed him down, Lawd, Lawd, an' dey blowed him down.

Ol' Laz'us tol' de deputy he had never been arrested,
Ol' Laz'us tol' de deputy he had never been arrested,
By no one man, Lawd, Lawd, by no one man.

So dey shot po' Laz'us shot him wid a great big number,
Dey shot po' Laz'us, shot him wid a great big number.
Number 45, Lawd, Lawd, number 45.

An' dey taken po' Laz'us an' dey laid him on de commissary
        county.
Dey taken po' Laz'us an' dey laid him on de commissary county,
An' dey walked away, Lawd, Lawd, an' dey walked away.

Laz'us tol' de deputy, "Please gimme a cool drink o' water."
Laz'us tol' de deputy, "Please gimme a cool drink o' water,
Jes' befo' I die, Lawd, Lawd, jes' befo' I die."

Laz'us' sister run an' tol' her mother,
Laz'us' sister run an' tol' her mother,
Dat po' Laz'us dead, Lawd, Lawd, po' Laz'us dead.

Laz'us' mother, she laid down her sewin',
Laz'us' mother, she laid down her sewin',
'Bout de trouble, Lawd, Lawd, she had wid Laz'us.

Laz'us' mother she come a-screamin' an' a-cryin',
Laz'us' mother she come a-screamin' an' a-cryin',
"Dat's my only son, Lawd, Lawd, dat's my only son."

Delia Holmes*

De-lia, De-lia, Why did'nt you run? See dat des—per-a-do, Had a for-ty-fo' smoke-less gun, Cryin', "All I had done gone."

Chorus

All I had done gone! All I had done gone! Good—by, Moth-er, friends and all; All I had done gone!

Now Coonie an' his little sweetheart
Settin' down talkin' low;
Axed her would she marry him,
She said, "Why sho'."

When the time come for marriage
She refuse' to go.
"If you don't marry me
You cannot live no mo'."

Shot her with a pistol,
Number forty-fo'.
"You did not marry me,
You cannot live no mo'."

Turned po' Delia over
On her side very slow.
She was cryin', "Coonie,
Please don't shoot no mo'."

Death had proceeded,
It wasn't so very long
Till her mother come runnin'
With a bucket on her arm.

"Tell me, my darlin',
What have you done wrong,
Cause Coonie to shoot you,
With that forty-fo' smokeless gun?"

From "Delia Holmes—A Neglected Negro Ballad," by Chapman J. Milling, *Southern Folklore Quarterly*, Vol. I (December, 1937), No. 4, pp. 3–7.

"Some give a nickel
Some give a dime,
Help to bury
This body of mine."

Threw down his pistol
An' tried to get away.
Officers picked him up
In just a few days.

Placed him in the jail
Till his trial should come.
"Tell me now, officer,
What have I done?"

They axed him did he remember this,
"A girl that you were in love,
An' spoken things unto her
That instantly taken her nerve?"

"She moved closely beside of me
An' threw her arms around."
"Do you remember little Delia Holmes
And which you shot down?"

"Have I now any bond,
Or can I get one,
For the crime that I am charged,
I plead guilty I have done?"

The judge that tried him,
Handsome with the time,
Say, "Coonie, if I don't hang you
I'll give you ninety-nine."

Coonie went to Atlanta,
Drinkin' from a silver cup.
Po' li'l Delia's in the cemetery,
I hope to never wake up.

Delia's mother
Taken a trip out west,
Just to keep from hearin' the talk
Of po' li'l Delia's death.

Everywhere the train would stop
You could hear the people moan,
Singin' dat lonesome song,
"Po' Delia's dead an' gone."

Rubber tire' buggy,
Rubber tire' hack,
Take you to de cemetery,
Don't never bring you back.

Coonie wrote to the Governor,
Asked him, "Pardon me,
I was charged with murder
In the first degree.

"The judge was liberal
In givin' me my time;
Happened that he didn't hang me
But he give me ninety-nine.

"I am now a murderer,
Servin' a long, long time;
And if you will pardon me,
I'll not be guilty of another crime.

"This is Coonie in Atlanta,
Workin' 'mong the stone.
Have been here for forty-five years,
And I'm now needed at home."

Take This Hammer*

Take this ham-mer, (huh!) car-ry it to the cap—tain, (huh!)
Take this ham-mer, (huh!) car-ry it to the cap—tain, (huh!)
Take this ham-mer, (huh!) car-ry it to the cap—tain, (huh!)
Tell him I'm gone, (huh!) tell him I'm gone. (huh!)

If he ask you (*huh!*) was I runnin', (*huh!*)
Tell him I's flyin', (*huh!*) tell him I's flyin'. (*huh!*)

---

* As sung by the Almanac Singers. Transcribed by Ruth Crawford Seeger.

If he ask you (*huh!*) was I laughin', (*huh!*)
Tell him I's cryin', (*huh!*) tell him I's cryin'. (*huh!*)

Cap'n called me, (*huh!*) called me "a nappy-headed devil," (*huh!*)
That ain't my name, (*huh!*) that ain't my name. (*huh!*)

I don't want no (*huh!*) peas, cornbread, neither molasses, (*huh!*)
They hurt my pride, (*huh!*) they hurt my pride. (*huh!*)

I don't want no (*huh!*) cold iron shackles (*huh!*)
Around my leg, (*huh!*) around my leg. (*huh!*)

Cap'n got a big gun, (*huh!*) an' he try to play bad. (*huh!*)
Go'n' take it in the mornin' (*huh!*) if he make me mad. (*huh!*)

I'm go'n' make these (*huh!*) few days I started, (*huh!*)
Then I'm goin' home, (*huh!*) then I'm goin home, (*huh!*)

Little Black Train Is A-Comin'*

God tole Hez-y—ki-yah In a mes-sage from on
high: Go set yo' house in or-dah, For
thou shalt sho-ly die. He turned to the wall an' a-
weep—in'. Oh! see the King in tears; He
got his bus'-ness fixed all right, God spared him fif-teen
years.   *Chorus*   Lit-tle black train is a—com-in',
Get all yo' bus'-ness right; Go set yo' house in
or-dah, For the train may be here to—night.

* From *The Negro Sings a New Heaven*, by Mary Allen Grissom, pp.
10–11. Copyright, 1930, by the University of North Carolina Press. Chapel
Hill.

Go tell that ball room lady,
All filled with worldly pride,
That little black train is a-comin',
Prepare to take a ride.
That little black train and engine
An' a little baggage car,
With idle thoughts and wicked deeds,
Must stop at the judgment bar.

There was a po' young man in darkness,
Cared not for the gospel light,
Suddenly a whistle blew
From a little black train in sight.
"Oh, death, will you not spare me?
I'm just in my wicked plight.
Have mercy, Lord, do hear me,
Pray come an' set me right."
But death had fixed his shackles
About his soul so tight,
Just befo' he got his bus'ness fixed,
The train rolled in that night.

Lord, Remember Me*

I want to die like-a Jesus die,
    And he die wid a free good will,
I lay out in de grave and I stretchee out e arms,
    Do, Lord, remember me.

---

* From *Slave Songs of the United States*, by William Francis Allen, Charles
Pickard Ware, Lucy McKim Garrison, p. 12. Copyright, 1867. Reprinted,
1929. New York: Peter Smith.

Boll Weevil Song*

Oh, de boll wee-vil am a lit-tle black bug, Come from
Mex-i-co, dey say, Come all de way to Tex-as, jus' a-
look-in' foh a place to stay, Jus' a-look-in' foh a home,
jus' a—look—in'. foh a home.

De first time I seen de boll weevil,
   He was a-settin' on de square.
De next time I seen de boll weevil, he had all of his family dere,
   Jus' a-lookin' foh a home, just' a-lookin' foh a home.

De farmer say to de weevil:
   "What make yo' head so red?"
De weevil say to de farmer, "It's a wondah I ain't dead,
   A-lookin' foh a home, jus' a-lookin' foh a home."

De farmer takes de boll weevil,
   An' he put him in de hot san'.
De weevil say: "Dis is mighty hot, but I'll stan' it like a man,
   Dis'll be my home, it'll be my home."

De farmer take de boll weevil,
   An' he put him in a lump of ice;
De boll weevil say to de farmer: "Dis is mighty cool an' nice,
   It'll be my home, dis'll be my home."

De farmer take de boll weevil,
   An' he put him in de fire.
De boll weevil say to de farmer: "Here I are, here I are,
   Dis'll be my home, dis'll be my home."

De boll weevil say to de farmer:
   "You better leave me alone;
I done eat all yo' cotton, now I'm goin' to start on yo' corn,
   I'll have a home, I'll have a home."

* From *The American Songbag*, by Carl Sandburg, pp. 8–10. Copyright, 1927, by Harcourt, Brace & Company. New York.

De merchant got half de cotton,
    De boll weevil got de res'.
Didn't leave de farmer's wife but one old cotton dress,
    An' it's full of holes, it's full of holes.

De farmer say to de merchant:
    "We's in an awful fix;
De boll weevil et all de cotton up an' lef' us only sticks,
    We's got no home, we's got no home."

De farmer say to de merchant:
    "We ain't made but only one bale,
And befoh we'll give yo' dat one we'll fight an' go to jail,
    We'll have a home, we'll have a home."

De cap'n say to de missus:
    "What d' you t'ink o' dat?
De boll weevil done make a nes' in my bes' Sunday hat,
    Goin' to have a home, goin' to have a home."

And if anybody should ax you
    Who it was dat make dis song,
Jus' tell 'em 'twas a big buck niggah wid a paih o' blue duckin's on,
    Ain' got no home, ain' got no home.

NOTES

INTRODUCTION

1. *Christian Science Monitor*, August 5, 1944, p. 3.
2. *The New York Times*, May 14, 1944, Book Review Section, p. 5.
3. *Saturday Review*, July 1, 1944, p. 18.
4. *Weekly Book Review*, May 7, 1944, p. 1.
5. *Journal of American Folklore*, 58, January-March, 1945, p. 57.
6. *Southern Folklore Quarterly*, 8, September, 1944, p. 250.
7. Richard M. Dorson, *Folklore: Selected Essays*, Bloomington, Ind.: Indiana University Press, 1972, p. 16.
8. *New Yorker*, May 31, 1944, p. 91.
9. Jan Harold Brunvand, *The Study of American Folklore: An Introduction*, New York: Norton, 1978, p. 2.
10. Richard M. Dorson, *American Folklore*, Chicago: University of Chicago Press, 1959, p. 1.
11. Archer Taylor quoted in Brunvand, *Study*, p. 1.
12. Quoted in Brunvand, *Study*, p. 2.
13. B.A. Botkin, *New York City Folklore*, New York: Random House, 1956, p. xv.
14. B.A. Botkin, *A Treasury of Western Folklore*, New York: Crown, 1951, p. xxix.
15. Richard M. Dorson, *Buying the Wind*, Chicago: University of Chicago Press, 1964, p. 1.
16. Brunvand, *Study*, p. 2.
17. Dorson, *Buying*, p. 1.
18. Dorson, *Folklore: Selected Essays*, p. 16.
19. Dorson, *American Folklore*, p. 4.
20. Herbert Halpert, "Some Undeveloped Areas in American Folklore," *Journal of American Folklore*, 70, October-December, 1957, p. 301.
21. Halpert, "Some," p. 299.
22. Bruce Jackson, *Folklore and Society: Essays in Honor of Benj. A. Botkin*, Hatboro, Pa.: Folklore Associates, 1966, p. xi.
23. Jackson, *Folklore*, p. xii.
24. Jackson, *Folklore*, p. xii.
25. Jackson, *Folklore*, p. xii.
26. The Associated Press, "Mighty Reggie," *El Paso Times*, October 13, 1978, p. 1-D.
27. "Some Cases Never Die, or Even Fade," *Time*, September 17, 1979, p. 63.
28. Haldeen Braddy to Joseph Leach, January 9, 1980.
29. John O. West, "The Professional-Amateur-Popularizer Feud in

Folklore," *Journal of American Folklore*, 88, July-September, 1975, p. 300.

30. V.S. Pritchett, "Books in General," *New Statesman and Nation*, 32, October 5, 1946, p. 248.

Part One: Heroes and Boasters

I. BACKWOODS BOASTERS

1. *A History of New York*, by Diedrich Knickerbocker (1809), Book VI, Chapter III.

2. The Salt River Roarer was so called from the Kentucky freshwater stream of that name, which was derived from the salt once made on its banks. Because of the difficulty of navigation, the river has also given rise to the phrase for a political or other defeat, *to row* (some one) up *Salt River*. Other explanations of the origin of the phrase are "that refractory slaves used to be punished by hiring them out to row keelboats up the river; that the saltboilers upon it were rough characters; that river pirates infested it; that after Kentucky summer elections, candidates, victor and vanquished alike, went up Salt River for a rest as far as Harrodsburg Springs. The story accepted in Kentucky, and repeated to me by state officials, is that when Henry Clay was candidate for President in 1832, he engaged a Jackson Democrat to row him up the Ohio to Louisville, where he was to speak. The boatman rowed him up Salt River instead, and he did not reach his destination until the day after election, when he learned of his own defeat. An intriguing picture, but one too full of geographic and logical improbabilities to credit." (*Sycamore Shores*, by Clark B. Firestone, 1936, p. 131.)

3. Wildfire was not Paulding's only attempt to portray backwoods character, for in Ambrose Bushfield, in *Westward Ho!* (1832), he created a burlesque Natty Bumppo.

4. It has also been suggested that the original of Wildfire may have been Florida's Governor William Pope Duval (father of John C. Duval), who supplied material for several stories by Washington Irving, Paulding's collaborator in the *Salamagundi* papers.

5. *Literary Life of James K. Paulding*, by William I. Paulding (1867), pp. 218–219.

6. See the plate facing page 504 in *Annals of the New York Stage*, by George C. D. Odell, Vol. III (1928).

7. *Ben Hardin, His Times and Contemporaries*, by Lucius P. Little (1887), p. viii.

8. *Life of Colonel David Crockett* (1860), p. 140n.

9. "A Neglected Epic," *Essays on Authorship* (1902).

10. *Sketches and Eccentricities of Col. David Crockett, of West Tennessee* (1833), pp. 77, 78.

11. Speech on the Fortification Bill, *Register of Debates in Congress*, Part IV of Vol. X, June 19, 1834, p. 4586.

12. For ten "Crockett" tall tales of hunting and shooting, see Vance Randolph's *Ozark Mountain Folks* (1932).

13. *Mark Twain's America* (1932), p. 60.

14. "The Last of the Boatmen," by Morgan Neville, *The Western Souvenir*, for 1829.

II. PSEUDO BAD MEN

1. *Underground, or Life Below the Surface,* by Thomas W. Knox (1873), pp. 680–684.
2. *A-Rafting on the Mississip',* by Charles Edward Russell (1928), pp. 189–190.
3. *Short Grass Country,* by Stanley Vestal (1941) p. 26.
4. "Justice in Early Iowa," by *George F. Robeson, The Palimpsest,* Vol. 5 (March, 1924), No. 3, p. 105.
5. *Cowboy Songs and Other Frontier Ballads,* Revised and Enlarged, collected by John A. Lomax and Alan Lomax (1938), p. 138 where it is ascribed to *Texas Siftings.*

III. KILLERS

1. *Wild Bill Hickok,* The Prince of Pistoleers, by Frank J. Wilstach, p. 242.
2. *Ibid.,* p. 162.
3. *The Bad Man of the West,* by George D. Hendricks (1941), p. 96.
4. *Memories of Buffalo Bill,* by his wife Louisa Frederici Cody, in collaboration with Courtney Riley Cooper (1919), p. 91.
5. *Belle Starr,* by Burton Rascoe (1941), pp. 9–10.
6. *The Saga of Billy the Kid,* by Walter Noble Burns (1925), p. 145.
7. *A Vaquero of the Brush Country,* by J. Frank Dobie (1929), p. 174n.
8. *Sweet Land,* by Lewis Gannett (1934), pp. 39–40.
9. An example of the ballad convention of "claim to authorship."
10. Cf. "Po' Laz'us" in Part Six.

IV. FREE LANCES

1. Compare Justice of the Peace Jim Burnett of Charleston, Arizona, in *Tombstone,* by Walter Noble Burns.
2. *Roy Bean, Law West of the Pecos,* by C.L. Sonnichsen (1943), p. 46.
3. *Law West of the Pecos,* The Story of Roy Bean, by Everett Lloyd (1936), pp. 74–75, 66–67.
4. The town of Big Foot in Frio County, Texas, is named for him.
5. "*John C. Duval: First Texas Man of Letters,*" by J. Frank Dobie, *Southwest Review,* XXIV (April, 1939), No. 3, pp. 277–278.

V. MIRACLE MEN

1. *Enjoyment of Laughter* (1936), p. 168.
2. *Paul Bunyan,* by James Stevens (1925), p. 1.
3. See his letter to Louise Pound in her article on "Nebraska Strong Men," *Southern Folklore Quarterly,* Vol. VII (September, 1943), No. 3, pp. 133–143. For Paul Bunyan bibliography see "Paul Bunyan Twenty-Five Years After," by Gladys J. Haney, *The Journal of American Folklore,* Vol. LV (July-September, 1942), No. 217, pp. 155–168.
4. In a note on "Paul Bunyan—Myth or Hoax?" in *Minnesota History,* Vol. XXI (March, 1940), No. 1, pp. 55–58, Carleton C. Ames places the burden of proof on "those who are presenting Paul Bunyan as a native product of the imagination of the shanty boy,

and who are making him, in a sense, the patron saint of the oldtime logger." On the basis of negative evidence that Paul Bunyan was unknown to old-timers in Wisconsin and Minnesota and of certain anachronisms in Esther Shepard's version, he reaches the "tentative conclusion" that "Paul Bunyan as the legendary hero of the shanty boy, as true folklore, is spurious. He may have appeared in the camps of a later day, possibly about the turn of the century when the true shanty boy had all but vanished. He may exist among the lumberjacks of the Pacific Coast, where logging is a far different operation than the Minnesota and Wisconsin jack ever knew, but he was a stranger to the loggers of the Middle West when logging was at its height."

5. Letter to Louise Pound, July 1, 1943, a copy of which, together with clippings from the Gothenburg, Nebraska *Times*, and other Febold data, is on file at the Archive of American Folksong, Library of Congress, Washington, D.C.

6. *Men and Steel*, by Mary Heaton Vorse (1920), p. 20.

VI. PATRON SAINTS

1. "The Return of Johnny Appleseed," by Charles Allen Smart, Harper's Magazine, Vol. 179 (August, 1939), pp. 233–234.

Part Two: Boosters and Knockers

I. TALL TALK

1. From *Westward Ho!* by James K. Paulding (1832).
2. From *Mike Fink: A Legend of the Ohio*, by Emerson Bennett (1848).
3. From "Fight with a Puke," in *Mince Pie for the Million*.
4. See "Speech of Colonel Crockett in Congress."
5. From *Col. Crockett's Exploits and Adventures in Texas*, Written by Himself (1836), p. 129.
6. From Paulding's *Westward Ho!*
7. From Bird's *Nick of the Woods*.
8. From *Travels on an Inland Voyage*, by Christian Schulz, Jr., Volume II, pp. 145–146. New York: Printed by Isaac Riley. 1810.

II. THE SKY'S THE LIMIT

1. Cf. "The Histrionic West," by Stanley Vestal, *Space*, Vol. I (June, 1934), No. 2, pp. 13–16.
2. Mr. Cathcart, of Indiana, in the House of Representatives, February 6, 1846. Cited by Thornton, in *An American Glossary* (1912), Vol. II, p. 985.
3. Cf. the similar nicknames of cities: The City Beautiful, the City of Magic, the City of Opportunities, the City of Prosperity, the Crown City, the Queen City.
4. *A Dictionary of American English on Historical Principles*, edited by Sir William A. Craigie and James R. Hulbert, Vol. II (1940), p. 646.

5. "Kentucky," *The Southern Guide*, Vol. I (January, 1878), No. 1, p. 59.
6. *The Resources and Attractions of Colorado for the Home Seeker, Capitalist and Tourist* (Union Pacific Railway, Omaha, 1888), pp. 61–62.
7. *California for the Settler*, by Andrew Jackson Wells (Southern Pacific Company, San Francisco, 1915), p. 62.
8. See *The Facts of Life in Popular Song* (1934), by Sigmund Spaeth.
9. "I saw a cowboy in California once who was a hundred if he was a day. It's astonishing how old these greasers get to be. I have traveled a great deal in Mexico, and it don't occur to me just now where I ever saw a graveyard. There's the Tombstone district in Arizona, and I know there isn't a tombstone in it. The people just dry up and blow away, and maybe you think it don't blow down there sometimes." . . . *Ten Wise Men and Some More*, by William Lightfoot Visscher (1909), p. 89.
10. See "The Wind," by Frank Neff and William Henry, Part Four.
11. Told by B. A. Trussell, of Miami, Florida, in *Tall Stories*, by Lowell Thomas (1931), pp. 236–237.
12. *Tall Stories*, by Lowell Thomas (1931), pp. 232–235.
13. *North America*, by J. Russell Smith and M. Ogden Phillips (1942), p. 349.
14. *Thomas W. Jackson with all the "Funny Ones,"* by Thomas W. Jackson (1938), p. 79.
15. *Report of the Commissioner of Patents for the Year 1851*, Part II, Agriculture (1852), pp. 3–7.
16. Although the author of this anonymous satire on land frauds maintains that "never could there be experienced just such another confounded take-in," Major Wilkey's misfortunes in "Edensburgh" may have furnished suggestions to Dickens (even to the name of the place) for the somewhat similar experiences of Martin Chuzzlewit in the city of "Eden," published four years later.
17. *The Grapes of Wrath*, by John Steinbeck (1939), p. 257.
18. *Pioneer Life in Nebraska*, Pamphlet One, *We Settled the Plains*, Series One, compiled by Workers of the WPA Writers' Program of the Works Project Administration in the State of Nebraska (Oct. 1941), p. 3.
19. "Legends of Febold Feboldson," by Paul R. Beath, in *Nebraska Folklore Pamphlets*, Number Eight, p. 7. Lincoln: Federal Writers' Project in Nebraska. September 15, 1937.
20. From *Iowa: The Home for Immigrants*, prepared by Secretary A. R. Fulton of the Iowa Board of Immigration, in 1870. Cited in *The Palimpset*. XVIII (July 1937), pp. 226–242.
21. From *The Iowa Handbook for 1857*, by Nathan H. Parker. Boston: J. P. Jewett and Company.
22. This tale, although oft repeated by Forty-Niners, was originally published by E. Bryant in 1848. Is it not the first California "booster" story?—A.B.H.
23. From *Beyond the Mississippi: From the Great River to the Great Ocean*; Life and Adventure on the Prairies, Mountains and Pacific Coast, by Albert D. Richardson, p. 202. Entered according to Act of Congress, in the year 1867, by Albert D. Richardson, in the Clerk's Office of the District Court of the Southern District of New York. Hartford, Conn. American Publishing Company.

24. From *Forty-Niners, The Chronicle of the California Trail*, by Archer Butler Hulbert, p. 41. Copyright, 1931, by Archer Butler Hulbert. Boston: Little, Brown & Company.

25. E. P. Hatheway, Ms. *Letters.*—A.B.H.

26. *Nebraska City News*, May 28, 1859. This item, showing the first use of the famous expression, was first given me by Dr. R. P. Beiber of Washington University, St. Louis. It was later found among the Willard items.—L.R.H.

27. *Jefferson Inquirer*, May 28, 1859; copied from the *St. Joseph Journal.*—L.R.H.

III. LOCAL CRACKS AND SLAMS

1. For the proverbial aspects of local witticisms—the French *blason populaire* and the German *ortsneckereien*—see *The Proverb*, by Archer Taylor (1931), pp. 97–105.

2. *Beyond the Mississippi: From the Great River to the Great Ocean, Life and Adventure on the Prairies, Mountains and Pacific Coast. . . . 1857–1867*, by Albert D. Richardson (1867), p. 132.

3. See Part Four.

4. *The Great Plains* (1931), p. 9.

5. Cf. "Brown's Descent, or, The Willy-Nilly Slide," by Robert Frost.

6. *The Truth About Arkansas*, by William H. Edmonds (1895), pp. 6, 15.

7. Cf. *Uncle Dudley's Odd Hours*; Being the Vagaries of a Country Editor; Also, as an Appendix, J. Proctor Knott's Famous Speech on Duluth, by M. C. Russell (Duluth, 1882), pp. 283–284; *Why We Laugh*, by Samuel S. Cox (1876), Chapter XII.

8. For discussion of Hall, see *Arizona, A State Guide*, compiled by Workers of the Writers' Program of the Work Projects Administration in the State of Arizona (1940) and *Desert Country*, by Edwin Corle (1941).

9. Cf. "Whimsical Dialogue between an Irish Innkeeper and an Englishman," *Wit and Wisdom; or The World's Jest-Book* . . . (London: Thomas Allman . . . , 1853), pp. 28–29; "A Musical Tennessee Landlord," by "Dresbach," *Spirit of the Times*, XVI (February 13, 1847), p. 603.

10. See "The Inquisitive Yankee Descendants in Arkansas," by Walter Blair, *American Speech*, XIV (February, 1939), 11–22, where Blair points out that whereas in the East the native is usually the questioner and the traveler the questioned, in the West the roles have been reversed in the West, *The Arkansas Traveler* being a case in point. Cf. " 'Old Sense' of Arkansas," Part Three.

11. Cf. *The Southern Poor-White from Lubberland to Tobacco Road*, by Shields McIlwaine (1939).

12. See *The Arkansas Traveler*, by Thomas Wilson (1900).

13. *The Arkansas Traveller's Songster, Containing the Celebrated Story of the Arkansas Traveller, with the Music for Violin or Piano, and Also an Extensive and Choice Collection of New and Popular Comic and Sentimental Songs* (New York: Dick and Fitzgerald, copyright 1863), which reprints, on pages 5–9, the Blodgett & Bradford version (Buffalo, *ca.* 1850) ascribed to Mose Case. Of the several newspapers of this name (see F.W. Allsopp's *History of the Arkansas Press*, 1922), the most famous is that founded and edited by Arkansas humorist, Opie Read. The first weekly issue

(June 6, 1882) reprinted Faulkner's *Arkansas Traveler*, together with the tune and the two Washburne paintings.

14. *The Arkansas Traveller and Rackinsac Waltz*, arranged by William Cumming (Louisville: Peters & Webster; Cincinnati: Peters & Field, copyright, 1847).

15. From "Vive la Bagatelle!" in *The Southern Literary Messenger*, Vol. VI (June, 1840), No. 6, p. 416.

16. From *Yankee Notions; or The American Joe Miller*, by Sam Slick, Junr., p. 47. London: Ball, Arnold, & Co.; Edinburgh: Fraser and Crawford; Glasgow: John Robertson. 1839.

17. That is, climb the windmill tower to turn the wheel by hand, and dig mesquite roots.—W.P.W.
    Cf. J. Frank Dobie, *The Flavor of Texas* (1936), p. 15: "Texas is where 'a man has to dig (mesquite roots) for wood and climb (go up gravely canyons) for water.'"

18. The word that went here was a corrupt form of *ajalote*—Texas-Mexican for that wondrous and hideous form of aquatic sala-mander, so common in the tanks and troughs of West Texas, known as water-dog or water-puppy.—G. H.

19. Sassafras tea.

20. Here is another version of what is supposed to have been the speech, delivered by Cassius M. Johnson, as printed in a pamphlet at Cleveland, Ohio. Printed by J.H. Philips, Cleveland, Ohio, no date—F. W. A.

Part Three: Jesters

I. PRANKS AND TRICKS

1. See *Thomas Chandler Haliburton*, by V.L.O. Chittick (1924).

2. *Here We Are Again*, by Robert Edmund Sherwood (1926), p. 191.

3. In addition to such April Fool stunts as tying a string to a pocket-book left lying on the sidewalk and jerking it away from the vic-tim who tries to pick it up, there are such time-honored gags as telephoning the zoo to ask for Mr. Wolf or Mr. Fox.

4. According to G.W. Orians, *Peck's Bad Boy* was inspired by Thomas Bailey Aldrich's *The Story of a Bad Boy*. It will be ob-served, however, that Tom Bailey was a "good bad boy."

5. See the stories of Ring Lardner, George Milburn, and Erskine Caldwell.

6. *A Song of the Pipeline*, by Daniel M. Garrison, *Folk-Say, A Re-gional Miscellany: 1930*, edited by B.A. Botkin, p. 110. See "Mirages," Part Four.

7. *Abraham Lincoln, The Prairie Years*, by Carl Sandburg (1926), Vol. II, p. 81.

8. See "Tricks and Catches," Part Six.

9. "Range Lore," by W.W. Adney, San Angelo, Texas. Manuscripts of Federal Writers' Project for the Works Progress Administration in the State of Texas.

10. *The Cowboy*, by Philip Ashton Rollins (1922), p. 184. For an example of a conversational sell "in the way of a string of plausibly worded sentences that didn't mean anything under the sun," see

"First Interview with Artemus Ward," in *Mark Twain's Sketches New and Old*, pp. 283–286.

11. *Hoaxes*, by Curtis D. MacDougall (1940), p. vi. Among the folkloric hoaxes treated by MacDougall are mythical monsters (the hodag), historical myths (Parson Weems' cherry tree myth), tall stories, and legendary heroes (Johnny Appleseed).

II. HUMOROUS ANECDOTES AND JESTS

1. The backwoods Lincoln has often been compared to Davy Crockett as a stump-speech story-teller. With Crockett, however, as has been pointed out above, the funny story was, chiefly a vote-getting expedient.

2. "High John de Conquer," by Zora Neale Hurston, *The American Mercury*, Vol. LVII (October, 1943), No. 238, pp. 450–458.

3. For a classification of "fool" motifs, see *Motif-Index* of Folk Literature, by S. Thompson, under "J. the Wise and the Foolish."

4. Panting.—Z.N.H.

5. With great difficulty.—Z.N.H.

6. From *Mules and Men*, by Zora Neale Hurston, p. 47. Copyright, 1935, by Zora Neale Hurston. Philadelphia and London: J.B. Lippincott Company.

7. *Ibid.*, p. 94.

8. "Blue Baby" was so black he looked blue.—Z.N.H.

9. From *Good Morning, America*, by Carl Sandburg, pp. 15–18. Copyright, 1928, by Carl Sandburg. New York: Harcourt, Brace & Company.

10. From *The People, Yes*, by Carl Sandburg. Copyright, 1936, by Harcourt Brace & Co. This and succeeding lines are from pp. 123–124.

11. *Ibid.*, p. 163.

12. *Ibid.*, p. 164.

13. *Ibid.*, pp. 165–166.

14. *Ibid.*, pp. 62–63.

15. *Ibid.*, p. 65.

16. *Ibid.*, pp. 83–84.

17. *Ibid.*, pp. 95–96.

18. *Ibid.*, pp. 111–113.

19. *Ibid.*, p. 9.

20. *Ibid.*, pp. 59–60.

Part Four: Liars

I. YARNS AND TALL TALES

1. *Humor of the Old Deep South*, by Arthur Palmer Hudson (1936), pp. 16–17.

2. *The Complete Works of Charles F. Brown, better known as "Artemus Ward."* (London: John Camden Hotten), pp. 316–317.

3. Five dollar bill.—J.C.

4. Rule forbidding excessive over time.—J.C.

5. Boiling of clothing to kill body lice.—J.C.

6. Satchel, resembling a rigid suitcase, in which itinerant sign painters keep their work materials and often their clothing as well.—J.C.

II. FROM THE LIARS' BENCH

1. "South-western Slang," by Socrates Hyacinth, *The Overland Monthly*, Vol. III (August, 1869), p. 125.
2. "An eastern visitor once wrote in a bread-and-butter letter to a Roundup newspaper editor: 'Out there every prairie dog hole is a gold mine; every hill a mountain; every creek a river; and everybody you meet is a liar.' "—Montana, A State Guide Book (1939), p. 258.
3. The "deacon's seat" was the lumberjack's name for the place on the "liars bench" occupied successively by the bunkhouse storytellers at the evening session of yarning. See *The Hodag, and Other Tales of the Logging Camps*, by Lake Shore Kearney (Wausau, Wisconsin, 1928).
4. *Hoosier Tall Stories* (Federal Writers' Project in Indiana, 1937), pp. 1–2.
5. *The Sazerac Lying Club*, a Nevada Book, by Fred W. Hart (Henry Keller & Co., San Francisco, 1878).
6. *Tall Stories*, the Rise and Triumph of the Great American Whopper, by Lowell Thomas (1931).
7. *The 25 Best Lies of 1933* (Burlington, Wisconsin, 1934), p. 1.
8. Scalped.—G.F.R.
9. Soles made of buffalo hide—G.F.R.

Part Five: Folk Tales and Legends

I. ANIMAL TALES

1. *Rumors and Hoaxes; Classic Tales of Fraud and Deception*, collected and arranged with an introduction by Peter Haworth (1928), p. xviii.

II. NURSERY TALES

1. "Mark Twain's Ghost Story," by E. P. Pabody, *Minnesota History*, Vol. 18 (March, 1937), No. 1, pp. 8–35.

V. DEVIL TALES

1. Cf. "The Devil and the Fiddle," by Herbert Halpert, *Hoosier Folklore Bulletin*, Vol. II (December, 1943), No. 2, pp. 39–43. For the Texas legend of "The Devil and Strap Buckner," see *The Coming Empire or Two Thousand Miles in Texas on Horseback*, by H.F. McDanield and N.A. Taylor, (New York, 1877), pp. 49–73.

Part Six: Songs and Rhymes

I. PLAY RHYMES AND CATCH COLLOQUIES

1. *Studies in Jocular Literature*, by W.C. Hazlitt (1890), p. 26.

II. SINGING AND PLAY-PARTY GAMES

1. Emma S. Backus, "Song-Games from Connecticut," *The Journal of American Folk-Lore*, Vol. XIV, p. 296.—W.W.N.

III. BALLADS AND SONGS

1. *English Folk Songs from the Southern Appalachians*, collected by Cecil J. Sharp, edited by Maud Karpeles (1932), Vol. I, "Introduction to the First Edition, 1917."
2. "Songs of the American Folk," *Modern Music*, Vol. XVIII (January-February, 1941), No. 2, p. 138.
3. *Our Singing Country*, collected and compiled by John A. Lomax and Alan Lomax (1941), p. xiii.
4. And so on for brother, sister, aunt, uncle, cousin, etc.—R.S.

INDEX OF AUTHORS, TITLES AND
FIRST LINES OF SONGS

583

INDEX OF SUBJECTS AND NAMES

ABOUT THE EDITORS

B. A. BOTKIN, a first-generation American and George Gershwin's first cousin, is one of America's most eminent folklorists. He has been president of the American Folklore Society and folklore expert and archivist for the Library of Congress.

DR. JOSEPH LEACH, who has provided a special introduction and abridgement for the Bantam edition of the *Treasury of American Folklore*, was Botkin's research assistant at the Library of Congress. Professor Leach currently teaches English at the University of Texas at El Paso, specializing in American social history. The descendant of pioneers who came to Texas in covered wagons in 1859, Professor Leach grew up in Wichita Falls, Texas, "surrounded by relatives who were farmers and ranchers, many of whom (including my grandparents) spun yarns and told me tales and taught me practical wisdom that only later, after I started college, did I learn to call 'folklore.' "

READ TOMORROW'S LITERATURE—TODAY

THE BEST OF TODAY'S WRITING BOUND FOR TOMORROW'S CLASSICS.

START A COLLECTION

With Bantam's fiction anthologies, you can begin almost anywhere. Choose from science fiction, classic litera- by both new and established writers in America and ture, modern short stories, mythology, and more—all around the world.

THE NAMES THAT SPELL GREAT LITERATURE

Choose from today's most renowned world authors—every one an important addition to your personal library.

Hermann Hesse

☐	13956	MAGISTER LUDI	$2.95
☐	13523	DEMIAN	$2.25
☐	14305	THE JOURNEY TO THE EAST	$2.25
☐	13855	SIDDHARTHA	$2.50
☐	14563	BENEATH THE WHEEL	$2.95
☐	14445	NARCISSUS AND GOLDMUND	$2.95
☐	14462	STEPPENWOLF	$2.75
☐	11510	ROSSHALDE	$1.95

Alexander Solzhenitsyn

☐	10111	THE FIRST CIRCLE	$2.50
☐	13441	ONE DAY IN THE LIFE OF IVAN DENISOVICH	$2.50
☐	13720	CANCER WARD	$3.95

Jerzy Kosinski

☐	14117	STEPS	$2.50
☐	14489	THE PAINTED BIRD	$2.75
☐	2613	COCKPIT	$2.25
☐	14661	BLIND DATE	$2.95
☐	13843	BEING THERE	$2.50
☐	14577	THE DEVIL TREE	$2.50

Doris Lessing

☐	13433	THE SUMMER BEFORE THE DARK	$2.95
☐	13675	THE GOLDEN NOTEBOOK	$3.95
☐	13967	THE FOUR-GATED CITY	$3.95
☐	14398	BRIEFING FOR A DESCENT INTO HELL	$2.95
☐	12581	MEMOIRS OF A SURVIVOR	$2.50

Buy them at your local bookstore or use this handy coupon for ordering

DISCOVER
THE DRAMA OF LIFE
IN THE LIFE OF DRAMA

☐	13434	**CYRANO DE BERGERAC** Edmond Rostand	$1.75
☐	12204	**FOUR GREAT PLAYS** Henrik Ibsen	$1.95
☐	13615	**COMP. PLAYS SOPHOCLES**	$2.95
☐	13307	**FOR COLORED GIRLS WHO HAVE CONSIDERED SUICIDE WHEN THE RAINBOW IS ENUF** Ntozake Shange	$2.50
☐	14559	**MODERN AMERICAN SCENES FOR STUDENT ACTORS** Wynn Handman	$3.50
☐	11936	**FOUR GREAT PLAYS BY CHEKHOV** Anton Chekhov	$1.75
☐	14674	**THE NIGHT THOREAU SPENT IN JAIL** Jerome Lawrence and Robert E. Lee	$2.25
☐	13390	**RUNAWAYS** Elizabeth Swados	$2.50
☐	12832	**THE PRICE** Arthur Miller	$1.95
☐	13363	**BRIAN'S SONG** William Blinn	$1.95
☐	14678	**THE EFFECTS OF GAMMA RAYS ON MAN-IN-THE-MOON MARIGOLDS** Paul Zindel	$2.25
☐	14161	**50 GREAT SCENES FOR STUDENT ACTORS** Lewy Olfson, ed.	$2.50
☐	12917	**INHERIT THE WIND** Lawrence & Lee	$1.75
☐	13102	**TEN PLAYS BY EURIPIDES** Moses Hadas, ed.	$2.50
☐	13902	**THE CRUCIBLE** Arthur Miller	$2.25
☐	14689	**THE MIRACLE WORKER,** William Gibson	$2.25
☐	14101	**AFTER THE FALL** Arthur Miller	$2.50

Buy them at your local bookstore or use this handy coupon for ordering: